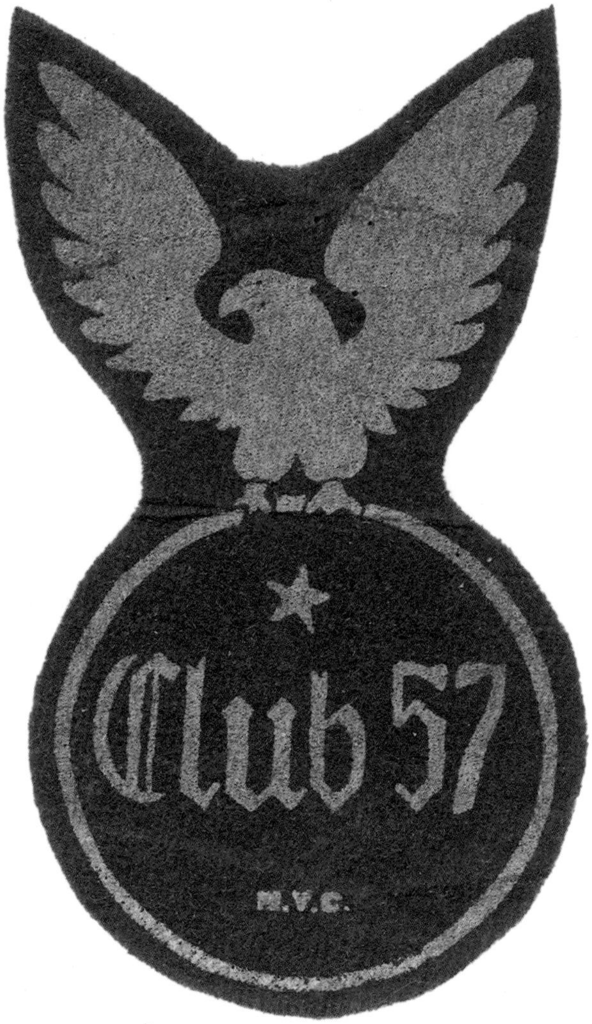
Club 57
N.Y.C.

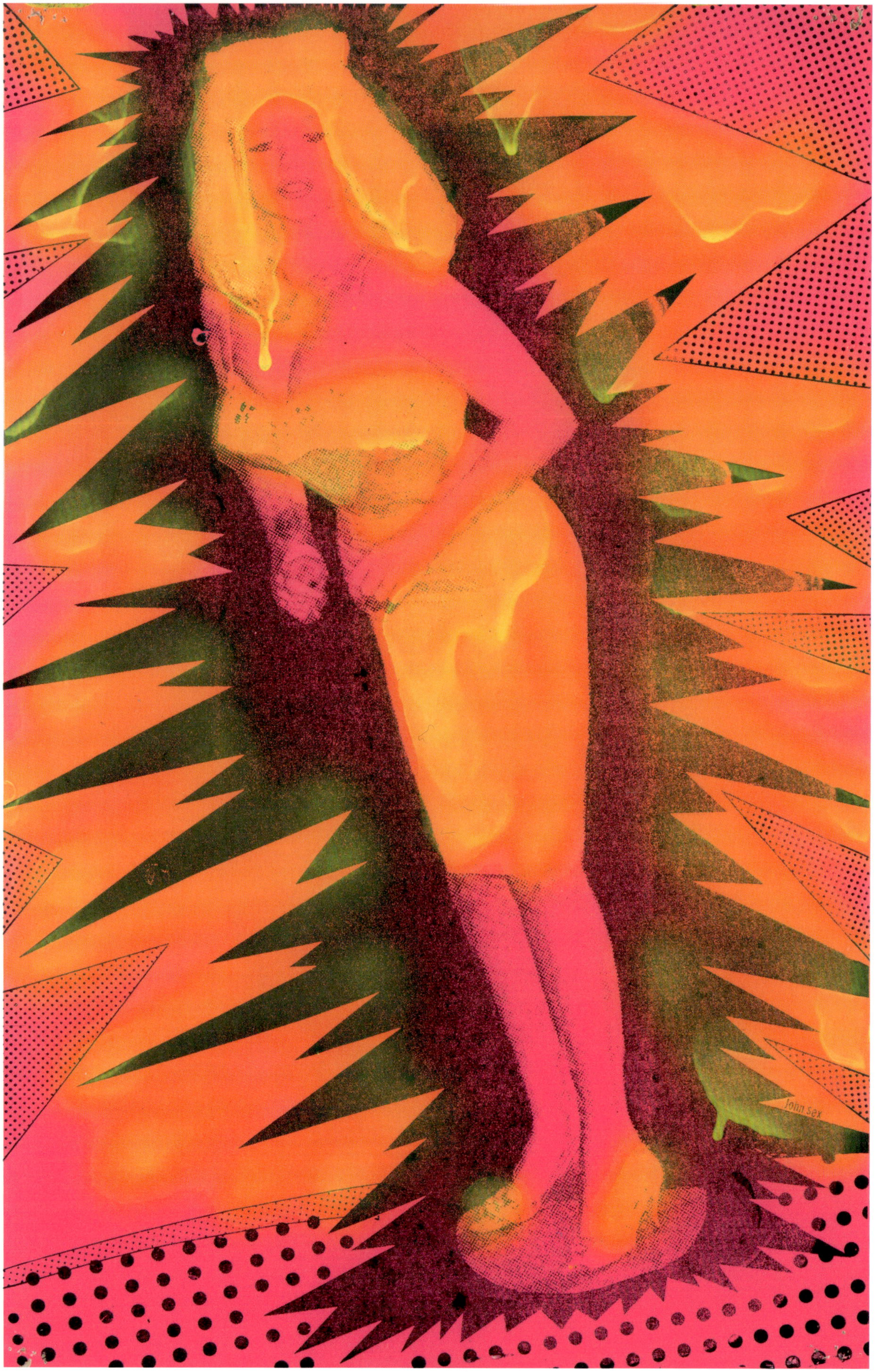
John Sex

Film, Performance, and Art in the EAST VILLAGE 1978–1983

Club 57
N.Y.C.

The Museum of Modern Art, New York

TODAY'S SPECIALS

T.V. Dinners	$3.00
Kielbasa w/boiled potato & sauerkraut	4.00

ANOUSHKA'S APPETIZERS

Cup of Chili a la Covert	$2.75
Putt Putt Green Salad w/vinaigrette	1.50
Montana Mozzarella & Tomato w/olive oil	2.75
French Onion Soup Scully	2.75

DISCO ITALIANO PASTA & ENTREES

Spaghetti Wittman w/Tomato Sauce Shaiman	$4.00
Spaghetti w/olive oil & garlic a la Stace Elkin	3.75
Spaghetti Alfredo Gremski	5.00
Spaghetti Alfredo Carbona San Marco Placo	5.25
Zany Dany's Angel Hair w/fresh vegetables	4.50
Astro Zombie Ravioli w/tomato sauce	4.50
Vegetarian Plate w/rice Kwong Chi	4.75
Tarragon Chicken Crucifixion w/rice & vegetables	5.75
Stanley Steak w/fries or rice & vegetables	8.75

JOHNNY CAFETERIA presents BREAKFAST

57 Eggs any style w/bacon or ham & Henry Jones English Muffin	$3.00

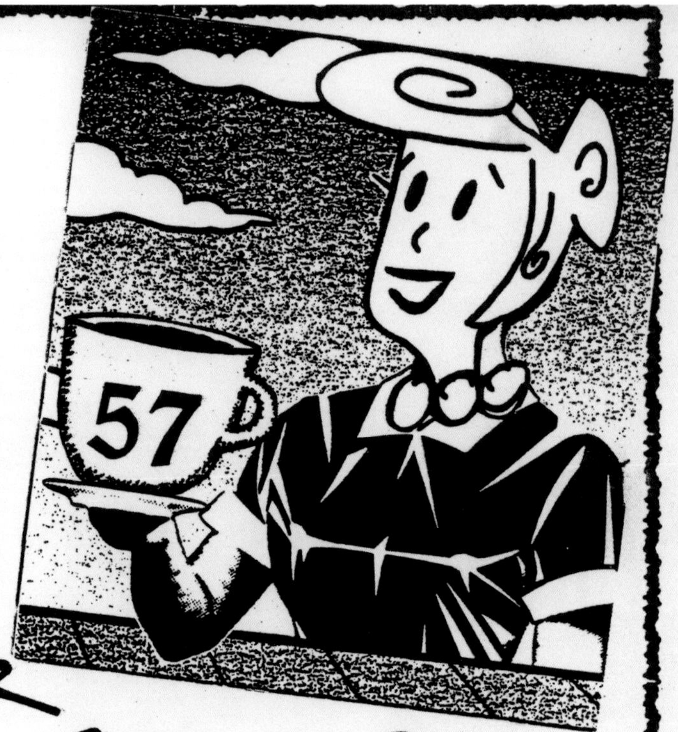

East Village Students Club

POT-LUCK PICNIC

Holy Cross Parish

57 VARIETIES BURGERS & SANDWICHES

Reesburger w/french fries	$3.75
Holliday Burger w/Swiss or Cheddar & fries	4.25
Shils & Brown Burger w/bacon, cheese & fries	4.75
Stromboli Pizza Burger w/fries	4.50
Wendy Wild Mushroom Burger w/day-glo fries	4.50
Christian Chili Burger w/fries	4.75
Kim Davis Triple-Decker Club Sandwich	4.25
Dale Ashmun Grilled Cheese Sandwich Swiss or Cheddar w/fries	3.00
Grilled Cheese w/tomatoes a la Bellomo	3.25
Lillig's Grilled Cheese w/bacon or ham	3.75
Katy K's BLT w/fries	3.75
Ira Abromovitz Tuna Salad Sandwich	3.50

SHAUN SALADS

Trojan Womens' Caesar Salad	$3.50
Salad Nicoise aux Bikini Girl	4.75
Bishop John's Chefs Salad Supreme	5.25
John Sex Hot Chilly Salad	4.75

LADIES AUXILIARY BAKE-OFF

Billy Harris' Carrot Cake	$2.00
Frankie Lymon's Nephew's Chocolate Cake w/fresh whipped cream a la Miss April 1963	2.50
Playboy Bunny Cheesecake du jour	2.50
Hot Apple Kai Pie w/fresh whipped cream	2.25
Lina HaagenDaszovich Chocolate, Vanilla or Strawberry	2.25
Ande Whyland Rice Pudding	2.00

5700 CLUB BEVERAGES

Tea, American Coffee, Sanka Jean Caffeine	$ .75
Pulasllama before (Carafe of Whine)	6.00
Pulsallama after (½ Carafe of Whine)	4.00
Glass of Sleazoid Whine	2.00
Alien Comic Cold or Hot Apple Cider	1.50
Tina Peel Milk Shakes & Malteds	2.90

Contents

A number of recent Museum of Modern Art exhibitions, such as the *Looking at Music* series (2008–11) and *Making Music Modern: Design for Ear and Eye* (2014–15), have explored the interplay of avant-garde and popular cultures across artistic disciplines, including music, design, and film. *Club 57: Film, Performance, and Art in the East Village, 1978–1983*, which examines the legacy of the seminal East Village artists' club, resumes this investigation. Yet the groundbreaking *Club 57* is distinguished by the collections initiative at its center, made even more essential by the Museum's 2019 renovation and expansion project, which has spurred staff across departments to reflect collectively on the institution's holdings.

As this volume attests, the exhibition takes an archival approach, with Club 57 as a historical case study through which to assess the New York City downtown arts scene in the late 1970s and early 1980s. *Club 57* celebrates the period's moving image culture, including its vibrant practice of small-gauge filmmaking (recalling our late colleague Jytte Jensen's influential film exhibition of 1998–99, *Big as Life: An American History of 8mm Films*), and chronicles the transition from film to early analog video. Thanks to the visionary support of the Committee on Film and Contemporary Arts Council, acquisitions of nearly one hundred Super 8, 8mm, 16mm, and video works bolster the exhibition's scope. The world-class Department of Film's preservation program and David Booth Conservation Department's media conservation team have digitized these outmoded formats for display in the galleries and projection in the related film series, and have also assured their long-term preservation. For many of these little-known but significant works, the Museum's preservation initiative was their first point of institutional contact, securing their accessibility for future scholarship and exhibition.

Club 57 has likewise relied on the acquisition of flyers, zines, animation process art, and other printed matter by the Department of Film Special Collections, the result namely of Curator Ron Magliozzi's career-spanning accomplishments in collections research and development. In recovering these ephemeral traces of artistic production, Magliozzi and Assistant Curator Sophie Cavoulacos have set the stage for a new generation of scholars to discover and study this rich period through the Celeste Bartos International Film Study Center. I thank them both for their exceptional scholarship and skilled organization of this complex exhibition and catalogue.

Club 57 reflects on the collaborative nature of artistic production across mediums during a period that is today considered to have played an essential role in establishing the modes and motifs of contemporary art. In light of this, it is especially rewarding to read essays in this catalogue by my esteemed colleagues Laura Hoptman, Curator, Department of Painting and Sculpture; Lucy Gallun, Assistant Curator, Department of Photography; and Jenny Schlenzka, formerly Associate Curator, MoMA PS1. I thank them, as well as writer J. Hoberman and guest curator Ann Magnuson, for their insightful contributions.

This exhibition brings together film, video, photography, performance, and painting, alongside print, sculpture, drawing, fashion, and artists' books, and I thank the artists and lenders who parted with artworks in their personal collections to make *Club 57* a revelation for our audiences. The hybridity of these works, along with the broad cross section of artists who produced them, is evidence of how social bonds inform and support art-making and viewing in crucial ways. The Museum's engagement with the local artist community has always been essential to our vision, not least through our vibrant dialogues with MoMA PS1, formerly P.S. 1, which was among the first venues to invite Club 57 artists to expand their reach. The legacies of Club 57 and P.S. 1 alike remind us that artists remain the Museum's first interlocutors.

Above all, I wish to extend my deep gratitude to the Keith Haring Foundation for their boundless support of this exhibition; I could not imagine a more meaningful partner in this endeavor.

Glenn D. Lowry, Director
The Museum of Modern Art

The making of *Club 57: Film, Performance, and Art in the East Village, 1978–1983* was a deeply collaborative endeavor. The web of artists and artist estates, who, over the course of several years, acted as generous and patient interlocutors, is central to the exhibition's success. In part through a series of oral history interviews recorded at the Museum, these former club participants have shed new light on the downtown scene and its experimentation with the era's mediums, recounting their own personal histories and giving voice to the artists and friends no longer with us.

Our journey alongside the East Village artistic community was an incredibly rewarding process of discovery. Each artist met the project with enthusiasm and support, and led us to other individuals across the disciplines of film, video, music, performance, visual art, zine-making, theater, and fashion. Stanley Strychacki, whose infectious joie de vivre and commitment to creative freedom led to Club 57's formation in 1978, was an essential, passionate supporter. We are also deeply indebted to Ann Magnuson, performance artist and one of Club 57's earliest programmers, who joined our team as a guest curator; her guidance was crucial throughout the exhibition's earliest stages, and it is on account of her that the project is as thorough and inclusive as the subject merits. Moreover, this exhibition would not have existed without John "Lypsinka" Epperson, whose conversations with Curator Ron Magliozzi in 2013 about drag performance in cinema, and Epperson's own drag debut at the venue, were the genesis of *Club 57*. We thank him for his singular perspective on movie-going at the club, expressed in the film series *You Are Now One of Us: Film at Club 57*, for which he is guest curator. Our film programming efforts are equally beholden to Susan Hannaford and Tom Scully, who, as early curators at Club 57, envisioned the space as an alternative screening venue. Within the film series *New York Film and Video: No Wave/Transgressive*, we are grateful to Tessa Hughes-Freeland for bringing to two of its screenings the discerning curatorship she displayed first at Club 57 and later at New York Film Festival Downtown. For our third film series, we are indebted to our colleagues at British Film Institute (William Fowler, Curator of Artists' Moving Image) and LUX (Matt Carter, Head of Distribution), with whom we collaborated to bring to New York the touring program *This Is Now: Film and Video after Punk 1978–1985*; its exploration of British club culture and avant-garde media serves as a vital and pleasing counterpoint to our investigations. The exhibition is likewise enriched by a program of performance and live events, still in formation at the time of writing. Even so, it is not too early to express our deepest appreciation to Marc Shaiman and Scott Wittman for agreeing to bring Club 57 to life with a performance at the Museum, and to all of the artists who will participate in the live programming, animating the galleries with the spirit of the club.

We are profoundly grateful to the artists, artist estates, and downtown alumni who have generously parted with works in their collections—both their own artworks and those exchanged with peers in the club era—so that we could share them with a wider public in our galleries. We are proud to have been able to assemble a checklist true to the venue's spirit. It is likewise a privilege to exhibit works that have not been shown publicly since the 1980s, as is the case for the majority on display. We warmly thank lenders Daniel Abraham, John Ahearn, Joey Arias, Donald Baechler, Ellen Berkenblit, Lina Bertucci, Fred Brathwaite (Fab 5 Freddy), Jef Bretschneider, Paul Bridgewater, Kitty Brophy, Robert Carrithers, Stefano Castronovo, Scott Covert, Parker Dulany, the Estate of Katherine Dumas, Daniel Durning, Patrick Fox, Henny Garfunkel, George Haas, the Keith Haring Foundation, Courtney Harmel, Bill Harris, Robert Hawkins, Frank Holliday, Peter Hristoff, M. Henry Jones, Katy K, Brant Kingman, Margaret Lanzetta, Marcus Leatherdale, Ann Magnuson, Eric Marciano, Natalya Maystrenko, Richard McGuire, John A. Mozzer, April Palmieri, Trix Rosen, John Rosis, Oliver and Min Sanchez, Robin Schanzenbach, Kenny Scharf, Anthony Scibelli, the Estate of Carlo Pittore, Jonathan Quinn, the Estate of Nelson Sullivan, Sur Rodney (Sur), Joseph Szkodzinski, Tabboo! (Stephen Tashjian), Bruno Testore Schmidt, Muna Tseng and the Estate of Tseng Kwong Chi, the Arturo Vega Foundation, Harvey Wang, Ande Whyland, and Christina Yuin.

We also acknowledge private lenders Irene Albright, Roger Cardinal, Lenny Kisko, and the Mugrabi Collection for the generous loans from their holdings. Securing loans from School of Visual Arts both bolstered our checklist and imbued it with special significance, the school having been a meeting place and site for experimental education for so many Club 57 artists; thanks are due to Gunars Prande at SVA for his assistance. We are furthermore appreciative of our colleagues at Alexander and Bonin (Kathryn Gile, Sabina Roslyakova), Anton Kern Gallery (Kristen Smoragiewicz, Amanda Singer, Grace Lerner), Gordon Robichaux (Sam Gordon and Jacob Robichaux), Honor Fraser (Corrina Peipon, Laura Watts, Jazmine Rivera), International Artists Manifest (Sarah Bouchard), and Martos Gallery (Ebony L. Haynes and Brooke Latham) for coordinating loans. We finally thank the studios, archives, and individual lenders who shared often-rare material with our film series; a complete account of these lenders will figure into the online program notes accompanying the screenings.

More than half of the exhibition was sourced from the Museum's collection, a result of the Department of Film's active moving image and documentation acquisitions over the past several years. This major archival initiative was made possible through the unfaltering support and enduring faith of Rajendra Roy, The Celeste Bartos Chief Curator of Film, the Committee on Film, chaired by the esteemed Ted Sann, and the Contemporary Arts Council. Thanks to their vision and active championship, the Museum has established a growing archive of materials related to Club 57 and its allied downtown venues, assuring the preservation and future study of New York's alternative art scene. This catalogue's filmography (page 177) includes all of the moving image work brought into the Museum's collection, along with other key titles from the period; the volume also includes a sample of period ephemera newly acquired to the collection.

We are grateful to the filmmakers, artists, performers, and downtown alumni who trusted us with their archives, and thus their legacies, and thank them for the cherished conversations. At the time of publication, acquisitions include film, video, and/or documentation from Stanley Strychacki, Frank Holliday, Dale Ashmun, Peter Kwaloff (Sun PK), Lisa Baumgardner, Kenny Scharf, Chris Gremski, Bill Doherty, Shawn "AMMO" McQuate, Tabboo! (Stephen Tashjian), Kestutis Nakas, Michael Oblowitz, Barry Shils, Eric Marciano, Esther Regelson, Anney Bonney, John Ahearn, Sur Rodney (Sur), Jonathan Quinn, M. Henry Jones, Stacey Elkin, Merrill Aldighieri, Harald Vogl, Jimmy Murray, George Haas, Julius Klein, Bill Harris, Jennifer T. Ley, Tessie Chua, Paul Dougherty, Alexa Hunter, Patti Astor, Steve Doughton, Joe Lewis, Frank Henenlotter, Glenn Andreiev, Jeorgia Anderson, Mykel Board, Linus Brant, Jean Caffeine, Rich Colicchio, David Schmidlapp, Paul Shapiro, Marlene Weisman, Animal X, Peter Zaremba, Scott Wittman, Melanie Monios, Kjeld Hylfelt, and Richard McGuire.

We must also thank all the individuals who shared their time, insights, and expertise with the project at various stages. Their contributions guided our development of both the exhibition and catalogue, allowing us to capture in detail the vibrancy of this singular community of artists. We extend our gratitude to Lary 7, Ira Abramowitz, Leonard Abrams, Charlie Ahearn, Joey Ahlbum, Lisa Altamore, Stuart Argabright, Larry Ashton, Beth B, Scott B, Jerry Beck, Snooky Bellomo, Tish Bellomo, Daniel Berglund, Karon Bihari, Richard Boch, Perry Brandston, Meg Brazill, Nancy Breslow, Amy Chaiklin, Christopher Chambers, Mike Colasuonno and Judy Nazemetz, Chris Cole, Jan Collins, William Coupon, Robin Crutchfield, Kimberly Davis, Edit DeAk, Jeffrey Deitch, Daria Deshuk, Vivienne Dick, Ray Dobbins, Gordon Edelstein, Steven Effinger, Kai Eric, Martha Fishkin, Coleen Fitzgibbon, Richard Flood, Jean Foos, Tony Frere, Simone Gad, Rodney Alan Greenblat, Andrew Gurian, Julie Hair, Richard Hambleton, Duncan Hannah, John Harris, Ula Hedwig, Tony Heiberg, John Held Jr., John Heys, Bob Holman, Michael Holman, AleXander Hirka, Holly Hughes, Pat Ivers and Emily Armstrong, Angela Jaeger, David Javelosa, John Jesurun, Dany Johnson, Christian Joiris, Tom Judson, Brian Kelly and Heather Spore-Kelly, Laura Kenyon, Richard Kern, Raghubir (Nancy) Kintisch, George Kirkikis, Chris Kraus, Jill Kroesen; Boris Kwaloff, Marc Waldman, Carol Pernelli, Susan Keane, Julia Deptula, and the entire Kwaloff circle; Art Labriola, Majka Lamprecht, Tom Langton, Beth Lapides, Zoe Leonard, Diana Lillig, Barbara London, Maripol, Steve Mass, Barry Masterson, Samantha McEwen, Peter McGough, Nancy McLoughlin, Mundy McLaughlin, Jeff McMahon, Larry Meltzer, Tim Miller, Eric Mitchell, Marjan Moghaddam, Alan Moore, Lori Montana, John Monteleone, Barbara Moore, Richard Murphet, Chuck Nanney, James Nares, Valery Oisteanu, Deb O'Nair, Deb Parker, Man Parrish, Robert Patrick, Clayton Patterson, Uzi Parnes, Cara Pearlman, Kembra Pfahler, Amos Poe, Rudi Protrudi, Howie Pyro, Blair Rainey, Naomi Walker Regelson, David Richardson, Christian Roebling, Robert Romagnoli, Lauren Rosati, Kathy Ruttenberg, Jim Self, Marc Shaiman, Frank Shifreen, Gregory Sholette, Amy Sillman, Charlotte Slivka, Peter Nolan Smith, Ryan Silveira, Robert Starkoff, Alan Steinfeld, Drew Straub, Betsy Sussler, Richard Toonkel, Michael von Uchtrup, Michael Wilk, Jonathan Williams, and Scott Wittman. Tim Lawrence, along with his book *Life and Death on the New York Dance Floor, 1980–1983* was a trusted companion during our research.

We are likewise indebted to colleagues at fellow institutions, and recognize first and foremost Marvin J. Taylor and his team at New York University's Fales Library & Special Collections for their pioneering scholarship and holdings on the downtown scene; our project greatly benefited from their work. Collections at New York Public Library for the Performing Arts were equally valuable. Julia Gruen, Anna Gurton-Wachter, and Annelise Ream at the Keith Haring Foundation were superlative supporters, and we thank them for the unforgettable experience of consulting Haring's archives in his final studio space, which today houses the foundation. Jane Friedman and Ted Riederer at Howl! Happening/the Arturo Vega Foundation offered encouragement in the form of spirited downtown programming. Maria Ilario, Ray Johnson Estate, Mark Manivong, Rare Book and Special Collections Division, Library of Congress, Stacy Szymaszek, Director, the Poetry Project, and Lois White, Getty Research Library, were all of great assistance.

Many esteemed collaborators were indispensable to the realization of this ambitious catalogue. We are profoundly grateful to writers Laura Hoptman, Curator, Department of Painting and Sculpture; Lucy Gallun, Assistant Curator, Department of Photography; and Jenny Schlenzka, former Associate Curator at MoMA PS1, for lending their time and expertise to this volume. Their contributions and collegial support enabled us to mirror Club 57's interdisciplinary spirit in the catalogue. J. Hoberman and Ann Magnuson each shared their unique perspectives, and we are most grateful for their terrific essays. In the Museum's Department of Publications, we offer thanks to Christopher Hudson, Publisher; David Frankel, former Editorial Director; Don McMahon, Editorial Director; Charles Kim, Associate Publisher; Marc Sapir, Production Director; Hannah Kim, Senior Marketing and Production Coordinator; and Doyin Samuel, Rights Coordinator. We are moreover appreciative of Matthew Pimm, Production Manager, and Emily Hall, Editor, for their skillful and patient shepherding of the book project. The book design, by Geoff Kaplan, perceptively and handsomely captures the essence of our project. The completion and success of the catalogue are due entirely to the talents of indefatigable text editor Sarah Resnick, who worked thoughtfully and meticulously with each writer and displayed grace under brutal deadlines. We were fortunate to have her as such a generous and dedicated interlocutor. Finally, we thank all those who contributed images to this volume, many of which are being reproduced for the first time.

This exhibition has involved every department across The Museum of Modern Art. Our deepest thanks go to Glenn D. Lowry, Director, through whose support and encouragement the exhibition has thrived. We are grateful to Kathy Halbreich, Associate Director and Laurenz Foundation Curator; Ramona Bronkar Bannayan, Senior Deputy Director, Exhibitions and Collections; and Peter Reed, Senior Deputy Director, Curatorial Affairs, all of whose guidance was essential in shaping and strengthening the exhibition. We have been fortunate for the backing of James Gara, Chief Operating Officer, and Todd Bishop, Senior Deputy Director, External Affairs, in assuring the successful execution of the project. The exhibition was notably enriched by thoughtful exchanges with Stuart Comer, Chief Curator, Media & Performance Art, and Peter Eleey, Chief Curator, MoMA PS1, particularly in considering the special history of P.S. 1 as a springboard for Club 57 artists.

Addressing the particularities and challenges of underground artwork and archives called on the superlative talents of our conservator colleagues. Erika Mosier, Paper Conservator, Roger Griffith, Associate Sculpture Conservator, and Michael Duffy, Paintings Conservator, lent their expertise in this regard. The preservation of more than one hundred recently acquired film and video works was undertaken with aplomb and great skill by Peter Williamson, Film Conservator; Katie Trainor, Film Collection Manager; and Peter Oleksik, Associate Media Conservator.

The exhibition's planning benefited from the abilities and thoughtful oversight of Chloe Capewell, Jaclyn Verbitski, Erik Patton, and Lizzie Gorfaine, in the Department of Exhibition Planning & Administration. Deputy General Counsel Nancy Adelson and Associate General Counsel Alexis Sandler offered guidance on the project's many complexities. In Collection Management and Exhibition Registration, Regan Hillman deftly coordinated our many loans, while the art handling team, led by Rob Jung and Sarah Wood, skillfully worked with us to install the show.

The exhibition's design emerged from a collaboration with our inspiring colleagues Lana Hum, Matthew Cox, and Peter Perez in Exhibition Design & Production; Aaron Louis, Aaron Harrow, Mike Gibbons, and Tal Marks, in Audio Visual; Claire Corey, Eva Bochem-Shur, and Damien Saatdjian, in Advertising and Graphic Design. The Imaging and Visual Resources team brilliantly imaged recent acquisitions, including many of the works that appear in this volume; our gratitude goes to Robert Kastler, Roberto Rivera, and John Wronn. The exhibition was enriched by research in the Museum Archives and Library. We thank Chief of Archives, Library, and Research Collections Michelle Elligott, along with colleagues Michelle Harvey and Lissie Thomas; Jennifer Tobias and Nathaniel Otting enthusiastically supported our archival discoveries in the Library's rich artist files.

A great many colleagues contributed to making our vision a reality and sharing it with varied audiences. In Development, our thanks go to Bobby Kean, Claire Huddleston Seifert, Genevieve Allen, Hillary Reeves; in Communications and Marketing, to Sara Beth Walsh, Rebecca Stokes, Victor Samra, Cortney Cleveland; in Special Events and Affiliate Programs, to Maggie Lyko, Jessie Cappello, Courtney Schaefer. In Retail, we thank Norman Laurila, Karen Hernandez, and Chay Costello. In Education, we extend our gratitude to Wendy Woon, Pablo Helguera, Sara Bodinson, Jess Van Nostrand, and Calder Zwicky.

We are grateful to the resourceful and enthusiastic Studio Museum in Harlem/MoMA Fellows Dessane Cassell and Adeze Wilford, who made significant contributions to the organization of the exhibition, and the interns who supported us in researching and organizing over several years: Emily Cohn, Jessica Fletcher, Manuel Goetz, James Widdicombe, and Brian Block. Department Assistant Brittany Shaw joined the department midway through the project and has brought crucial support and grace to our small team. Finally, the exhibition benefited from the company of our inestimable colleagues in the Department of Film: Sean Egan, Andy Haas, Pierre Vaz, Carson Parish, Ashley Swinnerton, Josh Siegel, Dave Kehr, Anne Morra, La Frances Hui, Kitty Cleary, Nancy Lukacinsky, James Layton, Thelma Ross, and Theo Harrison.

Ron Magliozzi, Curator, Department of Film
Sophie Cavoulacos, Assistant Curator, Department of Film

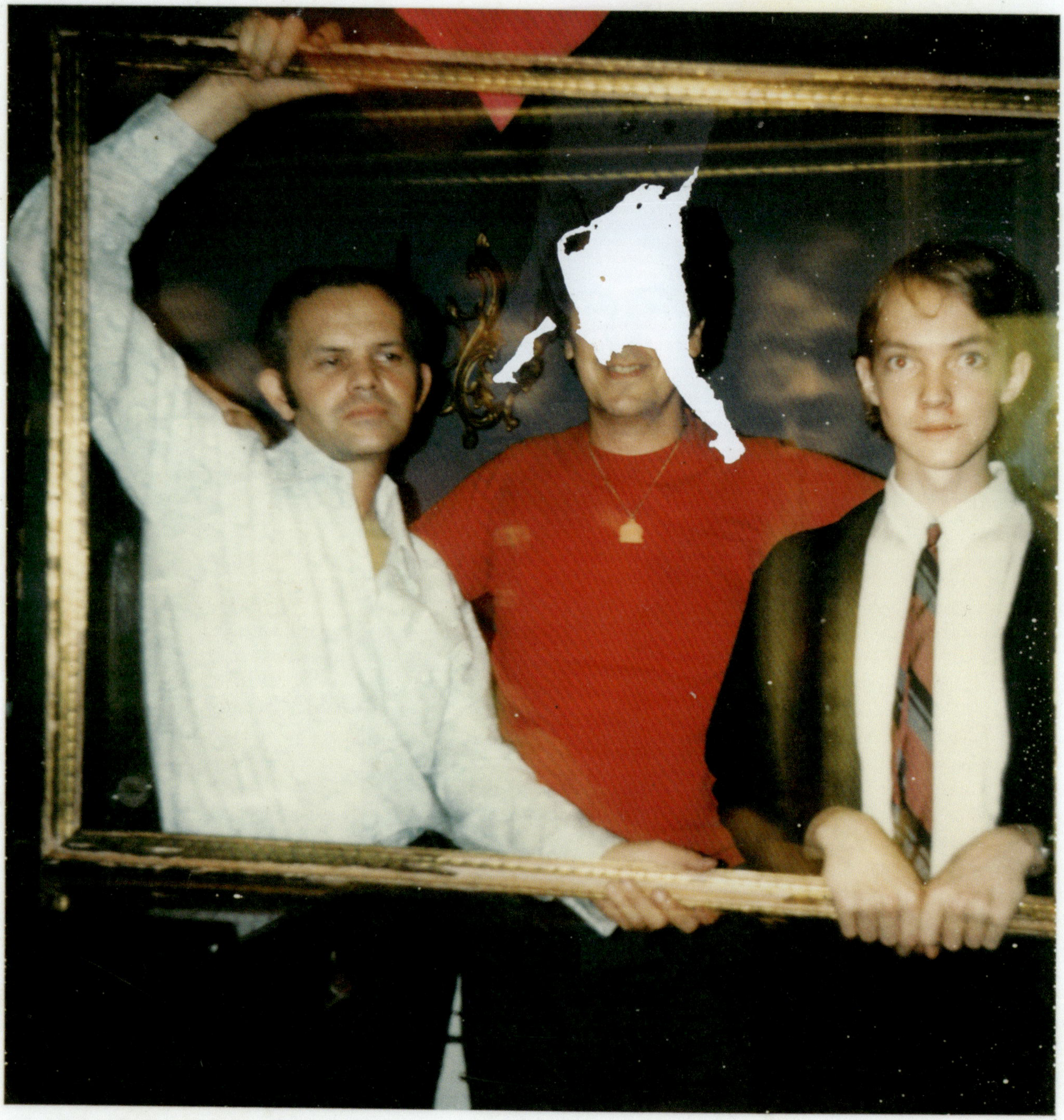

1. Stanley Strychacki, Robert Patrick, and painter Wally Edwards during the run of Patrick's *Kennedy's Children* at Club 57, June and July 1979. Unknown photographer.
The Robert Patrick Papers, T-Mss 1978-006. Billy Rose Theatre Division, the New York Public Library for the Performing Arts

Art Is What You Make It: CLUB 57 AND THE DOWNTOWN SCENE

Ron Magliozzi

We grow like trees amidst skyscrapers, not in one place but everywhere, hyper-hybridized not in one direction but equally upward and downward and inward and outward . . . we are no longer free to do only one thing, to be one particular thing.[1]
—Nicolas A. Moufarrege

A neighborhood club . . . shouldn't be anything bigger. It should always be there as some sort of funky weird thing. Ann, Susan, and I wanted to create a new art movement in New York . . . we were successful in creating a club for young artists to hang out in.[6]
—Tom Scully

In the late 1970s, New York City's downtown neighborhoods, including the East Village and Lower East Side, formed a fertile artistic environment and a new frontier for change in the social order. The area's tenement district had become a home to the disaffected from suburban America and Europe alike, looking to escape youthful boredom and do their own thing. These artists and artist wannabees, many of them graduates of the city's School of Visual Arts, found in the low-rent, off-the-grid environment opportunities for risk-free, creative expression. "It was a fascinating place—bankrupt, dangerous, run-down, and I loved it for that," recalls transplanted French scholar Sylvère Lotringer. "Shunned by the rest of America, New York radiated creativity and energy from afar."[2]

The downtown scene nurtured a community of alternative organizations that included clubs, artist collectives, theaters, and archives. The neighborhood's unregulated environment provided a context for art that was "more lively" and "more ritualistic than academic," as Rhys Chatham, director of performance space the Kitchen noted in 1980.[3] Performer Eric Bogosian explained the scene as having arisen on account of something more elemental: "The atmosphere is one of NEEDS: artists *need* new spaces which are congruent with the societal sources of their work. In turn, the new spaces themselves galvanize a *need* for new works, to be *used*, to function socially."[4] The people who were making work, the kinds of work they were making, and how these works were seen and heard—each was shaped by the city's influential club scene and its peer organizations.

Between 1978 and early 1983, Club 57, located in the basement of a church on St. Marks Place, joined other upstart clubs in challenging the practices of art, performance, and film as they were being presented in uptown museums and SoHo galleries. The club's busy mix of socializing and interdisciplinary art-making played an essential role in the creative life of this downtown scene. Its exceptional combination of young artists and their followers made the club a forum for questioning American values, gender politics, the mass media, and sexual identity. Although critics observed as early as 1983 that the spirit of the collective endeavor in which Club 57 took part was often more significant than the art it showcased,[5] the impact of the club goers' efforts would for some prove career defining. For many more, the club was a source of empowerment, steadying them to confront the crisis of AIDS that would soon enough bring the fun to an end.

Stanley Strychacki (fig. 1) first considered the space he ran in the church basement at 57 St. Marks a student social club, until in early 1978 he began renting it out as "Club 57" to garage bands and way-off-Broadway theater companies for five to twenty dollars a night. Roughly a decade older than the club members who would take over 57's management a year later, Strychacki superintended his "little" club like a benevolent parent.[7] With the support of his mother, with whom he'd moved from Poland in 1972, hominess became a lasting marker of Club 57, distinguishing the venue from rivals such as Mudd Club, which seemed elitist by comparison.[8] Writing in May of the club's first year, after attending a double bill with bands the Zantees and the Fleshtones, the music critic for *New York Rocker* enthused, "When was the last time you were hugged by anyone at Max's or CBGB's, let alone the bartender?"[9]

Hosting entertainment for the young generated its share of noise and sanitation issues,[10] irking the neighborhood's aging immigrant population, who were gradually being displaced. "The old Ukrainian and Polish people hated us,"[11] former club goer Shawn McQuate later remarked. Locals posted their complaints on the street, covering over wheat-pasted rock flyers, and frequently called the police. A disgruntled neighbor recalled how, if club goers were out late at night, he "would pour industrial-grade ammonia on the steps right behind them and start cleaning."[12] Strychacki was also forced to contend with the irreverent nature of club life as it occurred in a functioning church, with club goers occasionally performing antics like hanging raw meat over the front gates. Although these issues would never cease to trouble him, Strychacki was at the time on the lookout for something different.

In November 1978, recent School of Visual Arts graduates Susan Hannaford and Tom Scully, with the help of Ann Magnuson, organized the six-night variety show New Wave Vaudeville at Irving Plaza, which Strychacki also happened to manage. Hannaford and Scully had selected talent from the East Village's growing community of fledgling entertainers, culling the list "along the lines of Dadaism," according to Scully: "Anything that had the label of art—we wanted it. . . . We wanted to give it a slight slant, though."[13] Other cast and crew members essential to the show's success included Frank Holliday and Andy Rees, who, along with Hannaford, Scully, and Magnuson, would shape the future of Club 57.

New Wave Vaudeville's final program was an uncensored display of amateurism and low-budget inventiveness distinguished by strains of feminism and male burlesque that were singled out by reviewers in the downtown press: Tessie Chua and Gedde Watanabe's drag performance in which "a Catholic schoolgirl [is] systematically beaten by the pious sister Teresa for her vanity and impurity"; Annie Hickman, aka "Lady Bug," with a fluffy pink puppet on her arm demonstrating "perfectly controlled dance involving splits and twists without once losing her erotic posture"; a striptease by David McDermott to the music of Irving Berlin's standard "A Pretty Girl Is Like a Melody," for which he sang the altered lyric "A pretty boy is just like a pretty girl";[14] and Klaus Nomi's breakout number as an opera-singing alien creature of questionable gender, "the most effective piece of the night and the most disciplined."[15] The show's satiric roots in American popular culture, and its tendency

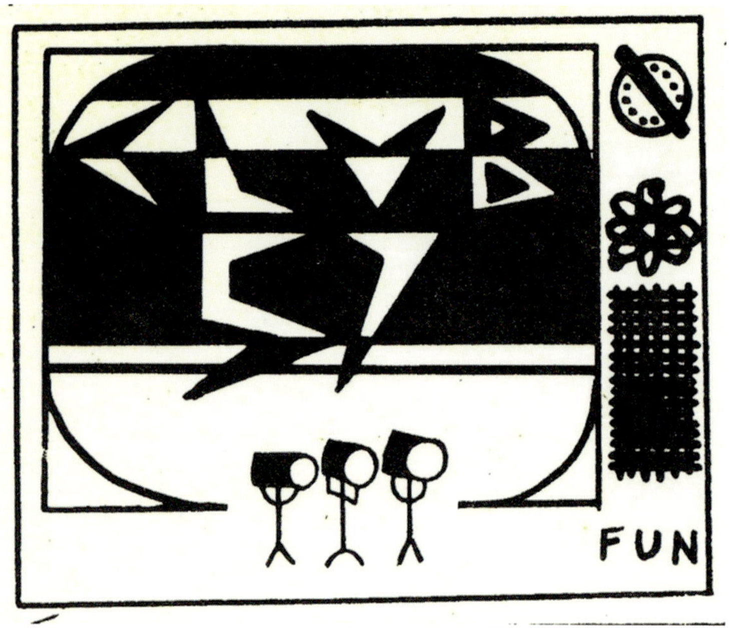

2. Club 57 logo designed by Kenny Scharf, 1979. Collection the artist. Strychacki had also designed a logo, in a font modeled on the *New York Times* masthead. (See page 1.) Meant to represent his concert series at 17 Irving Plaza as well as at 57 St. Marks, the pseudo-military badge was punk enough to look cool on shirts and jackets, but failed to reflect the nature of the pop-cult activities at the small club as well as Scharf's did.

toward self-parody, differentiated it from earlier downtown work "sanctified by artistic pretensions."[16] All of these characteristics would soon come to influence activities at the club.

At Strychacki's invitation, this formula of fun and subversion migrated to Club 57, as Hannaford, Holliday, Magnuson, Rees, and Scully began pitching in at the basement venue in January 1979. Hannaford and Scully quickly assumed responsibility for the film program,[17] while Magnuson presided over performance work.[18] What 57 St. Marks Place became after New Wave Vaudeville has been described by habitués as a mash-up of *Our Gang* comedy, "Let's put on a show" musical theater, Dada's Cabaret Voltaire, and a suburban living room,[19] and was pronounced in retrospect "the harbinger of the East Village club scene."[20] A five-dollar membership fee, instituted the following October to skirt an absent liquor license, retained the name's double meaning as both night club and social organization.

Notably, Hannaford and Scully were graduates of the nearby School of Visual Arts, as were a number of the club's earliest and most active participants; those who at the time of Strychacki's invitation had either recently left or were still enrolled included Frank Holliday, Bruno Testore Schmidt, John Sex, April Palmieri, M. Henry Jones, Peter Kwaloff, and Peter Hristoff. The club offered them an off-campus space to exercise the interdisciplinary interests that their SVA education had allowed them to explore and to show off their sharpened skills, knowledge of art history, and taste for visual wit.[21] When Holliday hung his 1979 painting *TVC15* (pages 54–55) behind the bar (where Jean-Michel Basquiat would later hang one as well, page 131), he could be confident that his art-savvy friends would appreciate its reference to a David Bowie song and the irony of its out-of-place minimalism in the kitsch setting of the club.[22] Artists Keith Haring and Kenny Scharf (fig. 2), who began attending club events in the summer of 1979, were also SVA students, and the two would soon join forces to organize video screenings, while Haring alone would take on organizing exhibitions of visual art.

Haring's interdisciplinary and egalitarian approaches to art-marking, and his multidirectional, unrestrained need to create, informed his curatorial discretion and are on the whole emblematic of the Club 57 ethos.[23] A contemporaneous autobiographical document he produced as a student includes a list of his obsessions: "MAKING video tapes audio tape experiments for multiple cassettes paintings performances writing video performance poetry reading dance film ideas sculpture ALL THESE FLOWING OUT IN EVERY DAY DIFFERENT."[24] The exhibitions he curated at the club expressed this same spirit of equal opportunity. An early invitational show he organized[25] promised an "unforgettable East Village event" with "a diverse group of artists: painters, poets, dancers, musicians, sculptors, photographers, designers, writers, filmmakers, etc."[26] Experimentation across mediums did not belong to Haring alone: primarily identified as performers, McQuate and Gerard Little were also designers; Little was also a sculptor (fig. 3).[27] John Sex, for example, was both performer and prolific silkscreen artist (pages 43–46), while Stephen Tashjian and Peter Kwaloff were both performers and painters (pages 58–59; 121). For club members, Club 57 became a place where they could define themselves as artists, spurred by the uncensored feedback of their peers.

Within a year of the New Wave Vaudeville team's arrival at Club 57, a kind of close-knit celebrity had emerged, as memorialized in artist Daniel Abraham's perceptive caricatures, *57 Drawings* (pages 150–51). By the time of their March 1980 exhibition, the club had developed a manic style of programming across a range of mediums that most resembled the daily changes in genre and audience seen in repertory cinemas of the period. Programming peaked in October 1980, when Haring's one-night exhibition *Anonymous Art* (page 127, fig. 3) and John Sex's Groovy Dada Lounge presents Acts of Live Art converged on a single day, summing up the club's curatorial initiatives. Upholding his belief that "'art' [is] a way of looking at things: not necessarily inherent in the things themselves," Haring displayed "street finds and propaganda by authors unknown."[28] For Sex and performance curator Magnuson, the evening merged all the elements of club members' talents into a single event with murals and graffiti, satirical and gender-based performances, fashion, dance, music, a sound installation, and even a light show.[29]

After Magnuson retired as manager in the fall of 1980, the club went through a series of managers—Dale Ashmun (who acted as manager briefly for some weeks in the summer of 1980, before Ann's official departure), Andy Rees, Tom Scully, and Kai Eric—before settling on its final management team of Pennsylvania-raised Ira Abramowitz and Belgian expatriate Christian Joiris.[30] Abramowitz was an aspiring performance artist known to appear on the East Village streets as an Adolf Hitler look-alike, provoking the local immigrant population and embarrassing club friends, and on the stage as Mendel the Rappin' Rabbi and Hasid Rocker in grotesque drag that exaggerated his Jewish heritage. Joiris, meanwhile, had been schooled in architecture and

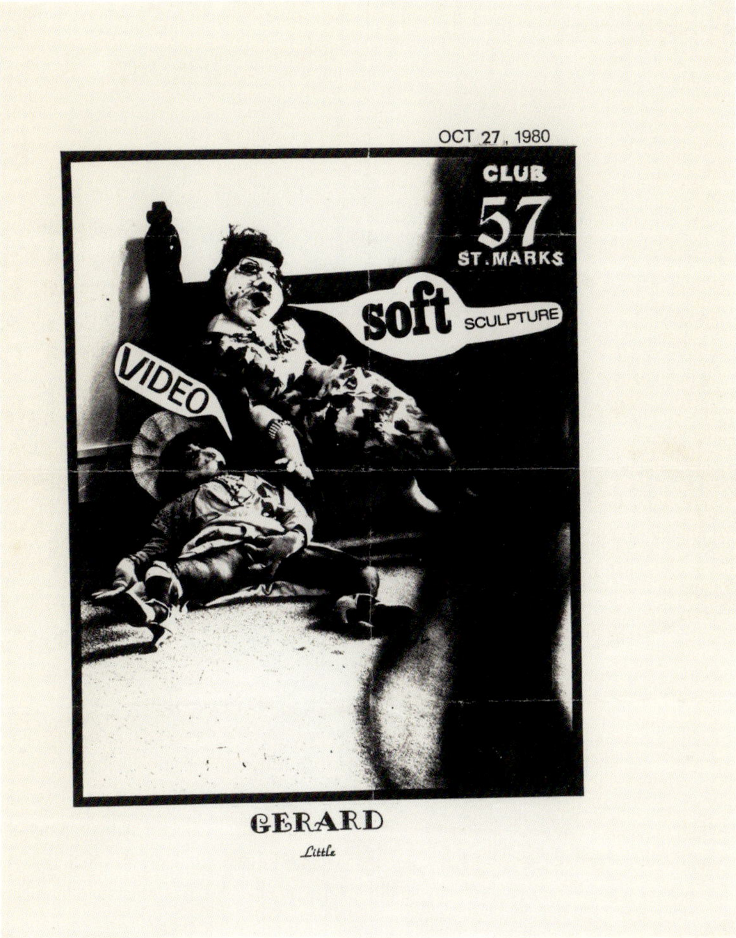

3. Flyer for Gerard Little's Soft Sculpture exhibition at Club 57, 1980. Design by Little. The Museum of Modern Art, New York. Department of Film Special Collections

the visual arts at the Institut supérieur des arts décoratifs in Brussels.[31] Together, he and Abramowitz continued to twist those same high-and-low performance threads into knots at the club. Joiris, for example, arranged for more experimentally conceived events, such as Poetes de l'invisible, Nude Theology, Club 57 Performance Expo (planned for video exhibition in Europe), and his own conceptual piece, *Evasion*, while Abramowitz organized bawdy entertainment programs, the likes of Vamps: The Art of Seductive Performing, Chateau 57: An Evening of Bondage Comedy, and Needle Jones + Perry Homo's Sleaze Review.

Club 57 was a model alternative to what critic Craig Owens described at the time as a nexus of studios, galleries, museums, and art press that ruled the New York art world.[32] Although it was said of downtown clubs that "nobody really thought about getting paid or selling work [because] it was about making work [and] being human,"[33] personal ambition remained important, and club members regularly invited curators from uptown museums and solicited press coverage. Several artists working seriously in visual mediums would soon see gallerist Tony Shafrazi, as well as collectors Donald and Mera Rubell and Jeffrey Deitch, take interest in their work.[34] For club members working in performance, many of whom had cultivated a repertoire of signature characters and thematic performance material the equal of *Saturday Night Live*, their success would spread first to other downtown clubs and then on to more prestigious venues, such as the Kitchen and the Whitney Museum of American Art.[35] Klaus Nomi and Joey Arias's No Wave fashion and robotic Dynamation[36] dance (which predated Michael Jackson's moonwalk), landed them a backup gig with David Bowie on *Saturday Night Live* in November 1979, and roles as alien "Jägerdudes" in a high-profile print campaign by the US importer of the German Jägermeister liquor.[37] In 1982, Magnuson united "the talents of performers on the nightclub circuit and those in the performance art world"[38] for her *Performance Rites* series at P.S. 1 and would later exorcize a gallery of the media-generated female characters that she'd mastered at Club 57 theme nights in *Made for TV* (1984) (pages 62–63), produced in collaboration with gay videographer Tom Rubnitz and with the support of Club 57 regulars William Fleet Lively and Gerard Little. By the time the club closed in 1983, those with careers in mind—Haring, Magnuson, Scharf, Joey Arias, John Epperson, Marc Shaiman, and Scott Wittman—had already begun making them.[39]

Reagan was elected commander in chief, Iran grabbed some hostages and we ran out of petroleum . . . if a movie star could be president then politics was performances.[40]
—Anthony Scibelli

Things happen to you, sickness, birth, death, war. These things are reality . . . but I don't think they are important really. What is important is the things we invent.[41]
—Anders Grafstrom

The group's closest antecedent, beyond the debt they owed to Dadaism and Surrealism, was the Detroit art collective Destroy All Monsters (1973–77),[42] whose members Mike Kelley, Jim Shaw, Niagara, and Cary Loren drew their inspiration from suburban angst, American deviance, religious irreverence, shape-shifting sci-fi creatures, and the alternative trinity of Andy Warhol, Jack Smith, and William S. Burroughs, just as their 1980s brethren would. The neglect-ravaged and abandoned setting of New York's East Village served as the ideal vantage from which to view mainstream America's value system and the cast of characters who had come to represent it.

George Haas's 16mm *American Shooting Series* (1979), which screened in installments over four weeks at the club (January 8–29, 1980), was inspired by the films of Rainer Werner Fassbinder. A riff on the United States' history of violence and homophobia, downtown scene-makers Haoui Montaug, Sean Cassette, and *New Yorker* cartoonist Roz Zanego starred in the series, acting in front of the simple backdrops of a photography studio the mildly erotic encounters and unsettling gunplay. The sleaze and gore films that programmer Bill Landis brought downtown from the grindhouses of the Forty-Second Street district, another still-ungentrified city neighborhood, were a rebuke of middle-class good taste. Jerry Beck's compilations Cartoons You Won't See on TV (November 15, 1979) and Television Nostomania (March 23, 1980) shed light on an entertainment history steeped in racism, sexism, and xenophobia. The suffocating nature of romantic love and the nuclear family were the subjects of Barry Shils and Ellie Nagler's 16mm *The Jones* (1977), shown at the club in 1979 and 1980, and *Love Comix* (1983), which was shot at Club 57 on video, as well as Scharf's *Radiation Family Dinner Murder* (1979), in which a dysfunctional family dining on mini-TVs is massacred. All three works were cast with performers from the club, many of whom, such as Magnuson and Joey Arias, would turn out to produce the scene's richest observations on the subject of American character.

Politics and an escalating culture of insecurity and violence added to club members' perspectives. The years 1978 and 1979 saw the Jonestown Massacre, the Three Mile Island nuclear meltdown, and the Iranian hostage crisis; the year 1980 the election of conservative president Ronald Reagan and the shooting death of John Lennon; and the year 1981 the attempts on the lives of Pope John Paul II, Reagan, and Egyptian president Anwar Sadat, the latter of which was successful.[43] For some, like club goer Carmel Johnson, "there seemed to be a definite fear of the future. People gave up on planning things."[44] For others, media coverage of current events was a trigger for social commentary. Headlines mixing political horrors and celebrity gossip on the front pages of the *New York Post* and *Daily News* became material for art projects and performances at clubs across the East Village, including at Club 57. More than thirty years later, in 2017, pertinent issues of tabloid newspapers from the period could still be found in the souvenir collections of club members like Magnuson, Kwaloff, and Kitty Brophy (see endpapers).

Creative activity at the club, for instance, responded to the Reagan presidency and its implications. Jef Bretschneider's *Shifting Borders* (1978), a six-foot-long, four-foot-wide sculptural map of the United States, each state a different colored mass of flashing Christmas lights, hung over the bar in the early fall of 1980 as a festive statement on the national debate over nuclear power, offering ironic commentary on the country's fractured electorate after Reagan's election in November.[45] Tseng Kwong Chi and Magnuson's "It's a Reagan World," a feature in a December 1980 issue of *SoHo Weekly News*, grew out of their club association and used members and occasional visitor Jack Smith (in what was likely the straightest drag of his career) as models in mock profiles of couples from middle America. Magnuson's ambitiously mounted 5700 Club (page 131) performance event in May 1981 fleshed out the spread's cast of characters, bringing biting satire of the new religious right to the club's stage. Other works reflected on the American experience from a historical perspective. Raghubir (Nancy) Kintisch's still-life paintings *Rio Grande Colorado* and *Rio Grande Gulf of Mexico* (page 65) represent the Wild West using children's color forms and animal action figures staged on a coffee table, their postmodern playfulness perfectly suited to 57's clubhouse aesthetic.

For all its focus on the American cultural landscape, race, admittedly, was less of a concern than it might have been. This can be linked in part to the makeup of early participants, who were largely a mix of white suburban kids from the New York area (Alexa Hunter, April Palmieri, John Sex, Wendy Wild), North Carolina (Frank Holliday, Andy Rees), Pennsylvania (Katy K, Drew Straub), West Virginia (Ann Magnuson), and the West Coast states (Kenny Scharf, Larry Ashton). Joining them were a handful of artists from abroad, including Brazil (Bruno Testore Schmidt), Scotland (Samantha McEwen), Italy (Stefano Castronovo), and Peru (Coco Ugaz). Although Black artists were involved in Club 57—Basquiat hung around, largely due to Haring, and heavy-hitting artists such as Fred Brathwaite (aka Fab 5 Freddy), Afrika Bambaataa, Michael Holman,

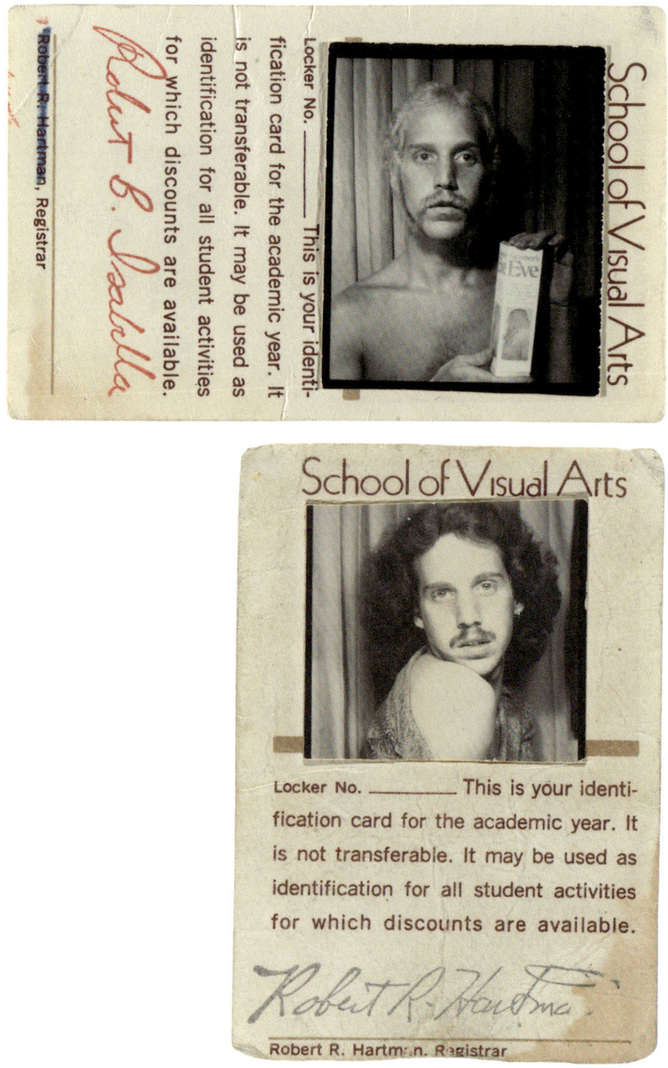

4. Peter Kwaloff's student ID cards for the academic years 1973–74 (bottom) and 1975–76 at School of Visual Arts. The Museum of Modern Art, New York. Department of Film Special Collections

Sur Rodney (Sur), Felice Rosser, Arlene Ramsey, and Julius Eastman occasionally appeared on the club's roster, as did Fashion Moda founder Joe Lewis—they did not make it their home. (The consistent presence at the club of Gerard Little, the nephew of rock music legend Frankie Lymon, was a notable exception.) And whereas films such as Steve Binder's *The T.A.M.I. Show* (1964), with picture-stealing performances by James Brown, Chuck Berry, Marvin Gaye, and the Supremes (October 20, 1979); David L. Weiss's *No Vietnamese Ever Called Me Nigger* (1968), an anti-war documentary protesting the exploitation of black soldiers (February 25, 1981); and Charlie Ahearn's *The Deadly Art of Survival* (1979), a martial arts drama using amateur black and Puerto Rican fighters from the inner city (July 31, 1981), screened at the club, works whose central themes were about race were more exception than rule. It would fall to later club neighbors 51X (at 51 St. Marks Place) and FUN Gallery (225 East Eleventh Street), both of which regularly mounted shows by graffiti artists, to craft a true cross-cultural mix. At Club 57, however, the interests of the artists who engaged there evolved less strategically, having emerged from the seeds of entertainment culture and a desire to explore alternative forms of expression and identity.

One's greatest project or work was one's self. It didn't matter if you were living in a squat or on someone's couch, or if you REALLY supported yourself by turning tricks or stripping, what mattered was that you looked INTERESTING.[46]
—Anita Sarko

The New York New Wave scene is . . . the only totally tolerant scene I know of—more even than any other bohemian scene—just completely tolerant of any kind of "perversion . . . it's integrated in an unbelievable fashion."[47]
—Edit DeAk

For many downtown artists struggling to refine their talent, explore their gender, or hide their less than savory endeavors to make ends meet, performing invented identities was a liberating rite of passage licensed by the neighborhood's unregulated nonconformity and informality. "Every time I left my apartment, it was a performance,"[48] recalled Shawn McQuate (page 136), aka "AMMO," a self-taught fashion designer and aspiring dancer who regularly practiced his moves before the large murals he painted on the walls of his apartment on Ninth Street between Avenues B and C. The culture of transformative performance was so widespread at the time that at SVA students were allowed to amuse themselves with a playful form of self-portraiture, creating different looks for their annual ID cards (fig. 4). When David McDermott, Peter McGough, Daniel Abraham, and Jeffrey Geiger formed the New York Dandies, and took to the devastated downtown streets in the high-style fashions of the 1920s, they became East Side celebrities, which in McDermott's case led to a significant career in No Wave films.[49] Performance was not merely something one undertook on stage—it was a way of life.

Within the walls of Club 57, acting out imaginary alter-egos characterized much of the original performance activity it helped to give birth to. Members took on names such as Bikini Girl, John Sex, Van Chrome, Wendy Wild, Becky Rockefeller, Mr. Fashion, Anoushka, the Batusi Brothers, Jean Caffeine, Needles Jones, Animal X, Johnny Cafeteria, and Tabboo!,[50] and slipped in and out of character in a social space where there was little to separate the thin slice of stage from their audience of peers. The names they took on indicated the character of their engagement with the "resurging emphasis on content . . . often absent from other avant-garde performance work,"[51] which commentators observed at the time.

At the club, performance was free to permeate every medium, and members embraced any discipline at their command in the pursuit of self-representation. Paintings were musically "performed" when artist Castronovo joined forces with composer Julius Eastman for Electric Renaissance (August 15, 1980); photography became *Pictures You Can Dance Too* (April 30, 1980); sculptures that were *Found in the Street* (May 3, 1982) were applauded if they fell off the wall; and film screenings were occasions for outspoken competitive commentary. Around the city, nighttime raids on buildings and subway stations by artists painting graffiti and club members pasting up flyers were similarly motivated: Haring, who with club pals John Sex and Drew Straub, plastered the gay West Village with political messages (page 113),[52] admitted that "the activity of posting itself usually becomes a performance."[53]

If the performance and exploration of identity at Club 57 had a defining agenda, it was promoting the politics of gender nonconformity. For those engaged, the transgender iconography of musicians like New York Dolls and David Bowie had given them permission, and critics on the scene like Nicolas A. Moufarrege put their desire into words: "the abrogation of masculine and feminine stereotype models, a certain sense of style that may incorporate a quirky aesthetic, a surrogate self, but ultimately and always a strong sense of personal affirmation. . . ."[54] The club was a space where fluid and heterogeneous expressions of sexual preference could be examined.

The mix of women and men, straight, gay, and undecided, in the club's homey setting was unique. For those fleeing the West Side bars, where men-only homosocial standards and clone attire were enforced, Club 57 was a refuge, a fact Haring celebrated with his facetious "Fags against Facial Hair" campaign and Sur Rodney (Sur) referenced in his 1980 pieces *Hal Living in the East Village* and *Ron Living in the West Village* (page 69). The club's intimacy allowed for the developing romantic relationship between club DJ Dany Johnson and photographer Ande Whyland (page 135) to be shared and documented by the membership. Open invitational events, such as Shawn McQuate's performance Universal Interaction (May 13, 1981), acted out by members on a floor-size checkerboard for "total audience participation," and Haring's *Erotic Art Show* exhibition (February 27, 1981; page 74), were opportunities for remarkably intimate physical and emotional juxtapositions. To wit, the contrasting perspectives on male genitalia between Kitty Brophy's diaristic drawings *Summer Time* and *At the Beach* (pages 84–85),[55] in which bloodied, armless women watch as men masturbate, and Peter Hristoff's celebratory illustration of autogratification, *Hand Job* (page 76).

The dismemberment motifs found in Brophy's work, and the peculiar "snake" drawings of Robert Hawkins (page 88), might be seen as signs of a gender self-examination process playing out at the club. In ways that were less about lamenting past sexism than they were defying the status quo and acting out alternative sexual identities, self-representation at the club followed currents of punk feminism and male burlesque across a range of mediums, and often centered on the use and misuse of the gendered body. The works brought together in MoMA's exhibition may be conveniently surveyed in these categories.

Everything was connected. The different media as well as the players—collaborations, cross-pollinations, and of course, sleeping together. . . . In some ways, everything that happened at [Performance Space 122] and the Kitchen and Club 57 is on Oprah *now.*[56]
—Beth Lapides

I was very much into feminist stuff. . . . I was pissed off a lot.[57]
—Animal X

The performances by women in the New Wave Vaudeville show augured the scene to come: Annie Hickman's cheery puppet-nibbling striptease, Tessie Chua's flagellation sketch, and Alexa Hunter's wild woman Polyurinsane dance, which was conceived by Andy Rees, announced that the traditional standards of behavior no longer applied. At Club 57, the woman performers carried on the revolt against anything limiting their powers of self-determination. "To strike a pose is to pose a threat,"[58] author Dick Hebdige observed of the politics of surveillance and display in the period. Performance, thus, was a strategy to combat the controlling male gaze of society, one already well underway in the feminist culture downtown. Tough, in-your-face scene makers like the musician Lydia Lunch, actresses Anya Phillips and Adele Bertei, and artists as diverse as Kiki Smith, Kathy Acker, Barbara Kruger, Jenny Holzer, Beth B, Vivienne Dick, Karen Finley, Nan Goldin, Ulrike Ottinger, Lizzie Borden, and Laura Kennedy gave unspoken encouragement and inspiration to the women of Club 57, whose stand against sexist stereotypes and pathologies took the form of ritual theme nights, homemade publications, and self-defining artwork. Performance was central to them all.

All-girl theme nights at the club were treated as occasions to satirize the outmoded forms of female socialization that influenced dress, manners, and sexual relationships, and, worse, that dampened women's will to change—which is why the antidepressant fun-factor of the evenings was so important. The faux women's organization, the Ladies Auxiliary of the Lower East Side, mocked American coming-of-age rituals and feminine role models, with events such as Stay-Free Mini-Prom (September 8, 1979), Gun Club Potluck Dinner (March 12, 1980), Amazon School of Modeling: Spring Meat Show (May 2, 1980; page 32, fig. 12), Debutante Ball (May 31, 1980), Beauty Pageant Exposé (July 27, 1980), and Bunny Lounge (July 28, 1980). This ironic role playing effectively inspired participants to more aggressive forms of playful self-expression—raw meat fashion shows, a "secret boyfriend file" that rated male partners' size and performance abilities. As exercises in empowerment, they were physically liberating to the degree that they led to the male-domain-busting Lady Wrestling nights in 1980 and 1981 (page 133) and the all-girl percussion band Pulsallama, conceived at the group's Rites of Spring Fertility Bacchanal (April 17, 1981), which joined Colab's 1982 video work *Cave Girls* as a manifestation of feminist tribalism downtown.[59] Adopting a similar approach, the lesbian collective Women's One World (WOW), in a series of fundraising events for their new theater space, hosted the Debutantes on Parade Coming Out Ball (February 11, 1983), Freudian Slip/Psychotic Underwear Bash, assuring those interested it was "another pure female production" (April 17, 1982), and post-Valentine's Day Women's Nite: Surgical Drag Ball (February 19, 1982), which picked up on the club's reputation for gore film programming to goof on the horrors of reassignment surgery with women dancing in bloody costumes and dripping IV catheters.

Homemade zines and copy art proved among the most useful and accessible mediums of choice on the downtown scene, and exhibitions such as *Watch These Girls: 19 Women Who Do Copy Art* (October 14, 1982), curated by artist Amy Chaiklin, confirmed that women had taken the lead in shaping the medium's creative uses.[60] Much as privately produced artists' books of the late 1970s served "as an inexpensive vehicle for feminist ideas" and a way around "the undependable museum and gallery system,"[61] so too did the print materials of the 1980s. The availability of the relatively new color-copier technology at places like Todd's Copy Shop on Mott Street accelerated the use of xerography (in use in black and white since the 1960s) as a means of promoting alternative opinion and programming. The undisciplined montage on flyers from the period, mostly created by unknown hands, is arguably the most expressive record of the irreverent, do-it-yourself attitude toward music, art, and film that prevailed at the time. An early reviewer summing up the appeal of copy art noted its "punk orientation . . . vivid industrial colors and [the] instant feedback of the copier process," which attracts "cultural satires, dada distortions, and experimentation."[62]

That xerography is an electronic process masks the complexity of these works and the ways that artists often intervened in them, manipulating the machine-made substrate in surprisingly innovative ways. Graphic artist Marlene Weisman used acetone to transfer toner ink from the original copy to illustration board or rag paper, hand-coloring the image with pencils, markers, and pastels, and adding collaged images. Using comparable techniques, Henny Garfunkel (page 122), Jennifer T. Ley (page 118), and Robin Schanzenbach (page 119) explored a variety of expressive ends, from direct feminist

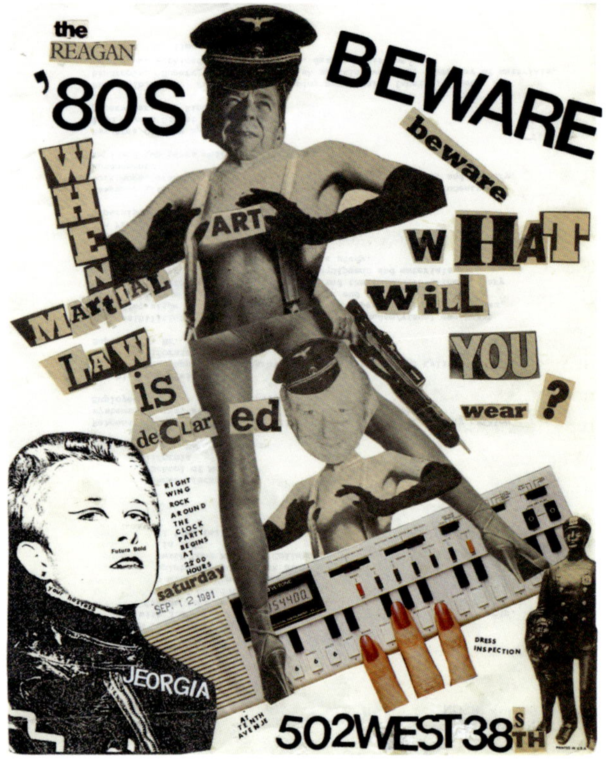

5. Original collage for a flyer for a performance event organized by Jeorgia Anderson at the loft of musician and writer Gabriel Rotello, 1981. Design by Anderson. The Museum of Modern Art, New York. Department of Film Special Collections

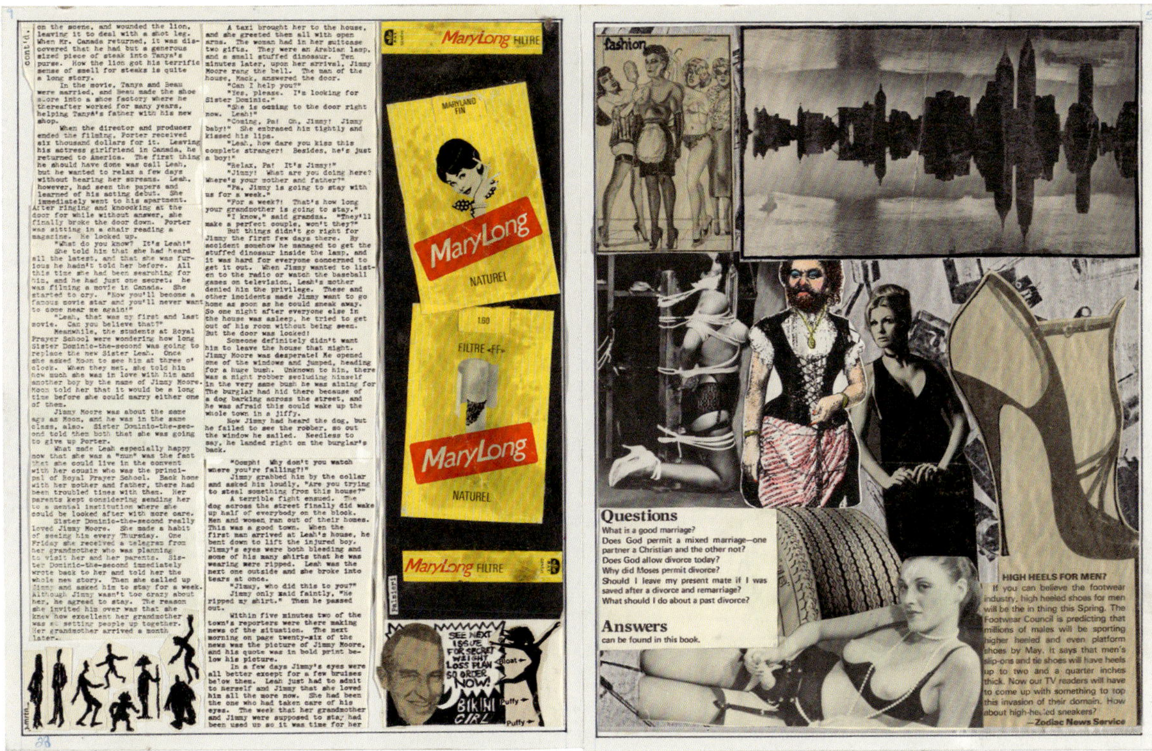

6. Original collage for issue two of Lisa Baumgardner's zine *Bikini Girl*, 1979. The Museum of Modern Art, New York. Department of Film Special Collections

messaging to impressionistic landscapes and self-portraits. Anney Bonney's process art from *Shattered (Cocktail Party on the Street)* (page 120), a color Xerox collage made for her 1978–79 stop-motion film, *Shattered*, captures the edgy character of downtown street life. Natalya Maystrenko's application of photo-copied elements to her 1979 pencil drawings enhances their punk sensibility (pages 66–67); and the agitprop cut-and-copy aesthetic of Jeorgia Anderson's concert flyer the Reagan '80s (fig. 5) expresses the female rocker's anger at the administrations of the president and then New York mayor Ed Koch.[63]

The preeminent proponent of punk-feminist practice at Club 57 was Lisa Baumgardner, whose zine, *Bikini Girl* (fig. 6), was a collage of printed female representation and text from the previous century on pink pages (an ironic reference to the feminine shade) done with vengeance and wicked wit. Declaring *Bikini Girl* "a book for everybody," she used it to benefit club friends, promoting the sculptural experiments of filmmaker friend M. Henry Jones (page 48), for instance, and to encourage men and woman alike to explore the perverse—high heels for men, S/M for women. Baumgardner herself was one of the practicing dominatrices on the downtown scene, a lifestyle she proudly documented in her self-made shorts *Girl Pack* (1978) and *Lisa in Bondage* (1978), and which informed her selections for the club's *Bikini Girl* film series, of 1979–80, including Luis Buñuel's *El (This Strange Passion)* (1953), on male sexual paranoia; and the Andy Warhol and Paul Morrissey collaboration, *The Loves of Ondine* (1968), about a gay man attempting to change his orientation.

Other club women, including a number working in print mediums, used short-form film, video, and slideshows to message their feminism. Merrill Aldighieri's sci-fi scratch video, *Skin Deep from Outer Space* (1982; page 177), set in an alien-invaded beauty parlor, and Anney Bonney's dance on downtown streets in her animated collage video, *Shattered* (1978–79), expressed female empower-ment, as did Jennifer T. Ley's *Such Sweet Dreams* (1981), with its criminal gang of gun-toting girls, and Tessa Hughes-Freeland's short documentary *Baby Doll* (1982), which gave voice to a critique of the sex trade by two topless dancers. In Tina L'Hotsky's *Barbie* (1977), the iconic doll is cooked and eaten. In *The Visitor* (1979), Jeorgia Anderson in extreme punk garb casts a critical eye through the gates of MoMA's Sculpture Garden toward the works of modernist female beauty on display.[64] Esther Regelson's films lampoon masculine behavior: in *Blih-Ah* (1981), a female hand obsessively squeezes a grotesque phal-lic toy (fig. 7),[65] and in *WMEN* (1981), a girl played by Charlotte Slivka dons male drag and hits the streets after being stimulated by a men's fashion spread. Perhaps the most sexually explicit work presented at the club was the 35mm slideshow *Maitresse*,[66] by Trix Rosen, a young photographer for the NBC television network assigned to cover "anything political or gay."[67] The slideshow, which premiered at *Pictures You Can Dance Too*, was an uncensored celebration of lesbian friendship and sexuality. In all of these works, there is no mistaking that women on the scene had taken charge of themselves and their image.

It was the first merging of the homosexual and hetero-sexual society into one. The first one that truly occurred and occurred so that it was no longer looked upon as anything but natural.[68]
—David McDermott

Before the mid-'80s, and Wigstock, and the Pyramid's drag hostesses, and Ru Paul, drag was a segregated performance art.[69]
—Shawn McQuate

For its homosexual members, liberation at the club took shape in a form of queer burlesque rooted in film, performance, and fashion. Gay-interest films, like the alternative programming of monster, sleaze, and gory slasher fare at the core of the club's reputation, were occasions to make fun of dramatic clichés, exaggerated

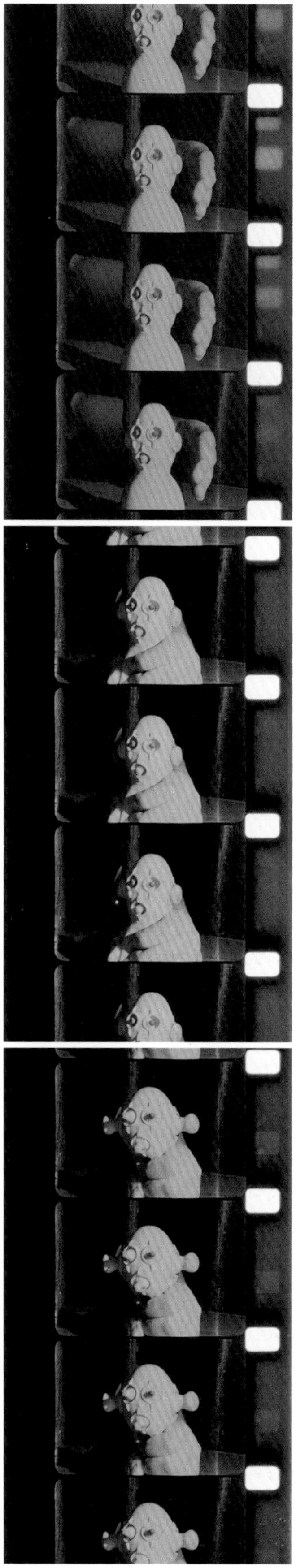

7. Film stills from *Blih-Ah*, 1981. Directed by Esther Regelson

forms of visual expression, and outmoded codes of gendered behavior that were inscribed in Hollywood films—motifs that future performers in the audience like John Epperson, Peter Kwaloff, and Stephen Tashjian would incorporate in their drag burlesque of feminine stereotypes. The competitive sport of shouting out sarcastic commentary during the films became a bonding exercise on par with that enjoyed by minority audiences at screenings of action films on Forty-Second Street.[70]

The club's defining queer event, and the key to understanding its overarching pop aesthetic, was its presentation of Russ Meyer's *Beyond the Valley of the Dolls* (1970), first screened at the club in May 1979. A satire of sexual liberation, *Valley* is a misbegotten digest of cinema and television clichés, lurid production values, pornography, and the horrors of the recent Manson Family murders, amounting to a work as unintentionally avant-garde as any made in the tradition of classical cinema.[71] Its mockery of good taste and celebration of the sensational had radical uses in the hands of a community seeking to stage its liberation.

The programming of films meant to serve as an open forum for the expression of a queer perspective and just plain fun was done by both gay and straight members. Aspiring gay theater writer-director Andy Rees was responsible for Let's Face the Music and Tap, which featured live "tap terror" choreography along with the stilted gothic thriller *What's the Matter with Helen?* (1971; April 2, 1980), with Debbie Reynolds and Shelley Winters. Aging glamour girl Lana Turner's psychedelic thriller, *The Big Cube* (1969), was paired with a selection of Hollywood Technicolor trailers (June 6, 1980), proving that color too could be claimed as queer by an audience that valued its kitsch excess. The cartoon sexuality of Jayne Mansfield and Mamie Van Doren in *Las Vegas Hillbillys* (1966), the girl-next-door, same-sex appeal of Doris Day in both *Calamity Jane* (1953) and *Midnight Lace* (1961), and the butch figures of Marlene Dietrich and Joan Crawford in *Rancho Notorious* (1952) and *Johnny Guitar* (1954), screened throughout 1980, fed the downtown scene's developing drag culture and entertained an audience at the club that, significantly, was not exclusively gay.

Bill Landis, self-described "sleaze civil service worker"[72] and a straight friend of Baumgardner's, organized programs under the rubrics Sex, Sin, and Sadism and the Other Sexes, which surveyed cinematic treatments of "Odd Combos" and "Transsexuals" with skepticism and delight. An authority on Forty-Second Street cinema, whose Club 57–based zine, *Sleazoid Express*, touted exploitation films, Landis got right to the point in his program notes: of Elizabeth Taylor's prestigious *Reflections in a Golden Eye* (1967), he wrote, "Homosexuality vies for a place with the fecund and glamorously oppressive South," and of the Italian sword and sandal epic *The Arena* (1974), "[It] pitches effeminacy against the rigors of ancient Rome's gladiatorial challenges." Queer-themed film programming and the subversive nature of its reception at the club cultivated an audience of straight and gay members who shared a minority point of view and were open to expanding their sense of difference from the mainstream.

The gender questioning given voice at club screenings, theme nights, and exhibitions was a marker of the difference celebrated there. Blurring the gender lines as Marcus Leatherdale did with his photography exhibition *Urban Women* (November 12, 1980), in which he placed images of female body builder Lisa Lyon and John Waters's drag "feminist" Divine side by side, was wholly appropriate (page 142). The club's cinema-fed strain of burlesque matured rapidly. The queer performance melodrama *Doris and Inez Speak the Truth*, written by club regular George Haas, was set in a downtown apartment wallpapered with images of female stars torn from movie magazines (fig. 8). Adapted to film in 1984 by Jimmy Murray from a Squat Theatre production, *Doris and Inez* features Warhol star Jackie Curtis in her final career performance as a weary, transgender drag character struggling to make her burlesque of heterosexual normality a reality.[73]

Although drag was never the major medium of entertainment activity at Club 57 that it became at Pyramid Club and the long-running Wigstock festival hosted by Lady Bunny,[74] legends Ethyl Eichenberger, John Kelly, Jack Smith, and Minette performed there, and it hosted the birth of drag impersonation with acts by Peter Kwaloff, Stephen Tashjian, Scott Covert, Gerard Little (page 136), Ira Abramowitz, Joey Arias, and John Epperson. Epperson's first appearance was a burlesque interpretation of popular television organist Jo Ann Castle in the club's Salute to Lawrence Welk (June 21, 1980); later renowned for his exquisitely tuned persona Lypsinka, Epperson ended his debut playing the piano with his feet.

Perhaps the performer most closely associated with Club 57 was John Sex (born John McLaughlin), who fashioned himself the figurehead for male burlesque downtown, and backed up his image

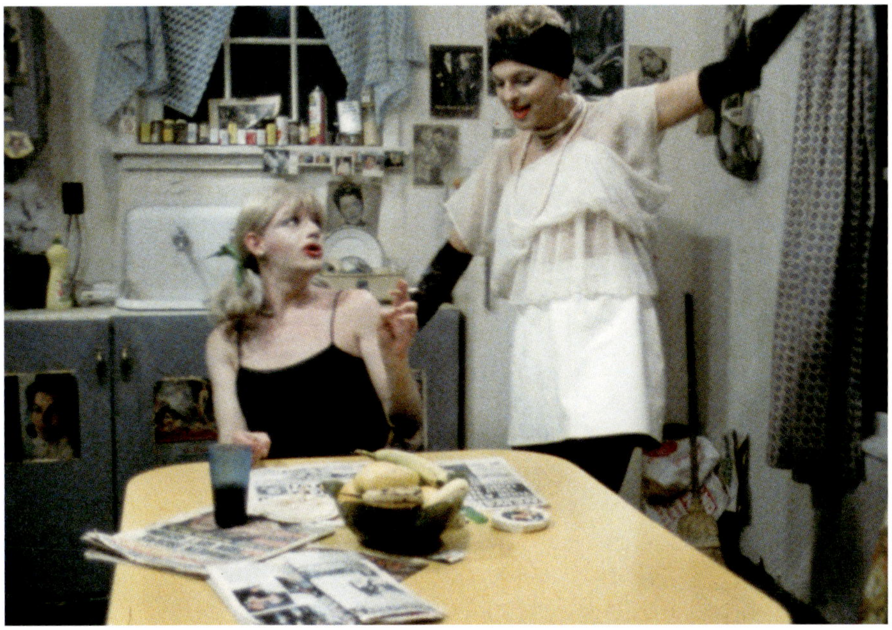

8. Jackie Curtis and Dennis Dyke in a still from *Doris and Inez Speak the Truth*, 1984. Directed by Jimmy Murray

with recurring events like John Sex Burlesque, an evening of male and female striptease with political overtones, which once included a nude Ronald and Nancy Reagan dance conceived by Larry Ashton. Occasionally partnered with drag icon Alexis del Lago,[75] he went on from the club to become one of downtown's leading men, performing in Scott Wittman and Marc Shaiman's revivals of *Peter Pan* (1983), *Bye Bye Birdie* (1986), and *The Sound of Music*, aka *The Sound of Muzak* (1986), at bigger clubs like Danceteria, the Saint, and Limelight. Inspired by Liberace and backed by showgirls he groomed from the club membership,[76] Sex developed a glitzy, Las Vegas alter ego with a two-foot-tall pompadour that flirted with androgyny.

Like drag, the androgyny that some on the scene were exploring was another way of challenging gender difference, which relied to a significant degree on fashion as a form of burlesque.[77] By the time Group Material mounted *Facere/Fascis* in May 1981, proposing to consider "high fashion as a dimension of the new fascist discourse,"[78] Club 57's designers, models, and drag performers were using fashion to reconsider gender norms. The impulse to define a new persona that so many club goers shared was manifest in a do-it-yourself East Side fashion movement spurred on by the presence of Tish and Snooky's punk fashion shop, Manic Panic, used clothing stores, and the number of cost-free design materials participants picked up off trash-strewn streets. For some, fashion allowed them to pointedly exaggerate gender difference. Patti Astor and Anya Phillips donned out-of-date fancy cocktail dresses to Mudd Club.[79] Stacey Elkin and Peter Kwaloff used retro fabrics, like period plaids, in their parodies of feminine design. Katy K created an original rockabilly clothing line. And Animal X assembled a line that she described in wildly unsettling terms as the "just-been-raped look."[80]

For others, design materials expressed social messages, such as Daniel Durning's use of repurposed plastic sheeting and pink fiberglass insulation for the coat he named *Self Contained Housing* (c. 1982), in reference to the harsh living conditions some on the scene were enduring. Shawn McQuate[81] and Gerard Little excelled at creating fashions from recycled packaging and industrial discards, producing work with remarkable structural qualities. McQuate's "wire dress," crafted from a few dollars' worth of hat wire purchased from a neighborhood shop (page 47), and Little's black plastic trash-bag gowns, which he modeled most effectively himself, were signature pieces.

Downtown fashion and performance had in fact found a retail outlet uptown early on, when the department store Fiorucci on East Fifty-Ninth Street employed budding actor Joey Arias in 1976 to bring gay attitude to straight America.[82] Acting as its host on the sales floor, Arias performed with sales items for props (page 52), staged live window displays with Club 57 members like Katy K and John Sex (page 135), gave Kenny Scharf his first formal painting exhibition, and brought in crafts, like jewelry, that club goers were fabricating on their kitchen tables.[83] With the exposure of queer burlesque and prop comedy that Arias instituted at Fiorucci and satellite presentations of club performance culture that Ann Magnuson had begun to curate in Queens at P.S. 1 and uptown at the Whitney Museum, a progressive blend of punk, feminist, and queer messaging was escaping from downtown.

A wild and funky figuration prevails.[84]
—Grace Glueck

Is it a crime, is it a crime, for you to fall in love with Frankenstein?[85]
—New York Dolls

Each painting, film, sculpture or page of writing I make represents to me a particular moment in the history of my body on this planet, in america.[86]
—David Wojnarowicz

During the punk and postpunk decades downtown, the body became the "scene." Across a range of creative mediums, the nature of the body itself was the centerpiece of live performance, film, video, fashion, and art, as well as a personal canvas (page 141) and an object of desire.

At Club 57, the body had always been a key subject. The success of its founding attraction,[87] the Tuesday-night Monster Movie Club (1979–80), tapped into an audience downtown that was eager to identify with ungodly characters and shape-shifting creatures. The *Sleazoid Express* and *Gore Gazette* screenings, in 1980 and 1981–82 respectively, upped the ante, celebrating the goriest excesses of exploitation films like *Doctor Butcher, M.D. (Medical Deviate)* (1980),[88] about which programmer Rick Sullivan wrote, "Limbs are hacked, eyes gouged, entrails devoured, throats slashed, skulls sawed and bodies mauled in a variety of sordid manners, all executed with top-notch special effects."[89]

Whether the appeal of monsters and gore was symptomatic of a loss of faith in society and politics, or a demand for change at any cost, disassembly and reconfiguration were recurring motifs in much of the work made and exhibited at Club 57. Haring's cutup texts, the collage technique used for calendars and flyers, the odds and ends of discarded materials cobbled together to create fashions, the personality and gender transformations executed by club performers on stage all fit the pattern. Kestutis Nakas was playing to the crowd when he described the cast of his production of Shakespeare's *Titus Andronicus* as severed body parts: "Chopped Hand [played by] Bill Rice" (page 158, fig. 8).

Despite all the fun, the expectation of impending fatality hung over the scene. Sculptor John Morton made a point of the fact with his *Suicide, Murder and Junk* show at ABC No Rio in the winter of 1980.[90] Manhattan Cable TV talk show host Kestutis Nakas kept a "nuclear button" on his desk and wore a clown nose when he read the news of the day to his audience. Scharf made the doomsday videos *Suicide Can Be Fun* (1980) and *The Sparkl End* (1980), and Haring drew nuclear silos blasted by alien flyers. Scott Covert's claustrophobic mixed-media drawings *Earth* and *Heaven* (pages 78–79), of 1979, pictured life and the afterlife as interchangeably troubling. Viewed today, the recurring images of the World Trade Center's Twin Towers in club-exhibited copy art (page 113) and No Wave films now appear to anticipate the apocalypse of 9/11 (fig. 9).[91]

Klaus Nomi's death from AIDS on August 6, 1983, approximately four months after Club 57 closed in 1983, signaled the real beginning of the end for many. Nomi's friend Stefano Castronovo left his deathbed portrait of the performer unfinished to commemorate the passing (page 93). The somber figuration in much of the work by the downtown artists who passed through the club may be seen now as a reflection of the ill-fated moment. The darkened palettes of Ellen Berkenblit and Paul Bridgewater paintings suggest grave business (pages 80–81). The male couple in Parker Dulany's circa 1982 painting *The World* (page 68), inspired by same-sex socializing at Club 57, might be enjoying the freedom of a Weimar cabaret, unaware their pink dance floor marks them for extinction.[92] Richard Hambleton's 1983 *Untitled (Shadowman)* (page 89) and the dismembered figure in Richard McGuire's 1980 *Sudden Anatomy* (page 92) appear to be caught in some noir melodrama. The photo collage and watercolors that artist Bruno Testore Schmidt created as studies for a sculpture project configure the vulnerable body of model Shawn McQuate in broken poses suggesting loss on the scale of a classical tragedy (page 77).

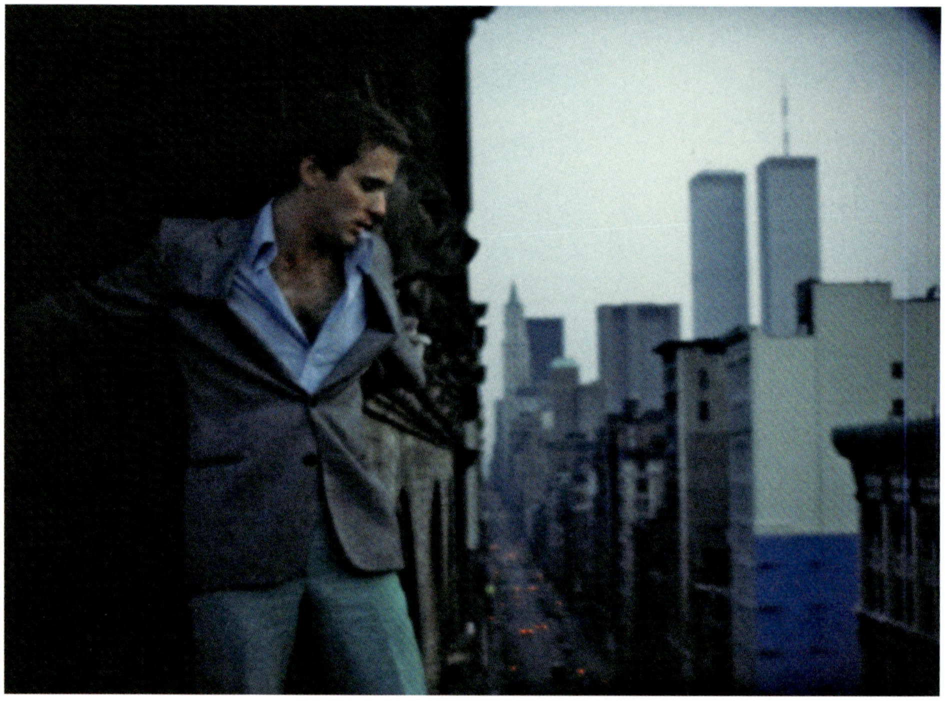

9. Jef Bretschneider in *OK Today Tomorrow*, 1982. Directed by Harald Vogl

The graffiti-inspired work of Dan Asher, painted over a newsprint advertisement from *USA Today* (page 90), and of Adolfo Sanchez, painted over a Bruce Weber pinup (page 91), express an urgent need to interrupt business as usual. The viral quality of these drawings, from 1983 and 1985 respectively, and the ephemerality of their recycled surfaces, give them added poignancy. Similarly moving are Sanchez's circa 1981 transgender self-portrait montage (pages 70–71) and Arch Connelly's 1981 faux-bejeweled sculpture *Self-Portrait*, which both reference queer performance, each in its way declaring the brave painted faces and superficial fashions of drag as spiritual armor against a disease that was taking no prisoners.

The body had become a scene of battle. Criticism that East Village artists had sacrificed political will for self-absorption was answered by their responses to the AIDS crisis.[93] The David Wojnarowicz and Tom Rubnitz video *Listen to This* (fig. 10), left unfinished at the time of their deaths in 1992, is a fiery denunciation of American government and media malfeasance, a blend of self-interest with political resolve memorializing the defiant anger that fueled the rise of ACT-UP and Queer Nation.[94] The downtown residents who resisted oppression at the historic Stonewall Inn riot in June 1969[95] would again emerge to fight back. Thanks to the creative nightlife of places like Club 57,[96] it was now a community feeling more empowered and self-possessed.

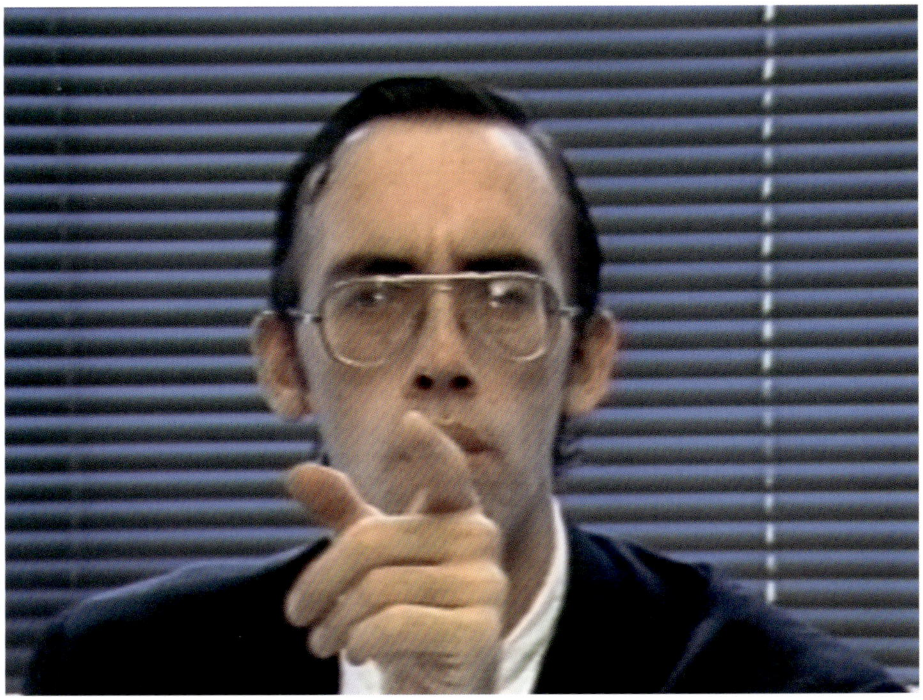

10. David Wojnarowicz in a video still from *Listen to This*, 1992. Created by Wojnarowicz and Tom Rubnitz. The Museum of Modern Art, New York. Purchase funds provided by The Contemporary Arts Council

1. "X Equals Zero, as in Tic-Tac-Toe," *Arts Magazine*, February 1983. Reproduced in *Duets: Dean Daderko & Elaine Reichek in Conversation on Nicolas A. Moufarrege* (New York: Visual Aids, 2016), 52.

2. Sylvère Lotringer, "Introduction to Schizo-Culture," *Schizo-Culture: The Event*, eds. Lotringer and David Morris (LA: Semiotext(e), 2013), 13.

3. Rhys Chatham, quoted in Tony Conrad, "At Last Real Movies: Super-8 Cinema from New York," *Southern California Art Magazine* (June–July 1980): 53.

4. Eric Bogosian, quoted in Conrad, "At Last Real Movies," 53. Emphasis in original.

5. Grace Glueck, "Gallery View: A Gallery Scene That Pioneers in New Territories," *New York Times*, June 26, 1983; Marc Stevens, "Everything Went," *New York*, January 3, 2005; Jerry Saltz, "Lost Horizon," *Village Voice*, December 24, 2004; Roberta Smith, "Looking Back at the Flurry on the Far Side," *New York Times*, December 10, 2004.

6. Tom Scully, unpublished memoir, c. 1983, copy of typed manuscript, The Museum of Modern Art, Department of Film Special Collections, New York.

7. Because Stanley Strychacki also booked a significantly larger concert series at 17 Irving Plaza under the same name, 57 St. Marks Place was referred to as "little" Club 57. Events like the Father's Day Celebration for Stanley dance party, June 15, 1980, testify to Strychacki's status in the eyes of members.

8. Steven Hager, *Art after Midnight: The East Village Scene* (New York: St. Martin's Press, 1986), 54.

9. David Koepp, "Fleshtones, Zantees: Club 57," *New York Rocker* (May 1978), unknown page number, The Museum of Modern Art, Department of Film Special Collections, New York.

10. A collection of materials documenting Strychacki's involvement with Club 57 holds seven official summons and sixteen typed correspondences/flyers that complain about Club 57 due to noise or sanitation issues. The Museum of Modern Art, Department of Film Special Collections, New York.

11. Shawn McQuate, email to the author, April 10, 2016.

12. Ada Calhoun, *St. Marks Is Dead: The Many Lives of America's Hippest Street* (New York: W. W. Norton & Co., 2016), 232.

13. Scully, unpublished memoir.

14. Pam Black, "Say Yes-Yes to the No-No-No-New Wave," *SoHo Weekly News*, November 16, 1978.

15. Leonard Abrams, "And Now for Something Completely Different," *Herald*, November 17, 1978.

16. Black, "Say Yes-Yes."

17. See J. Hoberman, "Come and Yell 'Marcello': Making Movies at Club 57," in this volume.

18. See Jenny Schlenzka, "Acts of Live Art: Performance at Club 57," in this volume.

19. Metro-Goldwyn-Mayer's *Our Gang* comedy series (1922–44) centered on a group of Depression-era, mixed-race American children and their misadventures; the same Hollywood studio teamed Judy Garland and Mickey Rooney in song-and-dance musicals like *Babes in Arms* (1939) and *Strike Up the Band* (1940); Cabaret Voltaire was founded in 1916 in Zürich, Switzerland, by writers and artists Hugo Ball, Emmy Hennings, Tristan Tzara, Sophie Taeuber, and Jean Arp; Dean Savard, who ran Civilian Warfare when it opened in 1982, described his gallery in similar terms: "I kind of think of the gallery as my living room." Quoted in Glueck, "Gallery View."

20. Uzi Parnes, "Pop Performance in East Village Clubs," *Drama Review* 29, no. 1 (1985): 7.

21. Michael Wilk, class of 1978, recalled in a conversation with the author a multiple-choice test for which one of the answers offered to the question "What is *Cubism*?" was "Ricky Ricardo," the fictional Cuban husband of Lucille Ball on the television show *I Love Lucy*.

22. Another of Holliday's notable paintings from the period was created in the carnivalesque style of James Ensor as a prop for club regular Eric Marciano's Super 8 sci-fi film, *The Age of Insects* (1983/1990).

23. At SVA, Haring took classes in film (with Amy Taubin), video (with B. Buckner and Keith Sonnier), and semiotics (with Bill Beckley).

24. "Autobiography: Self Portrait the Last Days of 1979 Written December 30 1979." Haring Foundation Archive.

25. Club "invitationals" were open calls for participation in art and performance events. Haring established the practice at the start with his Xerox art, black light, and erotic art shows, and it was used early on to assemble Acts of Live Art and other such performance occasions as well. Invitationals, so named or not, were a programming model at 57 St. Marks for the life of the club. See "Club 57 Chronology" in this volume (pages 160–77). Examples include *Found in the Street: Sculpture Invitational*, Monday, May 3, 1982; *Open Color Xerox Show*, September 15, 1980; Second Annual Club 57 Invitational: Keith Haring's Black Light Art Show with Fab 5 Freddy, June 3–4, 1981.

26. Club 57, "Club 57 Invitational Xeroxs [sic] Organized by Keith Haring," press release, May 29, 1980.

27. Gerard Little's To Be Drugged, Gifted, and Dressed in Black: Soft Sculptures fashion party in March 1981 was a privileged occasion for him to display his talents as performer, designer, and figurative sculptor in fabrics in one place (page 136).

28. Keith Haring, "Confronting Function: Street Works 79/80," SVA class paper, May 10, 1980. Haring Foundation Archive

29. Participants included Daniel Abraham, Dale Ashmun, Larry Ashton, Robert Carrithers, Daria Deshuk, Stacey Elkin, Dany Johnson, Haring, Lady, Bill Landis, Diana Lillig, Shawn McQuate, April Palmieri, Oliver Sanchez, Scharf, Bruno Testore Schmidt, Tom Scully, John Sex, Charlotte Slivka, the group Strange Party (with Joey Arias and Tony Frere), Min Thometz, Tseng Kwong Chi, and Wendy Wild.

30. Ann Magnuson, February 1979–summer 1980; Dale Ashman, summer 1980; Andy Rees, September–November 1980; Tom Scully, December 1980; Kai Eric, January 1981–mid-1982; Abramowitz and Joiris, 1982–83. Deb Parker also served briefly, dates unrecorded. As described in Scully, unpublished memoir.

31. Known as L'École de la Cambre, it was founded in 1927 by Henry Van de Velde.

32. "Representation, Appropriation, and Power," Craig Owens, *Beyond Recognition* (Berkeley: University of California Press, 1992), 91. In his essay "The Problem with Puerilism," Owens argued that the East Village had fallen in line with uptown art practice by the mid-1980s. See *Artforum* (Summer 1984): 162–63.

33. Julius Klein, "B4UGO," *Rivington School: 80's New York Underground*, ed. Istvan Kantor (London: Black Dog Publishing, 2017), 77.

34. John Gruen, *Keith Haring: The Authorized Biography* (New York: Simon & Schuster, 1992), 60, 62, 87.

35. Theme shows became standard fare in the East Village through the 1990s, spreading from immediate club heirs like Mudd Club and Danceteria to Limelight and Area, which had much larger budgets and a celebrity-heavy attendance. The Gracie Mansion gallery produced the *Famous Show*, about which Carlo McCormick commented, "Each exhibition was a concept, an event, an installation, a party." See McCormick, "On Gracie Mansion Gallery," *Artforum* (October 1999): 123. Among the more extreme examples was Kwok Gallery's *Shit Show* in March 1982, which boasted "Shit dance, shit food, shit Film, shit souvenir, shit noise"; see exhibition flyer reproduced in Kantor, *Rivington School*, 21.

36. "Dynamation" was the brand name for the stop-motion animation techniques of Ray Harryhausen.

37. "Klaus Nomi's Ad for Jägermeister (Circa 1980)," *Open Culture*, August 11, 2014, http://www.openculture.com/2014/08/klaus-nomis-ad-for-jagermeister.html.

38. "Performances at P.S. 1," press release, April 23, 1982. MoMA PS1 Archives, VII.B.33, The Museum of Modern Art Archives, New York.

39. By 1983, Keith Haring had mounted solo exhibitions at Westbeth Painters Space and Performance Space 122 in 1981 and at Rotterdam Arts Council and Tony Shafrazi Gallery in 1982; Ann Magnuson had performed with David Bowie and Catherine Deneuve in *The Hunger*, released in 1983; Kenny Scharf had shown work at Fiorucci, in 1979, *Times Square Show*, in 1980, P.S. 1, in 1981, and FUN Gallery, in 1982; Joey Arias had appeared with David Bowie on the December 15, 1979, broadcast of the popular late-night television program *Saturday Night Live*; and John Epperson, Marc Shaiman, and Scott Wittman were moving on to bigger and better appointed clubs like Danceteria and Pyramid.

40. Anthony Scibelli, email to the author, April 4, 2017. Photographer and club regular Scibelli contributed routinely to *Heavy Metal* magazine, for which he collaborated with William S. Burroughs.

41. Anders Grafstrom, from his script for the film *The Long Island Four*, 1979.

42. The collective named itself after the Japanese sci-fi film *Destroy All Monsters* (1968), which coincidentally Club 57 screened on November 6, 1979.

43. Jonestown, Guyana, November 18, 1978; Three Mile Island, Pennsylvania, March 28, 1979; Iranian hostage crisis, 1979–81; John Lennon shooting, December 8, 1980; Reagan shooting, March 30, 1981; Pope John Paul II shooting, May 18, 1981; Anwar Sadat assassination, October 6, 1981.

44. Carmel Johnson quoted in Hager, *Art after Midnight*, 51.

45. During its exhibition at Club 57, Bretschneider recalls curator Diego Cortez inviting *Shifting Borders* to be included in his *New York/New Wave* show at P.S. 1 (February 1981); unfortunately, they could not agree on the terms of the exhibition. Cortez, conversation and email correspondence with the author, July 7 and 13, 2017, respectively.

46. "Anita Sarko," *New York Noise: Art and Music from the New York Underground 1978–88* (London: Soul Jazz Publishing, 2007), 200–1.

47. Edit DeAk, "Liberals Can't Integrate," *Alive: The New Performance Magazine* 1, no. 1 (July/August 1982): 20.

48. Shawn McQuate, conversation with the author and Sophie Cavoulacos, July 7, 2016.

49. Kevin Gayer, "The East Village Dandy," *East Village 86: A Guide, A Documentary* (New York: Egret Publications, 1986), 16–20. McDermott's films include *Rome '78* (1978), directed by James Nares; *The Long Island Four* (1979), directed by Anders Grafstrom; *The Bogus Man* (1980), director Nick Zedd; *Downtown '81* (1980–81/released 2000), directed by Edo Bertoglio; *Measure Taken* (1983), directed by Harald Vogl.

50. These were the names assumed by, in order, Lisa Baumgardner, who also went by the names Deena and Lisa Herkowitz, John McLaughlin, Kenny Scharf, Wendy Andreiev, Scott Covert, Gerard Little, Ann Magnuson, Drew Straub and Kenny Scharf, Jean Leider, Ira Abramowitz, Kristin Xavier, Peter Kwaloff, and Stephen Tashjian. The practice of adopting evocative stage names was directly inspired by the preceding generation of punk musicians, such as Johnny Rotten (John Joseph Lydon); Siouxsie Sioux (Susan Janet Ballion); Sid Vicious (John Simon Ritchie); Lydia Lunch (Lydia Anne Koch); Richard Hell (Richard Lester Meyers); Johnny Thunders (John Anthony Genzale Jr.); Iggy Pop (James Newell Osterberg Jr.).

51. Parnes, "Pop Performance," 16.

52. John Gruen, *Keith Haring*, 56–57.

53. Haring, "Confronting Function."

54. Nicolas A. Moufarrege, "Lavender: On Homosexuality and Art," *Arts Magazine* (October 1982): 51–52.

55. In fact, few saw Brophy's autobiographical line drawings in the club period. Today the artist is unable to recall which work she exhibited at Haring's invitation.

56. "Beth Lapides," *New York Noise*, 201.

57. Animal X, in conversation with Sophie Cavoulacos, June 13, 2016.

58. Dick Hebdige, "Posing . . . Threats, Striking . . . Poses: Youth, Surveillance, and Display," *SubStance* 37/38 (1983): 86.

59. Cave Girls' performance activity was a collaboration by female members of Colab, led by Kiki Smith and Ellen Cooper, who in 1982 produced the short film *Cave Girls*, a fantasy of prehistoric female culture featuring dancers Cara Brownell, Rebecca Howland, Judy Ross, and Marnie Greenholz, with music by the Bush Tetras; Pulsallama's 1982 music video, "The Devil Lives in My Husband's Body," which satirized suburban angst, was directed by Paul Dougherty.

60. The 1979 George Eastman House exhibition *Electroworks*, curated by Marilyn McCray, established the dominant role of women in the field of copy art. The exhibition opened to New York City audiences at the Cooper Hewitt, Smithsonian Design Museum in New York on September 2, 1980.

61. Lucy R. Lippard, "Lucy R. Lippard," *Art-Rite* 14 (Winter 1976–77): 10.

62. Susann Boettger, "Copyrites and Wrongs," *ArtWeek* (July 5, 1980): no page. *Functional color* was the term used to describe the chromatic range of copiers, which did not produce natural colors and varied from machine to machine. See Marilyn McCray, *Electroworks* (Rochester, NY: George Eastman House, 1979), 8. Published in conjunction with an exhibition of the same name at George Eastman House.

63. By the late 1980s, both the president and the mayor would be just as angrily criticized by AIDS activists for their inadequate responses to the health crisis.

64. Anderson's attention is focused on the sculptures *Standing Woman* (Gaston Lachaise, 1932) and *The Mediterranean* (Aristide Maillol, cast c. 1951–53). *The Visitor* was produced as a collaboration between Anderson and director Andre Degas.

65. Called a "Martian Popping Thing," it was a childhood toy of the Regelson sisters, Naomi, Esther, and Mimi.

66. Rosen was a contemporary of Nan Goldin, whose slideshow *The Ballad of Sexual Dependency* showed at Club 57 in an early version in 1982; by contrast Rosen's *Maitresse* might have been subtitled *A Ballad of Sexual Independency*.

67. Trix Rosen, conversation with the author, May 13, 2017.

68. "Edit De Ak Talks with David McDermott," *ABC No Rio Dinero: The Story of a Lower East Side Art Gallery*, eds. Alan Moore and Marc Miller (New York: ABC No Rio with Collaborative Projects, 1985), 186.

69. Shawn McQuate, email to the author, October, 20, 2016.

70. The disruptive behavior at a club film showing wouldn't have been tolerated in the respectable repertory cinemas like the Thalia, the Elgin, or the Regency, which then ruled the city. By comparison, viewing habits at the club might be termed "post-repertory" and understood as another example of how the scene challenged critical norms and approved behavior. In a conversation with the author, October 9, 2016, club member Michael Wilk recalled his pleasure listening to the running commentary of a black audiences at screening of the "blaxploitation" pictures like *Abby* (1974).

71. The narration in the film's trailer states, "It's all here: rape, murder, dope, grass, abortion, suicide, something for everyone. . . . This is what life's all about." The Manson Family murders of actress Sharon Tate and four others took place in Los Angeles on August 8, 1969. At Pyramid Club in 1985, John Epperson would stage *Ballet of the Dolls* (page 37), a broad drag parody of *Valley of the Dolls* (1967), which Epperson wrote in the irreverent spirit of Meyer's unauthorized "sequel," *Beyond the Valley of the Dolls*. Meyer's film screened repeatedly at Club 57; the original *Valley of the Dolls* did not. Both films had cult followings, especially with gay audiences.

72. "Thirteen Mags for Moderns," *The Catalog of Cool*, ed. Gene Sculatti (New York: Warner Books, 1982), 97. Landis wrote a satire of the American television series *Ironsides* (1967–75) and its then-closeted star, Raymond Burr, which was performed at Club 57 as *The Life of Burr* (April 26, 1981), with Ondine and Gerard Little in the cast.

73. The film's cast of four was Curtis, Dennis Dyke, Tom Noonan, and Michael Santoro.

74. Wigstock (1984–2005) was an annual outdoor concert event for drag performers held on Labor Day weekend, first in Thompson Square Park and later in Union Square Park and the Hudson River piers.

75. Including in an adaptation of Tennessee Williams's play *Sweet Bird of Youth* (1959) as *Sweet Blondes of Youth*, which premiered at Danceteria on September 20, 1982.

76. Sex's backup group, known as the "Bodacious Ta Tas," were club members April Palmieri and Wendy Wild, with added support from Katy K, Micki French, Myra Schiller, Jane Alex, dancers Maggie McDermott and Jeani Filipini, and percussionists Dany Johnson and Sally Berg.

77. In an email to the author, October 20, 2016, Shawn McQuate wrote: "A big motivation for most of us was to be shocking, wild, [and] rebellious, and dressing slightly feminine was one way to do that. . . . Androgyny had become very popular and desirable, but Drag was still considered 'too gay' for serious artists."

78. Group Material held a sidebar event at Club 57, Dress/Dance/Dazzle with Mundy McLaughlin, on May 16, 1981.

79. Patti Astor, *FUN Gallery: The True Story* (New York: Pink Poodle Press, 2012), 112.

80. Hager, *Art after Midnight*, 10.

81. In an email to Sophie Cavoulacos, June, 28, 2016, model Jan Long Collins wrote of McQuate's design for the Ball Gown Show at Mudd Club, 1981: "Ammo's ball gown turned out to be a sort of big ribbon. White. Adding machine tape, a string of sequins, a hank of toule . . . braided. One going down the front of me, one going down the back with tiny little wires at my ribs, my waist and my thighs, holding the front and the back in place, it was pretty much like standing naked for four hours at the Mudd Club."

82. Arias was employed at Fiorucci in New York from its opening in 1976 through its 1988 closing. The performance side of his duties at the store gradually increased with the celebrity he incurred after his *Saturday Night Live* appearance in 1979.

83. Club goers who made jewelry from discarded cigarette packs, telephone wire, and bits of broken plastic and bones included Jeorgia Anderson, Alexa Hunter, Jennifer T. Ley, Samantha McEwen, Min Sanchez, Kenny Scharf, and Wendy Wild. Consumerism was a subject of interest in the disenfranchised Lower East Side community, evidenced by the Group Material show *Consumption: Metaphor, Pastime, Necessity*, on March 18, 1981, "an exhibition on the social relations of use, squander, absorption, and destruction." The show's press release is reproduced in *Show and Tell: A Chronicle of Group Material*, ed. Julie Ault (London: Four Corners Books, 2010), 43. Mykel Board, leader of the band ART, produced an anti-consumer-friendly album titled "The 'You'll Hate This Record' Record" in 1983, a compilation of politically incorrect music. Plastic vomit was glued to each front cover with the help of pals from Club 57.

84. Glueck, "Gallery View."

85. David Johansen and Sylvain Sylvain, "Frankenstein," on *New York Dolls*, New York Dolls, Universal, 1973.

86. David Wojnarowicz, *Close to the Knives: A Memoir of Disintegration* (New York: Vintage, 1991), 149.

87. Shortly before inaugurating Monster Movie Club, Tom Scully produced his play *The Moo Goo Guide Plan*, which included the stage direction "limbs scattered in a bloody heap upon the table, legs, arms, noses, etc. They all dig in, passing the salt and pepper and soy sauce." Scully, *The Moo Goo Guide Plan*, unpublished, no date, copy of typed manuscript, The Museum of Modern Art, Department of Film Special Collections, New York.

88. An Italian production whose original title was *Zombie Holocaust*.

89. *Gore Gazette* 25 (1981): 1.

90. "Suicide, Murder & Junk," *ABC No Rio Dinero*, 74–77.

91. *OK Today Tomorrow*, 1982, directed by Harald Vogl; *Minus Zero*, 1979, directed by Michael Oblowitz.

92. During the Second World War, pink triangle badges worn by men in Nazi concentration camps identified them as homosexuals.

93. Rosalyn Deutsche and Cara Gendel Ryan disparaged the tendency as a "retreat from political art practice into the expression of solipsistic feelings." See "The Fine Art of Gentrification," *October* (Winter 1984): 107.

94. ACT-UP (Action Committee to Unleash Power) was founded in 1987 and took to the streets with direct political action to address the Reagan administration's negligent response to AIDS; Queer Nation was established in 1990 as an advocate for the LGBT community on issues of prejudice and health care. Both organizations were initially created in New York City.

95. Members of the gay community fought back against police harassment at the Stonewall Inn, in Greenwich Village, in the early hours of June 28, 1969. The LGBT pride organizations and activities that formed in reaction were recognized today as the birth of the contemporary gay rights movement.

96. See Sophie Cavoulacos, "Downtown for Downtown," in this volume.

DOWNTOWN FOR DOWNTOWN

Sophie Cavoulacos

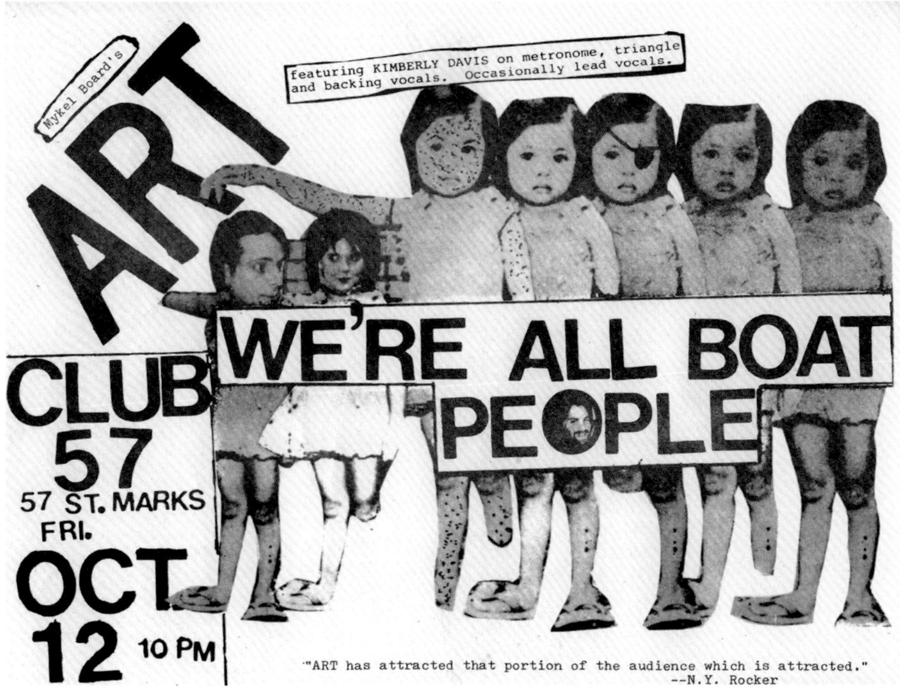

1. Flyer for the band ART, Club 57, 1979. Design by Mykel Board. The Museum of Modern Art, New York. Department of Film Special Collections

This text is a critical reading of the Club 57 chronology (pages 160–77) and one of any number of possible passages through the flyers, calendars, and programs that document the sequence of events at this interdisciplinary space.[1] The hybrid nature of Club 57, and the rich network of artists and venues it overlapped with, call for a nonlinear approach. Through the lens of music, theater, art exhibitions, and performance, this text alternately historicizes work that has not been previously chronicled in detail and situates Club 57 within the larger context of both its peer organizations and its predecessors, the latter a gesture undertaken by former club members when they compare the space to Dada's Cabaret Voltaire or Weimar Germany's nighttime club scene. Analyzing this ephemeral time interrogates the significance of any one night—a notion more plausible after giving life and texture to a one-line entry in a calendar—and assesses the impact of available, open, and democratic space on a generation of avant-garde artists. These proposed links remain poetic and fragile but they are essential nonetheless.

POSTPUNK MUSIC

By the time Club 57 opened in February 1978, the heyday of New York's punk era had passed. A year earlier, Washington Project for the Arts had mounted *Punk Art*, the first exhibition to chronicle the punk scene, which included contributions by future club goers Animal X and M. Henry Jones alongside those by punk musician Alan Vega, photographer Marcia Resnick, and *Punk* magazine founder John Holmstrom. Club 57 was firmly rooted in a postpunk moment. Before Mudd Club led the explosion of live music venues in downtown Manhattan, the landscape consisted of Max's Kansas City and CBGB.[2] For emerging acts, Club 57 offered an alternative to the area's limited and otherwise competitive options. Although it would be misleading to describe Club 57 as a major music venue within the overall history of downtown music, in its five years of operation, Club 57 programmed live music on a semiregular basis and supported several music subcultures within the New York scene.

In its earliest days, Club 57 was managed by Stanley Strychacki, who oversaw the basement space on behalf of the Holy Cross Polish National Church upstairs. Strychacki responded to the neighborhood youth's energy, booking in March and April of 1978 bands such as Nervus Rex, Foolish Virgins, the Fleshtones, and the Zantees, often in double bills. By May, *SoHo Weekly News* had taken note of the club, citing it as part of "a rejuvenated [N]ew York night life."[3] Club 57 did more than provide a space for bands to gig; it contributed to the formation of a postpunk aesthetic. While the punk scene had pitted itself against disco's commercialism (page 120), a slightly younger generation found interest, if not liberation, in melding the energies of both genres. If at CBGB dancing along to bands was discouraged, at Club 57 it was central—even when noise complaints forced the jukebox or DJs to replace live music. Peter Zaremba, Fleshtones front man and garage rock stalwart (page 48), has said he favored the basement club where the lack of a stage meant the band was dancing with the audience.[4]

Within a year, Strychacki had invited a group of young artists he had met through New Wave Vaudeville, a six-night variety show–style performance at Irving Plaza in November of 1978, to help program and run the club. Susan Hannaford and Tom Scully began organizing film screenings, while Ann Magnuson started curating performances and managing bookings. Soon bands formed by club members joined the eclectic program. The club's house band, led by Kai Eric, adjusted its name, lineup, and repertoire to suit the theme nights on offer. Mykel Board, a former Yippie, created ART: The Only Band in the World, which mixed punkish amateurism and absurdism to parody what he saw as the pretentiousness of art rock bands. Joining Board were Kimberly Davis, Lori Montana, and Bill Shor, the latter replaced in October 1981 by Dale Ashmun. ART favored the metronome as an instrument and performed numbers like "Ugly People with Fancy Hairdos (We Are All Boat People)," with Montana accompanying in sign language (fig. 1). The thirteen-strong girl group Pulsallama emerged out of a one-night act for an April 1981 event and soon after became a fixture at downtown clubs.

Perhaps most akin to the retro-inspired performance and theme nights that would feature regularly in its programming, Club 57 nurtured New York's garage rock bands, championing the Fleshtones' 1960s revivalism alongside the Zantees' punk-rockabilly and Certain Generals'[5] surf riffs.[6] In February 1980, Deb O'Nair presented a tribute to the Farfisa electronic organ; invented in the 1960s, the instrument was popular among New Wave and garage bands, including the bubblegum-punk group Tina Peel, which O'Nair had started with Rudi Protrudi. The bandmates appeared as Tina Peel for the last time in May of that year, returning in 1981

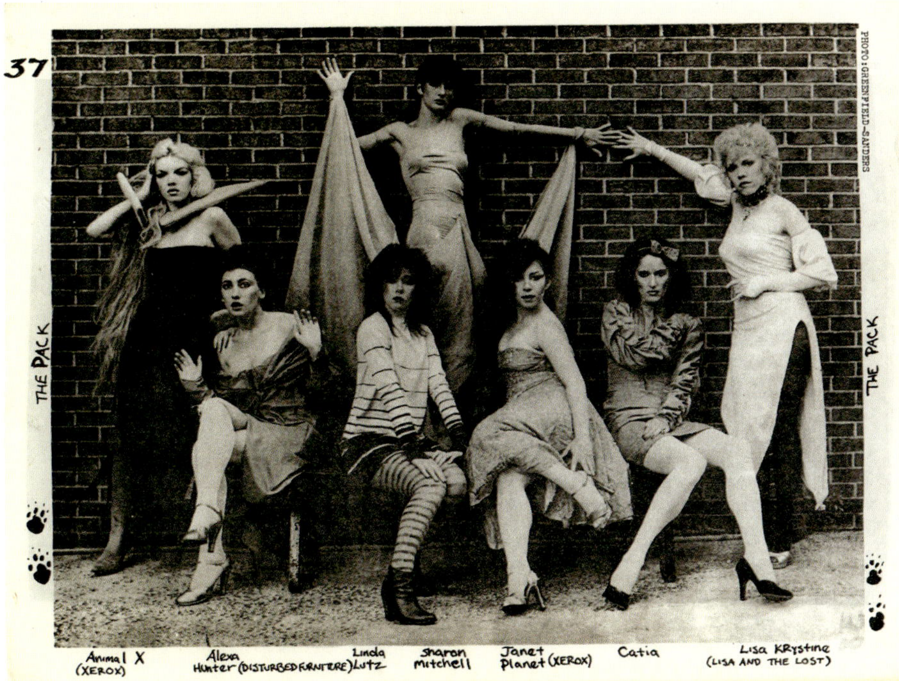

2. Members of the Pack, 1980. Photograph by Timothy Greenfield-Sanders, annotated and offset printed by Animal X for her artist's book, *Animal Skins*, in which the image appeared as the centerfold. The Museum of Modern Art, New York. Department of Film Special Collections

as the Fuzztones. Club 57 occasionally presented garage rock talents from outside New York: Brave Combo, billed as "nuclear polka," hailed from Texas, while punk-ska band the Offs came from San Francisco; they played shows in 1980 and 1981 respectively. The club's revivalist aesthetic was also one of its notable exports. By the end of 1981, Tom Scully was programming Psychedelic Weekend bills at West Side club the Cavern. Club members later formed bands like the psychedelic Mad Violets (Wendy Wild) and the polka-inspired Das Furlines (Wendy Wild, Deb O'Nair).

Club 57 also regularly showcased a subset of postpunk bands fusing percussion, dance music, and Latin and Afro influences. In October 1980, Strange Party, Joey Arias and Tony Frere's funk-infused New Wave extension of the Klaus Nomi Band, debuted in Acts of Live Art. (To the same event Man Parrish contributed a recording of crickets on audiocassette loop.[7]) In February 1981, Liquid Liquid and Dog Eat Dog performed in a double bill, while in September, Al Diaz, famed for having collaborated with Jean-Michel Basquiat on the SAMO tag, played handmade instruments in his loose-knit percussion ensemble, Elephant Dance. In February 1982, Los Microwaves, whose spry electronic sounds and deadpan lyrics (occasionally in Spanish) were described variously by critic Glenn O'Brien as "the theme to the world's best uninvented game show, Slavic disco, [and a] Bauhaus soap opera soundtrack," played weekly shows at Club 57.[8] The band's Meg Brazill, who described Club 57 as a "life raft for those of us . . . switching from music to visual arts to performance and back" created a separate performance with East Village designer Pilar Limosner. Their tap dance act, led by a local vaudevillian on an amplified stage, was combined live with sound effects and drums to create a multilayered work.[9]

Club 57 also presented various art bands. Disturbed Furniture, led by Alexa Hunter, whose background was in theater, played at Club 57 in fall of 1979, as did fashion designer Animal X's band, Xerox. Animal X also formed the Pack, a feminist alliance of women in punk bands (fig. 2). In February 1981, photographer Barbara Ess brought her all-girl band Y Pants to the club for an evening of music and videotapes. 3 Teens Kill 4, whose members included David Wojnarowicz and future Pyramid Club manager Brian Butterick, played a show in March 1981 that included their signature combination of audiotape samples, poetry, and toy instruments. A poetry evening in May 1981 saw one of the first gigs from a group that had recently taken on the name Sonic Youth. Jean-Michel Basquiat's Gray never played at Club 57, but the artist's bandmate, scene impresario Michael Holman, explored the group's structural aesthetics in a Super 8 film and audio-loop performance. The venue also booked avant-garde musicians associated with venues like the Kitchen: Jules Baptiste (January and March 1981), Rhys Chatham (March 1981), Elliott Sharp (April 1981), Glenn Branca (April 1981), and John Zorn (April 1982). In August 1980, painter Stefano Castronovo and iconoclastic minimalist composer Julius Eastman presented Electric Renaissance, an evening of art and music responding to seventeenth-century Baroque figure Heinrich Schütz.

DOWNTOWN THEATER

As it did with New York's music scene, Club 57 functioned as an unlikely site of convergence for experimental theater, with divergent groups turning to the venue as a place to try out their work. The first production at Club 57 took place in October 1978 and was directed by Gordon Edelstein, who had studied with Jerzy Grotowski in Poland before returning home to New York and immersing himself in the off-off-Broadway work of Richard Foreman, Charles Ludlam, the Wooster Group, and Mabou Mines. A young theater artist as enamored with the rock and roll bands at CBGB as he was his theatrical heroes, Edelstein sought out Club 57 to stage the virtually unseen 1971 play *Cowboy Mouth*, written and first performed by Sam Shepard and Patti Smith during their affair (fig. 3).[10] Edelstein's cast consisted of painter Jonathan Williams, Mabou Mines' L. B. Dallas, and writer Chris Kraus, who had written and performed a piece at the Performing Garage earlier in the year with Suzan Cooper, the production's codirector. The performers, none of whom were classically trained, called themselves Rock & Roll Theater.[11]

The confluence of Patti Smith and Sam Shepard made an impact.[12] Originally scheduled for three mid-week dates, the production attracted crowds and was held over. Rock critic Robert Christgau included it in a weekly roundup in the *Village Voice*, mostly noting the line down the street and the post-play set by Foolish Virgins. *SoHo Weekly News* theater critic Gerald Rabkin described it as "free-form Shepard in full bloom" in his review of a concurrent Shepard production at Theater for the New City.[13]

However welcome, exposure was not the goal: Kraus recalls how the show, for which she, Edelstein, and the other performers had prepared over many months, became an

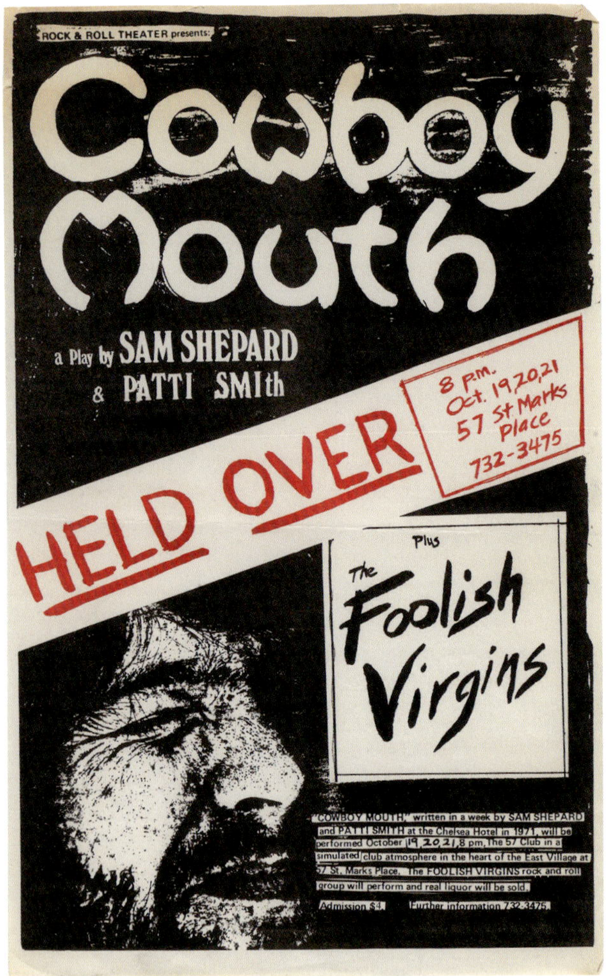

3. **Flyer for *Cowboy Mouth*, directed by Gordon Edelstein, Club 57,** 1978. Design by Jonathan Williams (pictured), who also acted in the play. The Museum of Modern Art, New York. Department of Film Special Collections

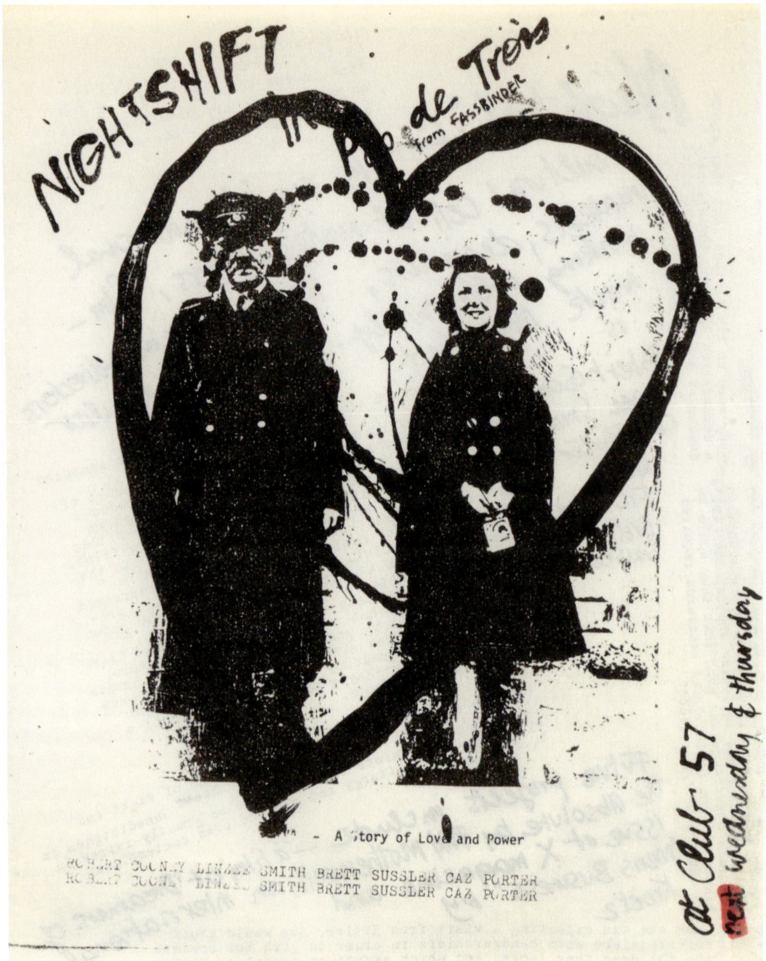

4. **Flyer for *Pas de trois,* directed by the Nightshift collective, Club 57,** date unknown, 1978. Design by Nightshift's Carol Porter. The Museum of Modern Art, New York. Department of Film Special Collections

extension of the group's interpersonal relationships and internal psychodramas.[14] Between the modest booking fee, attractive location, and creative freedom it offered, Club 57 was a boon—so much so, in fact, that in December 1980 Edelstein would return with a second production, *Home Bodies* (1980) by Michael Taav. His return is an example of the club's open model of curatorship, which began with Strychacki and extended through Magnuson, Andy Rees, Eric, and Ira Abramowitz. While other downtown spaces sought to do away with formal arbiters (Edelstein recently described Strychacki as the most "postmodern" of gatekeepers[15]), Club 57 was open to a constantly rotating ad hoc lineup of artists, distinguishing it from cooperative-based models run by and for a narrower, likeminded set.[16]

Club 57 provided a platform for theater artists of different stripes. The Australian theater group Nightshift mounted *Pas de trois* (fig. 4), a take on Rainer Werner Fassbinder's *Pre-Paradise Sorry Now* (1969), at the end of 1978, following a production earlier the same year in Australia. Announcing themselves "an international cultural cell of writers, actors, filmmakers, designers, theoreticians, directors working collectively," the group at Club 57 was made up of Robert Cooney, Lindzee Smith, Carol Porter, and Betsy Sussler.[17] Fassbinder's freeform piece used the story of the Moors child murders in the north of England in the 1960s to examine society's exploitative and alienating inherencies. More generally, Nightshift's productions explored the political and revolutionary potential of theater. Selecting works whose themes centered on fascism and violence, their staging relied on formalist and multimedia strategies that in their view articulated "the kind of energy that terrorism has."[18] The centerpiece of the Nightshift production was Super 8 footage shot by Sussler (who would later expand on it to make her film, *Menage*); the footage underlined how the murderers had compulsively documented themselves through Polaroids, tape recordings, and drawings.[19] Sussler's footage, which the play relied on to represent the murders, never showed the violent acts; instead it alluded to them with the sounds of screaming, gagging, choking, and spoken orders. A voiceover track portrayed the two murderers reflecting on the orchestrations of their past deeds and refining their aesthetics for the next. The mise-en-scène of the live sections treated the space as a flat, frontal plane, coalescing film and theater, all the while denying the audience the catharsis traditionally achieved through a moralistic treatment of violence and justice.[20] Nightshift would go on to perform in New York in the early 1980s in rotating configurations, including at Squat Theatre (*Tripe*, after Franz Xaver Kroetz's *Men's Business*, in 1979); *Times Square Show* (*The Hamletmachine*, by Heiner Müller, in 1980); and Pyramid Club (*Rancho Notorious*, a multiweek, serial piece after the Fritz Lang film and starring Club 57 member Alexa Hunter, in 1982).

The summer following *Pas de trois*, in 1979, seasoned playwright Robert Patrick presented another kind of social theater at Club 57: *Kennedy's Children*, his 1973 meditation on the 1960s. Patrick had sought out the club for the play, which was structured around monologues delivered by patrons of Bowery bar and artist hangout Phebe's. Over five weekends, actors performed *Kennedy's Children* without a stage or theatrical lighting, the club's atmospheric and immersive setting situating audience members and performers in an unfiltered relationship uniquely truthful to the work.[21] Patrick directed, the first time he had done so in New York City since 1973—and only the third time he had directed *Children*, among hundreds of productions worldwide. The production's press release outlines with remarkable clarity the avant-garde potential Patrick saw in Club 57. His vision for the conceptual staging cites the East Village roots of the 1960s protest movement and punk alike. Of mirroring the play's imagined setting with its actual one, Patrick wrote: "[Club 57] is a step in returning to the former purity of impulse of the original Off-Off Broadway movement."[22] A central figure at Caffe Cino, the Greenwich Village coffeehouse that pioneered underground and gay theater in the 1960s, Patrick's conceptualization of Club 57 places the space in this historical avant-garde lineage, if perhaps fleetingly.

On an evening in late June 1980, playwright and drag performer Ethyl Eichelberger performed his adaptation of *Medea* (fig. 5), accompanied by John Heys and Agosto Machado, in shows at 8 p.m., 10 p.m., and midnight. After a decade working in classical repertory theater, followed by several more years with Charles Ludlam's Ridiculous Theatrical Company, Eichelberger began developing solo work centered on

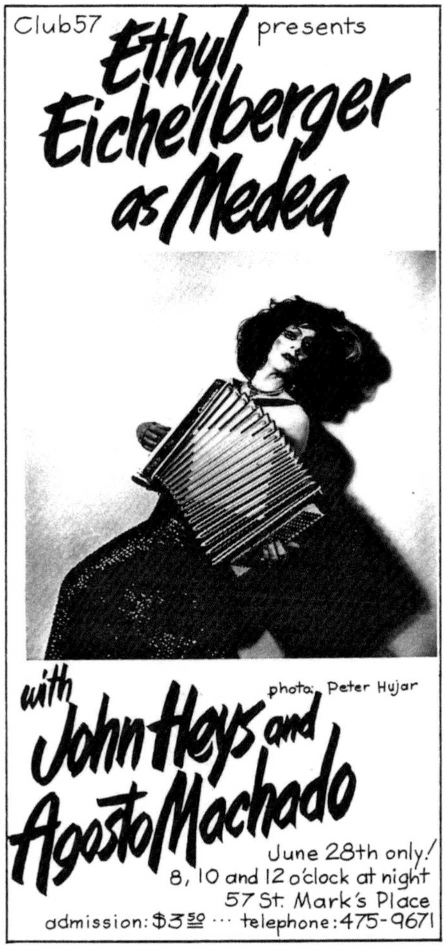

5. Flyer for Ethyl Eichelberger's *Medea*, at Club 57, 1980. Design by John Heys, who played Nerris the Nurse in the production. The Museum of Modern Art, New York. Department of Film Special Collections

Phèdre, Oedipus, and Nefertiti, which he presented at La MaMa, Dance Theater Workshop, and West Side bars that booked what were then called "transvestite acts." In a 1984 interview, Eichelberger noted that Club 57 was "the first club that I was aware of that did performance art."[23] The venue arguably occasioned a turning point in the performer's career, enabling him to discover an artistic space outside of both conventional and gay theater where he could develop a hybrid drag performance rooted in androgyny, burlesque, and vaudeville. Following *Medea*, Eichelberger gravitated toward the "unique performance environment" pioneered at Club 57 and by then proliferating in downtown spots such as Pyramid Club, 8BC, and others, where he would soon flourish as a regular performer.[24] Eichelberger's production attests to the significance that one night can have, and suggests that Club 57's free-flowing model fostered creative agency in ways participants did not necessarily anticipate.

Beyond its rich and varied links with the downtown scene, the core Club 57 membership developed its own pioneering theater. In September of 1980, Andy Rees replaced Magnuson as club manager. Today Rees is a theater artist who remains little known; yet under his tenure, theater took on a major presence at Club 57, marking a shift in theme but also in rhythm, as one-night happenings gave way to sustained runs. Rees was one of a cohort of friends who, along with Frank Holliday, hailed from the high school program at the University of North Carolina School of the Arts. A summer course in 1973 brought them both to New York—Rees to the School of American Ballet and Holliday to Joffrey Ballet School—and the two met in their shared dorm. A few years later, Holliday attended School of Visual Arts. When in 1978 Holliday got involved in the New Wave Vaudeville show being organized by his former SVA classmates Hannaford and Scully, he invited Rees, who had also moved to the city, to be part of the production.

Around the time he became manager, Rees teamed up with club member Scott Covert—who loved going to the ballet as much as staying out all night dancing—to bring dinner theater to the space under the aegis of Playhouse 57. In an ironic treatment of the medium's formalities, the "dinner" in Club 57's dinner theater consisted of mac 'n' cheese or peanut butter and jelly sandwiches, at times served in airplane vomit bags. Their first program, Summer Repertory Workshop (idiosyncratically hosted on September 17), included Marjorie Gross,[25] a comedian who would years later write for *Seinfeld*, performing from *Valley of the Dolls*; Covert and filmmaker Barry Shils's rendition of *Bent*, a 1979 play by Martin Sherman; and the Joan of Arc Bake-Off, featuring interpretations of the Maid of Orléans in works by Bertolt Brecht, George Bernard Shaw, Maxwell Anderson, and Jean Anouilh. In a punk gesture, Eileen Myles read Valerie Solanas's *Scum Manifesto*—the program advises "Don't Let the Joans-es Get You Down"—and was the fifth and winning Joan.

In some ways, Rees's theater works were extensions of performance nights mounted collectively at Club 57. For programs such as Salute to Lawrence Welk (June, 1980), A Night at the Opry (November, 1980), and iterations of 5700 Club performances (throughout 1981), Frank Holliday would create the sets, William Fleet Lively might

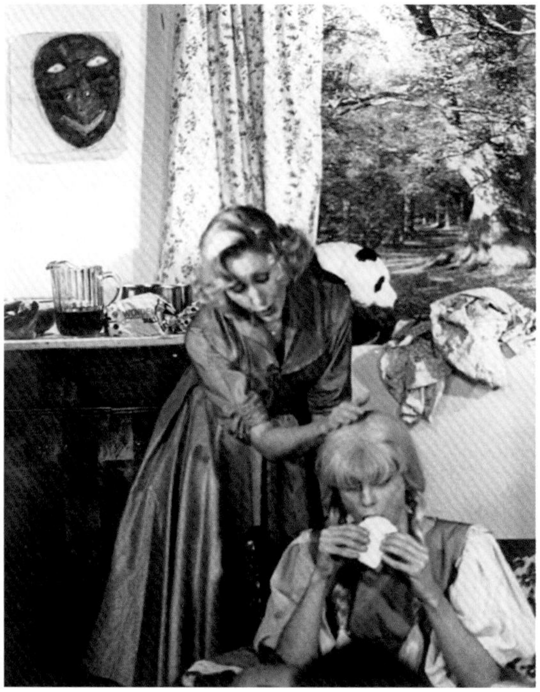

6. Georgia F. Wise and Scott Covert (as Becky Rockefeller) in *Bad Seed*, directed by Andy Rees, Club 57, October and November 1981. Set design (pictured) by Frank Holliday. Photograph by Victor Carnuccio

choreograph, and Rees would offer any combination of writing, performance, direction, or production.[26]

Yet, beginning in October 1981, with his adaptation of Maxwell Anderson's *Bad Seed*, Rees also honed a personal artistic vision. Rees's adaptation of the famous play was iconoclastic, with the model-child-turned-killer Rhoda Penmark played by Scott Covert in his Becky Rockefeller persona (fig. 6), outfitted in the blond lace wig that had become her signature adornment (a wheelchair was another frequent prop). Becky was a female character Covert acted out in semi-scripted public situations, following an acting class in which he had performed the female monologue from *Talk to Me Like the Rain and Let Me Listen*, a 1953 one-act Tennessee Williams play centered on melancholy and desperation. Favoring pathos over drag, Covert conceived of Becky as a "performance piece without an audience."[27]

The role of Monica Breedlove, neighbor to the Penmarks, was played by Lisa Altomare, a classically trained actor whom Rees had encountered at a summer stock program, and who would soon become his muse. Altomare, for her part, felt more at home in the East Village than in the uptown world of agents and auditions. She recalls Rees's urgent devotion to every part of the creative process, from precise props selected to elevate the production to scripts elaborately illustrated via hours of meticulously cutting, pasting, and xeroxing to communicate the visual language behind his direction.[28]

Rees's auteurism coexisted with a degree of anarchy, derived both from his mercurial temperament—albeit angelic in appearance, and by all accounts brilliant and adored by those close to him, Rees was said to be destructive with drink—and the dynamic between performers and spectators that the venue encouraged. Audience members, many of whom attended the production repeatedly, formed an unpredictable element of each performance. On any given night, a viewer might throw a sandwich at the stage or stand up and enact a scene with the actors; or the director might not show up, leaving the cast members to run the show. For Altomare, the essence of the work was the experience of its shared creation in the moment rather than a fixed performance executed by the cast and crew night after night. Working with Andy, she said recently, was "a celebration of the very reason I ever wanted to do theater, in the purest sense of the form."[29]

Rees would eventually take the theater he developed at the club to other venues. His original play *Webelos*—from "We'll Be Loyal Scouts"—was staged in conjunction with the P.S. 1 exhibition *Beast: Animal Imagery in Painting*, organized in 1982 by Richard Flood. Featuring Altomare and her fellow *Bad Seed* performer Georgia F. Wise in an exploration of "cub scouts, fascism and the family unit in America,"[30] the piece was presented in the museum's courtyard with the audience in the round. Rees's treatment of scouting rituals as a form of socialized "beast" traded the ironic treatment of suburban themes for an attempt at social satire centered on maladapted adults.

Rees's final project in the Club 57 period was an adaptation of Henrik Ibsen's 1881 play *Ghosts*, about a woman whose son is suffering from the patrimony of syphilis. Rees workshopped the play at Club 57 but presented it at the 18th Street Playhouse in January 1983. Described by its cast as "the first AIDS musical," Altomare played a Southern mother whose son, performed by Covert, contracts HIV. Rees's work recalls Jack Smith's adaptation of Ibsen in his epic and eccentric 1976 piece variously titled *Orchid Rot of Rented Lagoon* and *The Secret of Rented Island*. Smith's loft performance was experienced by its audience as a private ritual undertaken by the artist, a multihour affair achieving pathos that "belong[ed] more to the performing actor than . . . to the character he [was] allegedly creating."[31] The emotional immediacy at the center of Rees's production was equally raw, but by 1983 the ritual was no longer private, rather a shared experience of fear and grief during the AIDS crisis. Altomare recalls the project's heightened sense of urgency, likening it to a source of illumination within the surrounding darkness.[32] Club members attended *Ghosts* repeatedly to sing and cheer. The interactive and emotive theater experience was confounding to the Playhouse producer: Eighteenth Street was uptown by Club 57 standards.

Playhouse 57 also saw soon-to-be Broadway director Scott Wittman and composer-lyricist Marc Shaiman become creative forces after they were introduced to the space by Gross. Shaiman and Wittman, who recalled feeling "too rock and roll for theater, and too theater for rock and roll," found in Club 57 a creative outlet—and even a muse.[33] Their first production, *Boing Boing*, premiered in November 1980. The play was an adaptation of the French 1960s sex farce *Boeing Boeing*, "the worst play ever written" in their estimation, and which they transposed from Paris to Passaic, New Jersey. The cast included Covert alongside members of Shaiman and Wittman's theater circle, who would become Club 57 regulars over the five productions the pair staged there between November 1980 and December 1982. Tracey Berg, dressed as Joan Rivers, played the *Boing Boing* director, for which she sat in the front row with a script, prompting the actors if they forgot their lines.

After this first experiment, Wittman turned to more classical fare. The November 1980 fire at the MGM Grand Hotel and Casino in Las Vegas inspired him to stage Euripides's tale of the sacking of Troy amid the Sin City ashes. In *Trojan Women* (February to April 1981), Berg-as-Rivers returned as deposed Queen Hecuba and former Bette Midler backup singer Ula Hedwig emceed as Cher. J. P. Dougherty, an off-Broadway actor, played the messenger Talthybius in Elvis drag. Wittman spent the production's miniscule budget at the Eighth Street copy shop xeroxing scripts, flyers, and programs. The set consisted of dry ice, a bird bath, and a single hanging drop that created a makeshift backstage area. The chorus's show girls were encouraged to develop their characters with costumes from their closets. Wittman recalled how one evening, the drop fell and the chorus girls were doing the same thing offstage as they were on: eating watermelon, courtesy a fad diet.[34]

Despite the freewheeling nature of the weekly shows, *Trojan Women* brought a new level of ambition and scale to the venue. Its use of ironic mash-ups, today a major part of postmodern culture, resonated with audiences. After a favorable review in *SoHo Weekly News*,[35] the show was especially well-attended, with appearances by theater luminaries Joe Papp, Jay Presson Allen, and Allan Carr, who wanted to move the show to Las Vegas. Shaiman and Wittman's vision is also evidenced by the uptick in the club program's rhythm: at the start of 1981, *Trojan Women* ran on Mondays, beginning with its "preview" showing on February 23, while on Wednesdays *Boing Boing* showed in "revival"[36] (fig. 7).

Shaiman and Wittman's subsequent three shows at Club 57 further expanded the possibilities for the space and showcased the artists' increasingly mature creative vision. *Livin' Dolls* (September to December 1981) was an original musical: an homage to the beach party movies of the '60s starring Barbie and Ken,[37] it featured beach towels and pizza, synth music recordings by Man Parrish, and Barbie fashions by

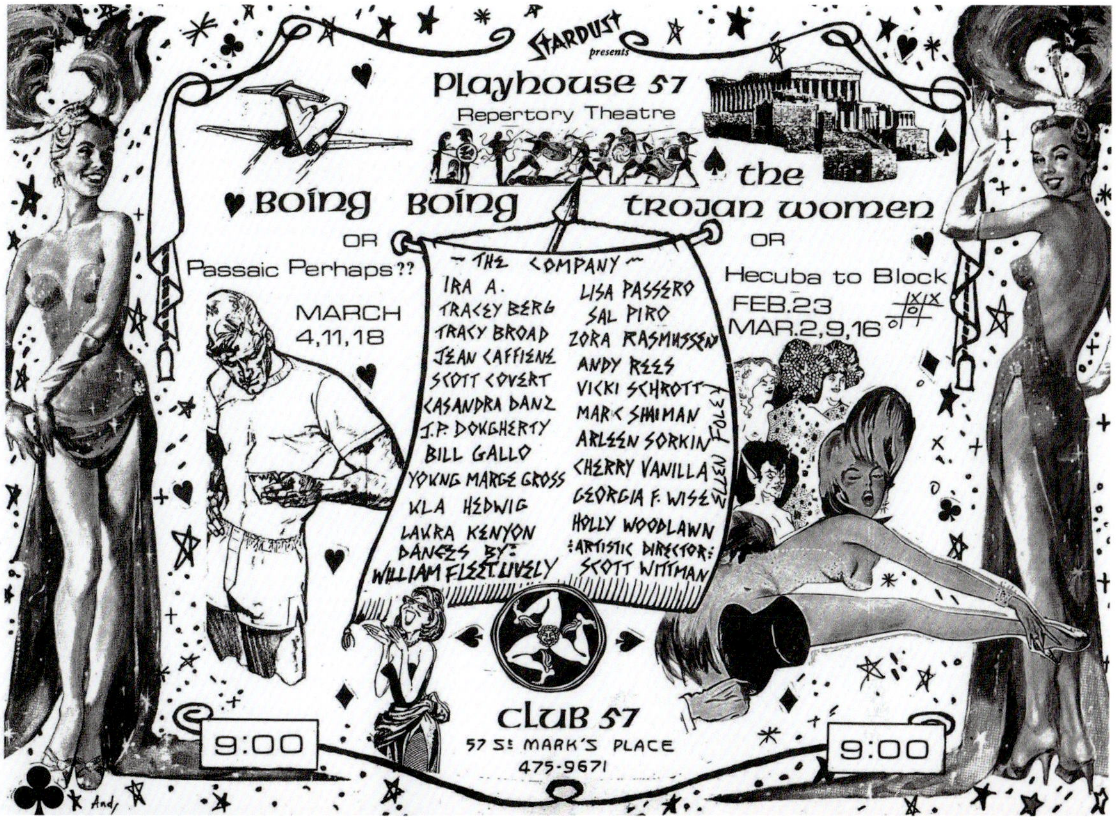

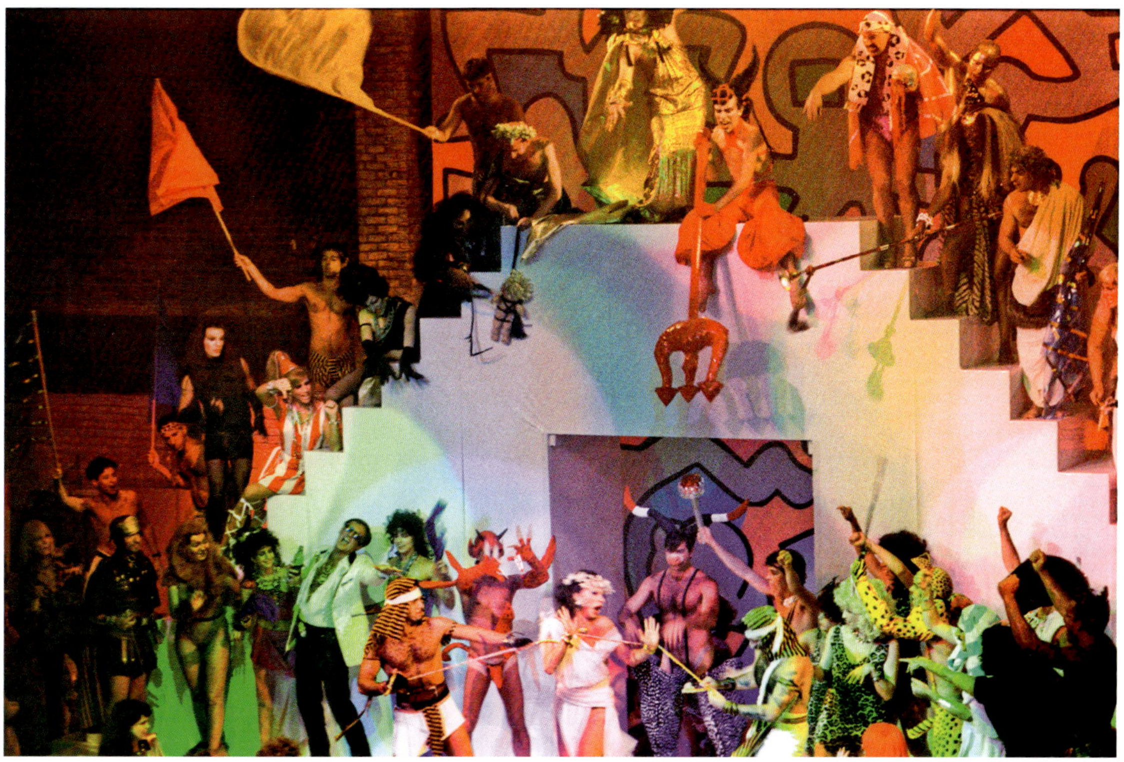

7. Flyer for Playhouse 57, February and March 1981, with Scott Wittman and Marc Shaiman's productions of *Trojan Women* and *Boing Boing* playing concurrently. Design by Andy Rees. The Museum of Modern Art, New York. Department of Film Special Collections

8. *Pagan Place*, directed by Scott Wittman, Palladium, August 7, 1985. Ascending stairs, left: Tabboo! (standing, in black), Peter Kwaloff, Lypsinka, Gerard Little, Marc Cato; top of platform: Alexis del Lago, Joey Arias (in red); descending stairs, right: Billy Gallo, Pony, Pepsi; front, from left: Lisa Altomare, Karen Mandelbaum, Craig Vandenburgh, Lyn Mandelbaum, Paul Zone, Bobby Siems, Holly Woodlawn (in white), Steve Rowe, Miki Zone, Tracey Berg, Mary Fulham, Gaylord. Photograph by Lynn M. Grabowski

Timothy Dunleavy.[38] A few months after its run at Club 57, the production moved to Manhattan Theatre Club, shedding the characters' trademarked names and much of the original team, and arguably losing its magic as a result.

The duo developed *The Sound of Muzak* (December 1981 to January 1982) around Warhol superstar Holly Woodlawn, who played the leading role. The limitations of the basement club necessitated a conceptual staging reminiscent of theater povera. The audience was seated in the middle of the club, with the Alps set on one side and the convent on the other; at the change of scene, Wittman would call out "Rotate," and the audience members would turn their folding chairs. The downtown-trash interpretation of the Julie Andrews film included a pair of McDonald's Golden Arches set among the scenic mountains that club member, artist, and performer Vicki Schrott painted on the club walls each week, as well as drugged-out lyrics to "My Favorite Things." Shaiman recalls arguing with agents demanding comp tickets to the sought-after show—Club 57 offered no such arrangement, not to mention that tickets were only five dollars to begin with—all the while being dressed in a makeshift nun's habit.[39] The final Shaiman-Wittman production at Club 57 was *Trilogy of Terror* (December 1982), developed with and starring Laura Kenyon, who was part of the Broadway show *Nine* at the time. Also in "Rotat-o-vision," the three vignettes covered conjoined twins and cool jazz amid tales of murder. The show's deadpan elements included child actor Cameron Johann (also in *Nine*) playing several adult roles and a dog sitting calmly on a barstool while being serenaded by Tom Waits's "The Piano Has Been Drinking."

Shaiman and Wittman figured among the many artists at Club 57 who quickly moved on to present work in more established venues. In September 1982, Wittman and Georgia F. Wise opened *Sweet Blondes of Youth*, a loose adaptation of Tennessee Williams's *Sweet Bird of Youth*, starring John Sex and drag icon Alexis del Lago, at the Twenty-First Street club Danceteria. The end of the following year, Wittman and Shaiman returned with a production of *Peter Pan*. While the scale of these performances was larger than those put on at the basement club, they remained more or less by and for a certain peer group and thrived on the energy of ad hoc stagecraft among friends and collaborators. For each production, Wittman's preshow ritual of walking the cast through the show might very well have been the first time all of the actors were in the same room. The backstage hangout and revelry in some cases lasted longer than the performance—as Shaiman recalls, "That *was* the show"[40]—and was often videotaped by Nelson Sullivan, whose camera was ubiquitous in downtown clubs in the mid-1980s. Danceteria provided the duo with an actual budget to realize projects, and shows there like their 1985 *Nude Faces of 85* boasted ambitious production values, as evidenced in its accomplished can-can number featuring petticoats designed by club alumnus Katy K.

Wittman and Shaiman also extended the legacy of Club 57 through their ongoing work with Sex, whose love of showbiz, generosity as a performer, and fundamental sweetness inspired Wittman to shape productions around him, including *Peter Pan*, *The Sound of Muzak* (revived in 1986 at the Limelight nightclub, with dozens of Von Trapp children played by club alum), and *Bye Bye Birdie* (at the Saint in 1986, with fashions by Patricia Field). By the mid-'80s, their productions began reaching an undeniably different scale. In 1985, Sex, Magnuson, and Joey Arias starred in a production of *Pagan Place*—"the Bible in twenty minutes"—with an extensive cast and elaborate sets, at the Palladium nightclub (fig. 8). Fearful of the vertiginous structures she was asked to climb, Holly Woodlawn reportedly superglued her high-heeled shoes to her feet; it was all light-years away from the watermelon-eating chorus line of *Trojan Women*.[41]

In its last year of operation, Club 57 intersected with a theater group itself on the rise. Peggy Shaw and Lois

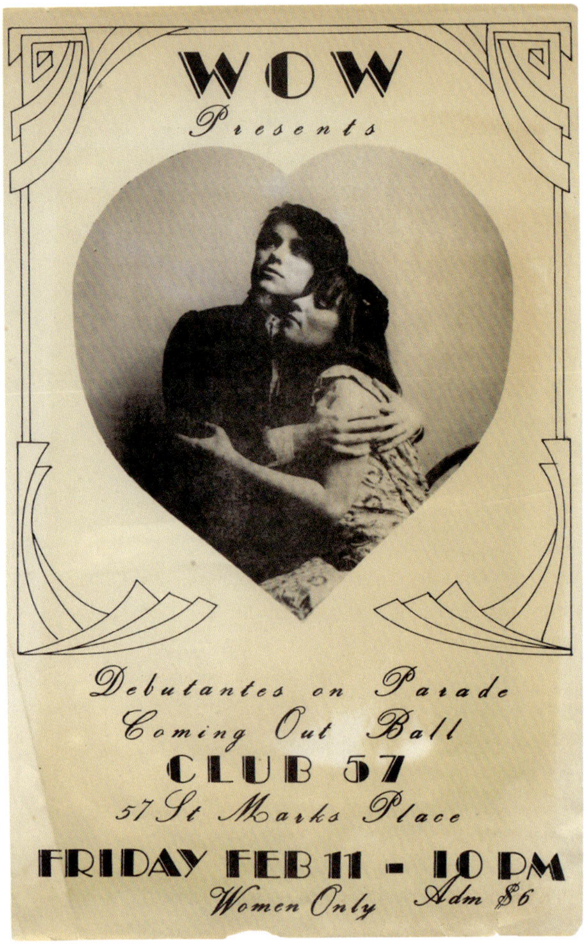

9. Flyer for Debutantes on Parade Coming Out Ball, organized by WOW, Club 57, 1983. Unknown designer. The flyer features Peggy Reynolds (left) and Holly Hughes (right) in a photograph by Eva Weiss. The Museum of Modern Art, New York. Department of Film Special Collections

Weaver, the organizers of the 1980 and 1981 Women's One World Performance Festival, sought to channel the momentum from their festival into a venue focused on women-centered and lesbian material. What would become WOW (Women's One World) hosted the women-only Freudian Slip/Psychotic Underwear Bash (April 1982), the military-themed Party to End All Wars (June 1982) and the XXXMAS Benefit (December 1982) at Club 57 to raise funds in the lead-up to the opening of WOW Café Theatre in a storefront on East Eleventh Street. Interviewed in 1986, Weaver reflected that the fundraisers were "an excuse to have a party, an excuse to have an event again, [and] a place to put that creative energy."[42] As part of the XXXMAS Benefit, Diane Torr, a performance artist, go-go dancer, and sex-worker organizer, set up rows of thrift store clothes from cocktail dresses to military gear, encouraging attendees to dress up, perform, explore, and transform their identities, if only for the night.[43] Even after inaugurating the café, the group continued to organize events at Club 57, such as Debutantes on Parade Coming Out Ball (February 1983; fig. 9). A gender-fluid space from the get-go, Club 57 members appreciated "WOW's purpose and zaniness,"[44] according to theater critic Alisa Solomon, and played a role in the group's early establishment. By the time Club 57 closed in spring of 1983, WOW Café had replicated the club's democratic form of curatorship and variety-style programming to form an incubator and open platform in its own right, which it remains to this day.

ART: OLD, NEW, AND COLLECTIVE

New York in the 1970s saw the flourishing of alternative venues and opportunities for artists outside of the commercial art system. On the heels of the 1960s-era artist-run galleries along Tenth Street and artist groups animated by political activism, organizations such as Artists Space, 112 Greene Street, the Kitchen, and P.S. 1 were among the multifarious new initiatives that took any number of forms, among them experimental visual art exhibition spaces, artist-run co-op galleries, small museums, performance spaces, and workshops or outreach programs.[45] The National Endowment for the Arts' support for local efforts, which began in 1972, catalyzed this generative period. Yet the new reliance on grant funding also saddled alternative venues with the bureaucratic obligations that accompany nonprofit tax status, such as an administrative staff and a board of directors. By the end of the decade, some of the most successful artists' rebellions had morphed into small-scale, vibrant institutions in their own right.[46]

By 1980, the downtown scene was made up of younger artists reacting against not only the commercial galleries but also the novel phenomenon of arts administration. This new crop of artists and artist groups adopted varying strategies. Colab, an artist collective, developed a cooperative model that disbursed grant funding to artists by artists, bypassing curators and arts administrators, albeit through lengthy member meetings. Political Art Documentation and Distribution began as a resource to artists with an emphasis on archiving and distributing socially engaged printed matter, borrowing from labor union strategies (fig. 10). An offshoot of Colab, ABC No Rio mounted the *Real Estate Show* in an occupied city building; the anti-gentrification initiative set the tone for its programming. Another collective, Group Material, sought to engage the community through critical theory. After manning a storefront gallery for a season on a Thirteenth Street block populated by Hispanic families, they admitted "the maintenance and operation of the storefront had become a ball-and-chain on the collective," and resumed itinerant programming.[47] Fashion Moda's similar community-oriented goal in the South Bronx was expressed through interdisciplinary and multicultural approaches.

Downtown New York's nightlife spaces merit consideration within this history. Their independence from inherited institutional structures is what unites them with art collectives, two orders of programming that might otherwise be separated into seriousness versus fun, daytime activity versus "art after midnight." Their shared outlook was best stated by musician, poet, and Fashion Moda director Joe Lewis: "Quality is no longer an issue. Quality is the concern of abstract art."[48] The period's collective experiments reclaimed artistic agency through inclusive and deliberately uncurated initiatives—epitomized by the invitational art shows replicated across the scene—and to varying degrees interrogated the artist's relationship to the urban and political context. Nightlife settings were also often more conducive to connecting peers and collaborators than were more formal art contexts, which is in part how the iconic White Street music and performance venue Mudd Club, for instance, came to be the unofficial headquarters of No Wave filmmaking.

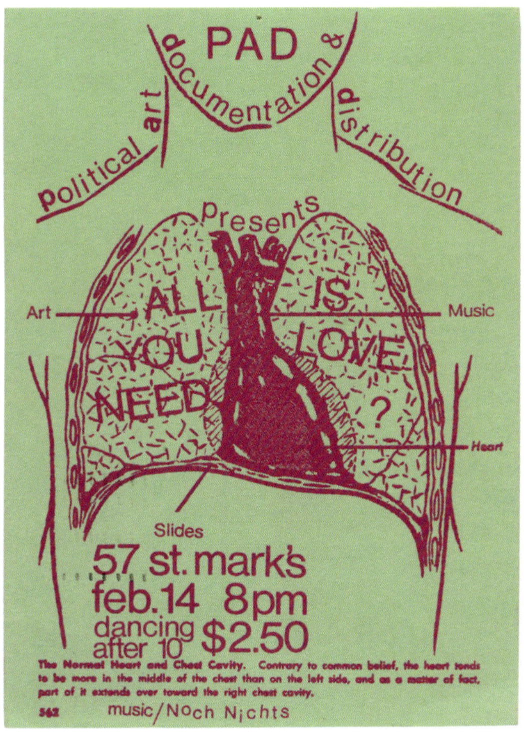

10. Postcard for All You Need Is Love, organized by PAD/D, Club 57, 1981. Unknown designer. This Valentine's Day event included slideshows, discussions, and music, and illustrates the overlap in programming between clubs and collectives. The Museum of Modern Art, New York, Library Collection, Political Art Documentation/Distribution (PAD/D) Archive

Club 57—a nightclub for all practical purposes—was less outwardly political than its art collective counterparts.[49] (As a whole the scene was arguably less political than its New York predecessors or its working-class British punk peers.) Yet the artists associated with Club 57 were working within a shared political context, often addressing the same topics as the collective-affiliated artists, albeit with different approaches. When in early December 1978 New Wave Vaudeville returned to Irving Plaza for a series of reprise performances, the new finale featured the cast drinking Kool-Aid and falling to the ground in front of a set piece by painter Frank Holliday. The performance was ripped straight from the headlines, a response to the November 18 Jonestown Massacre, in which more than nine hundred members of an American cult committed mass suicide in Guyana by drinking a concoction of cyanide and what historians now believe to be Flavor Aid (a sugary beverage similar to Kool-Aid). Two years later, Colab member Tom Otterness would create a newsprint piece depicting the Jonestown cult tragedy for the gift shop adjoining the Colab-organized *Times Square Show*, an exhibition staged in a Forty-Second Street massage parlor that brought together artists from Colab, Club 57, the graffiti scene, and beyond. Otterness's work reflected the collective's shared interest in the theme of violence.[50] It also adopted their shared interest in the artist multiple as a mode of dissemination, a method that would be formalized through Alan Moore's A. More store, which ran from 1981 to 1984. Whereas Otterness expressed a more somber take on the mass

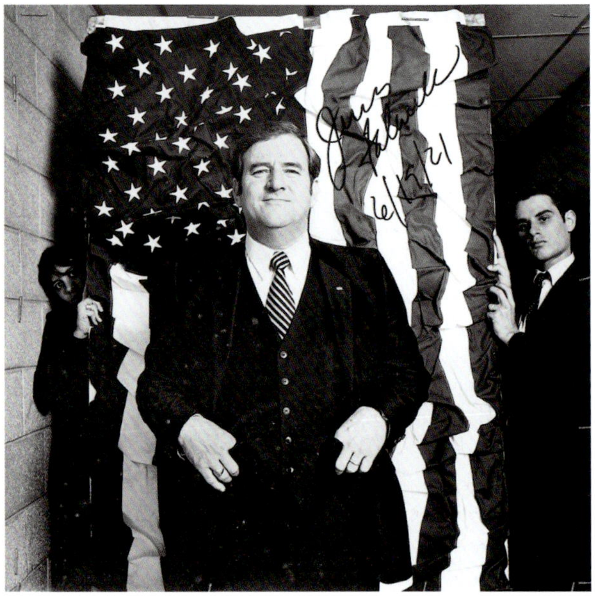

11. Tseng Kwong Chi (American, born Hong Kong, 1950–1990). Jerry Falwell with Jeanne Gianas and Bruno Testore Schmidt, from the Moral Majority series, 1981. Gelatin silver print, 10 × 10" (25.4 × 25.4 cm). Collection the Estate of Tseng Kwong Chi/Muna Tseng Dance Projects, Inc., New York

suicide, the Club 57 set had taken on the event in its own way, with irony and dark humor.

Similarly, artist groups across the scene reacted to the 1980 election of Ronald Reagan. On the day he was sworn in, ABC mounted the multimedia *It's War at No Rio*, while Mudd Club hosted its own inaugural ball. The affair boasted live entertainment organized by Ann Magnuson, including the newly formed Moral Majority Singers, an offshoot of the Ladies Auxiliary of the Lower East Side, Club 57's take on the women's organization Junior League; quotes from Reagan's speeches, researched by Mudd Club owner Steve Mass, served as décor.[51] Reagan's new conservatism delivered source material to Club 57 artists and defined in part their ongoing collaboration with *SoHo Weekly News*—and thus their reach to a wider audience. In December 1980, Magnuson and Hong Kong–born photographer and club member Tseng Kwong Chi created the satirical "It's a Reagan World," a spread featuring their downtown peers as buttoned-up, suburbanite couples, "exponents of the New Heterosexuality."[52] In the same issue, Animal X rounded up a government cabinet of her own in a fashion piece that included Joan Jett as the secretary of defense.[53]

In 1981, Tseng took this subversive energy further with his Moral Majority series, for which he orchestrated portrait sessions for the weekly with figures on the Christian right (fig. 11). Tseng used a wrinkled American flag as a backdrop and donned a seersucker suit for the sessions, staging a conceptual performance of American values in which a gay, foreign, and nonwhite artist undermined the unwitting sitter's conservatism and perceived control over the construction and meaning of images.[54]

The artists of the era also engaged cultural themes through different strategies. In May 1981, Group Material's Mundy McLaughlin organized *Facere/Fascis*, an exhibition reflecting on the tension between industry standards of beauty and fashion as street-level self-expression. McLaughlin hosted a party at Club 57 in conjunction with the show, which included club members April Palmieri, Jonathan Quinn, and Katy K—contributing one of her shower-curtain raincoat designs—alongside their Group Material cohorts. The exhibition's theoretical perspective reflecting on "high fashion as a dimension of the new fascist discourse"[55] differed from the club artists' explorations of the very same themes. Stacey Elkin called her fashion line "Amazon School of Modeling" to project a strong, confrontational female figure (fig. 12). One of Elkin's creations, a cocktail dress that left one breast exposed, channeled 1950s sophistication, while aligning it with the lived reality of gritty, post-punk New York. She made other garments from parachute nylon and whatever enticing fabric could be purchased on Orchard Street for less than one dollar per yard. One runway show even included fashions made of raw meat, a shock-value number that doubled as a comment on the objectification of women. Elkin staged her runway shows at Club 57 and Mudd Club (page 46), with Club 57 members Diana Lillig or Drew Straub as emcee. Lisa Baumgardner, Ann Magnuson, Min Thometz, Ande Whyland, and Elkin herself were among the models. The shows were free-flowing, semi-unconscious creations that Elkin never articulated as concepts.

Unlike its art collective peers, Club 57 never sought public funding. Nonetheless, it shared with these organizations a desire to exhibit avant-garde artists in a context outside the white cube model, a desire that set these venues apart from those that fostered

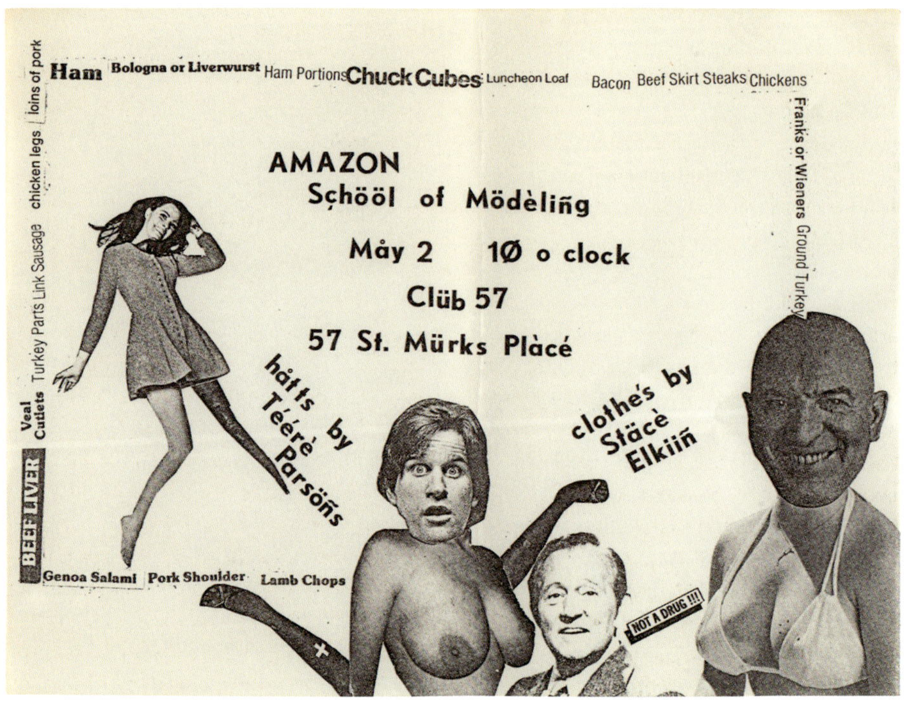

12. Flyer for Stacey Elkin's Amazon School of Modeling: Spring Meat Show at Club 57, 1980. Design by Elkin. The Museum of Modern Art, New York. Department of Film Special Collections

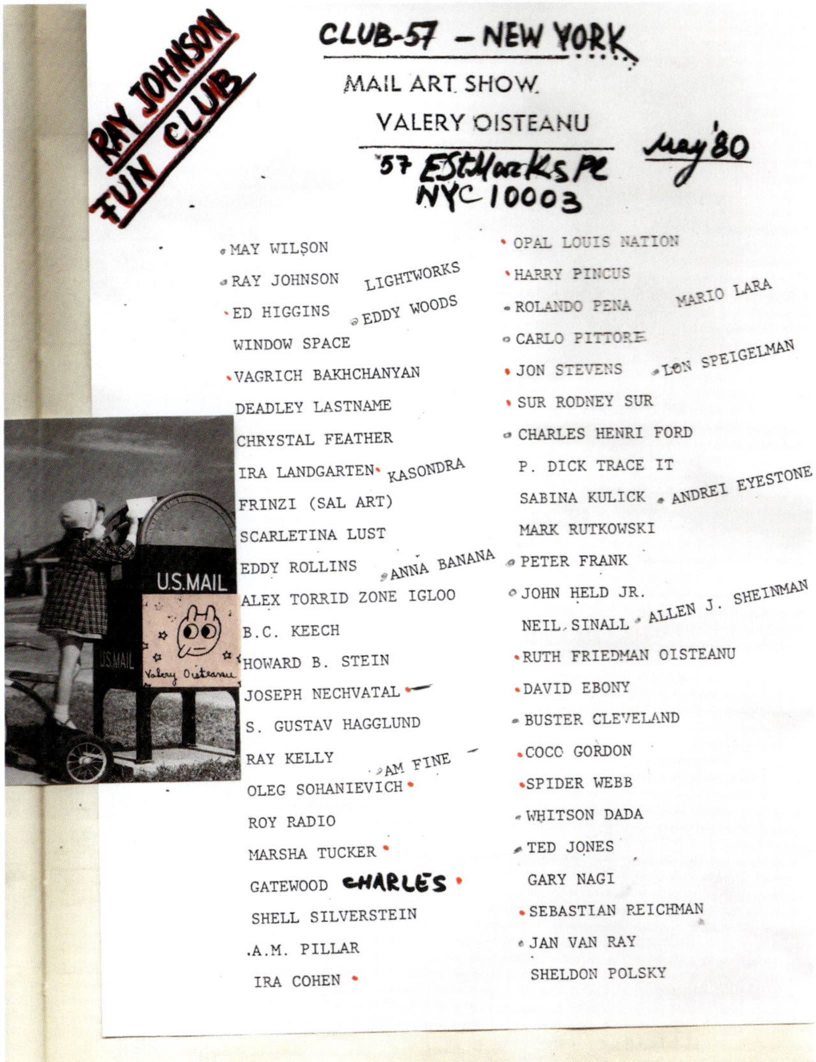

RAY JOHNSON FUN CLUB

CLUB-57 – NEW YORK
MAIL ART SHOW
VALERY OISTEANU
57 St. Marks Pl
NYC 10003
May '80

MAY WILSON	OPAL LOUIS NATION
RAY JOHNSON LIGHTWORKS	HARRY PINCUS
ED HIGGINS EDDY WOODS	ROLANDO PENA MARIO LARA
WINDOW SPACE	CARLO PITTORE
VAGRICH BAKHCHANYAN	JON STEVENS LEN SPEIGELMAN
DEADLEY LASTNAME	SUR RODNEY SUR
CHRYSTAL FEATHER	CHARLES HENRI FORD
IRA LANDGARTEN KASONDRA	P. DICK TRACE IT
FRINZI (SAL ART)	SABINA KULICK ANDREI EYESTONE
SCARLETINA LUST	MARK RUTKOWSKI
EDDY ROLLINS ANNA BANANA	PETER FRANK
ALEX TORRID ZONE IGLOO	JOHN HELD JR.
B.C. KEECH	NEIL SINALL ALLEN J. SHEINMAN
HOWARD B. STEIN	RUTH FRIEDMAN OISTEANU
JOSEPH NECHVATAL	DAVID EBONY
S. GUSTAV HAGGLUND	BUSTER CLEVELAND
RAY KELLY AM FINE	COCO GORDON
OLEG SOHANIEVICH	SPIDER WEBB
ROY RADIO	WHITSON DADA
MARSHA TUCKER	TED JONES
GATEWOOD CHARLES	GARY NAGI
SHELL SILVERSTEIN	SEBASTIAN REICHMAN
A.M. PILLAR	JAN VAN RAY
IRA COHEN	SHELDON POLSKY

13. Artist list for *Mail Art Show*, organized by Valery Oisteanu and dedicated to Ray Johnson, at Club 57, May 21, 1981. Design by Oisteanu. According to mail art bibliographer John Held Jr., the exhibition included contributions by a number of artists for whom the format was unusual, including May Wilson, Ray Kelly, Marcia Tucker (founder of the New Museum, name misspelled above), Charles Gatewood, Spider Webb, and A. M. Fine. Some artists appeared under aliases: Deadley Lastname (Bradley Lastname), Roy Radio (Roger Stevens), and Lightworks (editor Charlton Burch). Collection Valery Oisteanu

artistic experimentation while styling themselves after galleries or museums. In this way, Club 57 was situated within a network of alternative spaces that ran parallel to art institutions proper and served a set of artists seeking opportunity, unconventional contexts, or simply an offbeat energy.

As its first constituency of SVA students moved on to other outlets, the club remained a site of constant renewal and experimentation, bringing in a new roster of talent beyond its original membership.

In May 1981, Valery Oisteanu, a poet and artist of Romanian origin, organized a show in the spirit of Ray Johnson's New York Correspondence School (fig. 13). Oisteanu introduced what he perceived to be an untapped community of artists, his exhibition featuring individuals associated with mail art, such as Anna Banana, Buster Cleveland, E. F. Higgins III, Johnson, Scarlatina Lust, and Carlo Pittore; European conceptualists Vagrich Bakhchanyan and Achille Cavellini; downtown figures such as Charles Henri Ford, Ray Kelly (the Mark Rothko studio assistant who would go on to helm the Rivington School artist collective), Marcia Tucker, and May Wilson; and mail art bibliographer and curator John Held Jr.[56] Oisteanu had been part of Johnson's wider circle in the 1970s, creating moments of continuity between intergenerational avant-gardes at Club 57. In 1982, *Watch These Girls: 19 Women Who Do Copy Art* (October) and *Paintings at Club 57* (December) both brought in newcomers, the latter of which included Puerto Rican surrealist Angel Borrero and conceptual painter Brian Buczak, alongside organizer Bill Doherty, who made his painting directly on the club's wall. The same year, eccentric and prolific neighborhood fixture Dan Asher hung a solo show of his raw, evocative drawings (page 82).

The artists who gravitated to Club 57 also appeared around town in exhibitions at similarly unconventional spaces, attesting in a sense to the value that these spaces held for artists committed to nontraditional strategies. In February 1981, art enthusiast Mark Gildav put on a show of one hundred artists in the Department of Transportation garage windows in midtown.[57] Both he and artist Ken Kaczmarzyk had been individually curating shows in the garage's ten ground-level window displays overlooking Eighth Avenue since 1978. Teaming up as 10 on 8, they would replicate Gildav's hundred-artist format at Club 57 the following year. Also in 1981, in December, Doherty staged the month-long *Bank Show*, bringing together an array of artists' self-portraits at the Manufacturers Hanover Trust Bank at 682 Broadway. Richard Hambleton, Alice Neel, and Buczak were among the likenesses displayed in the teller windows and offices (fig. 14). In 1982, Buczak, who was part of Fluxus circles, and exhibited internationally in museums and galleries, hung a show at Todd's Copy Shop, the Mott Street xerox spot and ad hoc gallery run by Todd Jorgensen, who also cofounded the performance salon A's. In 1983, future East Village gallerist Patrick Fox began staging semipublic exhibitions featuring club members Scott Covert (pages 78–79) and Robert Hawkins (page 88) at the Anderson Theater Gallery, an empty theater house where he also lived; the theater marquee was deployed at times to exhibit sculpture.

The story of any alternative space, of any avant-garde perhaps, entails both how—and how well—it weathers the impact of external forces, be they bureaucratic pressures created by public funding institutions or commercial forces enticing artists to pursue individual careers. The Club 57 years, 1978 to 1983, saw artists constantly reshuffling their responses to the evolving externalities. In the early 1980s, the East Village saw an explosion of galleries, modeled in part after the exhibitions of Club 57 in terms of the artists they featured and the ethos they sought to embody. As historian and curator Brian Wallis observed: "Between 1981 and 1983, a third generation of artists founded *alternatives to the alternatives* in the form of commercial galleries."[58]

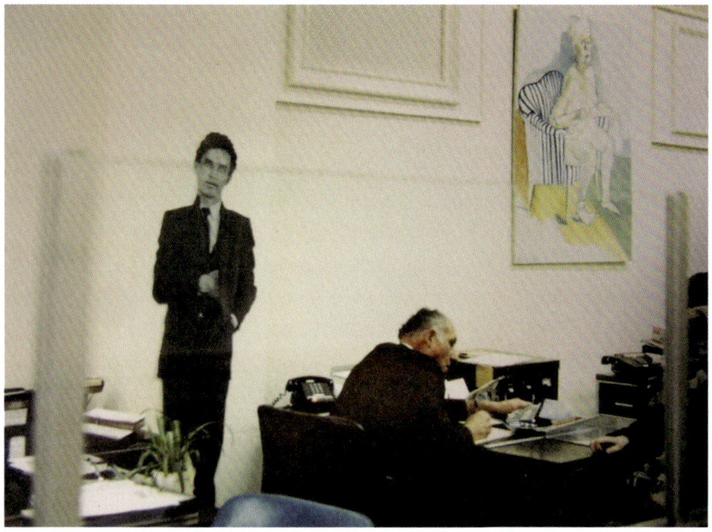

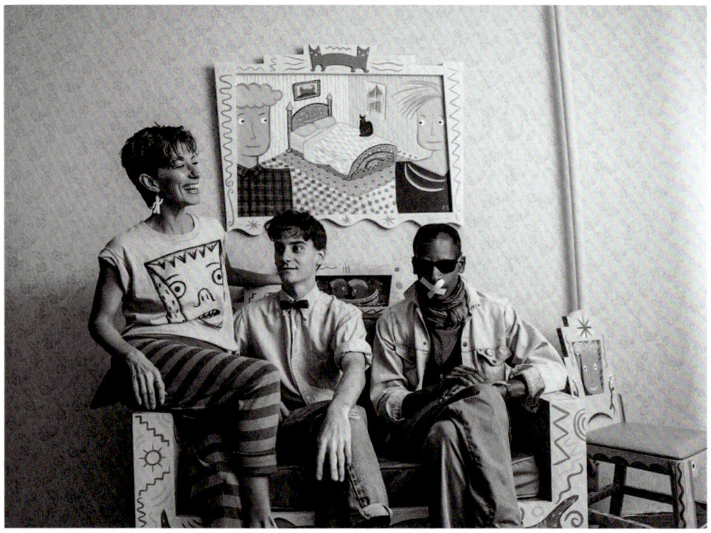

14. Installation view of *The Bank Show*, organized by ēpoch at Manufacturers Hanover Trust Co., 682 Broadway, December 22, 1981–January 31, 1982. Visible works are self-portraits by Richard Hambleton (left) and Alice Neel (right). Photograph by Bill Doherty

15. From left: Gracie Mansion, Rodney Alan Greenblat, and Sur Rodney (Sur) at Gracie Mansion Gallery on the occasion of the exhibition *Sofa and Painting*, in Andreas Sterzing's photograph *The Nuclear Family*, 1983. Visible are a customized sofa and painting by Greenblat.

FUN Gallery cofounder Patti Astor recognized White Columns, Artists Space, Fashion Moda, and Club 57 as precedents for the storefront space she opened with Bill Stelling in August 1981. The energetic program featured graffiti writers she had costarred with in Charlie Ahearn's *Wild Style*, including Lee Quinones and Fab 5 Freddy, alongside club affiliates Kenny Scharf (whose first show gave the space its name, *FUN*—a Club 57 tenet), Keith Haring, and Jean-Michel Basquiat. FUN's scene-defining openings saw the mingling of downtown regulars, hip-hop beat boys, and, for the first time, collectors.[59]

Painter-turned-gallerist Gracie Mansion put forth the exhibition itself as a happening and an ironic send-up.[60] In the 1981 *Limo Show*, she and partner Sur Rodney (Sur) staged a show of mail artist Buster Cleveland in a rented limousine parked on West Broadway at Spring Street, a stone's throw from Leo Castelli Gallery. In March of the following year, Mansion presented an exhibition of Timothy Greathouse photographs in her tenement apartment bathroom, dubbed "the Loo Division." A press release promised "the viewing at close range of intimate works of art by lower Manhattan artists."[61] At their later gallery space, Gracie Mansion Gallery, Mansion and Rodney (Sur)'s vision combined the small, affordable scale of their first ad hoc settings with media savvy and an offbeat, kitsch-inflected aesthetic.[62] Curator Dan Cameron identified Rodney Alan Greenblat, with his cartoonish innocence, as the artist in Mansion's roster who best embodied her sensibility.[63] Cameron, Greenblat, and Rodney (Sur) had each participated in invitational exhibitions at Club 57 as far back as 1980 (fig. 15).

In March 1982, painter Rich Colicchio turned his St. Marks apartment into exhibition space 51X.[64] Beyond showing his own work, and that of gallery partner Ed Kurpell, Colicchio's 51X took its cue from FUN, mounting one-man shows by graffiti writers Zephyr, Dondi, and Crash. The duo also exhibited AVANT, a collective founded by Christopher Hart Chambers that installed newsprint paintings in the streets of SoHo and empty lots in the Lower East Side. AVANT's assembly-line production methods entailed multiple artists producing handmade, "original" works in a preordained style.[65] AVANT's process and guerrilla-style installations referenced graffiti's energy as much as capitalist realism's negotiation of commodity in the work of Sigmar Polke. (The group also participated in group exhibitions at Club 57 in June 1982 and January 1983, having been introduced to the venue by occasional AVANT member Brant Kingman.)

Dean Savard and Alan Barrows's Civilian Warfare, which opened in 1982, was characterized by its grittier tone and direct intellectual and material relationship to the street, a historical precedent being Claes Oldenburg's evocation of the Lower East Side in *The Street* (1960) and *The Store* (1961–62). The same "easy artistic appropriation of all and any available media and material"[66] that animated art-making at Club 57—from Frank Holliday's theater sets to Kenny Scharf's detritus-filled Day-Glo assemblages to exhibitions such as *Found in the Street* (May 1982) and *The Matchbook Show* (March 1983), in which Savard participated—propelled the program at Civilian Warfare. Notably, David Wojnarowicz began exhibiting his paintings on supermarket posters and garbage can lids at the new gallery. For Keith Haring's Club 57 *Erotic Art Show* in February 1981 (page 74), Wojnarowicz had contributed an image of a naked man with a dog's face—a Minotaur motif staged with a stencil and spray paint in the abandoned buildings and cruising grounds of the Hudson River Piers.[67] The gallery's darker outlook and psychological rawness was also apparent in Richard Hambleton's ominous silhouettes (page 89) and Greer Lankton's cloth dolls exploring the mutability of gender, sexuality, and the body. For Lankton, the themes of her work were part of a lifetime investigation that included her own gender affirmation procedure. She occasionally showed at Club 57, notably in 57's Tribute to Motherhood (May 1982) organized by Cookie Mueller, who reflected her own postmodern female sensibility with simultaneous roles as a mother and scene impresario in the period.

Nature Morte, founded by artist-dealers Peter Nagy and Alan Belcher, opened on the same day as Civilian Warfare, and in some ways their initiative was aligned with their storefront gallery neighbors. Nagy, who cited the energy of *Times Square Show* as a touchstone, saw the gallery as "a direct route to action," while Belcher estimated that their audience was primarily fellow

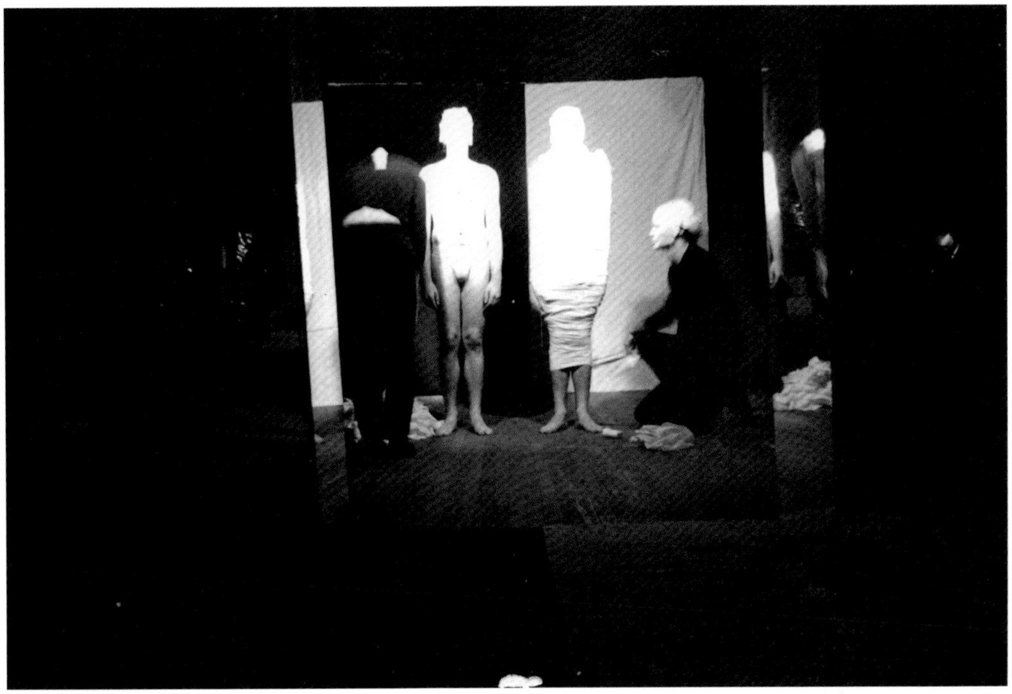

16. From left: Bill Sack, Josh and Dan Braun, Christian Joiris, and Robin Crutchfield in *Evasion*, a performance by Joiris, Club 57, June 28, 1981. Photograph by Ira Abramowitz

artists.[68] However, the gallery's interest in cool, intellectual, and media-based work, in the spirit of the Pictures Generation, stood in opposition to the neo-expressionism, punk angst, and kitsch alternately at play in much of the East Village. Most importantly, Nature Morte signaled that the scene would take multiple aesthetic directions as it grew.[69] And grow it did, with real estate values rising and galleries replacing ethnic businesses, empty blocks, or drug zones. At the end of 1982, there were six galleries in the East Village; at the end of 1983, there were thirty. Club 57 had already shuttered its doors that spring. The years 1984 and 1985 clocked in at 77 and 124 respectively.[70]

What to make of the church basement on St. Marks Place? The club's theme nights morphed into themed exhibitions such as Piezo Electric gallery's *The Wild West Show*, while art shows made their way into new nightlife venues like Limbo Lounge, one of many so-called art bars. But other aspects of what came to be known as the East Village scene at the height of the gallery boom—professionalism, the commercial market, and even Reaganomics[71]—were a departure from the ethos of Club 57 and similar spaces, as the scene moved beyond the initial scale of the neighborhood peer group.

PERFORMANCE: EVERY NIGHT OF THE WEEK

In October 1982, jazz composer Tony Heiberg wrote in *East Village Eye*, "Of course, everyone knows that theme parties began at Club 57."[72] While Mudd Club had introduced theme nights, often hosted by Tina L'Hotsky—Cold War Zeitgeist, Joan Crawford Mother's Day, and a beach party organized by Fred Schneider of the B-52's—such was the little club's reach, as epitomized by the participatory performance events under Ann Magnuson's curatorship. Yet, adding to this iconic history are lesser-known links with other genres, notably comedy and poetry. From November 1978 to April 1979, a comedy troupe by the name of the Other Leading Brand performed up to four times a week in the basement club. Styling themselves after *Saturday Night Live*, the group inhabited a transitionary period between the neighborhood "polka days" and its New Wave heyday.[73] In the years that followed, comedy was presented at Club 57 by New Wave Vaudeville alumni Tessie Chua, Robert Romagnoli, and Michael Peppe, among others. Frank Maya, later known for being the first openly gay comic to achieve mainstream success, appeared with his band the Decals and participated in a Bargain Monday poetry evening.

Poetry was also presented regularly at Club 57, notably when it provided the Poetry Project with a space following the 1978 fire at St. Mark's Church in-the-Bowery. While the church was under repair in summer of 1979, the Project's Bob Holman programmed readings at Club 57 that included Lee Breuer, Jill Kroesen (who returned with her 1974 play, *Fay Shism Began in the Home*, at the end of the summer), and Tim Miller (who recently reflected that Club 57 was "a kind of prep space for the huge [Performance Space] 122 footprint that began in fall of 1980").[74]

Nevertheless, the aesthetic core of performance at Club 57 was its mix of variety revue and postpunk performance art. Ira Abramowitz, who had first come to the club through Scott Covert as a dancer in *Trojan Women*, took over club management midway through 1981 (page 131). Under his tenure, the club's performance imprint shifted from the (musical) theater of Rees, Shaiman, and Wittman to something darker, a mix of irreverence and brassy cabaret. The turn can be attributed in part to changing patterns of harder-drug use in the club's midst and to a shift in zeitgeist, reflecting a new moment that contended with AIDS and the commodification of the neighborhood and artists alike. Abramowitz's Borscht Belt humor was the foundation for his recurring International Rap Night (beginning June 1981), which featured his Mendel the Hassid Rocker act alongside character riffs by "Chinese rappers, fat rappers, Lower East Side artist rappers and Dany Johnson . . . as the suburban rock head from the Meadowlands who rapped about David Bowie," according to Heiberg's report.[75] Under the moniker Needles Jones, Abramowitz organized Vamps: The Art of Seductive Performing and Chateau 57: An Evening of Bondage Comedy. These winter 1982 events brought erstwhile regulars, a flyer for Chateau 57 listing Wendy Wild, John Sex, and Lisa Baumgardner.[76] For his part, Abramowitz offered deadpan commentary over Bettie Page bondage films, salaciously castigating the furniture onscreen rather than the bound-and-gagged actors.[77]

Club 57's last eighteen months of programming were chaotic and bore signs of the venue's ultimate shuttering. Yet the program remained generative and influenced newer East Village clubs in its own way.[78] Christian Joiris, a Belgian transplant who roomed with Abramowitz, designed flyers and contributed

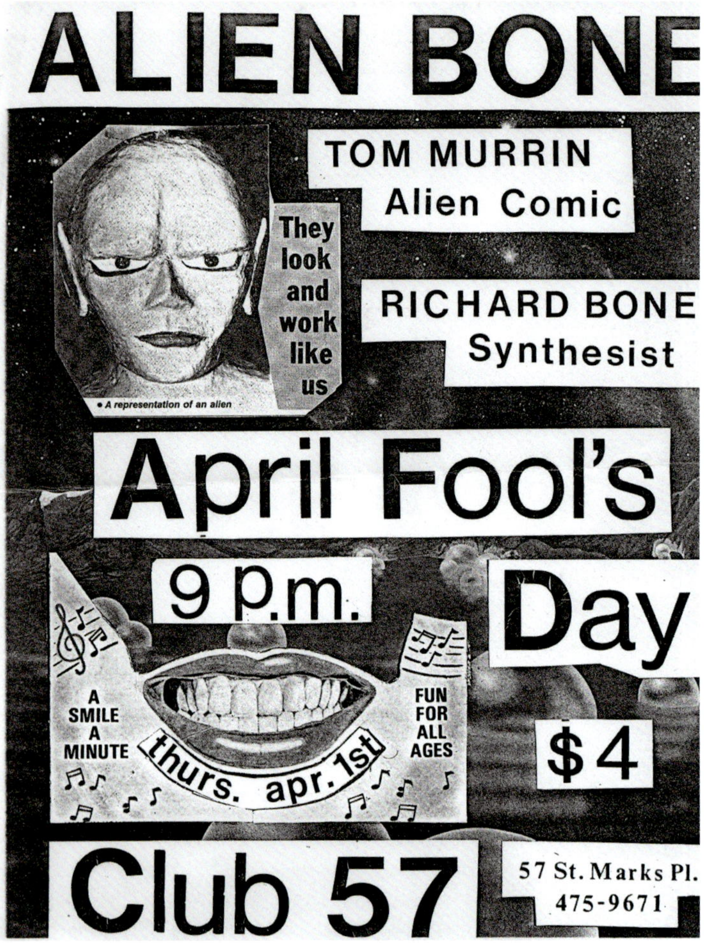

17. Flyer for a performance by Tom Murrin and Richard Bone, Club 57, 1982. Design by Murrin. The Museum of Modern Art, New York. Department of Film Special Collections

programming that was often conceptual in its approach. Joiris organized poetry readings (Poetes de l'invisible and Poetes du silence, in February and March 1982, respectively), screenings (International Super 8 Night, with avant-gardists such as Edit DeAk, Manuel DeLanda, and Arleen Schloss, in December 1981), and, most notably, performance evenings. In June 1981, Joiris presented his multimedia performance *Evasion*, which might have been at home in a SoHo loft some years earlier. Identical twins cast for the project became living sculptures around which the artist and fellow performers alternately staged props, screened Super 8 projections, and enacted ceremonial movements. In one segment, a twin wrapped head to toe in white gauze saw his bandages removed as his brother was simultaneously swaddled (fig. 16). Another segment employed film and paint to methodically transform an interplay of black-and-white imagery into a unified gray. A third used mirrors to create two singular images, half real, half reflection. Robin Crutchfield, who was in the foundational No Wave band DNA with Arto Lindsay, created an improvised score of ambient electronic sounds and spoken word.

The two-evening Club 57 Performance Expo in February 1982, according to Joiris, was conceived as a collage of interdisciplinary acts forming an ephemeral whole, each performance "a dream image that you put out there for a few minutes, maybe ten."[79] The audience was formed of friends and peers, more than a few of whom would perform themselves over the course of the evening. This assessment of club performance may ring familiar but the program distinguished itself on account of the participating artists, who hailed from across the performance art scene. Choreographers and Performance Space 122 (PS122) cofounders Charles Dennis and John Bernd were on the bill the first evening (cofounder Tim Miller returned to the club to perform with Dennis Cooper and Jeff McMahon in April 1982). Bill Doherty and Barb Lafferty Ferrari, under the moniker ēpoch, were also on the bill that first evening; they produced an installment of their Posture series, for which the duo would secure the closing slot on a performance bill and silently set up a scenario using an array of dissimilar props.[80] For Expo, Doherty laid out several pillows on the stage, covered them in white pillowcases handed to him by Lafferty Ferrari, piled them up, and poured aluminum silver enamel paint over the scene. Lafferty Ferrari's geisha makeup and street clothes intensified the scene's incongruousness. Then the duo walked out of the venue, leaving audience members to bring the performance to their own conclusion.

On the second night artists Beth Lapides and Arleen Schloss were among the participants, performing in their respective styles. Lapides was in fact no stranger to the club; in October 1981, she had performed a two-evening piece at Club 57 that used a jump-rope routine as a starting point for stories that integrated comedy, autobiography, and musical revue. Since the mid-1970s, Schloss had been making performance and film works centered on chance operation and text, most notably performative recitations of the alphabet. Since 1979, she had also been running the weekly performance salon A's in her Broome Street loft.

Performance artist Tom Murrin also performed regularly at Club 57, appearing half a dozen times between 1981 and 1982 as the Alien Comic, and once in March 1980 as the Suitcase Comic, before he had established his longtime moniker. A playwright for John Vaccaro in the late 1960s, Murrin had developed a lifetime interest in theatrical narrative. At Club 57, Murrin honed his imprint of object theater in the vein of Stuart Sherman, who, like Murrin, had performed on the street as much as he had on the stage throughout his career. Murrin's signature style saw him making rapid changes in costuming and props, formed from trash and found objects, and delivering quick-fire narrative entertainment and social parody. An

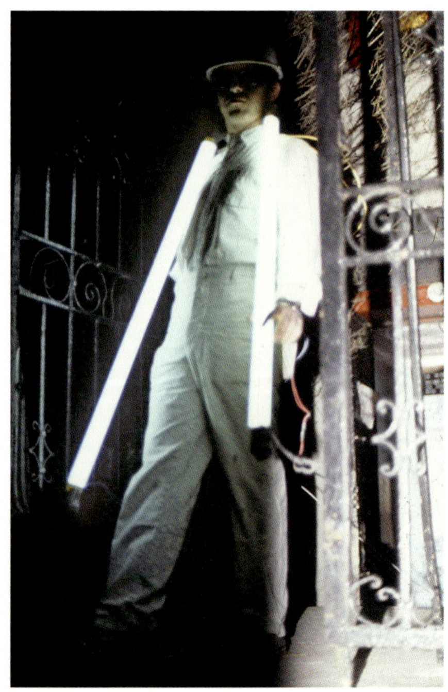

18. Julius Klein outside Club 57, 1983. Klein would later formalize his use of the fluorescent tube structure in a performance titled *Light Dances*. Photograph by Raken Leaves

April 1982 Club 57 performance began with music: to the sounds played by electronic musician and collaborator Richard Bone, Murrin sang of economic inequality under "save the rich economics" and the onset of a "drone society"[81] (fig. 17). After a break, he returned as the Alien Comic with a sketch that moved though the emotional properties of nine colors in the life of a character named Eve. For each of the colors, Murrin donned accoutrements as varied as masks, cardboard cutouts, and fruit jam, while varying the layers of costumes draped on his figure.[82]

Not all performances were as elaborate. On the occasion of a March 1983 exhibition of matchbook art, filmmaker and artist Julius Klein, without discussing the idea with the show's organizer, attached to his body a rig made of found fluorescent tubes and telephone wire, adding a spontaneous dimension to the evening (fig. 18). Klein had moved to New York in late 1981 and found in the venue a "ready-made scene"[83] where an artist could conceive of a work, book a timeslot, and put on a show, all in little time. This same spirit could be found in venues across the neighborhood, including No Se No, a Puerto Rican social club that became a venue for raw, even anarchic, underground performance, and ABC No Rio, which in 1983, once artists Jack Waters and Peter Cramer assumed the organizational reins, had shifted its focus from socially driven art to performance. Kembra Pfahler, a performance artist associated with the venue at the time, named the approach "availabism": the use of any materials that presented themselves as a source for performance-based work.[84] Venues like Pyramid Club, Limbo Lounge, and 8BC (where Murrin became a house favorite) were also part of the mix, but called for longer gestation periods and planning.

In June 1982, performer Stephen Tashjian moved to New York City with Boston pal and future gallerist Pat Hearn. Tashjian had attended Massachusetts College of Art, performed in '60s thrift-store drag with his New Wave band, Fuckin Barbies, and spent time in Provincetown, Rhode Island, with Jack Pierson and Mark Morrisroe, who would in 1981 immortalize Tashjian's drag character Popcorn in *The Laziest Girl in Town*. Soon after arriving in Manhattan, Tashjian moved to the East Village and ended up one night at Club 57, where he met Ira Abramowitz. Tashjian had recently started Wild and Wonderful, a band with Hearn, and asked to book a gig. In response, the club manager warned Tashjian that Club 57 was open only a few days a week; the venue was fizzling as the club scene exploded.[85] By then, Danceteria had reopened in its second location, four floors on Twenty-First Street, and launched No Entiendes, a weekly cabaret hosted by downtown doorman and impresario Haoui Montaug. Closer to the club, Bobby Bradley and Alan Mace had in December 1981 transformed a rundown bar on Avenue A into a vibrant mix of drag, theater, performance art, live music, and DJs: Pyramid Club. By the time Tashjian had encountered Abramowitz, Pyramid boasted programming seven nights a week, including the offbeat Cafe Iguana cabaret night hosted by Ann Craig. Much of the Club 57 set, including Ann Magnuson, John Sex, and Wendy Wild had already moved on to this new platform (fig. 19). In contrast to the basement venue, Pyramid offered a sound board, lights, a full bar, a stage, and the chance to make real money, especially on the weekends, which brought bridge and tunnel crowds as the club grew more successful.[86] Although Abramowitz would end up booking Wild and Wonderful at Club 57, he also directed Tashjian to Pyramid, where the performer's solo act, Tabboo!, would soon flourish alongside Club 57 drag performers Peter Kwaloff and Gerard Little (page 136).

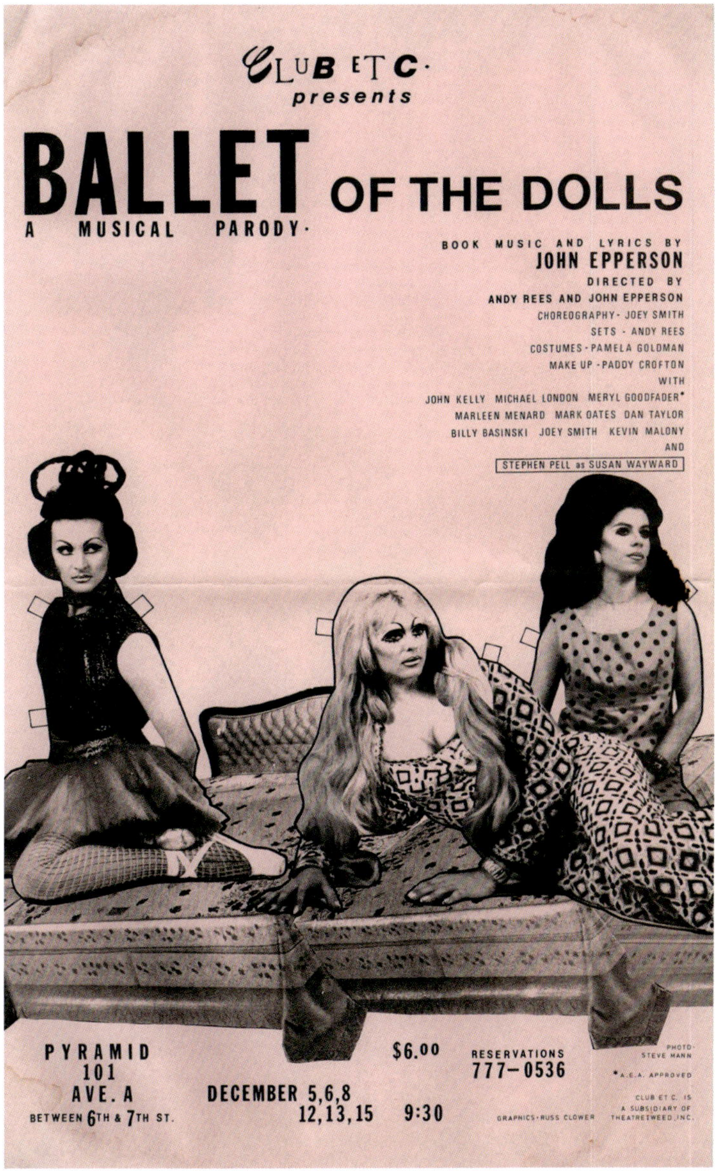

19. Flyer for *Ballet of the Dolls*, written by John Epperson and directed by Andy Rees, Pyramid Club, 1985. The original musical was a parody of *Valley of the Dolls* and the ballet world alike. Design by Russ Clower, featuring a photograph by Steve Mann. The Museum of Modern Art, New York. Department of Film Special Collections

That said, Club 57 was not over quite yet. It continued as a site of experimentation, as when theater artist John Jesurun presented *Non-Chang Pieces* in March 1983, distinct from the serial play *Chang in a Void Moon* that debuted at Pyramid in 1982. The last few months of the Club 57's programming provide a snapshot of its legacy, its final performance incarnations a return to the club's earliest days: over five years, New Wave Vaudeville had been transformed from a discrete event into a performance genre carried forward by a large and varied set of artists. In October 1982, classically trained jazz composer Tony Heiberg[87] presented On the Town, a series composed of three zany jazz revues emceed by filmmaker Tessa

Hughes-Freeland (who curated a regular bring-your-own Super 8 screening at the club); actor Irina Brook, only nineteen years old at the time, served as co-emcee on one occasion. The evenings featured Rockets Redglare's salty comedy; Abramowitz's Mendel, Needles, and Ira personas; and, in honor of Halloween, Haoui Montaug's rendition of "The Monster Mash." Chanteuse Phoebe Legere figured into the house band, which played themes from *West Side Story* and *Alfred Hitchcock Presents* and tunes from the Turtles, Johnny Cash, and Frank Sinatra.

Abramowitz helmed Needles Jonses's Red Light Café, his own rowdy cabaret, culled "from the heartland of America, from every roadhouse and Holiday Inn" according to the flyer.[88] Tashjian appeared in several Red Light events throughout early 1983 (fig. 20). At the time, Tashjian's performances ranged from his eclectic band to outré solo acts: one involved a stuffed poodle being set on fire (turning the circus act on its head); others centered on Americana or cowboy themes. In winter 1983, Rockets Redglare's *Taxicabaret*, a "three act valentine's play," starred Steve Buscemi. Buscemi was then a fireman and often performed with partner Mark Boone Jr. at PS122's Avant-Garde-Arama as well as at Pyramid Club and elsewhere. *Taxicabaret*'s February 6 flyer announces "Now Weekly!" but there is no known documentation of subsequent dates at the venue (fig. 21).

While chronologies strive to present a final entry, Club 57's has only a handful of unconfirmed stories. One anecdote tells of a padlock clipped by Guardian Angels so one last Super 8 screening could proceed (the date is unknown). Another relies on an unsigned flyer advertising a screening of David Cronenberg's *The Brood* on April 28, 1983. Yet another suggests the final event took place on May 1. It may be immaterial. Borrowing from music critic Greil Marcus, all that is left are lipstick traces.[89]

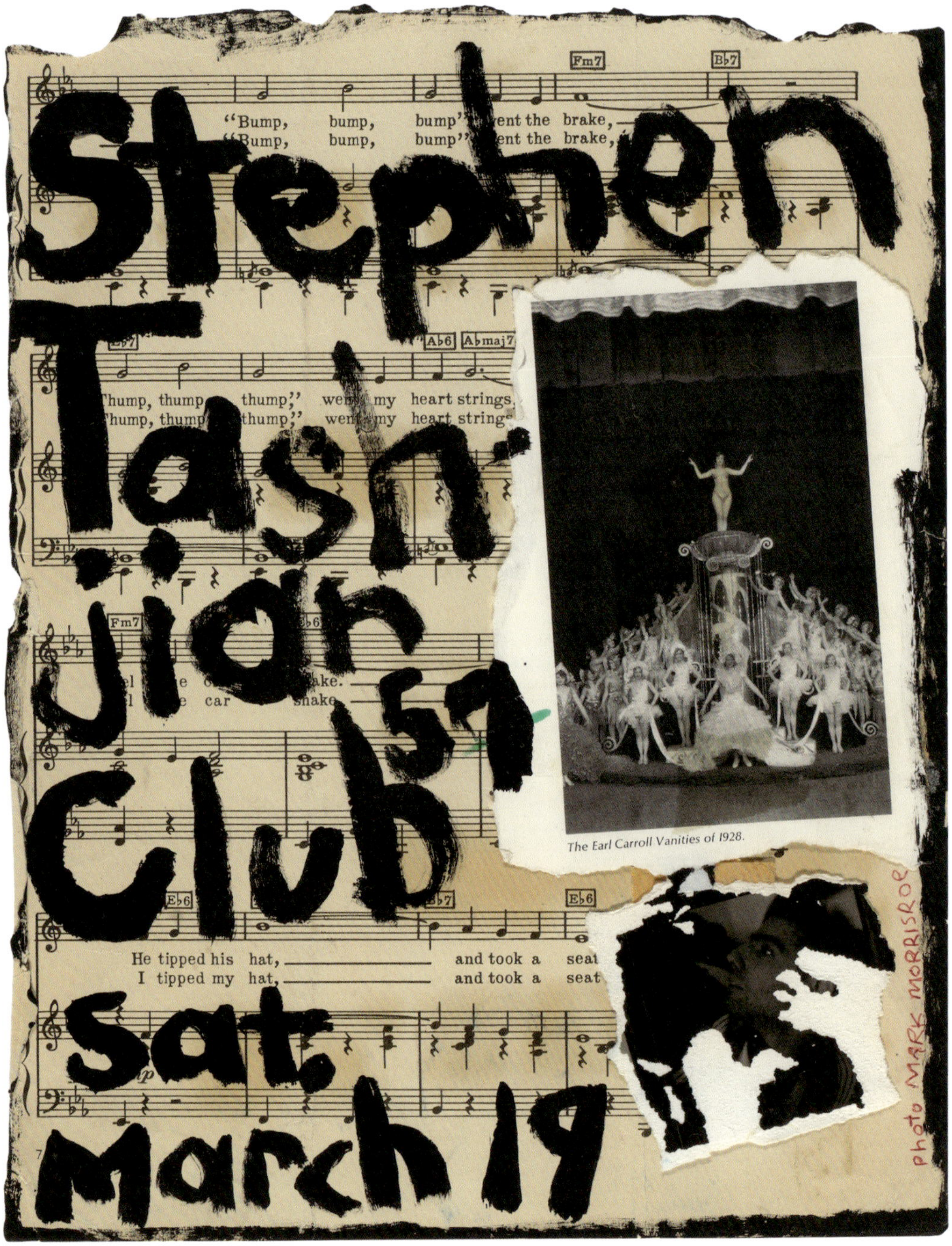

20. Flyer for a performance at Club 57, 1983. Design by Tashjian, with sheet music for Judy Garland's "The Trolley Song," from *Meet Me in St. Louis* (1954); a photograph of the 1928 Broadway musical *Earl Carroll's Vanities*; and a portrait of the artist by Mark Morrisroe. The Museum of Modern Art, New York. Department of Film Special Collections

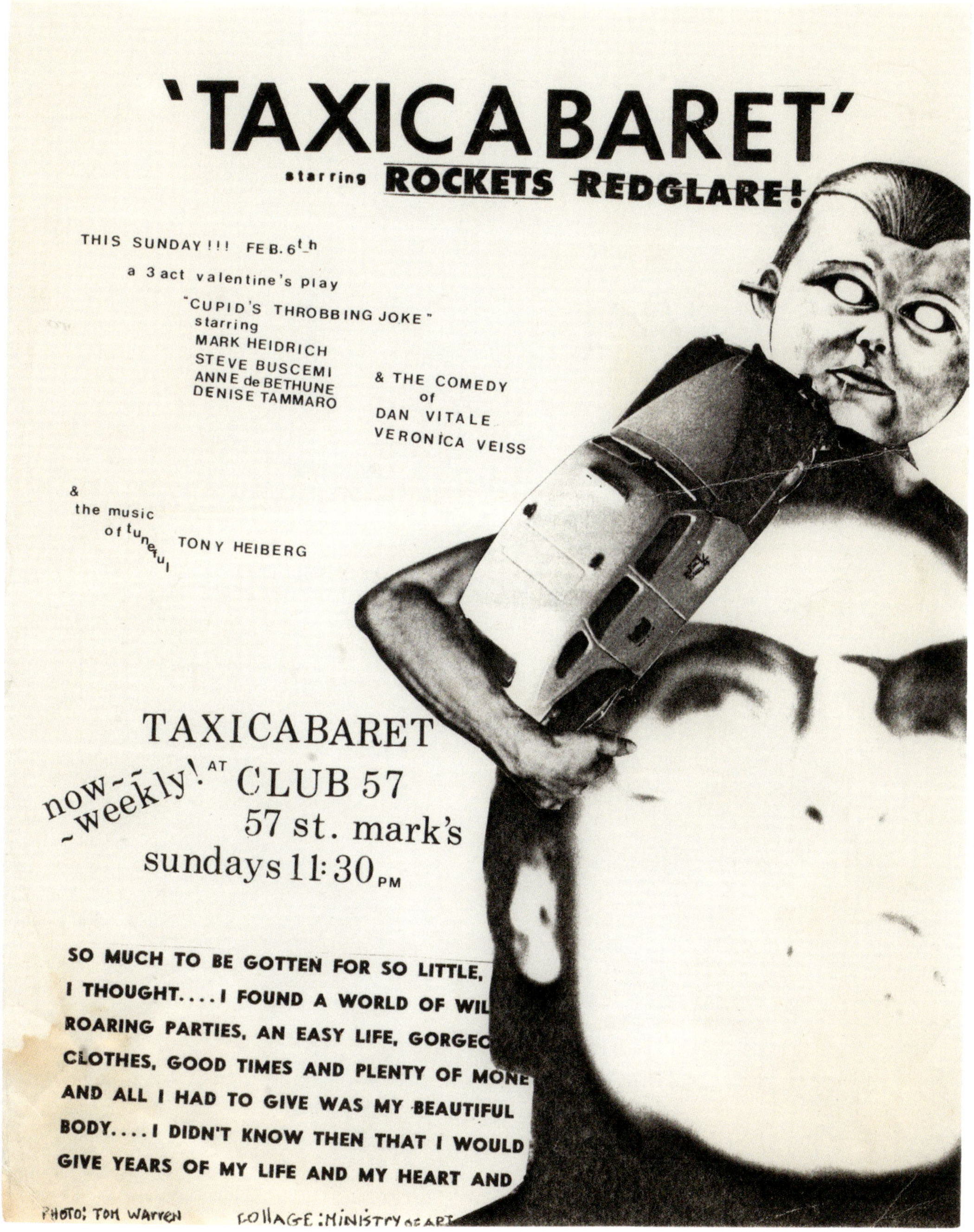

21. Flyer for Rockets Redglare's *Taxicabaret*, Club 57, 1983. Unknown designer. The Museum of Modern Art, New York. Department of Film Special Collections

1. The title of this essay was inspired by the flyer for the first performance hosted at Pyramid Club (December 10, 1981), which bears the original club slogan devised by Vincent Sapienza; it was not later used. "Downtown for Downtown" is emblematic of the scale and collaborative nature of the activities analyzed in this essay. Reproduced in Kestutis Nakas and Brian Butterick, "We Started a Nightclub: Building the Pyramid," *PAJ: A Journal of Performance and Art* (September 2015): 22–45.

2. One of the four bands that played at the February 8, 1978, kickoff event for Club 57—which had been operating previously as the East Village Students Club—was the New York Niggers. They took their name from New York Dolls and from Patti Smith Group's "Rock 'n' Roll Nigger." The heyday of 1970s rock and roll was already material to be reworked.

3. "The spirit of a raucous good-time night on the rock 'n' roll town is being preserved, though, but in the most unlikely of places. . . . An affable fellow named Stanley runs the place and handles the concessions at the shows, working the bar with a glee that reveals his affection for the kids and punks who jam the cave-like club and pogo into the night, barely avoiding smacking their heads on the low ceiling. The stage is eye-level, which encourages people to get off their two-dollar seats and makes for a pulsating mass of humanity backing the performers' efforts. In addition, Stanley is screening rare rock movies on Monday nights." Roy Trakin, "Punkclubbing," *SoHo Weekly News*, May 11, 1978.

4. Peter Zaremba, conversation with the author and Ron Magliozzi, October 5, 2016. Millennium Film Workshop likewise served as an alternate venue for the Fleshtones, who played there with Nervus Rex and the Mumps at a "New Wave Party" on April 15, 1978.

5. In 1982, after their first record, the band changed their name to Certain General.

6. A helpful overview of the garage scene can be found in Steven Blush, *New York Rock: From the Rise of the Velvet Underground to the Fall of CBGB* (New York: St. Martin's Griffin, 2016).

7. Parrish is best known for his 1982 synth-pop hit, "Hip Hop Be Bop (Don't Stop)."

8. Glenn O'Brien, "Glenn O'Brien's Beat," *Interview* 11, no. 11 (November 1981): 78.

9. Meg Brazill, email to the author, October 24, 2016.

10. For details on Shepard and Smith writing the mostly autobiographical play at the Chelsea Hotel, see Patti Smith, *Just Kids* (New York: Ecco, 2010), 185–86. According to Smith, Shepard skipped town after the third performance, after which the play lapsed into obscurity.

11. Richard Grabel, "Cowboy Mouth Rock & Roll Theater Company," *New York Rocker* 15 (November 1978): 53. While Grabel describes the performance as uneven, he praises the project as "a strange sort of hybrid creature, orphaned in a world where the two mediums of rock 'n' roll music and theater rarely meet." My understanding of this production was informed by conversations with Gordon Edelstein (March 16, 2017) and Chris Kraus (March 30, 2017).

12. Sam Shepard remained popular: in February and March of 1979, David Watkins, who would later appear in a recurring segment on Kestutis Nakas's Manhattan Cable show, *Your Program of Programs*, starred in a double bill of *Geography of a Horse Dreamer* (1974) and *The Holy Ghostly* (1969), mounted by his classmates at NYU Tisch School of the Arts. In May–June 1979, Watkin's would return with Shepard's one-act *Action*. An April 1980 run of *The Tooth of Crime* (1972) included Sharon Niesp, girlfriend of writer and John Waters star Cookie Mueller.

13. Robert Christgau, "A Little Night Music II: Ain't Got No Home," *Village Voice*, October 23, 1978; Gerald Rabkin, "The Bones Underneath," *SoHo Weekly News*, October 26, 1978.

14. Chris Kraus, conversation with the author, March 30, 2017.

15. Gordon Edelstein, conversation with the author, March 16, 2017.

16. Colab and Wow Café Theatre are two examples of spaces whose resources were more strictly reserved for their members.

17. Flyer, Nightshift in *Pas de trois* from Fassbinder at Club 57, 1978. The Museum of Modern Art, Department of Film Special Collections, New York.

18. Richard Murphet, quoted in Denise Varney, *Radical Visions 1968–2008: The Impact of the Sixties on Australian Drama* (Amsterdam/New York: Rodopi, 2011), 181. Murphet was part of Nightshift in Australia but not in the United States. An account of the Fassbinder production in Australia can be found in "Nightshift: Interviews of Two Members of the Group—Lindzee Smith & Betsy Sussler," *Cantrills Filmnotes* 29–30 (February 1979): 621.

19. The murderers were ultimately caught for this compulsion after they took it one step further, staging a murder for a one-man audience, who would later call the police.

20. Craig Gholson, "*Menage*: Interview with Betsy Sussler," *BOMB* 1 (Spring 1981): 12–13, 42; online at http://bombmagazine.org/article/9/betsy-sussler-s-em-menage-em. Sussler is the founder of *BOMB*.

21. Robert Patrick, email to the author, April 5, 2017: "The production allowed me to fulfill an ambition to present the play environmentally, that is, not on a fixed stage-space, but throughout a bar or bar-like space."

22. Press release, "The Fourth 'E' Company," no date. Robert Patrick Papers, T-Mss 1978-006, Billy Rose Theatre Division, New York Public Library for the Performing Arts.

23. Ethyl Eichelberger, quoted in Uzi Parnes, "Pop Performance, Four Seminal Influences: The Work of Jack Smith, Tom Murrin/the Alien Comic, Ethyl Eichelberger, and the Split Britches Company" (PhD diss., New York University, 1988), 278.

24. Ibid., 288. On drag as distinct from gay, Eichelberger is quoted as saying: "When I originally [put on a dress], I thought that I was associated with being gay. . . . I thought I was part of that world. But as soon as [gay men] got middle-class acceptance, they turned around and rejected us [drag performers]. I'll never forget when the Saint opened, they refused Holly Woodlawn entrance to it because she was a drag queen. It was like a symbol to me that they took away, and I had to reexamine everything. I realized it wasn't gay at all that I was a part of."

25. Ann Magnuson met her at an uptown improv show when scouting for a comedy night at Club 57.

26. Holliday, who studied semiotics with Keith Haring at SVA, envisioned his sets as environments performers would pass through. This same group of collaborators, joined by others like Tommy Hawk (sound) and Tim Dunleavy (costumes), would continue to work together as club-born projects went on to be presented at the Kitchen, P.S. 1, and beyond.

27. Scott Covert, email to the author, April 14, 2017.

28. Lisa Altomare, conversation with the author, May 20, 2016.

29. Ibid.

30. "Beasts Invade Alternative Space as Fall Season Opens October 17 at P.S. 1," MoMA PS1 Archives, II.A.381, The Museum of Modern Art Archives, New York.

31. *Village Voice* reviewer Dan Isaac, quoted in J. Hoberman, "The Theatre of Jack Smith," *Drama Review:* 23, no. 1 (March, 1979): 8.

32. Altomare, conversation with the author.

33. Marc Shaiman and Scott Wittman, conversation with the author and Ron Magliozzi, October 3, 2016.

34. Ibid.

35. Don Shewey, "Playing Around," *SoHo Weekly News*, March 11, 1981.

36. Shaiman and Wittman, conversation with the author and Magliozzi. Shaiman remarked on the ephemerality of performance. On the night Merrill Aldighieri and Joe Tripician videotaped *Trojan Women*, the blasting lights altered the performance itself. Paradoxically the performance had to be "ruined" to be archived.

37. Frank Rich, "'Livin Dolls': An Image from the 60s," *New York Times*, April 5, 1982.

38. Dunleavy, a high school classmate of Magnuson's, put on a Barbie Fashion Show featuring his designs at the uptown disco-turned-punk-club Hurrah in April 1980.

39. Shaiman and Wittman, conversation with the author and Magliozzi.

40. Ibid.

41. Ibid.

42. Lois Weaver, quoted in Parnes, "Pop Performance," 446.

43. Holly Hughes, email to the author, March 15, 2017. Hughes, the first manager of WOW Café Theatre, went on to say: "The implication was clear, you could check more than your coat. . . . The clothes as I remember were evening dresses, fifties sixties full skirts, military gear, men's suits and band jackets. You could layer it up, you could go back in time and fix what happened or remember—re remember what happened. Change genders."

44. Alisa Solomon, "The WOW Cafe," *Drama Review* 29, no. 1 (Spring 1985): 95.

45. This typology of various art spaces is borrowed from Sally Webster's *A Report: Alternative Spaces and the Crises Threatening Their Survival* (New York: RoseWeb Projects, 1982). Webster's description is quoted in Julie Ault, "For the Record," in *Alternative Art New York, 1965–1985*, ed. Ault (Minneapolis: University of Minnesota Press, 1996), 16, footnote 10.

46. Melissa Rachleff, "Do It Yourself: Histories of Alternatives," in *Alternative Histories: New York Art Spaces 1960 to 2010*, eds. Lauren Rosati and Mary Ann Staniszewski (Cambridge: MIT Press, 2012), 25.

47. Press release, "Caution! Alternative Space!," September 1981, reproduced in Arlene Goldbard's "When (Art) Worlds Collide," in *Alternative Art New York*, 186.

48. Joe Lewis, quoted in Steve Vincent, "Events," *East Village Eye* 2, no. 16 (Christmas 1980): 12.

49. Other nightclubs also engaged in political activities. In January 1980, Mudd Club hosted a mock hearing of grievances against the city as part of ABC No Rio's *Real Estate Show*. After graffiti artist Michael Stewart died in police custody, in 1983, Pyramid Club "served as a forum for political issues such as gentrification and police brutality," according to performance artist and ABC codirector Jack Waters. See "Other Venues: Performance at the Pyramid," in *ABC No Rio Dinero: The Story of a Lower East Side Art Gallery*, eds. Alan Moore and Marc Miller (New York: ABC No Rio with Collaborative Projects, 1985), 154. Lucy Lippard's *Get The Message?: A Decade of Art for Social Change* (New York: E. P. Dutton, 1984) offers perspective on the 1980s collectives from her vantage as a major figure of 1960s politically engaged art.

50. Alan Moore, "Models and Subjects," paper delivered at the Re-Membering Loisaida conference, Center for Puerto Rican Studies at the Clemente Soto Velez Cultural Center, November 20, 2009, available online at http://collaborativeprojects archive.wikispaces.com/Models+and+Subjects+11+09.

51. Tim Lawrence's *Life and Death on the New York Dance Floor, 1980–1983* (Durham, NC: Duke University Press, 2016) provides more detail on the Mudd Club event and the *SoHo Weekly News* crossover. See pages 135–36.

52. Ann E. Magnuson, "It's a Reagan World!" *SoHo Weekly News*, Style Supplement, December 10, 1980.

53. Animal X, "Inaugural Ball," *SoHo Weekly News*, Style Supplement, December 10, 1980.

54. Amy Brandt, "Tseng Kwong Chi and the Politics of Performance," in *Tseng Kwong Chi: Performing for the Camera*, ed. Brandt (Norfolk/New York: Chrysler Museum of Art/Grey Art Gallery/Lyon Artbooks, 2015), 42–50. When asked, Tseng told his sitters that the crumpled flag was meant to look as if it was blowing in the wind, when in fact the defiled backdrop was meant to destabilize the image. Artists Kenny Scharf and Bruno Testore Schmidt collaborated on the shoot and are at times seen peering out from behind the flag. Tseng was known for his Mao suit, itself a synecdoche for his Asian cultural identity (pages 138–39); the seersucker suit was a clear enactment of Southern Republicanism.

55. Postcard for exhibition *Facere/Fascis*, 1981, Group Material Archive, MSS 215, box 1, folder 22, Fales Library and Special Collections, New York University Libraries.

56. Valery Oisteanu, email to the author, March 17, 2017.

57. Grace Glueck, "Art People," *New York Times*, February 13, 1981. Gildav described his initiative as "unjuried and including—besides more conventional artists—children, [Gildav] and his mother."

58. Brian Wallis, "Public Funding and Alternative Spaces," in *Alternative Art New York*, 165. Italics the author's. In the same volume, Alan Moore and Jim Cornwell observe: "What artists chose to experiment with [in the East Village] in the 1980s were traditional forms of market presentation of art—that is, galleries." See "Local History: The Art of Battle for Bohemia in New York," 330.

59. "We were way too rock n roll to get any kind of grants," reflects Astor in her self-published memoir *FUN Gallery: The True Story* (New York: Pink Poodle Press, 2012), 112. Although FUN marks the beginning of the market explosion, Astor's work remained geared toward her artists. She recounts having a formal sit-down with the graffiti writers after their first sale to discuss managing their money and the associated pressures of the art world. She also called their parents. While Club 57 was radically off the radar, Don and Mera Rubell purchased an entire exhibition of Elvis Presley and Marilyn Monroe drawings by Keith Haring in 1981, save one piece that was acquired by Jeffrey Deitch. See John Gruen, *Keith Haring: The Authorized Biography* (New York: Simon & Schuster, 1992), 77.

60. Critic Nicolas A. Moufarrege even called the Loo Division "a form of graffiti art" and its name "a fun art-guerilla tactic." See "Another Wave, Still More Savagely than the First: Lower East Side, 1982," *Arts Magazine* (September 1982): 71.

61. Quoted in Phoebe Hoban, *Basquiat: A Quick Killing in Art* (New York: Viking, 1998), 154.

62. "Carlo McCormick on Gracie Mansion Gallery," *Artforum* 38, no. 2 (October 1999): 123.

63. Dan Cameron, "It Takes a Village," in *East Village USA*, eds. Julie Ault and Cameron (New York: New Museum of Contemporary Art, 2004), 52.

64. Collichio spoke about his gallery in 1983 to the *New York Times*: "All of us who deal in art here are friends. We're concerned to create an alternative gallery system to 57th Street and SoHo, with a different attitude, a system not so much commercial as artistic." Quoted in Grace Glueck, "Gallery View: A Gallery Scene That Pioneers in New Territories," *New York Times*, June 26, 1983.

65. Christopher Hart Chambers, email to the author, April 23, 2017. He added: "Once we started showing in nightclubs and then galleries the individual artists wanted to emphasize their own styles and agendas."

66. Carlo McCormick, "Boy in the Hood," *Artforum* 38, no. 2 (October 1999): 115.

67. Chuck Nanney, email to the author, May 4, 2017. While not a regular at Club 57, Wojnarowicz performed with 3 Teens Kill 4 and participated in invitational art shows as well as poetry readings. Nanney added: "[Club 57] was a viable venue that was most welcoming to almost anyone who wanted to do something and that's what David cared about. David took advantage of any avenue he could to present his work. I always liked that about him."

68. Peter Nagy, "Dual Nature," *Artforum* 38, no. 2 (October 1999): 129. Nagy echoes Astor on FUN: "The commercial gallery seemed to be a . . . way to forgo the hassle and dependencies associated with alterative spaces, and the nonprofit foundations with all of their paperwork and advisory boards." Belcher's reflection can be found in Glueck, "Gallery View."

69. Dan Cameron, "East Village, USA," in Phyllis Plous, *Neo York: Report on a Phenomenon* (Santa Barbara: University of California/University Art Museum, 1985), 13.

70. These numbers figure in the chronology compiled by Liza Kirwin in "The Wild East," *Artforum* 38, no. 2 (October 1999): 121–28.

71. As argued by Walter Robinson and Carlo McCormick in "Slouching toward Avenue D," *Art in America* 72, no. 6 (Summer 1984): 137.

73. Tony Heiberg, "Five Fab Years at Club 57," *East Village Eye* 4, no. 26 (October 1982): 21.

73. Mike Colasuonno, email to the author, April 3, 2017. They went on to venues like Dangerfield's in midtown and the Bitter End in the West Village rather than the clubs on the eastside circuit. The Other Leading Brand was made up of Colasuonno, Christine von Dohln, Fred Goehner, Dennis Lee, and Judy Nazemetz.

74. Tim Miller, email to the author, April 29, 2017. Miller was one of the cofounders of Performance Space 122.

75. Heiberg, "Five Fab Years at Club 57," 21.

76. Although Abramowitz was known to list people's names on flyers without first asking them.

77. Ira Abramowitz, conversation with the author and Ron Magliozzi, December 9, 2016.

78. See "8BC: From Farmhouse to Cabaret," *Drama Review* 29, no. 1 (Spring 1985), 109. Charles Tarzian names Club 57's 1981–83 seasons specifically as inspirations for 8BC; Uzi Parnes, in an email to the author, May 1, 2017, cites Club 57 as an influence on Club Chandelier.

79. Christian Joiris, conversation with the author and Ron Magliozzi, February 6, 2017. In an email to the author, April 27, 2017, Joiris further reflected that the artists' adaptions of their work to fit the compressed format resulted in "the great originality of the event." This was a departure from the free-wheeling, postpunk approach that was the basis of the performances in New Wave Vaudeville, for instance.

80. In November 1981, ēpoch had produced Artists Doing Comedy, a grouping of sketches bookended by screenings of the 1972 banned film *Lenny Bruce without Tears* (which packed the house). Writer Linda Frye-Burnham sang a song entitled "MFA," Italian mail artist Achille Cavellini covered artist Buster Cleveland in stickers, while Doherty's prop comedy involved a cream pie.

81. Videotape of Alien Comic/Tom Murrin at Club 57, April 1, 1982, documented by Merrill Aldighieri, 25 minutes, The Museum of Modern Art, New York.

82. In a 1984 interview with Uzi Parnes, Murrin recalled: "The club that really started it for me was Club 57, on 57 St. Marks Place. . . . That's where a lot of performance art got started—in a club scene." Quoted in Parnes, "Pop Performance," 177.

83. Julius Klein, email to the author, April 28, 2017.

84. Tessa Hughes-Freeland, "The Female Gaze," in *Deathtripping: The Cinema of Transgression*, ed. Jack Sargeant (London: Creation Books, 1995), 167.

85. Other pioneering venues were fading too. Tashjian described the audience at CBGB in 1982 as "four drunks at the bar." Stephen Tashjian, conversation with the author and Ron Magliozzi, April 18, 2016.

86. In its own way, Pyramid Club, home to the pioneering drag crowd behind Wigtsock (Pyramid regular Lady Bunny hosted the first festival in 1985) and garage rockers alike, fostered a tight-knit but eclectic community of artists. A half decade after they first gigged at Club 57 as an alternative to CBGB, the Fleshtones were regulars at Pyramid.

87. Heiberg discovered the club scene as a reporter for *East Village Eye*, a gig he took on after moving to the city and finding the jazz circuit staid. He found commonality with performers who turned to show tunes as the foundation for their comedy, such as Abramowitz. Heiberg would take On the Town to Pyramid Club and Danceteria, among other venues, and become John Sex's music director.

88. Flyer, Needles Jonses's Red Light Café December 18, 1982, The Museum of Modern Art, Department of Film Special Collections, New York.

89. Greil Marcus, *Lipstick Traces: A Secret History of the Twentieth Century* (Cambridge: Harvard University Press, 1989).

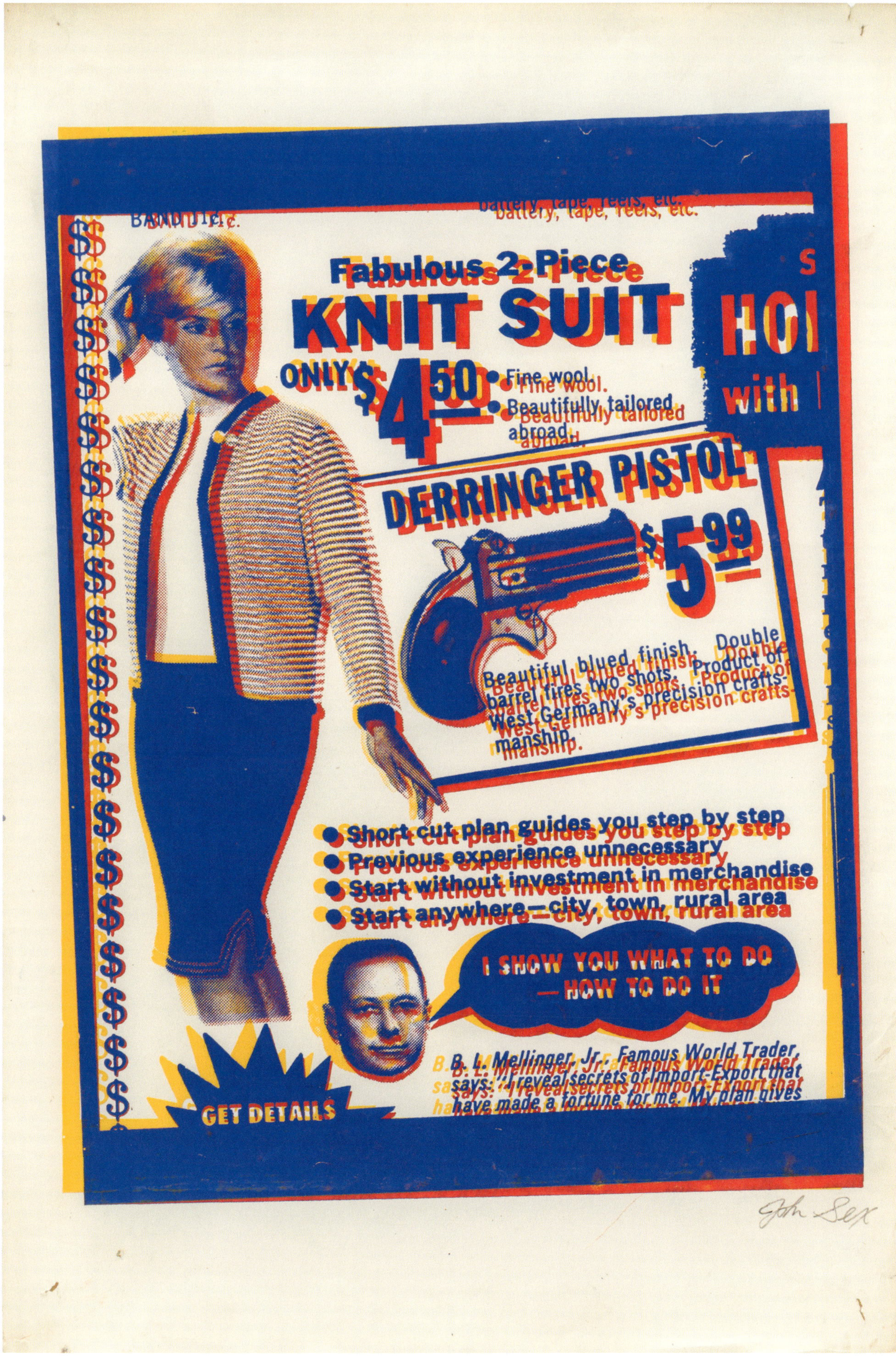

JOHN SEX (AMERICAN, 1956–1990). ***Knit Suit.*** c. 1980. Silkscreen, 35 × 23" (88.9 × 58.4 cm). Collection Kenny Scharf

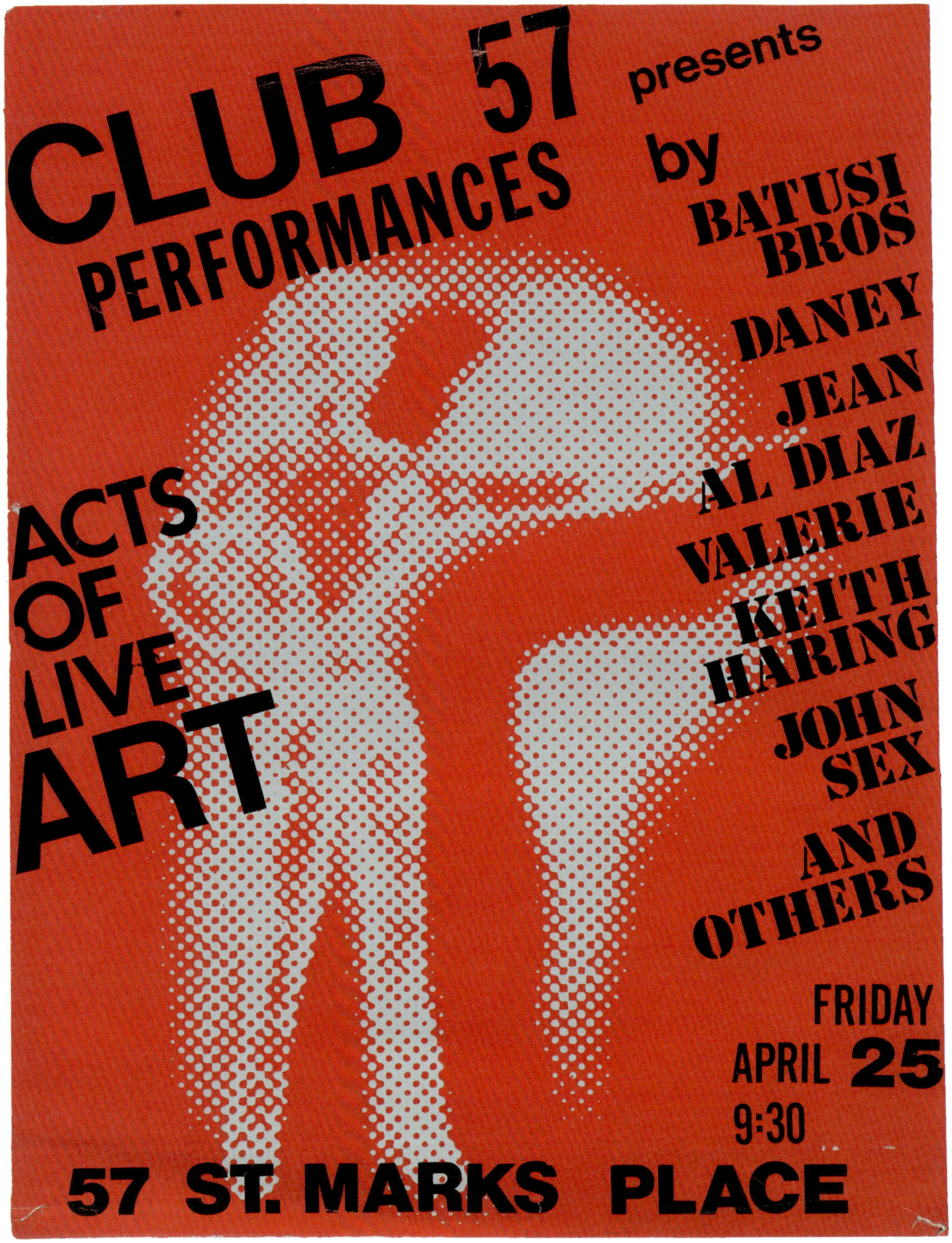
CLUB 57
presents
PERFORMANCES by
BATUSI BROS
DANEY
JEAN
AL DIAZ
VALERIE
KEITH HARING
JOHN SEX
AND OTHERS
ACTS OF LIVE ART
FRIDAY
APRIL 25
9:30
57 ST. MARKS PLACE

JOHN SEX (AMERICAN, 1956–1990). ***Acts of Live Art.*** 1980. Silkscreen, 22 × 17½" (55.9 × 44.5 cm). The Museum of Modern Art, New York. Department of Film Special Collections

JOHN SEX. ***Acts of Live Art.*** 1980. Silkscreen, 22 × 17½" (55.9 × 44.5 cm). The Museum of Modern Art, New York. Department of Film Special Collections

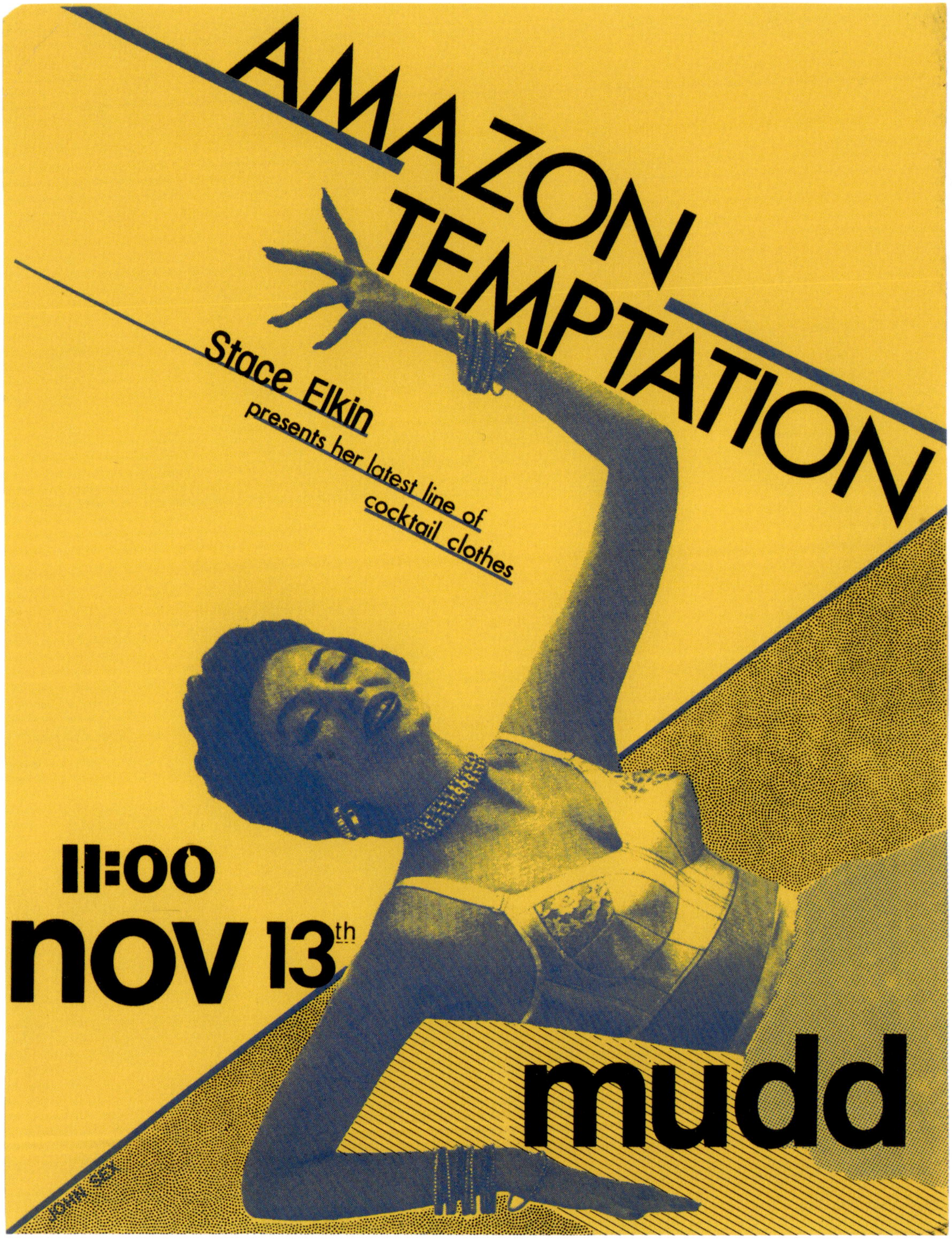

JOHN SEX. ***Amazon Temptation.*** 1980. Silkscreen, 22 × 17" (55.9 × 43.2 cm). The Museum of Modern Art, New York. Department of Film Special Collections

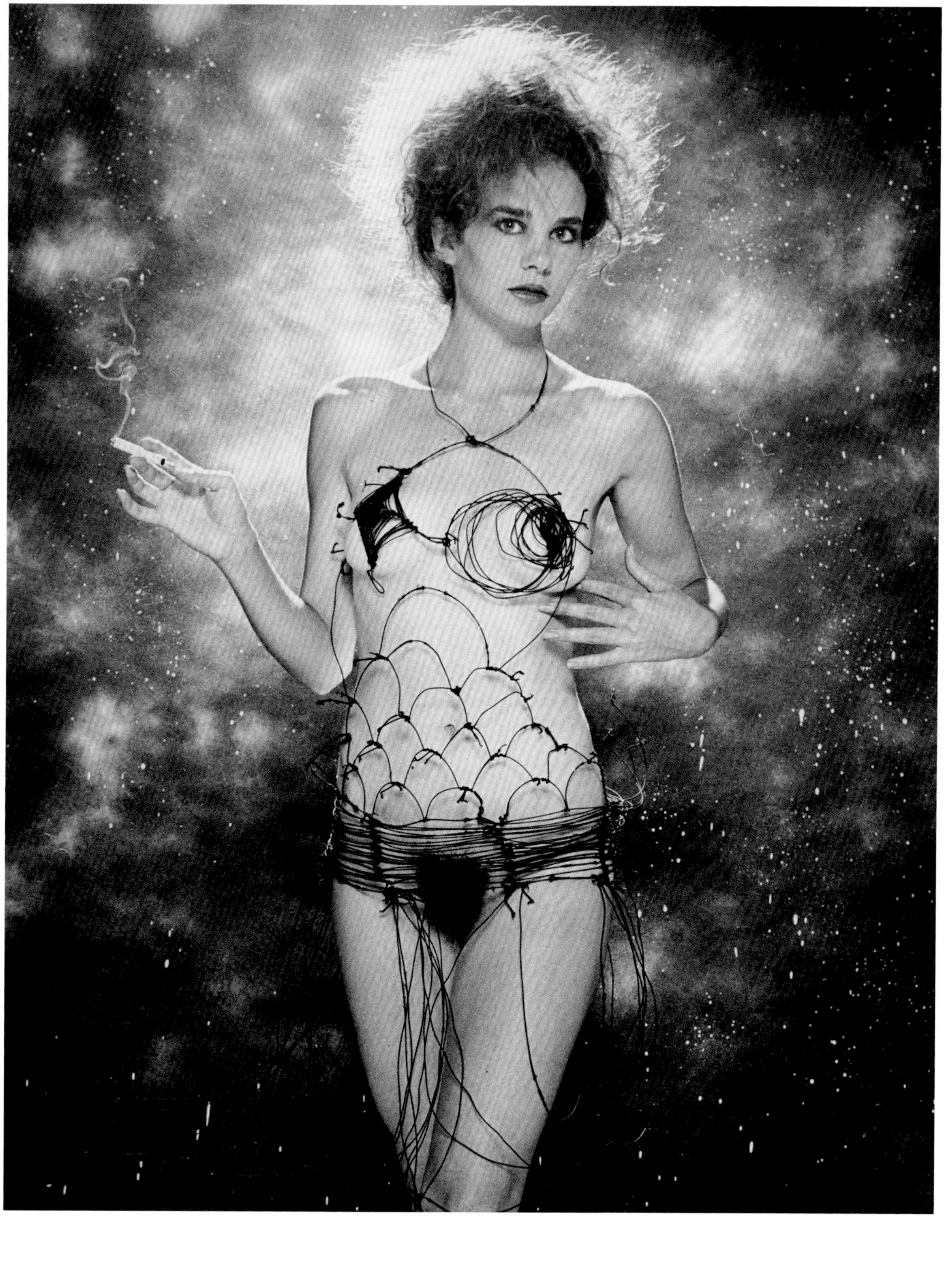

TSENG KWONG CHI (AMERICAN, BORN HONG KONG, 1950–1990). **Kitty Brophy in AMMO (Shawn McQuate) wire dress.** c. 1980. Gelatin silver print, 11 × 14" (28 × 35.5 cm). Collection Kitty Brophy

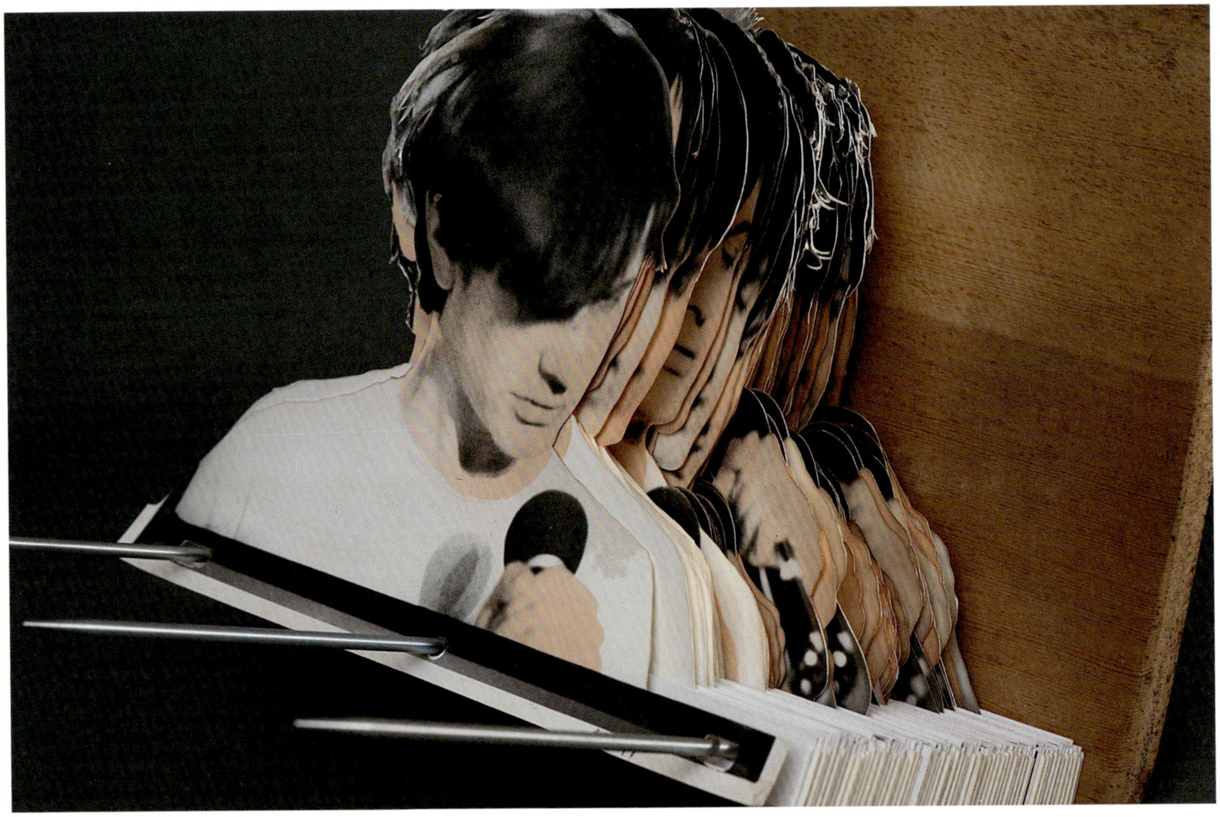

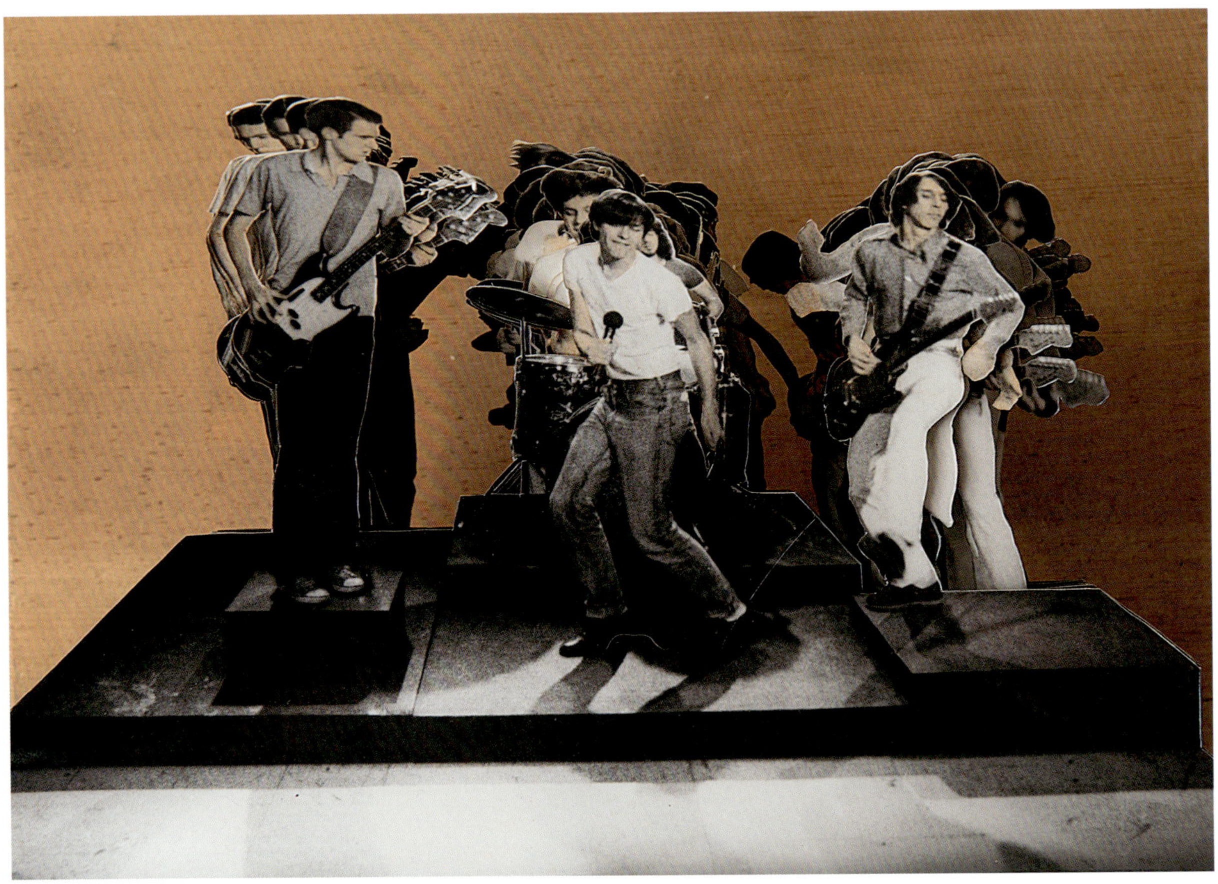

M. HENRY JONES (AMERICAN, BORN 1957). ***Soul City Animation Art (Peter Zaremba).*** 1977–79. Hand-colored photo-cutout sequence, 8 × 10 × 14" (20.3 × 25.4 × 35. 6 cm). Collection the artist
M. HENRY JONES. ***Soul City Animation Art (The Fleshtones).*** 1977–79. Hand-colored photo-cutout sequence, 8 × 10 × 14" (20.3 × 25.4 × 35. 6 cm). Collection the artist

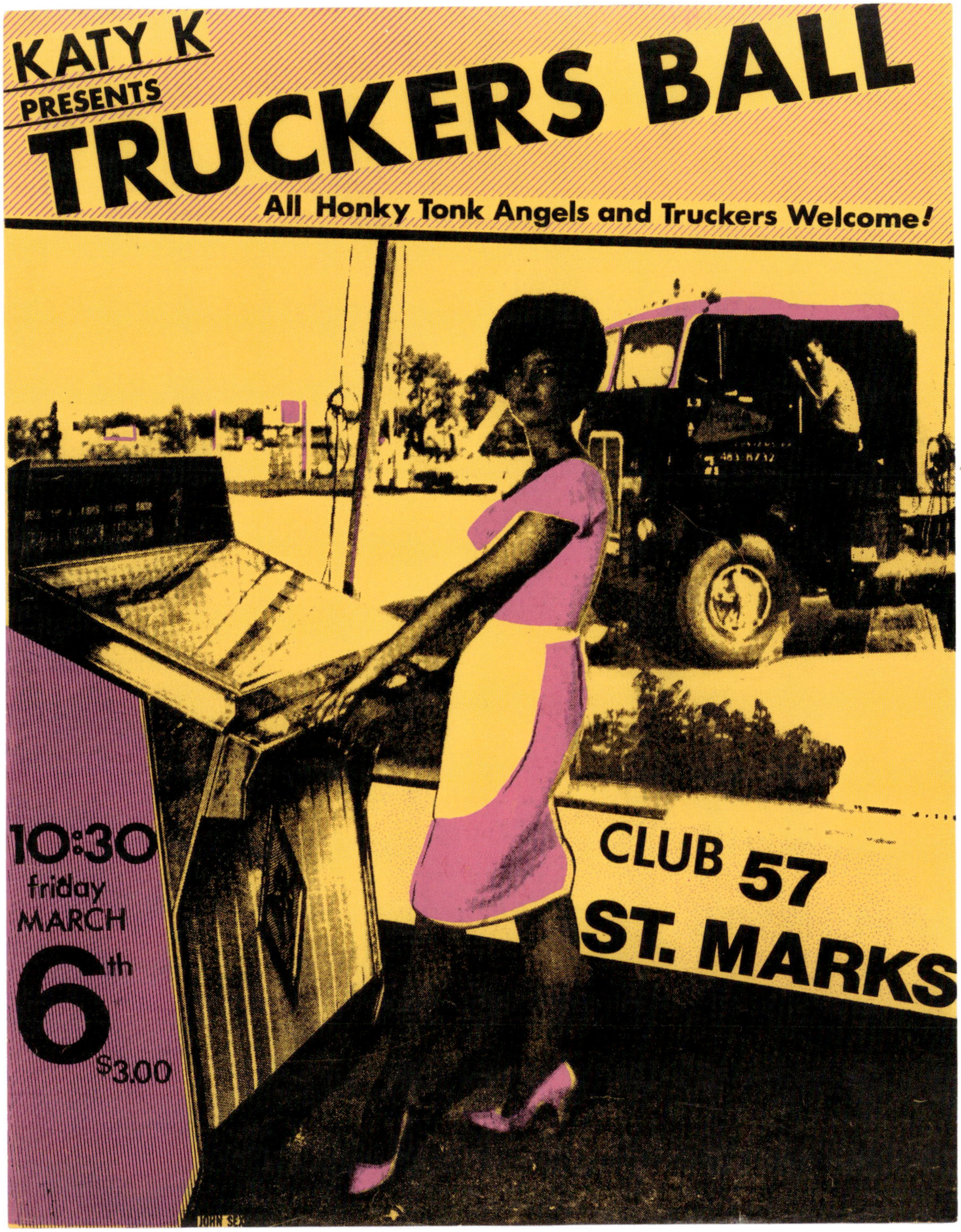

JOHN SEX. ***Truckers Ball.*** 1981. Silkscreen, 22 × 17" (55.9 × 43.2 cm). Collection School of Visual Arts

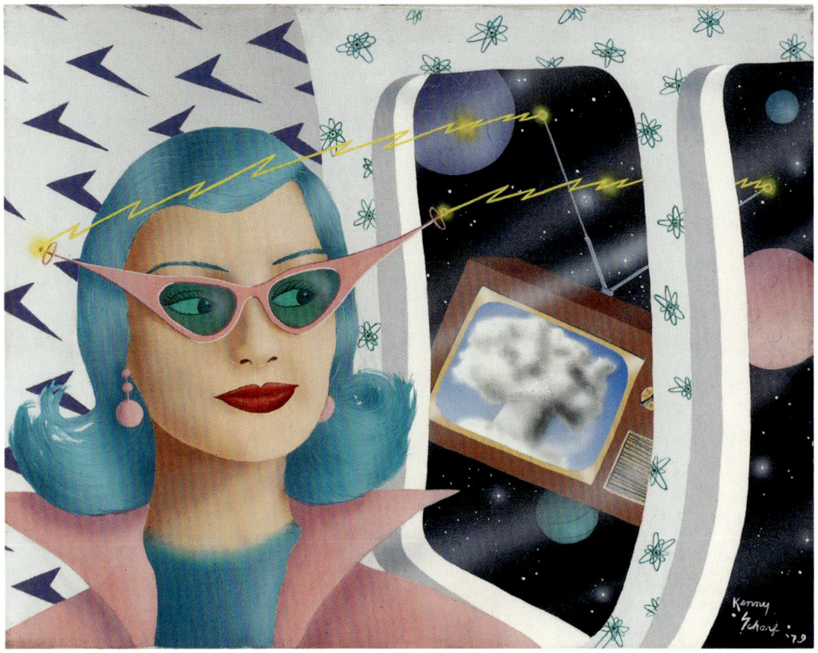
Kenny Scharf '79

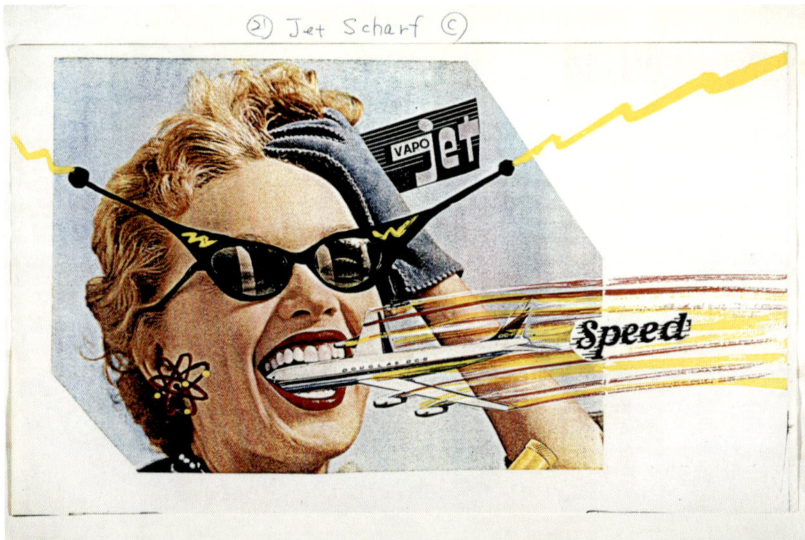
(2) Jet Scharf ©
VAPO
Jet
Speed

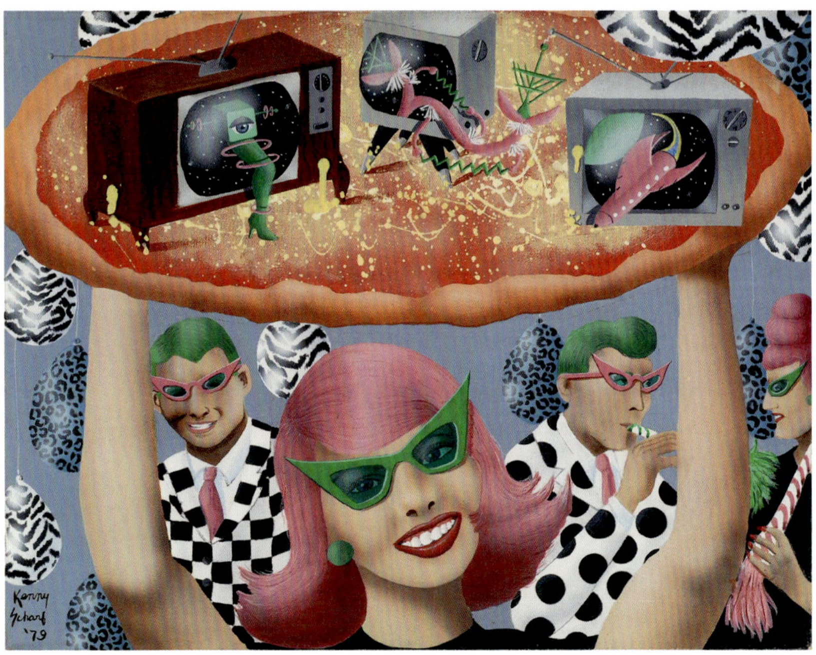
Kenny Scharf '79

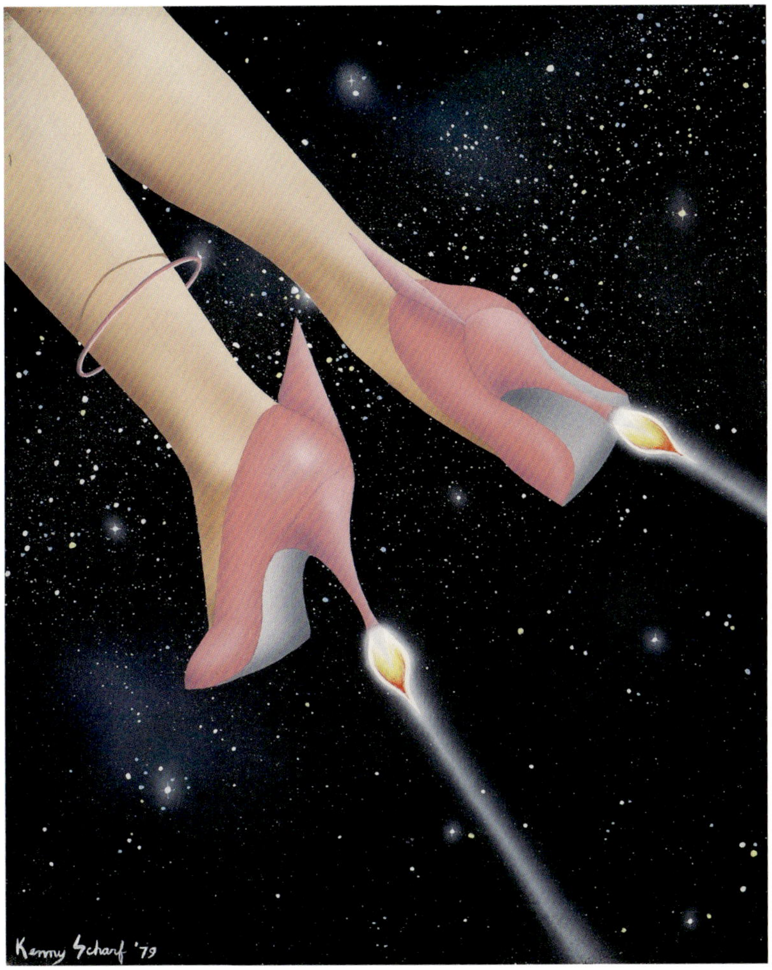

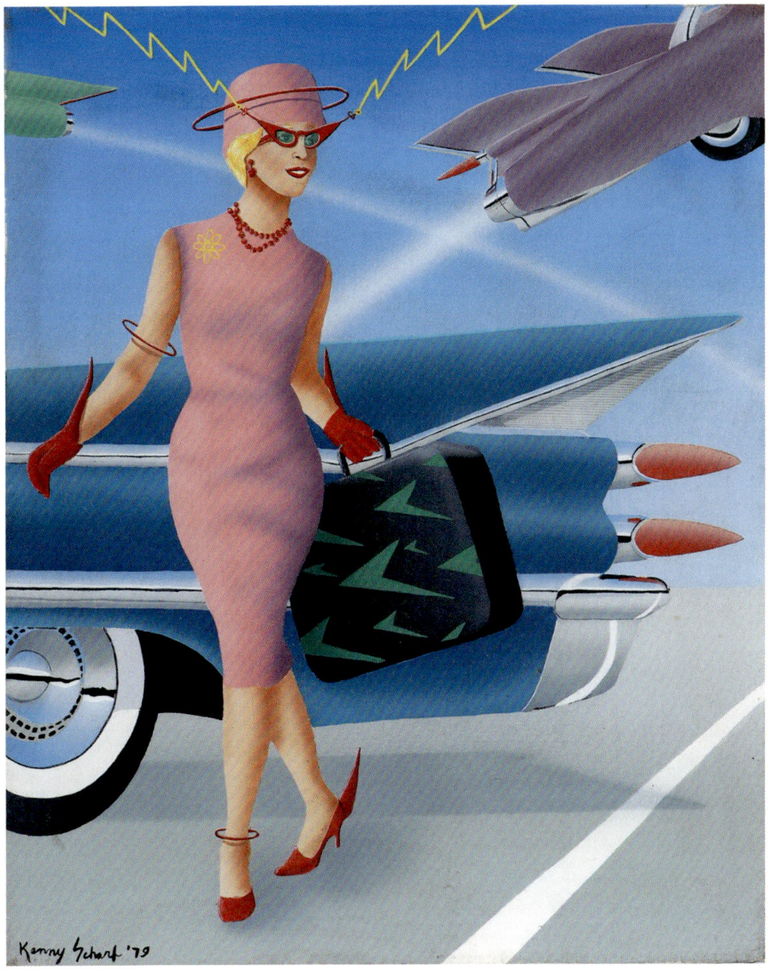

KENNY SCHARF (AMERICAN, BORN 1958). ***Escaped in Time, I'm Pleased.*** 1979. Acrylic on canvas, 16 × 20" (40.6 × 50.8 cm). Collection Bruno Testore Schmidt
KENNY SCHARF. ***Untitled #6 (Speed).*** 1979. Mixed media on board, 10 × 15" (25.4 × 38.1 cm). Collection the artist
KENNY SCHARF. ***Having a TV Pizza Party.*** 1979. Acrylic on canvas, 16 × 20" (40.6 × 50.8 cm). Collection Bruno Testore Schmidt
KENNY SCHARF. ***Having Fun.*** 1979. Acrylic on canvas, 20 × 16" (50.8 × 40.6 cm). Collection Bruno Testore Schmidt
KENNY SCHARF. ***I'm Off.*** 1979. Acrylic on canvas, 20 × 16" (50.8 × 40.6 cm). Collection Bruno Testore Schmidt

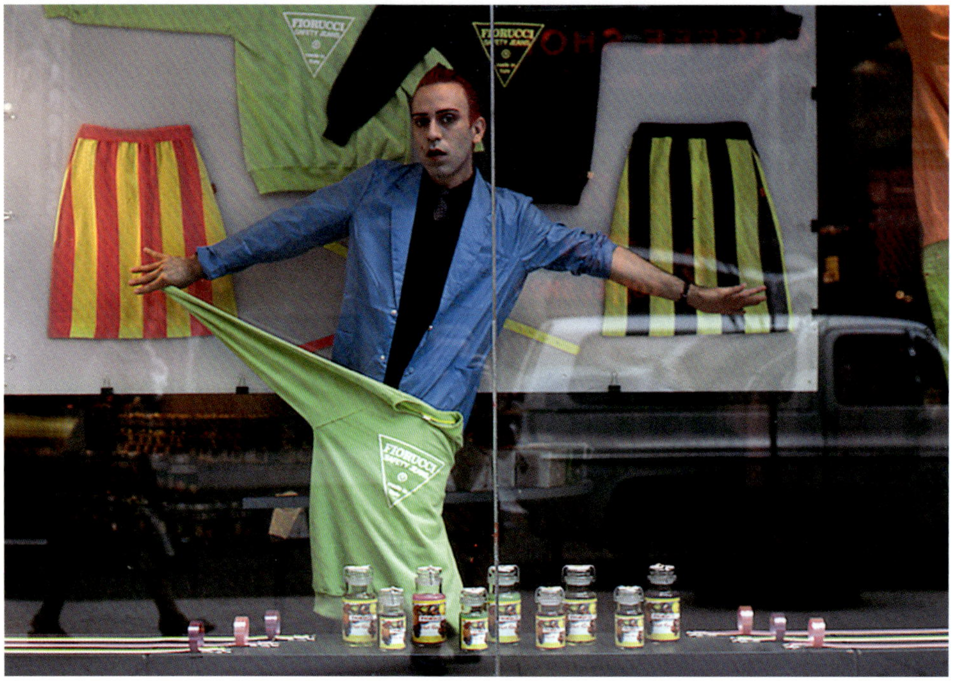

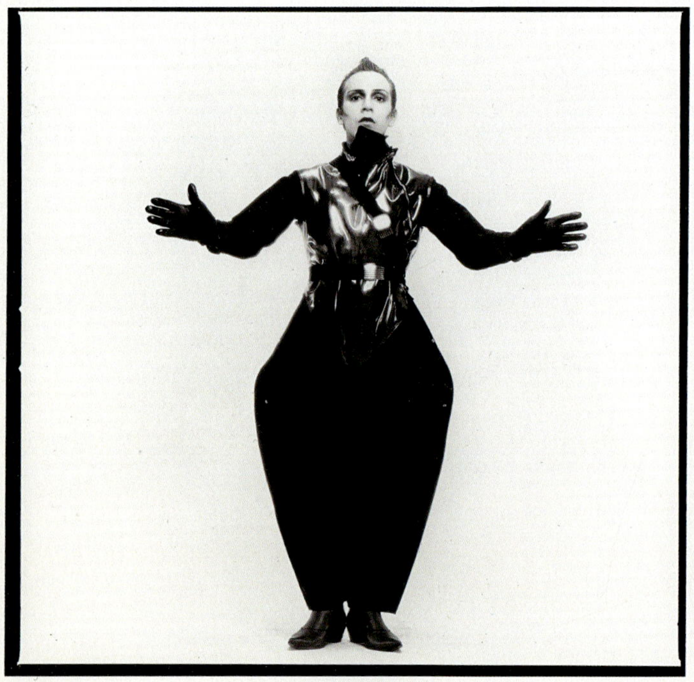

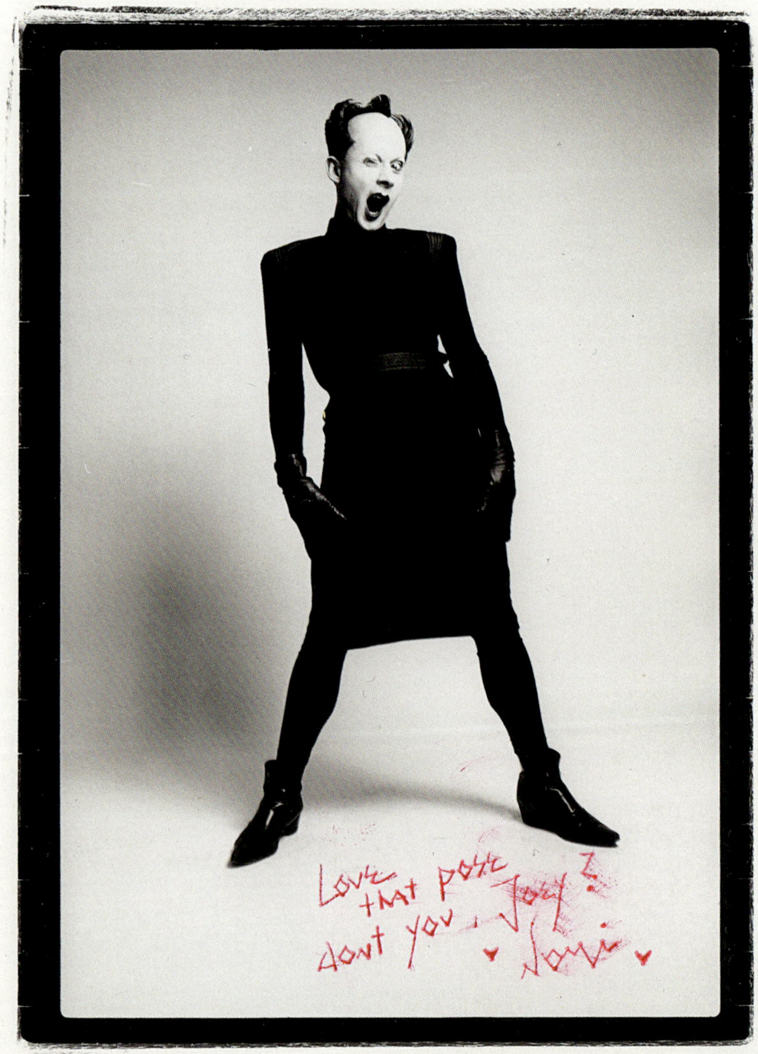

JOEY ARIAS IN THE FIORUCCI WINDOW, 1980. Photograph by Matthew Olszak
JOEY ARIAS, 1980. Photograph by Michael Halsband. Collection Joey Arias
KLAUS NOMI, 1980. Photograph by Michael Halsband. Collection Joey Arias

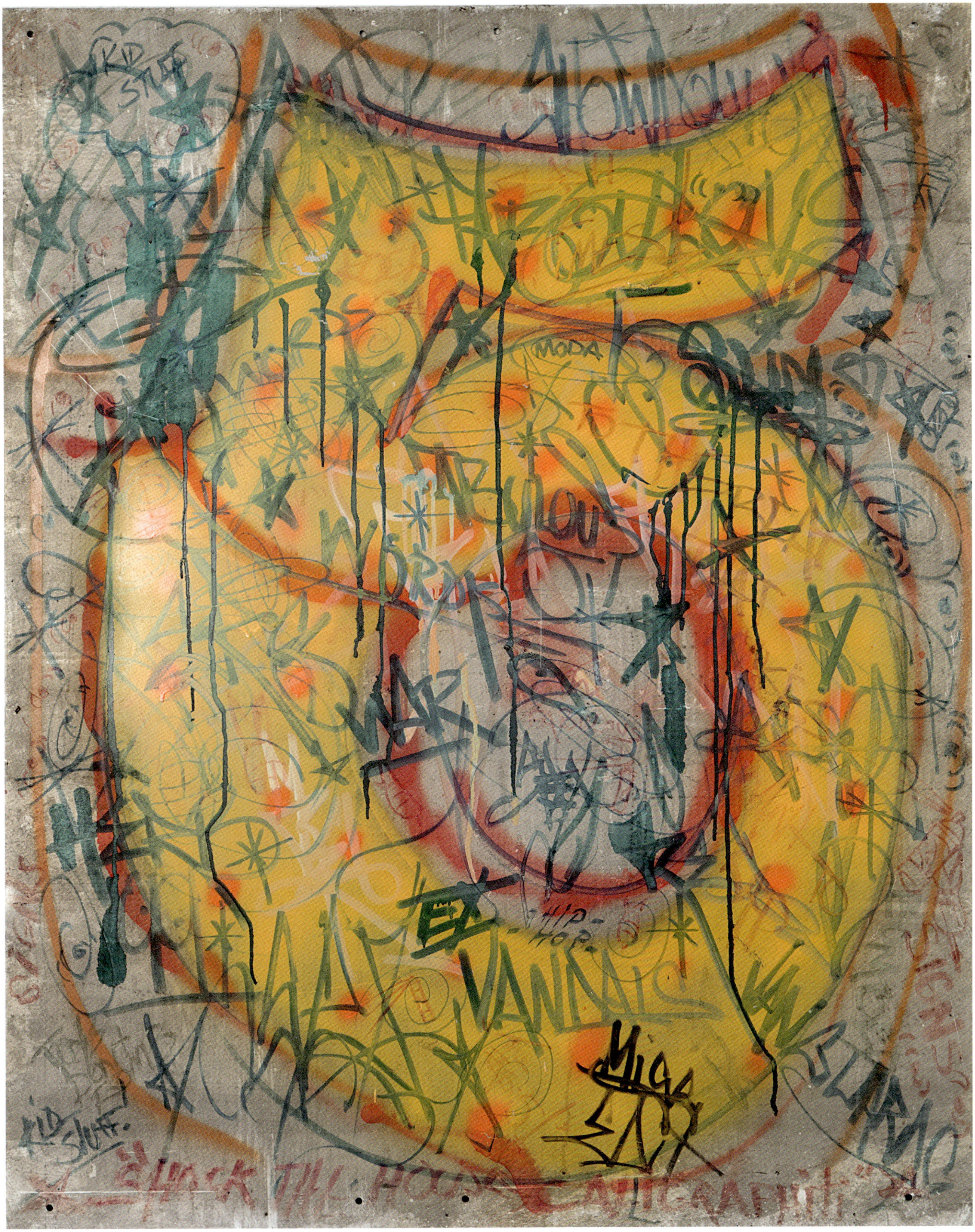

FRED BRATHWAITE, AKA FAB 5 FREDDY (AMERICAN, BORN 1959). *FIVE.* 1980–81. Spray enamel and marker on aluminum, 48¼ × 38" (122.6 × 96.5 cm). Collection Patrick Fox

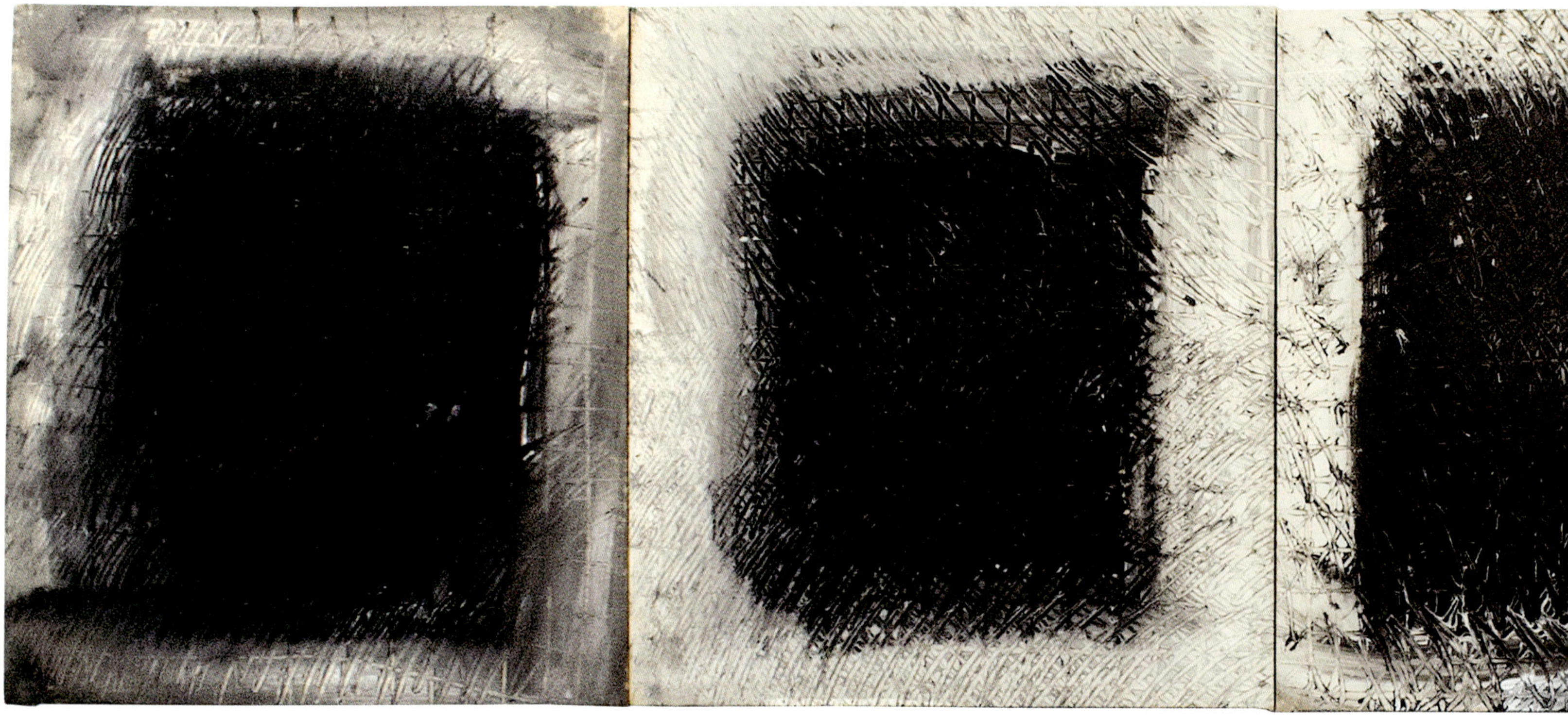

FRANK HOLLIDAY (AMERICAN, BORN 1957). ***TVC15.*** 1979. Acrylic on canvas, 25½ × 110" (64.8 × 279.4 cm). Collection the artist

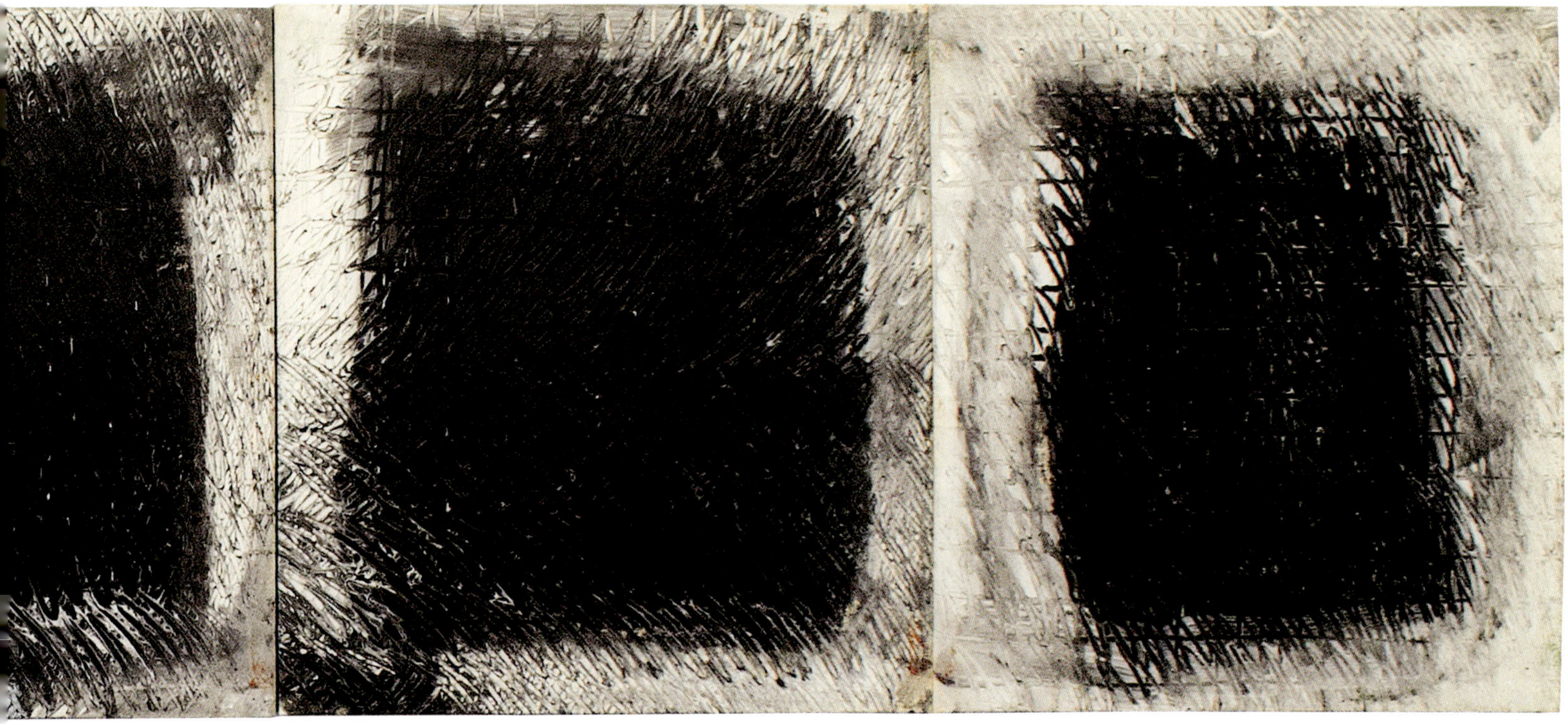

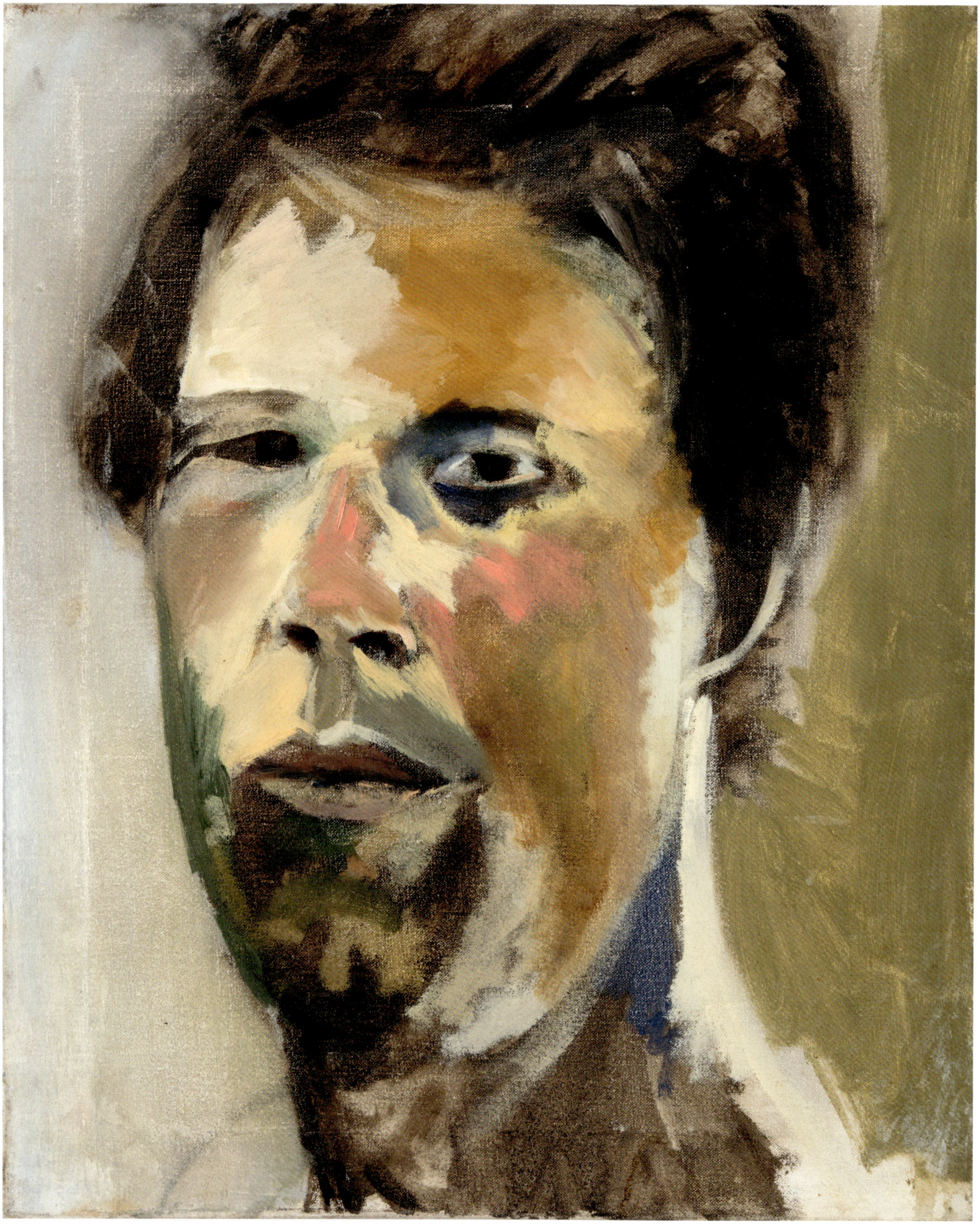

EDWARD BREZINSKI (AMERICAN, 1954–2007). ***Self Portrait.*** 1976. Oil on canvas, 20 × 16" (50.8 × 40.6 cm). Collection Lenny Kisko

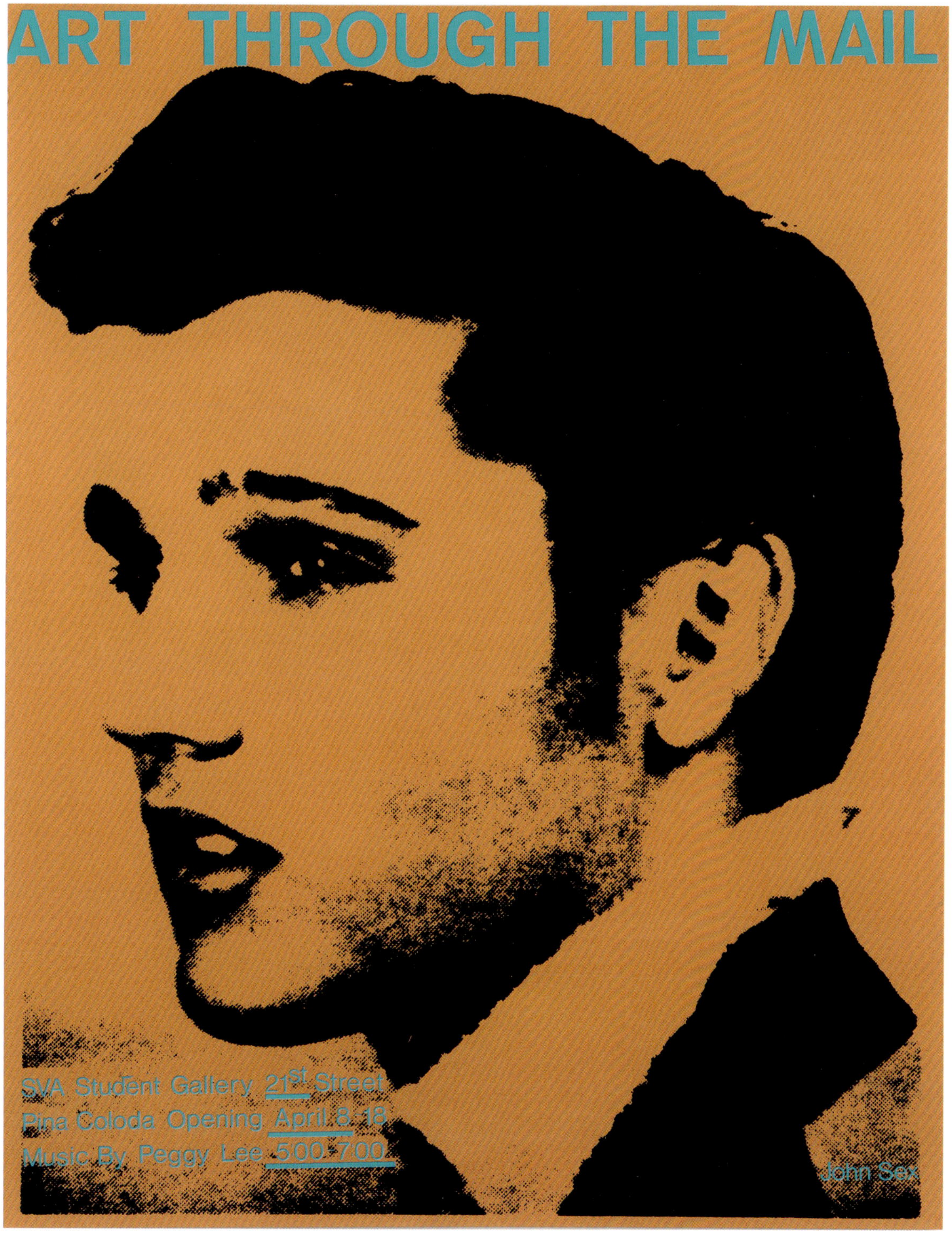

JOHN SEX (AMERICAN, 1956–1990). ***Art through the mail.*** 1980. Silkscreen, 23 × 17½" (58.4 × 44.5 cm). Collection the Keith Haring Foundation

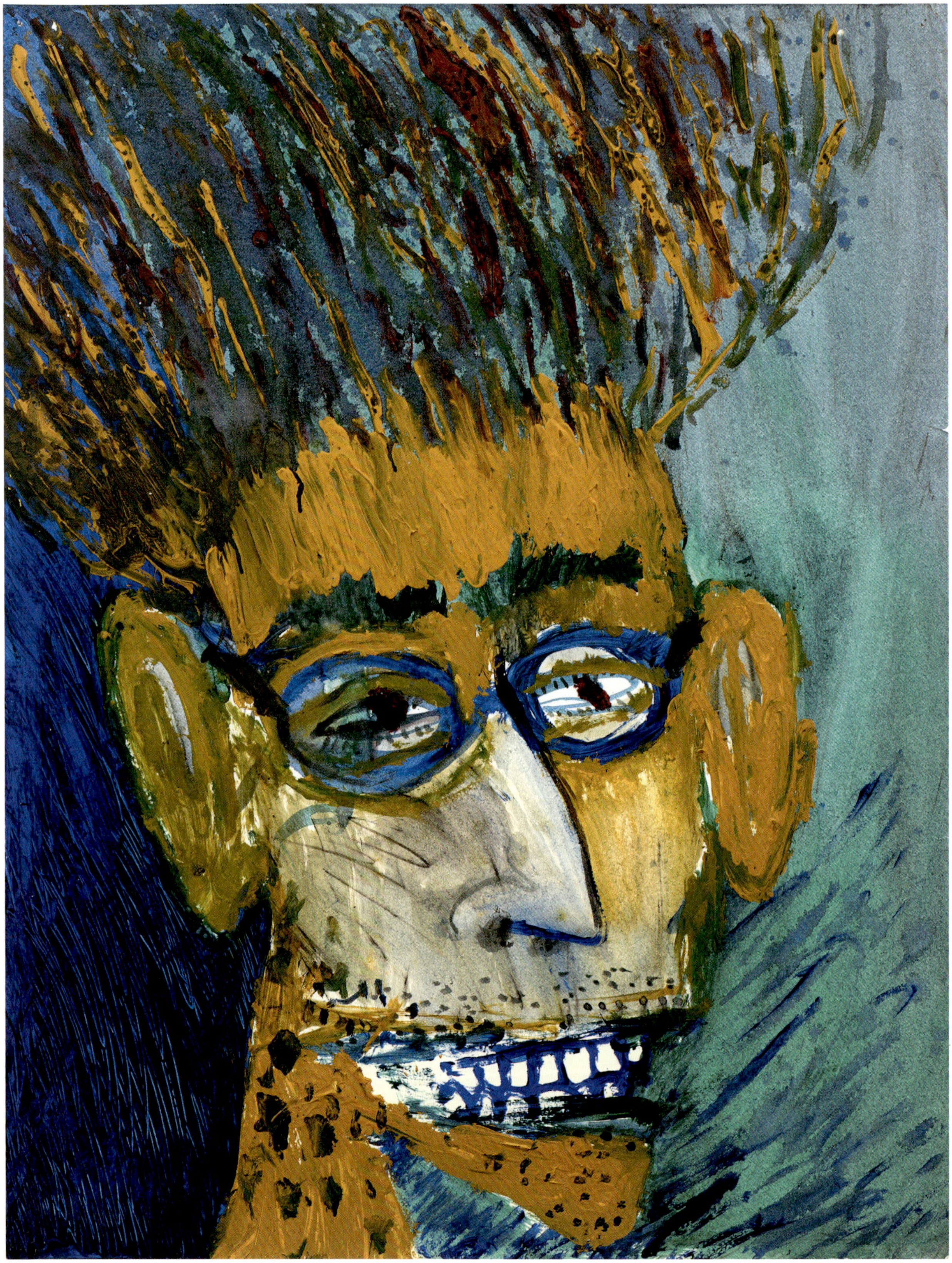

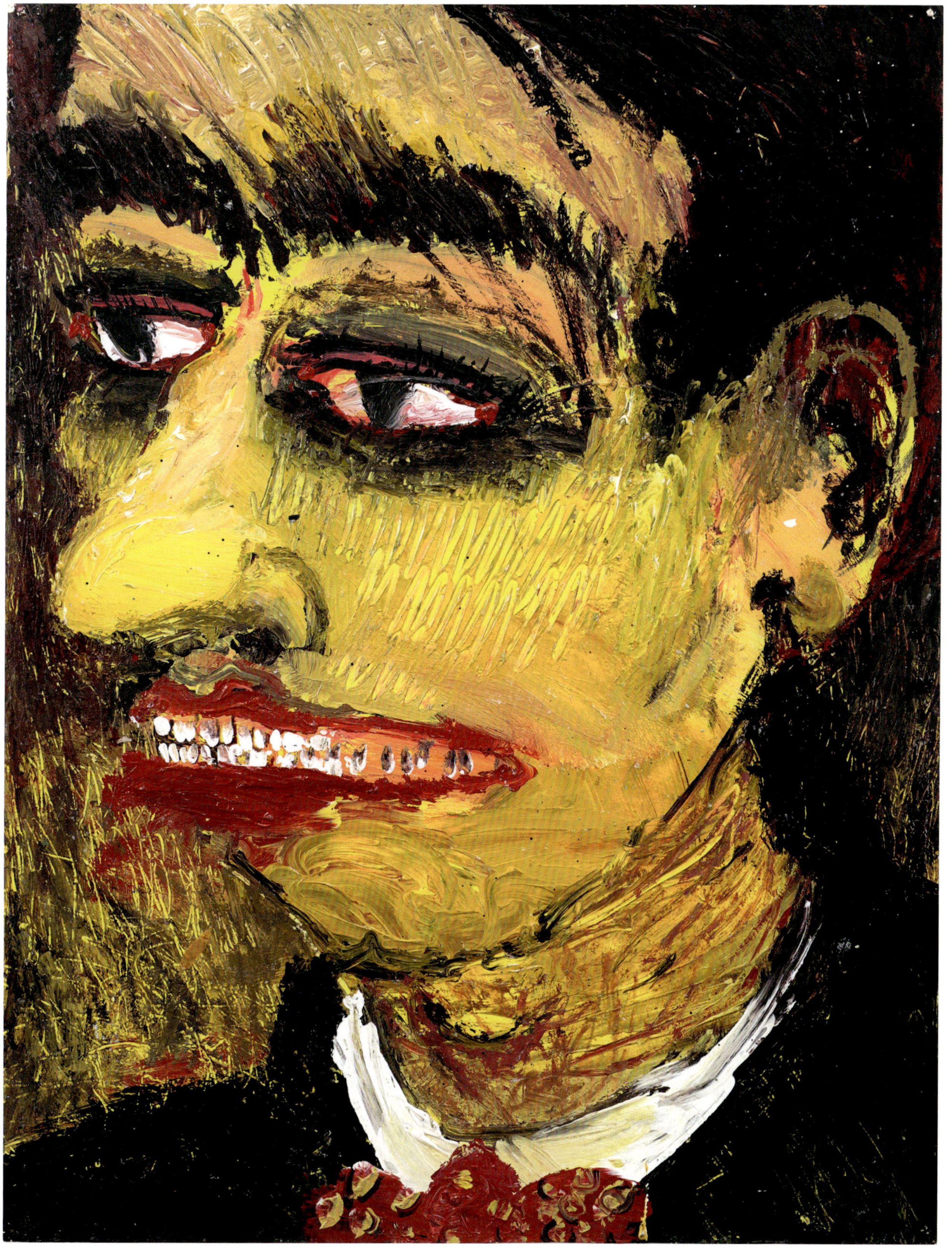

TABBOO! (STEPHEN TASHJIAN) (AMERICAN, BORN 1959). ***Untitled.*** 1982. Acrylic on found advertising paper, 27 × 20" (68.6 × 50.8 cm). Collection the artist
TABBOO! (STEPHEN TASHJIAN). ***Self-Portrait.*** 1982. Acrylic on found advertising paper, 27 × 20" (68.6 × 50.8 cm). Collection the artist

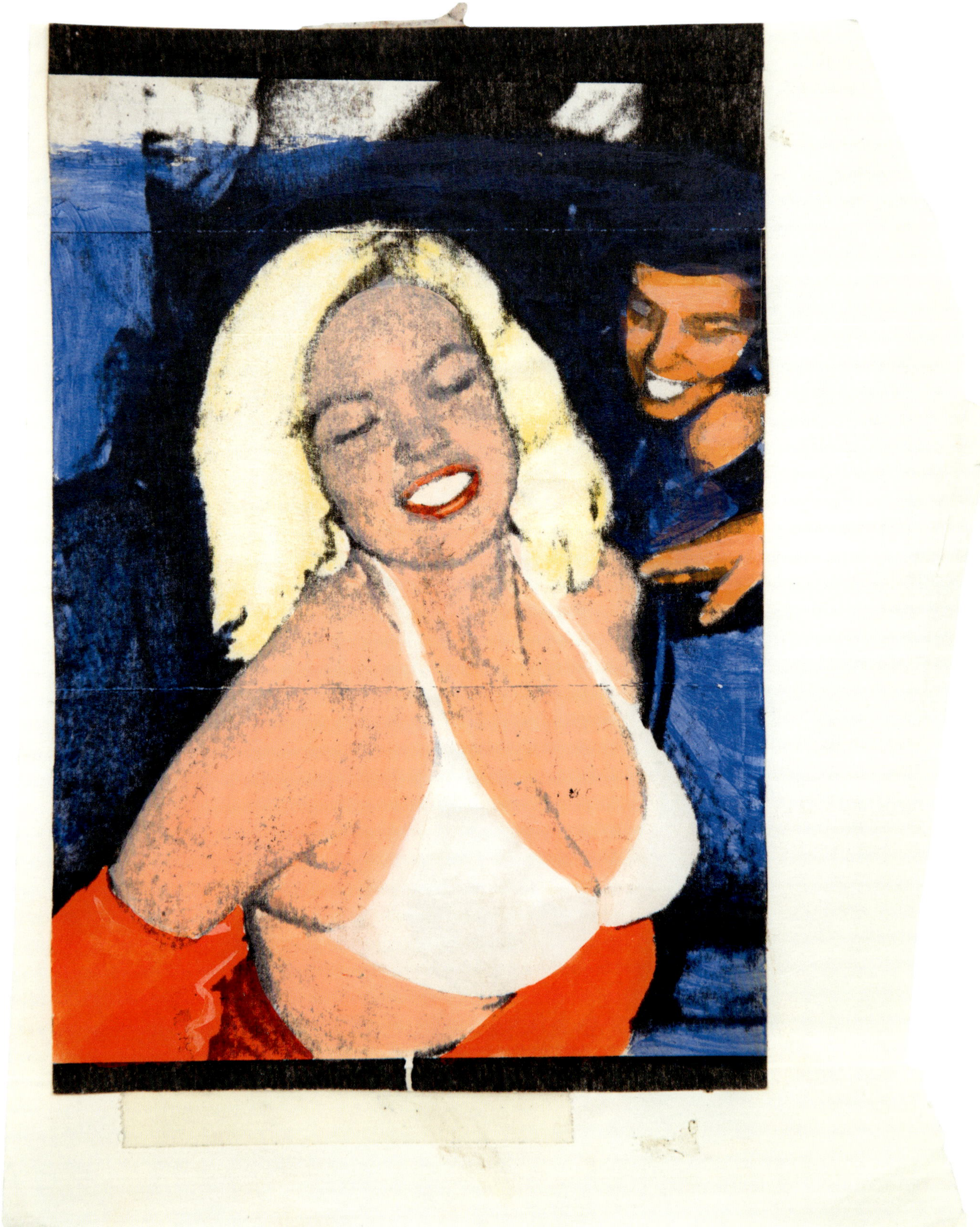

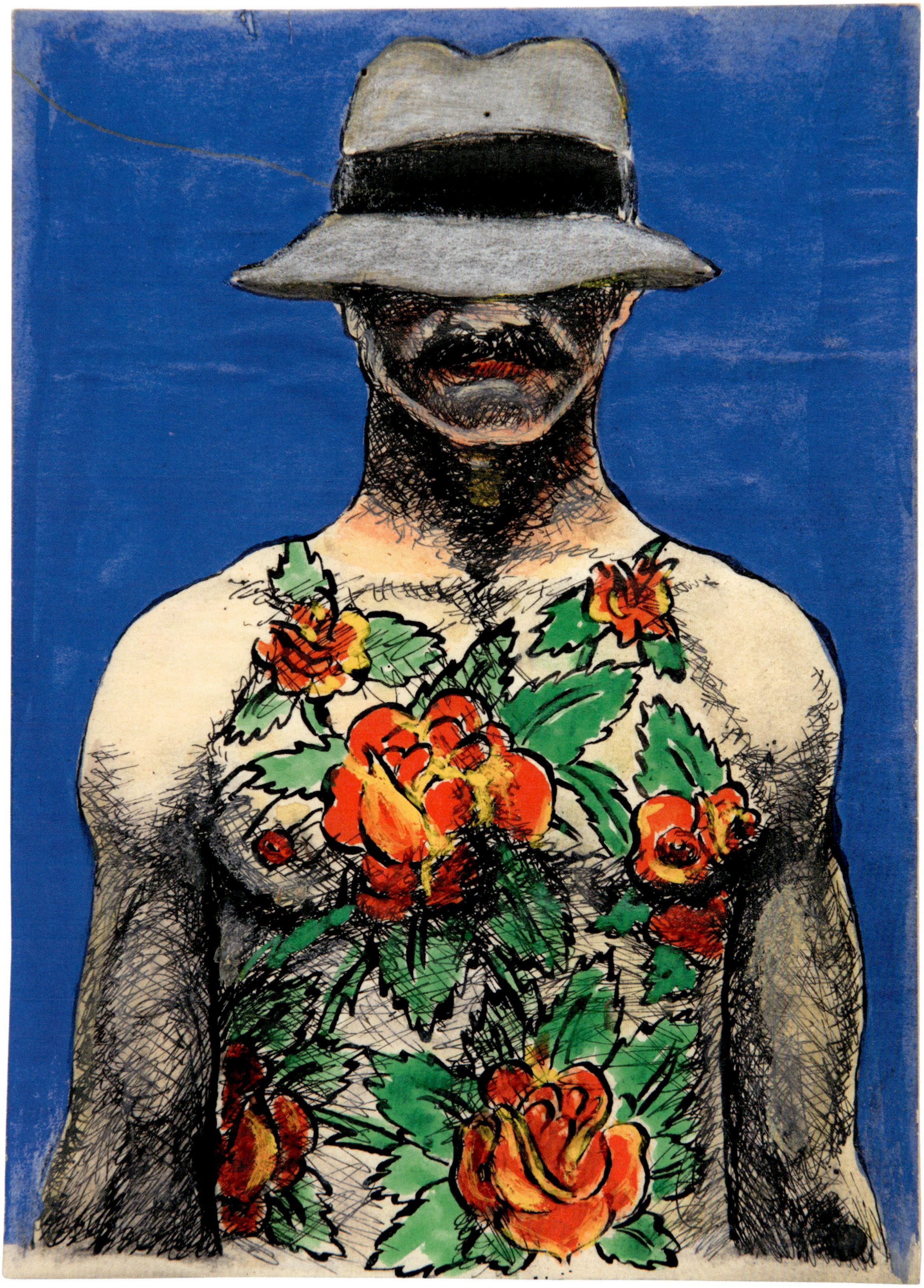

BRUNO TESTORE SCHMIDT (ITALIAN, BORN BRAZIL, 1954). ***Jane.*** 1981. Gouache on Xerox, 7 × 5" (17.8 × 12.7 cm). Collection the artist
BRUNO TESTORE SCHMIDT. ***Allan.*** 1981. Watercolor and ink, 7 × 5" (17.8 × 12.7 cm). Collection the artist

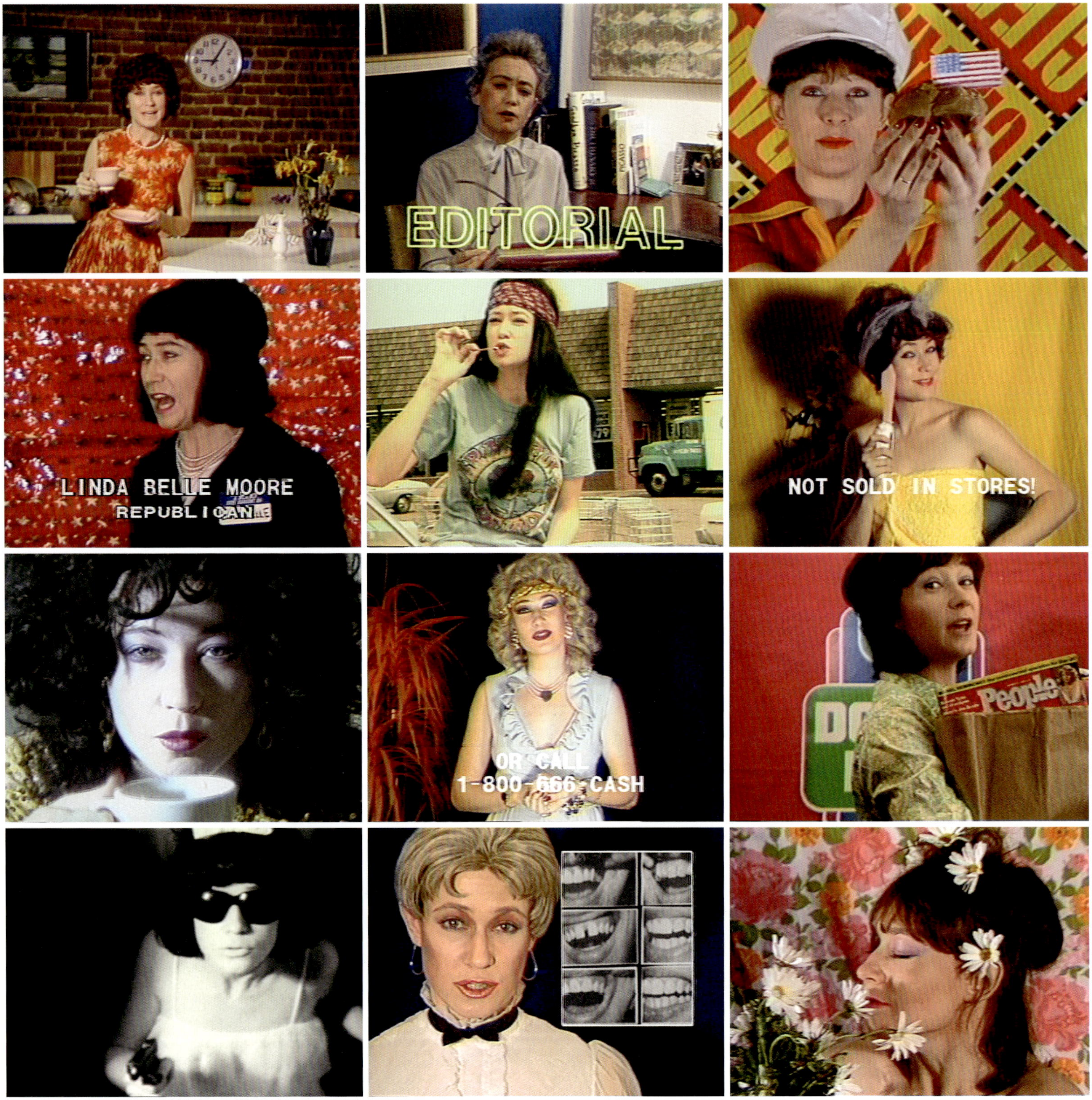
EDITORIAL
LINDA BELLE MOORE
REPUBLICAN
NOT SOLD IN STORES!
OR CALL
1-800-666-CASH
People

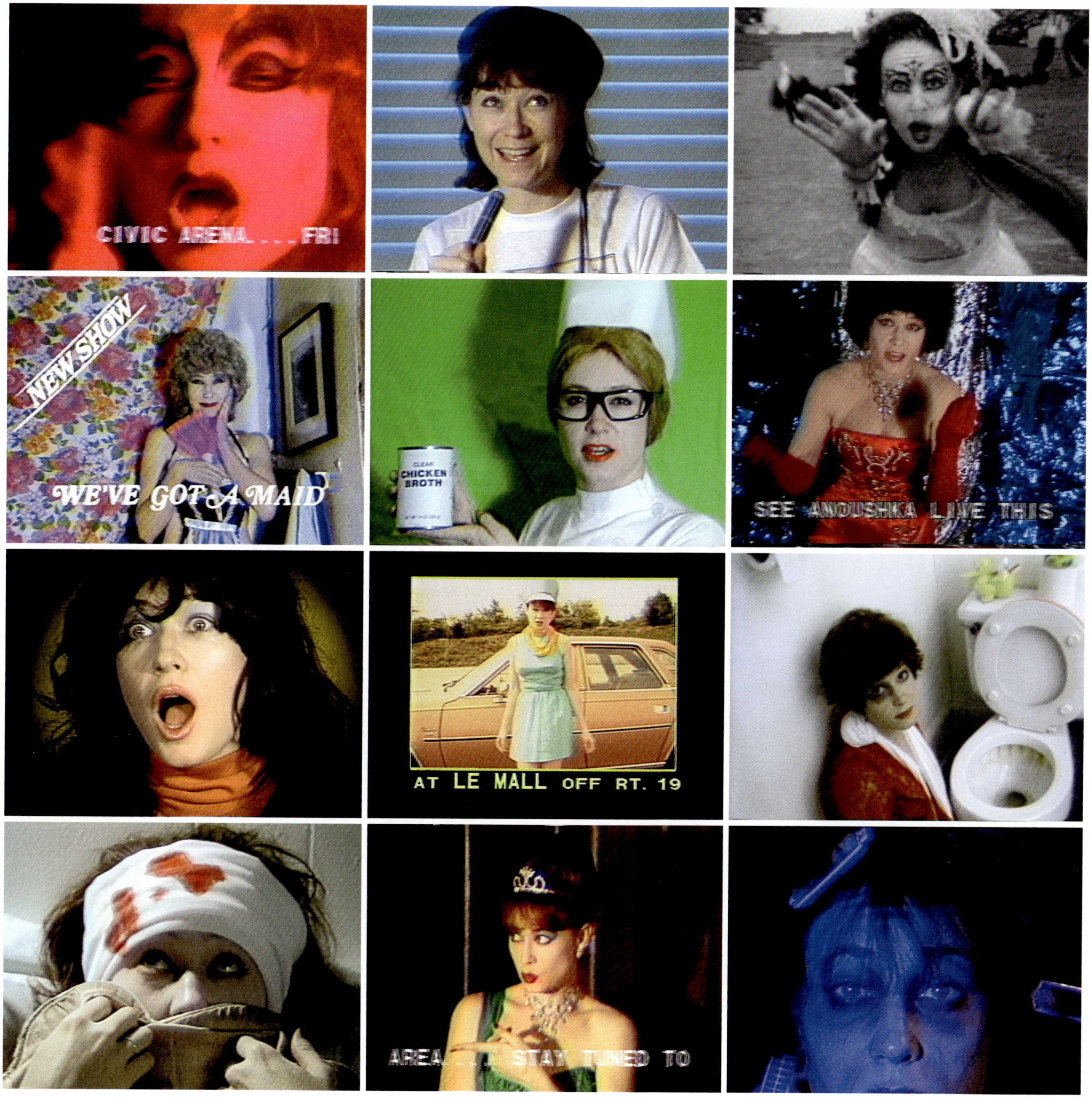

TOM RUBNITZ (AMERICAN, 1956–1992) AND ANN MAGNUSON (AMERICAN, BORN 1956). ***Made for TV.*** 1984. Video (color, sound), 15 min. The Museum of Modern Art, New York. Purchase funds provided by The Contemporary Arts Council.

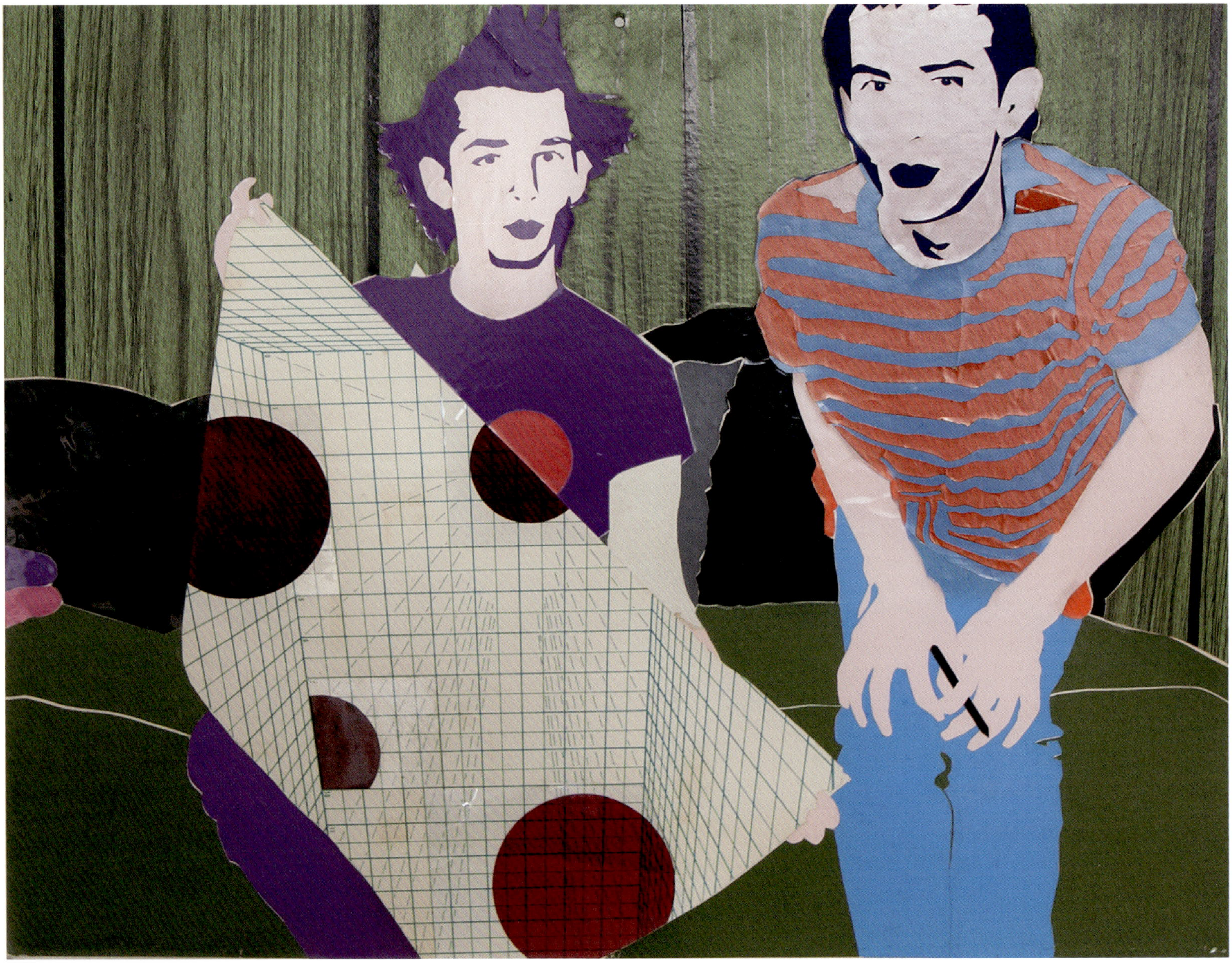

OLIVER SANCHEZ (AMERICAN, BORN CUBA, 1958). ***Untitled (Adolfo and Oliver).*** c. 1980. Paper collage on illustration board, 22 × 28" (55.9 × 71.1 cm). Collection Min and Oliver Sanchez

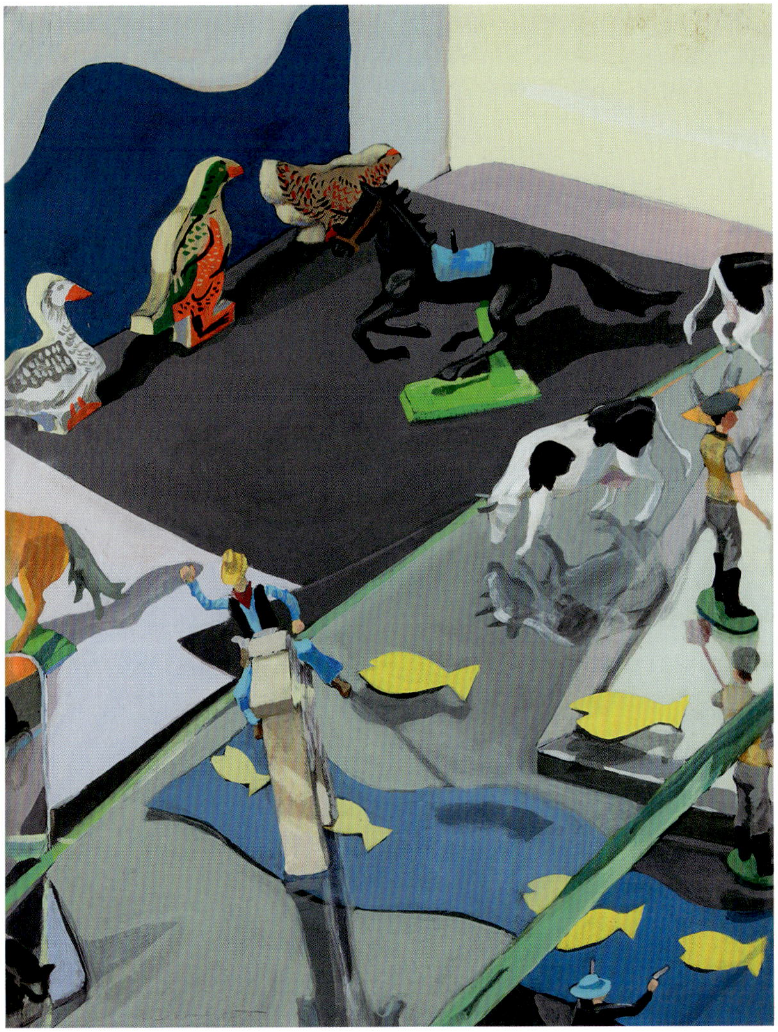

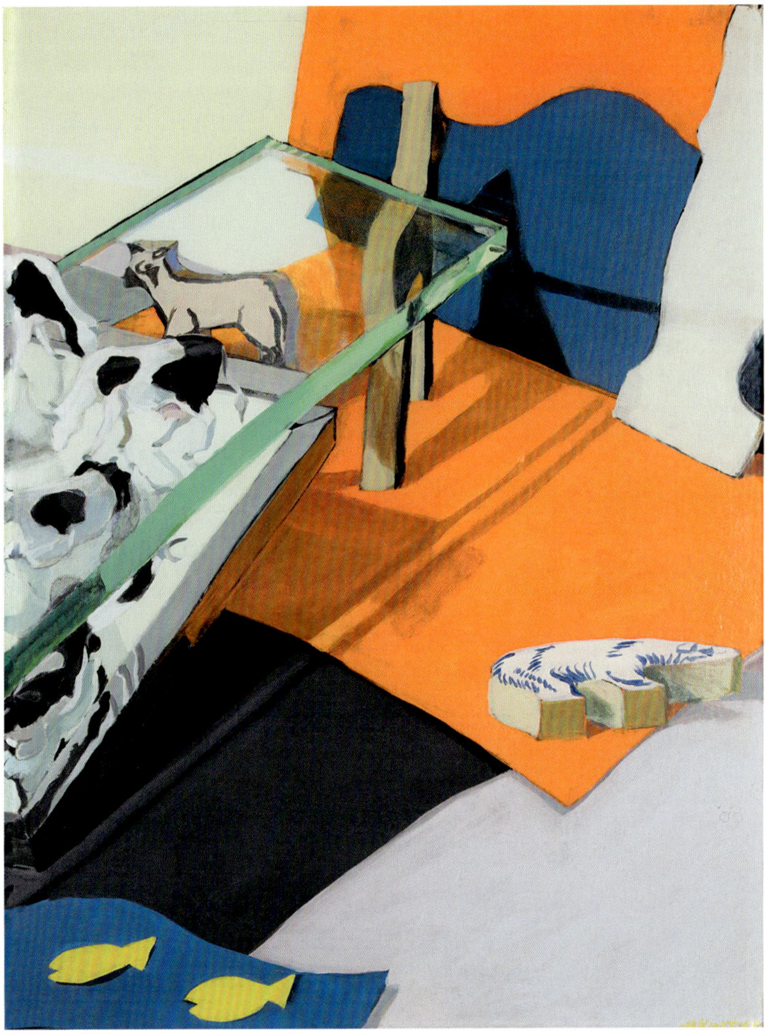

RAGHUBIR (NANCY) KINTISCH (AMERICAN, BORN 1955). ***Rio Grande Colorado.*** 1979. Acrylic on chipboard, 12 × 18" (30.5 × 45.7 cm). Collection Irene Albright
RAGHUBIR (NANCY) KINTISCH. ***Rio Grande Gulf of Mexico.*** 1979. Acrylic on chipboard, 12 × 18" (30.5 × 45.7 cm). Collection Irene Albright

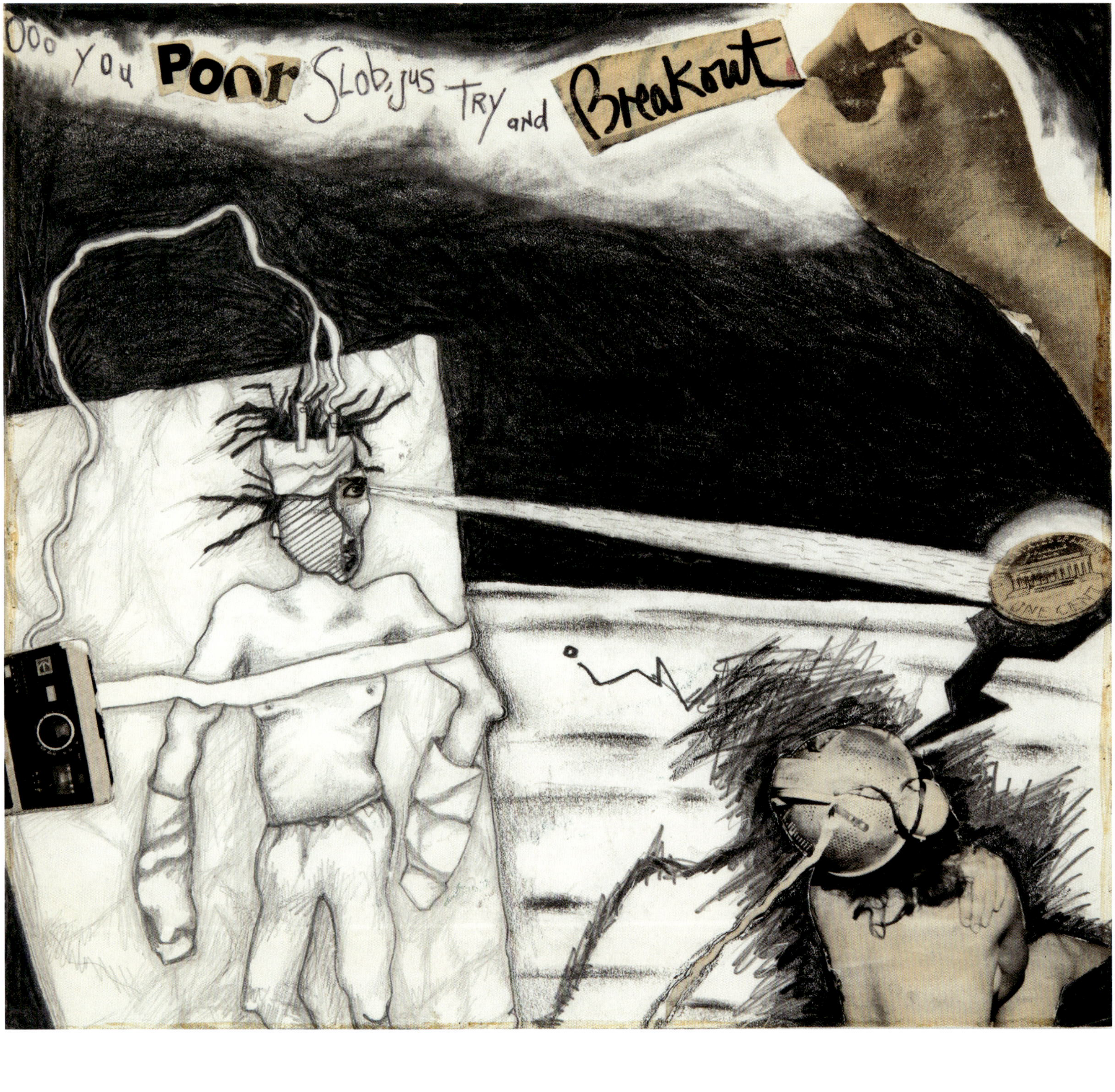
Ooo you Poor SLob, jus TRY and Breakout

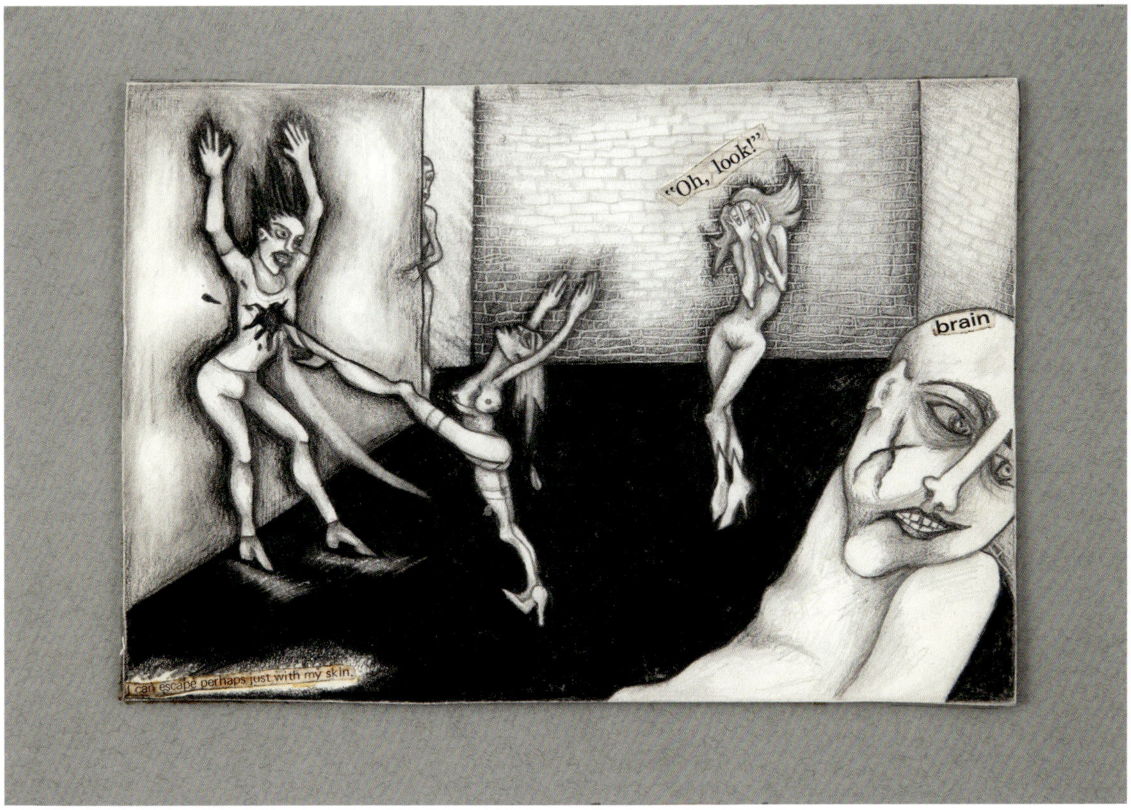

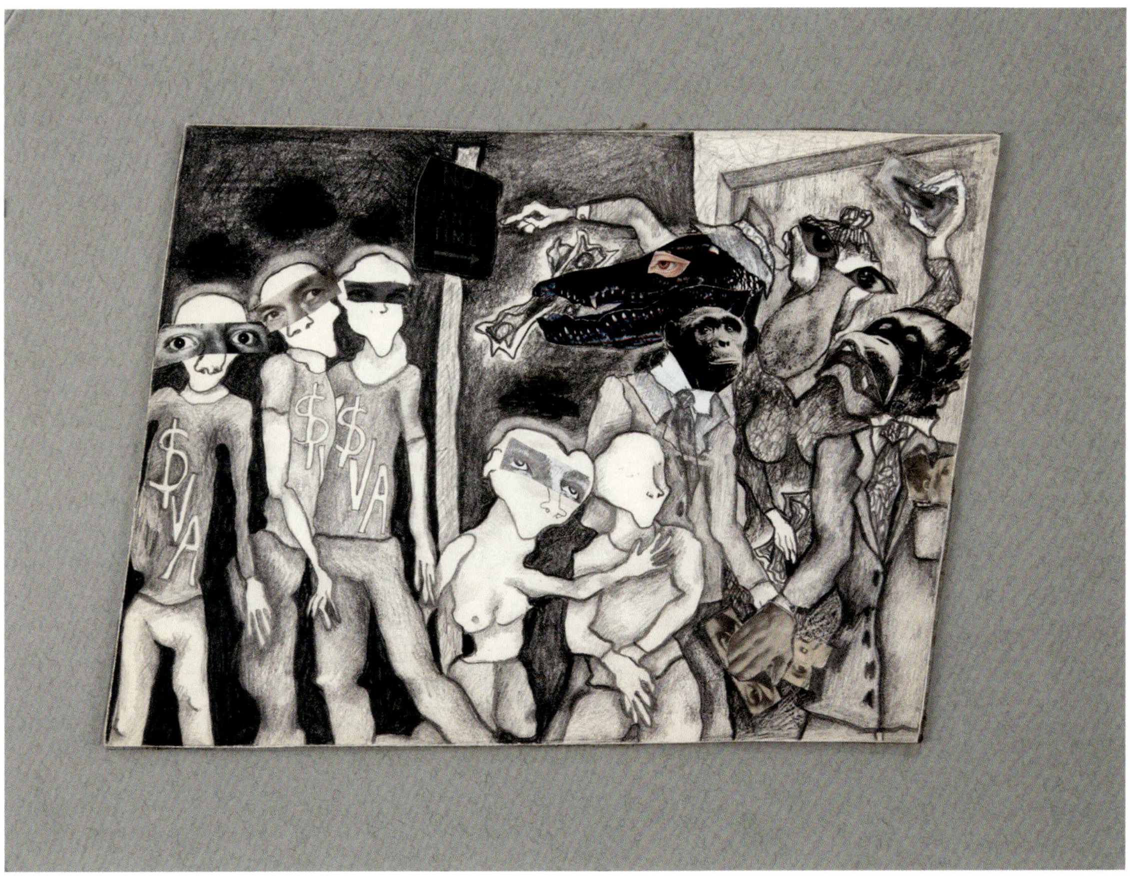

NATALYA MAYSTRENKO (AMERICAN, BORN 1957). ***Breakout.*** c. 1979. Collage and pencil on board, 9 × 10" (22.9 × 25.4 cm). Collection the artist
NATALYA MAYSTRENKO. ***Girl Gang.*** c. 1979. Collage and pencil on board, 8 × 6" (20.3 × 15.2 cm). Collection the artist
NATALYA MAYSTRENKO. ***SVA.*** c. 1979. Collage and pencil on board, 8 × 6" (20.3 × 15.2 cm). Collection the artist

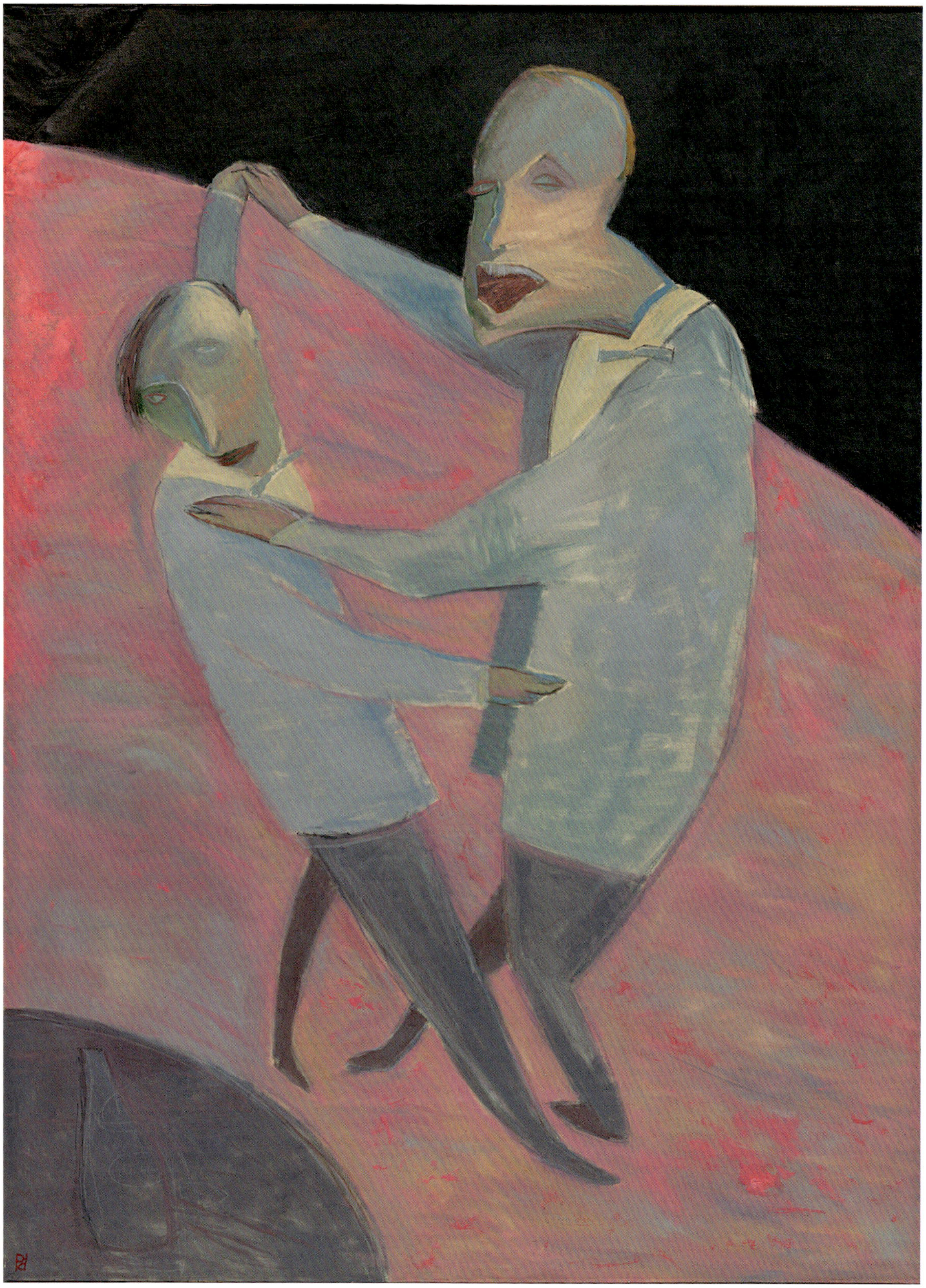

PARKER DULANY (AMERICAN, BORN 1958). ***The World.*** c. 1982. Oil on linen, 71 × 52" (180.3 × 132.1 cm). Collection the artist

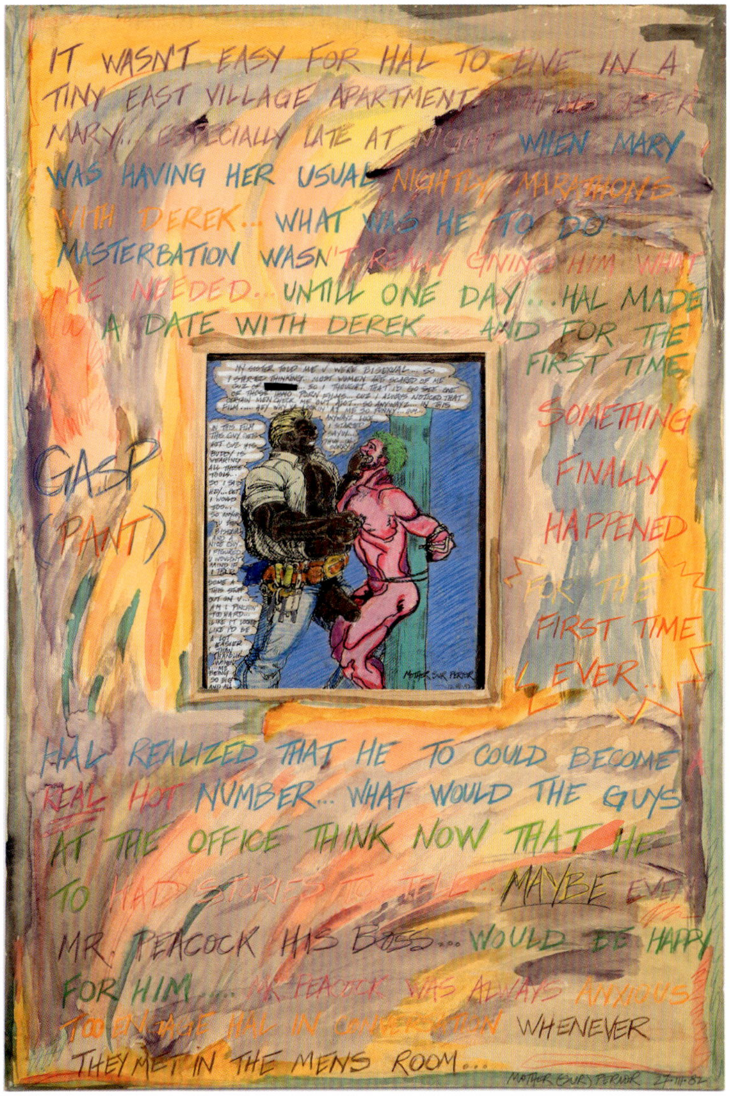

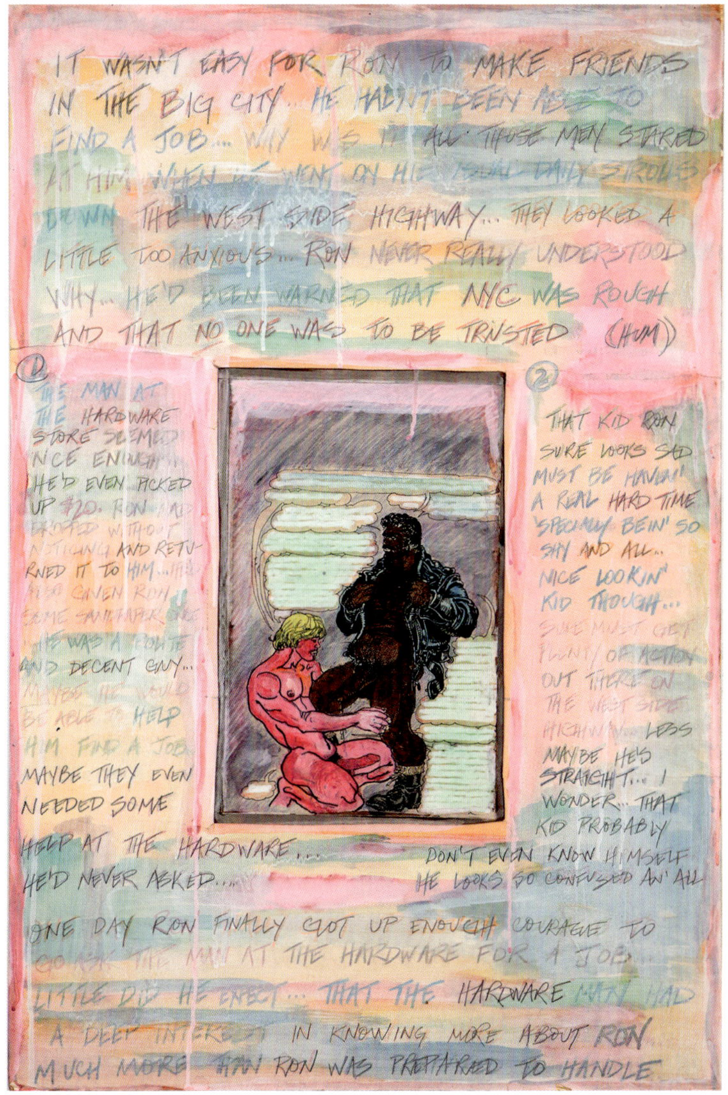

SUR RODNEY (SUR) (CANADIAN, BORN 1954). *Hal Living in the East Village.* c. 1980. Oil stick, color pencil, watercolor, and acrylic on Xerox and cardstock, 40 × 26" (101.6 × 66 cm). Collection the artist

SUR RODNEY (SUR). *Ron Living in the West Village.* c. 1980. Oil stick, color pencil, watercolor, and acrylic on Xerox and cardstock, 40 × 26" (101.6 × 66 cm). Collection the artist

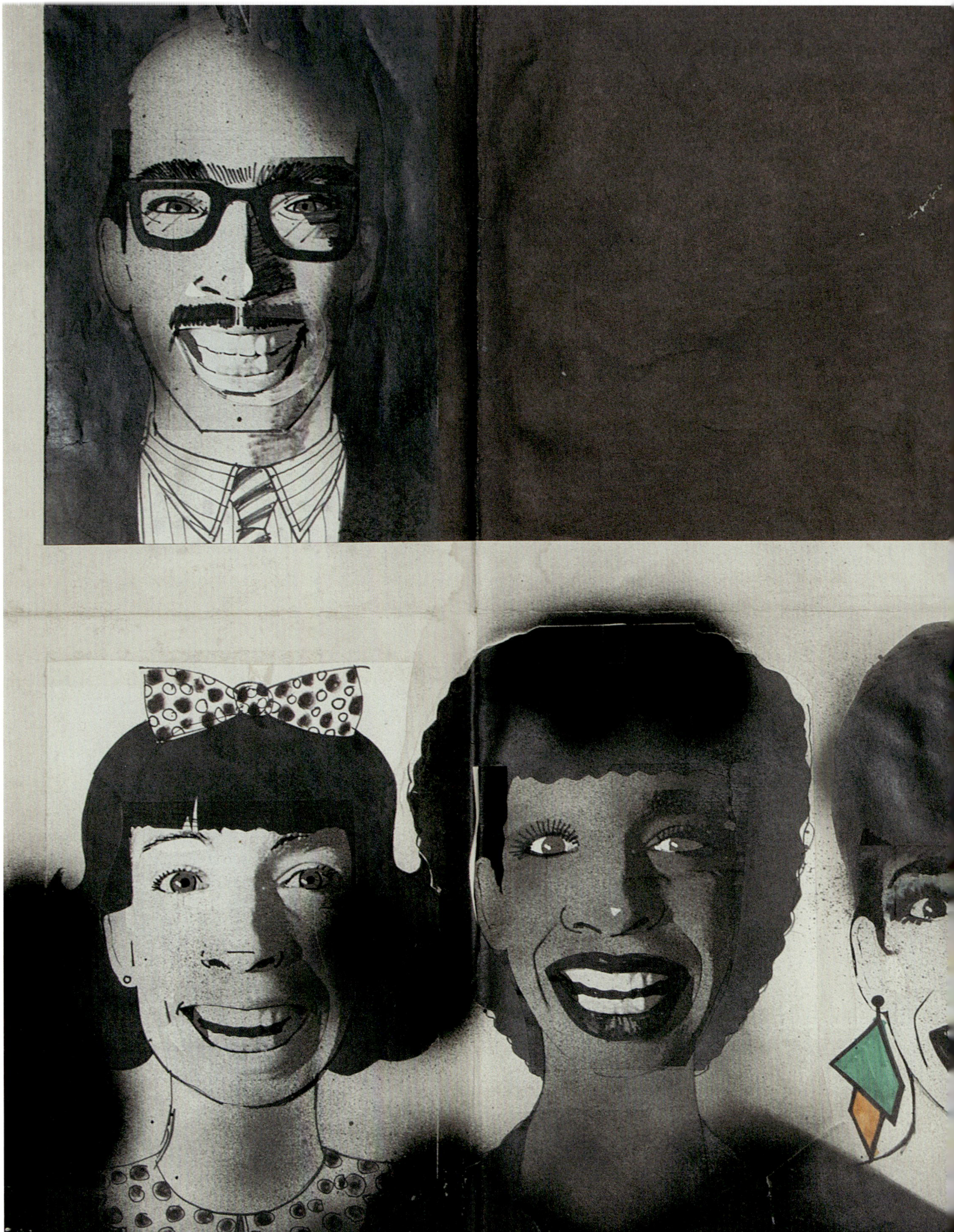

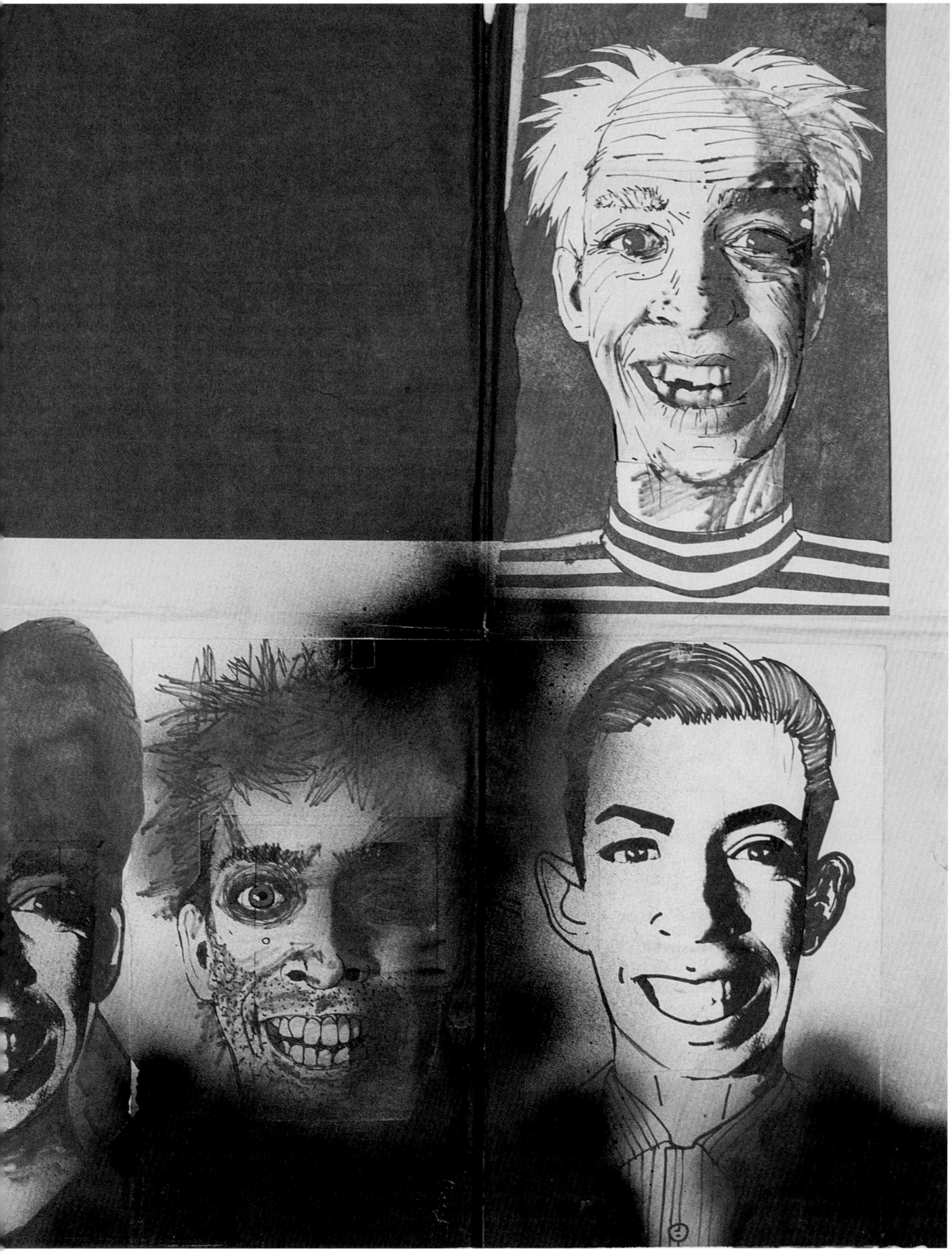

ADOLFO SANCHEZ (AMERICAN, BORN CUBA 1957–1990). Self-portrait montage. c. 1981. Enamel and marker on printed copy paper, 28 × 43" (71.1 × 106.7 cm). Collection Min and Oliver Sanchez

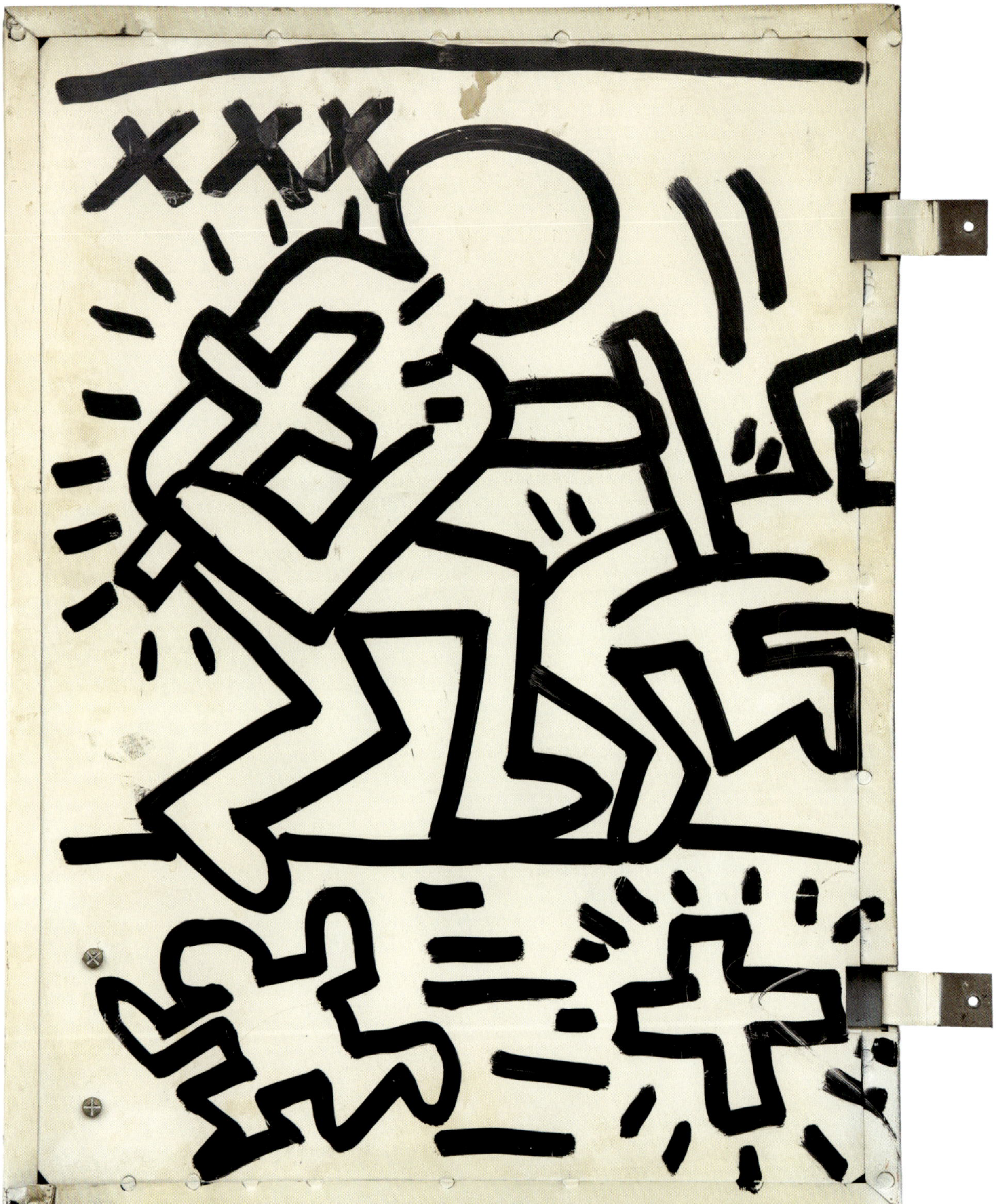

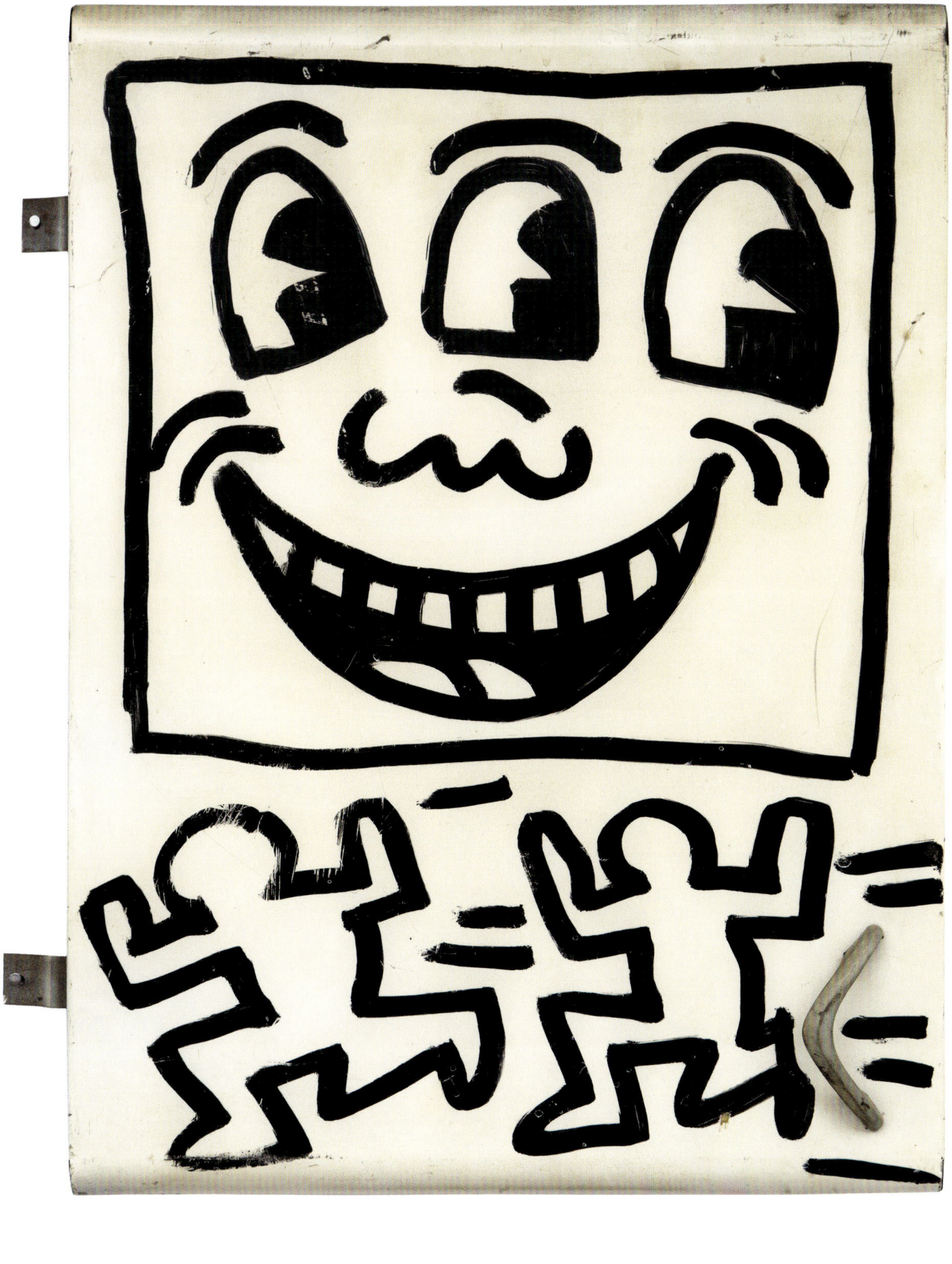

KEITH HARING (AMERICAN, 1958–1990). ***Untitled (Cabinet Door for Joey Arias).*** c. 1980. Acrylic on cabinet door, double-sided, 22 ¼ × 16 ¼ × 2" (56.5 × 41.3 × 5.1 cm). Collection Joey Arias

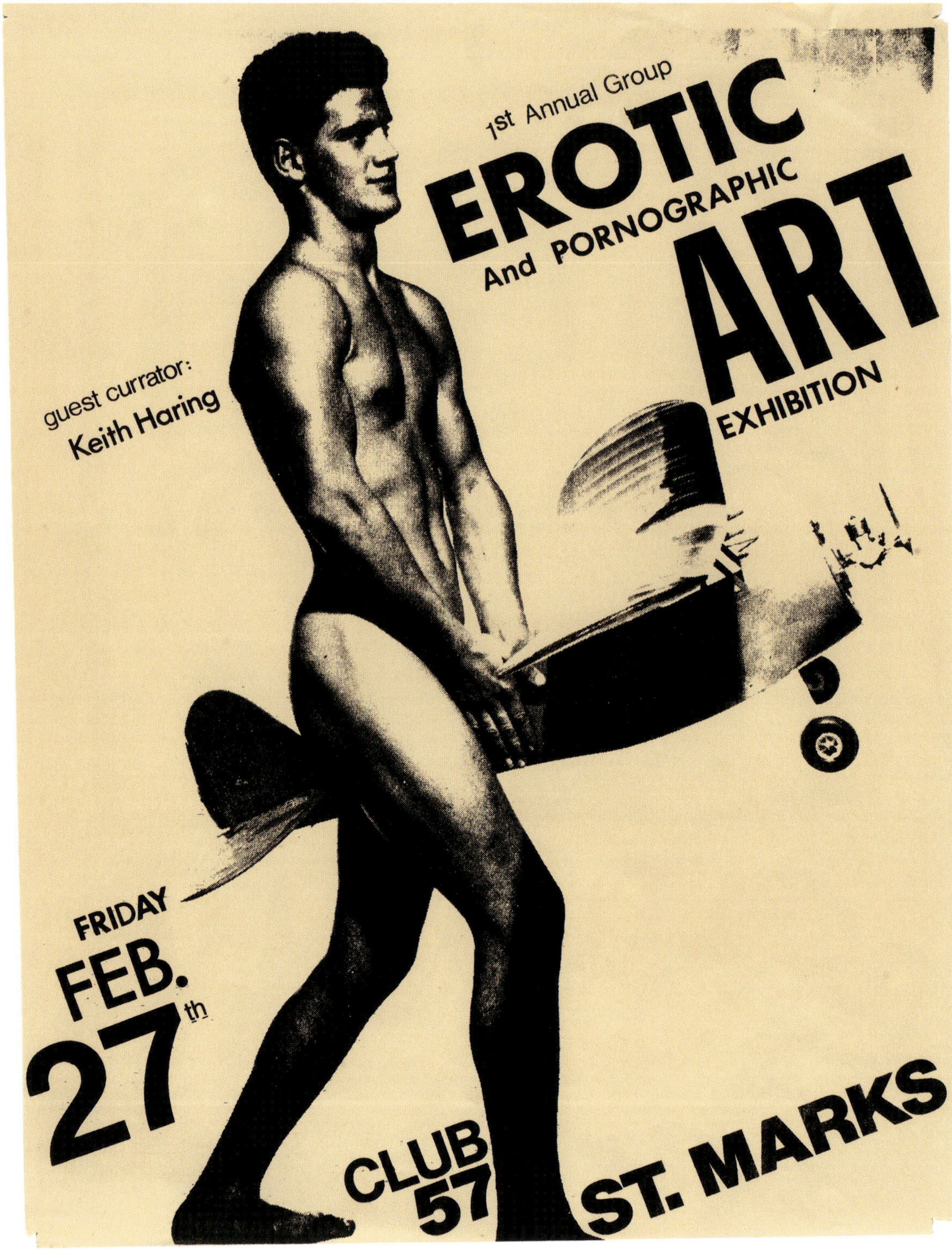

JOHN SEX (AMERICAN, 1956–1990). ***Erotic Art Show.*** 1981. Silkscreen, 22¾ × 17" (57.8 × 43.2 cm). The Museum of Modern Art, New York. Department of Film Special Collections

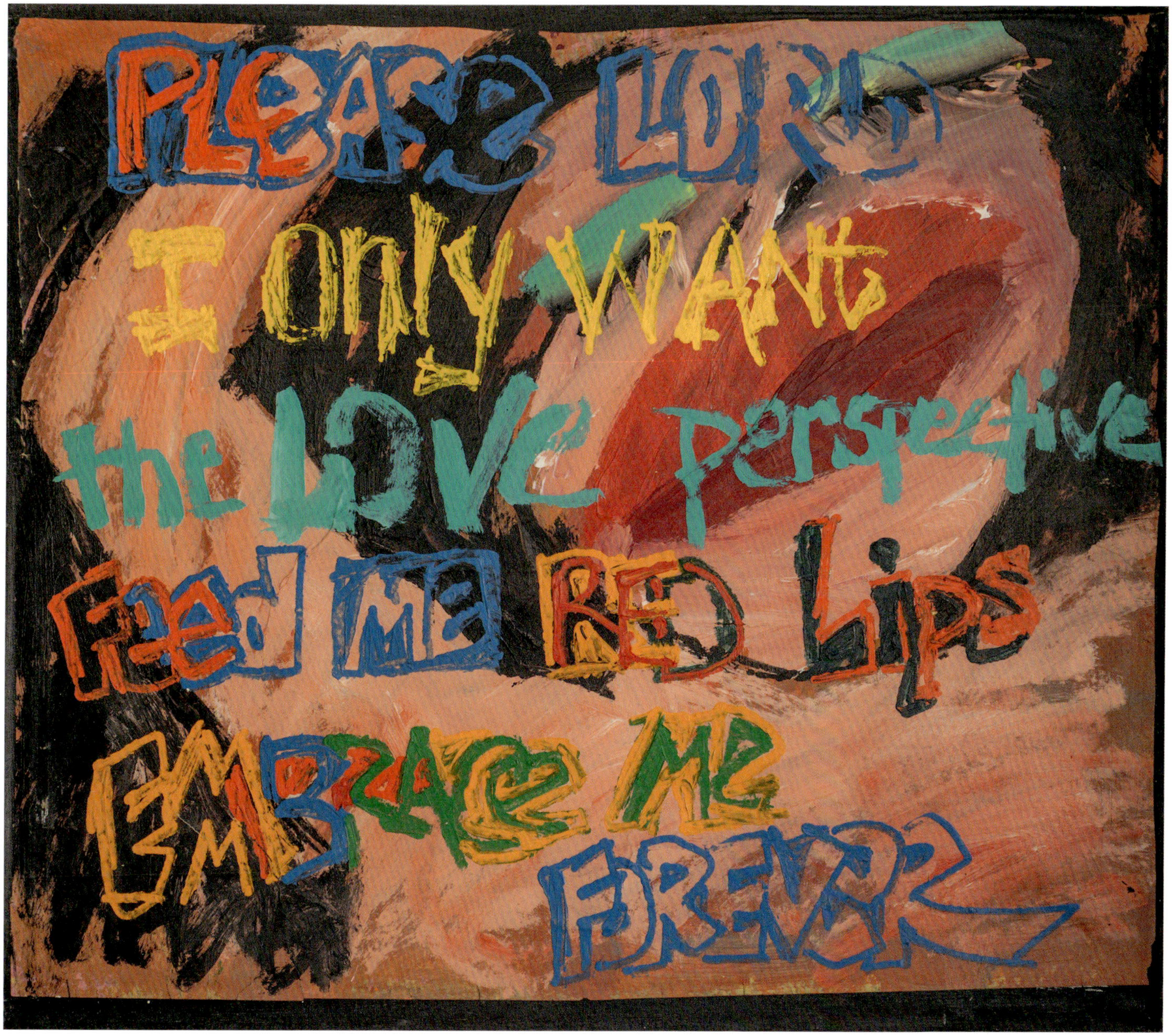

BRANT KINGMAN (AMERICAN, BORN 1953). ***The Love Perspective.*** 1982. Acrylic on newsprint, mounted on canvas, 32 × 36" (81.3 × 91.4 cm). Collection the artist

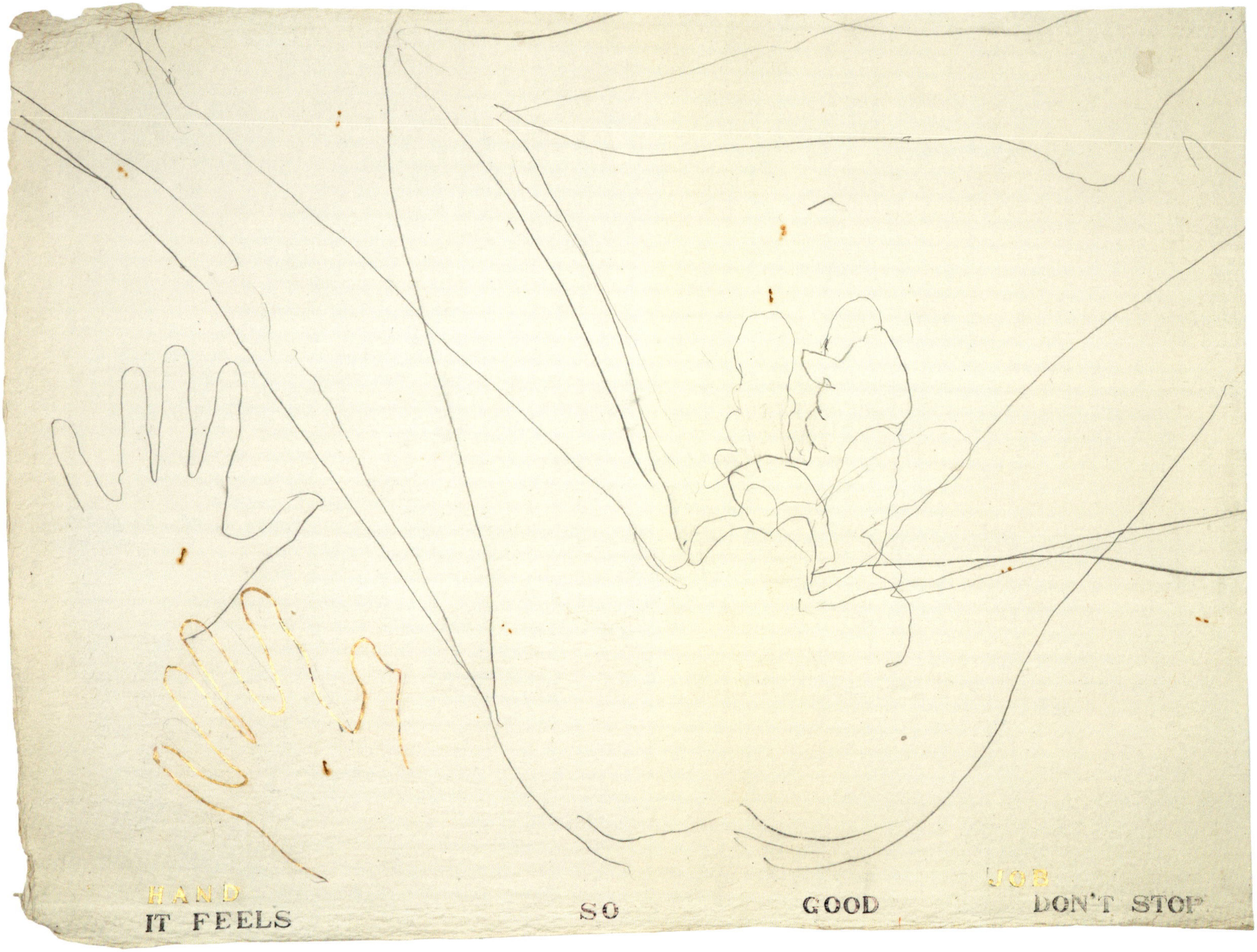

PETER HRISTOFF (BULGARIAN, BORN TURKEY, 1958). ***Hand Job.*** 1981. Pencil, gouache, gold leaf, rubber-stamped lettering, and rust on Indian cotton paper, 25 × 33 ¼" (63.5 × 84.5 cm). Collection the artist

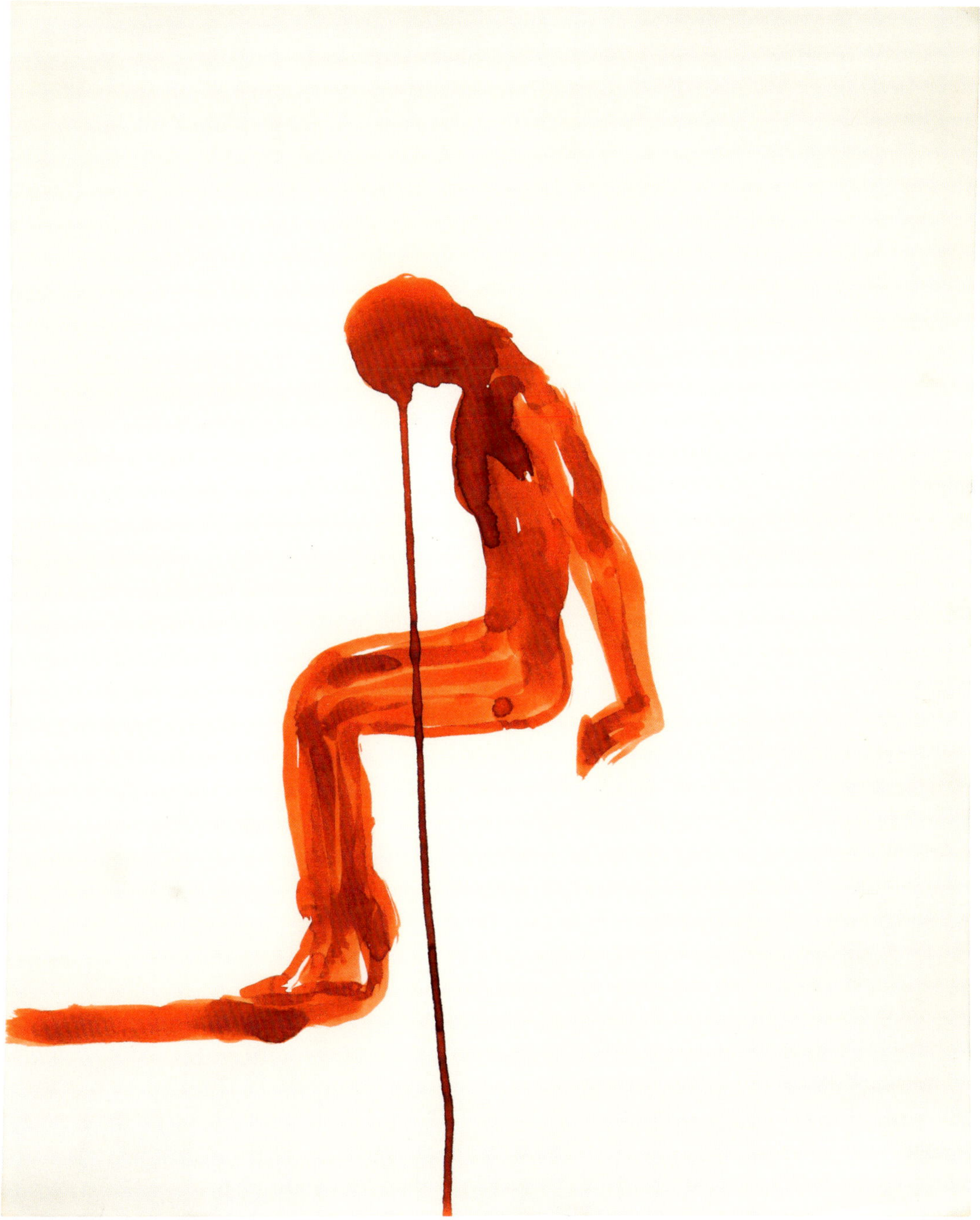

BRUNO TESTORE SCHMIDT (ITALIAN, BORN BRAZIL, 1954). ***Shawn Series.*** 1982. Ink on paper, 13¾ × 10½" (35 × 27 cm). Collection the artist

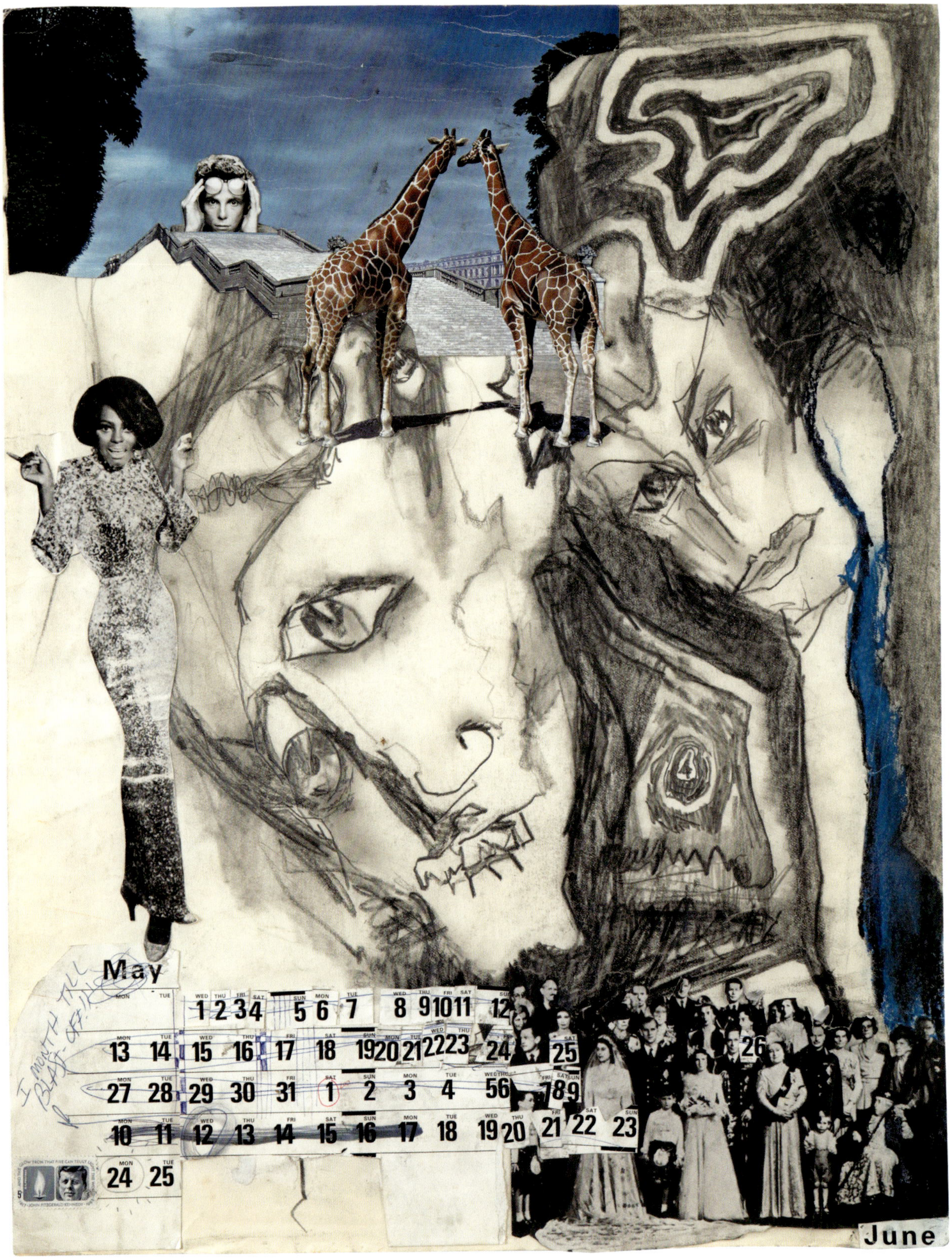
May
June

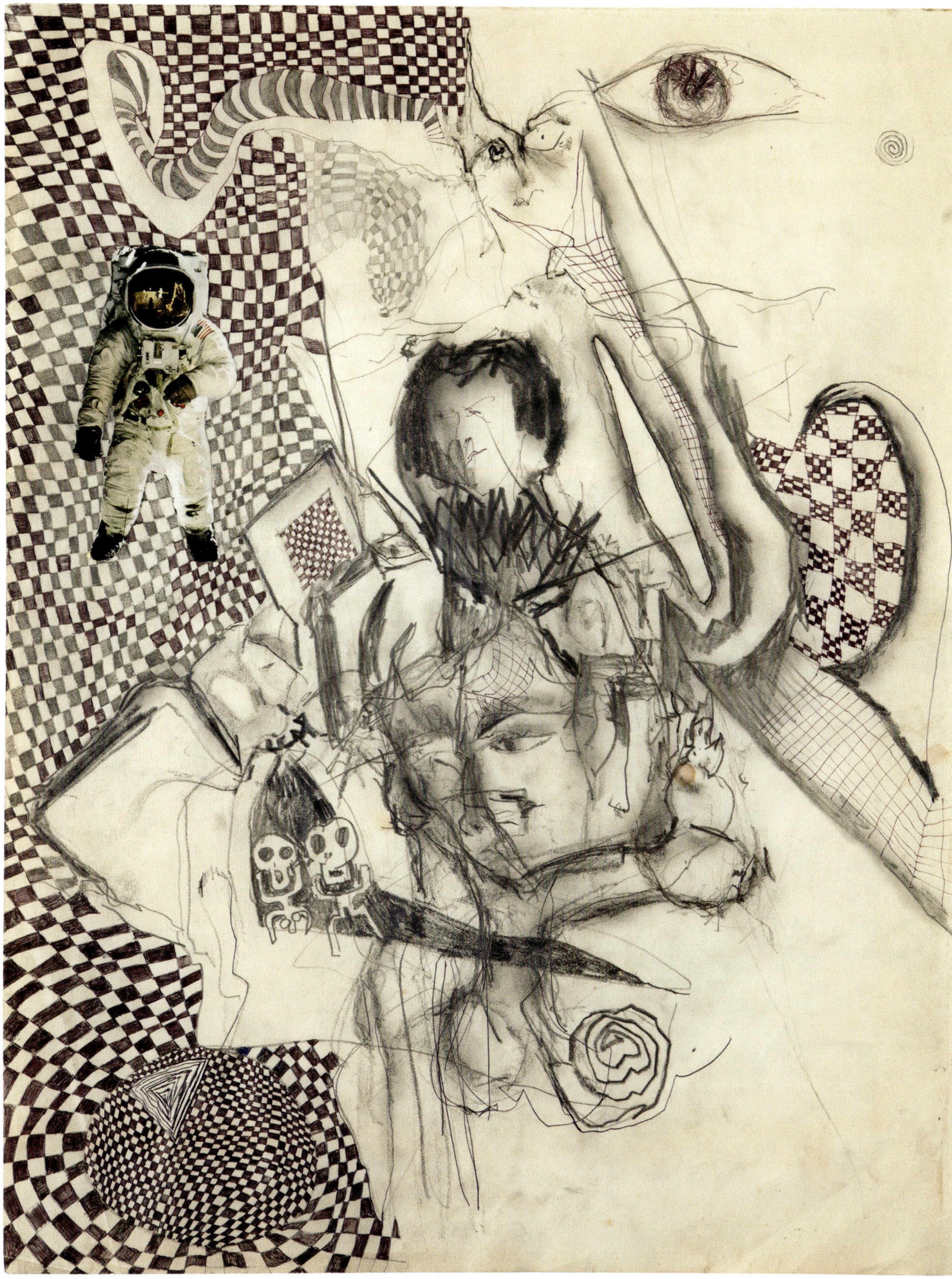

SCOTT COVERT (AMERICAN, BORN 1954). ***Earth.*** 1979. Collage on paper, 24 × 18" (61 × 45.7 cm). Collection the artist
SCOTT COVERT. ***Heaven.*** 1979. Collage on paper, 24 × 18" (61 × 45.7 cm). Collection the artist

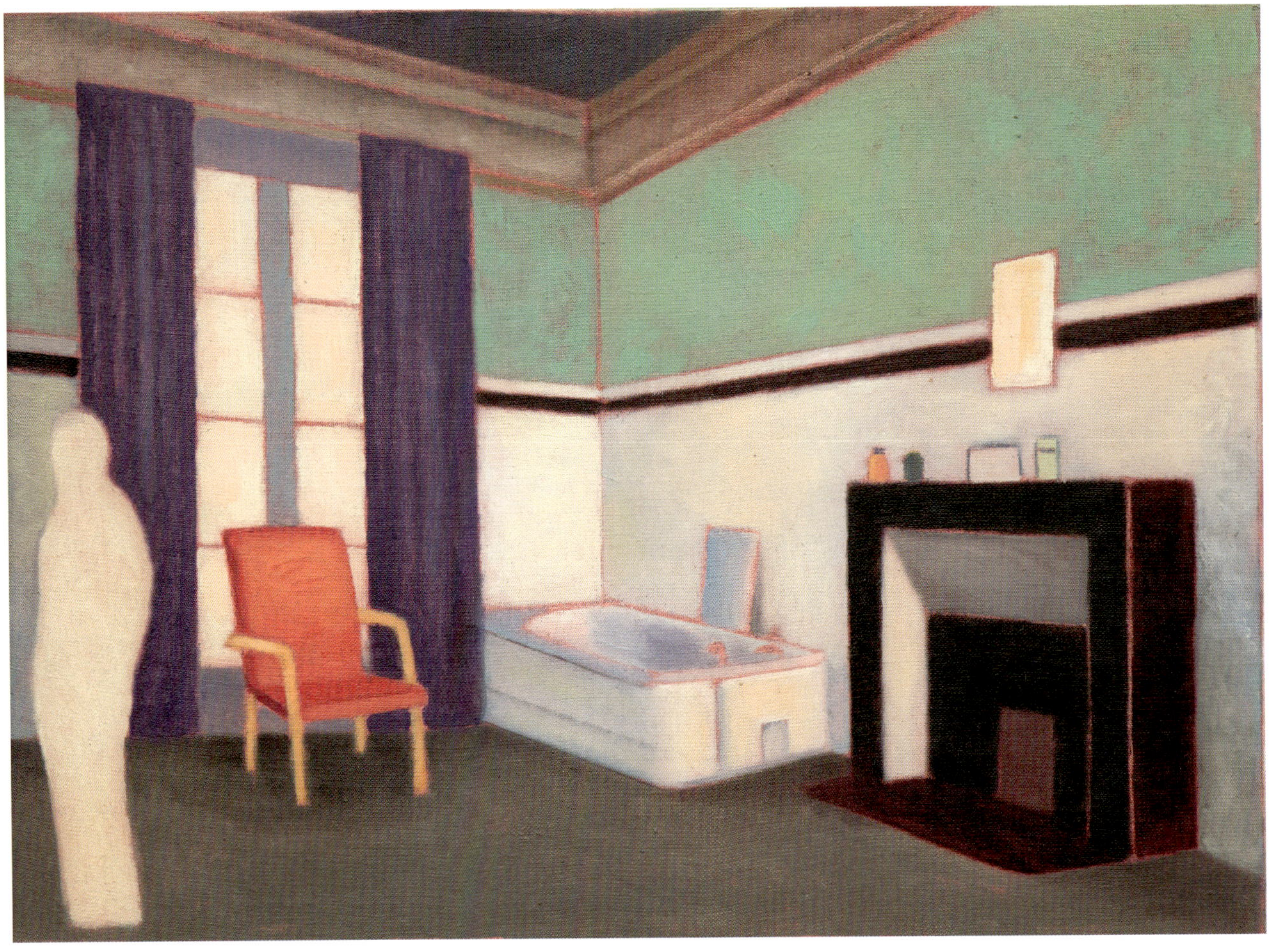

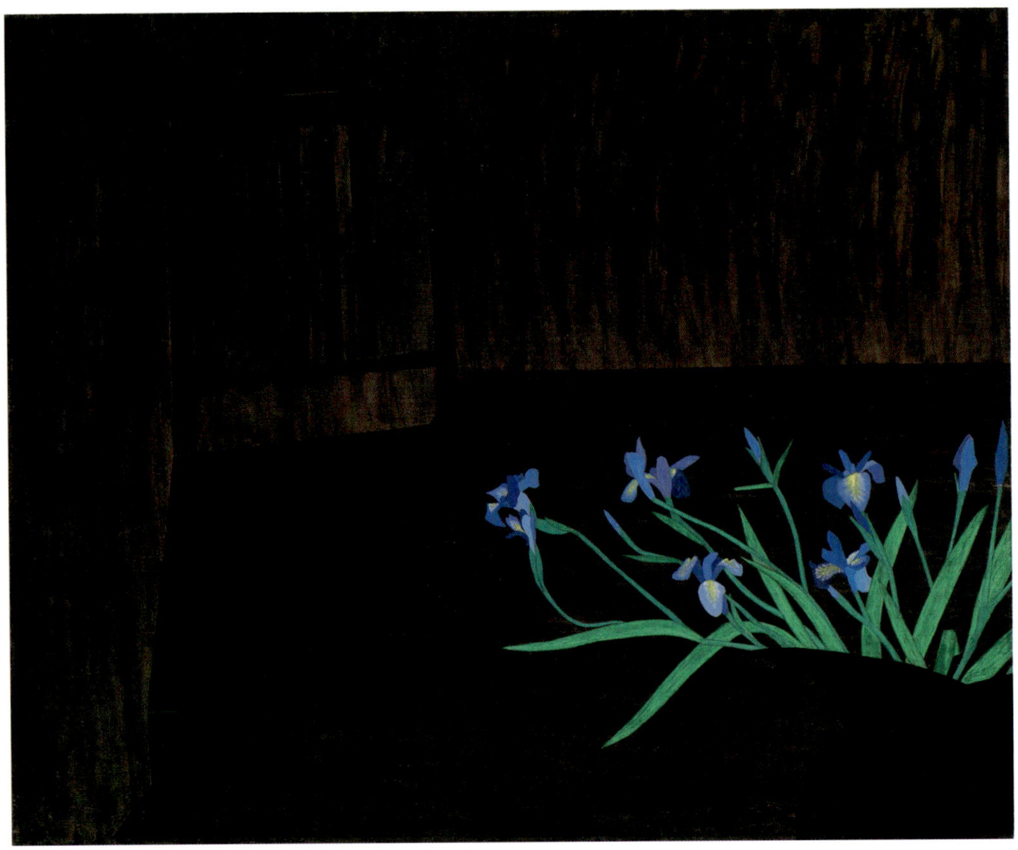

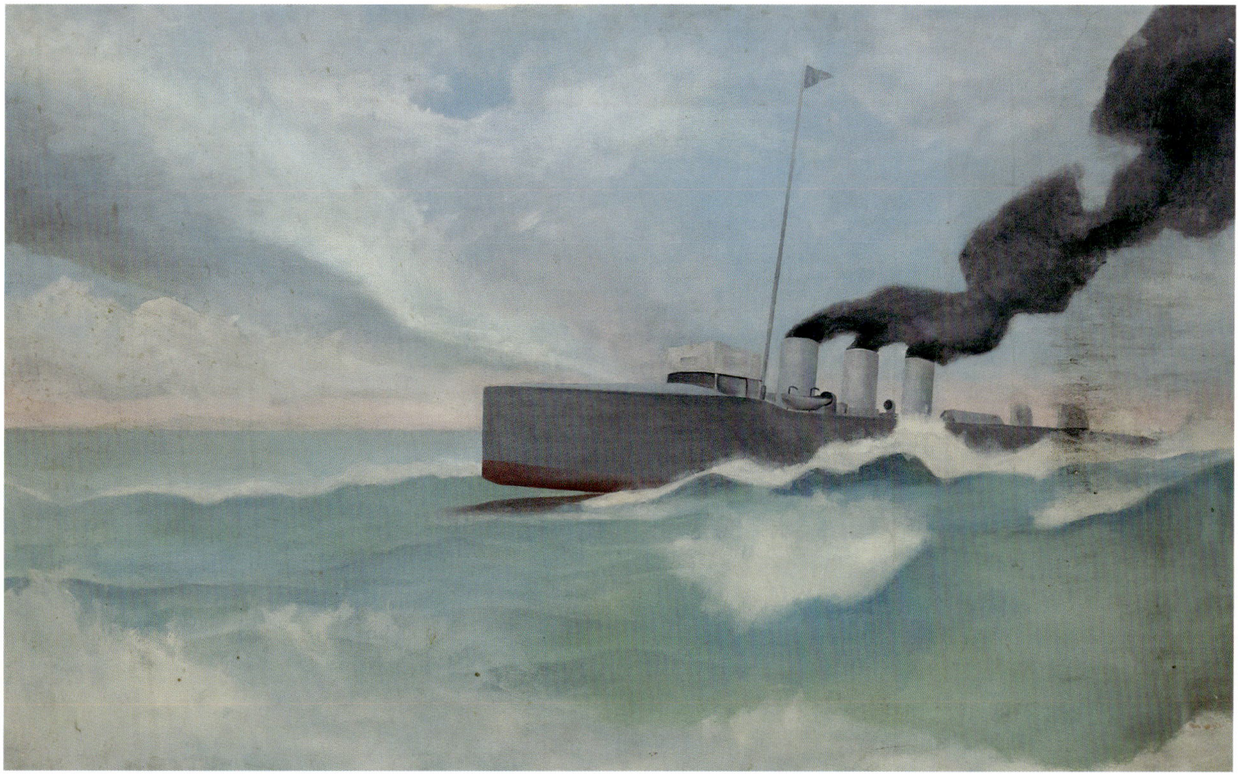

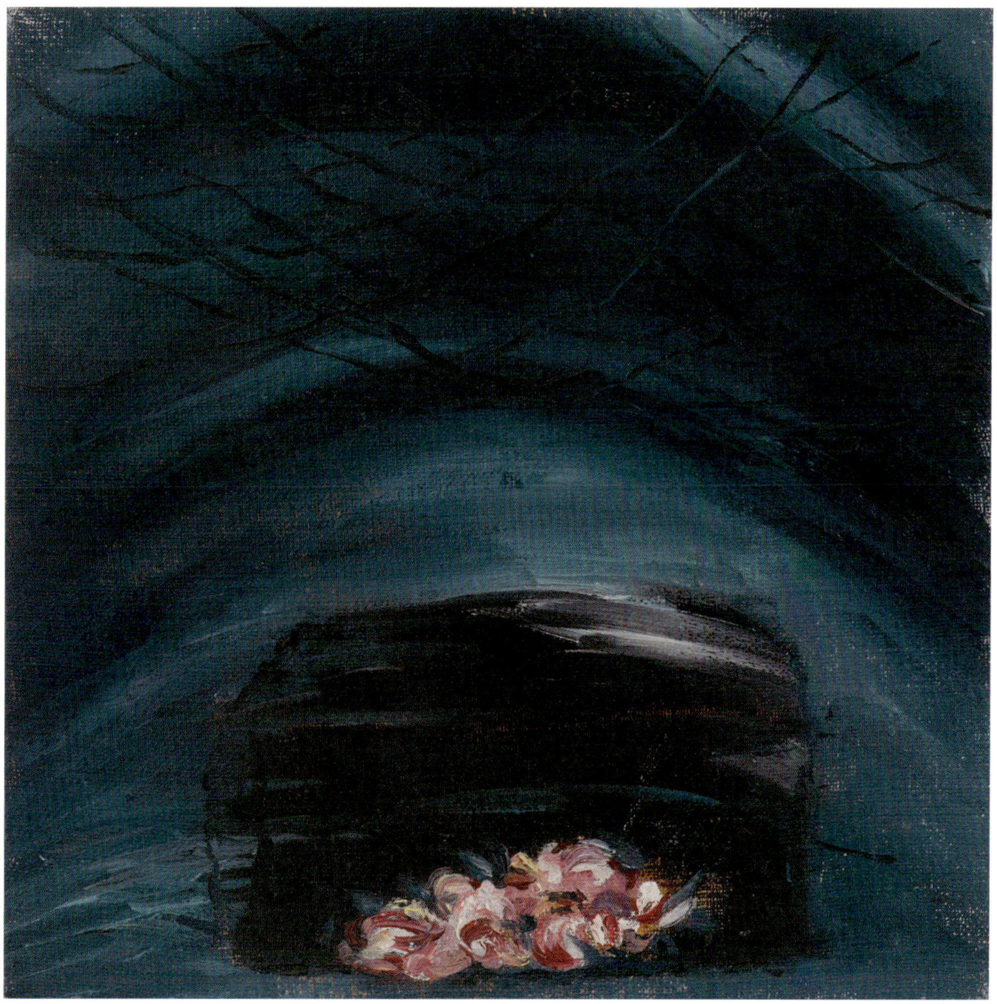

DUNCAN HANNAH (AMERICAN, BORN 1952). ***19 rue de Lille.*** 1980. Oil on canvas, 20 × 24" (50.8 × 61 cm). Collection Roger Cardinal
PAUL BRIDGEWATER (AMERICAN, BORN 1954). ***By the Light of the Night.*** 1978. Oil on canvas, 29 × 35" (73.7 × 88.9 cm). Collection the artist
JONATHAN QUINN (AMERICAN, BORN 1956). ***Turbinia.*** 1982. Oil on particleboard, 30½ × 48" (77.5 × 121.9 cm). Collection the artist
ELLEN BERKENBLIT (AMERICAN, BORN 1958). ***Untitled.*** 1983. Oil on linen, 8 × 8" (20.3 × 20.3 cm). Collection the artist

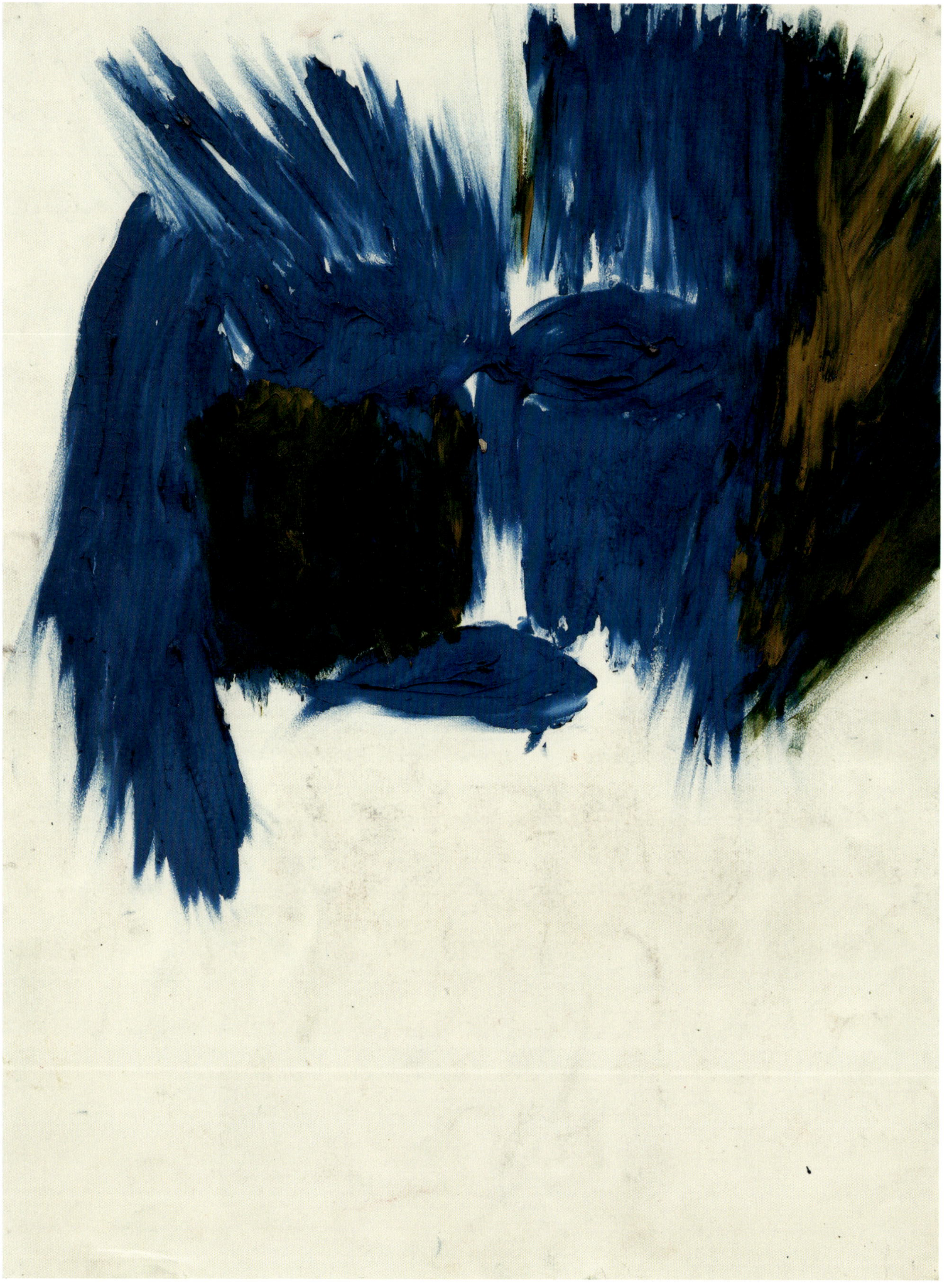

DAN ASHER (AMERICAN, 1947–2010). ***Untitled.*** c. 1983. Oil stick on paper, 22¾ × 17¼" (57.8 × 43.8 cm). Collection the Estate of Dan Asher/Martos Gallery, New York

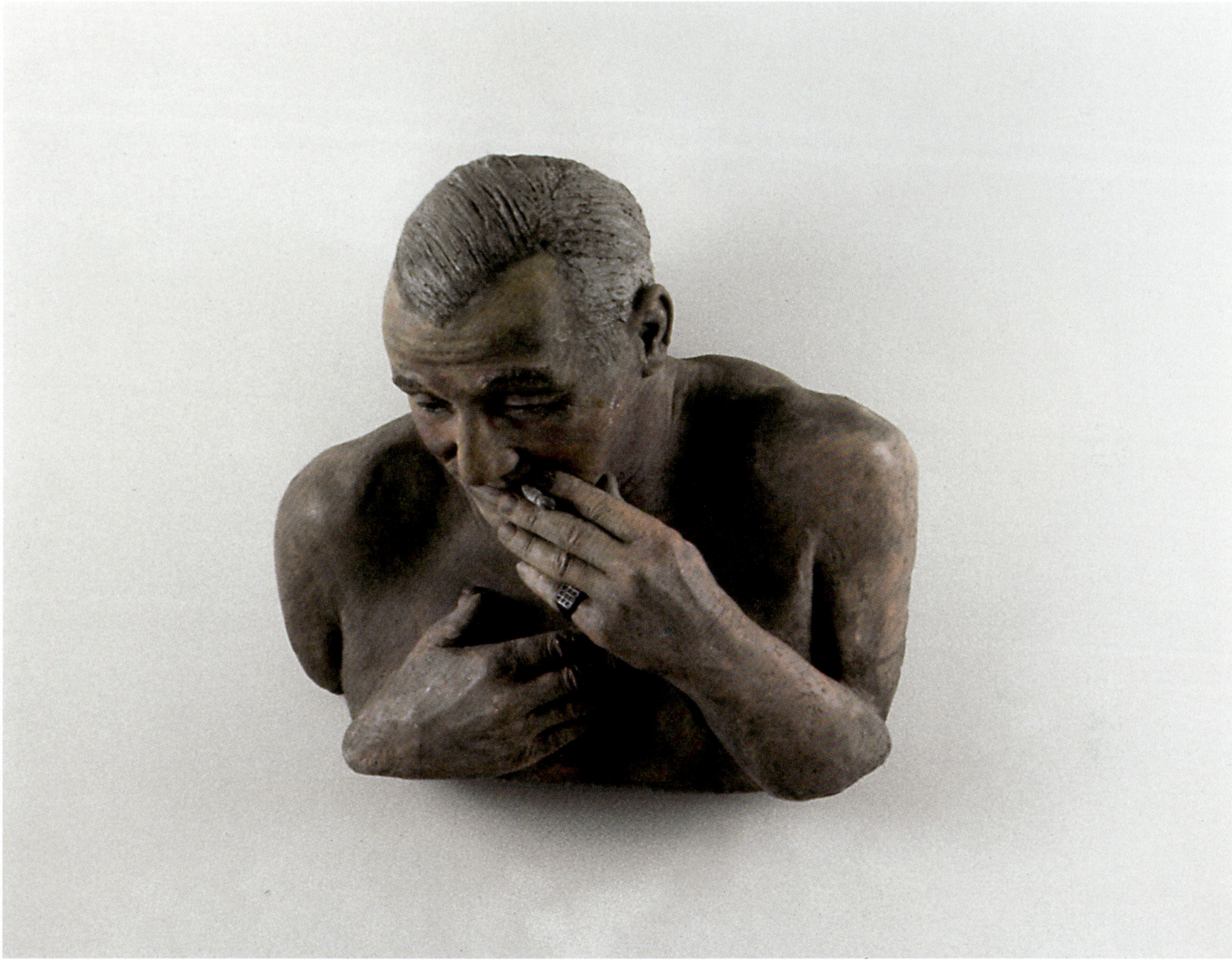

JOHN AHEARN (AMERICAN, BORN 1951). ***Eddie Moshier.*** 1979. Acrylic on plaster, 20 × 20 × 7" (50.8 × 50.8 × 17.8 cm). Collection the artist

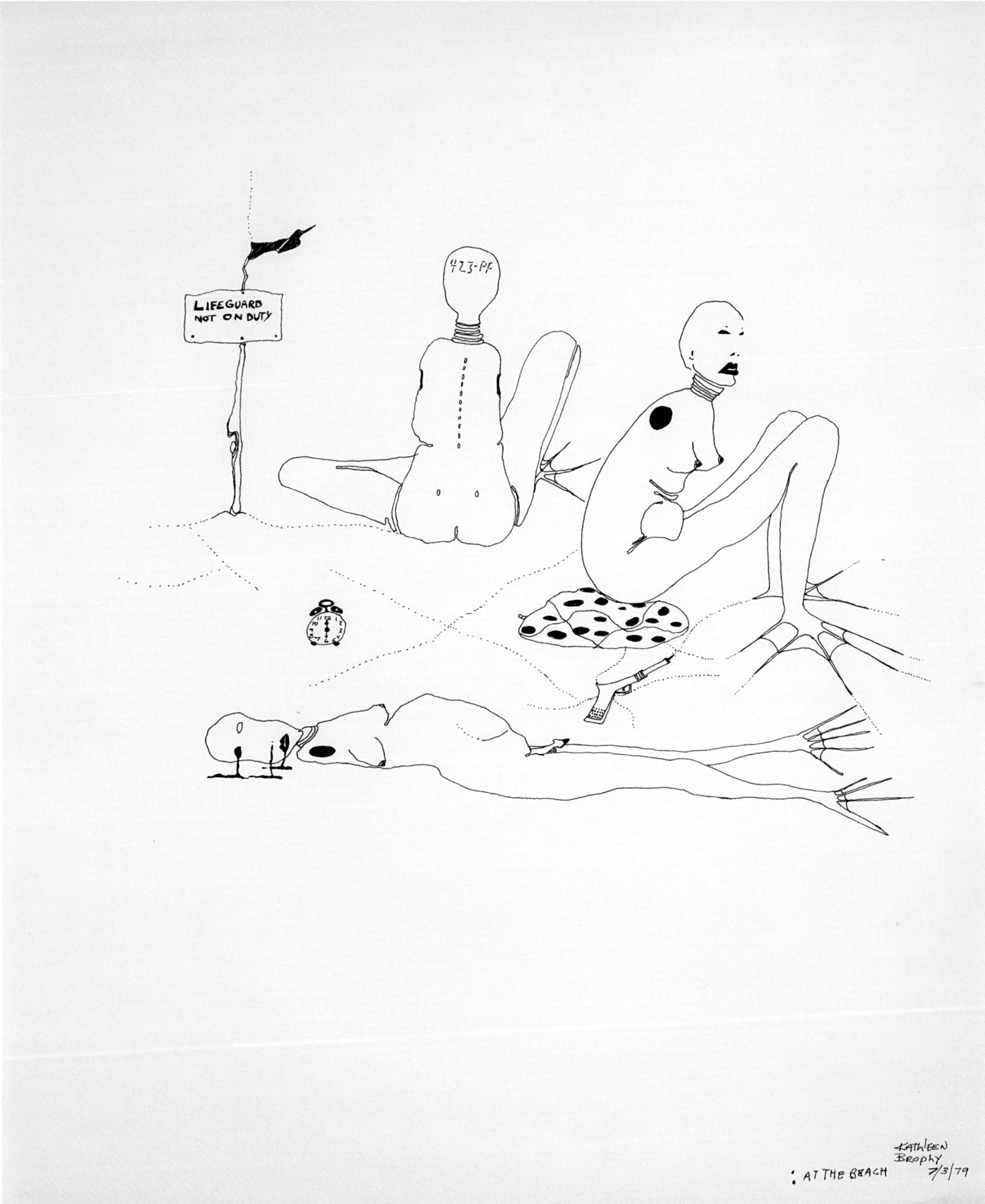

KITTY BROPHY (AMERICAN, BORN 1960). ***At the Beach.*** 1979. Ink on paper, 17 × 14" (43.2 × 35.6 cm). Collection the artist
KITTY BROPHY. ***Summer Time.*** 1979. Ink on paper, 17 × 14" (43.2 × 35.6 cm). Collection Kenny Scharf
KITTY BROPHY. ***She Cannot Draw.*** 1979. Ink on paper, 17 × 14" (43.2 × 35.6 cm). Collection the artist

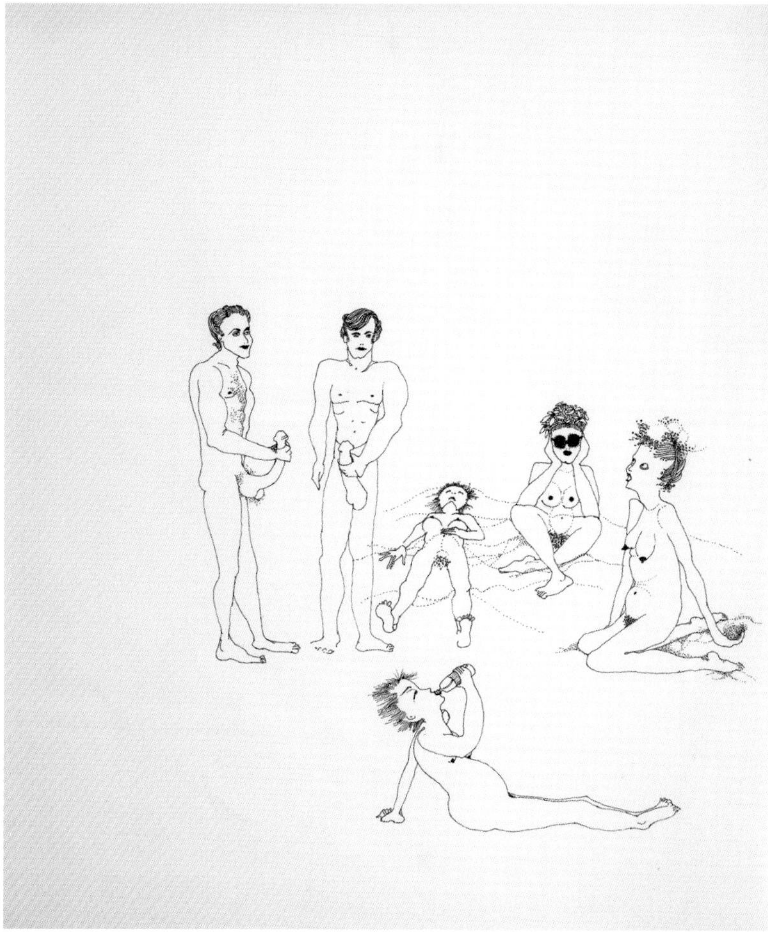

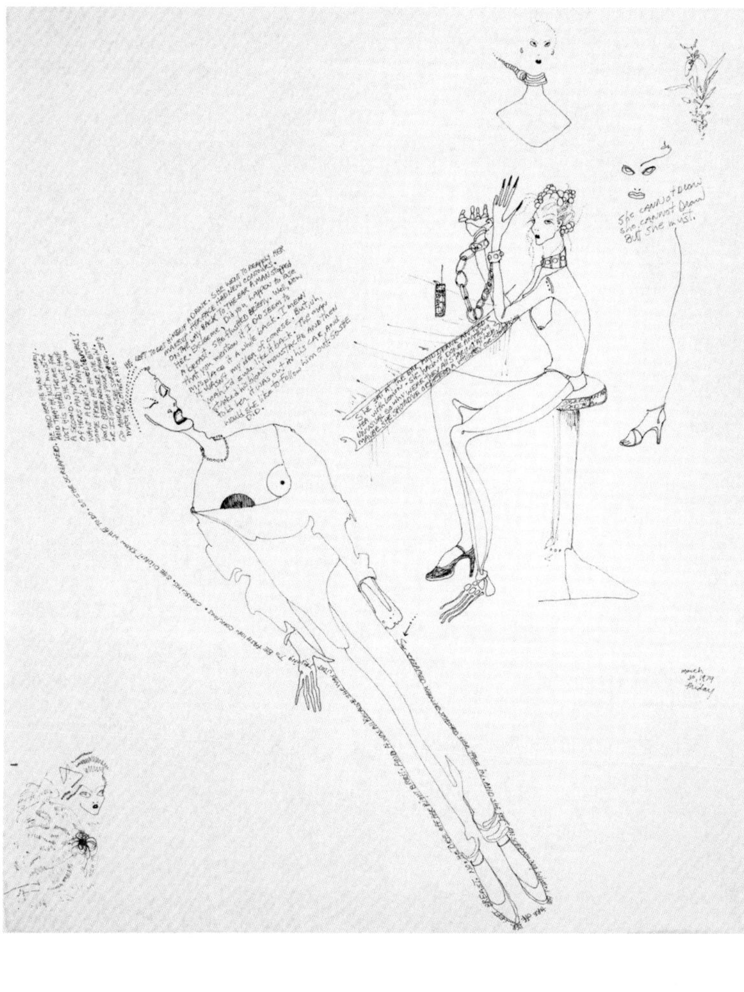
She cannot draw
she cannot Draw
But she must.

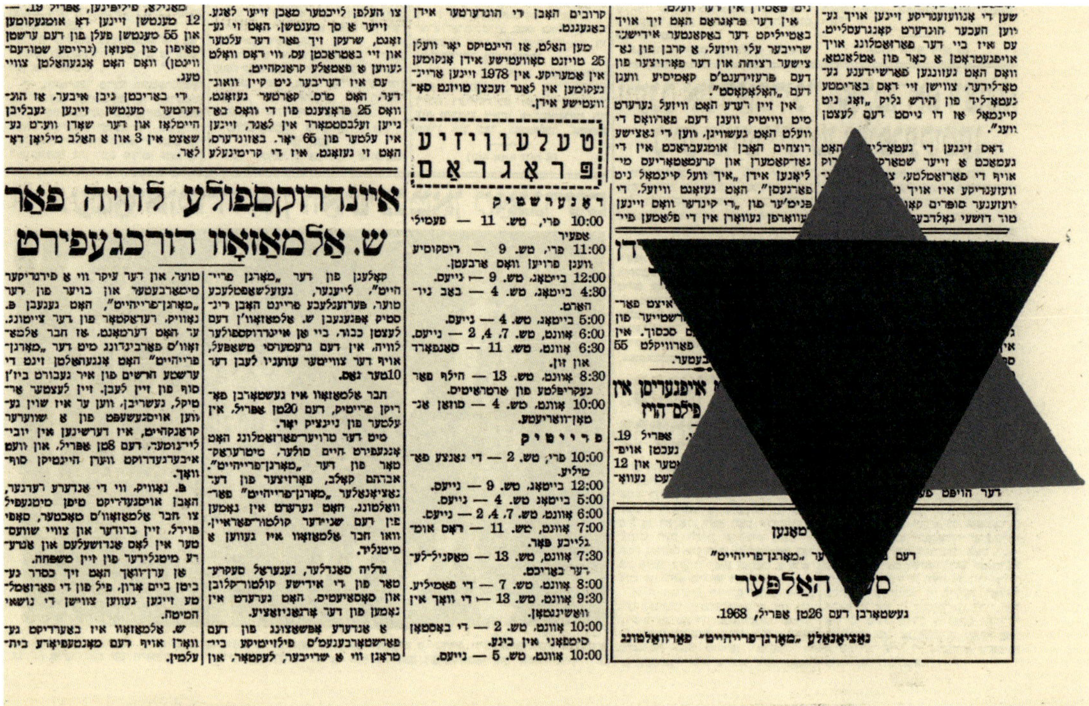

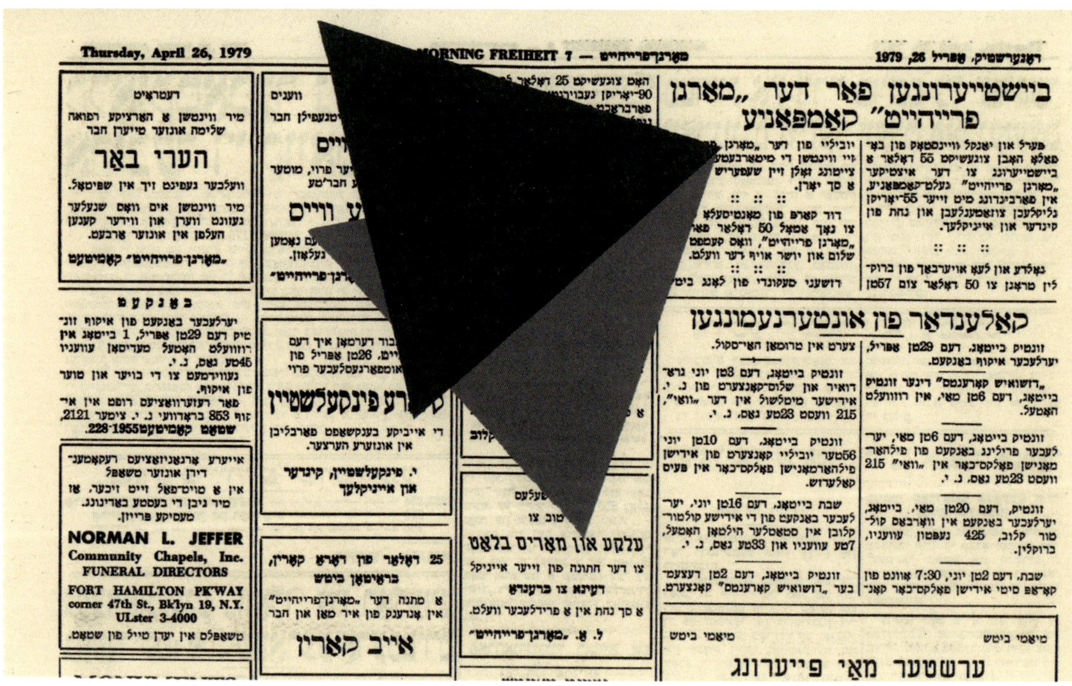

PETER HRISTOFF (BULGARIAN, BORN TURKEY, 1958). Untitled newspaper piece (star). 1979. Silkscreen on newsprint, 7 7/16 × 11¼" (18.9 × 28.6 cm). Collection the artist
PETER HRISTOFF. Untitled newspaper piece (flipped star). 1979. Silkscreen on newsprint, 7 × 11¼" (17.8 × 28.6 cm). Collection the artist

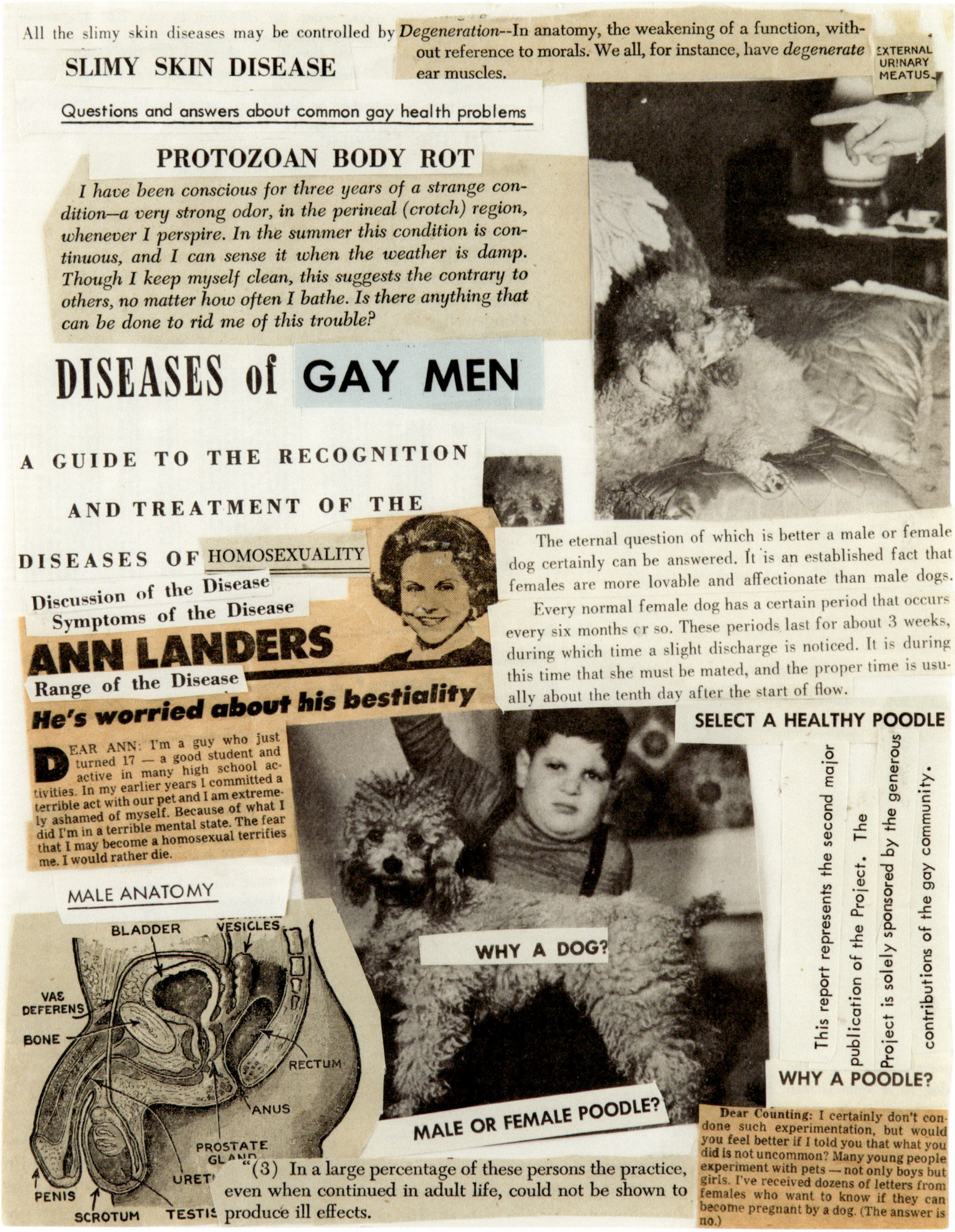

KEITH HARING (AMERICAN, 1958–1990). ***Untitled (Diseases of Gay Men).*** 1979. Collage on paper, 11 × 8½" (27.9 × 21.6 cm). Collection the Keith Haring Foundation

88–89

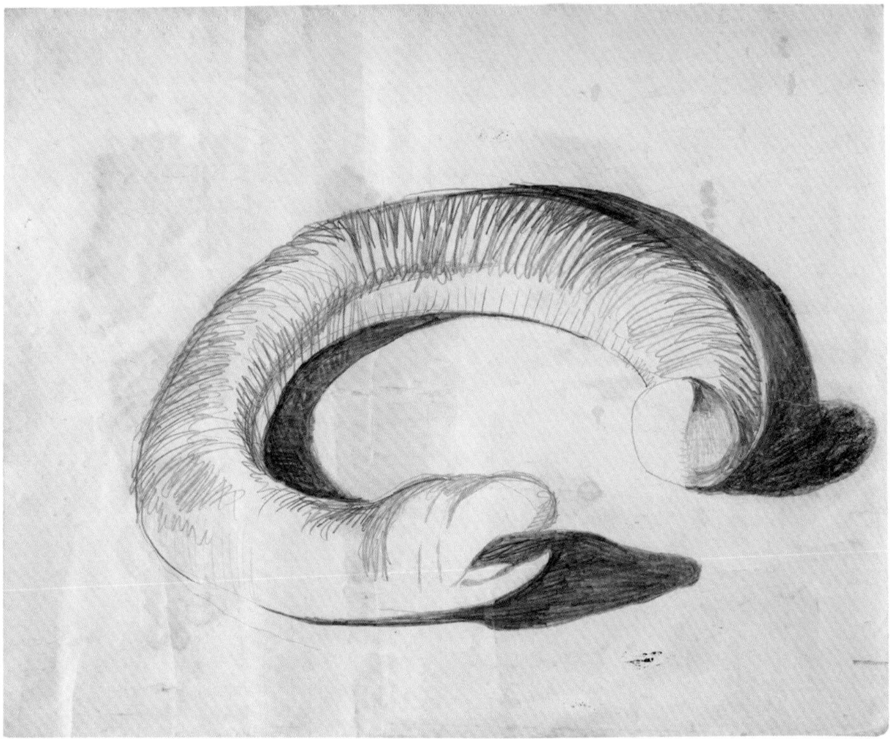

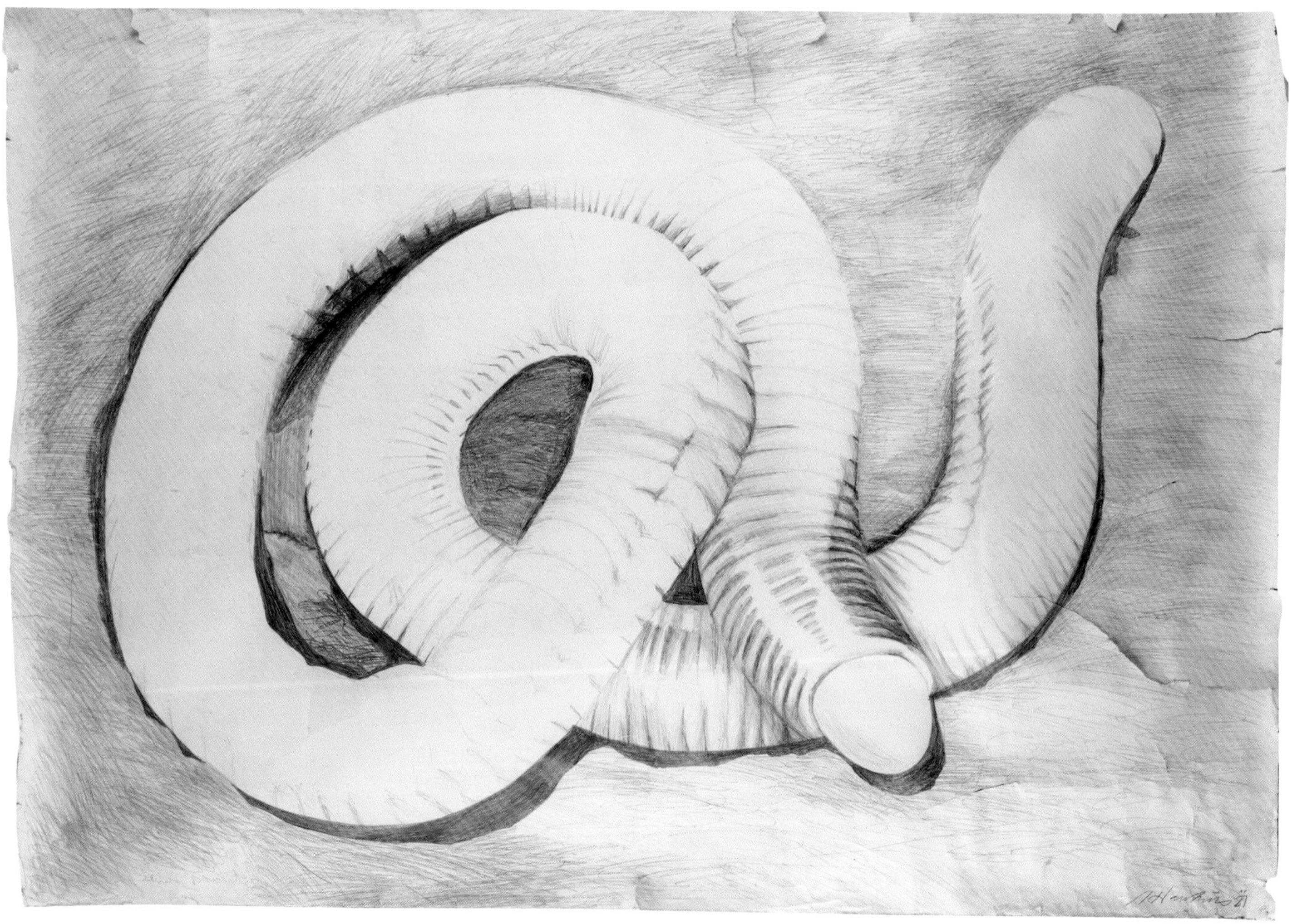

ROBERT HAWKINS (AMERICAN, BORN 1957). ***Eyeless Worm Snake.*** 1981. Pencil on paper, 14 × 16¾" (35.6 × 42.5 cm). Collection the artist, courtesy Patrick Fox
ROBERT HAWKINS. ***Shield Snout.*** 1981. Pencil on paper, 36 × 51" (91.4 × 129.5 cm). Collection the artist, courtesy Patrick Fox

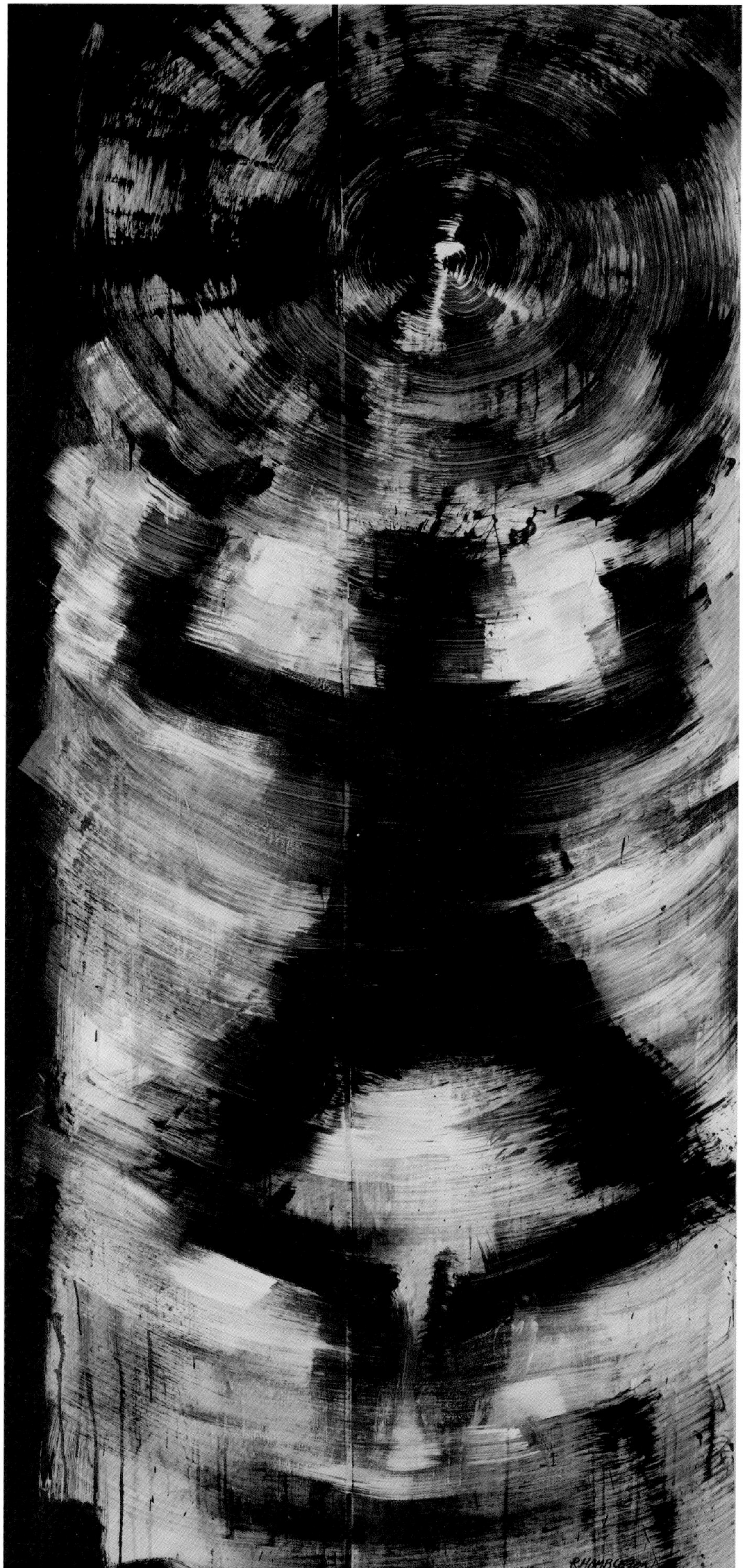

RICHARD HAMBLETON (CANADIAN, BORN 1954). ***Untitled (Shadowman).*** 1983. Acrylic on canvas, 95¾" x 43¼" (243.2 x 109.9 cm). Collection the Arturo Vega Archive

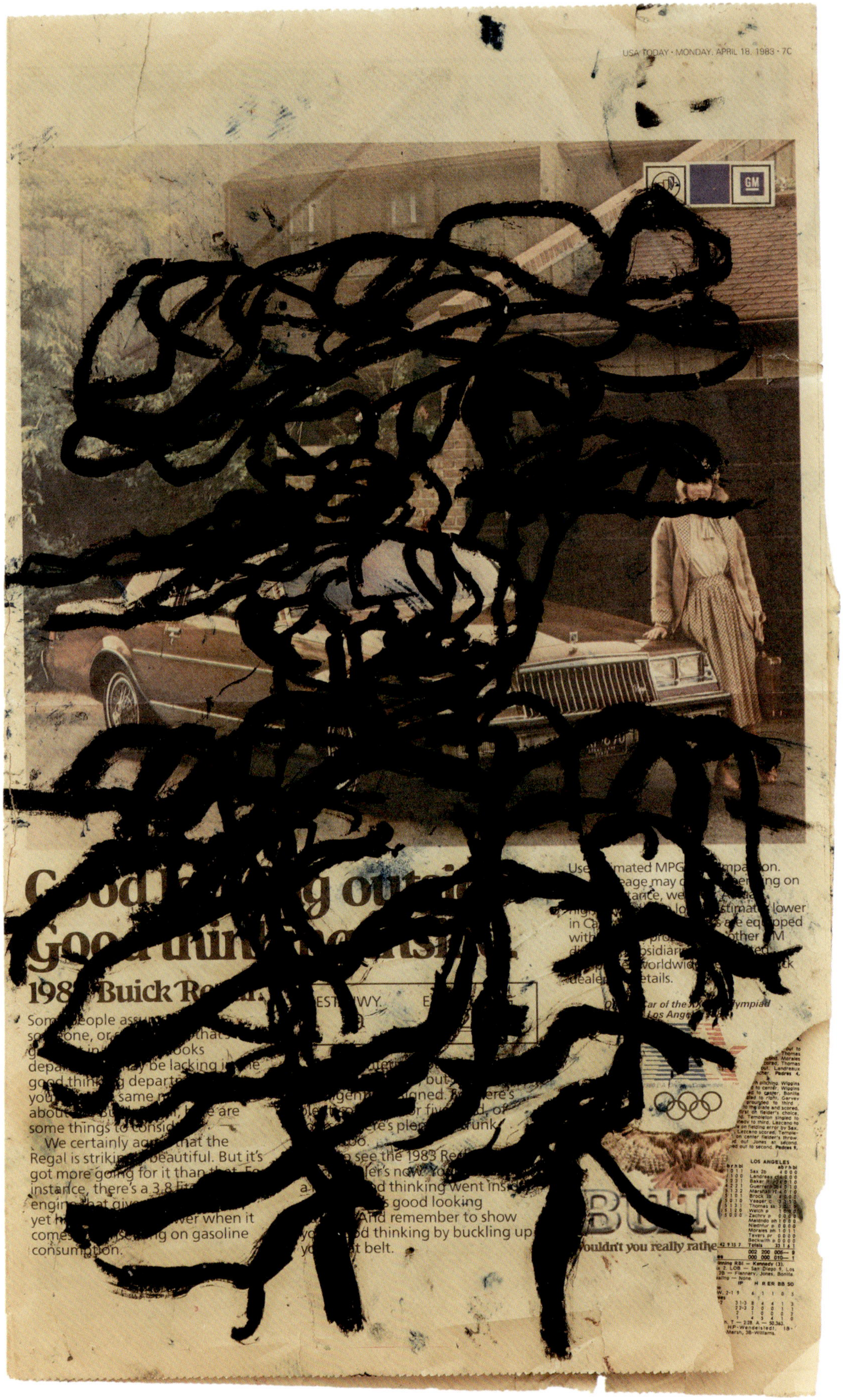

DAN ASHER (AMERICAN, 1947–2010). ***Untitled.*** 1983. Oil stick on newsprint, 22½ × 14½" (57.25 × 36.8 cm). Collection the Estate of Dan Asher/Martos Gallery, New York

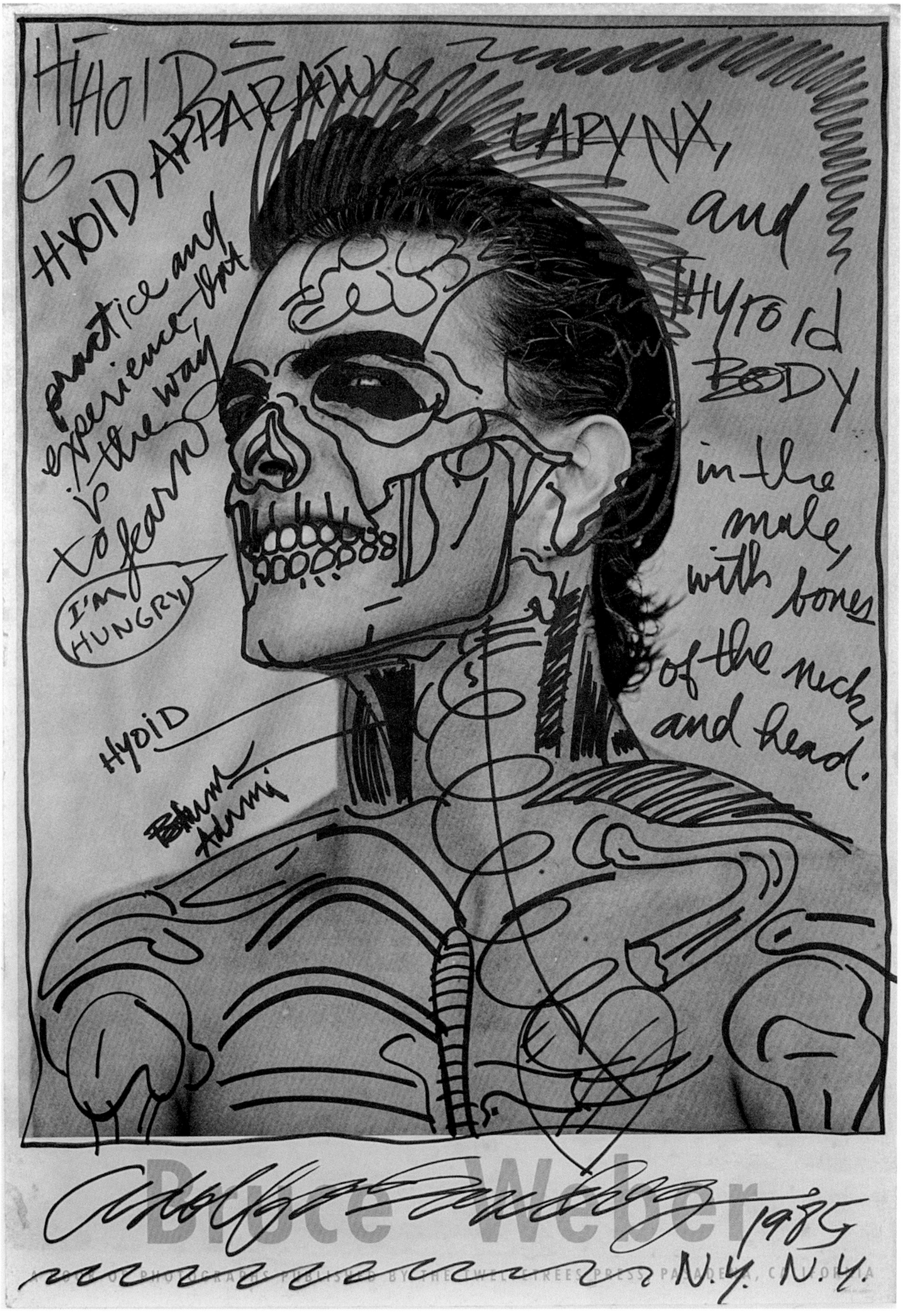

ADOLFO SANCHEZ (AMERICAN, BORN CUBA, 1957–1989). Embellished Weber poster. 1985. Marker on printed poster, 30 × 20½" (76.2 × 52.1 cm). Collection Min and Oliver Sanchez

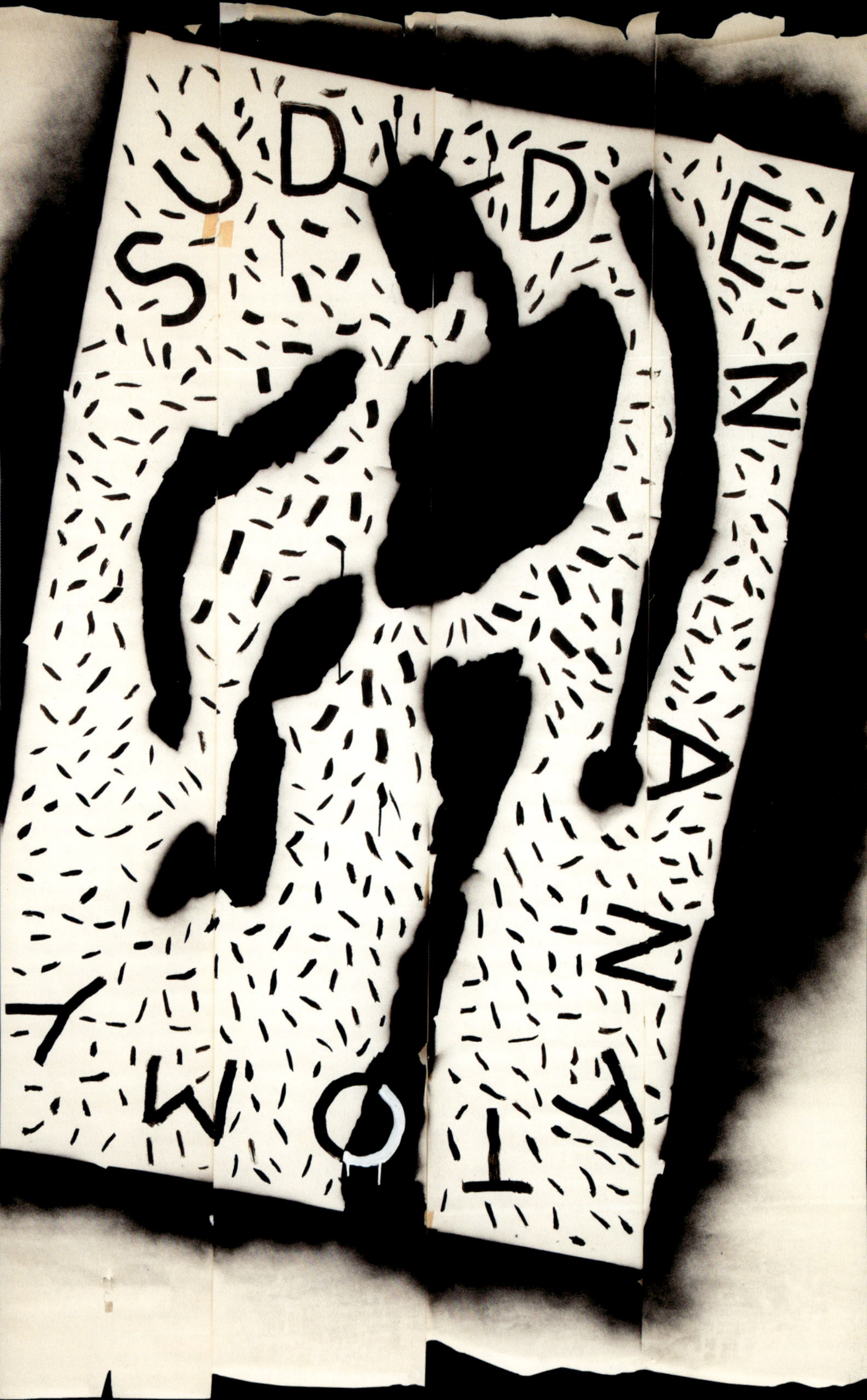
SUDDEN ANATOMY

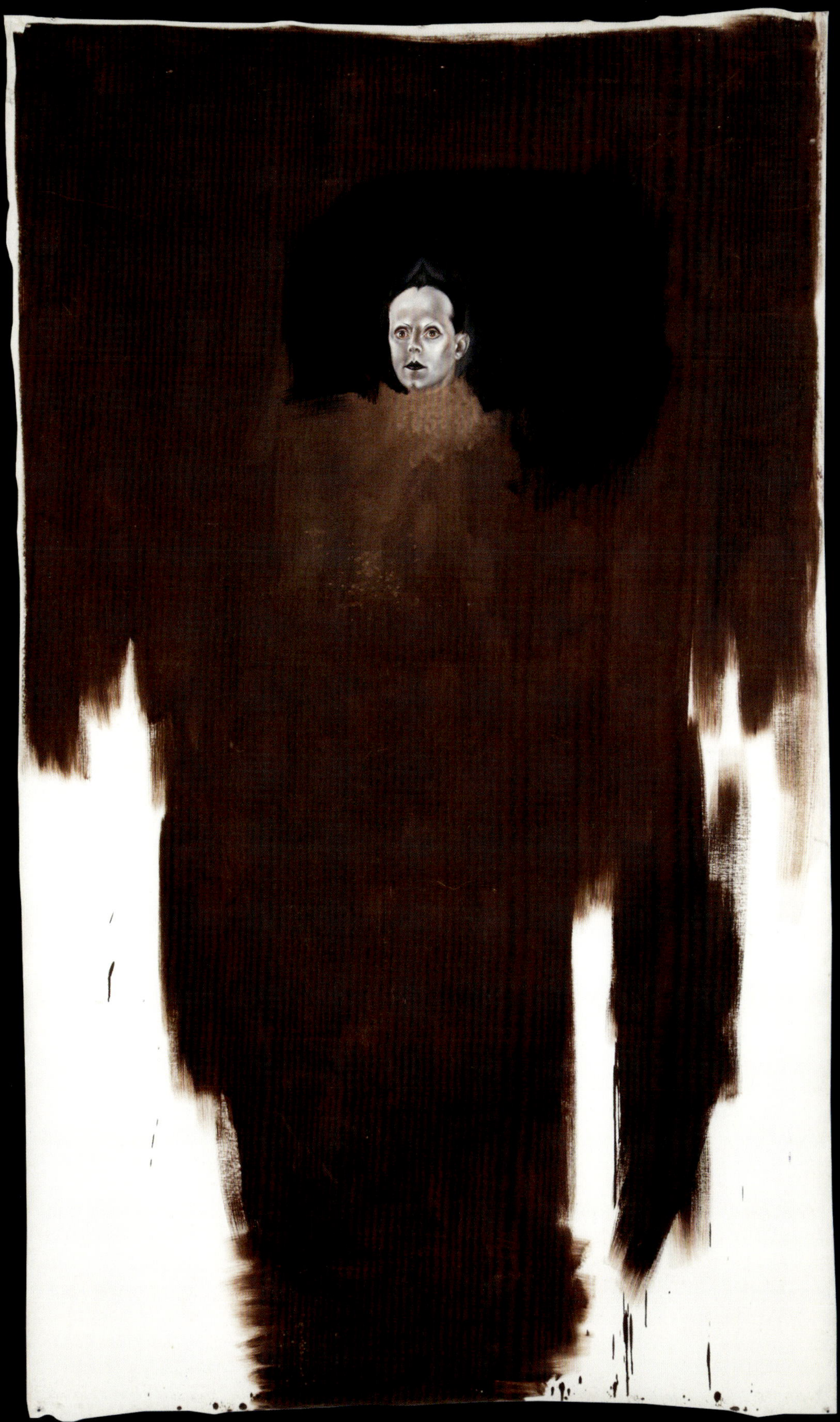

RICHARD MCGUIRE (AMERICAN, BORN 1957). ***Sudden Anatomy.*** 1980. Spray paint and acrylic on paper, 86 × 53" (218.4 × 134.6 cm). Collection the artist
STEFANO CASTRONOVO (ITALIAN, BORN 1950). ***Klaus Nomi.*** c. 1983. Oil on canvas, 90 9/16 × 51 15/16" (230 × 132 cm). Collection the artist

"Come and Yell 'Marcello'": MAKING MOVIES AT CLUB 57

J. Hoberman

Glory to the cliques in art. Cliques, movements, in art are concentrated wedges in the consciousness of man.[1] —Jonas Mekas

Performance, including participatory, costumed dance parties, was Club 57's privileged art form. The memory of (old) television programs served as its universal (or at least shared generational) language. But the approximately 350 movies shown (as well as TV shows watched as movies) were the club's aesthetic bread and butter.

The chronology found in *Artforum*'s special issue "The East Village 1979–1989: The Rise and Fall of an Art Scene" begins in the spring of 1979 with the first appearance of the monthly broadsheet *East Village Eye* and the opening of Club 57 in the basement of the Holy Cross Polish National Church at 57 St. Marks Place. Actually, the venue had been hosting events for more than a year. But May 1979 marked the beginning of a new era: the club's director, Stanley Strychacki, had recently brought on Susan Hannaford, Ann Magnuson, and Tom Scully, all in their early twenties, to program entertainment on the strength of New Wave Vaudeville, a six-night variety show they had organized at Irving Plaza—also managed by Strychacki—in November 1978. In a memoir accompanying the *Artforum* chronology, Magnuson noted that the club's first regular attraction was the Tuesday night Monster Movie Club, programmed by Hannaford and Scully (figs. 1–2).[2]

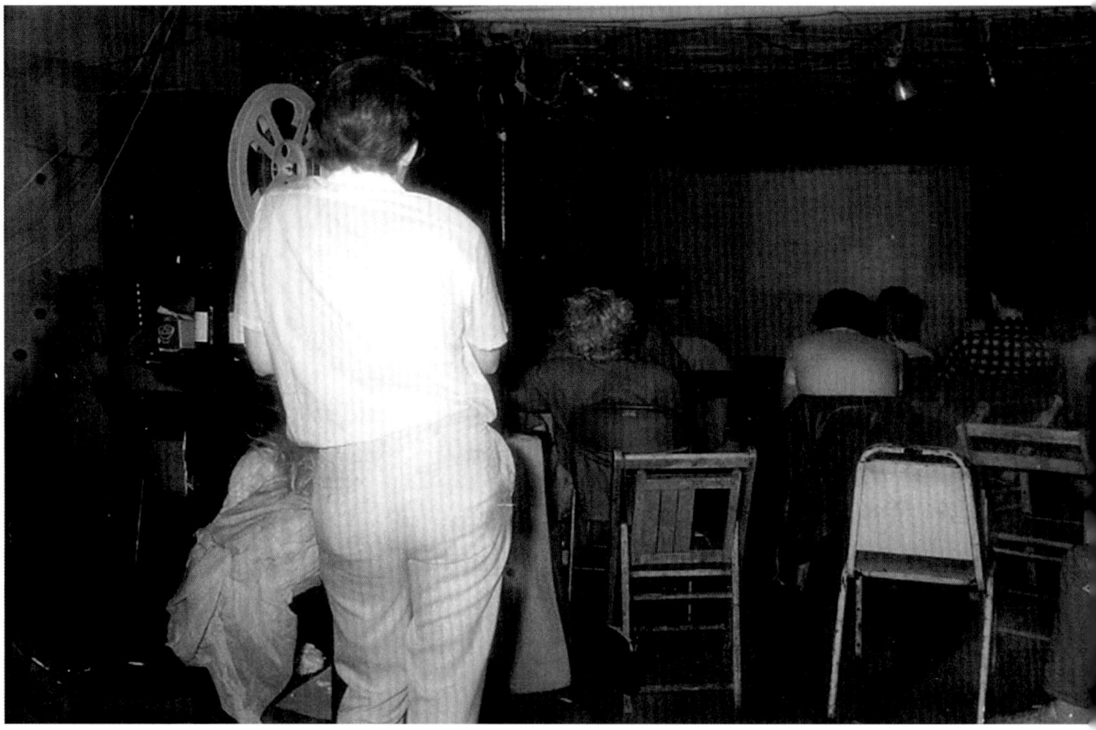

1. A Monster Movie Club screening at Club 57, October 1979. Photograph by Christina Yuin

Former School of Visual Arts students who had been active in the SVA film society, Hannaford and Scully were looking to create a populist neighborhood venue. In order to distinguish their film program from New York's other revival theaters, they decided to focus on horror and science fiction. Familiar with the taste of local cult heroes like Ramones, Scully intuited an audience for "strange films" and "trash": "You can hear it in the music. It fit into the East Village crowd, the postpunk crowd."[3]

Setting the table for all that followed, the first four films were the sort of cheesy genre flicks found once at drive-ins and subsequently on past-midnight television: American International Picture's (AIP's) teen sci-fi comedy *Invasion of the Saucer Men* (Edward L. Cahn, 1957), Mario Bava's first feature *Black Sunday* (1960), Edward D. Wood Jr.'s notoriously "bad" *Plan 9 from Outer Space* (1959), and *The Mysterians* (1957), a Japanese extraterrestrial-invasion film directed by Ishiro Honda and described as "a non-stop holocaust" in Susan Sontag's often anthologized essay, "The Imagination of Disaster."[4]

In addition to championing Wood and repeatedly screening the work of splatter pioneer Herschell Gordon Lewis (even hosting the New York premiere of his 1970 feature, *The Wizard of Gore*), MMC occasionally showed artier European fare, including Jean-Luc Godard's *Alphaville* (1964) and Roman Polanski's *The Fearless Vampire Killers* (1967). In its first few months, MMC showed more than a dozen movies, dominating the club's film program. With the exception of a mid-May "movie party," for which attendees were exhorted to bring their own Super 8 or standard 8mm films, and a screening of Frank Tashlin's 1956 Jayne Mansfield vehicle, *The Girl Can't Help It*, presented by clothing designer Katy K, most films through July 1979 were shown under the auspices of MMC.

Beginning in August, the film program began to expand, and would eventually include rockumentaries and various sorts of camp, both high

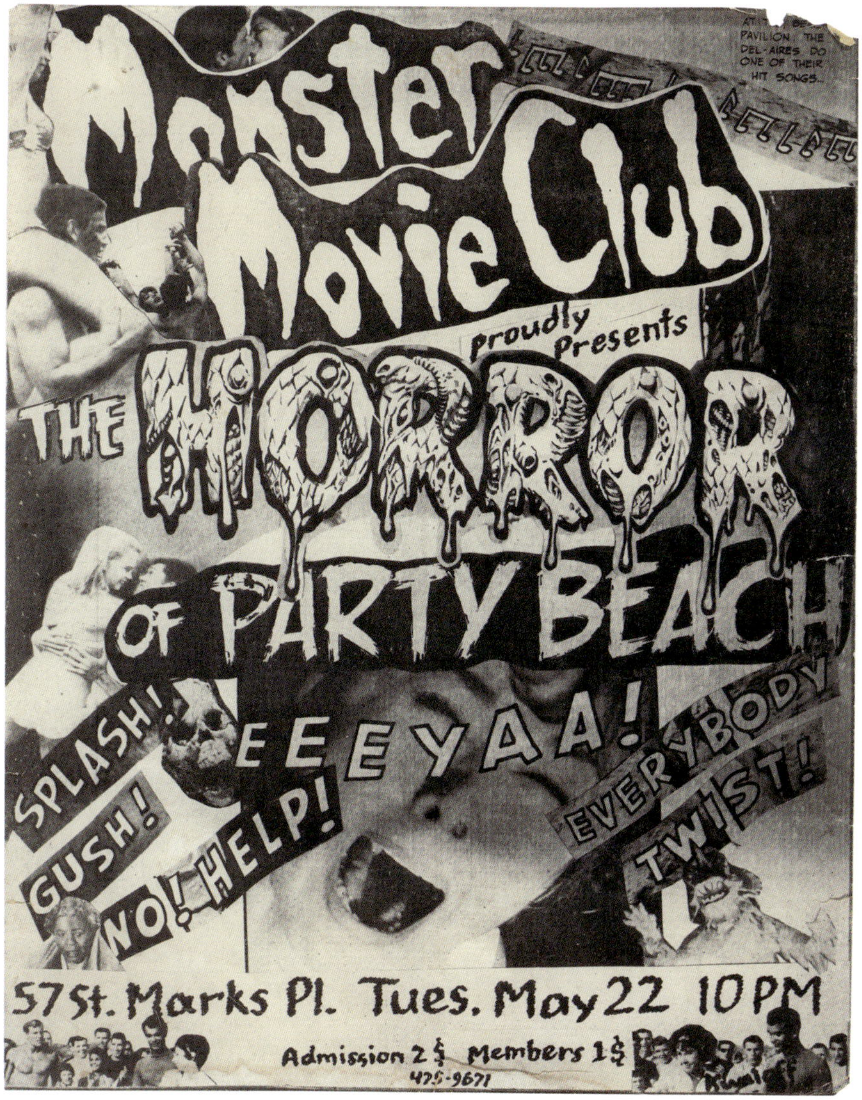

2. Flyer for a Monster Movie Club screening *of The Horror of Party Beach* at Club 57, 1979. Design by Peter Kwaloff. The Museum of Modern Art, New York. Department of Film Special Collections

'60s, like Joseph Losey's *Modesty Blaise* (1966) and Roger Corman's *The Trip* (1967), and, as programmed by club member and *East Village Eye* photographer Jeffrey Geiger, vintage (the 1934 musical thriller *Murder at the Vanities* and the 1944 Maria Montez vehicle *Cobra Woman*). Additional drive-in films were shown under the rubric Teenage Sex 'n' Violence.

Other series were organized by the editors of various zines. During the summer of 1980, for example, the sensationalist documentary *Mondo Cane* (1960), a pseudo-ethnographic series of shocking, mainly "primitive" practices, was screened under the auspices of Bill Landis's *Sleazoid Express*, a mimeographed one-sheet report on Forty-Second Street exploitation films that was initially distributed free at the club. Landis soon initiated a long-running series, sometimes known as the Sex, Sin, and Sadism Film Festival, which showcased outré documentaries, soft-core porn, and miscellaneous exploitation films. In late 1981, another zine, *Gore Gazette*, began programming films and sponsored a well-attended live appearance by Herschell Gordon Lewis (fig. 3), then in his early fifties and recently released after serving a three-year prison sentence for fraud. According to club member John Epperson, a drag performer later known as Lypsinka, Lewis took the club's adulation in stride: "[He] didn't seem surprised that all these young people were sitting on the floor of the basement of a Polish church. He didn't even seem amused!"[5]

Meanwhile, often in conjunction with *Sleazoid Express*, Lisa Baumgardner's feminist punk zine, *Bikini Girl*, sponsored work by established underground filmmakers Kenneth Anger (on hand to introduce his oeuvre), George Kuchar (fig. 4), and Andy Warhol (courtesy of the erstwhile Factory superstar Ondine, who had prints of several films in which he appeared). In March 1981, Jack Smith, a sometime club habitué, presented a "boiled lobster-color slide show" that to judge from its title, Penguin Rustling out by the Old Archives (fig. 5), was an attack on the nearby home for avant-garde cinema, Anthology Film Archives, and its cofounder, filmmaker Jonas Mekas. In October 1979, Abel Ferrara, whose independent feature *The Driller Killer* was released a month into the Hannaford-Magnuson-Scully era, used the club to direct live scenes from his unmade movie *Birds of Prey*—the story of a revolution against New York's corporate controllers.

Remarkable as they were, such shows were exceptional events. For the most part, Club 57 plumbed the catalogues of budget 16mm film distributors and the private collections of old television shows. Magnuson and Jerry Beck programmed an irregular series called TV Nostomania, projecting 16mm prints of 1960s programs like the debonair spy series *The Man from U.N.C.L.E.*, the sci-fi sitcom *My Favorite Martian*, and the surreal homage to Beatlemania, *The Monkees*. (Beck also organized animation programs of racially insensitive cartoons that could pointedly not be shown on TV.)

Theme nights often revolved around individual movies or television characters. As a performance artist, Magnuson developed a personal repertoire of TV types (pages 62–63). Television iconography figured in Kenny Scharf's paintings (not to mention the Club 57 logo he designed; page 12, fig. 2) as it did in Keith Haring's subway drawings. It was also a feature of the purposefully chaotic, regressive, and druggy videotapes the two artists produced, sometimes together. If the films were not themselves based on Club 57 performances, they were often shown at the club with their casts in attendance, and thus were something akin to home movies.

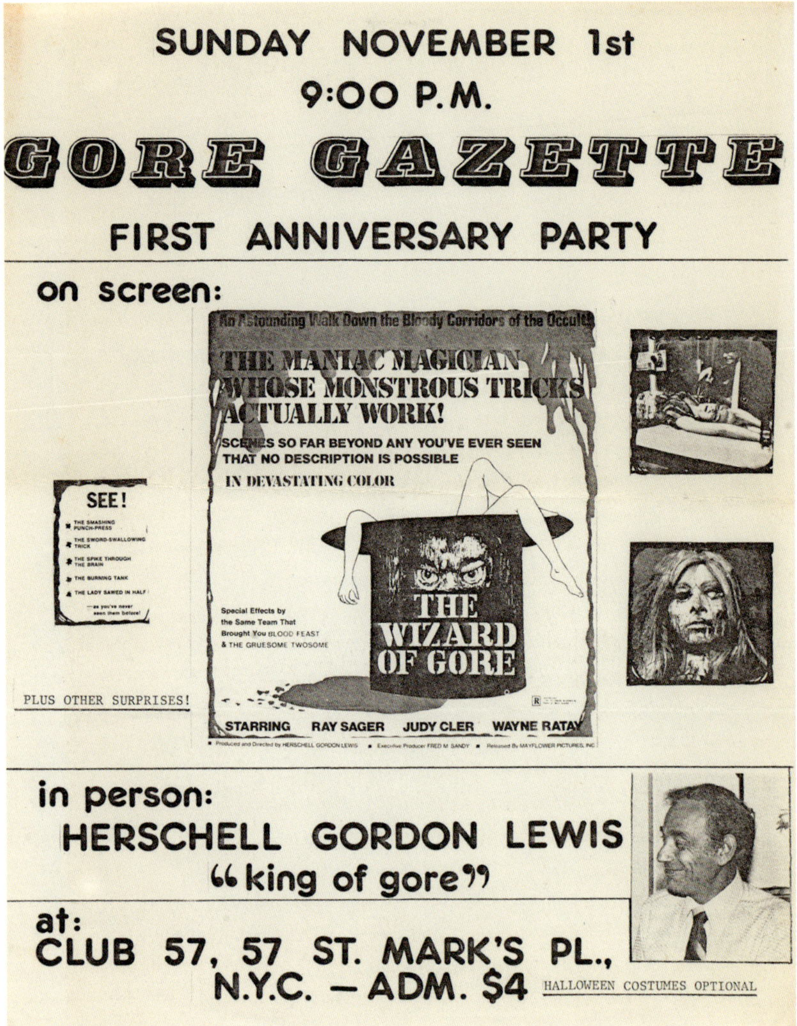

3. Flyer for *Gore Gazette*'s First Anniversary Party at Club 57, 1981. Design believed to be by *Gazette* editor Rick Sullivan. The Museum of Modern Art, New York. Department of Film Special Collections

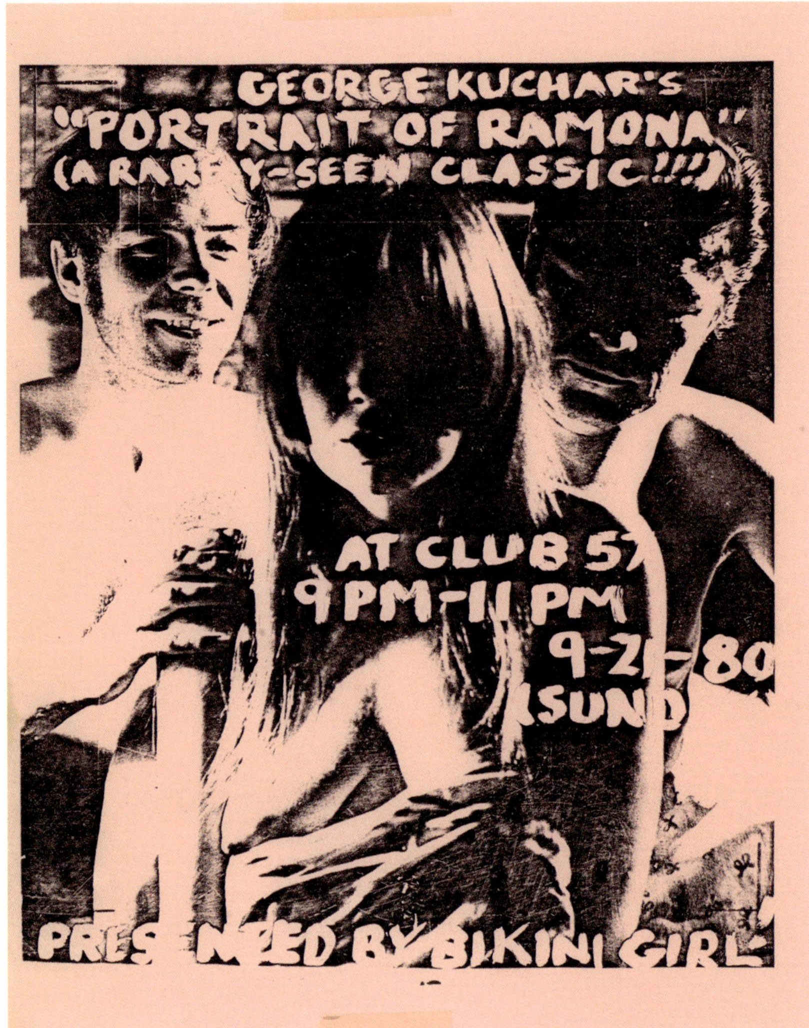

4. Flyer for *Bikini Girl*'s screening of George Kuchar's *Portrait of Ramona* at Club 57, 1980. Design by *Bikini Girl* editor Lisa Baumgardner. The Museum of Modern Art, New York. Department of Film Special Collections

While movies strove to educate club member's taste (Scully typically gave the MMC screenings a mock-scholarly introduction, at times in costume), TV shows confirmed it. In his memoir, Strychacki cites the poster advertising the March 1980 TV Nostomania: "Come over to our house and watch vintage '60s TV shows, with commercials, popcorn and Swanson TV dinners." These old sitcoms and half-hour dramas may have been "things that we had seen as kids," Epperson recalled, "but seeing them there gave them new meaning."[6]

Part of that new meaning undoubtedly derived from the audiences reexperiencing their past communally in the form of projected movies.[7]

Club 57 was hardly the lone film venue in Lower Manhattan. The Collective for Living Cinema, the Millennium Film Workshop, the Kitchen, Film Forum, and Anthology Film Archives were all nearby. Nor, during the spring of 1979, was Club 57 the only movie house on the block.

In January 1979, after nine months of activity by a group of Super 8 filmmakers, New Cinema—a project created under the auspices of the downtown artists' association Collaborative Projects (Colab)—opened at 12 St. Marks Place. (The street itself is a significant location in the history of American avant-garde cinema. On March 2, 1964, Mekas and others were arrested on obscenity charges for showing Jack Smith's sexually explicit *Flaming Creatures* at the New Bowery Theater, at 4 St. Marks Place, a venue which later became the Bridge and continued to show underground movies for several years thereafter.)

New Cinema's first attraction was *Kidnapped* (1978), a Super 8 talkie modeled on Warhol's *Vinyl* (1965) by one of the group's organizers, Eric Mitchell. Other films, all transferred from Super 8 to videotape and then shown on an Advent Video Beam Television, included New Cinema organizer James Nares's *Rome '78* (1978), a Manhattan-set costume travesty featuring David McDermott as the Roman emperor Caligula; Mitchell's second film, *Red Italy* (1979), a mock-neorealist cross-class love story set in Rome (though shot in Manhattan); John Lurie's *Men in Orbit* (1979), with Lurie and Mitchell as chain-smoking astronauts; and

Vivienne Dick's *Beauty Becomes the Beast* (1979), in which punk rocker Lydia Lunch plays a five-year-old child. By the time Club 57 began regularly screening films, both *East Village Eye* and the *Village Voice* had run lengthy articles on New Cinema.[8]

New Cinema was short-lived but the movies that opened there crossed over, almost immediately, to other venues. (By April 1979, *Men in Orbit*, *Kidnapped*, and *Red Italy* had been shown—as video—at the Kitchen.) The following spring brought the full flowering of the postpunk downtown aesthetic. Film Forum opened a 16mm blowup of Beth and Scott B's serial melodrama of cops and terrorists, *The Offenders*. A few months later, Mitchell premiered his first 16mm feature, *Underground USA*, at Theater for the New City. The film, an East Village *Sunset Boulevard* with local superstar Patti Astor playing a version of the Warhol superstar Edie Sedgwick, subsequently ran for seventeen weeks, from June to October, as a midnight attraction at St. Marks Cinema.

Club 57 was only one of several places, including clubs like Max's Kansas City and TR3, that showed work by downtown filmmakers—among them Charlie Ahearn, Amos Poe, and Nick Zedd, as well as Nares, Dick, and the Bs (figs. 6–7)—but it was seldom a place where their films premiered. In general, the club was apart from the larger world of independent and avant-garde film. (A rare exception was Poe's 1978 punk thriller, *The Foreigner*, which screened in January 1980, two years after showing at the Whitney Museum.) Club 57 programmers, for example, were oblivious to young Super 8 filmmakers like Ericka Beckman and Joe Gibbons, whose work was shown at the Collective, the Whitney, the Kitchen, and elsewhere. Valie Export's feminist variant on *Invasion of the Body Snatchers*, *Invisible Adversaries*, another notable avant-garde work that premiered in New York during the club's heyday, was never invited.[9]

In general, Club 57 was more interested in audiences than filmmakers. Still, in January 1980, Vivienne Dick showed a version of the Super 8 film she would eventually call *Liberty's Booty*, a work of sexual demystification, set in an invented Lower East Side brothel staffed by white, middle-class girls. A few weeks later, Irish filmmaker John Davis's fifty-minute documentary, *Shellshock Rock*, had its New York premiere, one of several films dealing with Northern Ireland that would be screened at Club 57. (Arthur MacCaig's documentary *The Patriot Game*, presented by Dick, and Nares's video *No Japs at My Funeral*, both showed during the spring of 1981.) Davis's documentary gave a utopian overview of Ulster's New Wave culture, suggesting that the province's local punk scene had united Catholic and Protestant teenagers in an affirmative force.

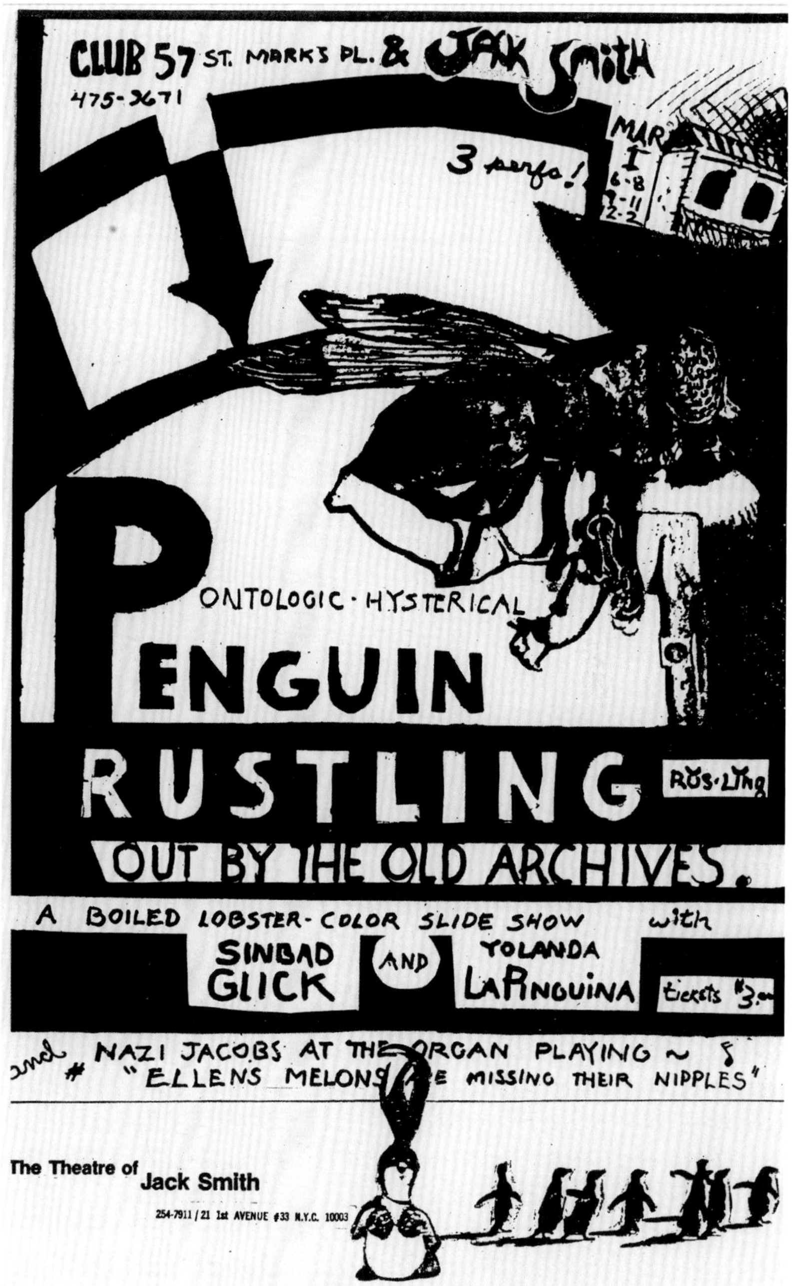

5. Flyer for Jack Smith's performance Penguin Rustling out by the Old Archives at Club 57, 1981. Design by Smith. The Museum of Modern Art, New York. Department of Film Special Collections

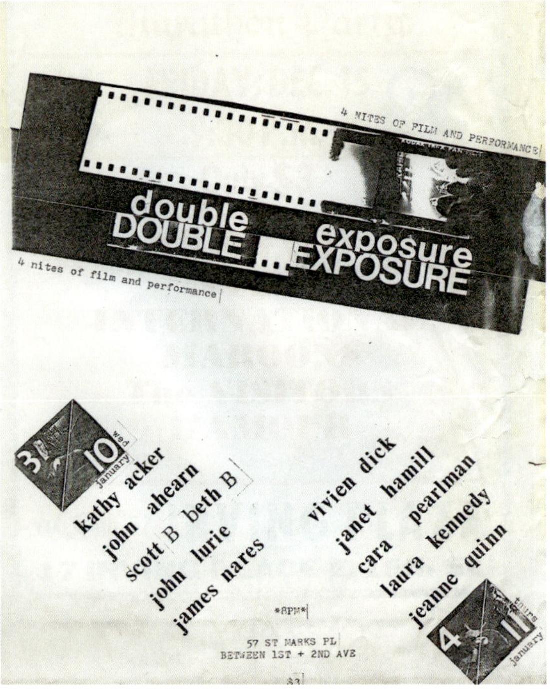

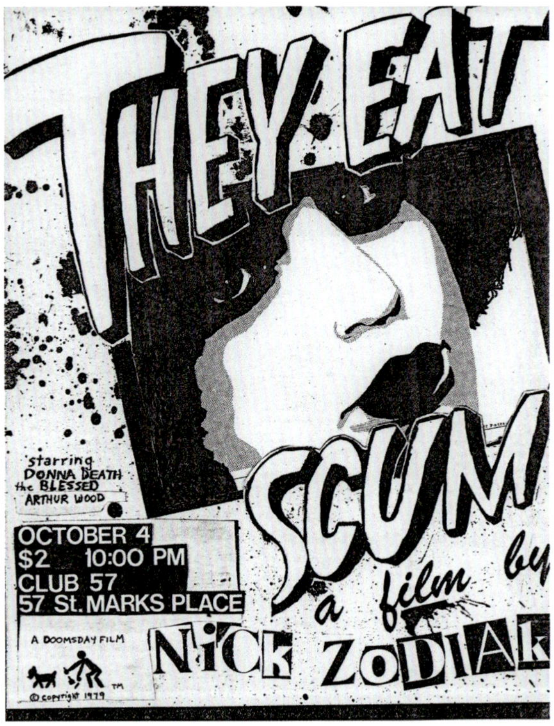

6. Flyer for Double Exposure: 4 Nights of Film and Performance at Club 57, 1979. Unknown designer. A *Village Voice* listing describes the January 4 program as having included films by Vivienne Dick (*She Had Her Gun All Ready*, 1978), Cara Perlman (*Topless*, 1979; surname misspelled above), and Bush Tetras's Laura Kennedy (*Les guérillères*, date unknown), along with poetry and performance by Janet Hamill, Jeanne Quinn, and Adele Bertei. The Museum of Modern Art, New York. Department of Film Special Collections

7. Flyer for Nick Zedd's *They Eat Scum* at Club 57, 1979. Designed by Zedd, who also went by Zodiak in the period. The Museum of Modern Art, New York. Department of Film Special Collections

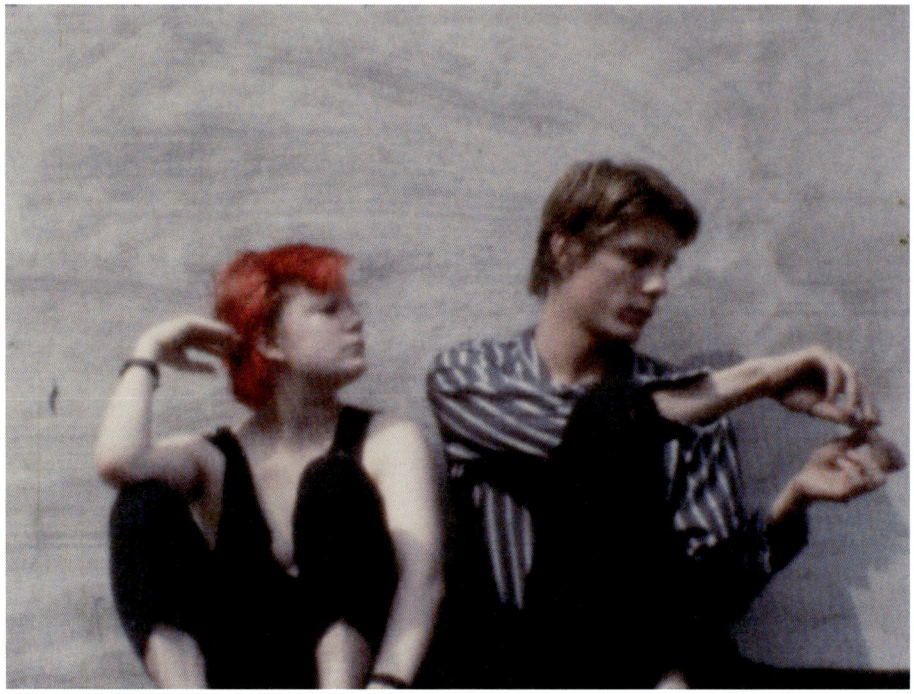

8. Trixie Salke and James Nares in a still from *Dear Jimmy*, 1978. Directed by Harald Vogl

Dear Jimmy (fig. 8), made by the Austrian-born filmmaker Harald V. Uccello under the name Harald Vogl, had its first public screening at Club 57 as part of the Classics of the New Cinema series organized by Patti Astor during the summer of 1981 (fig. 9). (Intentionally or not, the series postdated Anthology Film Archives' May-to-June survey of American 8mm and Super 8 movies, which included work by the Bs, Dick, Mitchell, and another New Cinema founder, Becky Johnston. The period was now historicized.) Shot in 1978, *Dear Jimmy* had not actually been shown at the New Cinema but, highly self-conscious, it both documented and commented on the East Village's burgeoning Super 8 scene, sharing the mix of melodrama and verité that characterized Nares's *Rome '78*.

Although *Rome '78* predated Club 57's heyday, the chaotic and hilarious thrift-store costume epic—which, among its many anachronisms was an obvious dependence on the 1976 BBC miniseries *I, Claudius*, telecast in New York during the 1977–78 season—was the film that most epitomized the club aesthetic. "What we all wanted to do was lift up the pop culture junk that had been drummed into our heads in the '50s, '60s, and '70s," Epperson recalled. "We needed to exorcise it. So that meant mocking it and loving it at the same time."[10]

In that sense, the most elaborate Super 8 feature to premiere at Club 57, and the one most closely associated with the venue, was twenty-three-year-old Swedish filmmaker Anders Grafstrom's *The Long Island Four* (fig. 10). Grafstrom, who died in a car accident several months after his movie was twice screened at the club in late 1979, used more or less conventional film language to recast, as camp myth, the story of the wartime German intelligence plan Operation Pastorius. The failed scheme saw a group of Nazi saboteurs (David McDermott, the star of *Rome '78*, Bradley Field, Kristian Hoffman, and Lance Loud) transported by U-boat to Amagansett, Long Island, in June 1942.

The low-budget, gross-out horror-comedy *Basket Case* (1982), shot in 16mm by Club 57 member Frank Henenlotter in New York City intermittently over a three-year period, represented the club's sleazoid sensibility. (It was premiered as a midnight movie at the Waverly in April 1982.) Henelotter previewed at least one clip at Club 57, but

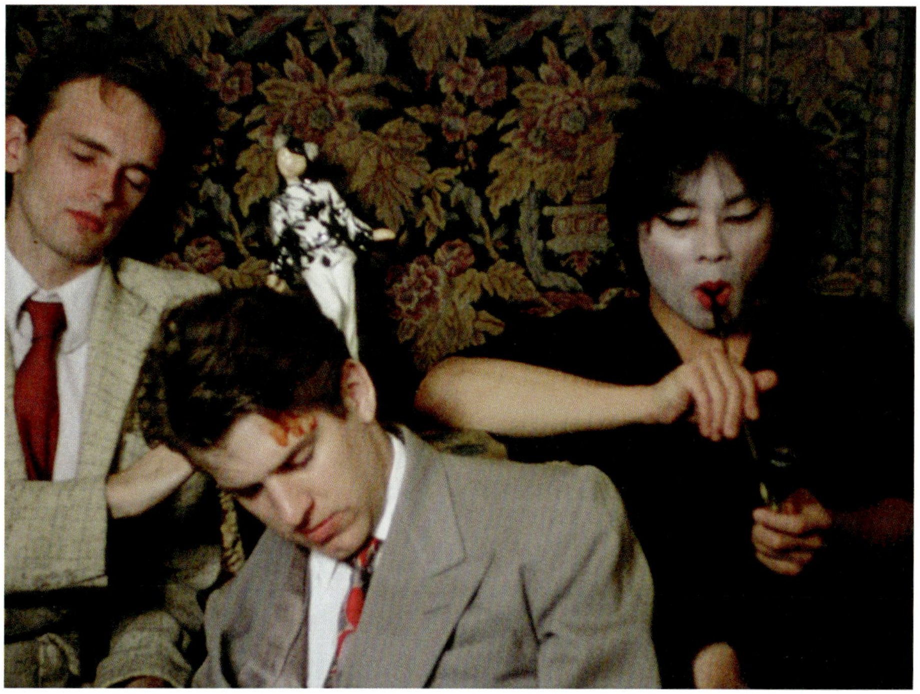

10. From left: Scott Gillis, Kristian Hoffman, and Tetsu Okuhara in a film still from *The Long Island Four*, 1980. Directed by Anders Grafstrom

The Long Island Four was closer to the club's "new wave vaudeville" performative aesthetic. Although set in the 1940s, rather than the '50s or '60s, and influenced more by contemporary German movies than old American television, it was a knowingly retro, crypto home movie, all about dressing up and role-playing. Nearly a musical, the film features a number of 1930s songs to accompany discreet scenes.

As if at Club 57 (or Mudd Club), the spies spend their time in New York fraternizing with East Village celebrities: Tina L'Hotsky plays McDermott's mistress, Astor appears as Loud's newly acquired girlfriend, Klaus Nomi and Eric Mitchell are present as Nazi agents, all resplendent in period dress. The party at L'Hotsky's apartment brings most of the cast together—albeit in far more decorous fashion than the ensemble scenes in Scharf's videotapes. Rendered elegiac with Grafstrom's untimely death, the movie's last end credit is "Special Thanks to Club 57."

Along with *Shellshock Rock*, *The Long Island Four* was one of the few Club 57 presentations for which press interest was solicited. Essentially the club was a revival house that, like the nearby Theatre 80 St. Marks, which showed mainly 16mm prints of pre–World War II Hollywood musicals, contributed to a particular revival.

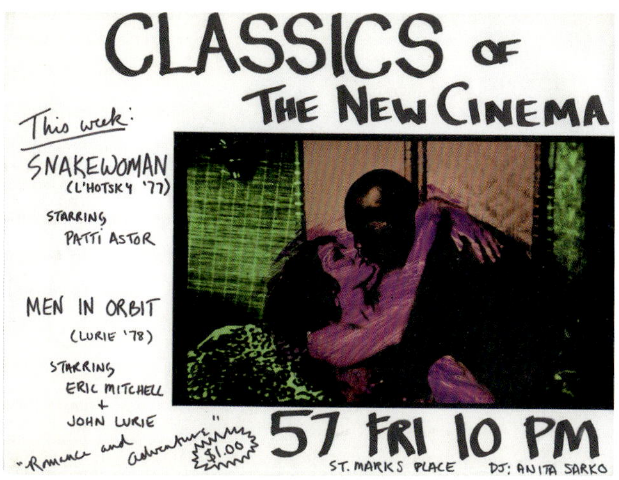

9. Flyer for a screening of Tina L'Hotsky's *Snakewoman* (1977) and John Lurie's *Men in Orbit* (1979) as part of the Classics of the New Cinema series at Club 57, 1981, organized by Patti Astor. Design by Astor. The Museum of Modern Art, New York. Department of Film Special Collections

The drive-in films of the 1950s and '60s were undergoing an enthusiastic revaluation during the summer of 1979. Both the punk-oriented broadsheet *New York Rocker* and the monthly culture magazine *East Village Eye* used their posters as art work. The season brought *Rock 'n' Roll High School*, a Roger Corman production that although featuring Ramones (who a year earlier had appeared along with Deborah Harry and Andy Warhol in the elaborate *fumetto* "Mutant Monster Beach Party," which took up virtually all of *Punk* 15) was a riff on the AIP youth pictures of the early 1960s, while a month-long AIP retrospective was held at The Museum of Modern Art.[11]

Del Tenney's *The Horror of Party Beach* (1964) was one Club 57 perennial, screened twice under the auspices of MMC and again as an example of Teenage Sex 'n' Violence during club manager Ira Abramowitz's 1981 reprise of the series. Historic in its own right as the first film to synthesize and satirize two quintessential drive-in genres (monster and beach party), it might also be considered a template for the club's performative mash-ups. Scully credits himself with the discovery of *Manos: The Hands of Fate*, a 1966 drive-in film concerning a demonic cult that was written, produced, and directed by an El Paso, Texas, insurance salesman, Hal P. Warren, who also appears in the movie. "It was garbage. It didn't have a crowd but the second time I showed it, it packed the house."[12]

Similarly, MMC screenings of *Plan 9 from Outer Space* and bad movies in general anticipated the World's Worst Film Festival, held at the Beacon Theatre in April 1980. In the context of Club 57, however, these films were not simply entertainment but usable culture. According to Hannaford, although Scully "always wanted the movies to be taken seriously," she saw them as a stimulus for performance: "Ann and I would think of the victim in the movie that week and dress the part."[13]

VCRs had not yet saturated the market. Club 57 showed 16mm and as there was only a single projector, the time taken for reel changes encouraged such active spectatorship—as did the venue's somewhat rowdy café atmosphere. "People would shout, talk to the people on screen, or even do a monologue," Scully recalled. Club member Drew Straub compared the screenings to karaoke and claimed to have been "the king of the Monster Movie Club" because of a distinctive shriek that he would save "until the exact moment you needed a blood-curdling scream." On the other hand, Epperson recalled that audience members commenced screeching even as the opening credits rolled.[14]

Insofar as the movies were an excuse for audience participation, they were an analogue to the midnight screenings of *The Rocky Horror Picture Show* that, having begun at Waverly Theater, had been held at 8th St. Playhouse since the summer of 1978. Like *Rocky Horror*, Club 57—which privileged hallucinogenic drugs and delighted in parodic hippie impersonations—might be considered a continuation of the counterculture by other means. Indeed, the screening parties at Club 57 were a hipper, more aesthetically self-conscious (and anarchic) version of the *Rocky Horror* cult.[15]

Many Club 57 movies were enjoyed by an appropriately costumed audience. *The 10th Victim* (1965), an Italian sci-fi spy satire starring Marcello Mastroianni, occasioned a Super-Ultra Mod Night. Spectators for a showing of spy comedy *Casino Royale* (1967) were directed to dress their "favorite 007 character."[16] An MMC presentation of the 1956 British adaptation of George Orwell's dystopian classic, *1984*, provided the occasion for a "No Future" party.[17] Movies also served as backdrops as when the June 1981 event Disco Italiano featured the coming-of-age vacation romp *Gidget Goes to Rome* (1963) or when a few months later the Psychedelic Freak-Out incorporated the band the Fuzztones plus AIP's sensational, rock-fueled youth drama *Riot on Sunset Strip* (1967). The audience for Fellini's *8½* (1963) was invited to "come and yell 'Marcello'—Italiano gear appropro."[18]

Films by artists were secondary or even tertiary at Club 57. If various programmers created a canon, the audience produced the movie. All movies became performances, and, according to Scully, all performances featured movies—some people simply let the projector run and put on a shadow play. "*Incorporating* film," he recalled, "was the essence of what we tried to do."[19]

1. "Long Live Cliques in Art," *Village Voice*, November 26, 1970, reprinted in *Movie Journal: The Rise of a New American Cinema* (New York: Collier Books, 1972), 405.

2. Ann Magnuson, "On Club 57," *Artforum* 38, no. 2 (October 1999): 121. Film screenings at Club 57 predate the Hannaford-Magnuson-Scully era. In April 1978, an entity called Reel Classics held a weekly Reelin' & Rockin' Film Festival, which included D. A. Pennebaker's *Keep on Rockin'* (1969); *Revolution* (1968), by Jack O'Connell; and *The Big TNT Show* (1966), by Larry Peerce. In January 1979, the club hosted Double Exposure: 4 Nights of Film and Performance, with underground Super 8 filmmakers Scott B and Beth B, James Nares, and Vivienne Dick among the listed artists. Following New Wave Vaudeville, Hannaford, Magnuson, and Scully began occasional programming—including, in January 1979, Magnuson's Movie Party, a format that returned in May. Magnuson departed as Club 57 manager in the fall of 1980. Andy Rees, Kai Eric, and later, Ira Abramowitz, took her place in succession.

3. Tom Scully, conversation with Sophie Cavoulacos and Ron Magliozzi, May 16, 2016.

4. Susan Sontag, *Against Interpretation* (New York: Delta Books, 1966), 219.

5. John Epperson, conversation with Ron Magliozzi, April 25, 2016.

6. Stanley Strychacki, *Life as Art: The Club 57 Story* (Bloomington, IN: iUniverse, 2012), 117; Epperson, conversation with Cavoulacos and Magliozzi.

7. As Marc H. Miller noted in the catalogue to the 1986 Queens Museum exhibition *Television's Impact on Contemporary Art*, "Club 57 heralded the arrival of the TV generation into the art world." See *Television's Impact on Contemporary Art* (New York: The Queens Museum, 1986), 24.

8. Bethany Haye, "Cine Stars Spill," *East Village Eye*, May 1979, 7; J. Hoberman, "No Wavelength: The Para-Punk Underground," *Village Voice*, May 21, 1979, 42–43.

9. There was some traffic the other way. The Collective for Living Cinema may or may not have been influenced by MMC when in late October 1979 it programmed a double bill of *Voyage to the Planet of Prehistoric Women* (1968) and *Cat-Women of the Moon* (1953). *Cat-Women* was first shown at Club 57 the previous July; *Voyage*, a remarkable concoction pseudonymously directed by Peter Bogdanovich for AIP, and which inserted Mamie Van Doren into footage culled from the Soviet film *Planeta Bur*, appears to have never been screened there.

10. Epperson, conversation with Cavoulacos and Magliozzi.

11. The aesthetic seemed ubiquitous. Observing that "sleazy monster movies alternate with super-8 at Max's or Club 57" at the conclusion of a write-up for the *Village Voice* (July 2, 1979), I asked MoMA curator Laurence Kardish if the museum had "gone punk." "That's the one thing we didn't think of," he replied.

12. Scully, conversation with Cavoulacos and Magliozzi. A dozen years later, *Manos* was revived after a fashion as a particularly popular episode of the cable television series *Mystery Science Theater 3000*.

13. Susan Hannaford in Steven Hager, *Art after Midnight: The East Village Scene* (New York: St Martin's Press, 1986), 67–68.

14. Scully, conversation with Cavoulacos and Magliozzi; Drew Straub, conversation with Sophie Cavoulacos and Ron Magliozzi, June 15, 2016; Epperson, conversation with Magliozzi.

15. While there may not have been much of an overlap between Club 57 and Eighth Street habitués, the club did host a *Rocky Horror* Fan Club Christmas Party in December 1980 and subsequently booked *Rocky Horror*'s de facto master of ceremonies, offering An Evening with Sal Piro on October 1, 1981.

16. Club 57 newsletter (November 1979). The Museum of Modern Art Department of Film Special Collections.

17. Club 57 newsletter (January 1980).

18. Club 57 newsletter (June 1980).

19. Scully, conversation with Cavoulacos and Magliozzi, emphasis mine.

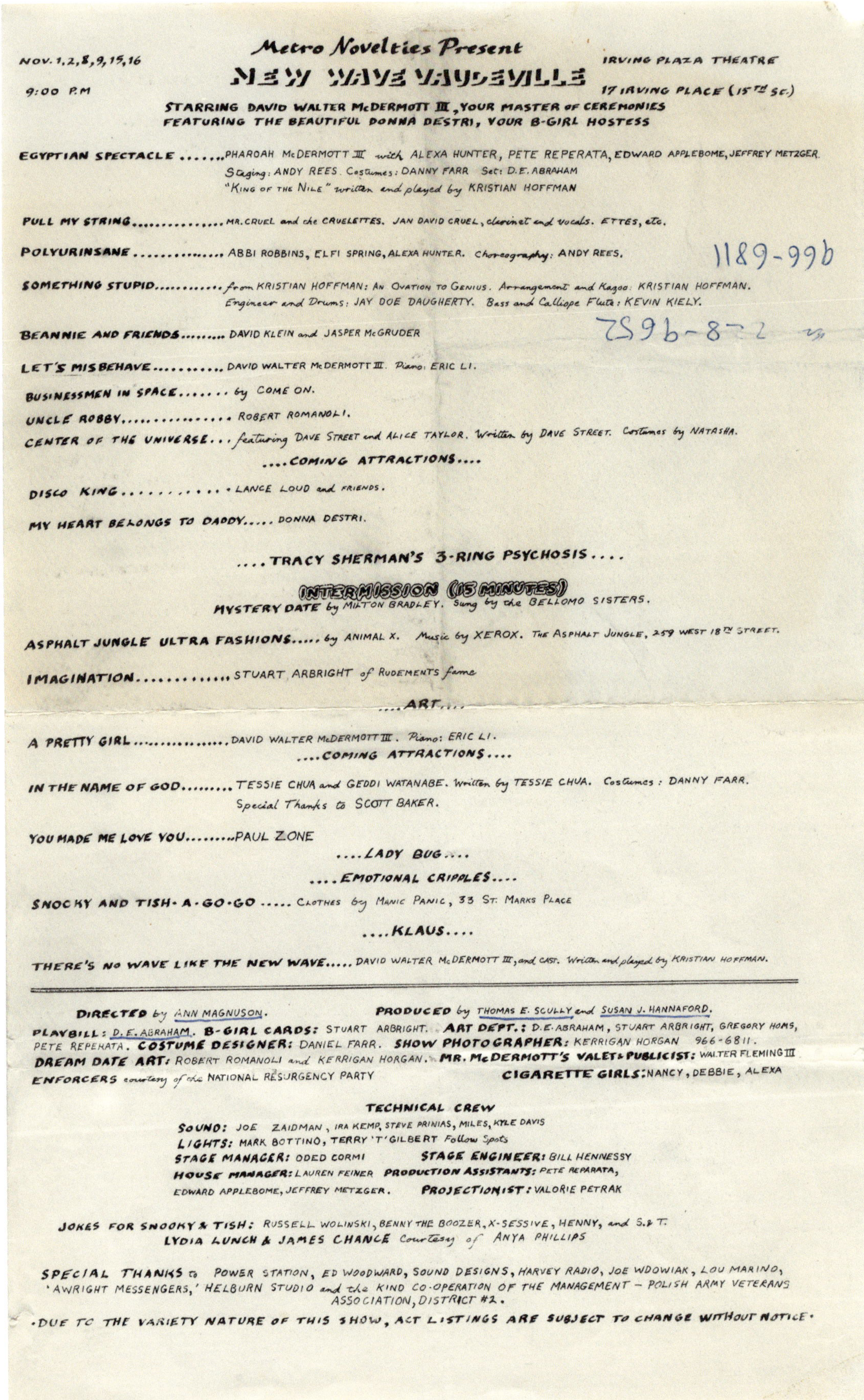

Metro Novelties Present

NOV. 1, 2, 8, 9, 15, 16

9:00 P.M

NEW WAVE VAUDEVILLE

IRVING PLAZA THEATRE

17 IRVING PLACE (15TH St.)

STARRING DAVID WALTER McDERMOTT III, YOUR MASTER OF CEREMONIES
FEATURING THE BEAUTIFUL DONNA DESTRI, YOUR B-GIRL HOSTESS

EGYPTIAN SPECTACLE .... PHAROAH McDERMOTT III with ALEXA HUNTER, PETE REPERATA, EDWARD APPLEBOME, JEFFREY METZGER.
Staging: ANDY REES. Costumes: DANNY FARR Set: D.E. ABRAHAM
"King of the Nile" written and played by KRISTIAN HOFFMAN

PULL MY STRING............... MR. CRUEL and the CRUELETTES. JAN DAVID CRUEL, clarinet and vocals. ETTES, etc.

POLYURINSANE .... ABBI ROBBINS, ELFI SPRING, ALEXA HUNTER. Choreography: ANDY REES.

1189-99b

SOMETHING STUPID........... from KRISTIAN HOFFMAN: An Ovation to Genius. Arrangement and Kazoo: KRISTIAN HOFFMAN.
Engineer and Drums: JAY DOE DAUGHERTY. Bass and Calliope Flute: KEVIN KIELY.

BEANNIE AND FRIENDS........ DAVID KLEIN and JASPER McGRUDER

2-8-9652

LET'S MISBEHAVE.......... DAVID WALTER McDERMOTT III. Piano: ERIC LI.

BUSINESSMEN IN SPACE....... by COME ON.

UNCLE ROBBY................ ROBERT ROMANOLI.

CENTER OF THE UNIVERSE... featuring DAVE STREET and ALICE TAYLOR. Written by DAVE STREET. Costumes by NATASHA.

....COMING ATTRACTIONS....

DISCO KING............ LANCE LOUD and FRIENDS.

MY HEART BELONGS TO DADDY..... DONNA DESTRI.

....TRACY SHERMAN'S 3-RING PSYCHOSIS....

INTERMISSION (15 MINUTES)

MYSTERY DATE by MILTON BRADLEY. Sung by the BELLOMO SISTERS.

ASPHALT JUNGLE ULTRA FASHIONS..... by ANIMAL X. Music by XEROX. The Asphalt Jungle, 259 West 18th Street.

IMAGINATION............ STUART ARBRIGHT of RUDEMENTS fame

....ART....

A PRETTY GIRL............... DAVID WALTER McDERMOTT III. Piano: ERIC LI.

....COMING ATTRACTIONS....

IN THE NAME OF GOD......... TESSIE CHUA and GEDDI WATANABE. Written by TESSIE CHUA. Costumes: DANNY FARR.
Special Thanks to SCOTT BAKER.

YOU MADE ME LOVE YOU........ PAUL ZONE

....LADY BUG....

....EMOTIONAL CRIPPLES....

SNOOKY AND TISH-A-GO-GO ..... Clothes by Manic Panic, 33 St. Marks Place

....KLAUS....

THERE'S NO WAVE LIKE THE NEW WAVE..... DAVID WALTER McDERMOTT III, and CAST. Written and played by KRISTIAN HOFFMAN.

DIRECTED by ANN MAGNUSON. PRODUCED by THOMAS E. SCULLY and SUSAN J. HANNAFORD.
PLAYBILL: D.E. ABRAHAM. B-GIRL CARDS: STUART ARBRIGHT. ART DEPT.: D.E. ABRAHAM, STUART ARBRIGHT, GREGORY HOMS, PETE REPERATA. COSTUME DESIGNER: DANIEL FARR. SHOW PHOTOGRAPHER: KERRIGAN HORGAN 966-6811.
DREAM DATE ART: ROBERT ROMANOLI and KERRIGAN HORGAN. MR. McDERMOTT'S VALET & PUBLICIST: WALTER FLEMING III
ENFORCERS courtesy of the NATIONAL RESURGENCY PARTY CIGARETTE GIRLS: NANCY, DEBBIE, ALEXA

TECHNICAL CREW

SOUND: JOE ZAIDMAN, IRA KEMP, STEVE PRINIAS, MILES, KYLE DAVIS
LIGHTS: MARK BOTTINO, TERRY 'T' GILBERT Follow Spots
STAGE MANAGER: ODED CORMI STAGE ENGINEER: BILL HENNESSY
HOUSE MANAGER: LAUREN FEINER PRODUCTION ASSISTANTS: PETE REPARATA, EDWARD APPLEBOME, JEFFREY METZGER. PROJECTIONIST: VALORIE PETRAK

JOKES FOR SNOOKY & TISH: RUSSELL WOLINSKI, BENNY THE BOOZER, X-SESSIVE, HENNY, and S. & T.
LYDIA LUNCH & JAMES CHANCE Courtesy of ANYA PHILLIPS

SPECIAL THANKS to POWER STATION, ED WOODWARD, SOUND DESIGNS, HARVEY RADIO, JOE WDOWIAK, LOU MARINO, 'AWRIGHT MESSENGERS,' HELBURN STUDIO and the KIND CO-OPERATION OF THE MANAGEMENT – POLISH ARMY VETERANS ASSOCIATION, DISTRICT #2.

• DUE TO THE VARIETY NATURE OF THIS SHOW, ACT LISTINGS ARE SUBJECT TO CHANGE WITHOUT NOTICE •

1–2. This page and opposite: Playbills for New Wave Vaudeville at Irving Plaza, November 1–2, 8–9, 15–16, 1978. Design by Daniel Abraham. The two playbills advertise slightly different lineups. The right-hand playbill was embellished (independently of Abraham) by *Smegma* zine editors Scarlatina Lust and Alex TorridZone Igloo for publication in *A Supple Mint 1* (1978), a supplement put out between zine issues. The Museum of Modern Art, New York. Department of Film Special Collections and Library Collections, respectively

ACTS of LIVE ART: PERFORMANCE at CLUB 57

Jenny Schlenzka

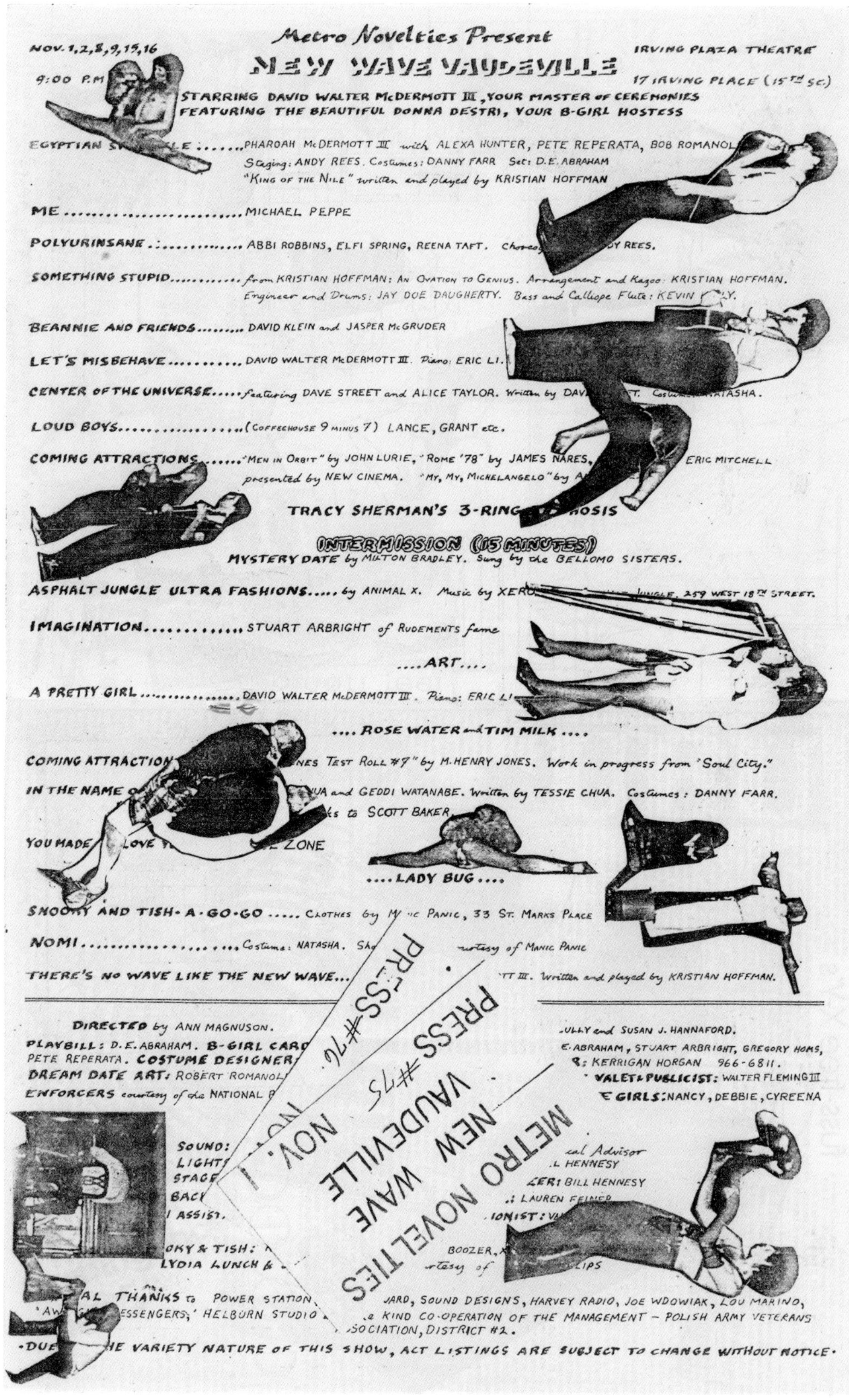

After visiting the first big Dada survey show in Paris in 1967, Max Ernst warned that trying to distill the movement's spirit by exhibiting a series of art objects in a museum is like trying to capture the violence of an explosion by presenting a singular piece of shrapnel.[1] It feels equally futile to attempt to write about the extraordinary accumulation of talent and creativity in the small East Village basement that became the epicenter of an immensely rich and prolific period of art production in postwar America. How does one translate into words the events and performances that took place almost forty years ago, many of them last-minute endeavors meant to last no longer than a night? What is the right form to represent the many friendships and encounters, the long alcohol- and drug-infused nights, the dancing and flirting and laughing, that were elemental to the subterranean space? How best to portray the plurality of ideas exchanged when all that remains are pictures, home videos, flyers, and many hours of audio interviews, their subjects reminiscing about one of the most exciting periods of their lives? One way to go about this conundrum might be to describe the circumstances that made the remarkable phenomenon that was Club 57 even possible.

In January of 1978, Ann Magnuson was still a senior in college when she arrived in New York City's East Village. She was one of any number of young artists who, lured by the promise of a bohemian lifestyle (and, for some, the stories of Andy Warhol's notorious Factory), poured into the neighborhood from all over the country, crowding into its one-mile radius. The apartments were smaller and more rundown than the spacious lofts of SoHo, the neighborhood called home by the previous generation of New York artists, but the rents were much cheaper—about one hundred dollars per month. This meant the artists who lived there didn't have to work very much to get by, their time freed up for creative activities and for idling in the dilapidated streets, where one would inevitably run into one's peers. That the neighborhood dwellings were more ruinous and cramped made them less than favorable for hosting performances and happenings (unlike their SoHo counterparts) and forced social life into the streets, alternative spaces, bars, and, most important, nightclubs—unlike today, to meet people, to get news of the latest social developments and art-related happenings, you had to be out in the world.[2] The neighborhood's unprecedented density of artists, all of whom shared the same desire to make art outside of institutional and commercial realms, sparked one of the biggest art explosions in American history.

Like Magnuson, many of the artists descending on the East Village were white college graduates with suburban, middle-class upbringings.[3] Born into the Eisenhower era of the 1950s, they came of age during the Vietnam War; night after night, over family dinner, they watched as news of the war and the spirited antiwar movement beamed into their homes through the television set.[4] Their adolescence profoundly shaped by these images, these artists were media savvy and instinctively aware of the hidden power structures embedded in television and other mass media. What stimulated their ideas more than art school, experimental theater, or the New York arts milieu was punk rock. The punk movement, initiated in the early 1970s by downtown bands who performed at the club CBGB—among them New York Dolls, the Patti Smith Group, Ramones, and Television—rejected the commercialized music industry and any form of elaborate musical production or virtuosity. Instead punk celebrated raw expression and DIY culture, and taught younger artists that anyone, no matter how inexperienced, can pick up a guitar, a paint brush, or a video camera to make art right here and now.[5] In this atmosphere, live performance quickly evolved into the go-to artistic form: not only could performance accommodate a diverse spectrum of mediums and styles, it could be made collectively, then instantaneously staged in front of an audience of friends. By the late 1970s performance had become key to the downtown community's strong interconnectedness.[6]

Several months after arriving in the city, Magnuson met Susan Hannaford and Tom Scully during one of her routine visits to music hotspot CBGB. Hannaford and Scully were former film students at School of Visual Arts, and the three became fast friends; recognizing their mutual love for vaudeville theater, Scully and Hannaford began plotting a modern-day show with Magnuson, who was eager to help them make it a reality. Their idea was to "define the growing energy everyone felt in the air"[7] as well as to have fun. A variety show as a choice of format was a nod to the history of American vaudeville that had flourished in the Eastern European and Yiddish immigrant Lower East Side at the turn of the twentieth century and would transfer to television in the 1950s and '60s. Magnuson, whose heroes were David Bowie and Alfred Jarry, was increasingly less excited by her internship at a more traditional off-Broadway theater and jumped at the opportunity to be the event's director. The trio, with help from friends such as SVA classmate and future drag performer Peter Kwaloff, plastered flyers for an open call all over the East Village, making sure to hit the hot spots. Hannaford recalls: "We got a lot of strange responses. Just about anyone could be in it, as long as their act was under five minutes."[8]

New Wave Vaudeville (figs. 1–2) ran for six nights at Irving Plaza in November 1978. Artist David McDermott emceed the show dressed as an Egyptian pharaoh with a crown and two scepters. To mark his entrance, McDermott was hoisted onstage on a wacky sedan chair by several slaves in loincloths, preceded by a dancing slave girl played by Alexa Hunter, who would later become an active member of Club 57. His rather amateurish rendition of an Egyptian-themed number, composed for the occasion by Mumps songwriter Kristian Hoffman, took place in front of a gigantic Camel cigarette advertisement created by future Club 57 member Daniel Abraham. Punk singer Donna Destri (sister of Blondie member Jimmy Destri), dolled up like a 1950s showgirl, carried a placard to announce the various acts, of which there were more than twenty. The evening encompassed every conceivable form of performance: art band Come On brought out suitcases stuffed with wobbly foam guitars to perform their "Businessmen in Space"; an act called Beannie and Friends involved a singing dog; Andy Rees, a future Club 57 manager, choreographed one of a few dance pieces, a New Wave number called Polyurinsane, which Hunter danced in; a performance of "Asphalt Jungle Ultra Fashion," with the band Xerox, featured frontwoman Animal X (the owner of one of the first punk rock boutiques) smashing a pink guitar; a sweet-natured stripper performed a duet with a dancing bird puppet; Tish and Snooky from Manic Panic sang '60s girl group harmonies; and Lance Loud, star of the PBS-TV documentary series *An American Family*, reinterpreted the Sex Pistols' "Anarchy in the UK" as a disco song. The program's two intermissions featured trailers from *Beneath the Planet of the Apes* (1970), accompanied by Jimi Hendrix's psychedelic guitar sound. The entire mix could not have been more bizarre and haphazard—and the cheering crowd loved it!

Although accounts of the show's run vary widely, there are two facts everyone seems to agree on: First, New Wave Vaudeville had tapped into an aesthetic sensibility that was percolating all over town—indeed all over the nation, as cities like San Francisco and Devo's own Akron, Ohio, were creating their own homegrown brand of New Wave. Second, its final act, a debut by the little-known German singer Klaus Sperber, is the reason the revue made pop cultural history. Toward the end of each night, the lights would go off and McDermott would announce: "Klaus Nomi!" The room would fill with a thundering musical ovation, the curtains would open, and the spotlight would fall on a "strange, unearthly presence,"[9] a little figure wearing black under a clear plastic cape, along with white makeup, black lipstick, and an angular hairdo. When the orchestral refrain of one of the most romantic arias ever composed, "Mon coeur s'ouvre à ta voix," from Camille Saint-Saën's opera *Samson et Dalila,* would start to play, the "strange Weimar version of Mickey Mouse" would begin to sing in an angelic soprano voice.[10] (At performances later in the run, McDermott had to reassure audiences that the classically trained Sperber was in fact singing.) "I still get goose pimples when I think about it," remembers performance artist Joey Arias, who was in the audience.[11] (Arias was one of Nomi's most important collaborators.) The unfamiliar mélange of "New Wave, Kabuki, and Bauhaus"[12] mesmerized the auditorium full of punks who, boisterous throughout the evening's previous performances, listened quietly until the last note. Then smoke machines would go off, strobe lights would flash, and the ear-shattering sound of a spaceship landing would reverberate through the room. The otherworldly figure would bow and recede into the cloud of smoke, while the audience would go berserk calling for an encore. When the smoke cleared, Nomi was gone, but a downtown star was born.

The show was a grand success. Hannaford, Magnuson, and Scully were spotted by Stanley Strychacki, the building manager of Irving Plaza, which was back then run by a Polish veterans' club. Strychacki liked the crowd the show attracted and invited the trio to look at a smaller venue he ran in the basement of the Holy Cross Polish National Church at 57 St. Marks Place. If they liked it, he proposed, they could organize events there. Hannaford, Magnuson, and Scully accepted the offer, sporadically putting on events over the next few months.

In many ways, New Wave Vaudeville laid the groundwork for the particular ethos and aesthetic vivacity that Hannaford, Magnuson, Scully, and their friends would bring to Club 57. For one, several of the artists who would soon become club regulars performed together at Irving Plaza for the first time. And, much as the revue offered an open path to the stage, so too would the club: everybody who wanted to perform would be invited to do so. Moreover, New Wave Vaudeville's interactive setting; its variety-style presentation of disjointed short acts and Hollywood B movies; its self-conscious juxtaposition of highbrow and lowbrow (opera and sci-fi), past and present (ancient ruins and contemporary advertising), mainstream and alternative (Cole Porter and punk rock), would each become characteristic of Club 57 programs. "We were against any kind of labels, any kind of confinements, and did not want to be fenced in," explains Magnuson.[13] This new formal language was blatantly different from the highly cerebral Minimalism taught to young artists in art school at the time, as well as from the pedestrian performance works that a generation earlier emerged from the movement around Judson Dance Theater and were staged in loft concerts in SoHo. The only rule at Club 57 was to keep it short and, most importantly, not to be boring.[14]

Throughout the winter and spring of 1979, much of the New Wave Vaudeville gang ramped up their involvement in the club, with Magnuson acting as manager, and Scully and Hannaford launching the weekly Monster Movie Club in May. Magnuson understood instinctively how to reap her friends' unbound creative energy, and she invited them to transform their ideas into actualities. "We were all kinetic pinballs bouncing off each other in this crazy, dangerous, exciting pinball machine known as Downtown New York."[15] Because few other venues existed in that part of town, and no one wanted to spend time in their small, decrepit apartments, people tended to hang around after screenings and events, partying and dancing to songs playing on the jukebox or to those supplied by club DJs, such as Scully and Kwaloff. Early theme nights were developed collectively around shared musical genres, including Motown and British Invasion.

By September 1979, Strychacki had charged Ann with creating a more formalized monthly schedule and filling the evenings with additional events, for which she would solicit ideas from club regulars, encouraging them to show their work untested. A brief glance at the club's printed calendar, which Magnuson meticulously pasted together with tiny cutouts from old magazines (pages 156–57, fig. 5), attests to the devotion and ingenuity with which she ran the entire operation. Magnuson, who channeled into the job her desire to be a theater director, found influence for the Club 57 program in the work of other theater-makers. Shortly after moving to the East Village she met avant-garde playwright and impresario Jeff Weiss, who ran serial plays out of his Tenth Street storefront apartment. Over several years of weekly performances, a dedicated community of performers and spectators had flourished and coalesced around his home. Magnuson also often attended performances hosted by Squat Theatre, a collective of Hungarian emigré artists and musicians who lived together in a building on West Twenty-Third Street. They famously staged their plays in the storefront against the backdrop of the street, the performances bleeding into everyday city life. The ways that both Weiss and Squat Theatre blurred public and private spaces was for Magnuson a revelation, and she embraced these models when thinking about what to host at the club.

Magnuson booked events nearly every night of the week, and although many were not performance events outright, rather themed nights with their own titles, decorative motifs, costume advisories, and participant lineups, they integrated performance and other theatrical and dramatic elements. Celebrity tribute nights (Elvis Presley Memorial Party, Dick Clark Tribute, and Salute to Lawrence Welk); genre-themed parties (Casino Royale, Playboy Bunny Club Party, and A Night at the Opry); fashion fêtes (Exclusive Fashions by Amazon and AMMO and Amazon School of Modeling); and events like Lady Wrestling (page 133), Stay-Free Mini-Prom, and Rites of Spring Fertility Bacchanal (these last three were mounted by the Junior League–inspired Ladies Auxiliary of the Lower East Side) rendered previous distinctions between staged productions and spontaneous presentations, performers and spectators, more fluid.

Moreover, that the floor-level stage lacked a proscenium made it more or less indistinguishable from the rest of the space, while the dense atmosphere left young artists uninhibited enough to try new things without contemplating them too much. Video documentation from the time captures how people constantly moved back and forth between stage and audience: spectators spontaneously became performers and performers spectators.[16] The frequency of events also often meant that artists did not have much time in advance to reason through or prepare their contributions, adding another element of spontaneity. With some exceptions, each night was

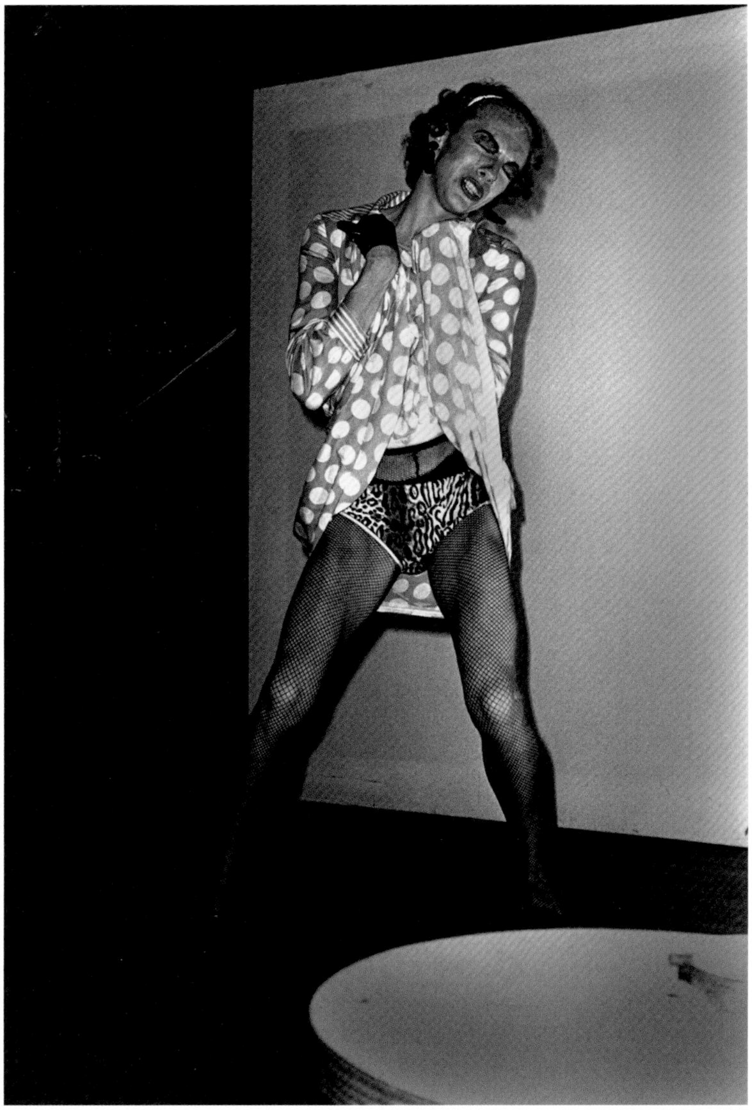

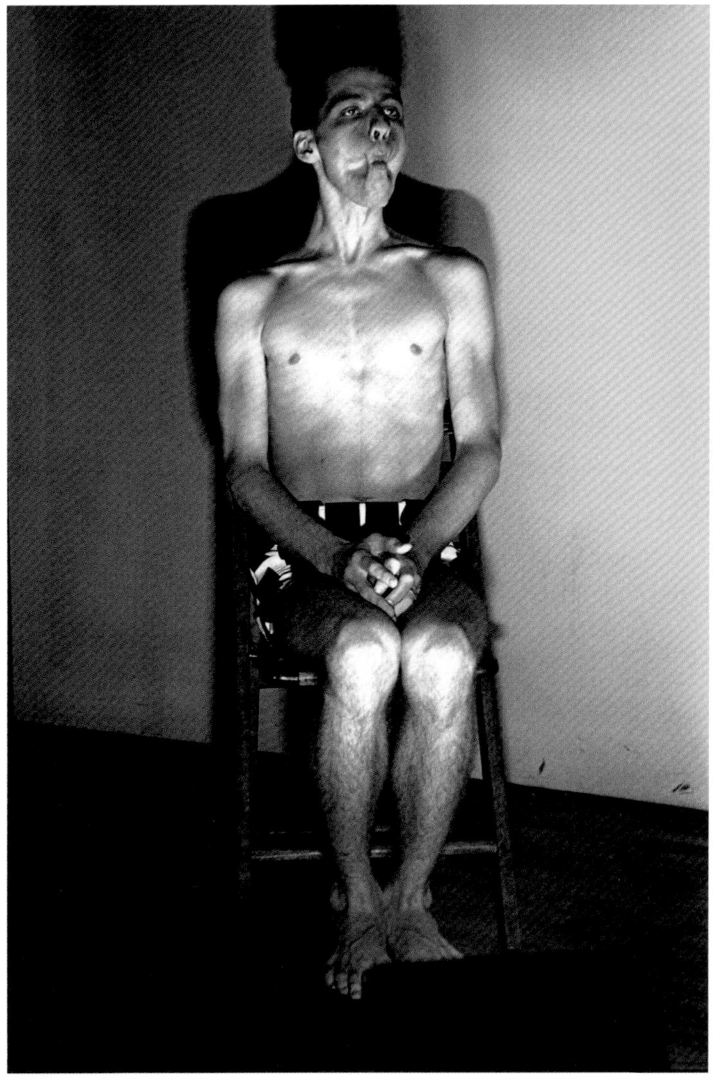

3–4. John Epperson (above) and Larry Ashton (right) in *Acts of Live Art at Club 57*, 1980, organized by John Sex. Photographs by Harvey Wang

different from the one before and happened only once. The ephemerality of the events added to the excitement, unleashing a well of new ideas and pushing club members to "live in the moment."[17]

In a short time, Club 57 drew a substantial number of regulars, many of whom would also become contributors. The New Wave Vaudeville gang welcomed everyone who wasn't afraid of being silly or goofy and rejected only those who took themselves too seriously, with few exceptions. Exclusivity and coolness were reserved for other venues, like Mudd Club. People came to see and be seen, to support their friends, or to find ideas and collaborators for their own art projects. They also came to chase romantic adventures (and had a good time doing so!). More often than not, they came for all of the above. The club's small size—it measured approximately twenty feet by fifty feet—and low-hanging ceiling contributed to its explosive energy.[18] When fifty people showed up, the place felt full. When one hundred people showed up, it was body-to-body packed.[19] In hindsight, the genius of Club 57 lay less in the individual projects that took place there and more in its setup: the compressed event calendar and closely packed space generated a creative pressure cooker, bringing together some of the generation's most imaginative young artists and offering them opportunities to make new work collectively, and in front of supportive audiences, night after night.[20]

In April 1980, John Sex organized a variety show called Acts of Live Art (page 44), which turned out to be significant for the direction the club was taking. Sex's evening was loosely inspired by Cabaret Voltaire in Zurich, in 1916, the venue that gave birth to the Dada movement. Founded by Hugo Ball, Tristan Tzara, and others, Cabaret Voltaire was a riotous gathering place for artists, hosting improvised music, noise machines, and simultaneous poetry readings in which a number of voices merged in a polyphonic cacophony. Like the Dada artists, Sex and his collaborators were interested in destroying the notion that art has meaning.[21] They were also interested in television and the way channel-surfing could flatten the viewer's experience—of watching the news, say, followed by a chewing-gum advertisement, followed by a classical music program. Acts of Live Art borrowed from Dada, television, and the vaudeville tradition, leveling disparate modes of performance by juxtaposing them one after the other under the banner of a single show.

Sex's show was emceed by club member Drew Straub, who announced the various acts wrapped in an American flag and wearing a life vest around his neck, and opened with Dany Johnson, Club 57's resident DJ, dancing and singing in a wheelchair and driving it into the audience. She was followed by John Sex, who lasciviously swung his hips and fired up the audience by undressing himself in what was the first in a long series of stripteases. For her part, Magnuson tap-danced and juggled twirling batons to the 1979 hit "Hot Stuff," by Donna Summer. She also played synthesizer as dancer and fashion designer AMMO (Shawn McQuate) prepared a salad made from lettuce, tomatoes, onions, and other ingredients spread out on a tabletop. Judging from the video artist Kenny Scharf made that night, the show seems to have consisted mainly of twenty-somethings undressing and showing off their attractive bodies, a testament to the highly sexual and drug-induced atmosphere of the time.[22] Scharf remembers looking around and realizing that he had slept with everyone in the room. Sex had likewise earned his moniker for good reason. Today the show is considered a critical moment in Club 57's history, having launched the careers of various performance artists[23] and ushered in the performance-dominated program that would broaden and evolve after Magnuson retired as manager in September of 1980. It was so successful that Sex restaged it with different acts in June (Acts of Live Art II)—here artist Keith Haring recited poetry through a television cutout held to his face (page 130), in the vein of his experiment with permutation poetry, *Lick Fat Boys*—July (Acts of Live Art III), and October (the Groovy Dada Lounge presents Acts of Live Art) of the same year (figs. 3–4, see previous spread).

Magnuson insists that the club members' main motivation was to have fun: "It helped us *not* to think of [what we were doing] as art."[24] Yet the period's satiation with irony and play often obscures the wit and ingenuity with which the artists were making their work. What at first glance appears self-referential and superficial is on closer examination full of personal investment and social commentary. The dance party Iran, Iraq, and Iroll, inspired by news headlines, was a light-hearted critique of the Iran hostage crisis and featured newspaper covers as décor and costumes for attendees. One John Sex Live Burlesque night (another recurring performance) featured an undressed couple sporting oversized masks of Nancy and Ronald Reagan; created by club member Larry Ashton, these unflattering likenesses were meant to deride the conservative values the new administration represented. Scharf once hosted a lecture—initially he had invited SVA professor Luis E. Navia, who taught a class in cosmology, to give the lecture, but Navia didn't show—that related to Scharf's deep-seated notion "about the promise not delivered that we grew up with. In the '60s . . . we were going to go to space. . . . The '70s came around and it wasn't going that way."[25] A dance party to "Fly Me to the Moon" followed the talk. The works were playful, to be sure, but their humor also served to shield them from their disappointment over the shattered utopian dreams of the 1960s and the dark undercurrent left by the Cold War and the conflict in Vietnam. As club photographer Tseng Kwong Chi would later note, the performances seemed a kind of purge or cleanse or catharsis.[26]

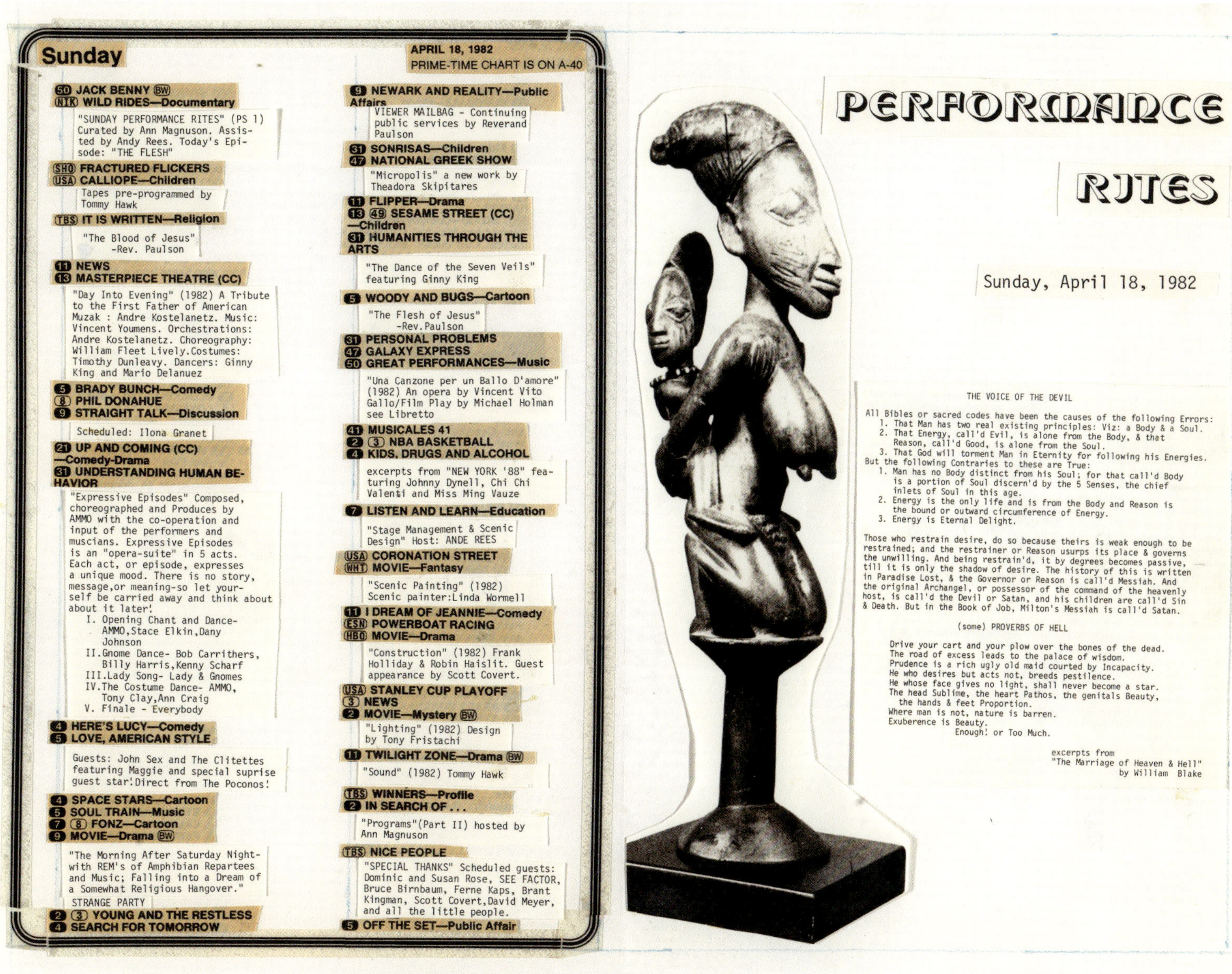

5–6. Above and next spread: Original collages for a program for *Performance Rites* at P.S. 1, 1982. Design by Ann Magnuson. MoMA PS1 Archives, I.A.730. The Museum of Modern Art Archives, New York

Around September of 1980, Magnuson left her position as club manager to pursue her interests as a performer and curator at other venues, including P.S. 1, where in April 1982 she organized *Performance Rites* (figs. 5–6), a four-part series that brought together a cast of Club 57 members, downtown pals, and collaborators, along with established folks, such as Ilona Granet, Theodora Skipitares, and Fran Lebowitz. At the club, management was turned over first to Andy Rees, then to Kai Eric, and then to Ira Abramowitz; each would leave his own imprint on the 57 program. Under Rees, the performance work leaned toward more traditional theater, with proper scripts and scheduled rehearsals. (Most notable: the Barbie-themed *Livin' Dolls*, by Scott Wittman and Marc Shaiman, who would go on to write the music and lyrics for *Hairspray* on Broadway. The pair also put on the parody musical *The Sound of Muzak*, which featured Holly Woodlawn and John Sex.) Under Ira Abramowitz's tenure, drug- and drag-infused cabaret performers cut their teeth before transitioning to the multifaceted drag, theater, and theme nights produced at Pyramid Club, a once-sleepy Avenue A joint that became a major interdisciplinary nightclub. Soon Club 57's short-lived tenure of spontaneous, raw, and wacky performance art in downtown New York, and the free spirit of those times, would take on mythic proportions.

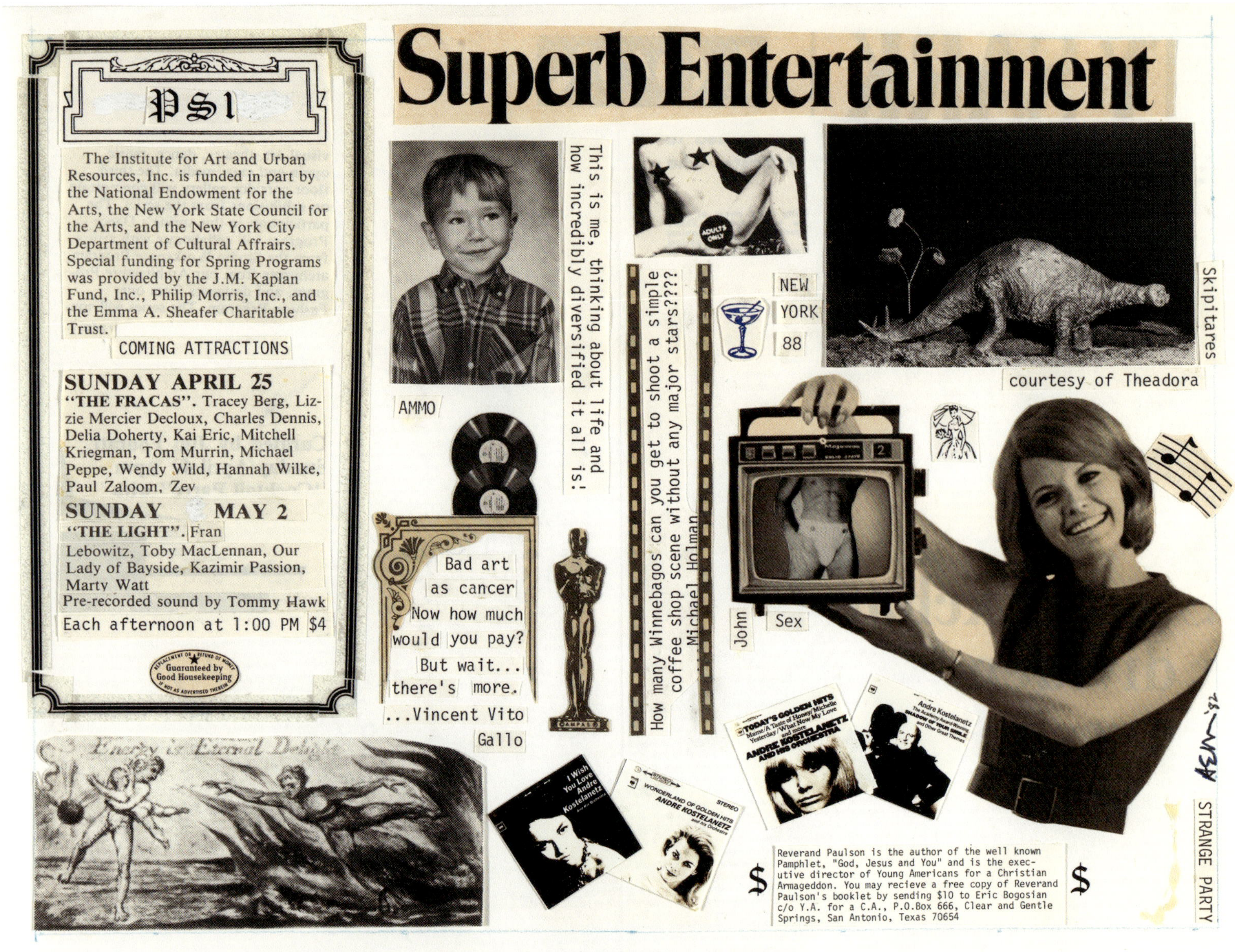
Superb Entertainment
PS1
The Institute for Art and Urban Resources, Inc. is funded in part by the National Endowment for the Arts, the New York State Council for the Arts, and the New York City Department of Cultural Affairs. Special funding for Spring Programs was provided by the J.M. Kaplan Fund, Inc., Philip Morris, Inc., and the Emma A. Sheafer Charitable Trust.
COMING ATTRACTIONS
SUNDAY APRIL 25
"THE FRACAS". Tracey Berg, Lizzie Mercier Decloux, Charles Dennis, Delia Doherty, Kai Eric, Mitchell Kriegman, Tom Murrin, Michael Peppe, Wendy Wild, Hannah Wilke, Paul Zaloom, Zev
SUNDAY MAY 2
"THE LIGHT". Fran Lebowitz, Toby MacLennan, Our Lady of Bayside, Kazimir Passion, Marty Watt
Pre-recorded sound by Tommy Hawk
Each afternoon at 1:00 PM $4
Guaranteed by Good Housekeeping
This is me, thinking about life and how incredibly diversified it all is!
AMMO
ADULTS ONLY
How many Winnebagos can you get to shoot a simple coffee shop scene without any major stars????
Michael Holman
NEW YORK 88
Skipitares
courtesy of Theadora
Bad art as cancer
Now how much would you pay?
But wait... there's more.
...Vincent Vito Gallo
John Sex
Energy is Eternal Delight
I Wish You Love Andre Kostelanetz
WONDERLAND OF GOLDEN HITS ANDRE KOSTELANETZ
TODAY'S GOLDEN HITS ANDRE KOSTELANETZ AND HIS ORCHESTRA
Andre Kostelanetz
Reverand Paulson is the author of the well known Pamphlet, "God, Jesus and You" and is the executive director of Young Americans for a Christian Armageddon. You may recieve a free copy of Reverand Paulson's booklet by sending $10 to Eric Bogosian c/o Y.A. for a C.A., P.O.Box 666, Clear and Gentle Springs, San Antonio, Texas 70654
$
$
STRANGE PARTY

1. Werner Spiess, *Max Ernst—Retrospektive zum 100. Geburtstag* (Munich: Prestel, 1991), 19. Translation the author's.

2. According to Ann Magnuson, a precious few had apartments worth staying home for but most did not. Conversation with the author, October 18, 2016, and May 15, 2017.

3. For a discussion of suburbia's major influence on the East Village art scene, see Robert Siegel, "Writing Downtown," in *The Downtown Book* (Princeton, NJ: Princeton University Press, 2006), 132–33. "For it was from suburbia that many Downtown artist fled to Manhattan, looking for something that was more real than what Kathy Acker calls the nicey-nicey-clean-ice-cream-TV society."

4. Magnuson, conversation with the author, October 18, 2016.

5. "The punk bands at CBGB opened everybody's eyes and made us think 'Yeah, pick up an instrument, pick up a paintbrush, there's nothing to stop you!'" Ann Magnuson, quoted in Tim Lawrence, *Life and Death on the Dance Floor, 1980–1983* (Durham: Duke University Press, 2016), 30.

6. "Imagine how different the way of life would have been if artists had sat alone making only objects," performance-art historian Roselee Goldberg noted in "Art after Hours: Downtown Performance," *The Downtown Book*, 103.

7. Steven Hager, *Art after Midnight: The East Village Scene* (New York: St. Martin's Press, 1986), 26.

8. Susan Hannaford, quoted in ibid.

9. Hager, *Art after Midnight*, 30.

10. Ibid.

11. Joey Arias, quoted in ibid.

12. Hager, *Art after Midnight*, 37.

13. Magnuson, conversation with the author, October 18, 2016.

14. Ibid.

15. Ibid.

16. Kenny Scharf, *Acts of Live Art*, 1980. Video (color, sound), 35 min. The Museum of Modern Art, New York.

17. Magnuson, conversation with the author, October 18, 2016.

18. See Uzi Parnes, "Pop Performance," *Drama Review* 29, no. 1 (Spring 1985): 7; and Merle Ginsberg, "(Night) Life Imitates Art," *Alive* (July/August 1982): 7.

19. Lawrence, *Life and Death*, 34.

20. It may be interesting to note the simultaneity of the downtown vaudeville scene with Harlem's ballroom culture, which, ongoing since the 1960s, consisted mostly of Black and Latino youths adopting fashion-media representations of glamour and affluence as a form of aspirational drag. In their own version of drag, Club 57's predominantly white, middle-class crowd performed a self-conscious mockery of those same mainstream ideals. The two scenes were therefore united by their burlesque parodies of whiteness, heteronormativity, and gender binarism, as perpetuated by popular culture.

21. Dominic Johnson, "Capricorn on Fire: An Interview with Ann Magnuson," *The Art of Living* (London: Palgrave MacMillan, 2015), 158.

22. Scharf, Acts of Live Art.

23. According to Shawn McQuate, "It was a real turning point—a lot of people got their performance careers started that [first] night." McQuate, quoted in Hager, *Art after Midnight*, 74.

24. Magnuson, conversation with the author, October 18, 2016.

25. Kenny Scharf, conversation with Ron Magliozzi and Sophie Cavoulacos, November 3, 2016.

26. Tseng, a club regular who frequently enlisted members to model in his editorial work, remarked: "I got the impression every time Ann did a performance it was like a purge for her. She seemed to be pouring out all these things from her childhood. In the early days it was like they were spilling their guts. And I think it was totally unconscious." See Tseng, quoted in Hager, *Art after Midnight*, 81.

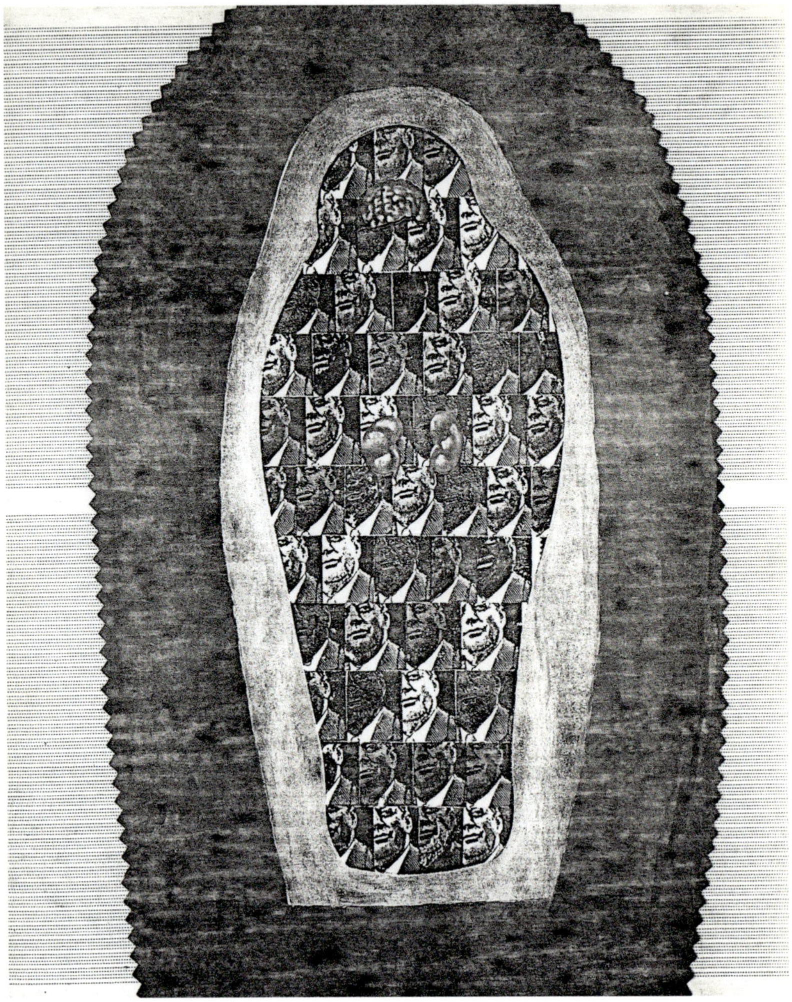

om for it in Paris (no room
ure dicotomy?) it must have an edge. The
point of criticism of concept-en elaborated and transformed
of the spoken, the idea of this not merely "touched" "shore",
of language; of the subject, changing , as in Mallarmé's declar-
s that perhaps performance l those boundaries that form
metalanguage or paralanguage be called a text, of what
e) are taking place in the artdentify,i.e., the supposed end
object of consumption. ... of a corpus, the title, the
referential realm outside the
The Text (if only beppened, is a sort of overrun
decants the work from its con- se boundaries and divisions and
, task, production, and activity concept, the dominant notion of
! Burroughs for the petit-boin contemporary art) as being
uss, Straub, Barthes, et al. by Levi-Strauss when he says
that the work in mythology (IBM)
If we are to approach a text , in America because there is no ro
question of the text, as it has been in the European painting/scul
in the last dozen or so years, ha Rosalind Krauss stated that the
le bord (scandalously tampering, ual, performance art, etc. is one
ation, "On a touché au vers"), alanalysis is one of the convention
the running border of what used tmaker of the art. Ms. Krauss fee
we once thought this word could iart is the place where the ideas
and beginning of a work, the unit(criticism and literature being o
margins , the signatures, the ref (6) The work is ordinarily an o
frame, and so forth. What has ha
(débordement) that spoils all the
forces us to extend the accredite of its frequent "unreadability")
The question of structuralism (sumption and gathers it up as play
American in nature was predicted Who owns words? Make them gush.
Derrida for the Yale learned. Kraus

ne·ol·o·gism \nē-ˈäl-ə-ˌjiz-əm\ n 1 : a new word, usage, or expression 2 : a meaningless word coined by a psychotic — ne·ol·o·gist \-jəst\ n — ne·ol·o·gis·tic \(ˌ)nē-ˌäl-ə-ˈjis-tik\ adj

Storyness Drew Straub 3 26 80

112–113

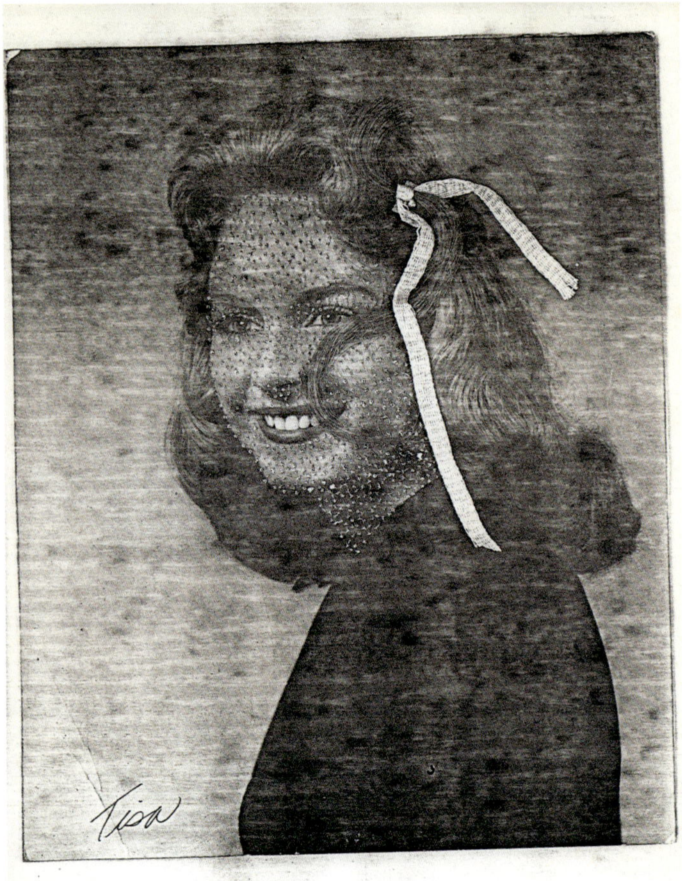

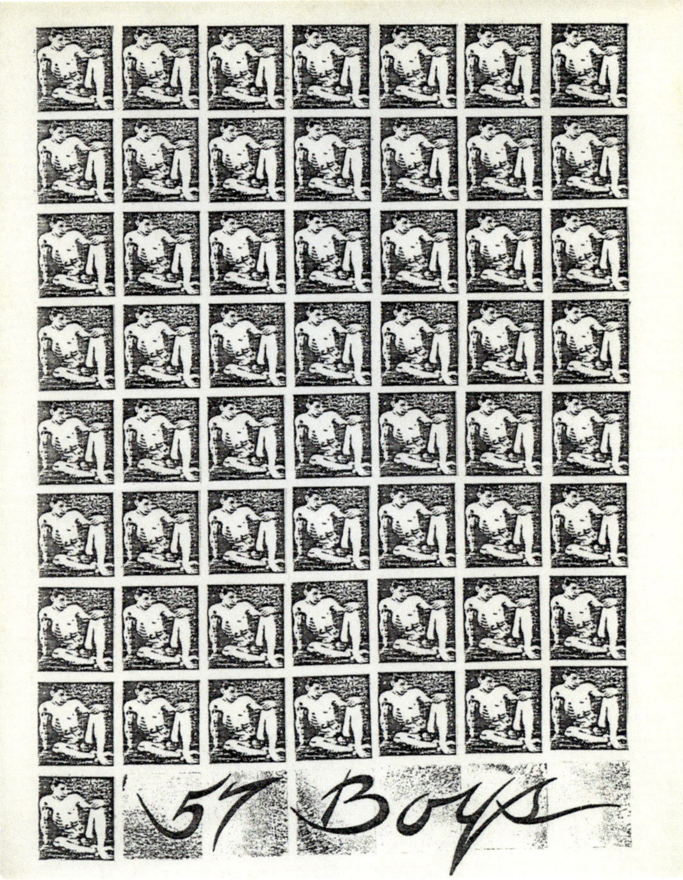

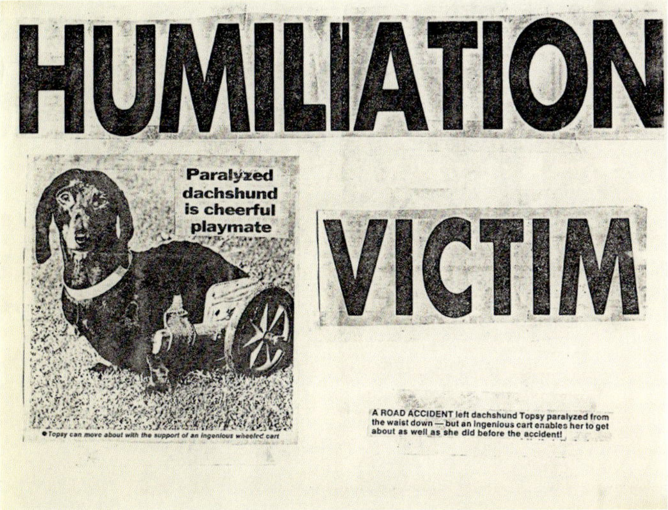

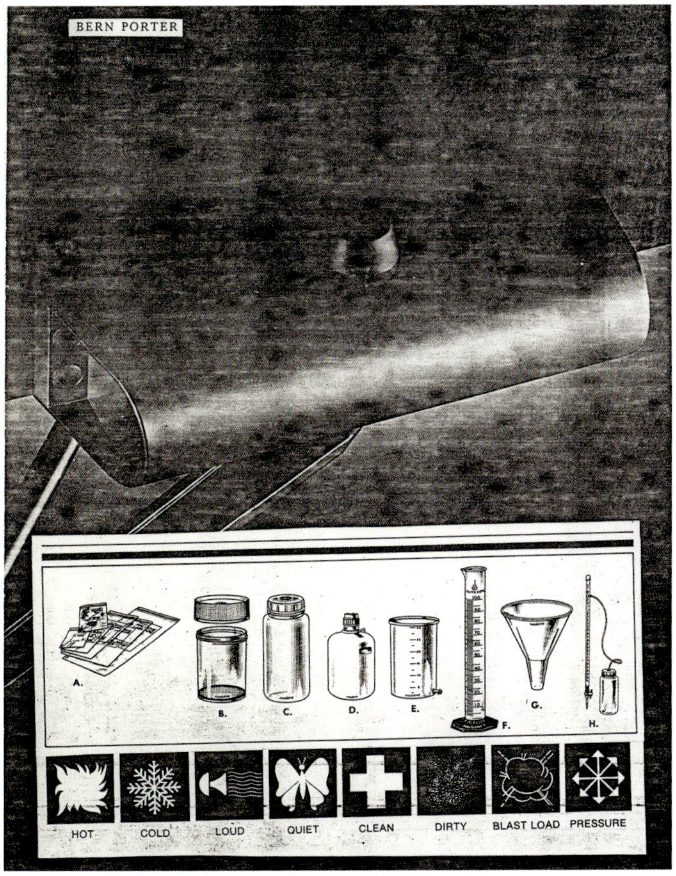

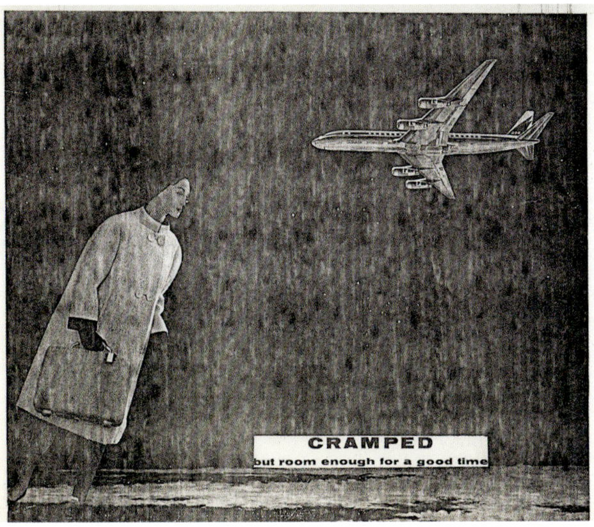

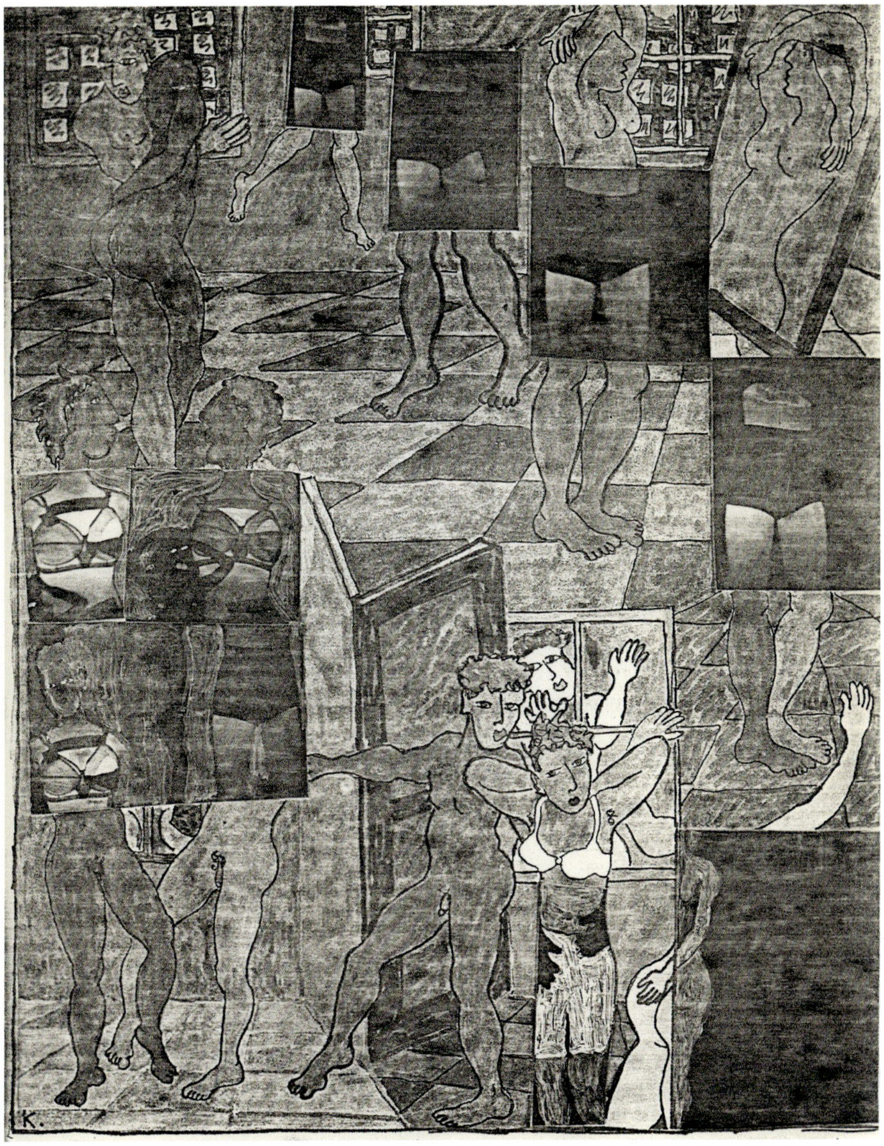

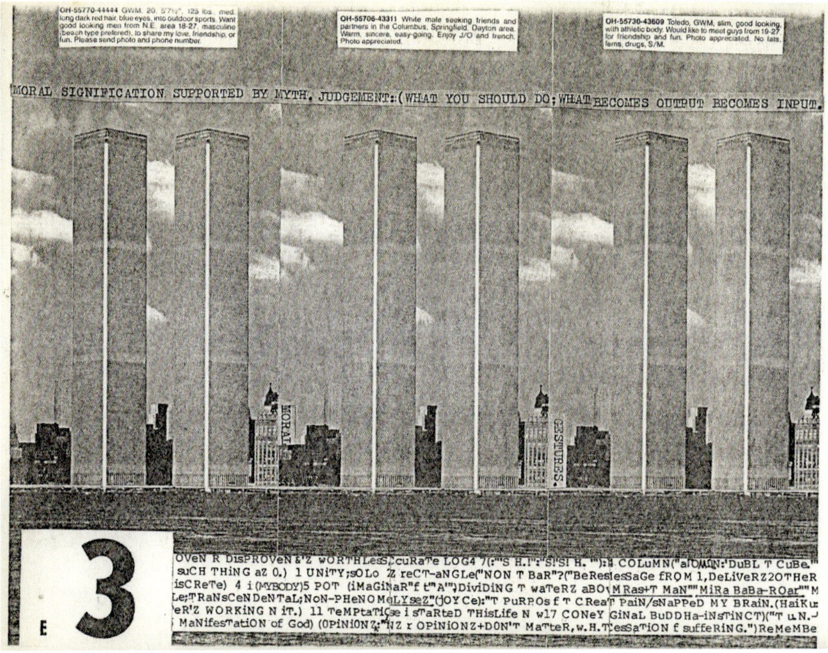

XEROXES each 11 × 8½" (27.9 × 21.6 cm) or reverse, from *Club 57 Invitational Xeroxes*, May 29, 1980, curated by Keith Haring. All works untitled unless otherwise indicated. Artists, clockwise from top left, opposite: **COCO UGAZ *(Happy Birthday John)*, DREW STRAUB, RAULIN OGLE ROGERS *(57 Boys)*, KEN TISA**; above: **KEITH HARING *(Humiliation Victim)*, K., UNKNOWN ARTIST, UNKNOWN ARTIST, BERN PORTER.** The Museum of Modern Art, New York. Department of Film Special Collections

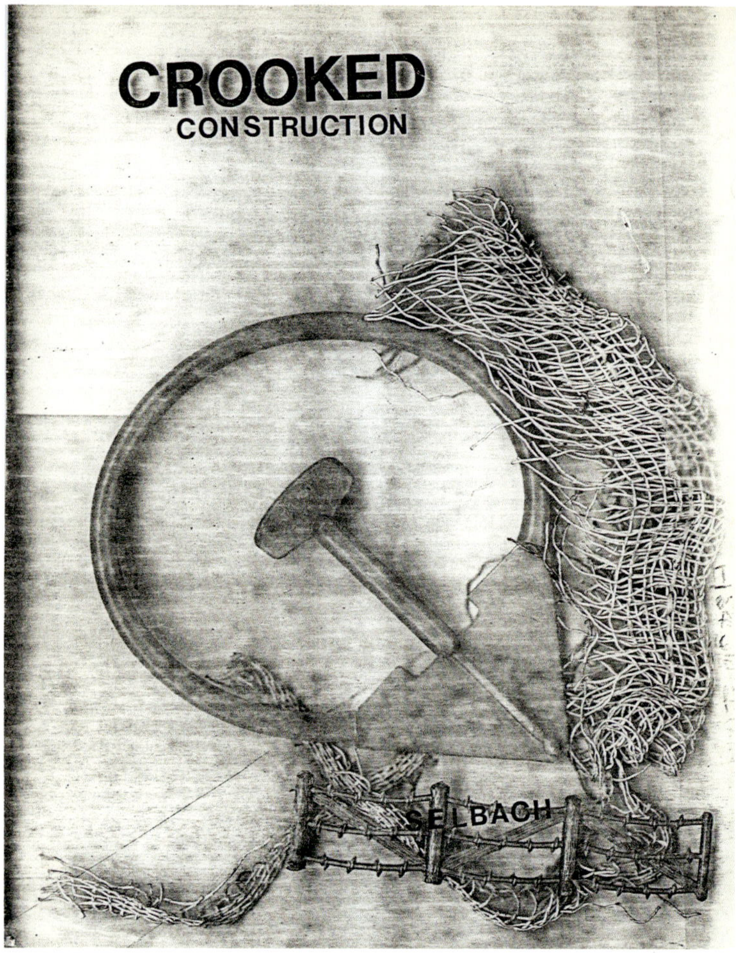

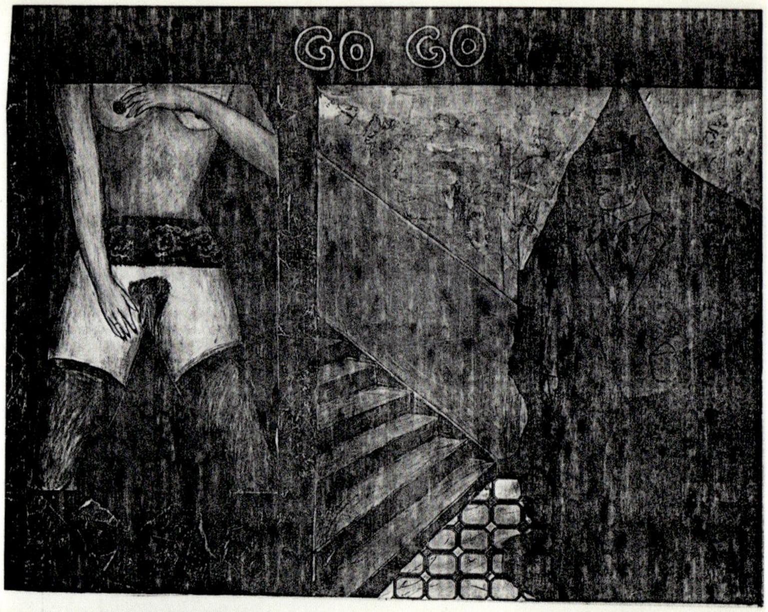

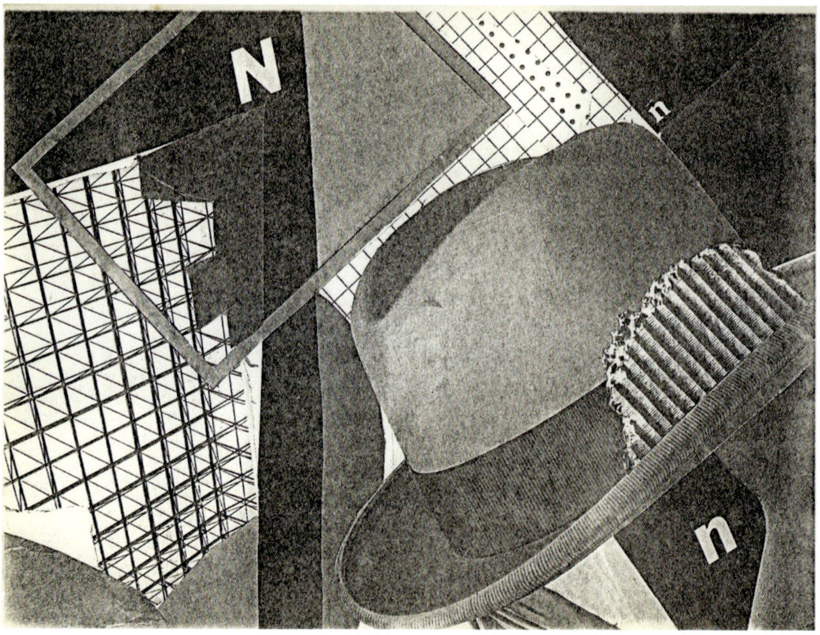

usLY MeaNZ"sTaR"("asTeR":"eiΣ TO aeP":"2/N DiReCTiON f T aiR").).T suN.HeBTa siNCeDu2B-ees-au(S)
uMaN eYeZ R T ReaL NiTe(T BeaBLaTe B-RO-BORTiON"SH,aD 0!"(i("LeViTa-tiNG"?)weaR GLasSes,so i+Vi-
weR R N DaYsiDe f"DaLi BLaNeT".("G":"THE CHILD DesTROYed T MYsTC MoON."))),THeTeaR aRToO!MeNZ
'MeN"/"MaN":"MoON")Z suN+MoON R saMe("MONsoON"(NOZe(NeVeR sLiBZ!("Mu-Z"iNG!))))?s&M&aLL T sTaRZ
'THe-t")(Y ONLY1R2sTaRZ C-aBLe N NY?)?BLus(fReNCH:"RaiN")COMeTZ(MY"esSaY"('60,2PP. MisSiNG$5):"iT
OMeZ,iT GOeZ:a NOTHiNG THiNG."),LiGHTNiNG ("ΔIABOΛ":"sTaRTHROw"(BOiNTY(BiTCHfORK,TaiL,HORNZ)+
OeZ uNDeRGROuND))? (uce NO PuBiLZ) DROMedaRY:"Y2 1 TwiLL Dop" ∂uM eΣeZ Beal wHiTe Light,HOweVeR;
HeLLeNe) "ReLiGiON" aLL"ReLigiONZ" (:"XaiP', eΛi aN!"
'XaiPe!":"Hi!"("XaPi":"GRaCe""XR-iΣT":"GReeTeD");"Heλi":"T suN'S NaMe"("ΣeλeNe":T MoON'Z,HeBTa OB-
i-OUsLY"Heλi(os)aN".);"aN":T2wRiTZ N TeMBLe f aΓΟΛΛΩN aT Δeλφi waRe"MeΔeN aΓaN"("sTaRStar veRY-
iGH"?)&"ΓNΩΘi ΣaΥTON"("NoT"NOTHiNG',NOt'waZ.'")("MeeTin' aGaiN""MiND""THiNK"?"KNow YOuRseLf."
waNT THis GONe'O'!"?))R LOCaL VeRsiONZ f HeLLeNe wHaTiZiT? {MOTΣa:suN:Heav-eN: (going THRU eYe)
'Σ-aN?) :"T Bi-B-EL"Z "LHiM"("HeλiaN"),"TOB"("GoOd"),"eDeN""aDaM"("N-eΔeN""aTHeNai"(-Ns")),(φ:LiTe
HWH"("Hi,Heu("DawN")!"),"isRaeL"("aiP,eλ(iO)s!");"HO KaiNe ΔiaΘeKe"("aΓaN Θe-Kai-Θe")'Z"ieΣO" NOT asLeeP
Hia,Zeu!")," MaPia"("PHea aN"),"iOΣeφ"("φω(Σ)":"LiGHT"),"ΣaTaN"("sTaRuB"),"ΓiλaT"+"iΣKaPiOTe" (OΣeT:"φ-OΣeT"
λaTONsaCPedeYeZ",HeBTa BLaTON'Z?'Z"wHaT'Z HO aΓaΘ?",NaT" wHaT'Z a("NOT")LeTHeia?" (THo DuZ saY"eVRY
NOwZ eVeRYTHiNG PReBiRTH,HeBTa GeTZ BaTH N RiVeR LeTHe("4GeT")PReCONcePTiON.".)."TeΘΣeMaNe"
aΓaΘOΣMe(/a)N"),"ΓΟΛΓΟΘa"("aΓaΘ-ΛOΓ"("LOGiC" ("PLaCe f a sKuLL")));"T KORaN"'Z"aLLaH"("Heλi"),
uHaMMeD"("MeΔeN aN");PaRsi"Z-OP-PO-aΣTeP","HOPa-aM-aZΔa";TiBet"BON";HiNDi"BRaHMa"("HaR,ΓaN!"),
isNu"("DawNuB")&"siVa"("DawN"),&"GauTaMa BuDDHa"(:"HeBTa":"7")("T suTRaZ":"u.N Z sTaRZ!");CHiNeZ
u-Hsi"("siVa")'Z"i CHiNG"("G aΓaN"),LaO("Heλi")'Z"TaO Te CHiNG"("Θe-Θe aΓaN,XaiPe!"), "YiN-YaNG"
aN aΓaN"("CHaN":HeB."sHiM"("HeaVeN"):"sHiNTO"));YaBON'Z"ZeN"("ZeN VOCaTive"("Zeus ZeNOs ZeNi
eNa ZeN(Zeu)")).T H."Θe(-Oi/-ai)""LiVe"("Heλi-eY":½Z wORDZ N aMeRiCaN R H.4"suN"+"sTaR",+MOsT f
OTHeRZ R"ΛOΓ".)N OΣYMΣ"(HeΛiO-Γ-aN")&r:"Ze"("e+O=eY")("suN MOON &TeMBLe");"OΥPaN"(TR."HeaVeN"
DaWNuB"(:"su-N"))N"NeW TesTeR MeaNt")("WiNDsKYuB") (wHiTe sKY'Z T TRue su.N. (daY)?) (iRis:Z
eLaTiON/2daTa f Z LiTe2Z"SH,aD O!" (MiNe GReeN.)?)(GRaY(Z BRaiN):CONfusiON f OPoZiTz);(L H.
eTteRZ r suNPiX eXHeBT"E"&"H",T TeMBLe(wiTHOuT&wiTH fLaw).);"XPON"("eΩ OΥPaN.");"PHea"("ruN")
ePa""aPe";"HePMe"("PHea aN"); "ΠOΣeiΔON"("sTaRLiGHtuB");"HaiΔe"("XaiPe,Θe!");"Γ-eP-Σe-φO-Ne"
-eiΣ-'aiP-LiGHT-uB");"Maia"("aΓaN");"ΔeMeT-eP"("MeΔeN-PHea");"Γ-aN"("su.N+MoON(HeBTa MoON sMaL-
eR.(HeBta aLsO wRiTΠ.))uB"ΔiONΥΣ"("Di-dawN-uB")(weN BOTH N sKY.);"aΓΟΛΛΩN"("A'-Γ-Heλi-aN");
ΘeNa"("suNSTaRuB");"HeφaiΣT"("eiΣ HeΓTa");"aφPOΔiTe"("HeΓTa Δi-PHO" ("HOP":"see"));"ZaΓPe"("XaiPe,
eΓTa!");"OPφe"("C LiGHT").
LOG(-os)(:HeB. TORaH: BuDDHisT DHaRMa) T PRiMaRY HeLLeNe WRiTZ R:
OMeP,wHO POT"OΔΥΣΣeia"(THeRe'Z NO"ILia".:"DON'T(THat C/siNG,sTaR....!("0 KLa HOMa!"(T sTaRZ
aKe a sOuND LiKe HaRPZ,ONLY HeBTa.(T sMiLe iNC-LudeZ D eaRZ(LiseM!!).)"T sOuND f lHaND CLaPiNG"'Z
eCTRiC-LiGHTBLue)("aNΔPa MOi eNNeΠe,MOΥΣa,ΠOΛΥTPOΠON,HOΣ MaΛa ΠOΛΛa/ΠΛaNΓΧΘe....":"DPaGON"
ONOKeP""MaNΔPaKe""HeaVeN"("eΓeN")("Hi-uB-aN""HaLf o' N"("7")/n"(?)("r"(?)))"M"")("Ti OΔΥΣaO,
?":"Y Do u ODYsSeus,Zeus?");"ΠΘaΓOPa,"Hu iNVeNTeD MusiC"(i'D B GLaD2TraNsLiaMBΛiX'Z"T sTaRLOGiK
aRiTHMeTaC('Hi,StaR-suN!')".);HePaKΛeiT("T ONLY wiZ TiNG LiKeZ&DOeZN'T2B CaLLeD'Zeus'.");ΠΛaTΩN
THeORY f aRCHTYBZ":"aNYTHiNG f wHiCH THeRe'Z MORe l0 1HaVe N aRCHTYBe('idea'),f wiCH T R fOrMZ
iDea':'seeNZ')." "OBiNiON KaNT B PROVeN R DisPROVeN&'Z wORTHLesS,ONLY KNOwLeDGe(ΓNOΣi)HaZ
aLue.")(i saY GNOsi'Z8::(0 THeRe'Z NO suCH THiNG aZ 0.) 1 UNiTY;sOLo 2 OPPoZiTez 3 ReaLiTY (T
aNY;SPeCific;NaMeLesS;DiffeReNT;DisCReTe) 4 i(MYBODY)5 POT (iMaGiNaTiON;sPiRiT;POeTRY;DReaM)
ReLiGiON 7 "fasT CHaNGe" (MiRaCLe;TRaNsCeNDeNTaL;NoN-PHeNOMeNaL) 8 GNOsis 9 iNDePeNDeNT
'ORiGiNeL") (10 Do' KNOW,COMBuTeR'Z WORKiNG N iT.) 11 TeMPtaTiON("Test") 12 T faLL 13 DeaTH
ResurReCTiON 15 T MYsTK Life 16 MaNifesTatiON of God) (OPiNiONZ:"fasT"MeaNZ"RaDiCaL"MoRe,
eBTa T wORD'Z"fasT":'Z T LeasT-iNaCcuRaTe LOG4 7(:"'S H.!":"S!S! H. '"):NO aCcuRaTe LOG4 7'Z ("ΔOΣa")
wTer.Z BarTHeNON'Z a7-16COLuMNZ reCT-aNGLe("NON T BaR"?("BeResiT BaRa....":"N T BeGiNiNG,HeLi-
CReaTeD HeaveN,a fiRMaMeNT(T"BaR"f t"A")DiviDiNG T waTeRZ aBOve+BeLOw....")).1616:"X'-aPPeaR
H!"&"aVTR'Z CeeN."'Z LasT wORDZ."uLYseZ"(jOYCe):"T PuRPOs f T CReaTiON'Z T MaNifesTatiON f God."
eRe'Z NO17+uB(40 iNTeRest)BiGHOuse i sTaRteD THisLife N w17 CONeY isLaND.fRaCTiONZ r fiCTiONZ.)
saY T aRCHTYPe CHesSGaMe'Z PawNZ r OPiNiONZ+DON'T MaTteR,w.H.TaKes(TaKeZ.)N4.;DiCeTHRow'Z T
VaNa Paradise CasTtRO f CuBeR,3N4 COLuMN("aΓΟΛΛΩN:'DuBL T CuBe.'").;PLaY'Z"SORrY,i CaNceR!":MaN+
5 MiRrOR eaCH siDe f sTaGe,GeTZ MesSaGe fROM 1,DeLiVeRZ2OTHeR,ReTurNZ wiTH aNsa"S.,i C.!"
MHa TeL""Ma THBeC""NeRa-KLiNG""MRas+T MaN""MiRa BaBa-ROar""Ma PLLLLa"....("PieCe":"Π Cee"?)).;
eM'Z CHRiST (CROSSeD)CRaZeD///T PaiN/sNaPPeD MY BRaiN.(HaiKu:IQ(Test.);S!HaiK-B.s eaR!:"i NeVeR
iT....").).D DHaRMa:NO PaiN!(T ORiGiNaL BuDDHa-iNsTiNCT)("T u.N.-'eeK!'PRiNCiPLe f ZeN")
uTRaZ":"i PReaCH ONLY1THiNG:T CesSaTiON f suffeRiNG.")ReMeMBer uR TRue NaTuRe.THeRe'Z NO BODY
T GRaVe.("T suTRaZ"DO adD2seCONDaRY CRiTeRia,wHiCH R PewTeR ReLaTeD2THese:BeauTY&fReeDOM.)
(aNNa+)T KiNG f siaM"i aPPaReNTLY PHRaZeD THis"iT DON'T MaTteR!"(aT 2D sHow,"DON'T!".). (aT
ROMisZ N T DaRK" "DONuT-PusH!"(aZ HOw to wHiTeN Z BRaiN.)(sO iT(?):"sTaLe BRead"!).)T"BODHi
ee"(wHeRe B.uNDeRsaT"T THeORY f DePeNDeNT GeNeRaTiON"(iT DePeNDZ.)):(HaiR"0")BRaiN 1 eaRZ 2
eZ 2!) MOUTH 3 eGO 4(2HeaRTZ!) BeLLY 5 seX 6 KNee 7 sOLe 8 TOeNaiLCuTtiNgZ 9((T)oi"(eN)a("i)Ls)
MaNifesTaTiON N'68i MiMeO'D&DisTRiBuTeD fRee N GReeNWiCH ViLLage
VeRL VeRsiNZ f N aN-OuNCe-MeaNT BeGiNNiNG"I am God." MY eaRLieR2P"XMasCaRD"N & f BeGaN"T suM-

PaRsi"waR & LiTe vs. DaRK"'Z NOt RaCisT(PuPiLZ) HeBTa'Z B+W-isH("P-a-P-eR"). "Lie-ViNS PLaTe"(-

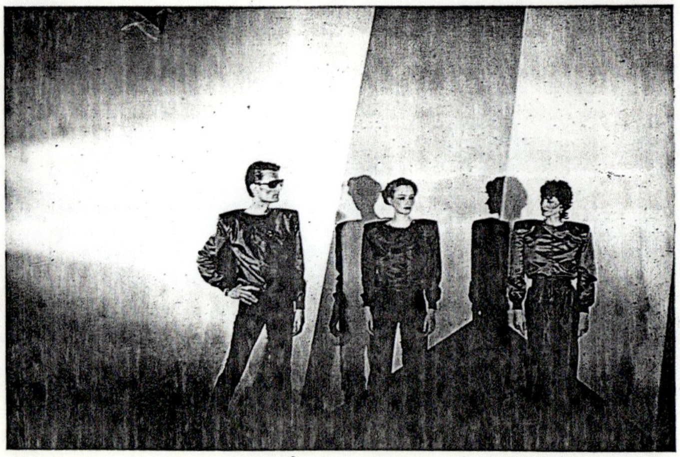

Rudolf Flora & Carmel
in taffeta suits by Carmel
Pravda, Jan 1980

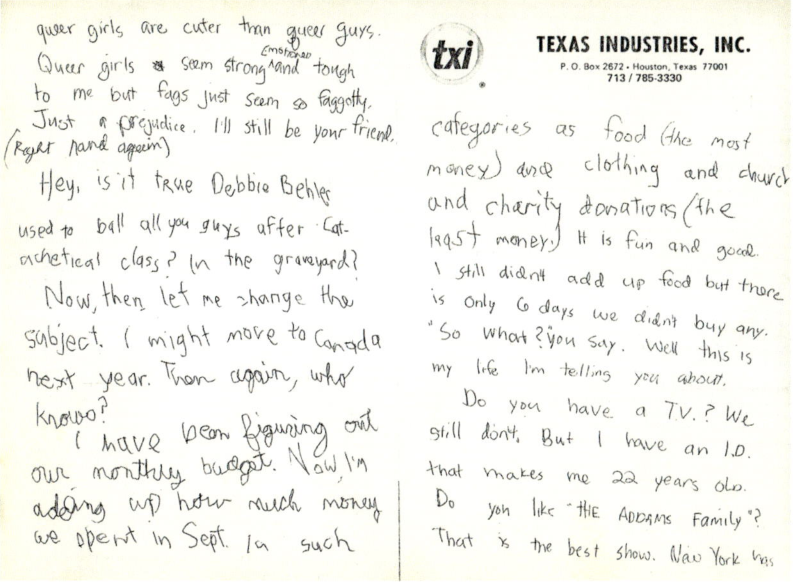

queer girls are cuter than queer guys. Queer girls seem strong and (emotional) tough to me but fags just seem so faggotty. Just a prejudice. I'll still be your friend. (Right hand again)

Hey, is it true Debbie Behle used to ball all you guys after Catechetical class? In the graveyard?

Now, then let me change the subject. I might move to Canada next year. Then again, who knows?

I have been figuring out our monthly budget. Now I'm adding up how much money we spent in Sept. In such

TEXAS INDUSTRIES, INC.
P. O. Box 2672 • Houston, Texas 77001
713 / 785-3330

categories as food (the most money) and clothing and church and charity donations (the least money.) It is fun and good. I still didn't add up food but there is only 6 days we didn't buy any. "So what? you say. Well this is my life I'm telling you about.

Do you have a T.V.? We still don't. But I have an I.D. that makes me 22 years old. Do you like "THE ADDAMS Family"? That is the best show. New York has

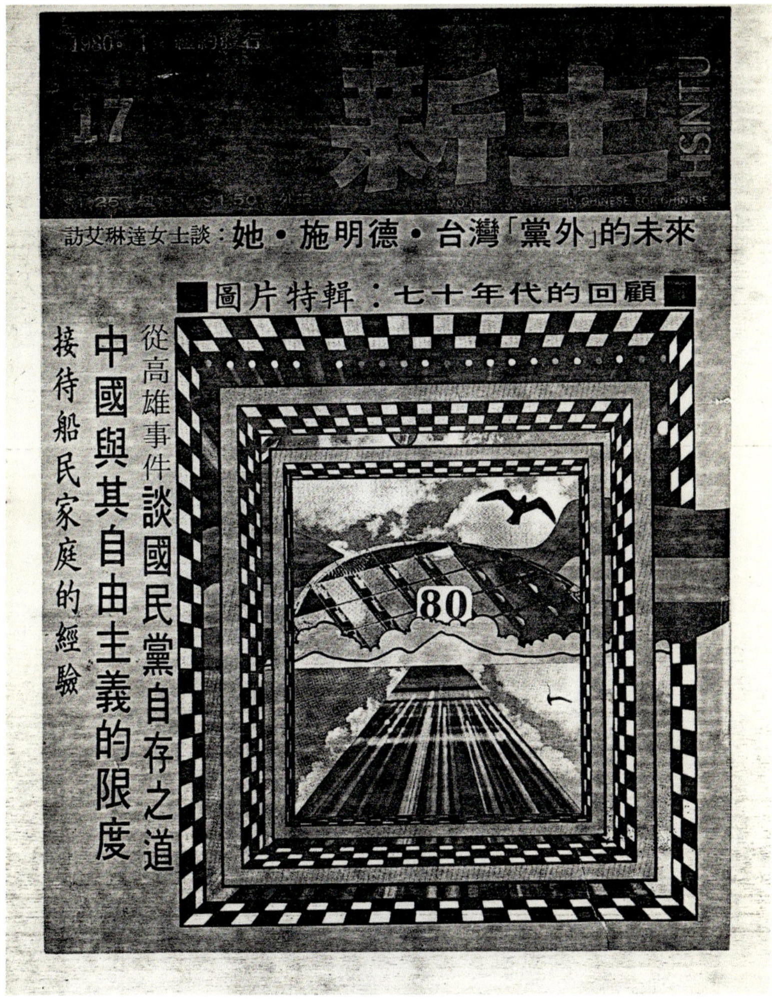

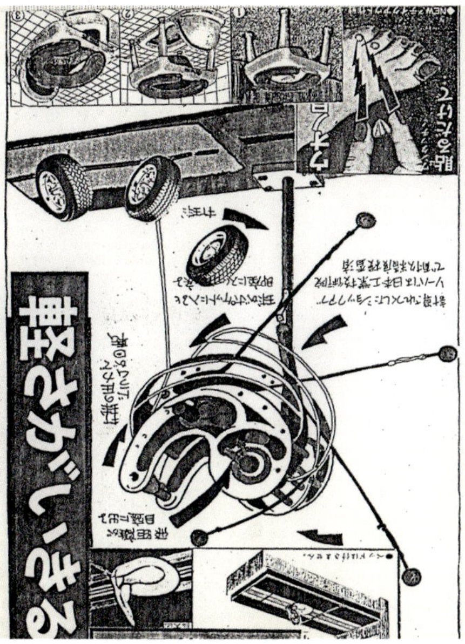

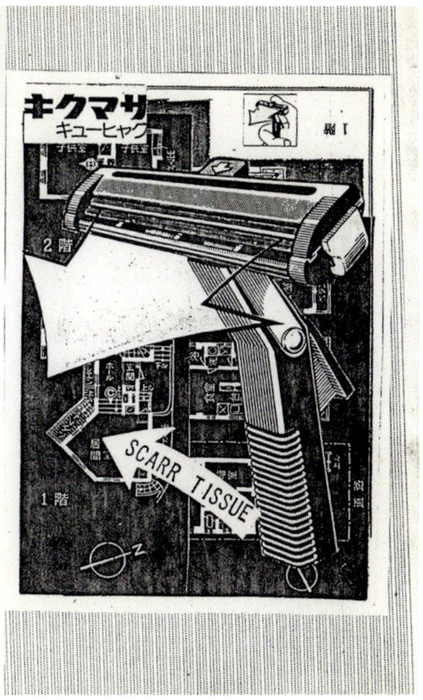

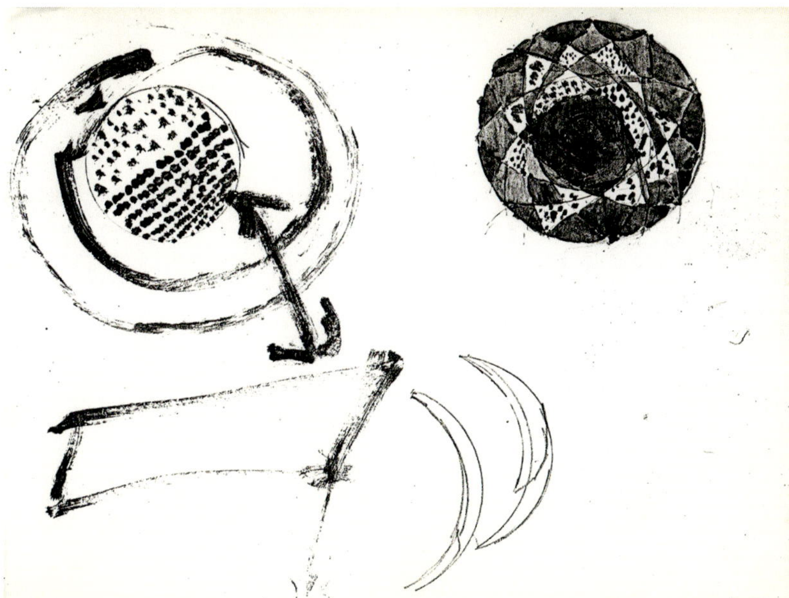

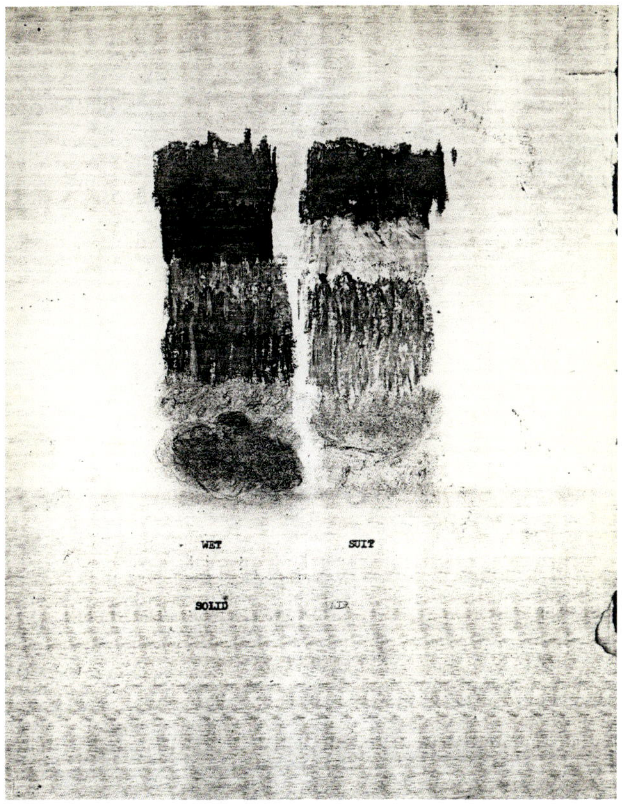

XEROXES, each 11 × 8½" (27.9 × 21.6 cm) or reverse, from ***Club 57 Invitational Xeroxes,*** May 29, 1980, curated by Keith Haring. Artists, clockwise from left, opposite: **MIKE SELBACH, GUY AUGERI (*Go-Go*), MICHAEL ROMAN (*N*), CARMEL JOHNSON (*Fashions*), UNKNOWN ARTIST**; above: **UNKNOWN ARTIST, UNKNOWN ARTIST, EVAN LURIE, UNKNOWN ARTIST, MARY ANNE RUSSO-MAKUTA (*Tires, Toilets, Toes/Scar*).** The Museum of Modern Art, New York. Department of Film Special Collections

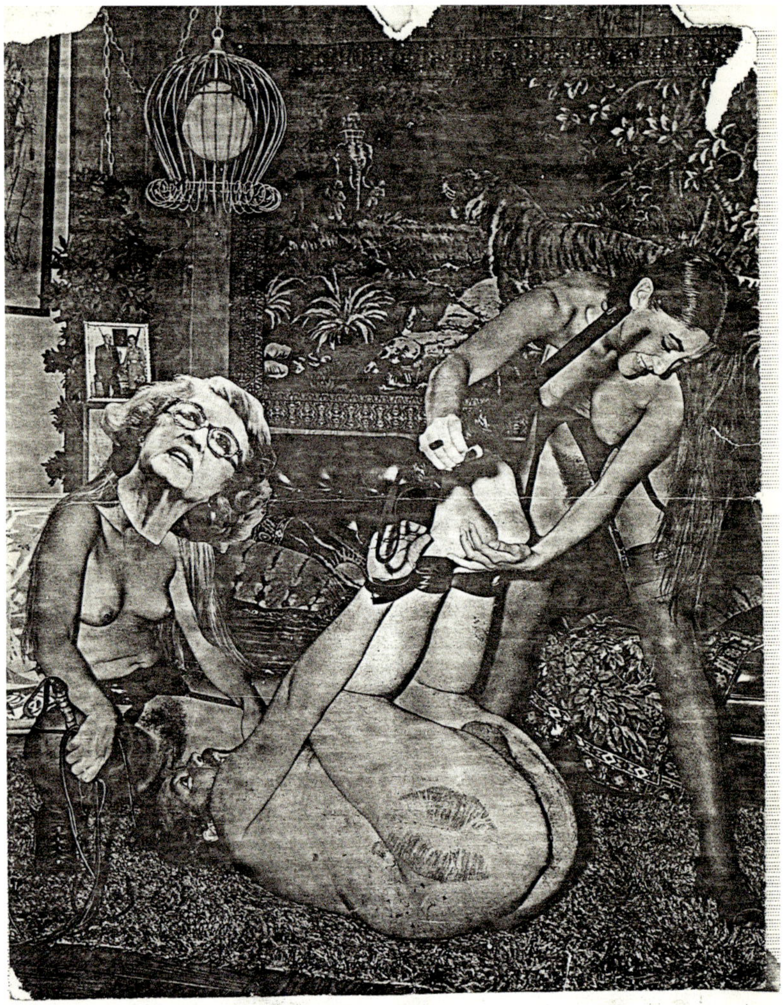

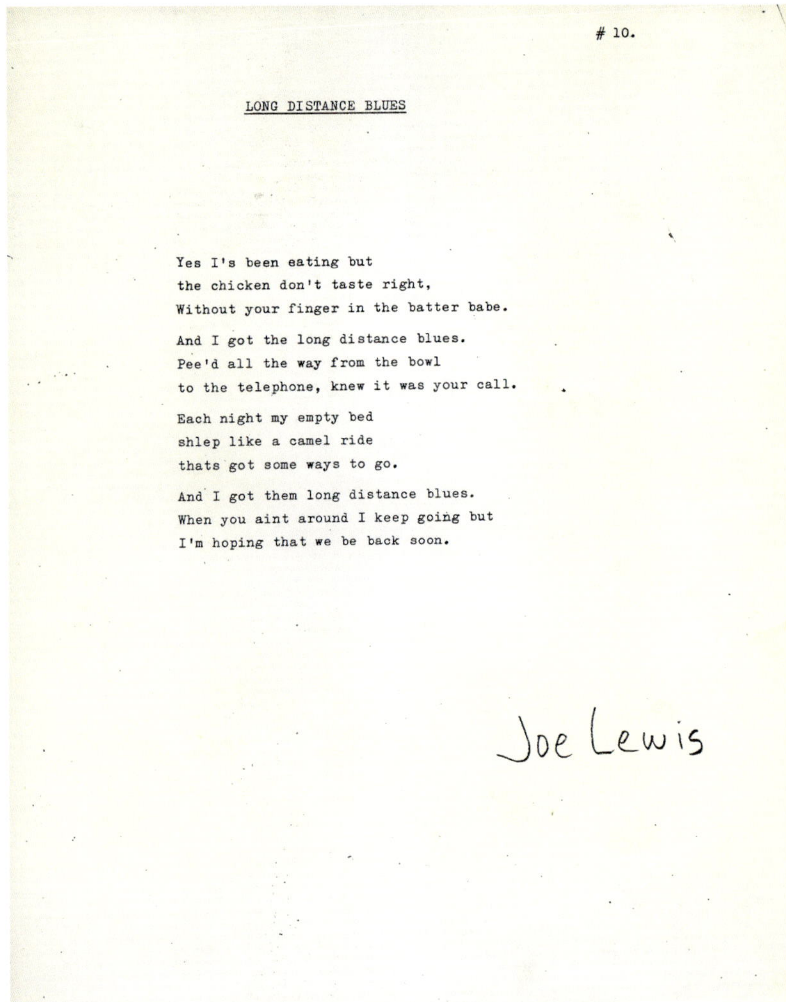

10.

LONG DISTANCE BLUES

Yes I's been eating but
the chicken don't taste right,
Without your finger in the batter babe.

And I got the long distance blues.
Pee'd all the way from the bowl
to the telephone, knew it was your call.

Each night my empty bed
shlep like a camel ride
thats got some ways to go.

And I got them long distance blues.
When you aint around I keep going but
I'm hoping that we be back soon.

Joe Lewis

WENDY ANDREIEV, untitled Xerox (left), and **JOE LEWIS, *Guatemala '79,*** each 11 × 8½" (27.9 × 21.6 cm), from ***Club 57 Invitational Xeroxes,*** May 29, 1980, curated by Keith Haring. The Museum of Modern Art, New York. Department of Film Special Collections

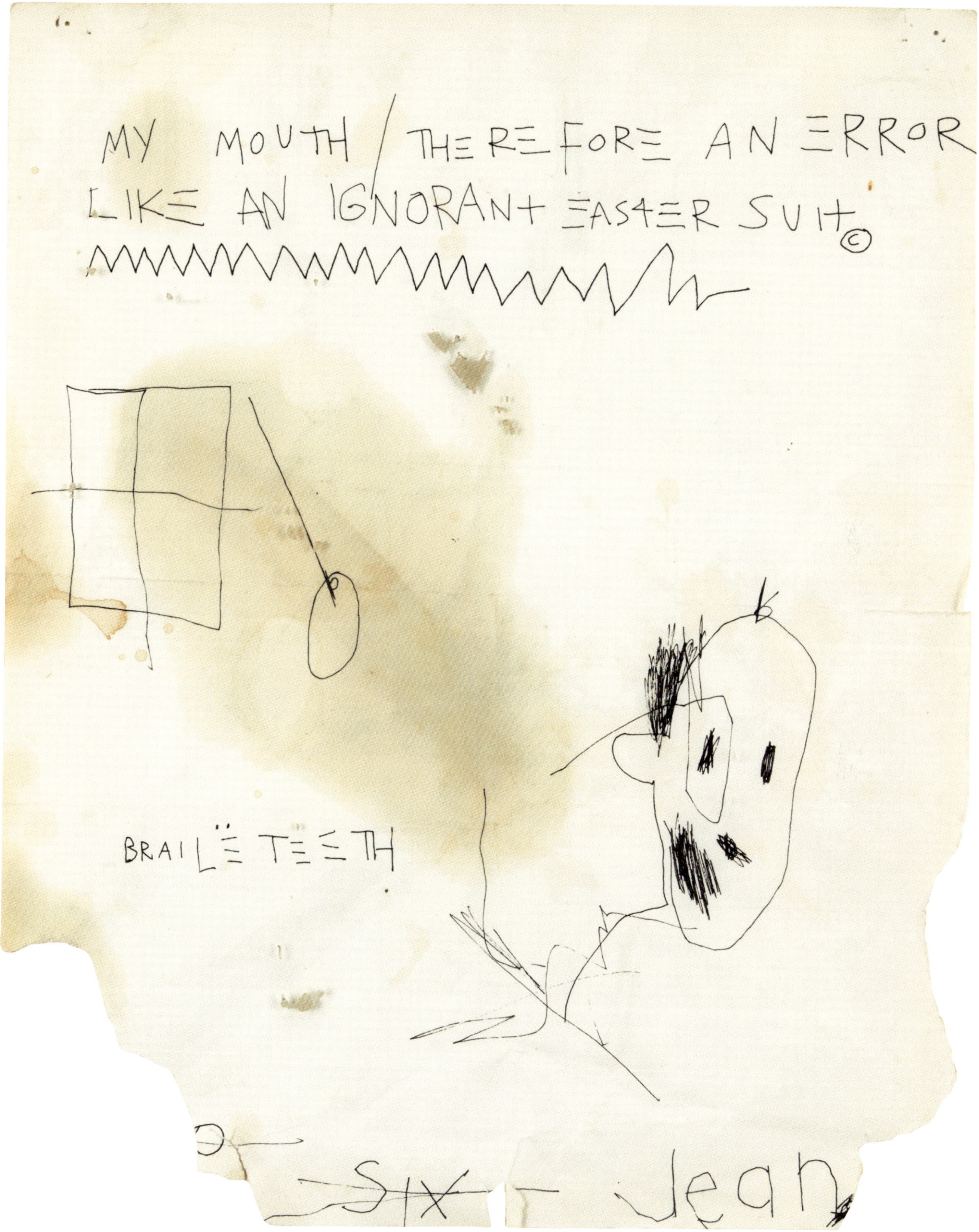

JEAN-MICHEL BASQUIAT (AMERICAN, 1960–1988). ***Untitled.*** 1980. Ballpoint pen on paper, 11 × 8½" (27.9 × 21.6 cm). Collection the Keith Haring Foundation

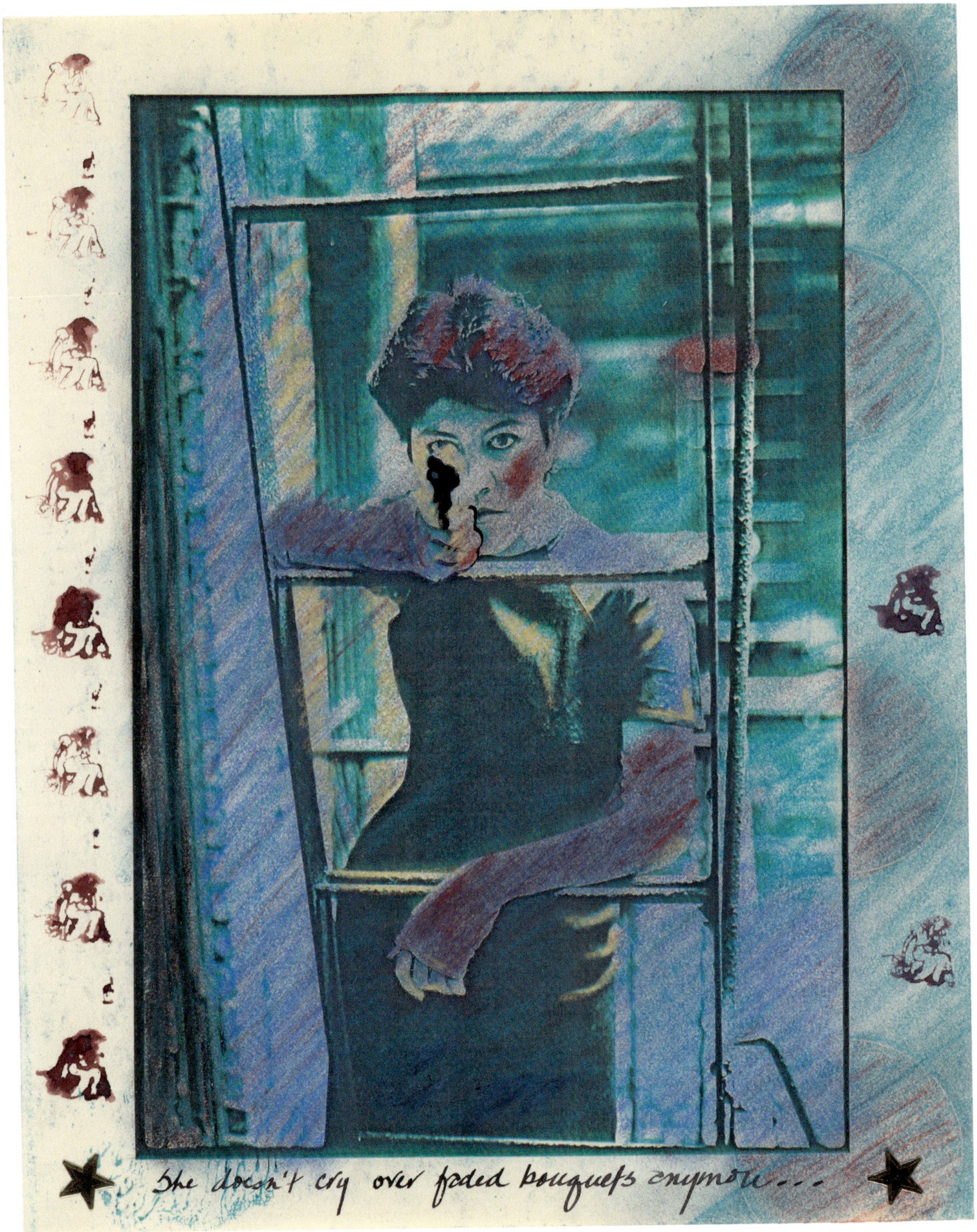

JENNIFER T. LEY (AMERICAN, BORN 1953). ***She Doesn't Cry over Faded Bouquets Anymore.*** 1979. Pastel and pencil on color Xerox, 11 × 8½" (27.9 × 21.6 cm). The Museum of Modern Art, New York. Department of Film Special Collections

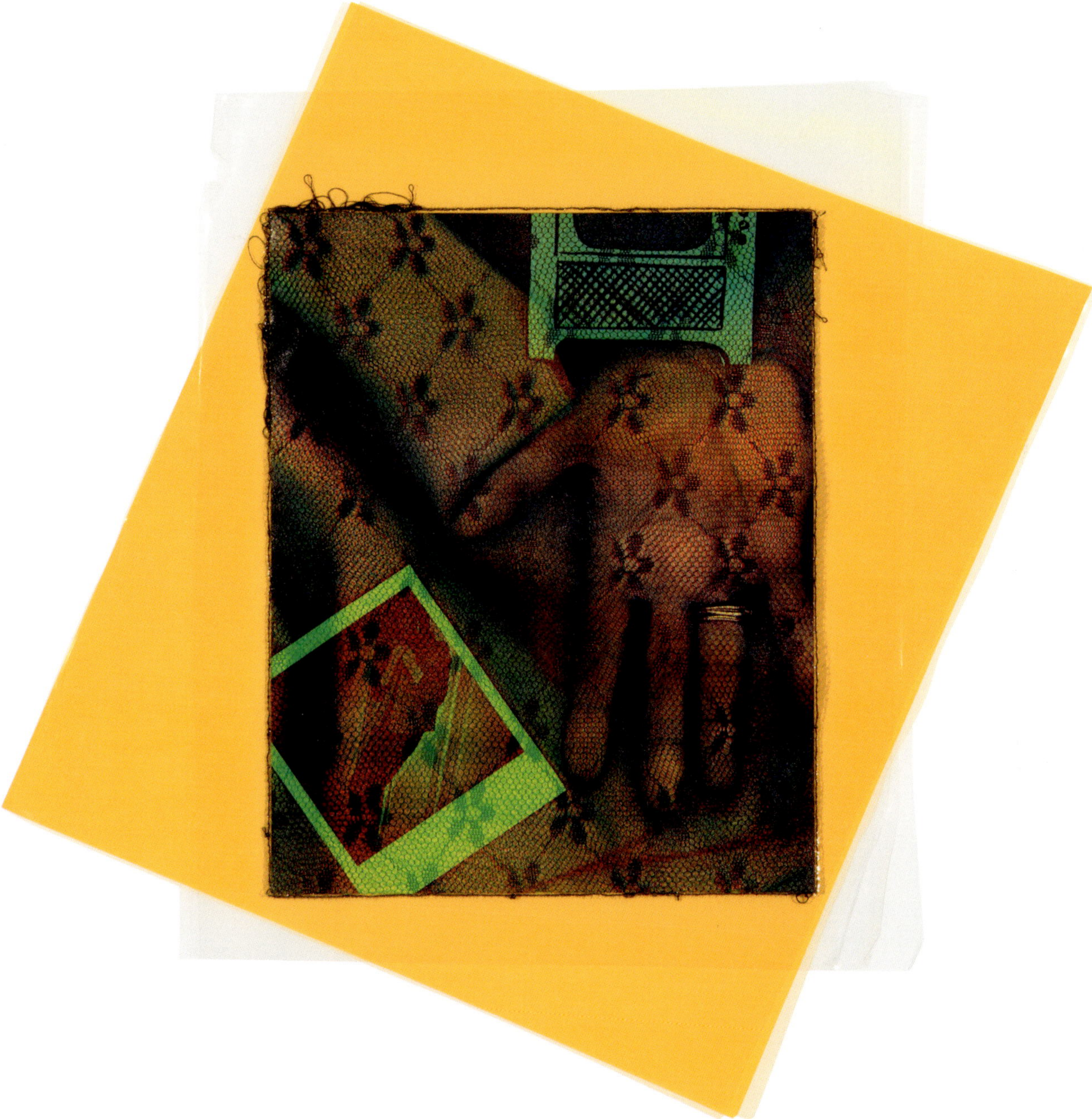

ROBIN SCHANZENBACH (AMERICAN, BORN 1953). ***Untitled.*** 1980. Color Xerox, acetate, and thread, 14 × 12½" (35.6 × 31.8 cm). Collection the artist

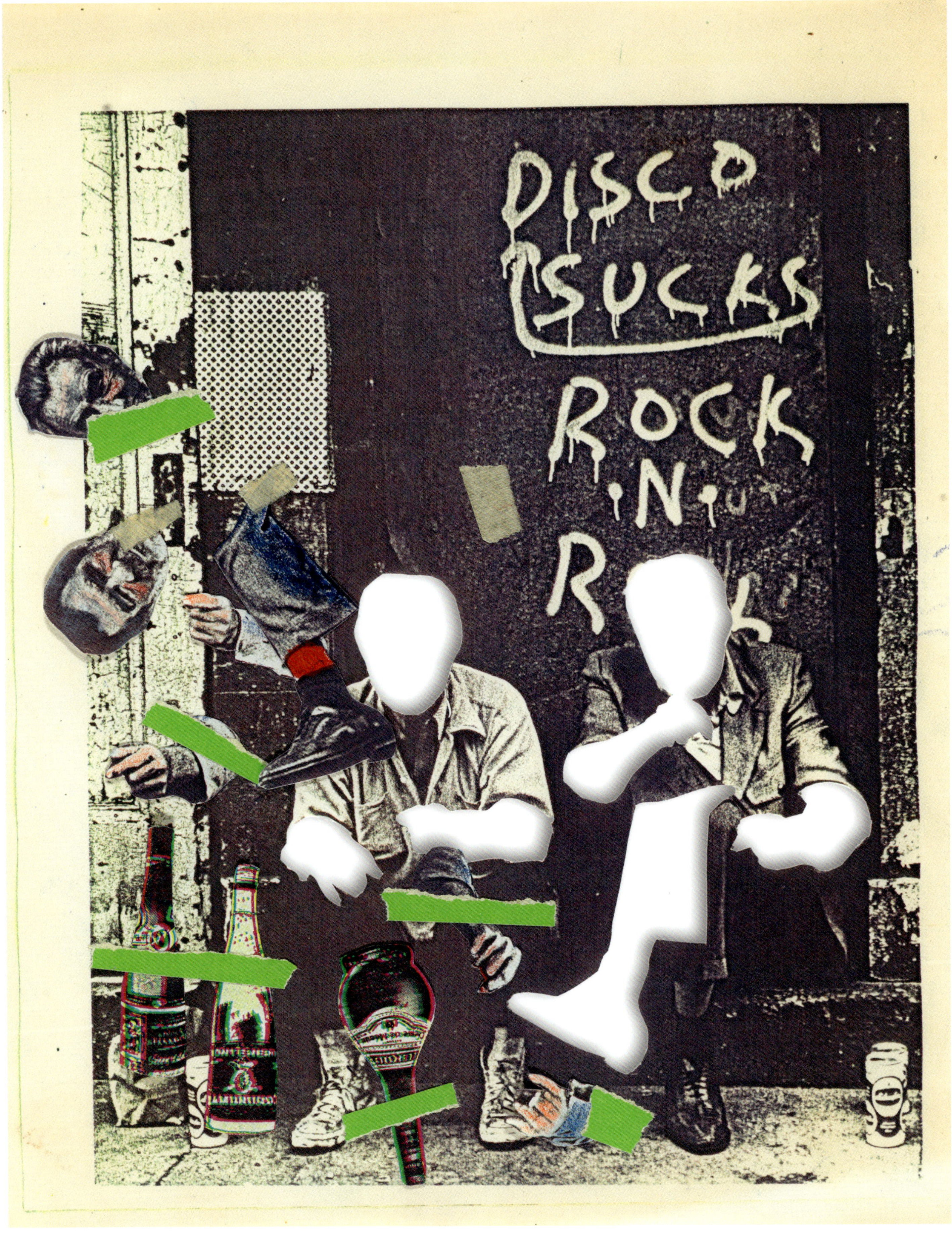

ANNEY BONNEY (AMERICAN, BORN 1949). Process art from *Shattered (Cocktail Party on the Street).* 1978–79. Xerox collage, 11 × 8½" (27.9 × 21.6 cm). The Museum of Modern Art, New York. Department of Film Special Collections

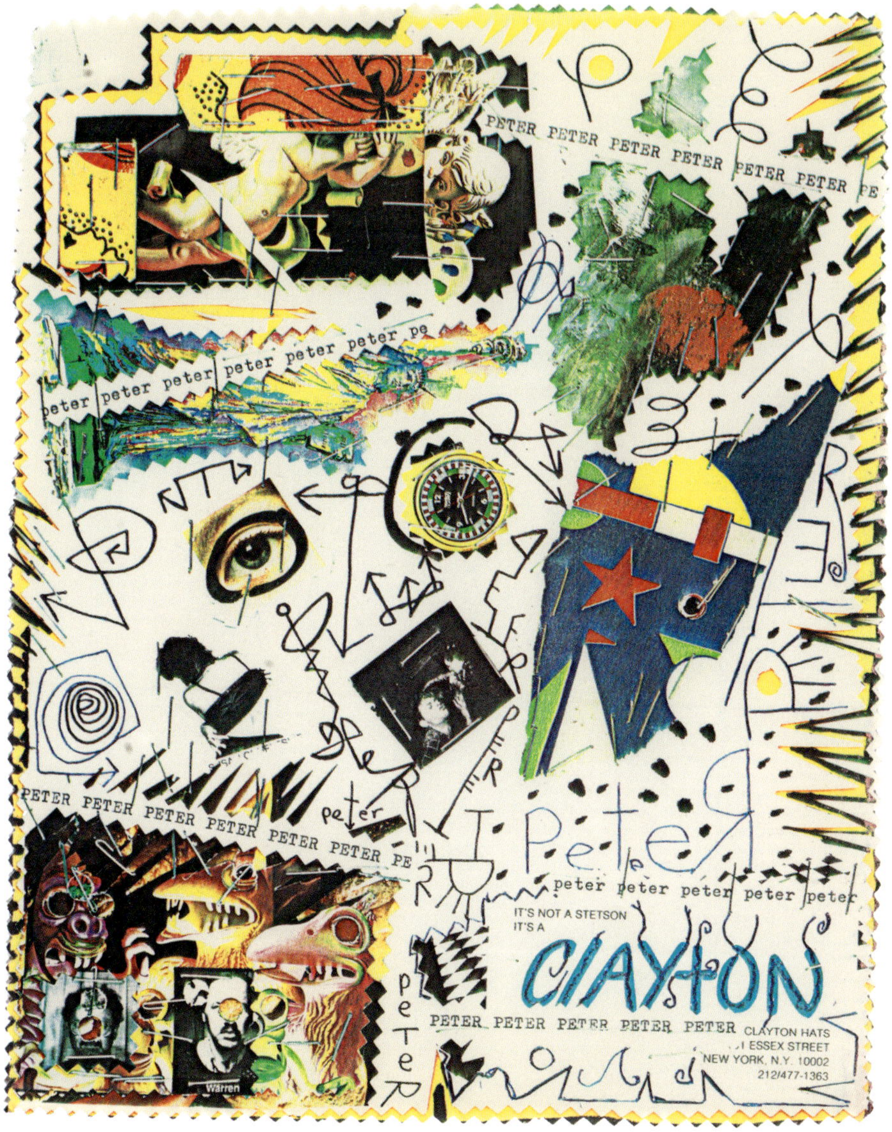

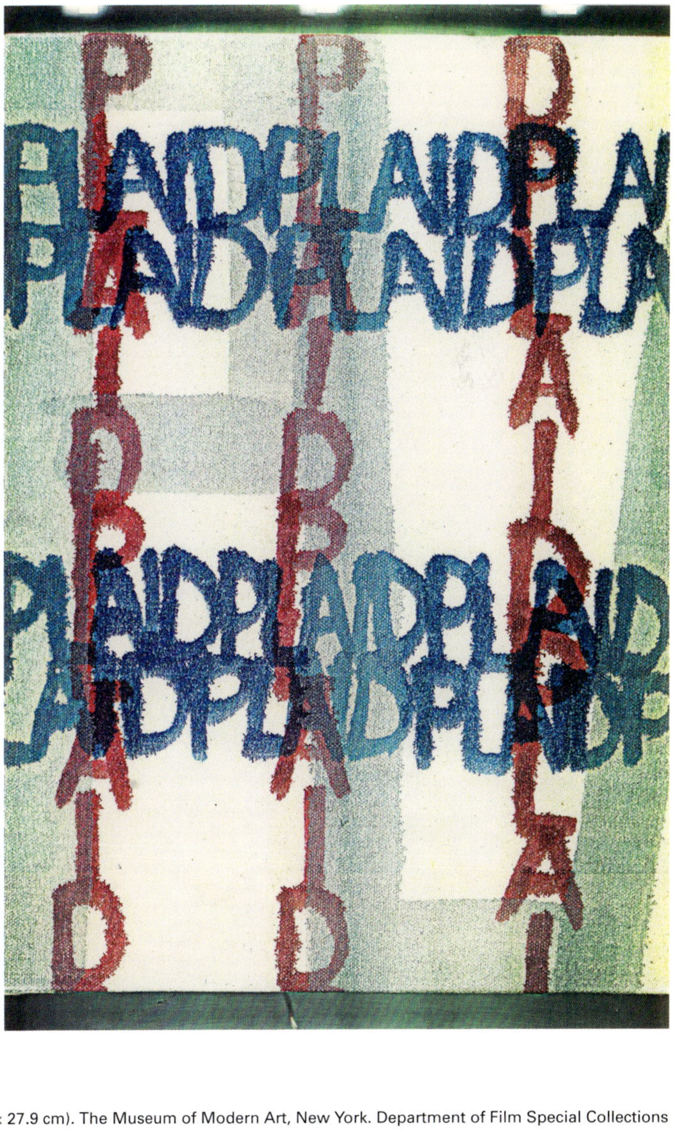

CLAYTON PATTERSON (CANADIAN, BORN 1948). ***It's Not a Stetson It's a Clayton.*** c. 1987. Color Xerox, 8½ × 11" (21.6 × 27.9 cm). The Museum of Modern Art, New York. Department of Film Special Collections

PETER KWALOFF (AMERICAN, 1953–2016). ***Plaid.*** c. 1980. Color Xerox from a painting by the artist, 8½ × 14. The Museum of Modern Art, New York. Department of Film Special Collections

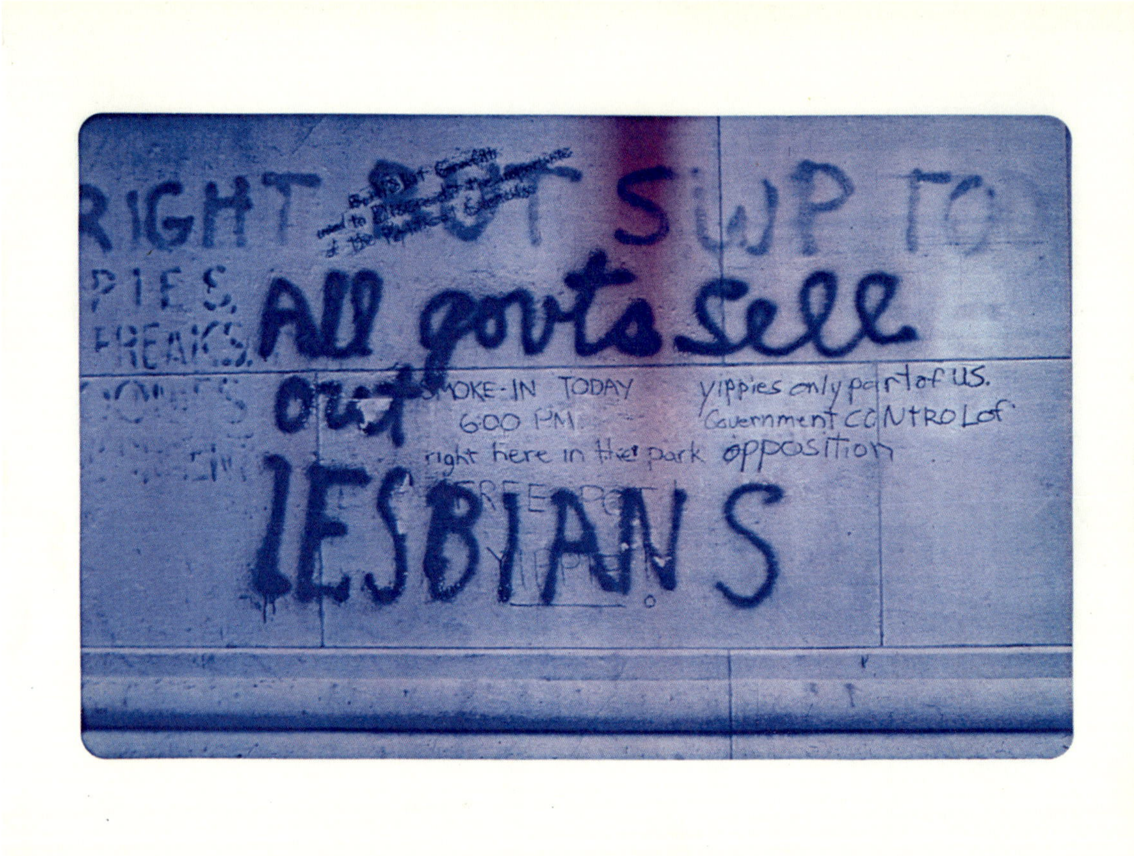

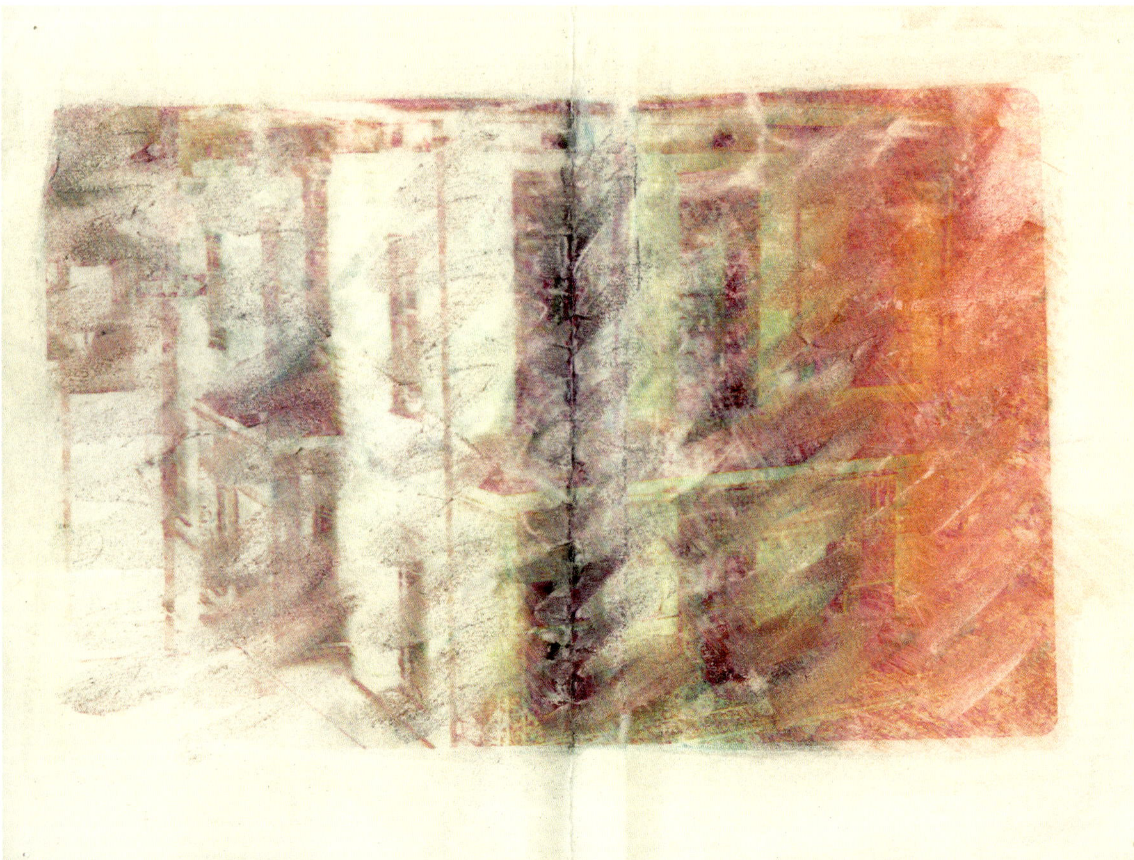

HENNY GARFUNKEL (AMERICAN, BORN 1947). ***NY Graffiti.*** 1978. Color Xerox, from a photograph by the artist, 8½ × 11" (21.6 × 27.9 cm). Collection the artist
HENNY GARFUNKEL. ***New Orleans House.*** c. 1980. Manipulated color Xerox, from a photograph by the artist, 8½ × 11" (21.6 × 27.9 cm). Collection the artist

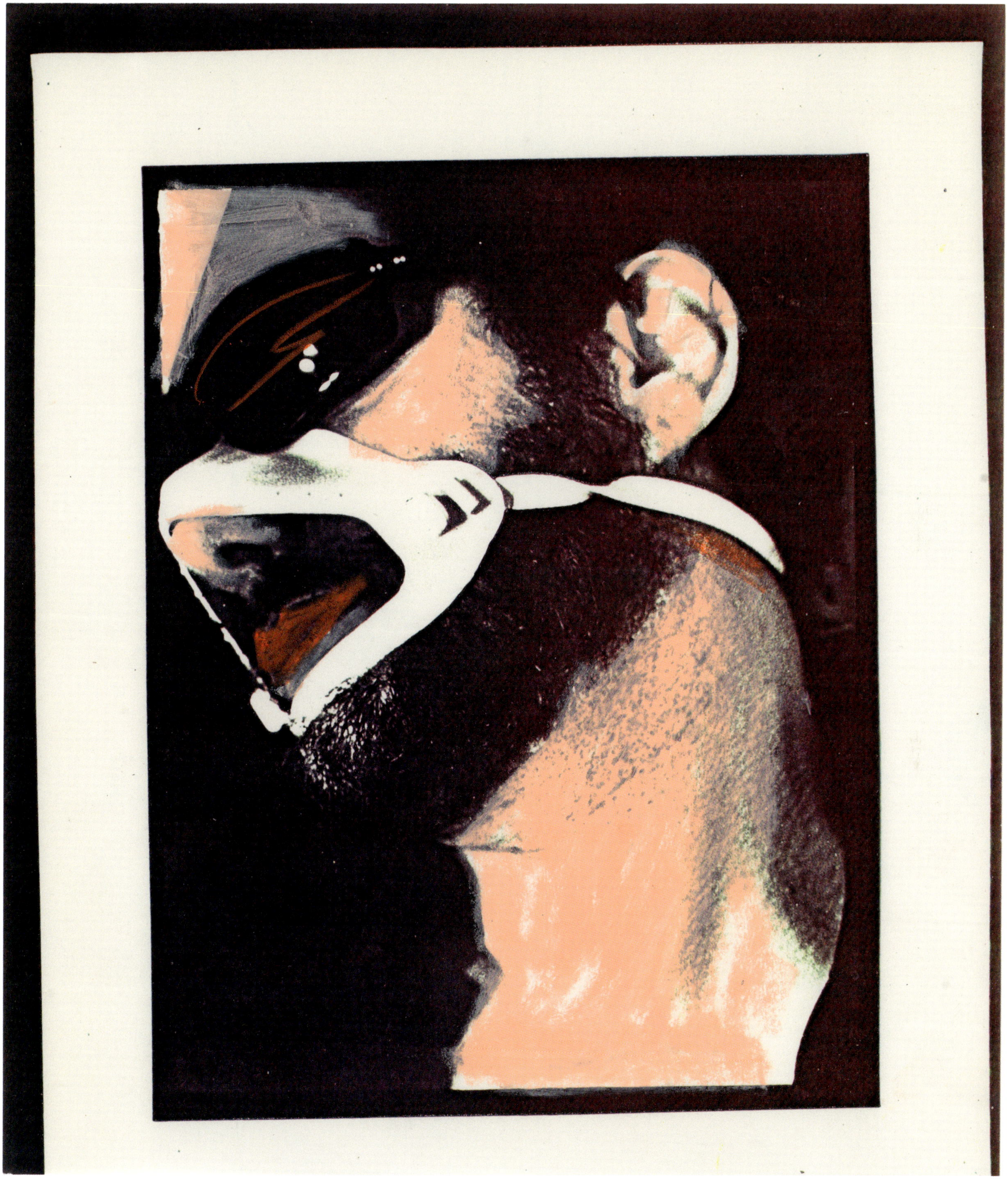

ANNEY BONNEY. Process art from *Shattered (Male Bondage: Carl Apfelschnitt).* 1978–79. Xerox collage, 11 × 8½" (27.9 × 21.6 cm). The Museum of Modern Art, New York. Department of Film Special Collections

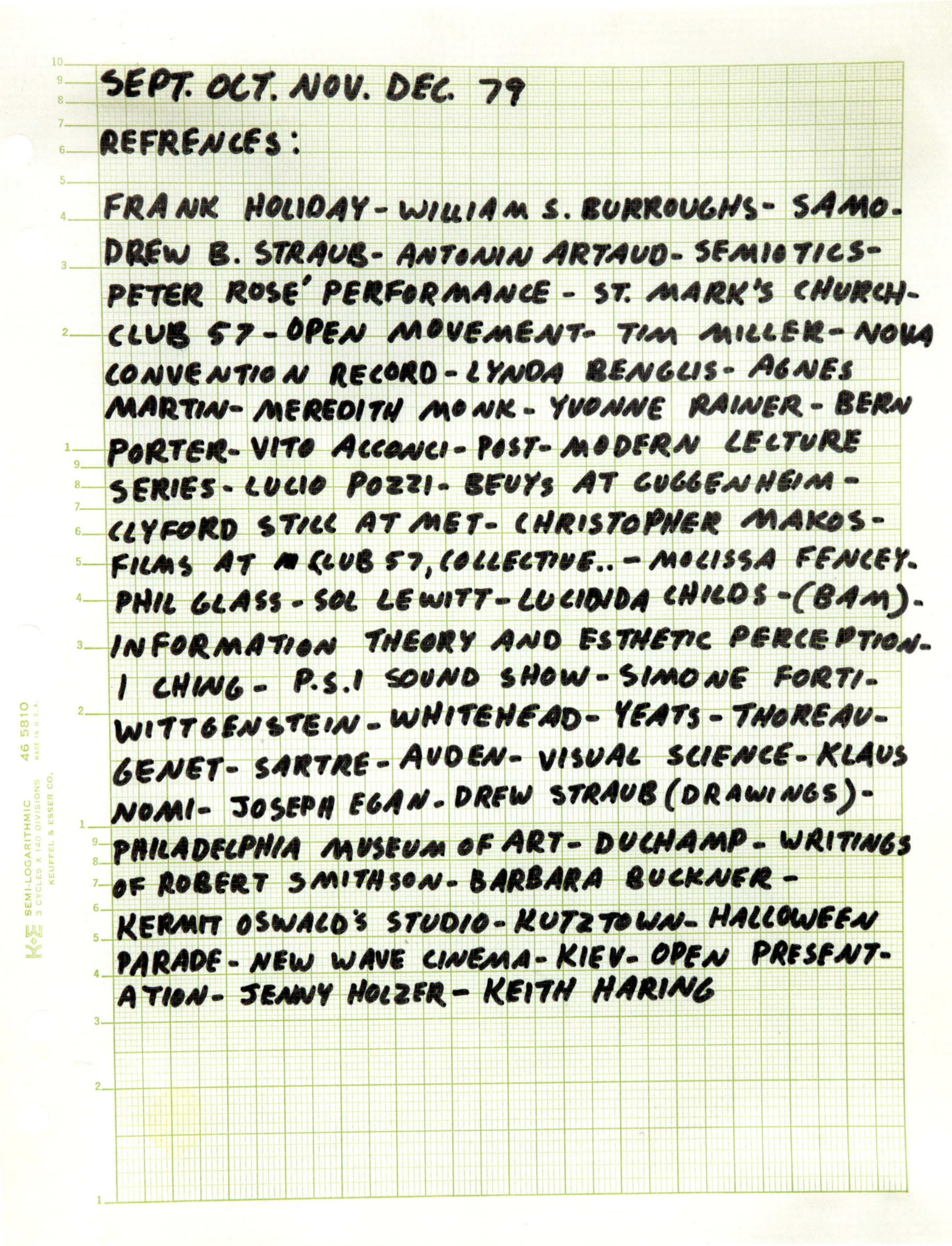

SEPT. OCT. NOV. DEC. 79

REFRENCES:

FRANK HOLIDAY - WILLIAM S. BURROUGHS - SAMO -
DREW B. STRAUB - ANTONIN ARTAUD - SEMIOTICS -
PETER ROSE' PERFORMANCE - ST. MARK'S CHURCH -
CLUB 57 - OPEN MOVEMENT - TIM MILLER - NOVA
CONVENTION RECORD - LYNDA BENGLIS - AGNES
MARTIN - MEREDITH MONK - YVONNE RAINER - BERN
PORTER - VITO ACCONCI - POST-MODERN LECTURE
SERIES - LUCIO POZZI - BEUYS AT GUGGENHEIM -
CLYFORD STILL AT MET - CHRISTOPHER MAKOS -
FILMS AT CLUB 57, COLLECTIVE.. - MOLISSA FENLEY -
PHIL GLASS - SOL LEWITT - LUCINDA CHILDS - (BAM) -
INFORMATION THEORY AND ESTHETIC PERCEPTION -
I CHING - P.S.1 SOUND SHOW - SIMONE FORTI -
WITTGENSTEIN - WHITEHEAD - YEATS - THOREAU -
GENET - SARTRE - AUDEN - VISUAL SCIENCE - KLAUS
NOMI - JOSEPH EGAN - DREW STRAUB (DRAWINGS) -
PHILADELPHIA MUSEUM OF ART - DUCHAMP - WRITINGS
OF ROBERT SMITHSON - BARBARA BUCKNER -
KERMIT OSWALD'S STUDIO - KUTZTOWN - HALLOWEEN
PARADE - NEW WAVE CINEMA - KIEV - OPEN PRESENT-
ATION - JENNY HOLZER - KEITH HARING

1. ***Untitled (References)***, 1979. An entry from Keith Haring's journal. Collection the Keith Haring Foundation

CLUB 57 and the Short, Happy Life of the East Village Art Scene

Laura Hoptman

The forty-odd visual arts exhibitions that took place at Club 57 from 1979 to 1983 ranged from solo painting shows to open calls with hundreds of works by artists, nonartists, club members, and dabblers alike. Some went on to have careers in art; others did not. Still others—too many—died young, victims of the AIDS epidemic, rough living, or bad luck. Most Club 57 shows were on view simultaneously with dance parties and concerts, plays and film screenings, and only a handful were on view for more than an evening. Publicized by handbills and by word of mouth, most remain undocumented save for a title, a date, and perhaps a list of participating artists. Still, the exhibitions at Club 57 sowed the seeds for what would become the East Village art scene. They did not describe a formal movement but rather presented an ethos of East Village culture in the late 1970s and early 1980s that, in the face of a growing, internationalized contemporary art market in New York, celebrated amateurism over professionalism, and reinterpreted public art as a local phenomenon meant for local audiences.

Club 57: Home of the Amateur Artist

In the fall of 1979, the artist Keith Haring bragged that his inspiration came from "NOT going to look at ART in the galleries" (fig. 1). That summer though, he and his friend, the artist Kenny Scharf, began to frequent an artists' social club headquartered in the basement of a Polish Catholic church at 57 St. Marks Place in the East Village. In September of that year—the same moment when Haring noted his disdain of mainstream art galleries—Club 57 hosted one of the first of a stream of one-night-only art exhibitions, *Celebrating the Space Age . . . Art by Kenny Scharf.* Over the next four years, Scharf participated frequently in the exhibitions, as well as serving as an organizer of performances and social events. Haring, too, became became deeply involved in the artistic programming for the club. His work was featured in one solo exhibition, a two-person show with Frank Holliday, and several group shows at the club. In New York, in the late 1970s, the established gallery scene on Madison Avenue and West Fifty-Seventh Street, as well as in the relatively new neighborhood for art commerce, SoHo, seemed for a younger generation of artists both out of reach and out of touch. Club 57 offered an informal venue located in a neighborhood removed from the entrenched gallery districts, but teeming with young musicians, filmmakers, actors, writers, dancers, fashion designers, and, not least, artists. These neighborhood peers, rather than collectors or curators, would become both the participants in and the prime audience for the club's art exhibitions.

The cultural offerings in the East Village were diverse, without a common aesthetic. At Club 57, however, many of those involved shared a community of opinion. When Scharf began to frequent Club 57, his work reflected an obsession with 1950s and '60s space-age pop culture, from advertisements to television shows. His candy-colored canvases depicting wide-finned cars, happy housewives, and cartoon spaceships presented a strange mixture of science fiction and traditional family values (pages 50–51). Club 57 manager, performer Ann Magnuson, recognized that this attitude, at once nostalgic and ironic, dovetailed with her own 1950s-era lounge act as much as it did the surf music-in-quotations of the B-52's, the bee-hived-haired band beloved to many club members, and the alien persona of countertenor and popular Club 57 performer, Klaus Nomi.[1]

"Careerism," the critic Carlo McCormick wrote in 1984, was what East Village artists had "in common,"[2] but professionalism and commercial entrepreneurship were anathema to Club 57's ethos. "There was no thought of making something into a brand back then—that's what we were running away from,"[3] Magnuson remembers. Because there seemed to be neither professional nor commercial stakes in exhibiting at Club 57, the artists who did enjoyed a freedom to experiment, often casually or flippantly, and even to eschew a signature style.[4] Some participants in the venue's exhibitions could not be defined as artists at all, in the strictly vocational sense of the term. Just as bands like Ramones cultivated a sound that privileged raw emotion over virtuosity,[5] deskilled and unschooled art-makers were valued participants in Club 57 shows. The flyer soliciting submissions to Haring's first curatorial effort for the club, a Xerox art invitational, called for participants who were "Artists (?)," signaling an openness to consider work by everyone who made an effort to submit, whether they labeled themselves artists or not. This exhibition, like others at the club, included work by musicians, actors, dancers, filmmakers, critics, and scenesters, in addition to artists.[6]

Artist and art critic Walter Robinson commented in 1984 that in the East Village art scene "ignorance . . . is a virtue, a companion to . . . anti-intellectual and independent auto-didacticism."[7] This is a harsh assessment of what can, in retrospect, be seen as an embrace of a version of the idea of the *amateur*, defined as an individual who pursues an activity for pleasure rather than for professional acclaim or financial benefit. The Club 57 version of this gentile, Enlightenment term valued curiosity and adventurism in the creative process over traditional artistic abilities. Underlying it was a decidedly punk passion for revivalism

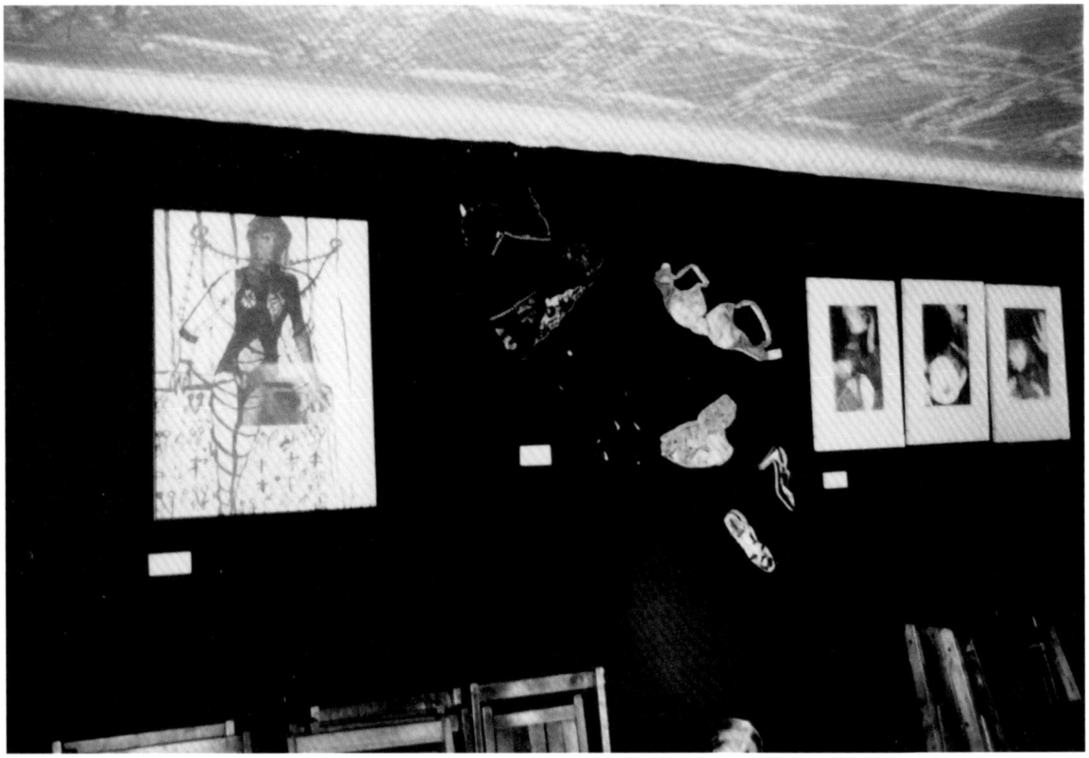

2. Installation view of *Watch These Girls: 19 Women Who Do Copy Art*, Club 57, October 14–17, 1982, organized by Amy Chaiklin. Visible are works by (from left) Chaiklin, Barbara Wyeth, and Miriam Jacobs. This exhibition was rare insofar as it was on view for more than one day. Photograph by Chaiklin

as an antidote to the tiresome progressivism of the current artistic avant-garde.[8] The embrace of this counter-aesthetic made for exhibitions crowded with great, good, and some frankly unserious work. "The major thing about Club 57 was that everything had to be entertaining," Kenny Scharf recalls,[9] and this translated into exhibitions that were slapdash, eclectic, and ephemeral; a hodgepodge of artwork, sometimes identified, frequently not, taped to the club's walls (fig. 2). Some shows featured Xeroxes, or work made from disposable objects like matchbooks. In keeping with the "everyone is an artist attitude," others featured works by self-taught or anonymous artists (fig. 3). One exhibition featured "found in the street" sculpture. Stripped of the elements that traditionally confer value—preciousness, virtuosity, attribution—artwork in Club 57 shows offered stark contrasts to the exhibitions of huge, portentous oil paintings filling the galleries a few blocks away in SoHo.[10] If dilettantism was a virtue for Club 57 participants, badness—judged by criteria of the mainstream artistic mores—could be one as well. The embrace of amateurism, even to the point of showcasing infuriating ineptitude, was both a democratic lark and a strategy, a counter to the notion of an artist as a professional and art as a career, like law or banking.[11]

If the Club 57 scene was goofy and ad hoc, the crowd at Mudd Club was cooler, more fashionable, and aspiring to professionalism. The advent of the club's gallery program in 1981 was a challenge to the punky, outlaw charm of Club 57 art exhibitions, primarily because it called into question the viability of amateur versus professional exhibition-making. In 1981, after haunting Club 57 and meeting Haring there, Steve Mass, owner of Mudd Club, hired him to curate its first exhibition. *Lower Manhattan Drawing Show* inaugurated a string of multiweek-long shows of thoughtfully curated, professionally presented works by invited artists. The gallery was nicely painted, properly lighted, and even included someone minding the show and dispensing price lists. The presentation of *Lower Manhattan Drawing Show* was a conscious counter to a Club 57–type show, as its press release reveals. "The new gallery space will exhibit the works of some of the most talented young artists in lower Manhattan, many as yet unrepresented by dealers," it reads. "They will now have the advantage of the convenience of Soho as well as a full length THREE WEEK EXHIBITION with gallery hours extending as late as 2 am."[12]

Public Art for a Local Audience

In retrospect, the Mudd Club endeavor seems misguided, as the notion of creating art not only *from* the neighborhood but *for* it was central to the East Village ethos. Throughout the 1970s, as the neighborhood's housing stock deteriorated, groups of young people, joined in some cases by older residents, homesteaded and rehabbed abandoned buildings and planted guerrilla gardens in empty lots.[13] Collectives of artists, musicians, poets, and the like commandeered derelict storefronts, making exhibition and performance spaces to show and distribute their own work. One of the largest artists' collectives to emerge from the neighborhood was Collaborative Projects, or Colab. Incorporated as a nonprofit in 1978, the same year as Club 57 came into being, Colab defined itself as an umbrella organization under which members could apply for grants from the city, state, and federal governments to make exhibitions. It was also dedicated to the idea of creating local exhibitions of local art for a local audience. According to James Nares, a founder, like Club 57 Colab "consciously stood against what was happening in SoHo"[14] and many artists participated in exhibitions organized by both groups.

One of Colab's early exhibitions, the January 1980 *Real Estate Show*, took as its subject the neighborhood's most pressing problem: the creeping gentrification of the East Village. The group's best-known exhibition though, did not take place in the neighborhood but in an abandoned massage parlor on Times Square, geographically and ideologically distant from "the elite art-world system."[15] The *Times Square Show* (or *TSS*) opened in June 1980 with work by one hundred artists installed over four floors and the basement of the building (fig. 4). Colab invited groups of artists from other organizations and neighborhoods to participate, including not only Club 57 but also White Columns, a nonprofit in the far West Village; Harlem Workshop uptown; and most notably, Fashion Moda, a scrappy storefront gallery in the South Bronx that showed artwork

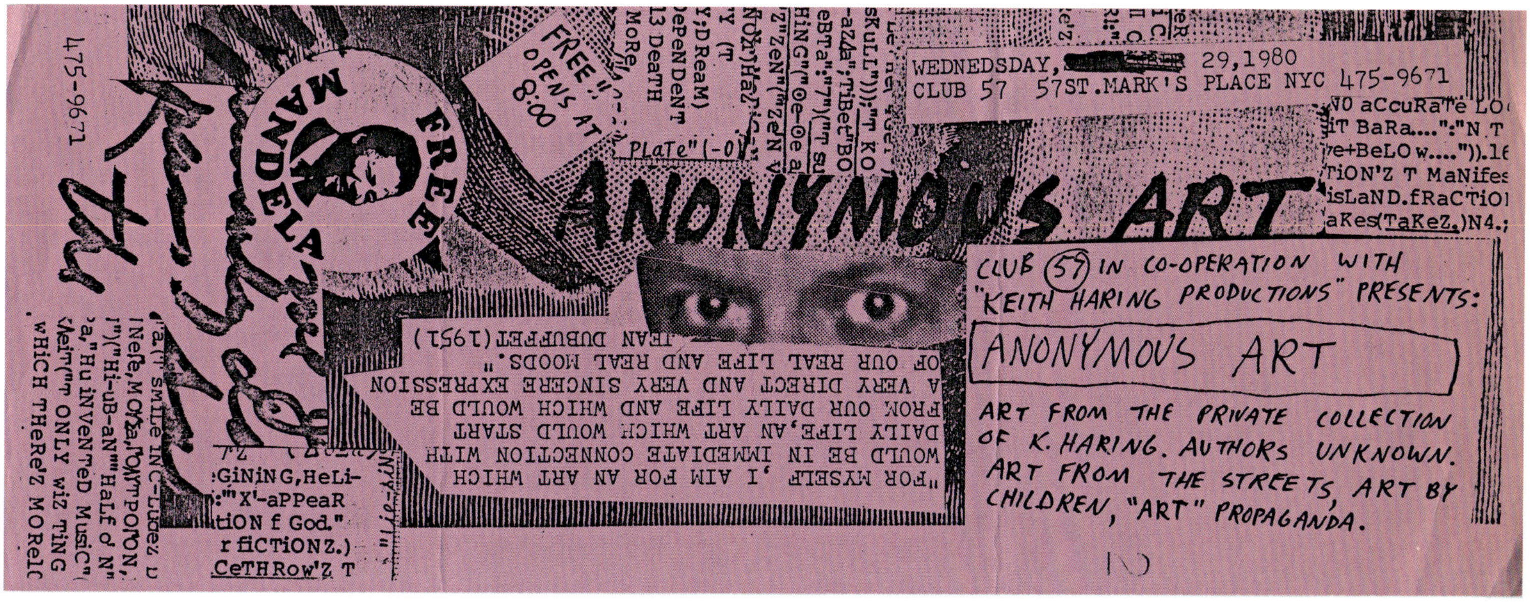

3. Flyer for *Anonymous Art*, curated by Keith Haring at Club 57, 1980. Design by Haring. The flyer features a quote by painter and sculptor Jean Dubuffet, an early influence on Haring. The Museum of Modern Art, New York. Department of Film Special Collections

by graffiti writers. The influence of these outer-borough imports, whose canvases were subway trains, and whose stages were sidewalks, cannot be overstated: when soon after *TSS* downtown artists began bringing art out into the city for a general audience, the entire notion was inspired by the graffiti artists' example.

Of his peers, Haring was most affected by the graffiti writers. His style, and, more importantly, his idea of public art, were deeply indebted to them. The desire to move beyond the conventional art system was reflected in the exhibitions Haring curated at Club 57. They showcased reproducible and distributable art as well as kinds of art made by participants who were outside of the art system, like children, the self-taught, and anonymous artists. These shows were a preamble to Haring's more radical push to broaden his artistic practice to include audiences beyond the insular ones of Club 57 or even the art world.

Haring had started to develop a vision for an art accessible to a more general public as a student, with the goal of creating what he called the "most direct art experience for an un-selective audience . . . outside of the shelter of 'art' contexts."[16] Already under the influence of the writings of William S. Burroughs and Brion Gysin,[17] whom together advocated for the complete merging of word and image, Haring was inspired by graffiti's perfect conflations of language and image. With these examples in mind, Haring developed a hieroglyphic type of outline drawing of recognizable images and patterns that was as immediately readable as signage as it was identifiable as signature (pages 72–73). By the time he met the artist Fab 5 Freddy (Fred Brathwaite) at *TSS*, Haring had already started to use this language to draw on walls and on empty advertising frames on subway platforms. As Haring's fame grew, he began to exhibit large canvases and drawings. Within a few short months, Haring's remarkable images exploded into the popular culture, penetrating public consciousness through murals, posters, books, and, eventually, a line of products that were distributed worldwide. At the time of his death, in 1990, Haring's work had already traveled beyond the East Village's community of artists and SoHo's firmament of art stars and into mass culture. Today, his work is emblematic of the East Village moment in American art.

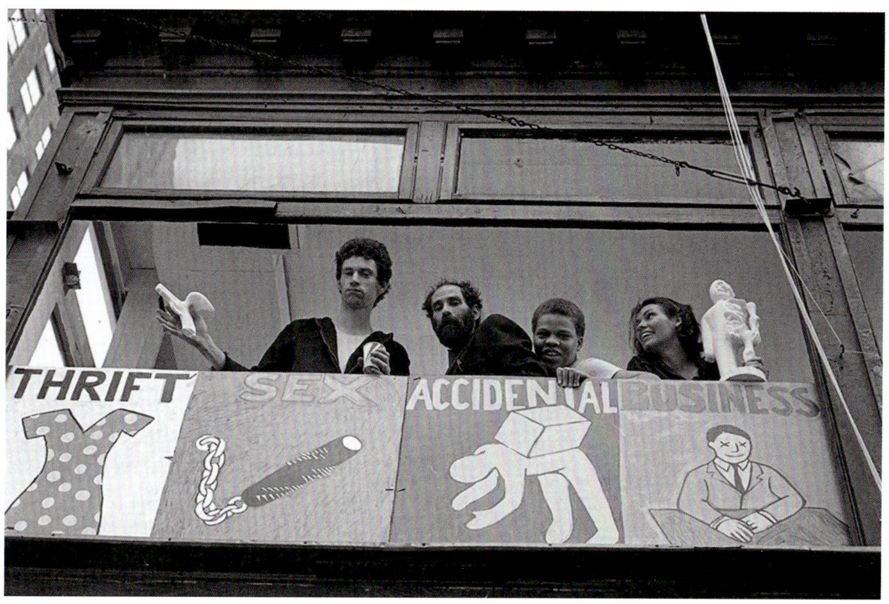

4. From left: Alan Moore, Scott Miller, William Scott (junior director of Fashion Moda), and Coleen Fitzgibbon look out the window from the second-floor Open Air Fashion Lounge at *Times Square Show*, June 1–30, 1980. Plywood signs and sculptures, from the show's first-floor store, are by Tom Otterness. Photograph by Francene Keery

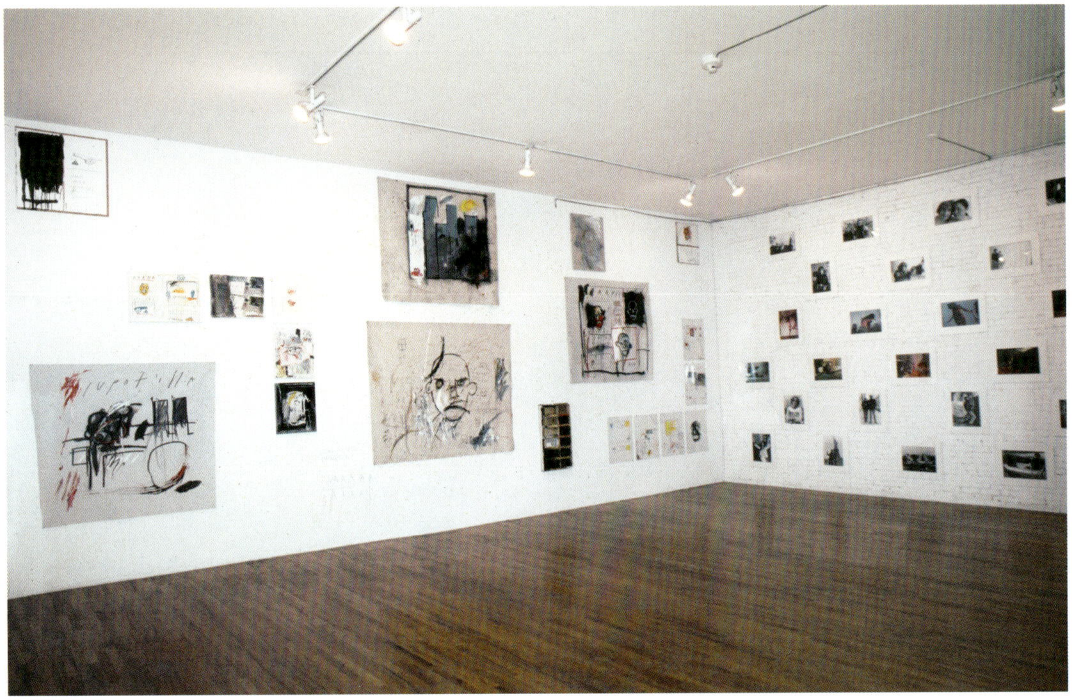

5. Installation view of *New York/New Wave*, P.S. 1, February 15–April 5, 1981. Visible are works by (from left) Jean-Michel Basquiat and Bob Gruen. MoMA PS1 Archives, III.A.18. The Museum of Modern Art Archives, New York

No Future

The brevity of the existence of the non-careerist, ad hoc, and multidisciplinary community created by Club 57 is remarkable. As if to reinforce the Sex Pistols declaration "No Future!," the club created kinds of art experiences meant to be enjoyed for a single evening before fading into imperfect memory. The advent of Mudd Club's gallery in 1981 signaled the end of this fragile moment when a local, public art danced between the underground and the art world, the purposefully amateur and the professional. That year also saw the opening of *New York/New Wave*, an exhibition at P.S. 1, an alternative art space located in a refurbished public school in Long Island City, Queens. It is generally recognized that it was with this omnibus exhibition of downtown New York artists that the marketing of the East Village as the context for a kind of art, rather than a kind of community, began. Curated by Diego Cortez, *New York/New Wave* included generous selections of work by Jean-Michel Basquiat, Keith Haring, and Kenny Scharf as well as the work of more than a dozen artists associated with Club 57 (fig. 5). These were joined by contributions by South Bronx graffiti writers and downtown musicians such as David Byrne of Talking Heads, Chris Stein of Blondie, Brian Eno, and Alan Vega. Documentary photography of concerts, fun, and mayhem at clubs like CBGB and Mudd Club was also foregrounded in the show.

Although *New York/New Wave* featured more than six hundred discrete objects in every medium, the works were arranged with a curatorial coherence that built a case for a community of artists of all stripes held together not by a shared style but a shared experience. Despite this, and the exhibition's nonprofit venue, the show was eagerly mined by "smart dealers and hungry collectors and investors."[18] The "discovery" of Basquiat served as encouragement to collectors and nascent art dealers to find other unknown artists whose work might give huge returns on small investments. When FUN Gallery opened soon afterward, it was merely the first of what would by the end of the decade become several hundred contemporary art galleries in the East Village.

The End and After

"The irony of street or, by extension, club aesthetics is that they cannot in themselves be introduced into the art world of galleries, collectors or museums,"[19] curator and critic Dan Cameron observed in 1984, but the explosion of the East Village commercial gallery scene endeavored to prove him wrong. FUN demonstrated that even the art most dependent upon the street—the "graffiti prototype"—could adhere to "salon aesthetics,"[20] and its early success inspired galleries of all kinds to proliferate, each selling its version of "East Village Art." As for the ethos that began at Club 57—that celebrated participation over product, audience over market—it died in the face of ambitious professionals who rapidly became the identity of the East Village art scene. For Peter Nagy, founder of the gallery Nature Morte, as well as for subsequent art dealers who, wave after wave, came into the area to turn storefronts into well-lit, white-walled, climate-controlled galleries, the East Village art community did not really begin until the art market arrived. "In the end," Nagy recalled in the late 1990s, "it's really the collectors whom we all have to thank for creating the scene."[21]

Club 57 exhibitions were not made for the new commercial art context that had overtaken the East Village, and by 1983 the obsolescence of its exhibition program had become clear. *New Year's Resolutions*, a group show that opened in January, was accompanied by a price list that mordantly reflected the anachronism of a show of art by amateurs. One artist listed the price of her work at $0.43, another at $1.50. Instead of a price, someone else just wrote "cheap." Haring, Basquiat, and Scharf did not participate. Their responsibilities had changed along with their status as artists. As Scharf recalled recently, "All of a sudden it wasn't for fun."[22] Though the actual date is hazy, Club 57 stopped programming at some point in the spring of 1983. It left its living participants, as Magnuson wrote, to "go forth and multiply." "And they did," she reports, "creating a pantheon of divinities and developing the Ultimate Philosophy of Grooviness"[22]—but for the most part, not in the East Village, which, much as Cinderella's coach transformed back into a pumpkin, lost its galleries and turned back into a neighborhood by the end of the decade.

1. When Klaus Nomi saw Kenny Scharf's painting series dedicated to the 1960s futuristic cartoon *The Jetsons*, he is reported to have said, "You and I are working on the same thing." Quoted by Steven Hager, in *Art after Midnight: The East Village Scene* (New York: St. Martin's Press, 1986), 34.

2. Carlo McCormick, "Guide to East Village Artists," supplement to Phyllis Plous, *Neo York: Report on a Phenomenon* (Santa Barbara: University of California/University Art Museum, 1984), 1.

3. Ann Magnuson, "If the World Has You Asking 'Seriously, WTF?!' Ann Magnuson's Show Is for You," *LA Weekly*, March 15, 2017.

4. The exceptions to this, obvious even at this early point in their respective careers, were Haring, Scharf, and Basquiat.

5. Hager, *Art after Midnight*, 5.

6. The zeal for the amateur at Club 57 was not limited to artists. Amateur actors performed there, and amateur writers read at events such as Non-Writers Reading Their Writing.

7. Walter Robinson, "The East Village Goes to School: History, Geography, Civics, Economics," in Plous, *Neo York*, 14.

8. Ibid.

9. Kenny Scharf, quoted in Hager, *Art after Midnight*, 88.

10. In April 1981, Julian Schnabel's exhibition of expressionist paintings opened simultaneously in two powerhouse galleries in SoHo: Leo Castelli Gallery and Mary Boone Gallery. Both exhibitions sold out before their openings, with the paintings going for record prices. This display of selling power became as much a reason for the wild press attention as the artworks in the show.

11. Jean-Michel Basquiat, a peripatetic participant in Club 57 activities, never bought into this strategy of undermining the prevailing artistic status quo. He is quoted in a 1985 interview as having admitted, "Esthetically I really hated Club 57. Thought it was silly. All this old and bad shit. I'd rather see something old and good." See Hager, *Art after Midnight*, 40.

12. Adam Purple (1930–2015), an East Village resident, radical ecologist, and activist, spent five years, from 1975 to 1980, creating a community garden located in an empty lot at 184 Forsythe Street. Called the "Garden of Eden," it gave joy to the neighborhood until 1986 when the city demolished it.

13. James Nares, quoted in Hager, *Art after Midnight*, 15.

14. Shawna Cooper, "The Times Square Show," in *Times Square Show Revisited: Accounts of the Landmark 1980 Exhibition*, eds. Cooper and Karli Wurzelbacher (New York: Bertha and Karl Leubsdorf Art Gallery, Hunter College, 2012), 12.

15. The Keith Haring Foundation Archives.

16. Keith Haring, *Journals* (New York: Viking Press, 1996), 106–7. Haring met Burroughs and Gysin in 1978 when he attended the Nova Convention in New York, a weekend of performances and readings by Beat poets.

17. Robert Becker, "Corporate Culture," *Manhattan, inc* (June 1985): 131.

18. Dan Cameron, "East Village, USA," in Plous, *Neo York*, 13.

19. Ibid.

20. Ibid.

21. Kenny Scharf, conversation with Ron Magliozzi and Sophie Cavoulacos, November 3, 2016.

22. Ann Magnuson, "I Dreamed I Was an Androgynous Rock Star in My Maidenform Bra," *ZG* 8 (Winter 1982). Reprinted in *ABC No Rio Dinero*, eds. Alan Moore and Marc Miller (New York: ABC No Rio, 1985), excerpt available at http://98bowery.com/return-to-the-bowery/abcnorio-the-neighborhood.php.

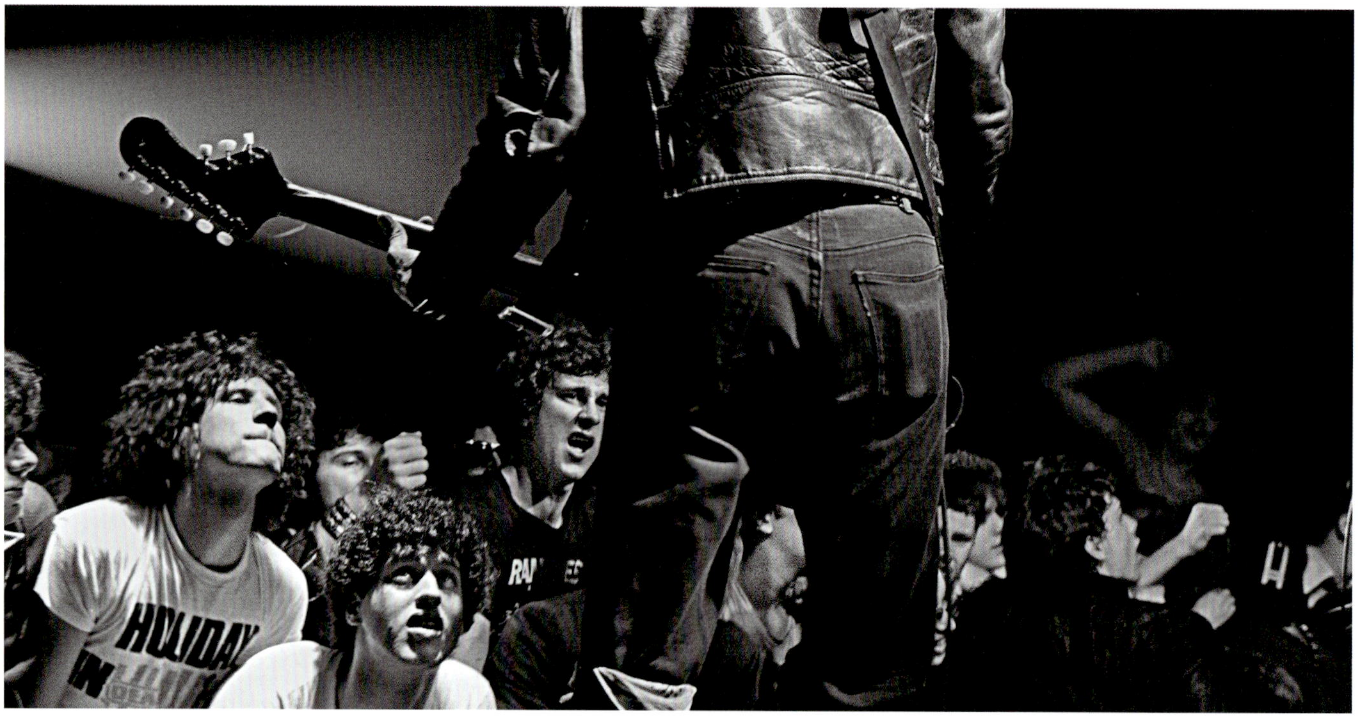

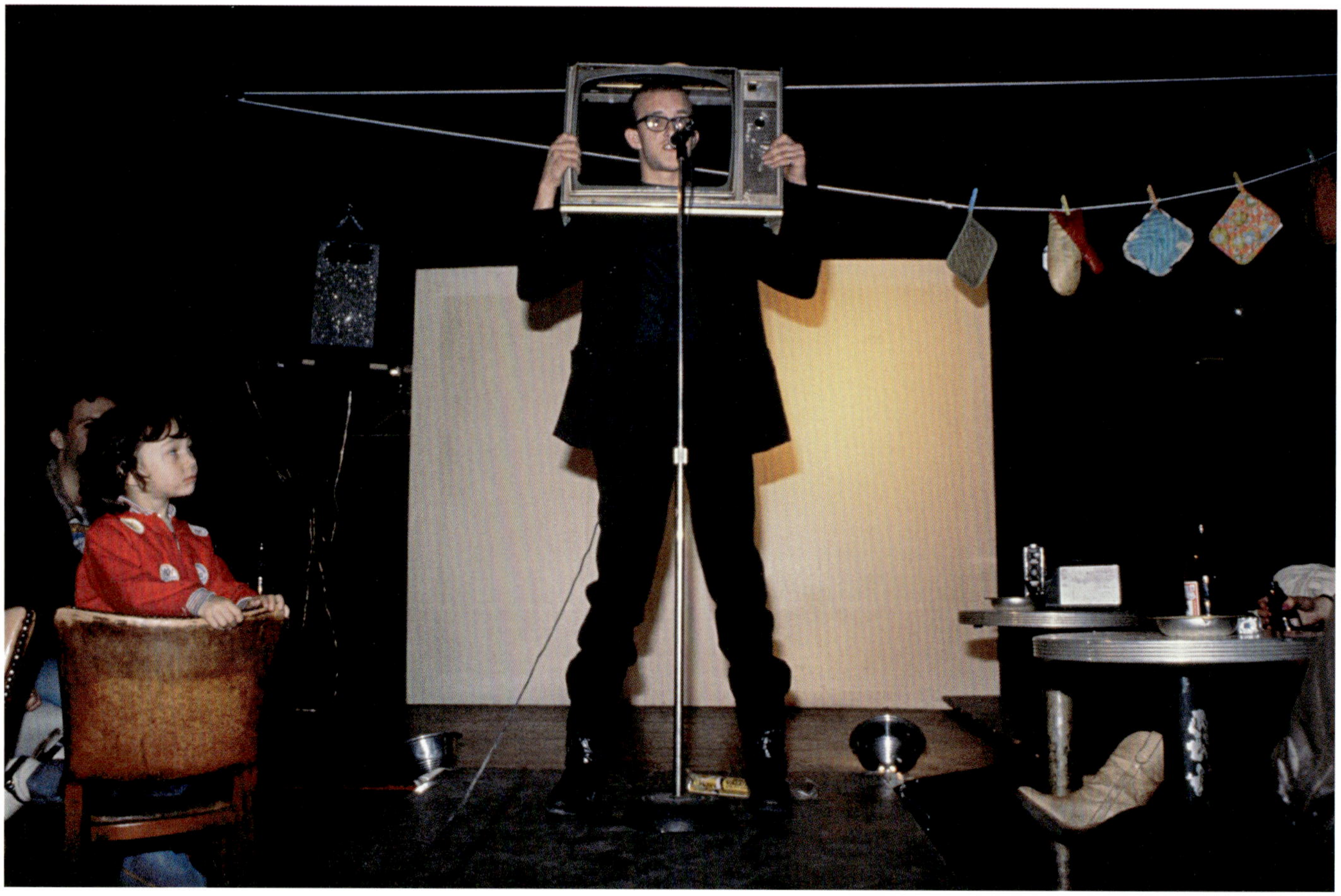

JOSEPH SZKODZINSKI (AMERICAN, BORN 1954). ***Dead Kennedys at Club 57 Irving Plaza.*** 1981. Digital image from 35mm negative. Collection the artist
JOSEPH SZKODZINSKI. ***Keith Haring, Acts of Live Art at Club 57.*** 1980. Digital image from 35mm negative. Collection the artist

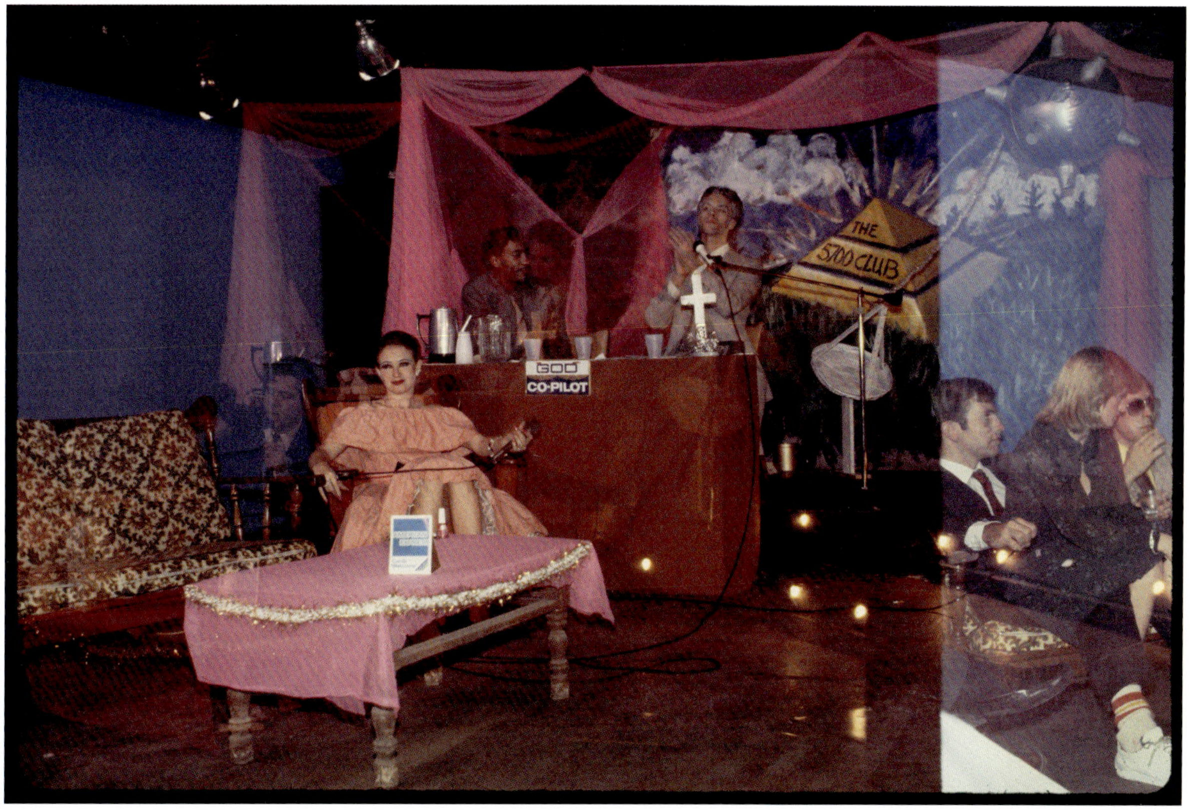

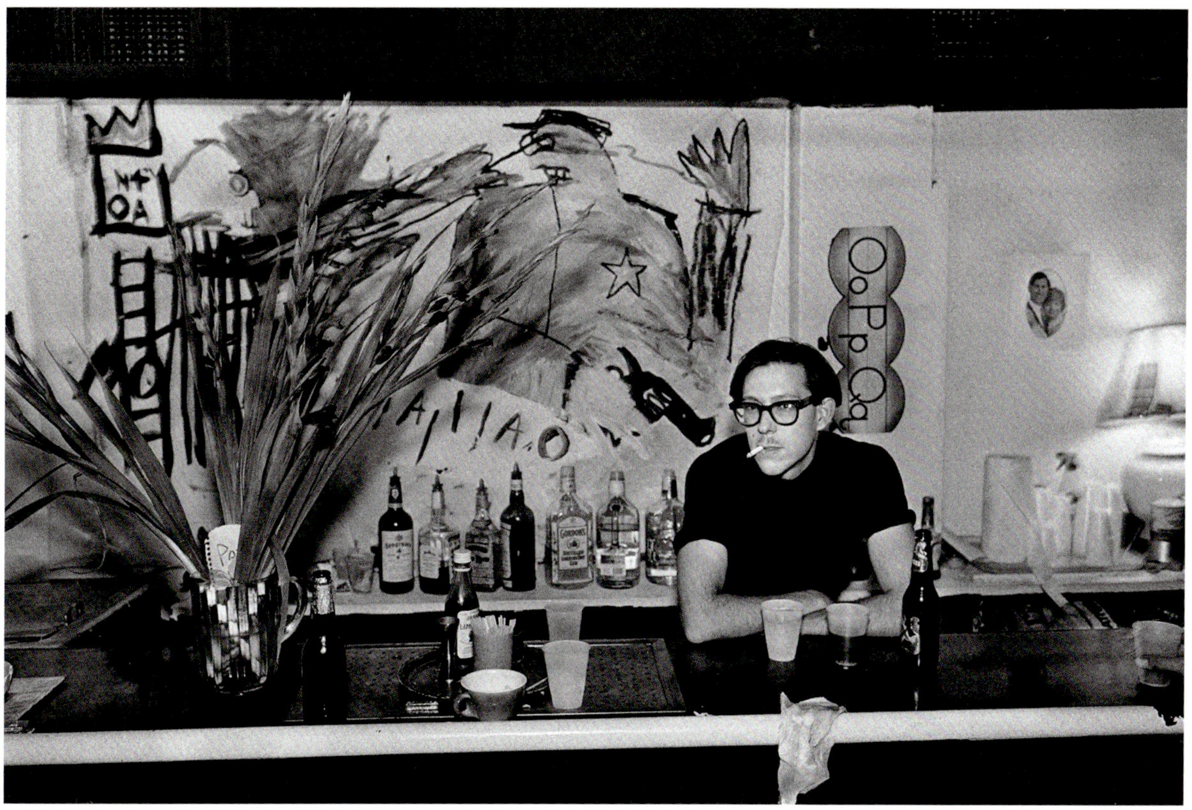

LINA BERTUCCI (AMERICAN, BORN 1958). *5700 Club, "Praise the Lord."* 1981. Digital image from 35mm Ektachrome slide. Collection the artist. Clockwise from left: M. Henry Jones (in camera double exposure), Ann Magnuson, Gerard Little, Andy Rees, Kenny Scharf, Wendy Wild, and Ira Abramowitz

LINA BERTUCCI. *5700 Club, Ira Abramowitz behind the Bar.* 1981. Digital image from 35mm negative. Collection the artist

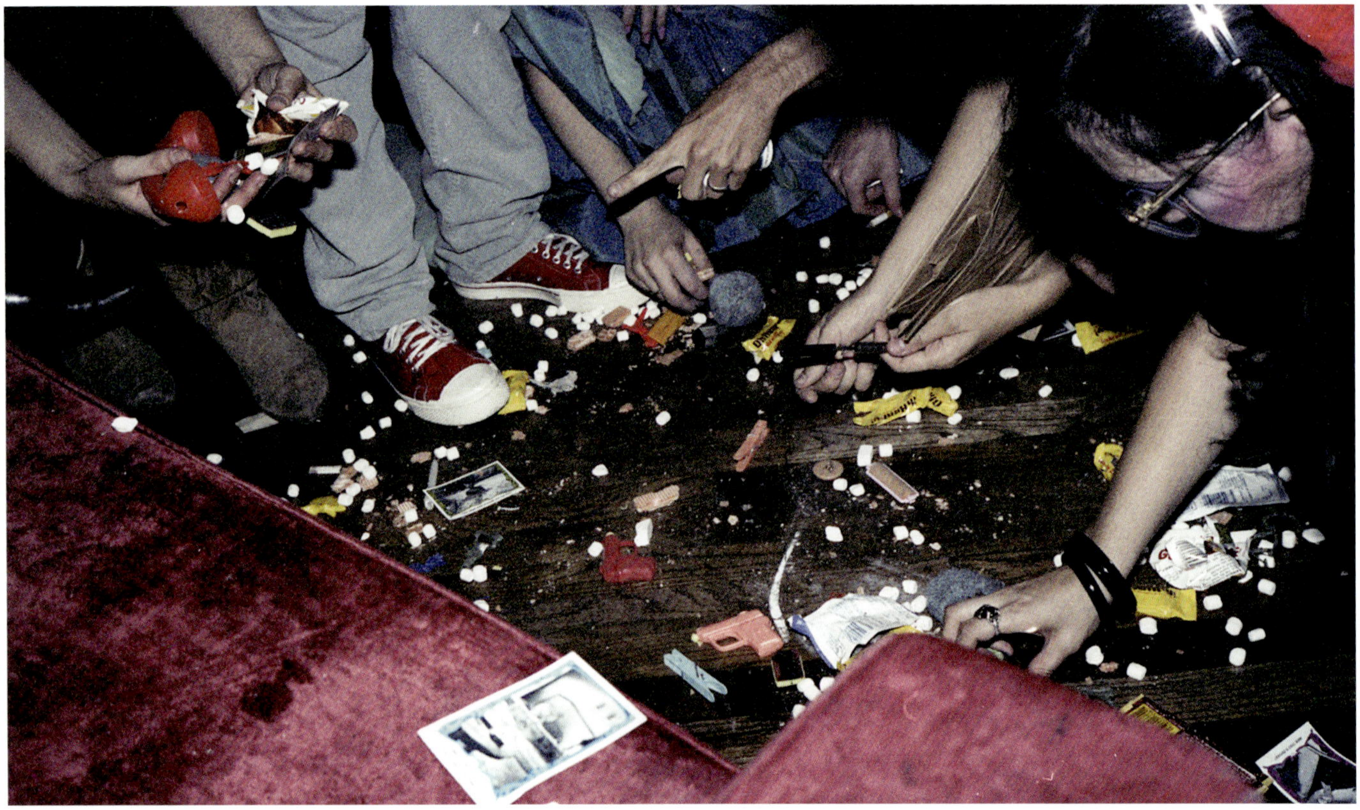

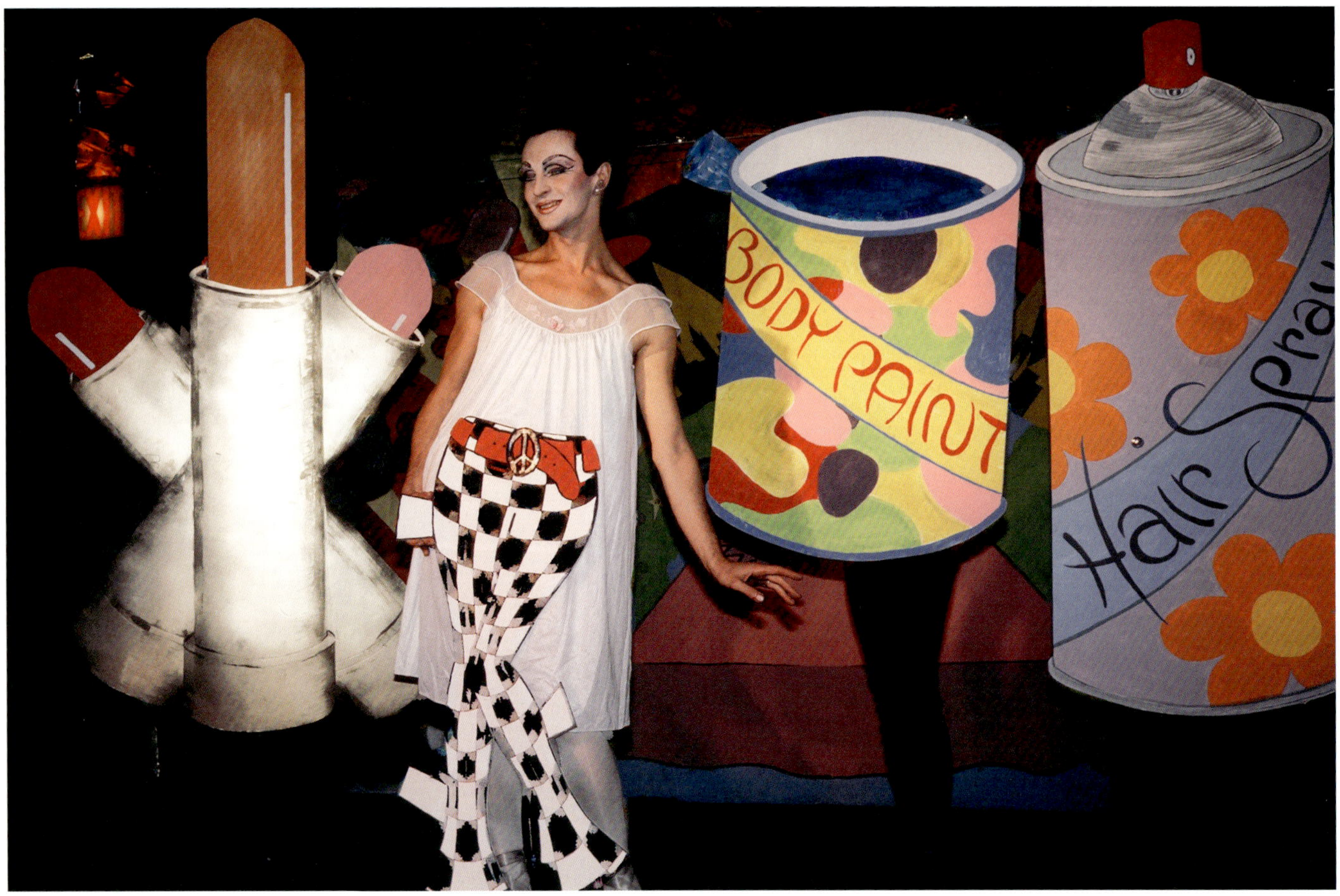

ANDE WHYLAND (AMERICAN, BORN 1950). ***Unidentified Birthday Party, Club 57.*** c. 1979. Digital image from 35mm Kodachrome slide. Collection the artist
ANDE WHYLAND. ***Ballet of the Dolls, Pyramid Club.*** 1985. Digital image from 35mm Kodachrome slide. Collection the artist. Pictured: John Kelly

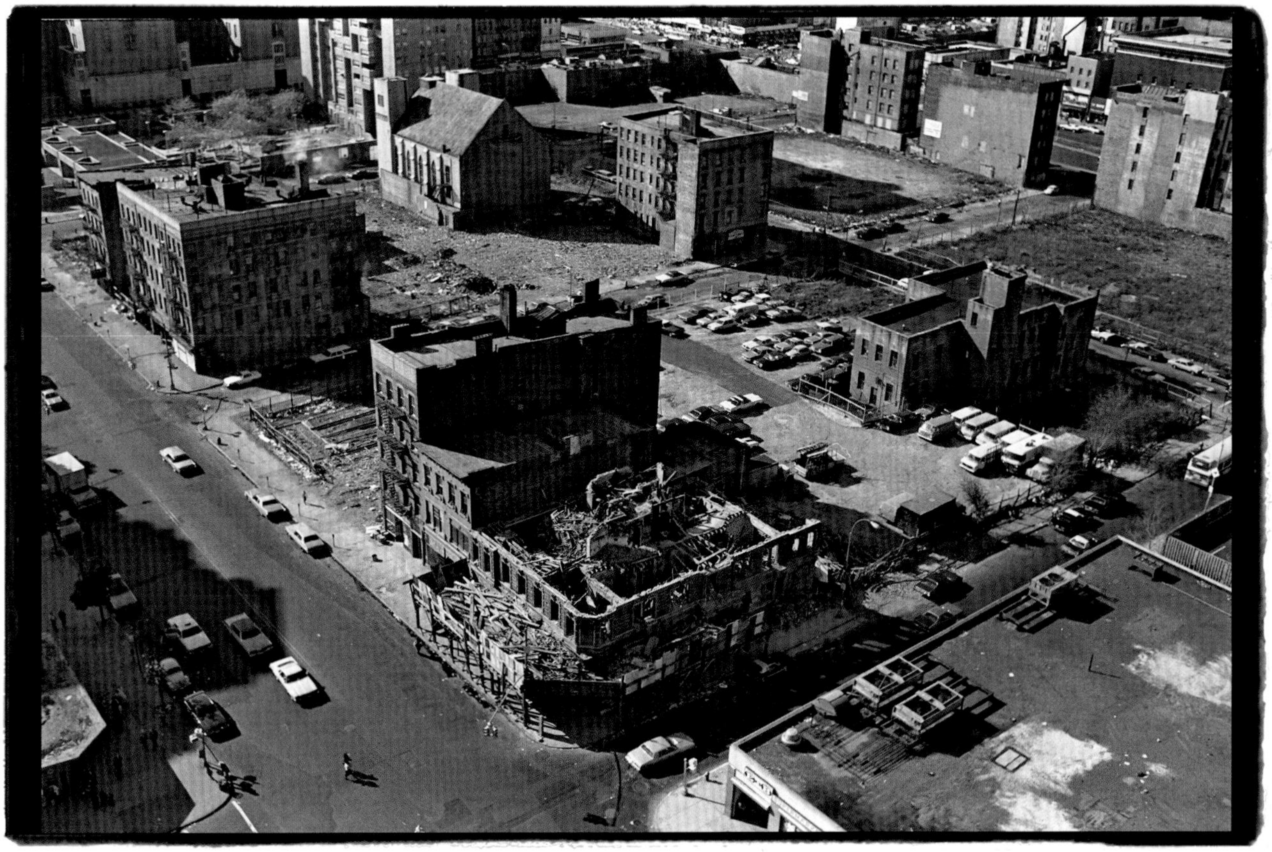

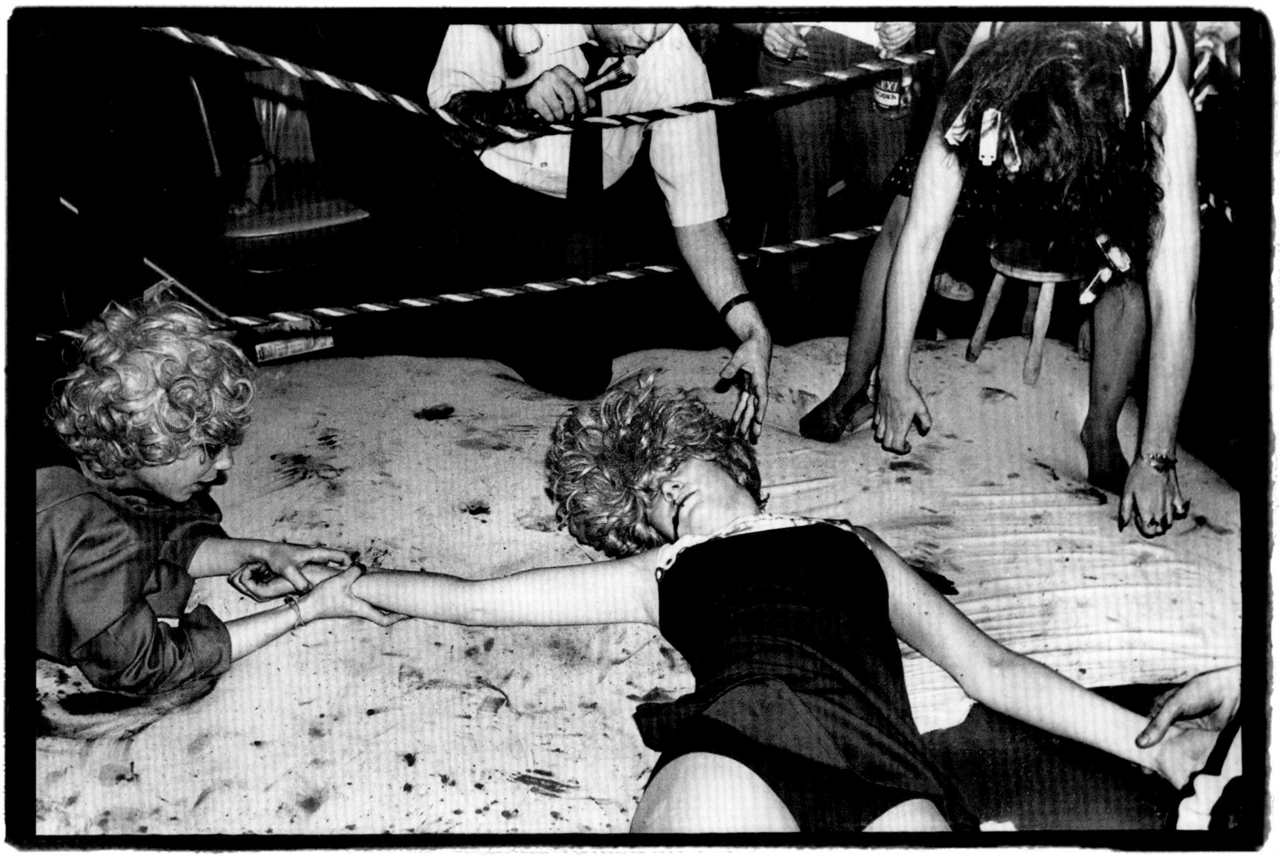

HARVEY WANG (AMERICAN, BORN 1956). ***Grand & Clinton.*** 1980. Digital image from gelatin silver print. Collection the artist

HARVEY WANG. ***Ladies' Wrestling at Club 57.*** 1980. Digital image from gelatin silver print. Collection the artist. From left: Stacey Elkin, Ann Magnuson, Bill Landis, and Tish Bellomo

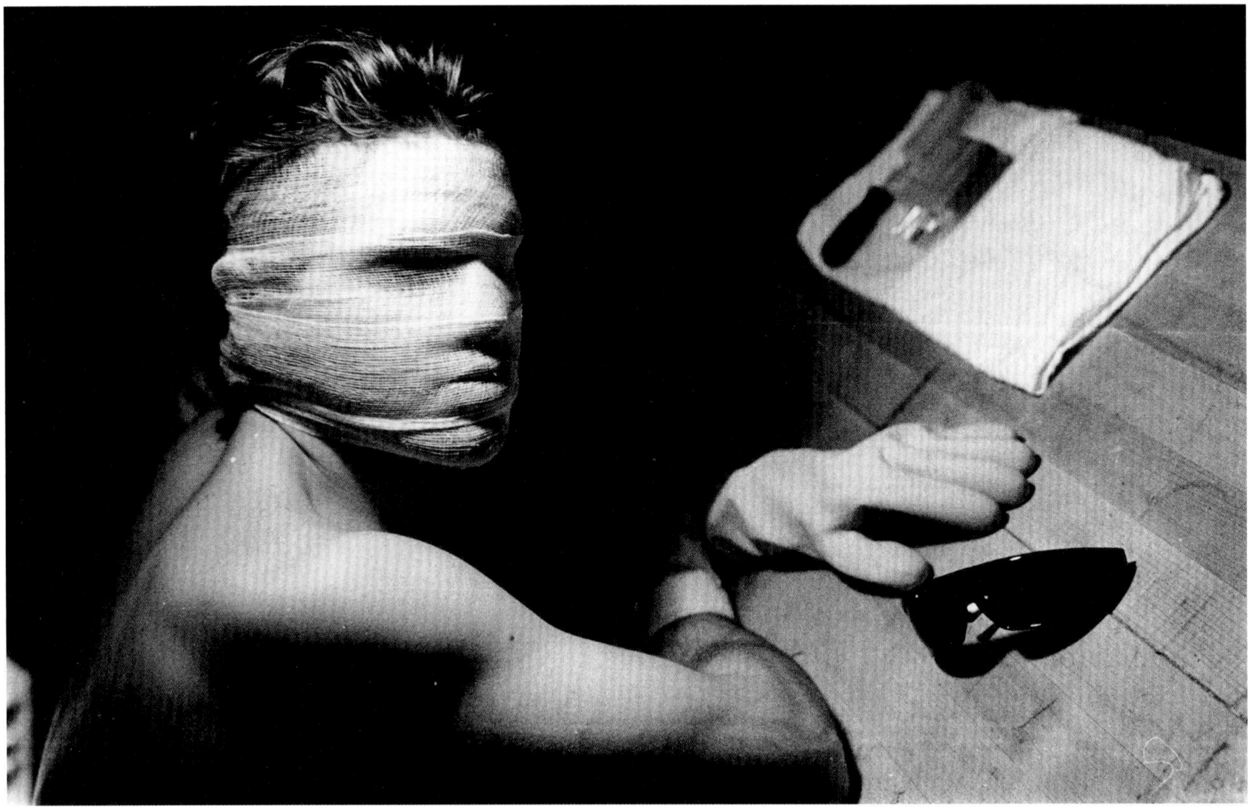

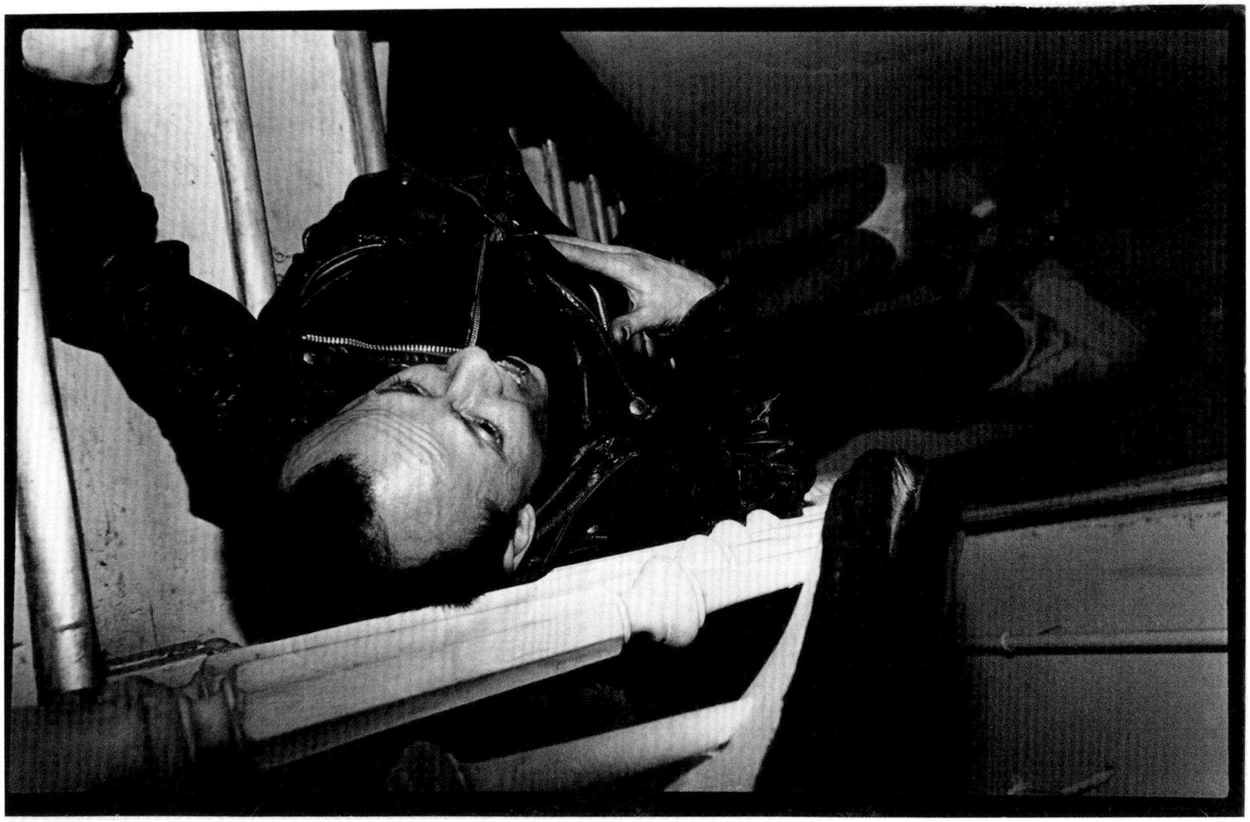

ANTHONY SCIBELLI (AMERICAN, BORN 1953). *The Rule of Mr. Klaus #19,* from a series for a photo-roman written by Peter Nolan Smith (pictured). 1980. Digital image from gelatin silver print. Collection Peter Nolan Smith
ANTHONY SCIBELLI. *The Rule of Mr. Klaus #23,* from a series for a photo-roman written by Peter Nolan Smith. 1980. Digital image from gelatin silver print. Collection Peter Nolan Smith

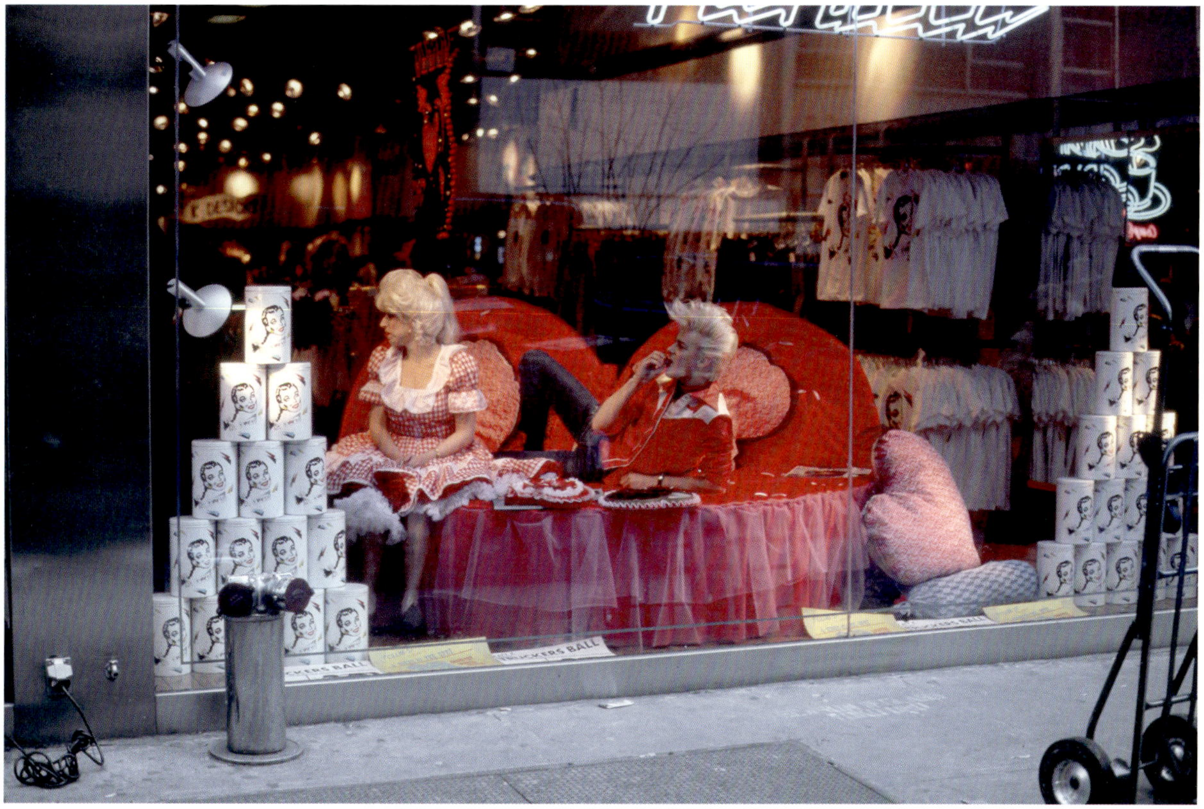

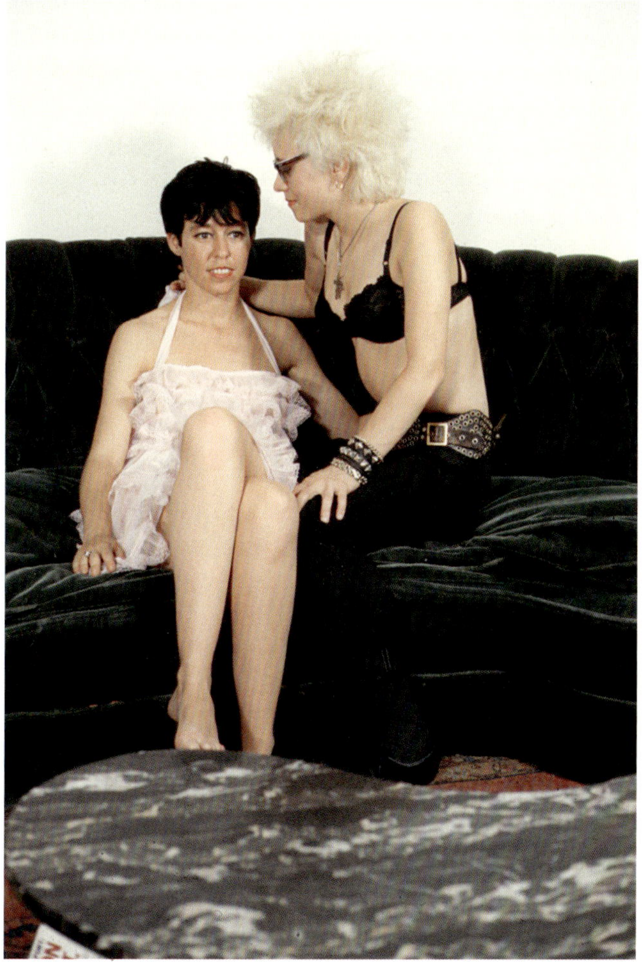

APRIL PALMIERI (AMERICAN, BORN 1956). ***Valentine's Day Repose.*** 1982. Digital image from 35mm Kodachrome slide. Collection the artist. From left: Katy K and John Sex in the window of Fiorucci

APRIL PALMIERI. ***Ande and Dany.*** 1981. Digital image from 35mm Kodachrome slide. Collection the artist

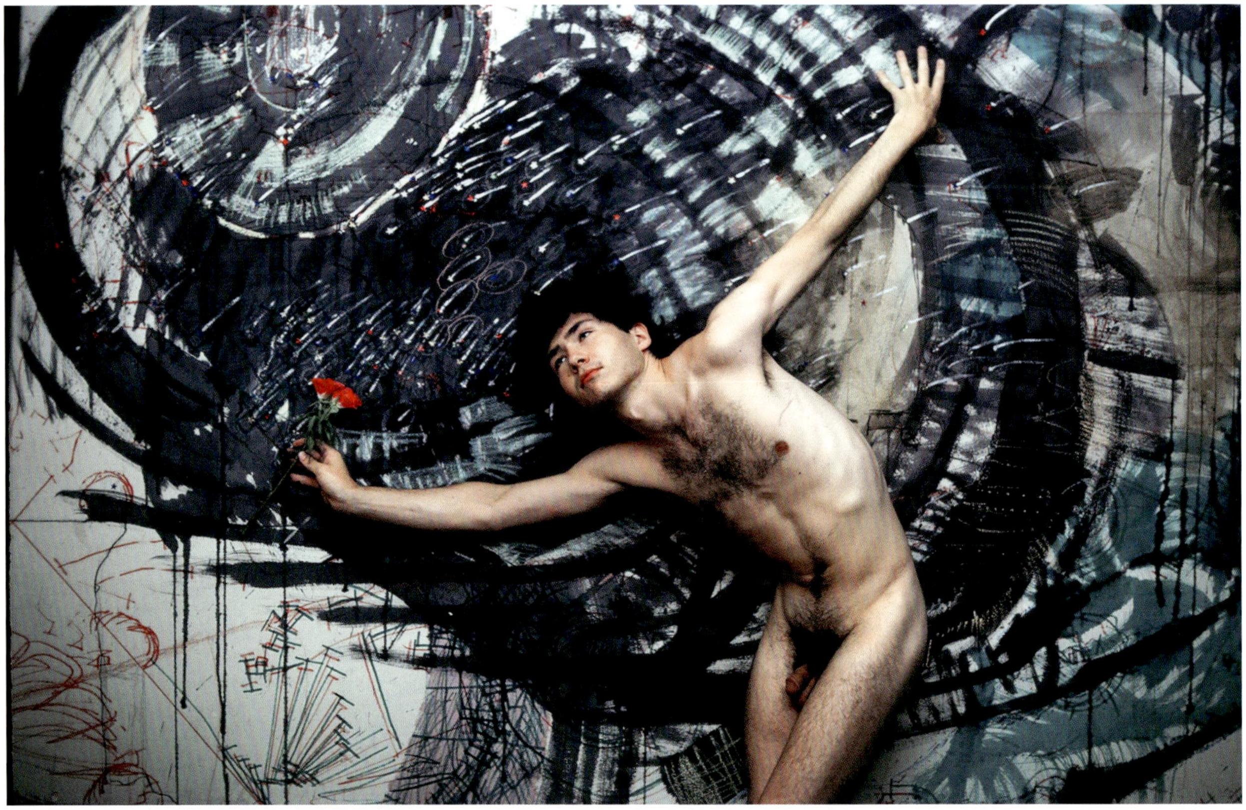

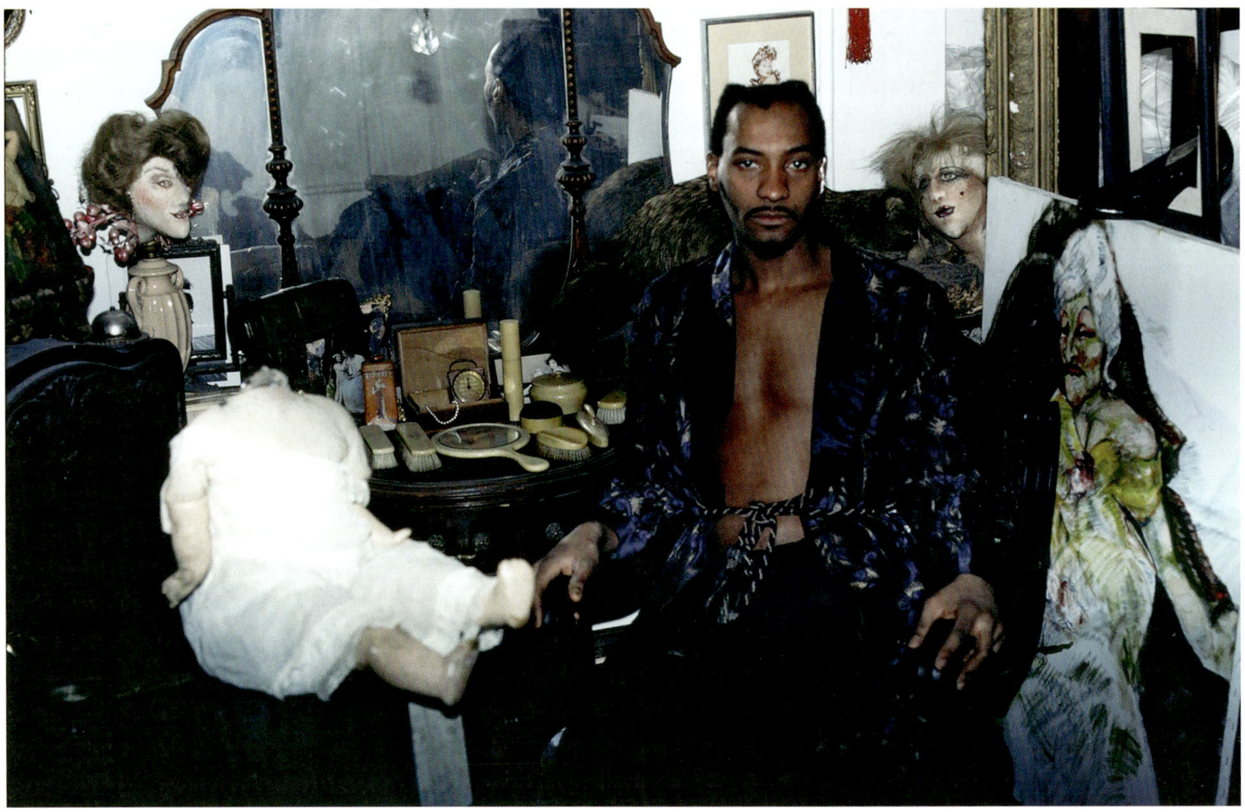

ROBERT CARRITHERS (AMERICAN, BORN 1954). ***AMMO/Shawn McQuate.*** 1980. Digital image from 35mm Kodachrome slide. Collection the artist
ROBERT CARRITHERS. ***Gerard Little.*** 1980. Digital image from 35mm Kodachrome slide. Collection the artist

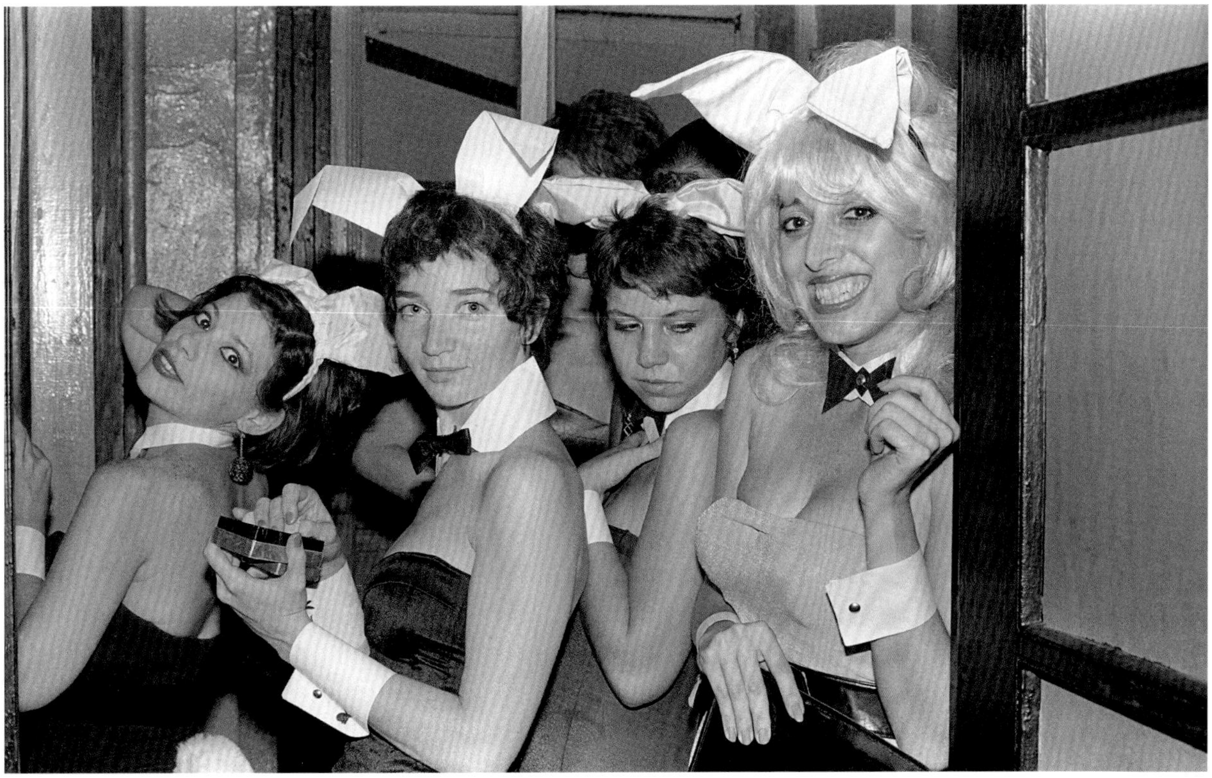

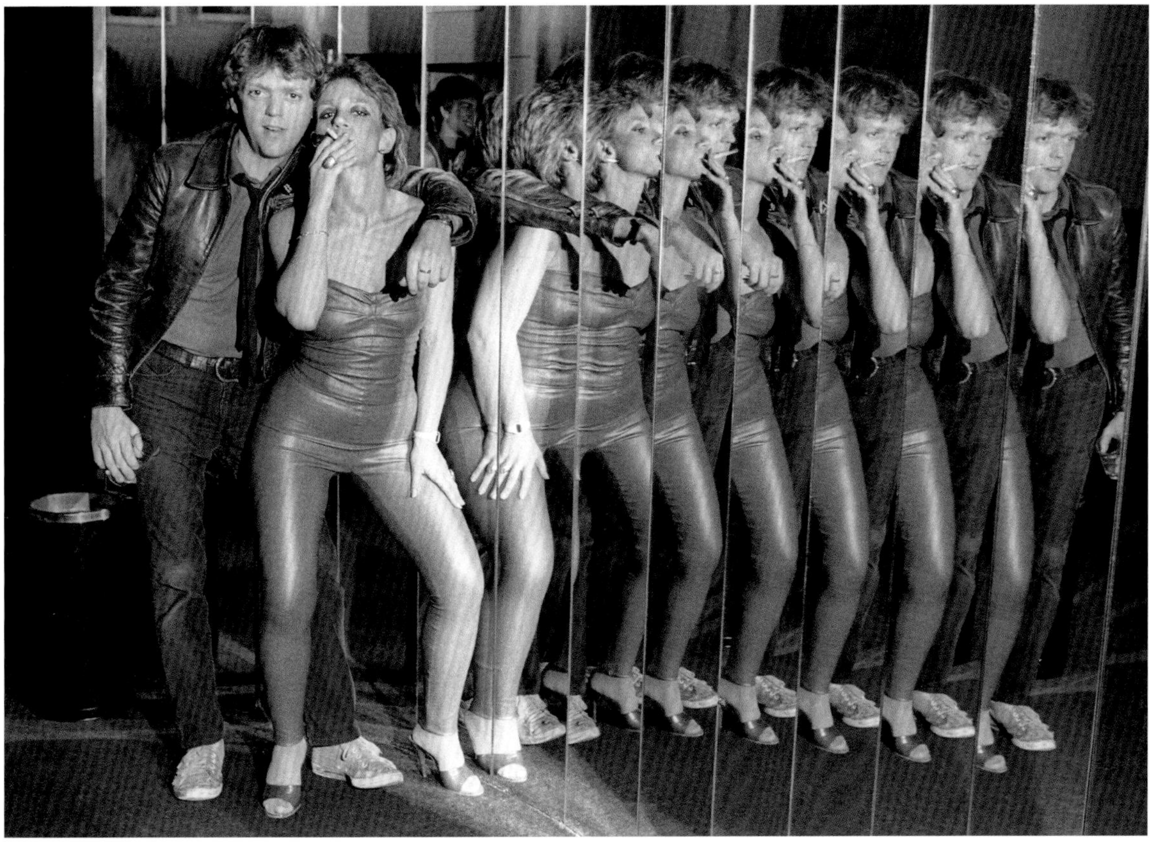

TRIX ROSEN (AMERICAN, BORN 1947). ***Playboy Bunny Club Party at Club 57.*** 1980. Digital image from 35mm negative. Collection the artist. From left: Stacey Elkin, Diana Lillig, Charlotte Slivka, and Katy K

TRIX ROSEN. ***Jackie and Jimmy at Hurrah.*** 1979. Digital image from 35mm negative. Collection the artist

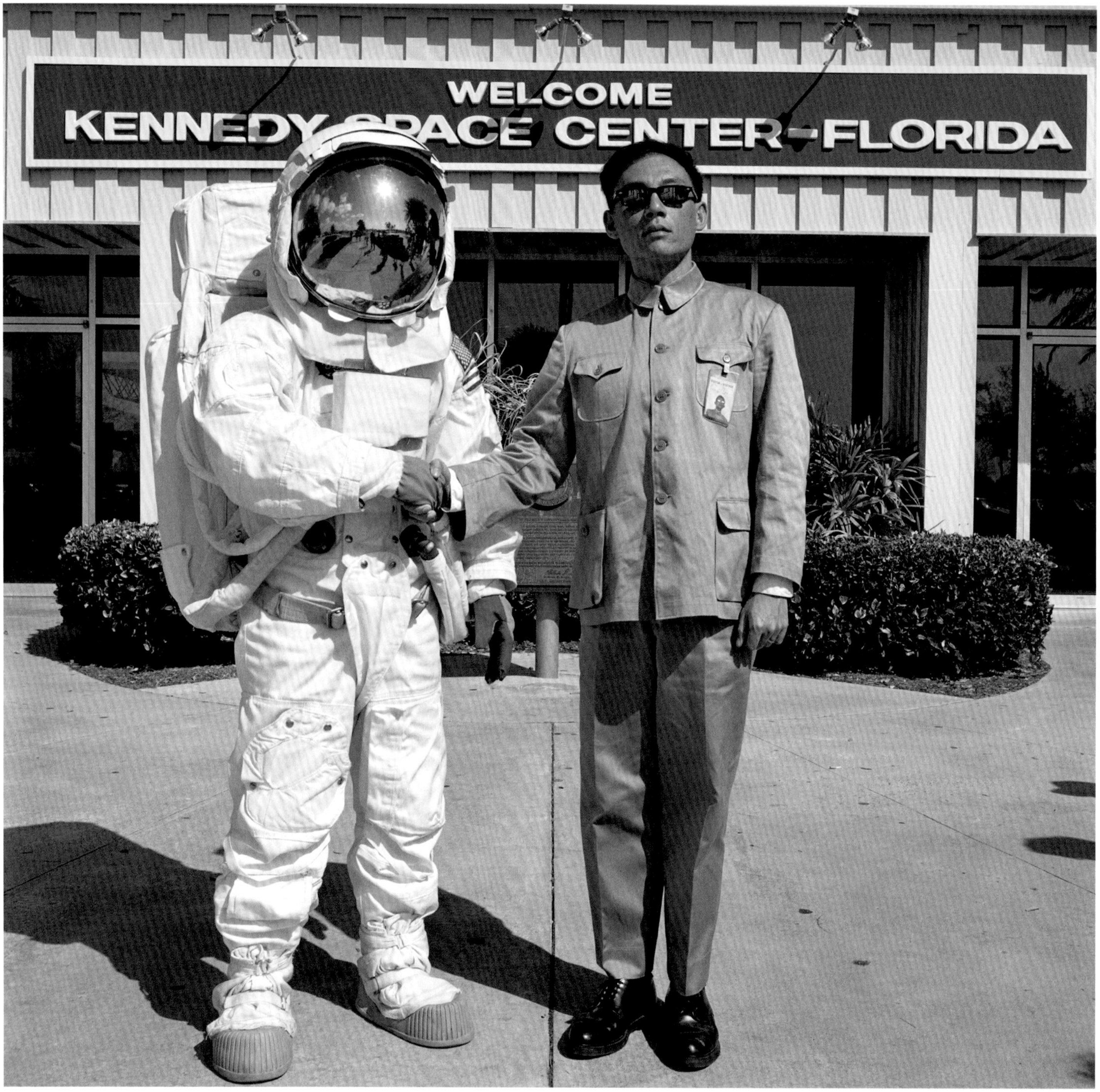

TSENG KWONG CHI (AMERICAN, BORN HONG KONG, 1950–1990). ***Cape Canaveral, Florida (Astronaut).*** 1985. From the East Meets West self-portrait series, 1979–89. Gelatin silver print, 36 × 36" (91.4 × 91.4 cm). Collection Kenny Scharf

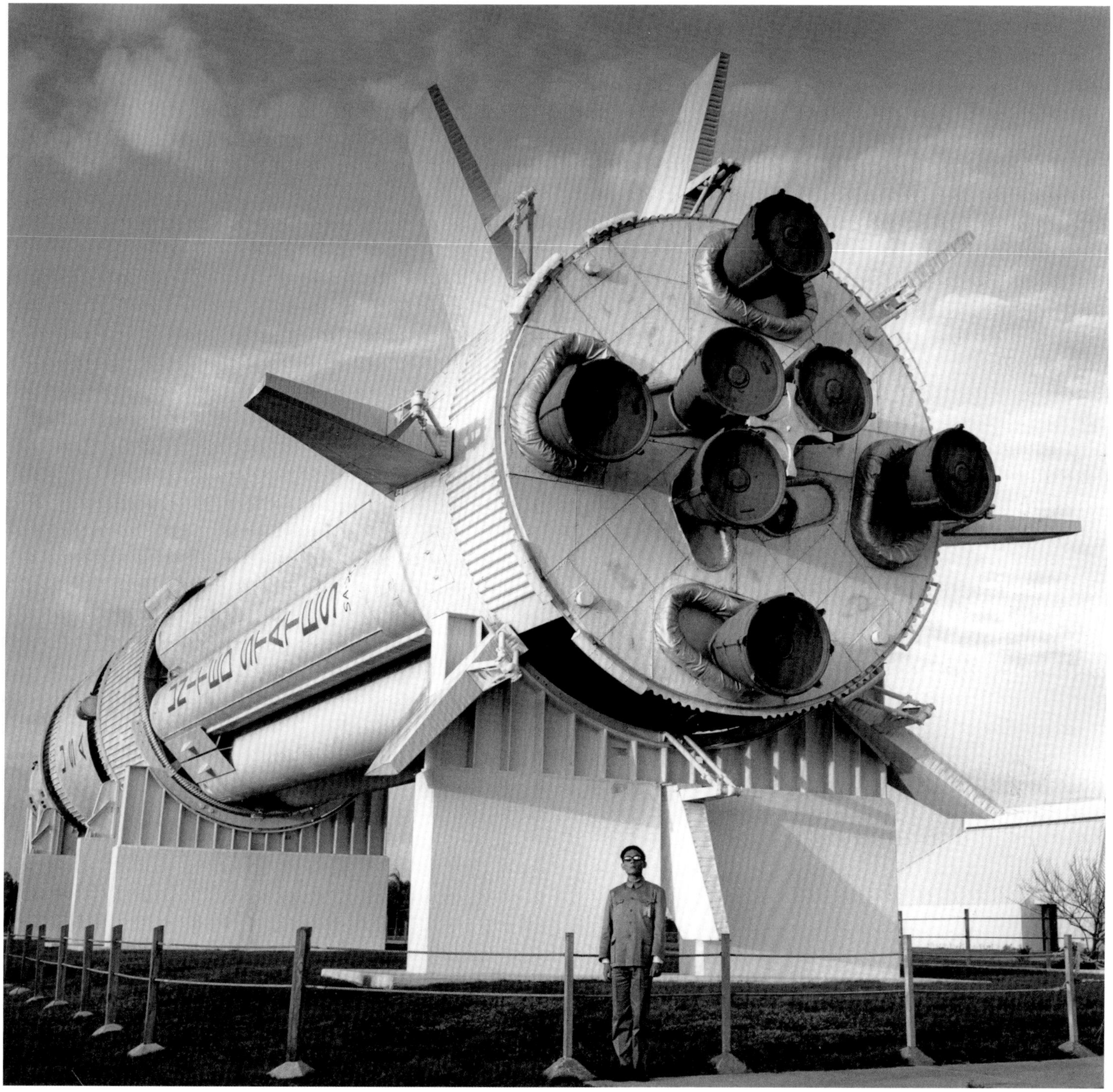

TSENG KWONG CHI. ***Cape Canaveral, Florida (Missile Base).*** 1985. From the East Meets West self-portrait series, 1979–89. Gelatin silver print, 36 × 36" (91.4 × 91.4 cm). Collection Kenny Scharf

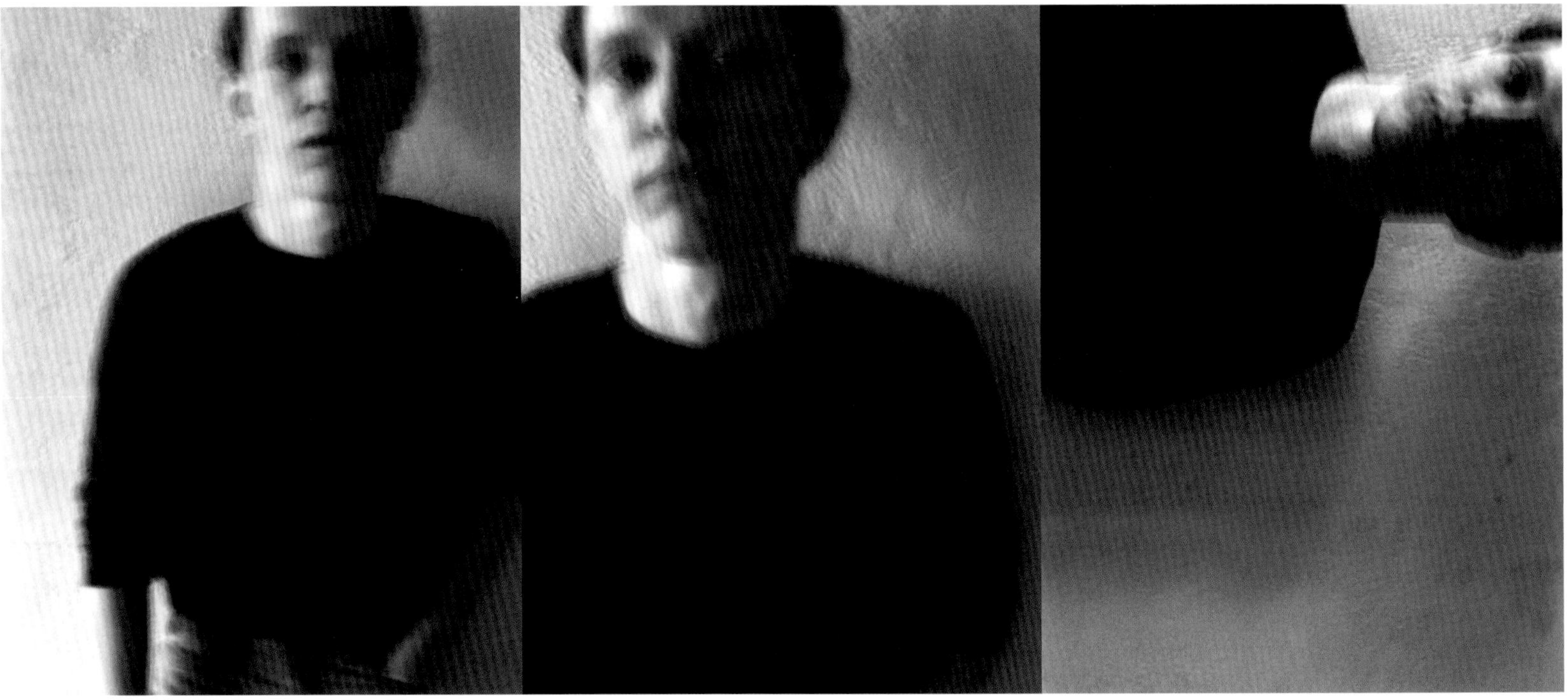

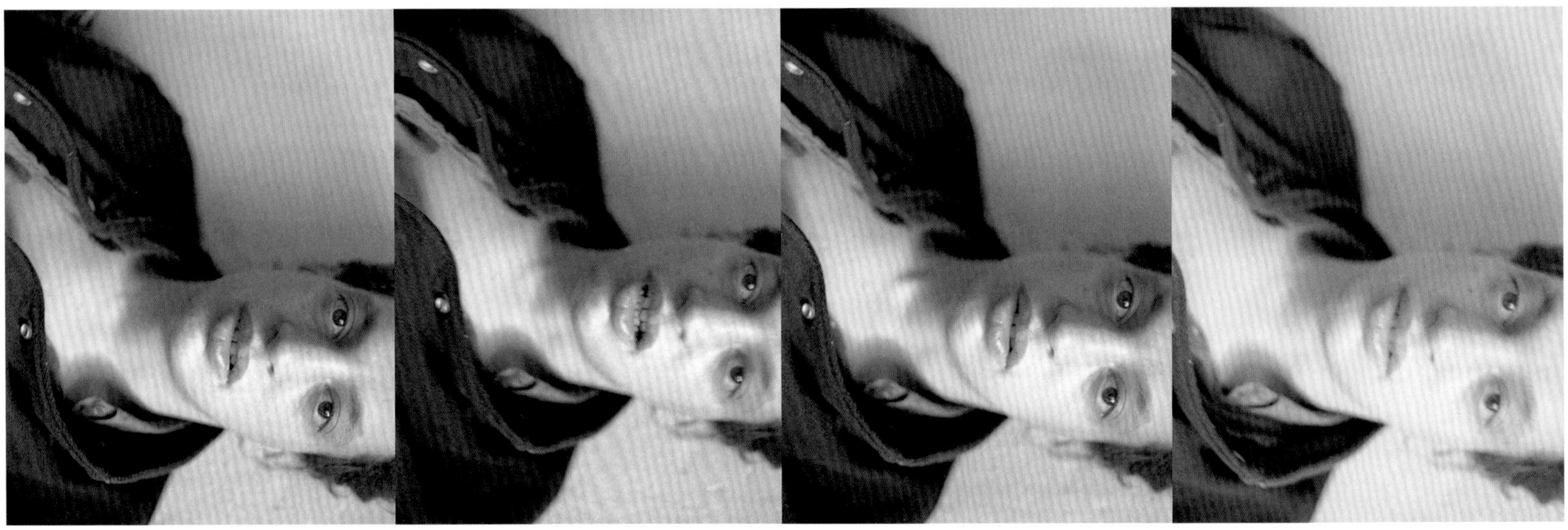

GEORGE HAAS (AMERICAN, BORN 1953). ***Haoui Montaug.*** 1979. Digital image from 120mm negative. Collection the artist
GEORGE HAAS. ***Andrew.*** 1979. Digital image from 120mm negative. Collection the artist

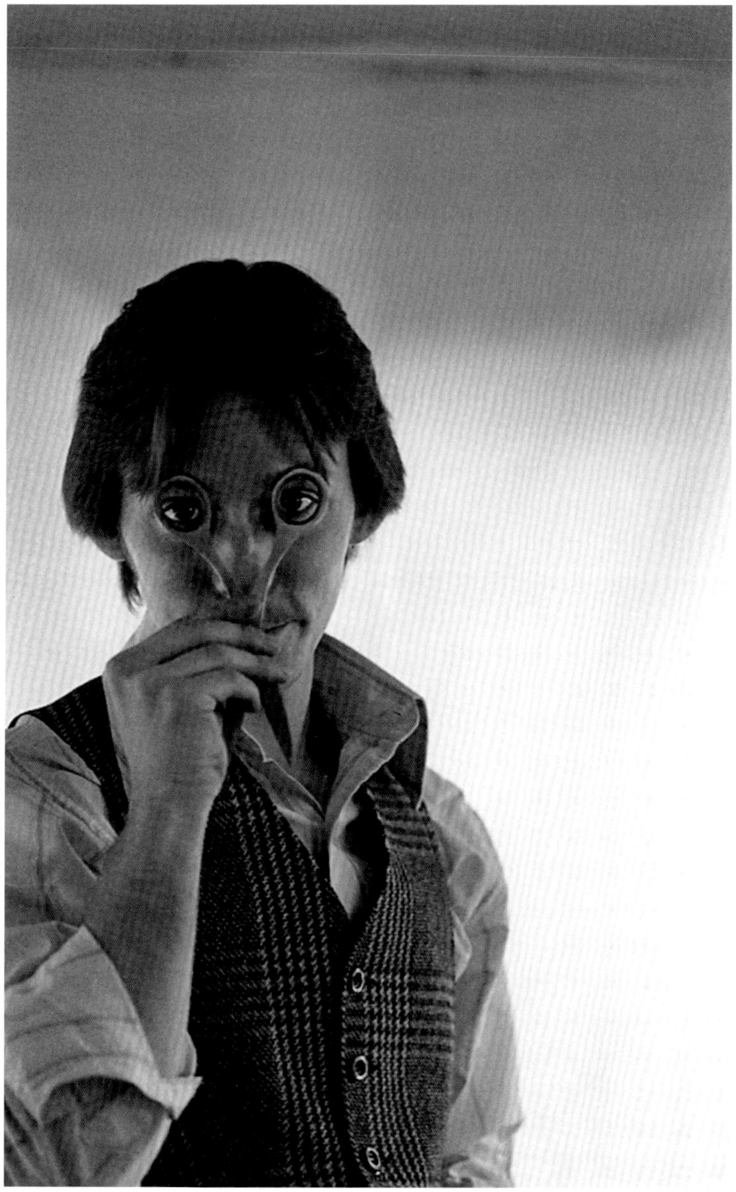

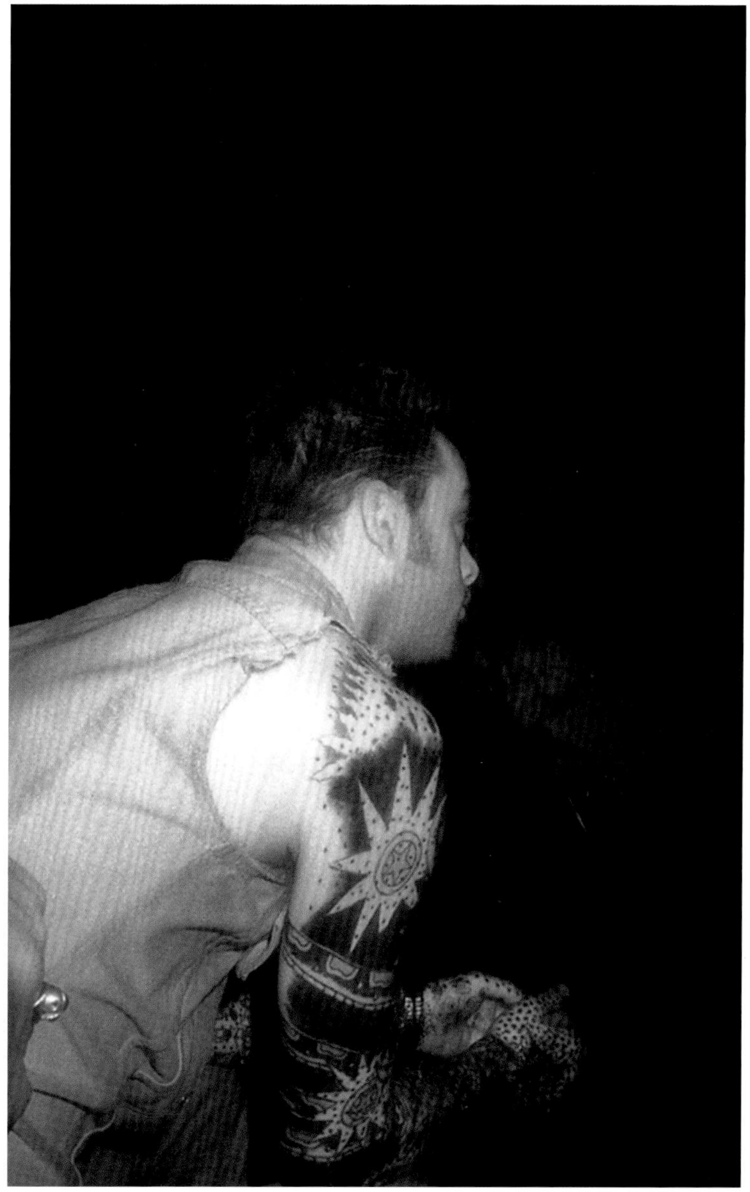

CHRISTINA YUIN (AMERICAN, BORN TAIWAN, 1950). ***Tom Scully.*** 1978. Digital image from 35mm negative. Collection the artist
CHRISTINA YUIN. ***Man Seated, Porn Film Party, Danceteria.*** 1980. Digital image from 35mm negative. Collection the artist

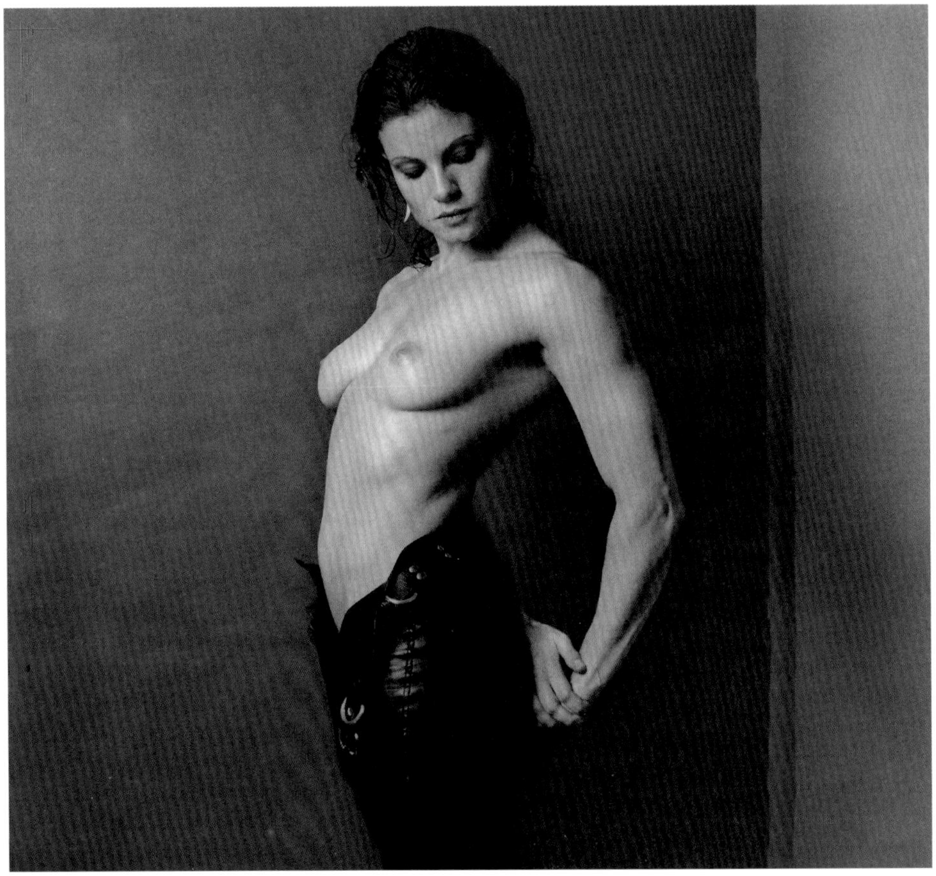

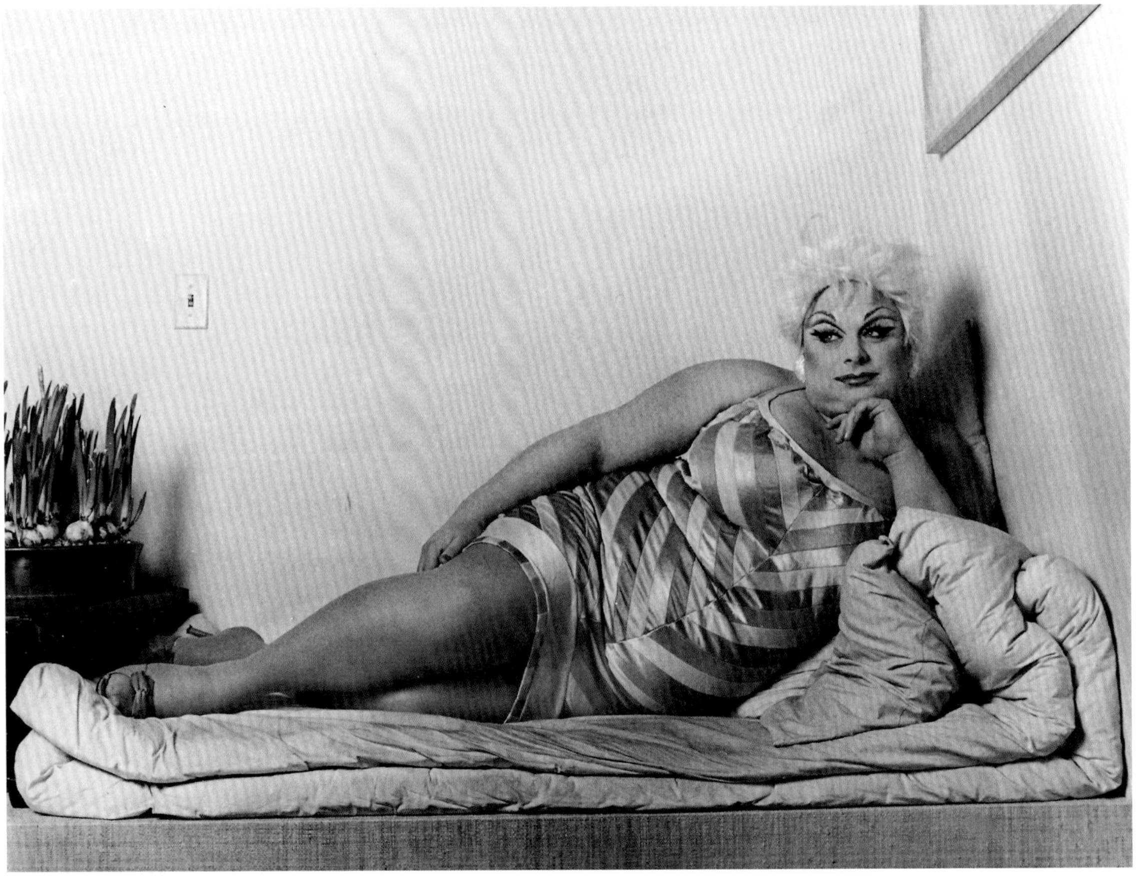

MARCUS LEATHERDALE (CANADIAN, BORN 1952). ***Lisa Lyon***. 1980. Gelatin silver print, 13 × 13" (33 × 33 cm). Collection the artist
MARCUS LEATHERDALE. ***Divine.*** 1980. Gelatin silver print, 13 × 15" (33 × 38 cm). Collection the artist

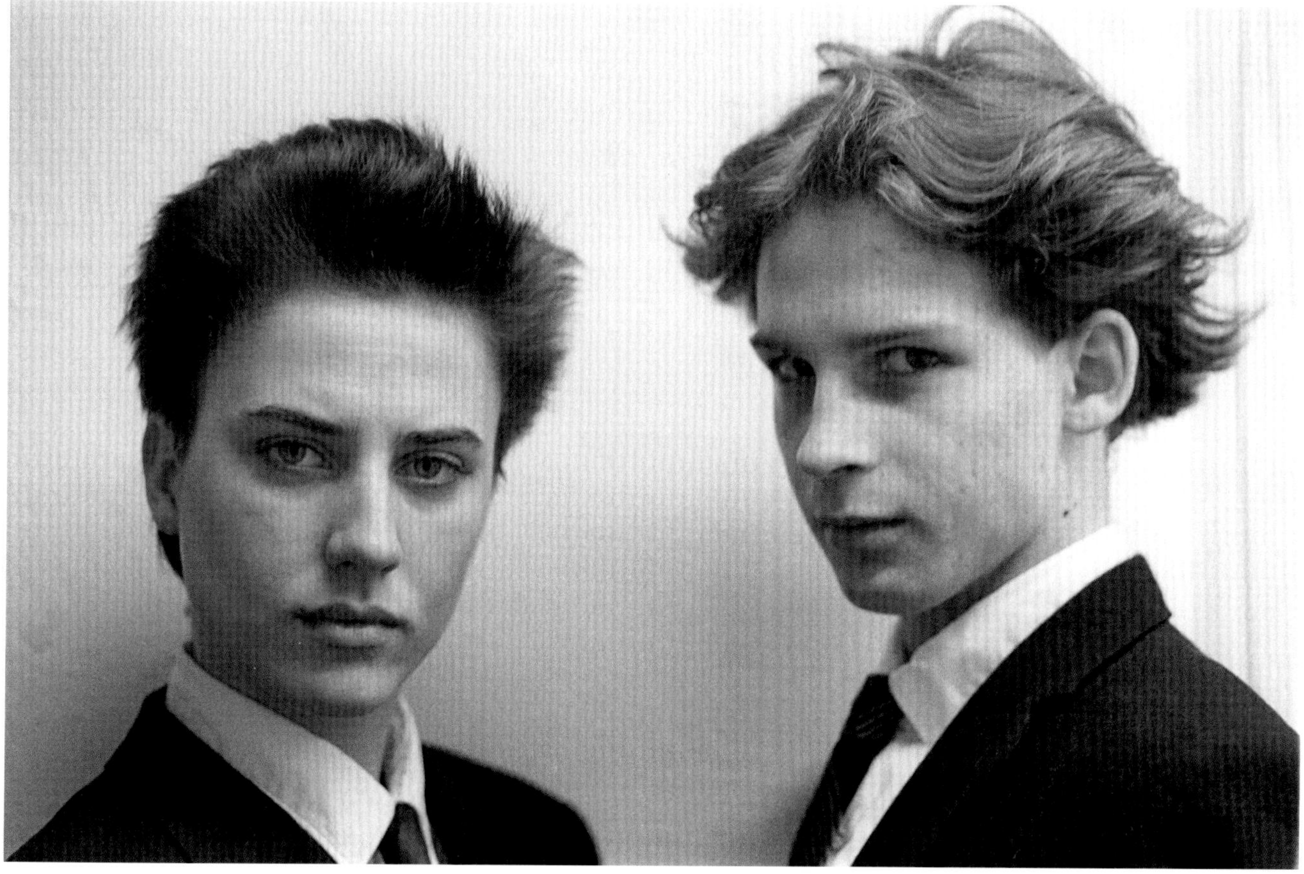

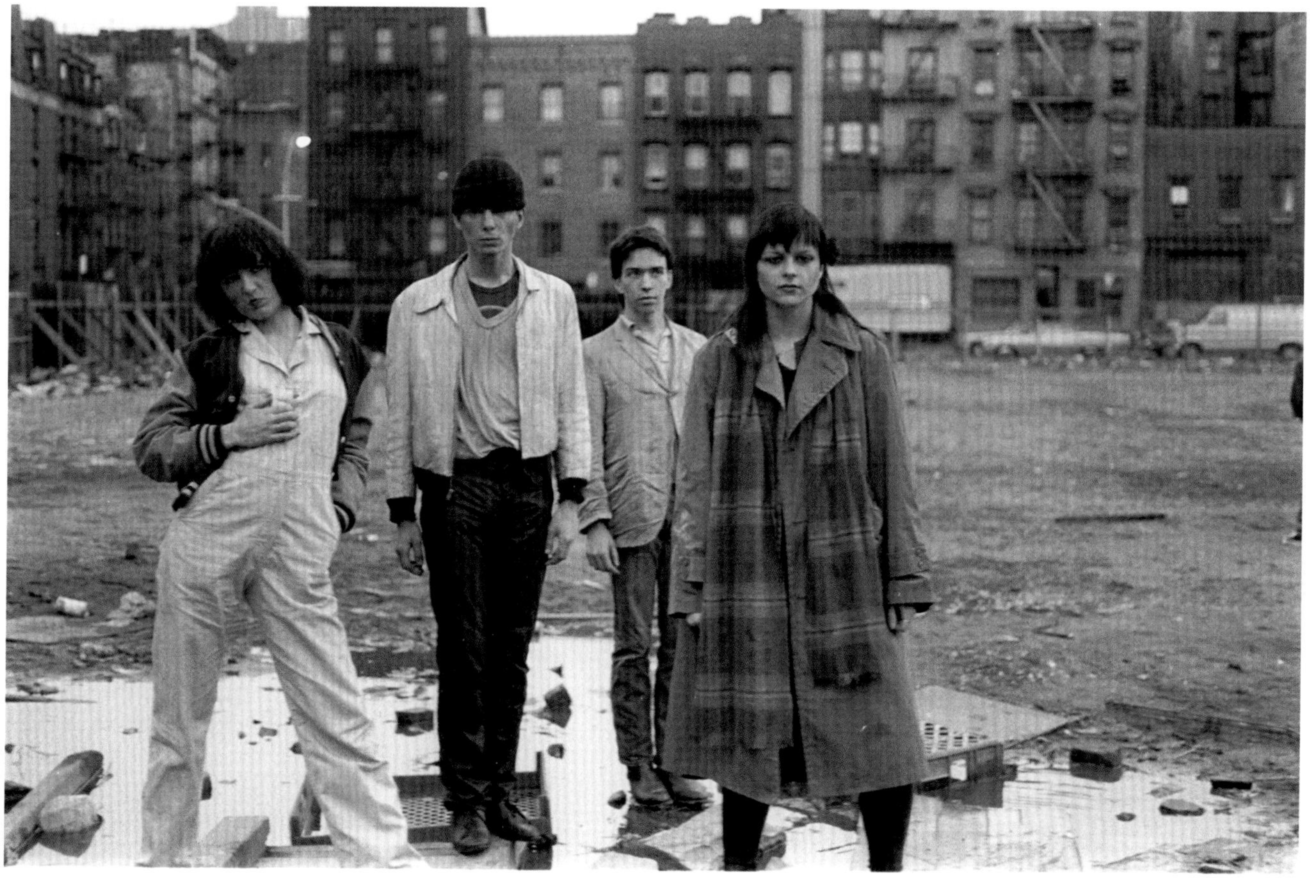

KATHERINE DUMAS (AMERICAN, 1956–2012). ***Rhonda Waggoner and Christophe Hameon.*** 1979. Digital image from 35mm negative. Collection the Estate of Katherine Dumas

KATHERINE DUMAS. ***Youth against Death.*** 1980. Digital image from 35mm negative. Collection the Estate of Katherine Dumas. From left: Natalya Maystrenko, Scott Covert, Frank Holliday, and Nancy Ulrich

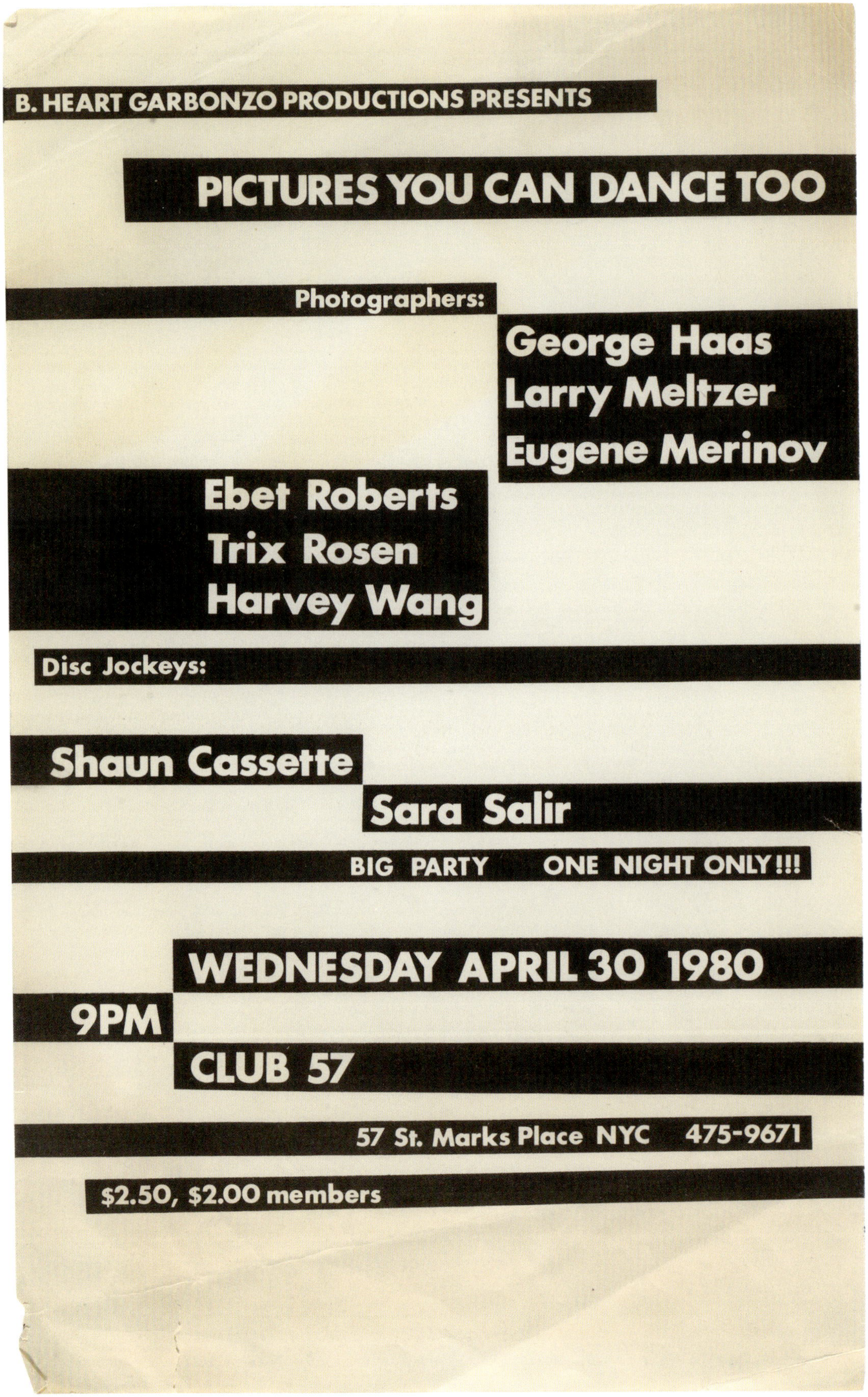

1. Flyer for *Pictures You Can Dance Too*, organized at Club 57 by George Haas, 1980. Design by Haas. The Museum of Modern Art, New York. Department of Film Special Collections

Dancing to Pictures

Lucy Gallun

On the last night of April in 1980, Club 57 hosted an evening of pictures (fig. 1). You could dance, too.[1] Hung from the ceiling, six 35mm carousel slide projectors clicked through image after image, beaming pictures onto white paper adhered to the club's black walls: here were New Yorkers embracing on the sidewalk; portrait subjects posing in studios; musicians performing exuberantly on stage. This one-night event gave top billing to the photographers, though they shared the program with DJs Sean Cassette and Sara Salir, each of whom regularly spun an eclectic mix of punk and New Wave records at nightclubs including Danceteria and Hurrah; if you showed up, you could also expect a dance party. This was a night when imagery comingled with sound; when club goers could absorb a diverse array of photographic art practices while reveling in a dynamic mix of music, a combination of multiple forms that was not atypical for downtown clubs like Club 57.

The show was organized by George Haas, whose own images were also included in one of the six projectors. Haas showed his work alongside pictures by Larry Meltzer, Eugene Merinov, Ebet Roberts, Trix Rosen, and Harvey Wang. Though portraiture was a predominant genre (though by no means the only genre—Meltzer, for instance, showed abstract enlargements of Super 8 film frames), the artists approached the figural subject from a range of positions. Roberts, for example, captured bands performing: amalgams of extraordinary energy, sweat, and ego. Rosen produced imagery of women's nude bodies from a lesbian perspective in which dignity and self-possession were paramount. And Wang, who regularly shot documentary images of the club and its scene (page 133), brought for this project a rollicking DIY sensibility through hand-painted color applied to black-and-white slides, many featuring New York City dwellers generally enjoying life out in the city (fig. 2).

As with many of the club's programs, there was a feeling of spontaneity and happenstance to the whole event. Haas sought a mash-up of images, selecting artists whose images he believed would complement one another without selecting the individual images that would be included or the order in which they would be loaded into the carousels. Moreover, the carousels were not synchronized, so new combinations of images would appear in successive cycles over the course of the night. The DJs also hadn't seen the images in advance, so any associations drawn between image and song were likely to have been unintentional and coincidental.

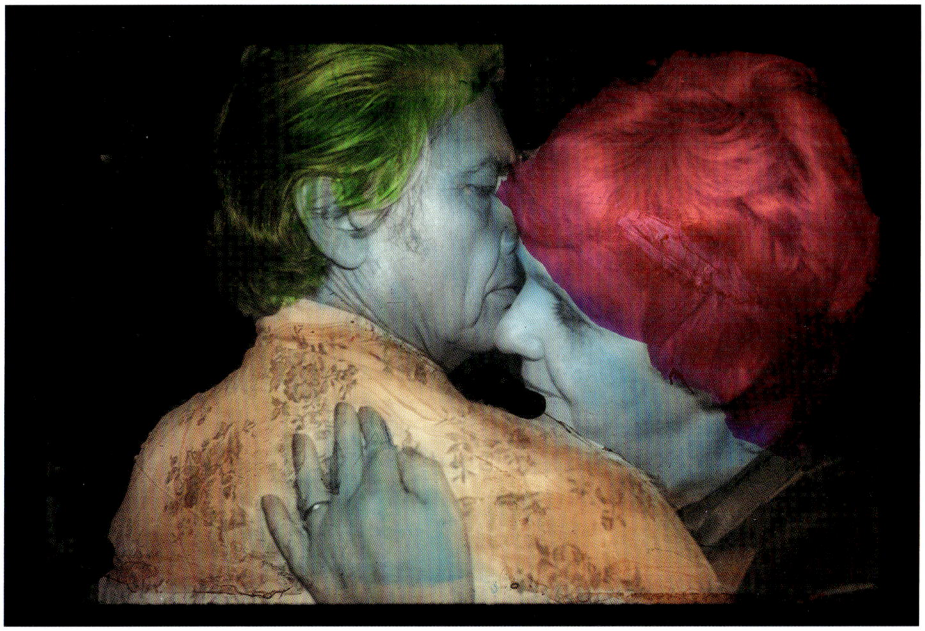

2. Harvey Wang (American, born 1956). Untitled. 1980. Hand-painted 35mm slide. Exhibited in *Pictures You Can Dance Too*, 1980

The first two sentences of this short text have reworked Haas's title for the event: *Pictures You Can Dance Too*. What initially might appear to be a typographical error (an extra *o* added to the word *to*) is actually a bit of clever word play.[2] When read out loud, the title sounds similar to "music you can dance to," though in the case of Haas's event we imagine the attendees moving their bodies to the tune (or the tone) of the pictures, which, clicking by successively, also had a percussive or rhythmic sensibility. Yet if the extra *o* is considered, and some punctuation added (perhaps a period or an em dash after *Pictures*), we might recognize that this was first and foremost a show of pictures, specifically of projected photographic images.

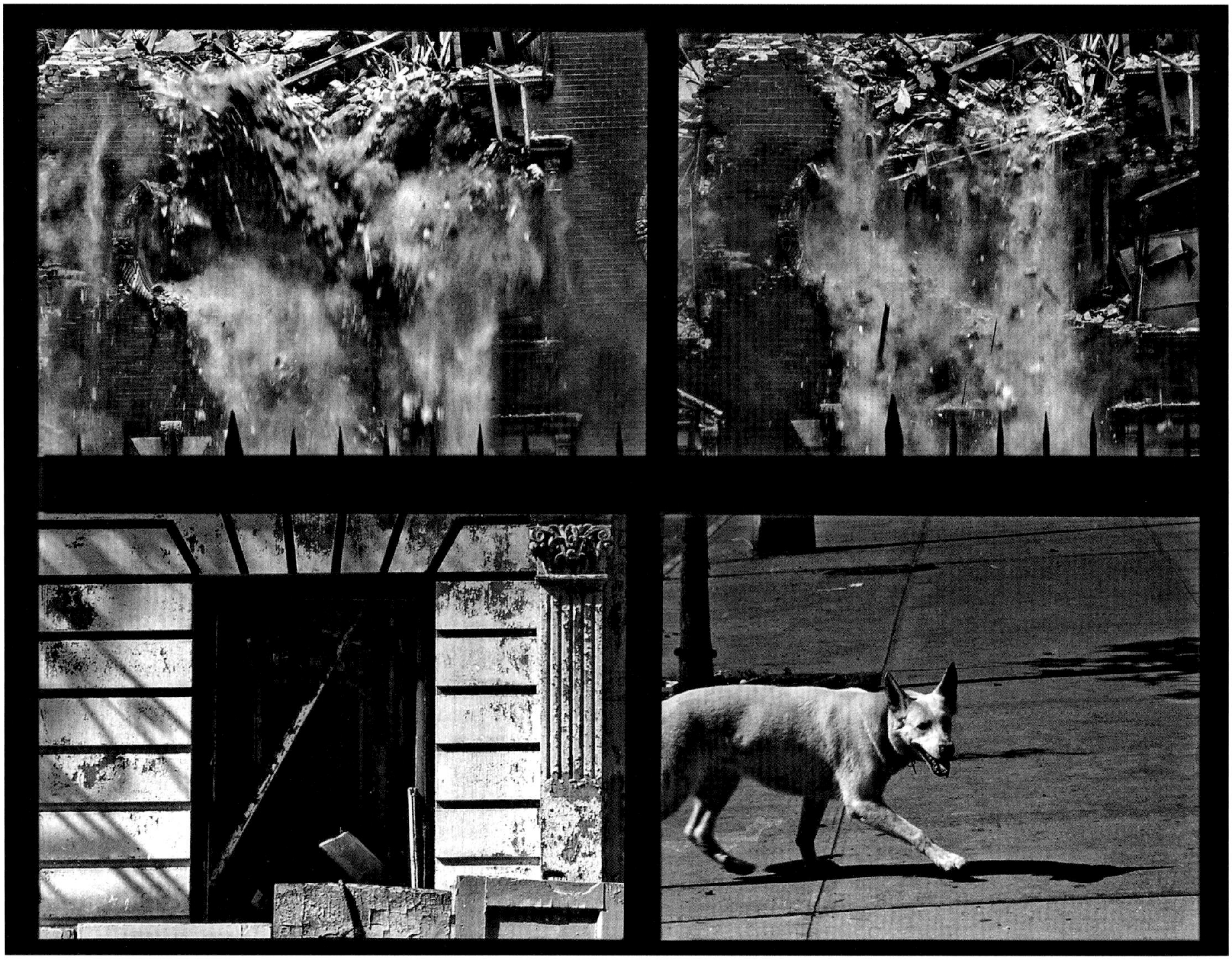

3. **Anthony Scibelli (American, born 1953).** ***Cluster Doorway.*** 1978. Photomontage, gelatin silver print, 11 × 14" (27.9 × 35.6 cm). The work, which features the artist's apartment at Ninety-Eighth Street and Madison Avenue as it was being torn down, was exhibited in *At Long Last Photos*, a two-person show with Katherine Dumas, Club 57, September 29, 1980. Collection the artist

Pictures You Can Dance Too was neither the first nor the last presentation of photography at Club 57. Throughout the five years of its existence, many exhibitions either were devoted entirely to photo-based practices or included photography within presentations of work in multiple mediums. Yet despite an expanding interest in photo-based art-making during this period—including the image-scavenging practices of the so-called Pictures Generation, and the emergence of an alternative gallery scene in the East Village—painting still dominated the wider art scene, making alternative venues like Club 57 especially crucial for exhibiting photography in its many forms.

The slideshow format also proved natural for the club environment. By the late 1960s, projected slide images had become a crucial component of musical events in downtown New York City. The Joshua Light Show, a troupe of resident artists at Fillmore East (just a couple blocks from where Club 57 would later open), mesmerized rock-concertgoers with the psychedelic liquid effects of their projected imagery, which included hand-painted slides and appropriated reproductions of works from throughout the history of art. Andy Warhol's Exploding Plastic Inevitable merged imagery from multiple film and slide projections with live music from the Velvet Underground to produce a multisensory experience. The slide format had also been repurposed in a fine art context by conceptual artists, including Robert Smithson and Dan Graham (and even appeared in the Photography Galleries at MoMA, in exhibitions like *Projects: Helen Levitt in Color*, of 1974), so its availability as an art medium was certainly not unprecedented.

Historically, slides were associated with lectures or with family travel snapshots, and indeed such a medium was appealing to artists who were actively rejecting traditional art professionalism and polish in favor of the layperson's materials. In addition, given the prohibitive expense of printing and preparing photographic prints for exhibition, and the limited wall space—Club 57 was tiny—the inexpensive slideshow format was ideal. Sequential projected slides provided an easy way to show many more images in a smaller space. As art historian Charles Harrison has noted, "Slides, of course, offered a virtually infinite range of cheap pictures, easily accumulated."[3] Projected images can also be understood as part of a reaction or backlash on the part of artists to the object fetishization that proliferated in an ever-more market-driven environment.

While the entire program of *Pictures You Can Dance Too* stretched beyond the parameters of club scene as subject, many of the photographs were also representations of the extended East Village club community, including Merinov's images of bands on stage and Haas's own multifaceted portraits of distinctive individuals, such as the legendary nightclub doorman Haoui Montaug (page 140).[4] The tendency to picture the community itself, for a club's attendees to see images of themselves represented in large-scale on a venue's walls, had significant appeal and power. Indeed, one of the best-known works to emerge from the era—also an amalgam of projected slides set to recorded music—was undoubtedly Nan Goldin's *The Ballad of Sexual Dependency*, which the artist started developing throughout the early 1980s during live performances at small clubs and independent performance spaces, including Collective for Living Cinema, O-P Screening Room, 8BC, and many others. In April 1982, in fact, Goldin participated in a multidisciplinary event at Club 57, in which she presented slides of photographs from a sojourn in Mexico, some of which would also be incorporated into *The Ballad*. Calling the work, "the diary I let people read,"[6] Goldin compiled poignant and searing images of her private life, including herself and her friends in moments of aching grief or ecstatic love, all projected in vibrant color in front of the subjects themselves or the members of their communities.

Indeed, much as with *Pictures You Can Dance Too* or *The Ballad*, a significant portion of the photo-based work featured at Club 57 over its five-year run might be categorized generally as documentation of the scene and its denizens. Later in 1980, for example, visitors to the club might have found scenes from the East Village in a two-person exhibition of photographs by Katherine Dumas (page 143) and Anthony Scibelli (fig. 3; see also page 134). In November of the same year, Marcus Leatherdale presented prints in *Urban Women*, a solo exhibition that included studio portraits of Jean Caffeine, Divine, Anita Sarko, and others (pages 142). Club members April Palmieri (page 135), Ande Whyland (page 132), and Robert Carrithers (page 136) all photographed the downtown scene and showed their photographs in slide form at the club. Artist David Schmidlapp presented his work in what the club calendar

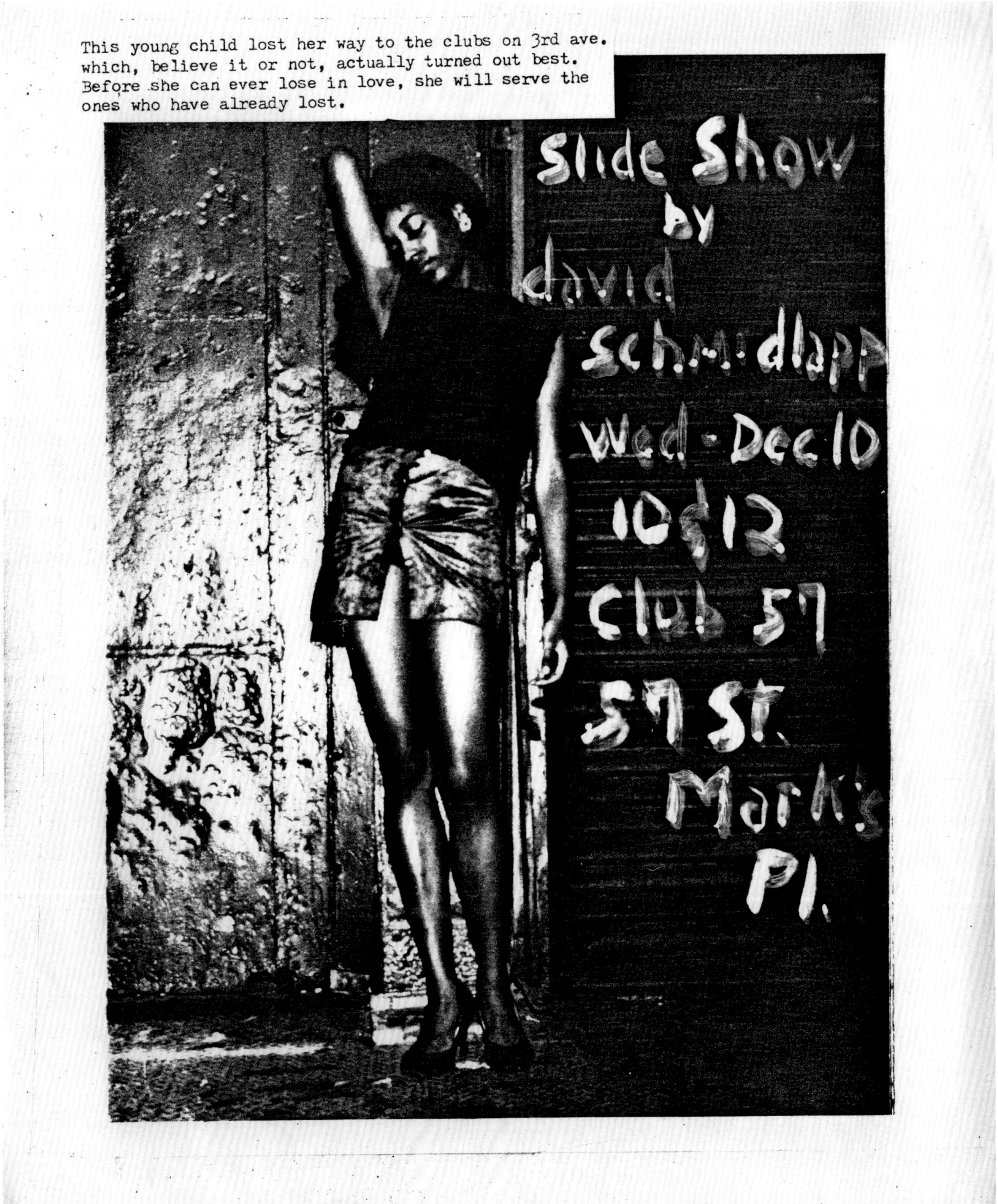

4. Flyer for David Schmidlapp's slideshow performance at Club 57, 1980. Design by Schmidlapp. The Museum of Modern Art, New York. Department of Film Special Collections

called an evening of Slides of Politics and Fashion (fig. 4). And Tseng Kwong Chi (pages 138–39)—now widely recognized for his witty self-portraits dressed in a "Mao suit" at tourist sites in New York City and around the world—was also a regular and prolific documenter of Club 57 through his studio and editorial work, which put club cohorts in the pages of *SoHo Weekly News* among other venues, and in the thousands of photographs he took of Keith Haring's work in a wide variety of locations.

The flyer for *Pictures You Can Dance Too* proclaimed "One Night Only!!!" and indeed there would be no subsequent iterations of this particular visual-sonic party. Haas recalls the event as having been very successful—the dance floor was packed, and he was asked to restage the program. But by then he had begun work on other projects and the show never materialized. Nonetheless, the heterogeneous elements brought together in this event provide an apt model around which to consider how photographic images were integrated into the club's multidimensional program. The slideshow format enabled multiple images by multiple artists to be shown together and experienced against a backdrop of dance music spun by DJs. Yet unlike typical nightclubs at which the dancing was central, here the pictures themselves were the main event.

1. I am indebted to George Haas and Harvey Wang for their generous recollections of this event.

2. During this period, Haas and Sean Cassette collaborated continuously using word play, employing snippets of overheard conversations in the poetic verses they exchanged.

3. Charles Harrison, "Saving Pictures," in *SlideShow*, ed., Darsie Alexander (Baltimore and University Park, PA: Baltimore Museum of Art and Penn State University Press, 2005), 43. Alexander's book offers an extraordinary overview and history of 35mm slides as art medium.

4. Haas himself also worked as a doorman, an integral and exceedingly influential role. In his recollections of the scene, critic Gary Indiana likened club doormen to artists in the way they shaped the culture: "Many artists made no objects but did things that were art, like keeping dull people out of the Mudd Club." He then went on to add that "Ann Magnuson and a cohort of appealing freaks turned Club 57 into a breezy retort to the Mudd Club's manic-depressive door policy." Gary Indiana, "One Brief, Scuzzy Moment," *New York* (December 6, 2004): 48–52.

5. Nan Goldin, *The Ballad of Sexual Dependency* (New York: Aperture Foundation, 1986), 6.

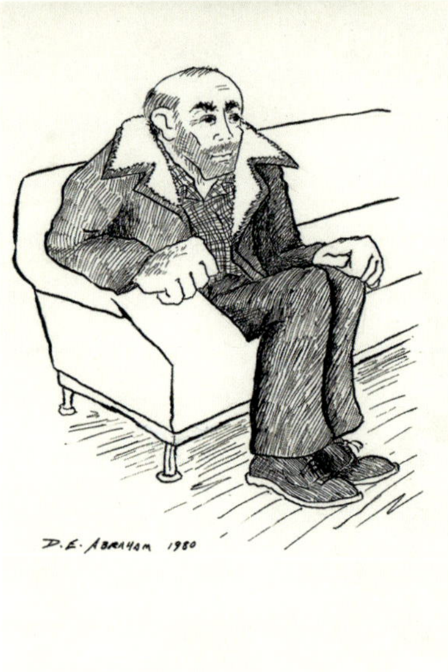

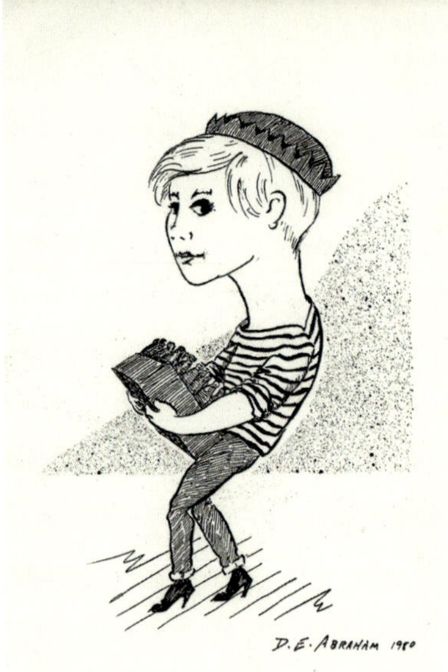

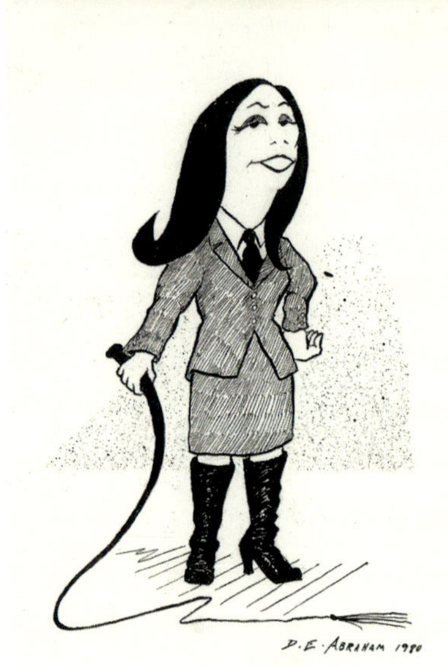

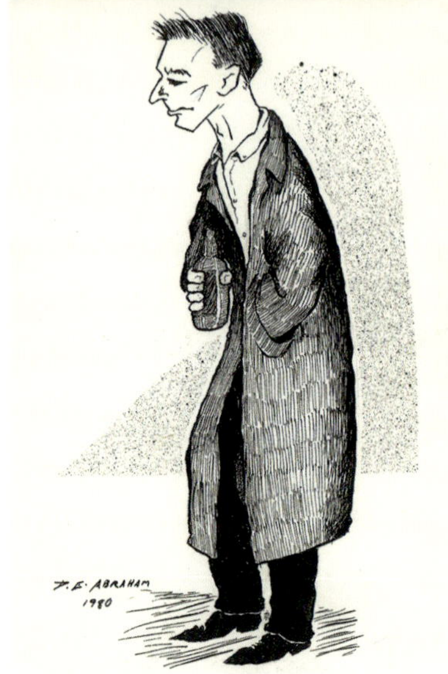

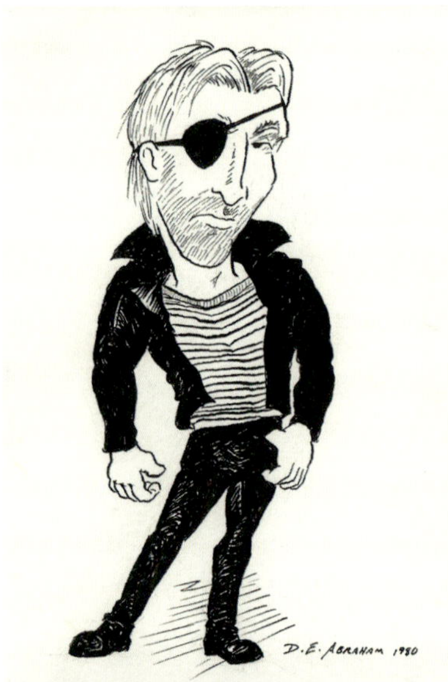

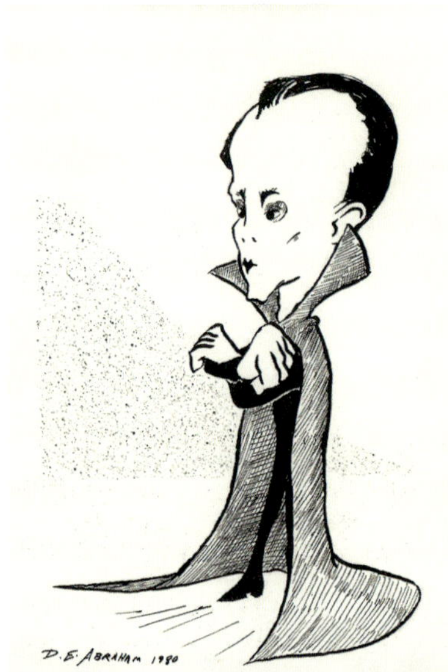

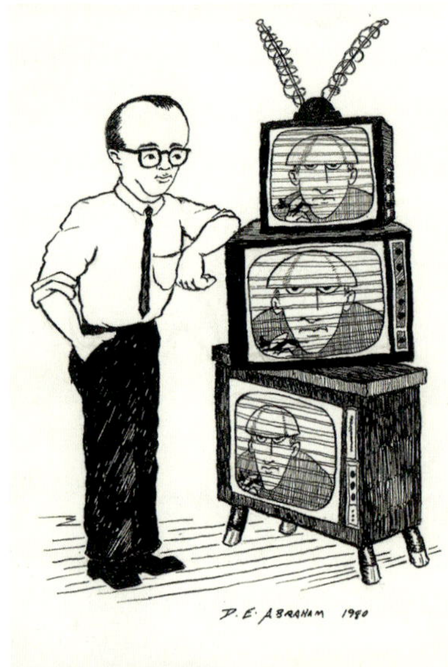

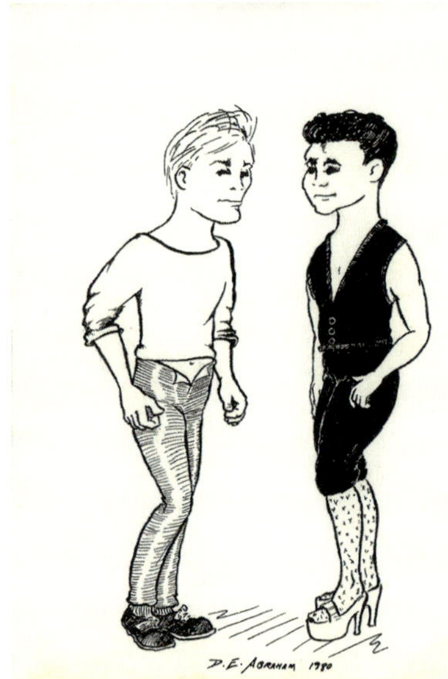

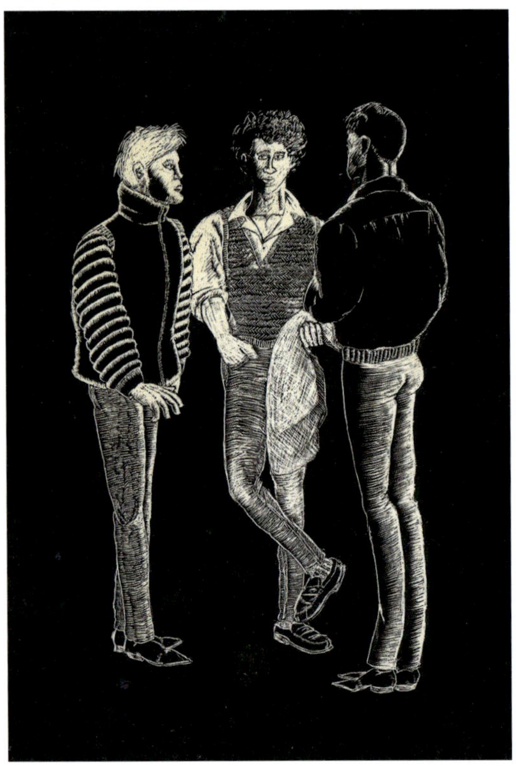
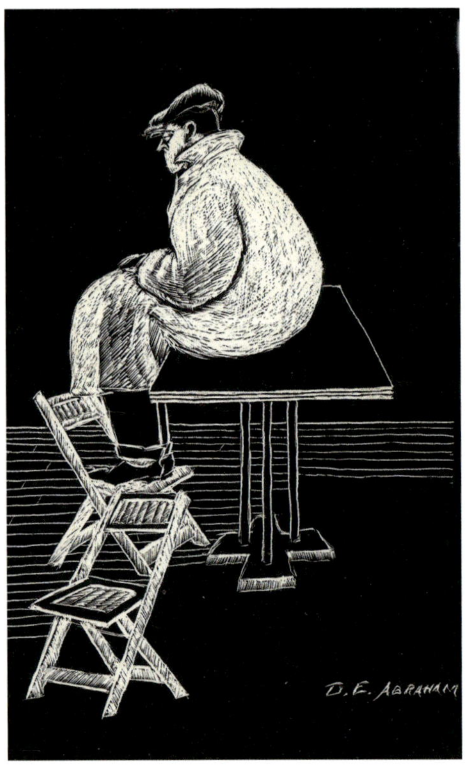

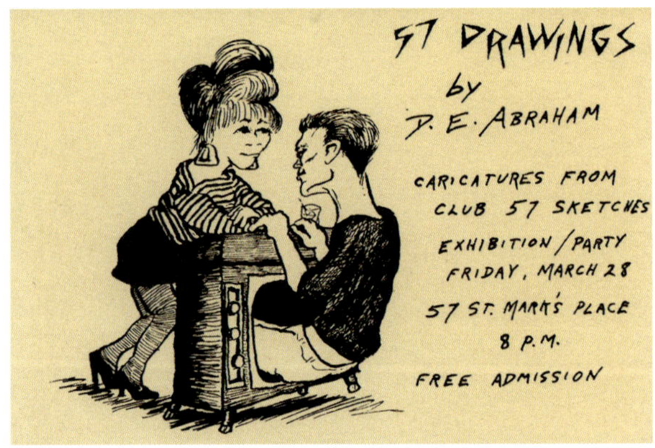

DANIEL ABRAHAM (AMERICAN, BORN 1952). **Works in top two rows are from the series *57 Drawings,*** 1980. Ink on paper, 9 × 6" (22.9 × 15.2 cm). Collection the artist. Clockwise from top left: Stanley Strychacki, Min Thometz, Tessie Chua, Evan Lurie, John Sex and AMMO, Keith Haring and Kenny Scharf, Klaus Nomi, and John Spacely. **Preparatory sketches for *57 Drawings,*** 1980. Pen on scratchboard. Left: 9 × 6½" (22.9 × 16.5 cm). Right: 5 × 3" (12.7 × 7.6 cm). Collection the artist. **Postcard for 57 *Drawings* by D. E. Abraham at Club 57,** 1980. Design by Daniel Abraham. Collection the artist. Pictured: Ann Magnuson and Drew Straub

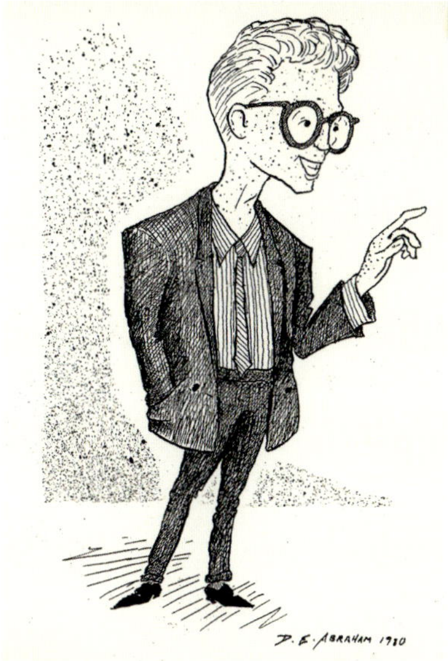

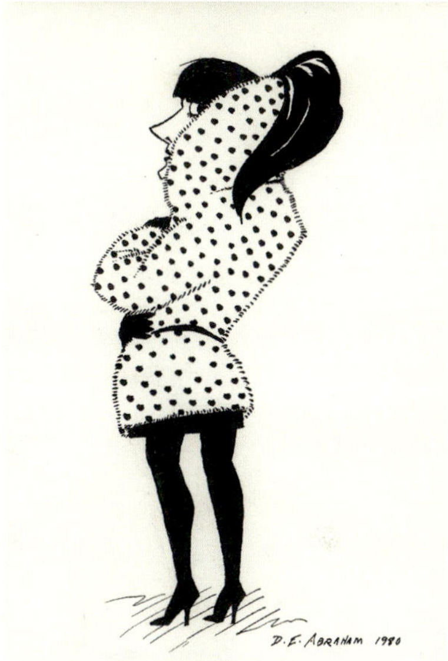

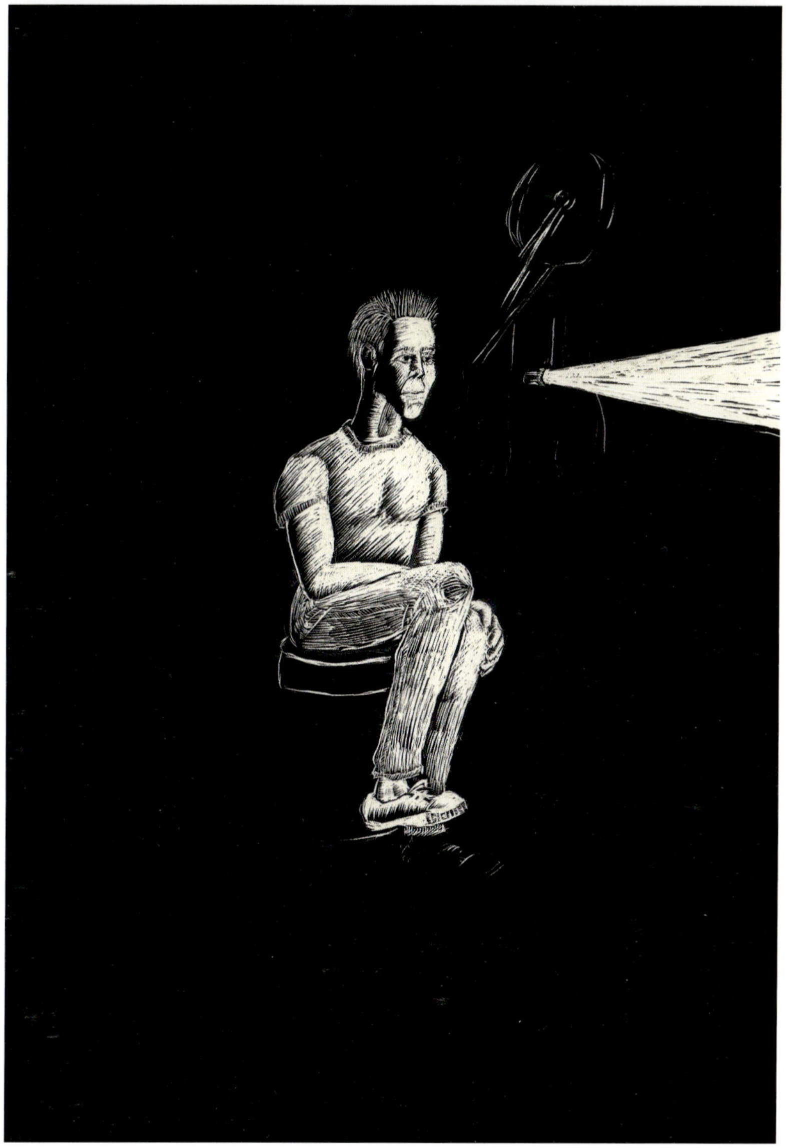

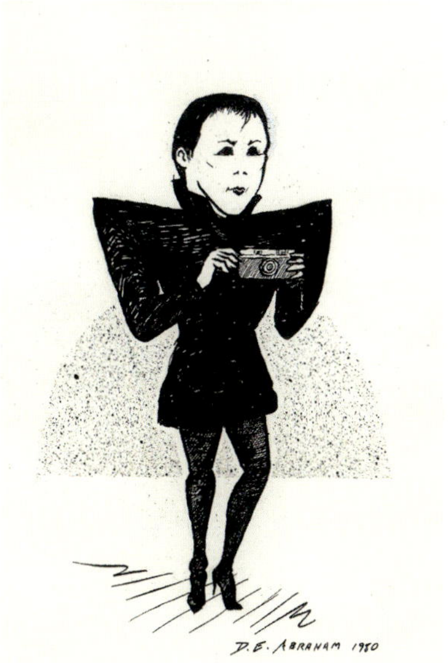

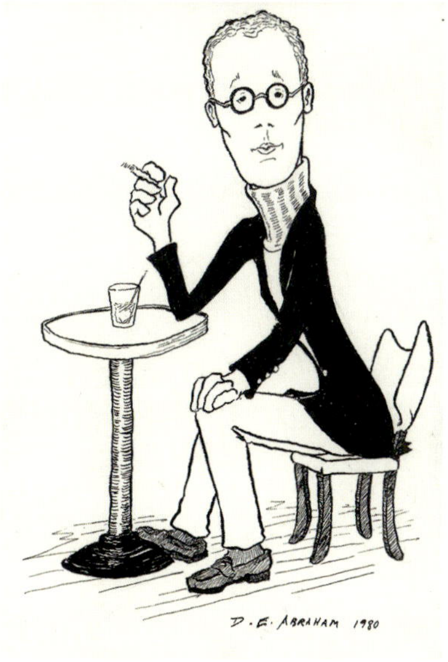

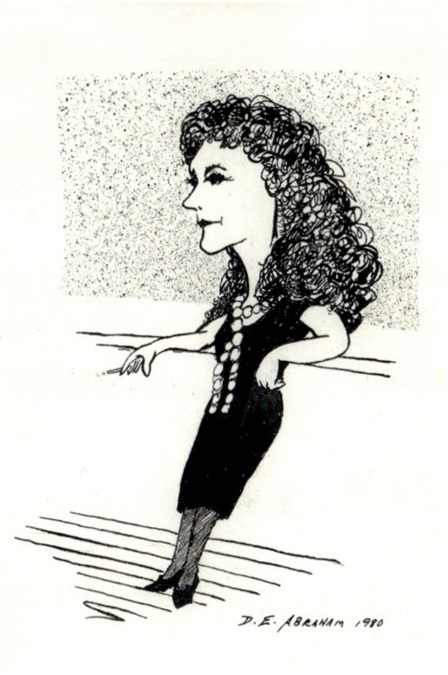

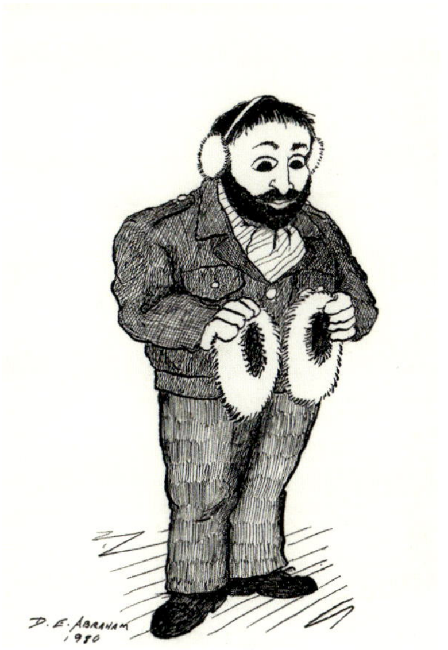

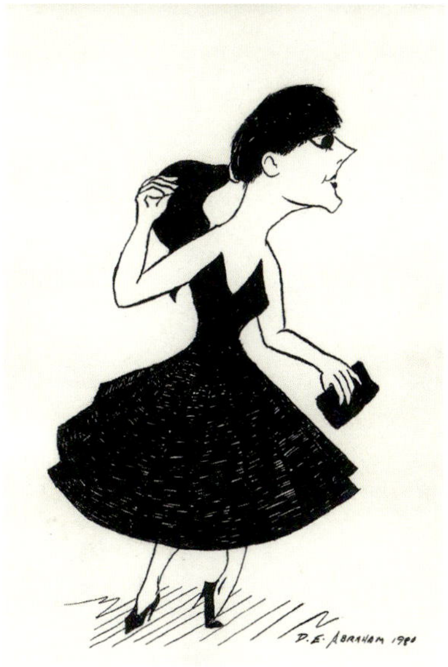

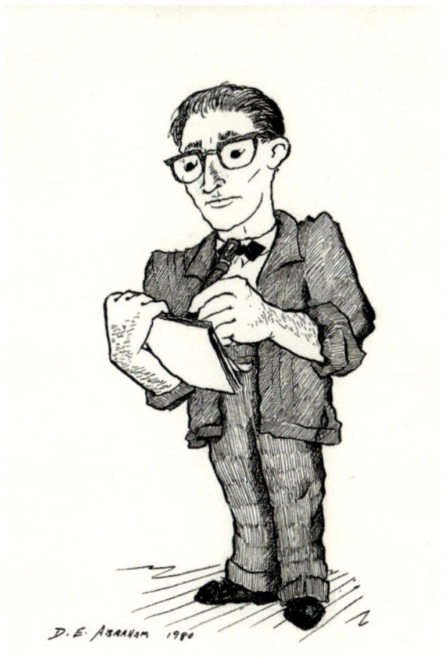

Top right: **Preparatory sketch of Tom Scully for *57 Drawings,*** 1980. Pen on scratchboard, 6¾ × 4" (17.1 × 10.2 cm). **Other works on the page are from the series *57 Drawings,*** 1980. Ink on paper, 9 × 6" (22.9 × 15.2 cm). Collection the artist. Clockwise from top left: Scott Covert, Susan Hannaford, Mark Upton, Daniel Abraham, Susan Hannaford, Bruce Edelman, Alexa Hunter, and Judith Wong

IT TAKES AN EAST VILLAGE

Ann Magnuson

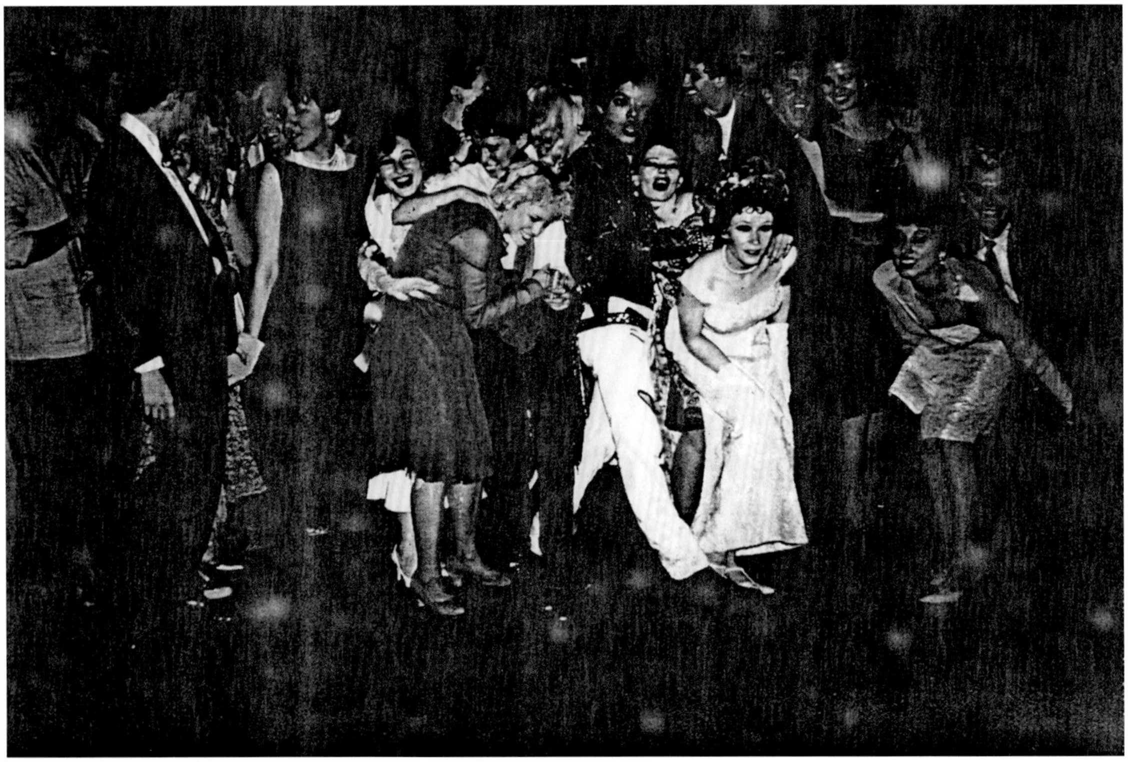

1. Ladies Auxiliary Debutante Ball at Club 57, 1980, from a xeroxed booklet made for the group's members by April Palmieri. Photograph by Palmieri. The Museum of Modern Art, New York. Department of Film Special Collections

The gritty songs of Lou Reed taught me that "Noo Yawk" wasn't the safest place for a lil' West Virginny gal to aimlessly roam. Although I'd spent my junior year abroad in London in 1976 and 1977, where I witnessed disaffected teens co-opting the aesthetics of punk pioneer Richard Hell, I wasn't sure of what I might encounter on the mean streets of this particular Asphalt Jungle. Plus, the traumatic memory of having a switchblade held up to my throat within an hour of first stepping foot in Manhattan (in 1975 for a quick visit to see my first Broadway play) was still fresh in my mind.

It was November 1977, and I was in New York City for Thanksgiving weekend, having temporarily escaped the staid Ohio liberal arts college where I was a theater and cinema major. I threw caution to the wind and walked bravely down St. Marks Place. Traveling east from Third Avenue, I passed shady characters, shabby storefronts, and psychedelic graffiti fading on the front of the Dom (which housed a cavernous ballroom where the famous Electric Circus nightclub used to be).

I hadn't yet reached Second Avenue when I stopped dead in my tracks in front of the Manic Panic display window. There, alongside ripped T-shirts and stiletto-heeled boots, was the Farrah Fawcett pinup poster from 1976—the one featuring the actress in a red bathing suit so tight that the shape of her erect nipples showed through. That damn poster was everywhere back then, and it represented the dominant culture of the time: *Charlie's Angels*, denim flares, mullets, and bland, boring polyester conformity. Except this particular poster had a paper bag taped over Farrah's head, obscuring her perfect toothsome smile. I laughed out loud and thought, I'm *home*!

I quickly got my frustrated ass out of Ohio and moved to NYC in January 1978, where I spent my final semester on a work-study program. I was given an internship at Ensemble Studio Theatre (EST), which was located on Fifty-Second Street and Eleventh Avenue, in the then-desolate wilds of Hell's Kitchen, which was just as sketchy as the East Village but with none of the outrageous élan. While EST was a highly respected professional theater that produced new work, it was fairly traditional (i.e., square) and nowhere close to the avant-garde fare I loved. While I learned a lot at EST, I learned more spending nearly every night downtown discovering much wilder stuff like Squat Theatre and bands like Suicide and James Chance and the Contortions.

Vagabond writer Peter Smith immediately became my first New York boyfriend, playing Virgil to my Dante as we explored the subterranean world of New York together.

I had first met Peter at Timothy Dunleavy's uptown apartment. Tim was a high school friend two years my senior and the first person I knew who ran off to New York City to pursue his artistic dreams. I met a lot of fun people at Tim's, including some of his former classmates from North Carolina School of the Arts. Andy Rees, William Fleet Lively, and Frank Holliday were among the smartest, funniest, most ribald raconteurs I had ever met and all would become central figures in creating the future Club 57 ethos (fig. 1).

Early on, Tim took a group of us to Studio 54. Since he was a regular, we easily got past the velvet rope and into the club. Tim whisked me down the hallway past the potted palms and straight onto the dance floor. As a disco beat pounded and confetti fell from above, the infamous moon-with-the-coke-spoon set piece descended from the ceiling. It was all very exciting until I remembered, Wait a minute. . . . I *hate* disco. I want to go to CBGB!

Peter obliged and we soon became regulars at the infamous punk rock venue where I would meet many future Club 57 cohorts. CBGB was the undisputed center of cool in 1978, even if many of the bands, like Ramones, Blondie, and Talking Heads, had moved on to the big time. No matter, there were plenty of new cool people arriving every day.

I made fast friends with a golden-haired stranger with the unusual name of Kestutis Nakas. I brazenly gushed over his beautiful blond hair, admittedly loosened up from the many free drinks I'd received from my new best friend and CBGB bartender, Kimberly Davis. But more than the booze, the greatest icebreaker was the excitement of meeting like-minded people who shared the same passions, young people who wouldn't be caught dead at Studio 54. Kestutis, a drama student at NYU, immediately turned me on to way-out downtown theater folk, including Jeff Weiss, whose epic neo-Brechtian improvised theater pieces would open my eyes to a whole new way of breaking down the fourth wall. Weiss would also end up being my neighbor on East Tenth Street, when Peter and I moved in together. The actor Willem Dafoe lived in the same building, and he invited us to see him perform in his first show with the Wooster Group. I was dazzled.

When things were slow at CBGB, Peter and I would walk up to Max's Kansas City, Andy Warhol's former hangout just off Union Square. It was there that we met Klaus Sperber. World Trade Center pastry chef by day and flaming creature by night, Klaus's alien Nomi persona would come later. But Klaus already looked otherworldly: his sharp Germanic features and tight, shiny vinyl outfits made him stand out from the crowd. Peter and I made a beeline to this mysterious stranger and we became instant friends.

Peter and I would hang out with Klaus a lot in early 1978 (page 134), when massive snowstorms transformed Manhattan into a glittering Arctic tundra. One night the three of us were walking back to the East Village when Klaus jumped up on a filthy snow mound and began to sing an operatic aria in a high soprano voice, reminding me of the Baroque castrati I had learned about in theater history class.[1]

There was no doubt about it, downtown was a lot more interesting than uptown, and soon I was loath to venture north of Fourteenth Street.

I was introduced to Tom Scully at CBGB a bit later, in early spring. Tom was very friendly and soon we were deep in conversation, discovering we loved the same things: Dada, monster movies, and vaudeville. Tom wanted to revive vaudeville by producing a modern-day variety show featuring the punk and New Wave talent of the day. Impulsively I blurted out "Can I direct it?"[2] Tom immediately said "Sure!" and then introduced me to his beautiful comrade-in-arms, Susan Hannaford. Like everyone I'd met that year, we became fast friends.

Andy Rees was one of the few of our gang who lived uptown, on Ninety-Sixth Street, sharing an apartment with his partner David Richardson from American Ballet Theatre. The wild and wildly funny North Carolina native immediately won me over with his exuberant southern charm. Andy and I spent many nights together watching TV evangelists like Pat Robertson and Jim and Tammy Faye Bakker (at his place since you could only get those cable channels uptown). Christian television was a shared guilty pleasure that reflected our respective Bible Belt roots. Andy and I would later mount our own improvised marathon productions of Jim and Tammy's "Praise the Lord" show (i.e., *The PTL Club*) at Club 57, calling ours "The 5700 Club" (page 131).

Peter Smith soon started his self-styled anticonservative "political" group, the National Resurgence Party (NRP), and every Sunday our ever-growing group of party people (including Anthony Scibelli, Haoui Montaug, Kimberly Davis, and Steve Brown) met around our kitchen table chasing away hangovers by drinking copious amounts of Café Bustelo, while discussing ways to subvert the mainstream.

I didn't bother going back to Ohio for my graduation ceremony in June. I never wanted to leave Manhattan for fear of missing something. After my internship at EST was up, I was hired as assistant to their artistic director. But I yearned to quit and only do "weirdo" theater downtown. When Tom and Susan finally secured the funds to mount their vaudeville show in the fall of '78, I was overjoyed. Daniel Abraham, a charming illustrator who looked and dressed like a young Walt Disney, created the retro neo-vaudevillian flyers that put out the call for unique talent. I excitedly told everyone I encountered about the show, dutifully passing Tom and Susan's number to all I thought worthy of an audition.

New Wave Vaudeville was straight out of the Judy Garland/Mickey Rooney 1939 film, *Babes in Arms*, where a group of discouraged show-biz-loving teens pull themselves up by their Depression-era bootstraps with the rallying cry, "Let's put on a show in the barn!" Our barn was an old Polish-American meeting hall and ballroom called Irving Plaza. Tom and Susan encouraged their friends and acquaintances to participate, while I did the same. Our scenes began to comingle and word spread fast, with many local performers, bands, and miscellaneous oddballs responding to the flyers.

New Wave Vaudeville was Tom and Susan's baby, but everyone involved came up with ideas and pitched in, wearing multiple hats. Like all theater, it was a very collaborative (if frequently uneven) effort.

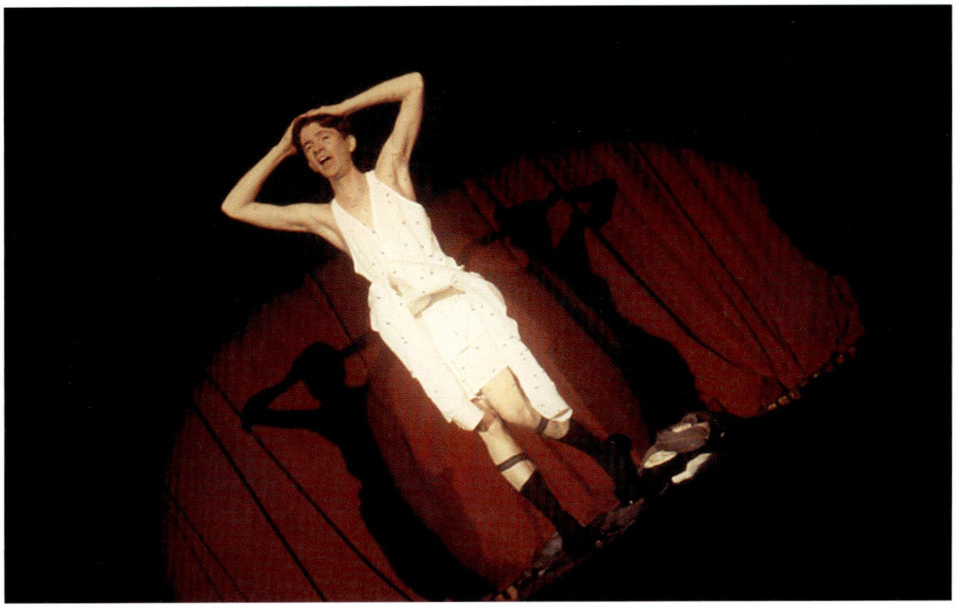

2. David McDermott at New Wave Vaudeville, Irving Plaza, 1978. Photograph by Ande Whyland

I must admit, I wasn't "directing" so much as herding cats. Very cool cats (see pages 102–3, figs. 1–2).

Tom and Susan brilliantly cast the artist/performer David McDermott—the most genuine eccentric in town—as the emcee (fig. 2). Dressed in a King Tut costume that featured old-fashioned sock garters, the delightfully (and stubbornly) anachronistic David made his entrance on an Egyptian-style litter to the soundtrack of *Land of the Pharaohs* (1955). Then he sang in his signature high-pitched 1920s crooner voice, and introduced the acts like a wayward but excited time traveler. David stole the show every time he appeared. That is, until the finale, when Klaus debuted as Nomi, a New Wave opera-singing alien. Klaus/Nomi stopped the show with the heartbreaking mezzo-soprano aria "Mon coeur s'ouvre à ta voix" from Camille Saint-Saëns's 1877 opera *Samson et Dalila*. The raucous, cynical punk crowd sat in stunned silence, shocked that what they were hearing was real. Nomi brought tears to more than a few eyes, then dramatically disappeared into a cloud of smoke bombs.[3]

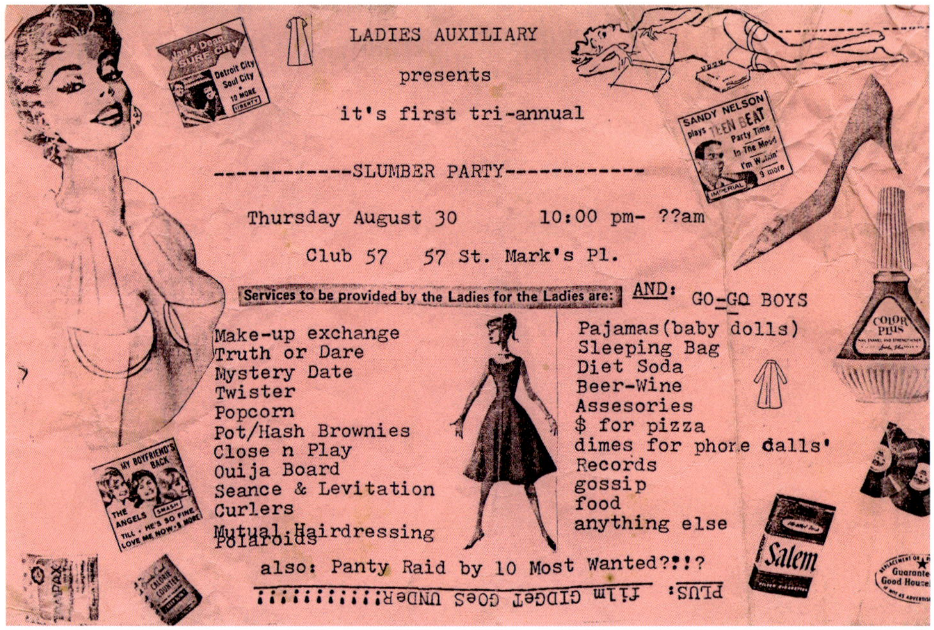

3. Flyer for Ladies Auxiliary First Triannual Slumber Party at Club 57, 1979. Design by the author. Collection Charlotte Slivka

Stanley Strychacki recognized the value of this new vaudeville energy right away. Stanley was an older Polish émigré (old to us although he was probably just in his late thirties) who worked odd jobs, including as a show promoter at Irving Plaza (page 130). But it was Stanley's "small club" at 57 St. Marks Place that he was anxious for us to see. Club 57 was a subterranean space located in the basement of the Polish National Church. It was essentially a church fellowship meeting room with a small built-in bar that used to host Polish polka parties.[4] Various punk rock bands and theater groups had sporadically rented the place before our arrival but Stanley was seeking an infusion of new creative blood.

Stanley had initially asked Tom to manage the small venue but Tom declined, preferring to focus on a weekly Monster Movie Club and miscellaneous film screenings, which he and Susan would organize at the venue. However, Tom suggested me for the job. I leapt at the chance! I had read all about Le Chat Noir, the nineteenth-century cabaret and artists' salon that was often called the birthplace of the avant-garde, and knew in my bones that Club 57 could be our twentieth-century version!

The first event I recall happening at Club 57 that involved our gang was held on January 19, 1979. An old datebook reads: "Movie Party." Many folks from the vaudeville show (and beyond) were invited and several brought their films to show. I was excited to screen my college student films, including *One God, One Singer*, a Super 8 film I had made in 1976, when Elvis performed in my hometown of Charleston, West Virginia. The club was packed, the party a hit, and it was clear to everyone that something great was in the making.

The early bookings were scattershot with little thematic consistency. All of us spent a lot of time and energy cleaning and repainting the place. Peter moved his Sunday NRP meetings to the club and the Poetry Project temporarily used the space while their regular space, the St. Mark's Church, was being renovated after a fire. Various outside groups occasionally booked the space, and I was thrilled when the playwright Robert Patrick walked in and asked to stage his play *Kennedy's Children* at the club. (I had done the play in college four years earlier.)

Because Stanley only paid me sporadically per event, my job as club manager had to be shared with other part-time work. In May 1979, the Wall Street stock brokerage firm I had been occasionally temping at offered me a full-time job. The pay was great but I declined, telling them my heart was really in the theater. Actually, I had fallen head over heels with the potential of Club 57 and wanted to focus on it full-time. Thankfully, Stanley agreed to pay me a pittance of a monthly salary, just enough to get by. Which wasn't much—you literally could live on five to ten dollars a day back then. He also helped me find a new apartment since my romantic relationship with Peter had come to an end.

Monster Movie Club premiered in May 1979 and attracted fantastically fun people to the club every Tuesday night. Susan and Tom's frequent weekend film series, with themes like 1950s juvenile delinquents, did the same. Tom helped fill the jukebox with his stellar collection of 45s, including retro dance tunes from Motown and the British Invasion, as well as current New Wave hits (such as "Money" by the Flying Lizards) and singles by local bands like Tina Peel and ART (who were also our friends). Soon the current crop of SVA art students was on the scene, including Keith Haring, Kenny Scharf, Drew Straub, John McLaughlin (soon to morph into John Sex), and Wendy Wild, along with Parsons students Kitty Brophy, Larry Ashton, and Katy K.

Stanley got around not having a liquor license with the excuse that we were a church youth group operating as a private club, which we really (kind of) were. For five dollars you could become a member and get in free to nearly every event. Plus you got a customized membership card and mailings of the monthly calendar, flyers, and an occasional newsletter. As time went by the membership grew and more new members booked nights at the club. Nearly every address on the membership list was in Alphabet City, and people started dropping by just to go-go dance to the jukebox—and guzzle the cheap drinks, which always featured overgenerous amounts of alcohol.

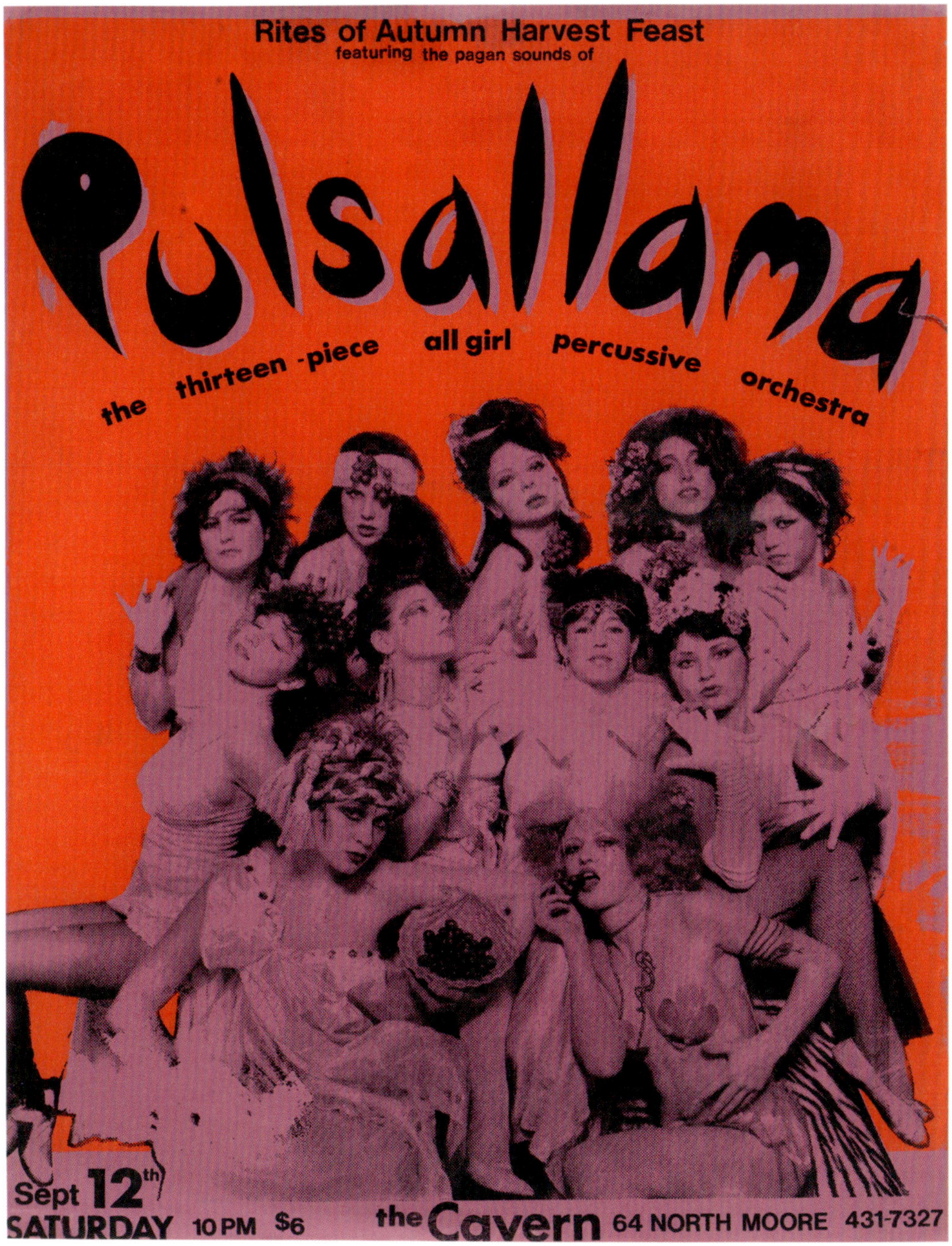

4. Poster for Pulsallama at the Cavern, 1981. Design by John Sex, from a photograph by Tseng Kwong Chi. The Museum of Modern Art, New York. Department of Film Special Collections

In no time, Club 57 became everyone's collective rec room, a place where you could not only escape your cramped and crappy apartment, but also find safety and inspiration among kindred spirits. The club became our new home and the membership our new surrogate family. This new family was different from the one most of us had run away from. This new family let everyone be authentically and freakishly themselves.

In the summer of 1979, the Ladies Auxiliary of the Lower East Side formed and met regularly at the club (or in my new apartment), mostly for laughs and potluck dinners. Conceived as a punk rock/New Wave counterpart to my mother's Junior League meetings, we sought the same kind of coffee-klatch fellowship that previous generations of women enjoyed. But while the motivations were identical—empowerment in numbers—we gave it a playful punk feminist twist. Soon we were hosting our own crazy events at the club.

We threw a pot- and hash-brownie slumber party with go-go boys (fig. 3), which Bishop John T. Jakubik, the rector of the upstairs church, accidentally walked in on while we were sleeping it off. We held a thrift-store prom for us misfits who had skipped our real high school proms; staged a "debutante ball"; and mounted two separate Lady Wrestling nights where we built a wrestling ring in the middle of the club and took on the roles of different battling female personae (page 133). The latter was such a hit that curator Joe Lewis invited us to repeat the madness at his South Bronx gallery, Fashion Moda. The Auxiliary's Rites of Spring Fertility Bacchanal led to the formation of the all-girl pagan cacophony band Pulsallama (fig. 4).

In spite of women's lib, the gender dynamic at the time (especially uptown) was very much an oppressive *Mad Men* man's world, where women were still expected to kowtow to male authority figures. But there were so many young women—and young men—itching to get out from under that, and Club 57 was a place where we could.

In October 1979, I started making monthly calendars using collage (fig. 5). Stanley had given me a blank calendar template with the request to "make program." Here was the chance to fully control the programming and create a consistent vibe! I encouraged everyone to book shows or host events and spent many a happy hour in Tom and Susan's Chinatown loft hatching ideas for thematic dance parties. Those first dance parties were built around basic genres—Motown, Rockabilly, British Invasion—but quickly mutated. Everyone got into the act and made up their own to boot. Andy Rees, Anthony Scibelli, and Scott Covert hosted a debauched punk rock night. Min Thometz threw an evening of Bongo Voodoo (with "frenzied ceremonial dancing"). Lisa Baumgardner's *Bikini Girl* magazine threw numerous events. And everyone put on formal wear and played a giant Twister game laid out on the dance floor in Twistin' in High Society (a night named after my favorite thrift store record). Peter Kwaloff, who had gone to SVA with Tom and Susan, and had been deeply involved with New Wave Vaudeville, was one of our first DJs, although Tom DJ'd most of those early dance parties. Naomi Regelson, who had been working at the club helping Stanley before the vaudeville

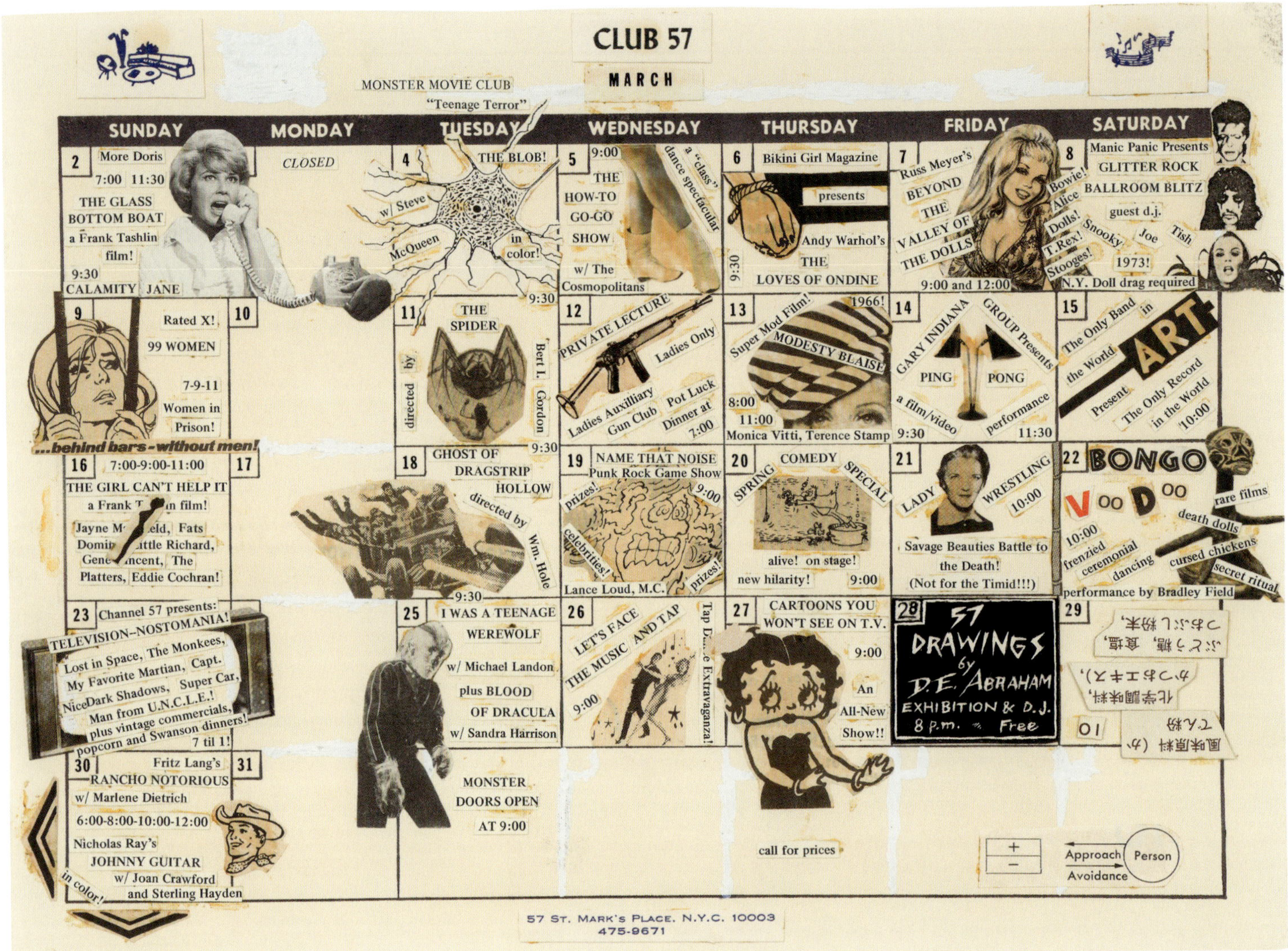

5. Original collages for Club 57 calendars, March and July 1980. The author, who scoured for imagery and text in vintage magazines such as *House & Garden*, *MAD*, *Playboy*, and *Vogue*, created twelve calendars from October 1979 through September 1980. Collection Ann Magnuson

group showed up, also played great sets, usually featuring new bands she discovered before anyone else while working at the college radio station WNYU. Club regular Dany Johnson soon became a frequent DJ as did my new boyfriend, Kai Eric, whom I had met at Mudd Club. In the ensuing months, the themes got wackier and wackier, and were often mashups.

My favorite one has to be Putt-Putt Reggae, where we created a Jamaican shantytown miniature-golf course with trashed cardboard boxes we dragged in off the street, and played dub reggae music. I distinctly remember seeing future Area masterminds Eric Goode and Shawn Hausman, whom I had met much earlier via Kimberly Davis, looking over our nutty DIY installations with interest.

Casino Royale was another early hit with the membership. Tom and Susan screened the film and brought in gambling tables, and somehow we managed to run an illegal gambling joint for a night. Everyone dressed in formal attire or as Bond characters, with Dany Johnson and me painted entirely in gold. My fellow exchange student from London, Alexa Hunter, who had returned to her native New York and quickly become part of the gang, captured it all on Super 8 film.

Alexa also shot footage of one of my favorite Tom Scully dance parties, Iran, Iraq, and Iroll. We decorated the club with tabloid covers from the *New York Post* and *Daily News*, whose headlines were continually screaming about the American hostages being held in Tehran, and wore flags and tablecloths as head gear. PC this was not.

Stanley let us do whatever we wanted, essentially letting the inmates run the asylum. Incredibly, Bishop John defended us at every turn, especially when irate neighbors kept trying to close us down—mostly over the noise but also because we were "evil." Obviously, the Polish National Church prayed to a very tolerant and forgiving God.

No doubt Stanley's experiences in Soviet-controlled Poland gave him a special appreciation for all forms of freedom, and he gave us the kind of carte-blanche creative license *no one* uptown ever would. As far as I was concerned, uptown, where I had witnessed desperate actors auditioning for scraps from the table, was the world of "No!" Downtown was the world of "Yes!" and Club 57 soon became the world of "Yes! Yes! Yes!" Or, in Polish, *Tak! Tak! Tak!*

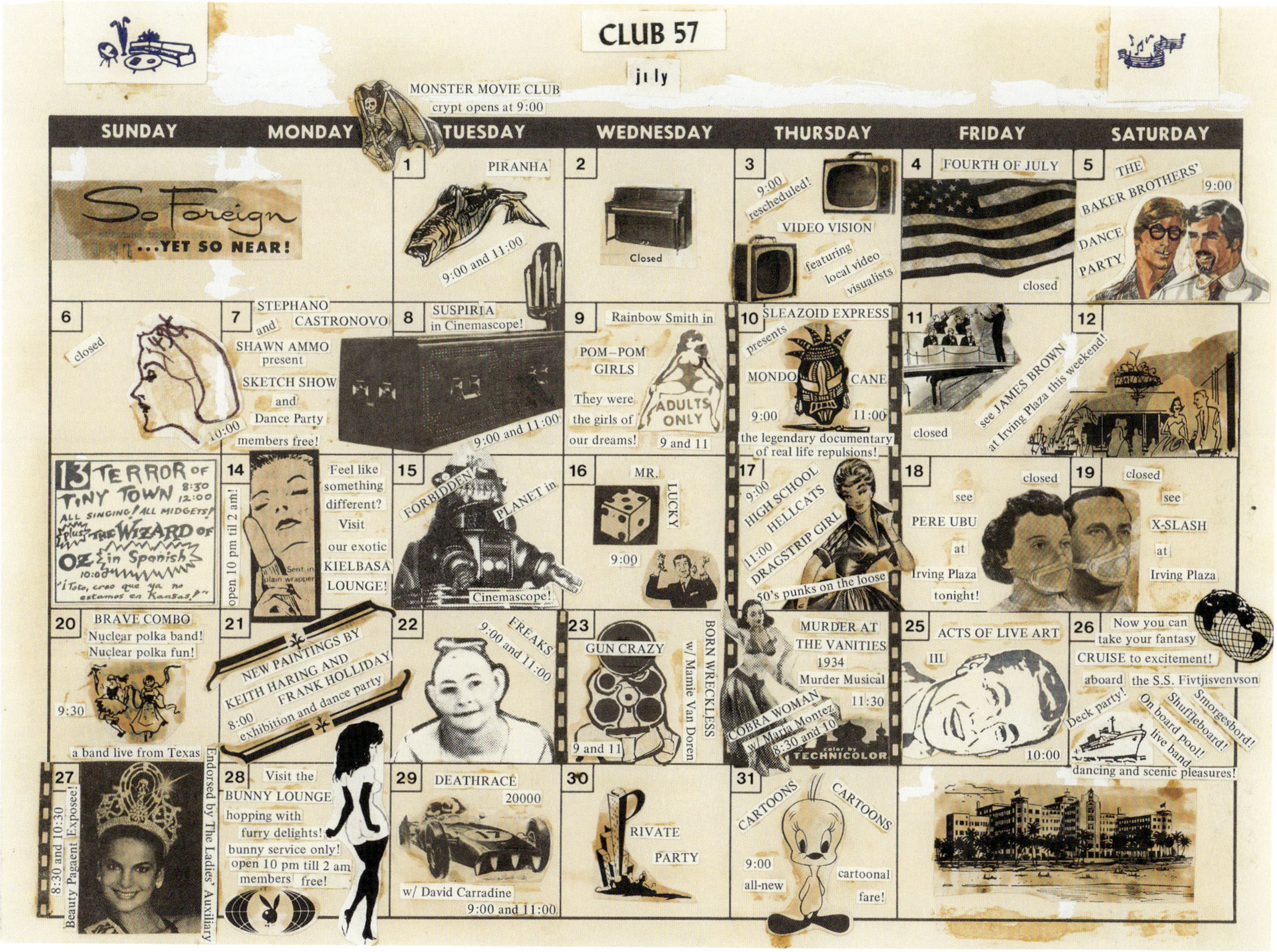

At any given time, the club was a dance hall, a screening room, a watering hole, a theater lab, an art gallery, or a self-styled "let it all hang out" encounter group. Sometimes it was all those things at once. Mostly it was a shamanic black box where we could ritualistically shape-shift and make any crazy dream into a reality—albeit with no-budget, *Little Rascals*–style production values. Besides being a fresh take on the Surrealist cabaret, I also saw the club as a giant TV set, where every night was a different channel. For our generation, the first weaned on television, it was also a place to collectively exorcise the TV demons we had grown up with—the most harrowing having been broadcast on the nightly news. To reflect this, I asked artist Kenny Scharf to design a TV-themed New Wave logo for the club (page 12, fig. 2).[5] We were all "made for TV"—just not the *Charlie's Angels* kind.

Soon many of us were making our own TV. Kestutis Nakas, inspired by Ernie Kovacs's surreal TV show from the late 1950s, and Glenn O'Brien's more recent *TV Party* on Manhattan Cable, hosted *Your Program of Programs*, a

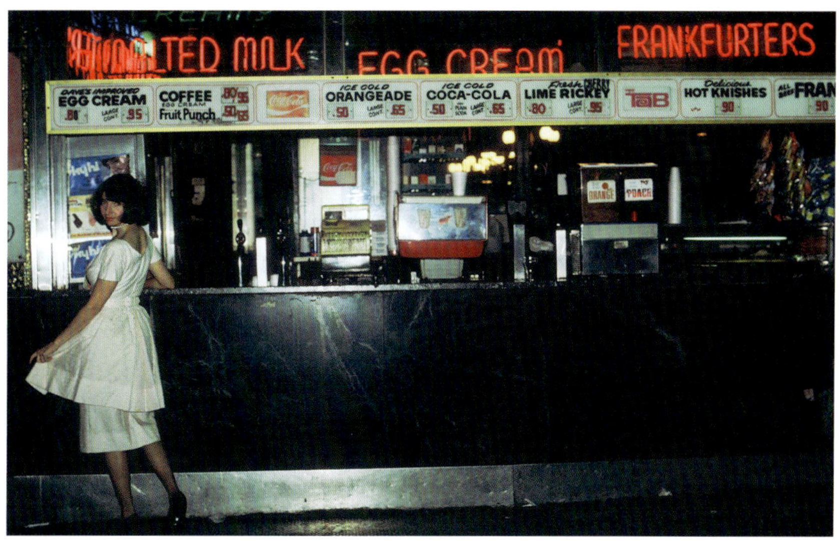

6. Diana Lillig in front of Dave's Luncheonette, at Broadway and Canal Street, 1981. Photograph by Robert Carrithers

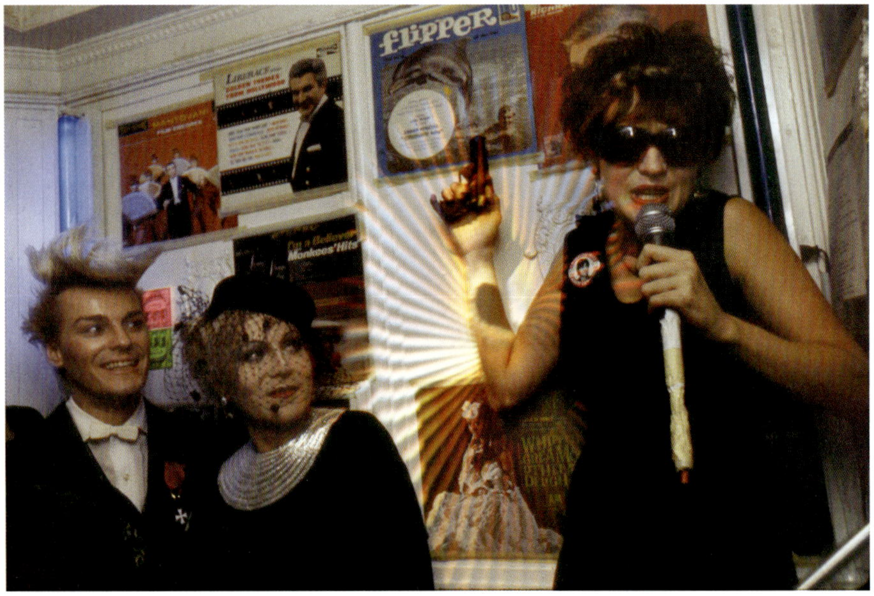

7. The author performing in the elevator at Danceteria, 1982. Also pictured are John Sex and Alexis del Lago. Photograph by Tseng Kwong Chi

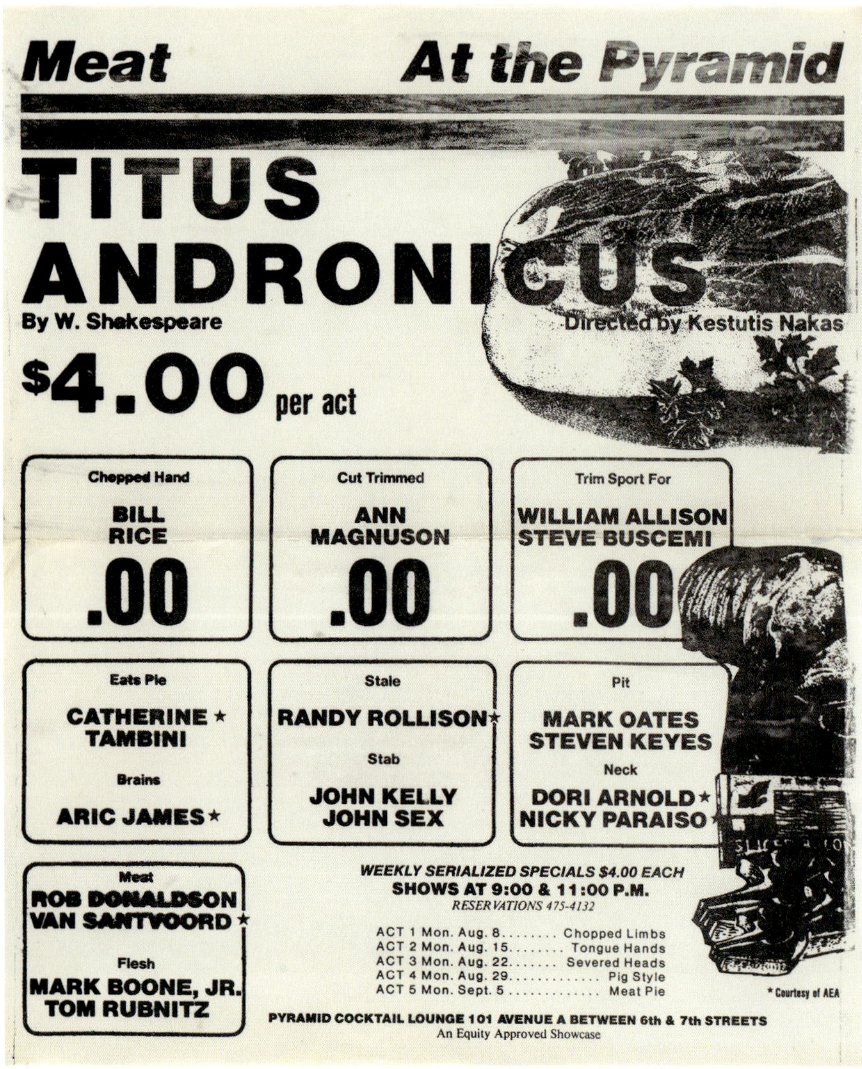

8. Poster for *Titus Andronicus*, directed by Kestutis Nakas at Pyramid Club, 1983. Design by Marta Huszar and Nakas. The Museum of Modern Art, New York. Department of Film Special Collections

cable-access talk and variety show, whose title referenced Sid Caesar's vintage '50s *Your Show of Shows*. Many Club 57 members appeared as guests.

The collective reanimation (and deconstruction) of pop-cultural elements from America's optimistic postwar era also acted as an antidote to the bleakness of our surroundings. Much of the East Village looked like bombed-out London after the Blitz (page 133), and most of us were completely broke, living a hand-to-mouth existence. Hence a colorful, goofball riff on *Laugh-In* was more appealing than another dreary *Naked Lunch*. Besides, some of us needed respite from the surly meanness favored by the older, black-clad, heroin-loving snobs who frequented other clubs. (Even if some of our members could snarl with the best of them, while others, sadly, were starting to experiment with the all-too-available opiate.) But while downtown New York was full of rivalries and high school–style cliques, there was some fluidity between the borders. Even the too-cool-for-school No Wavers and New Cinema folk showed their work at Club 57, while the 57 kooks became regulars at Mudd Club. At the end of the night, we all ate the same greasy potato knishes at Dave's Luncheonette (fig. 6).

As 1980 progressed—carrying with it the stark reality that former actor Ronald Reagan was indeed our new president—the monthly calendars got more jam-packed. We were fully convinced Reagan was going to start a nuclear war with Russia, so we were creating at a frenetic pace and living every day like it was our last. I was happier than ever, but by September, the nonstop activity was burning me out. I decided to quit as manager, sometimes wondering if I'd made a mistake. But I was writing and performing more and wanted to branch out to work in other milieus. Steve Maas was hiring a lot of us to do things at Mudd Club and Jim Fouratt and Rudolf Piper were inviting us to work and create at their various clubs as well, particularly Danceteria (fig. 7).

I started performing in art spaces like the Kitchen and, in early 1982, after returning from shooting the film *The Hunger* with David Bowie, I curated the *Performance Rites* series at P.S. 1, which featured many of the Club 57 gang (see pages 109–10, figs. 5–6), as did my shows at the Kitchen and new spaces such as Life Cafe. Other club members were branching out too. Keith Haring was becoming a bona fide art star, Klaus Nomi was becoming an international sensation, and more 57 performers and DJs were moving their acts over to Pyramid Club. There, Kestutis Nakas directed many of us in his wild production of Shakespeare's *Titus Andronicus* (fig. 8), each act presented in weekly installments and performed with raucous audience participation.

Video artist Tom Rubnitz was one of my fellow *Titus* castmates, and he asked if I wanted to collaborate on a video. I loved *Undercover Me!*, the secret agent spoof

Tom had made with John Sex, featuring Dany Johnson and Tseng Kwong Chi as hilarious Bond-style villains. Tom and I shot *Made for TV* (pages 62–63) through 1983, and it was a nonstop party of improvisatory fun—especially when we spent a weekend at the upstate home of the B-52's and raided Kate and Cindy's closets for costumes and wigs!

I constantly collaborated with my club friends (especially William Fleet Lively, Joey Arias, and Kristian Hoffman) and cast many downtowners in the shows I did for the Serious Fun! Festival, at New York's Lincoln Center, and my 1987 Cinemax/HBO special, *Vandemonium*. So much was happening, so many opportunities were opening up, and we all felt we were riding this New Wave to something really, *really* big.

Then AIDS hit.

For a long time, looking back was difficult. Whenever I would think of Club 57, every face from that time, every event, every moment of hilarity and camaraderie was tinged with deep sorrow. AIDS killed so many of our family members, and it decimated the entire New York arts community. None of us could have predicted we'd experience such soul-sickening sadness while still so young. True, we *did* grow up thinking we'd all die in a nuclear war with Russia, but no one had imagined the Bomb would turn out to be a plague straight out of a sci-fi movie that might have played at Monster Movie Club. Those of us who miraculously survived AIDS—or alcoholism, drug addiction, Hepatitis C, bad romances, or just plain old bad luck—had to keep on keepin' on . . . often without looking back for fear of being engulfed in another tsunami of grief. "It's as if we are all survivors of an earthquake," Frank Holliday told me decades later, when we reunited at the dawn of social media networking, "emerging dazed out of the rubble."

Now, nearly forty years on, it finally feels safe to look back. There is Klaus Nomi, swaddled in latex and wearing black plum lipstick (so outré for its time); John Sex in his signature sky-high Mr. Softee–style pompadour taking his pet boa constrictor Delilah on a walk down St. Marks Place; Tseng Kwong Chi dressed in his "Slut for Art" Mao suit, gleefully fooling people into believing he really was an ambassador from "Red" China; William Fleet Lively making me laugh so hard I would literally roll on the ground; Peter Kwaloff excitedly turning us onto super-obscure psychedelic tunes and his beloved girl groups; Wendy Wild shaking those ridiculously huge fake boobs that she used to knock out her opponents while impersonating Dolly Parton on Lady Wrestling night; Andy Rees improvising for hours as a TV evangelist while, as I would learn much later, tripping on LSD; a still-nerdy, eager-to-be-corrupted Bill Landis loudly plopping his school books down on the table in the first row at Monster Movie Club; a baby-faced Keith Haring angering the serious-minded St. Marks poets by endlessly repeating and reshuffling the words *fat, boy, lick*; even the image of my soft-spoken younger brother, visiting from out of town, getting caught up in the improvised fake-blood ritual during Pulsallama's chaotic debut at the Ladies Auxiliary Rites of Spring Bacchanal—all these faded memories begin to emerge with greater clarity, deeper love, and fewer tears.

1. My interview in the film *The Nomi Song* (2004) mistakenly conflated two events: Klaus singing on the dirty snow mound in early 1978 and Klaus performing in New Wave Vaudeville later that same year.

2. Part of my internship at EST involved directing a modern adaptation of a Molière play, staged as a sitcom. I was eager to do more.

3. See Jenny Schlenzka, "Acts of Live Art," in this volume for additional details on New Wave Vaudeville.

4. Decades later my Polish-American mother-in-law would tell me that she and her sister had gone to dances there in the 1940s.

5. Kenny's logo was used only occasionally. Stanley clung doggedly to his earlier design: an emblem featuring the Polish eagle.

CLUB 57 CHRONOLOGY

The following timeline of events at Club 57 has been compiled from official club calendars, event flyers, and press releases created by individual artists; *SoHo Weekly News* event listings; datebooks held by club managers; and event documentation. The entries at times combine descriptions from various sources to offer a more complete or evocative representation of a given event. Passages in quotes preserve typos, inconsistencies, and other errors in the original documentation unless otherwise indicated. Programs listed here that took place at other venues mark events that were initiated by Club 57 artists and members; occasions that were scene-wide and likely to have had club members in attendance; and programs that were indicative of the scene's shifting landscape toward the club's final days.

Between October 1979 and June 1982—except January, July, and August 1981, as well as May 1982—the club's management team generated monthly calendars. A missing date within this nearly three-year window indicates that the club was either closed (this was often the case on Mondays) or booked for a private event. Outside of these three years, we have documented the events that took place at Club 57 to the best of our ability, relying on approximate dates where necessary. Beginning in summer 1981, the club was closed intermittently for soundproofing and repairs, which accounts for the number of dates where no event took place. Although the document represents our best effort at total representation, no such effort can ever be complete.

1978

● Wednesday, February 8 **Free Party with 4 Bands: The Tears, the Communists, the Blessed, and the New York Niggers**

● Sunday, March 19 **Foolish Virgins**

● Friday, March 31 **Nervus Rex and Foolish Virgins**

● Friday, April 7 **The Fleshtones and the Zantees**

● Monday, April 10 **Reel Classics presents Reelin' & Rockin' Film Festival: *Keep on Rockin'*, a film by D. A. Pennebaker.** "Presenting classic films of yesteryear, plus live bands of today (2 shows each nite). Not seen in NYC in 5 Years. Live on stage: Pyramid (1rst N.Y.C. Appearance)"

● Monday, April 17 **Reel Classics presents Reelin' & Rockin' Film Festival: *Revolution***

● Friday, April 21 **The Zantees, the Fleshtones, and Foolish Virgins**

● c. Saturday, April 22 ***Moo Goo Guide Plan: A Short Plague* by Tom Scully at St. Mark's Church-in-the-Bowery.** Starring Jackie Curtis, Peter Kwaloff, Susan Hannaford, Ann Magnuson, Amos Poe, Christina Yuin, and Casey Wayne. [No comprehensive artist list has been found]

● Monday, April 24 **Reel Classics presents Reelin' & Rockin' Film Festival: *The Big T.N.T. Show***

Sunday, April 30 **Fun Productions presents Baseball and Cleve Trevor**

● Friday, May 12 **The Misfits**

● c. Friday, September 8 **40th Annual Edit DeAk Fast + Furious Surprise Birthday Party**

● Wednesday, October 4–Friday, October 6 **Rock & Roll Theater presents "Solitude," *Cowboy Mouth*, plus Foolish Virgins. "Solitude."** A song written and performed by Suzan Cooper. ***Cowboy Mouth***. Written by Sam Shepard and Patti Smith. Directed by Gordon Edelstein and Suzan Cooper. Starring Jonathan Williams, Chris Kraus, and L. B. Dallas. "Written in a week by Sam Shepard and Patti Smith at the Chelsea Hotel in 1971 . . . will be performed in a simulated club atmosphere in the heart of the East Village." **Foolish Virgins**. Drums by Sam Joe. Telephonic keyboards by Paul Laroid. Bass by John Piccarella. Guitar and vocals by Angel Rivera. "Special thanks to the Labor Theater, Fanfare Theatre Ensemble & Ralph Lee for inspiration on lobster costume & Allen Frey"

● Thursday, October 12–Saturday, October 14 **Rock & Roll Theater presents "Solitude," *Cowboy Mouth*, plus Foolish Virgins**

● Thursday, October 19–Saturday, October 21 **Rock & Roll Theater presents "Solitude," *Cowboy Mouth*, plus Foolish Virgins**

● Friday, October 27–Saturday, October 28 **Rock & Roll Theater presents "Solitude," *Cowboy Mouth*, plus Foolish Virgins**

● Tuesday, October 31 Mudd Club opens

● c. November Fashion Moda opens

● c. November, two nights (Wednesday–Thursday) **Nightshift, in *Pas de trois* from Fassbinder.** "A story of love and power . . . Robert Cooney, [Lindzee] Smith, [Betsy] Sussler, [Carol] Porter. Nightshift is an international cultural cell of writers, actors, filmmakers, designers, theoreticians, directors working collectively. On this particular night Nightshift is Robert Cooney, [Lindzee] Smith, [Carol] Porter with film by [Betsy] Sussler"

● Wednesday, November 1 **Metro Novelties presents New Wave Vaudeville** at Irving Plaza. Starring David Walter McDermott III as Master of Ceremonies. Featuring the Beautiful Donna Destri as B-Girl Hostess. Produced by Thomas E. Scully and Susan J. Hannaford. Directed by Ann Magnuson. **Egyptian Spectacle**. Performed by Pharaoh McDermott III, with Alexa Hunter, Pete Reperata, Edward Applebome, Jeffrey Metzger. Staging by Andy Rees. Costumes by Danny Farr. Set by D. E. Abraham. "King of the Nile" written and played by Kristian Hoffman / **Pull My String**. Performed by Mr. Cruel and the Cruelettes. Clarinet and vocals by Jan David Cruel, ETTES, etc. / **Polyurinsane**. Performed by Abbi Robbins, Elfi Spring, and Alexa Hunter. Choreography by Andy Rees / **Something Stupid**. By Kristian Hoffman: An Ovation to Genius. Arrangement and kazoo by Kristian Hoffman. Engineering and drums by Jay Dee Daugherty. Bass and calliope flute by Kevin Kiely / **Beannie and Friends**. Performed by David Klein and Jasper McGruder / **Let's Misbehave**. Performed by David Walter McDermott III. Piano by Eric Li / **Businessmen in Space**. Performed by Come On / **Uncle Robby**. Performed by Robert Romagnoli / **Center of the Universe**. Performed by Dave Street and Alice Taylor. Written by Dave Street. Costumes by Natasha / **Disco King**. Performed by Lance Loud and friends / **My Heart Belongs to Daddy**. Performed by Donna Destri / **Three-Ring Psychosis**. Performed by Tracy Sherman / **Mystery Date**. By Milton Bradley. Sung by the Bellomo Sisters / **Asphalt Jungle Ultra Fashions**. Performed by Animal X. Music by Xerox / **Imagination**. Performed by Stuart Argabright of Rudiments fame / **ART: The Only Band in the World** / **A Pretty Girl**. Performed by David Walter McDermott III. Piano by Eric Li / **In the Name of God**. Performed by Tessie Chua and Gedde Watanabe. Written by Tessie Chua. Costumes by Danny Farr. Special thanks to Scott Baker / **You Made Me Love You**. Performed by Paul Zone / **Lady Bug** / **Emotional Cripples** / **Snooky and Tish-a-Go-Go**. With clothes by Manic Panic / **Nomi**. Costumes by Natasha / **There's No Wave Like the New Wave**. David Walter McDermott III and cast. Written and played by Kristian Hoffman

● Thursday, November 2 **Metro Novelties presents New Wave Vaudeville** at Irving Plaza. Starring David Walter McDermott III as the Master of Ceremonies. Featuring the Beautiful Donna Destri as B-Girl Hostess. Produced by Thomas E. Scully and Susan J. Hannaford. Directed by Ann Magnuson. **Egyptian Spectacle**. Performed by Pharaoh McDermott III, with Alexa Hunter, Pete Reperata, Edward Applebome, Jeffrey Metzger. Staging by Andy Rees. Costumes by Danny Farr. Set by D. E. Abraham. "King of the Nile" written and played by Kristian Hoffman / **Me**. Performed by Michael Peppe / **Polyurinsane**. Performed by Abbi Robbins, Elfi Spring, and Alexa Hunter. Choreography by Andy Rees / **Something Stupid**. By Kristian Hoffman: An Ovation to Genius. Arrangement and kazoo by Kristian Hoffman. Engineering and drums by Jay Dee Daugherty. Bass and calliope flute by Kevin Kiely / **Beannie and Friends**. Performed by David Klein and Jasper McGruder / **Let's Misbehave**. Performed by David Walter McDermott III. Piano by Eric Li / **Center of the Universe**. Performed by Dave Street and Alice Taylor. Written by Dave Street. Costumes by Natasha / **Loud Boys**. Performed by (Coffeehouse 9 minus 7), Lance, and Grant / **Coming Attractions**. *Men in Orbit* by John Lurie. *Rome '78* by James Nares. *Red Italy* by Eric Mitchell. *My, My, Michelangelo* by Amos Poe. Presented by New Cinema / **Three-Ring Psychosis**. Performed by Tracy Sherman / **Mystery Date** Milton Bradley. Sung by the Bellomo Sisters / **Asphalt Jungle Ultra Fashions**. Performed by Animal X. Music by Xerox / **Imagination**. Performed by Stuart Argabright of Rudiments fame / **A Pretty Girl**. Performed by David Walter McDermott III. Piano by Eric Li / **Rose Water and Tim Milk** / **Coming Attractions**. Fleshtones Test Roll #7 by M. Henry Jones. Work in progress from *Soul City* / **In the Name of God**. Performed by Tessie Chua and Gedde Watanabe. Written by Tessie Chua. Costumes by Danny Farr. Special thanks to Scott Baker / **You Made Me Love You**. Performed by Paul Zone / **Lady Bug** / **Emotional Cripples** / **Snooky and Tish-a-Go-Go**. Clothes by Manic Panic / **Nomi**. Costumes by Natasha / **There's No Wave Like the New Wave**. David Walter McDermott III and cast. Written and played by Kristian Hoffman

● Wednesday, November 8–Thursday, November 9 **Metro Novelties presents New Wave Vaudeville** at Irving Plaza

● Friday, November 10–Saturday, November 11 **The Comedy of the Other Leading Brand. A Regular Riot**. Shah of Iran / **Packs a Punch**. Billy Martin / **A Hit**. Donald (Don) Corleone / **Haven't Seen It Yet**. Clive Barnes

● Wednesday, November 15–Thursday, November 16 **Metro Novelties presents New Wave Vaudeville** at Irving Plaza

● Friday, November 17–Saturday, November 18 **The Comedy of the Other Leading Brand**

● Friday, November 24–Saturday, November 25 **The Comedy of the Other Leading Brand**

● Friday, December 1–Saturday, December 2 **The Comedy of the Other Leading Brand**

● Friday, December 8–Saturday, December 9 **The Comedy of the Other Leading Brand**

● Film, video, and TV ● Performance, theater, poetry, and comedy ● Exhibitions ● Music, social events, and theme nights ● Events at other venues

Friday, December 8–Saturday, December 9 **Metro Novelties presents New Wave Vaudeville Reprise** at Irving Plaza

Friday, December 15–Saturday, December 16 **The Comedy of the Other Leading Brand**

Friday, December 22–Saturday, December 23 **The Comedy of the Other Leading Brand**

Thursday December 28–Saturday, December 30 **The Comedy of the Other Leading Brand**

Sunday, December 31 **New Year's Eve Party with the Nails and the Metros**

1979

c. January New Cinema opens under the auspices of Colab (Collaborative Projects), founded September 1977

Wednesday, January 3–Thursday, January 4 **Double Exposure: 4 Nights of Film and Performance**. Featuring Kathy Acker, John Ahearn, Scott B, Beth B, Vivienne Dick, Janet Hamill, Laura Kennedy, John Lurie, James Nares, Jeanne Quinn, and Cara Pearlman

Friday, January 5–Saturday, January 6 **The Other Leading Brand**. "Currently held over. The funniest comedy group this side of the International Date Line stars Anne Paul, Judy Nazemetz, Dennis Lee and Fred Goehner, written by Mike Colasuonno, Mark Daponte, Gary Goldstein, and Jean Harte, and is directed by Max Bloom"

Wednesday, January 10–Thursday, January 11 **Double Exposure: 4 Nights of Film and Performance**. Featuring Kathy Acker, John Ahearn, Scott B, Beth B, Vivienne Dick, Janet Hamill, Laura Kennedy, John Lurie, James Nares, Jeanne Quinn, and Cara Pearlman

Friday, January 12–Saturday, January 13 **The Other Leading Brand**

Friday, January 19 **Movie Party**

Saturday, January 20 **The Other Leading Brand**

Wednesday, January 24–Thursday, January 25 **Nightshift: New Films and Performance**. "Nightshift is Carol Porter, Lindzee Smith, Robert Smith. Also featured: Tom Otterness, Mitch Corber, Charlie Ahearn"

Friday, January 26–Saturday, January 27 **The Other Leading Brand**

Thursday, January 25 *Where It's At* Awards includes New Wave Vaudeville in best shows of 1978

Friday, February 2–Saturday, February 3 **The Other Leading Brand**

Friday, February 9–Saturday, February 10 **The Other Leading Brand**

Friday, February 16–Saturday, February 17 **The Other Leading Brand**

Thursday, February 22–Sunday, February 25 **Cool Theater presents Sam Shepard's *Geography of a Horse Dreamer* and *The Holy Ghostly***. Costumes by Maura Clifford. Technical work by Jean Rasenberger. ***Geography of a Horse Dreamer***. Directed by Bill Rennie. Cast: Cody / David Watkins. Beaujo / John Murray. Santee / John Monteleone. Fingers / Rainer Uebersezig. Doctor / Allen Williamson. Waiter / Duncan Hutchison. ***The Holy Ghostly***. Directed by David Watkins. Cast: Pop / David Garvin. Ice / John Monteleone. Witch / Jean Rasenberger

Thursday, March 1–Sunday, March 4 **Sam Shepard's *Geography of a Horse Dreamer* and *The Holy Ghostly***

Thursday, March 9–Friday, March 10 **The Other Leading Brand Grand Finale II**

Sunday, March 18 **National Resurgence Party Meeting**

Friday, March 23–Saturday, March 24 **The Other Leading Brand Grand Finale II**

Friday, March 30–Saturday, March 31 **The Other Leading Brand Grand Finale II**

Thursday, April 5 **The Coalition**. "An evening of poetry featuring Akua Lezli Hope, Esther Louise, Mbembe, Benjamin McFall, Rick McKoy, Carmen Rosario, Victor Rosa, Weatherly"

Saturday, April 14 **Vivienne Dick Party and Screening**

Wednesday, April 18 **Lady Bug**

Friday, April 20–Saturday, April 21 **The Other Leading Brand Grand Finale II**

Saturday, April 28–Sunday, April 29 ***La Villa de Voix de Ville de Vie, or Through de Broken Glass***. "A mythical, musical vaudeville show"

Tuesday, May 1 **Monster Movie Club: *Invasion of the Saucer Men***

Thursday, May 3–Sunday, May 6 ***La Villa de Voix de Ville de Vie, or Through de Broken Glass***

Friday, May 4 **Molissa Fenley and Keith Haring: Video Clones** at SVA Amphitheater

Tuesday, May 8 **Monster Movie Club: *Black Sunday***

Tuesday, May 8 **Fiorucci Celebrates the New Wave** opens at Fiorucci. Paintings by Kenny Scharf. Performance by Klaus Nomi

Saturday, May 12 **Movie Party**. "Bring any of your 8 mm (super or standard) and/or 16 mm films—this means anything"

Tuesday, May 15 **Monster Movie Club: *Plan 9 from Outer Space* and *The Mysterians***

c. Wednesday, May 16 **Ruth Ansel and Chas Churchward present *Beyond the Valley of the Dolls***

Friday, May 18–Saturday May 19 **Robin Holcomb, White Noise**

Tuesday, May 22 **Monster Movie Club: *The Horror of Party Beach***

Friday, May 26–Saturday, May 27 **Sam Shepard's *Action*, with David Watkins and Valley Hendrickson**

Tuesday, May 29 **Monster Movie Club: *The Vampire Lovers***

c. Thursday, May 31 **Screening of *The Jones***

Friday, June 1–Saturday, June 2 **Sam Shepard's *Action*, with David Watkins and Valley Hendrickson**

Tuesday, June 5 **Monster Movie Club: *A Bucket of Blood***

c. Thursday, June 7 **Steve Brown presents *The Green Berets***

Friday June 8–Saturday June 9 **Sam Shepard's *Action*, with David Watkins and Valley Hendrickson**

Tuesday, June 12 **Monster Movie Club: *The 7th Voyage of Sinbad***

Tuesday, June 19 **Monster Movie Club: *White Zombie***

Wednesday, June 20 **Poetry Project Reading**. "Preceded by an open reading of 15–30 artists . . . directed by Bob Holman . . . including Lee Breuer, Charles Borkhuis, and Ruth Landowne"

Friday, June 22–Sunday, June 24 **The Fourth E presents *Kennedy's Children***. Written and directed by Robert Patrick. With Paul Carlin, Sharon Ferry, Denise Galonsky, Carol Nelson, Steve Nelson, Bonnie Young

Friday, June 22–Sunday, June 24 ***Jet Paintings* by Wally Edwards**. In conjunction with the opening of *Kennedy's Children*

Tuesday, June 26 **Monster Movie Club: *Murder by Television* and *Invasion of the Star Creatures***

Wednesday, June 27 **Poetry Project Reading**. "Preceded by an open reading of 15–30 artists . . . directed by Bob Holman . . . including Maureen Owen, Nathan Whiting, and David Zimmer"

Friday, June 29 **Jet Paintings by Wally Edwards** at Fashion Moda

Friday, June 29–Sunday, July 1 **The Fourth E presents *Kennedy's Children***. Written and directed by Robert Patrick

Tuesday, July 3 **Monster Movie Club: *Teenage Caveman, The Lost World*, and *Space Patrol*: "The Man Who Stole a City"**

Wednesday, July 4 **Poetry Project Reading**. "Preceded by an open reading of 15–30 artists . . . directed by Bob Holman . . . featured Frontward Books Poets Neil Hackman, Daniel Krakauer, and Susie Timmons, introduced by Rochelle Kraut, with a guest set by Regina Beck at the piano"

Friday, July 6–Sunday, July 8 **The Fourth E presents *Kennedy's Children***. Written and directed by Robert Patrick

Tuesday, July 10 **Monster Movie Club's Vampire Triple Feature: *Horror of Dracula, Dracula Has Risen from the Grave, Taste the Blood of Dracula*, and *Space Patrol*: "The Brain Machine."** "Vampire Festival. Count Dracula rises to unleash his reign of terror on the East Village . . . Until sunrise!"

Wednesday, July 11 **Poetry Project Reading**. "Preceded by an open reading of 15–30 artists . . . directed by Bob Holman . . . including *The Judgement*, a play by Mitchell Redmon, with Poetry Dance Bands: Cindi Haring, Tim Milk, the Moroccan Green March Army, Tom Carey with Mark Breeding and the Bar-ettes, Ace-in-the-Hole, and Jeff Wright reading *Employment of the Apes*"

Friday, July 13–Sunday, July 15 **The Fourth E presents *Kennedy's Children***. Written and directed by Robert Patrick

Tuesday, July 17 **Monster Movie Club: *Cat-Women of the Moon* and *Space Patrol*: "The Alien Invasion"**

Wednesday, July 18 **Poetry Project Reading**. "Preceded by an open reading of 15–30 artists . . . directed by Bob Holman . . . including Susan Cataldo, Kate Hammon, Gary Lenhart, Jim Brodey, and Mark Breeding doing poetry/jazz"

Friday July 20–Sunday, July 22 **Held Over: The Fourth E presents *Kennedy's Children***. Written and directed by Robert Patrick

Tuesday, July 24 **Monster Movie Club: *The Abominable Dr. Phibes* and *Space Patrol*: "The Iron Fist"**

- Wednesday, July 25 **Poetry Project Reading**. "Preceded by an open reading of 15–30 artists . . . directed by Bob Holman . . . including Jame-Maceo Camier, Sandra Esteves, and Cliff Fyman. Guest star Stacey Erra"

- Saturday, July 28 ***Bikini Girl* Magazine presents An Evening of Music and Film.** "Special performance by the Futants . . . Deena requests pink attire"

- Monday, July 30 **Katy K's Rainwear presents *The Girl Can't Help It*.** Starring Jayne Mansfield

- Tuesday, July 31 **Monster Movie Club: *Two Thousand Maniacs!* and *Space Patrol*: "Mystery of Planet X"**

- Wednesday, August 1 **Poetry Project Reading**. "Preceded by an open reading of 15–30 artists . . . directed by Bob Holman . . . including John Batki, Maggie Dubris, and Mark Fisher. Midnight show: Jill Kroesen"

- Saturday, August 4 **Teenage Sex 'n' Violence presents *High School Confidential***

- Sunday, August 5 **Ladies Auxiliary of the Lower East Side**. "Organizational meeting: potluck dinner, election of officers, definition of goals . . . men admitted after 11:00 pm"

- Tuesday, August 7 **Monster Movie Club: *The Little Shop of Horrors* and *Space Patrol***

- Wednesday, August 8 **Poetry Project Reading**. "Preceded by an open reading of 15–30 artists . . . directed by Bob Holman . . . Frank Murphy, Allen Planz, and Chuck Wachtel"

- Saturday, August 11 **Teenage Sex 'n' Violence presents *The Cool and the Crazy***

- Sunday, August 12 **Ladies Auxiliary Meeting**

- Tuesday, August 14 **Monster Movie Club: *Queen of Outer Space* and *Space Patrol***

- Wednesday, August 15 **Poetry Project Reading**. "Preceded by an open reading of 15–30 artists . . . directed by Bob Holman . . . including Enid Dame, Simon Schuchat, and James Sherry"

- Thursday, August 16–Friday, August 17 **Jill Kroesen's *Fay Shism Began in the Home*.** With Kenny Deifik, Alfred Heller, Alexander Peck, Brenda Wismer

- Saturday, August 18 **Teenage Sex 'n' Violence presents *Wild for Kicks***

- Sunday, August 19 **Ladies Auxiliary Meeting**

- Tuesday, August 21 **Monster Movie Club: *Dr. Goldfoot and the Bikini Machine* and *Space Patrol***

- Wednesday, August 22 **Poetry Project Reading**. "Preceded by an open reading of 15–30 artists . . . directed by Bob Holman . . . including Yolanda Garcia, Michael Lally, and Rose Lesniak"

- Thursday, August 23 **Monster Movie Club Haunted Mansion and Beach Party Field Trip**

- Thursday, August 23–Friday, August 24 **Jill Kroesen's *Fay Shism Began in the Home***

- Saturday, August 25 **Teenage Sex 'n' Violence presents *Teenage Doll***

- Tuesday, August 28 **Monster Movie Club: *The Astro Zombies* and *Space Patrol***

- Thursday, August 30 **Ladies Auxiliary First Tri-Annual Slumber Party**. "Services provided by the Ladies for the Ladies are: make-up exchange, Truth or Dare, Mystery Date, Twister, Popcorn, Pot/Hash brownies, Close n Play, Ouija Board, Séance and levitation, Curlers, Mutual Hairdressing, Polaroids, Pajamas (baby dolls), Sleeping Bag, Diet Soda, Beer, Wine [. . .] pizza, dimes for phone calls, Records, gossip, food, anything else. AND Go-Go boys . . . Also: panty raid by 10 most wanted?!!? . . . Plus film *Gidget Goes Under*"

- Friday, August 31–Saturday, September 1 Scott and Beth B's ***The Offenders***. "Originally shown in serialized form, the film is a satire of the underworld mind and method, starring Adele Bertei, Bill Rice, John Lurie, Judy Nylon, and Robin Winters"

- Monday, September 3 **Go-Go Painting Show Party**. *Celebrating the Space Age . . . Art by Kenny Scharf*

- Tuesday, September 4 **Monster Movie Club: *The Last Man on Earth* and *Space Patrol***

- Saturday, September 8 **The Ladies Auxiliary Stay-Free Mini-Prom**. "A special evening of dance and romance accentuated by the sound of the Furors. Punch and bar. Formal wear mandatory. Prom Queen and Court to be elected"

- Monday, September 10 **Anders Grafstrom *The Long Island Four* Film Shoot**

- Tuesday, September 11 **Monster Movie Club: *Attack of the 50 Foot Woman* and *Space Patrol***

- Tuesday, September 18 **Monster Movie Club: *House of Dark Shadows* and *Space Patrol***

- Thursday September 20–Friday September 21 **Target Video presents California New Wave: Dead Kennedys, Sex Pistols, Avengers, Screamers, Mutants, Weirdos, Ramones**

- Tuesday, September 25 **Monster Movie Club: *I Was a Teenage Frankenstein* and *Space Patrol***

- c. October Group Material is formed

- Tuesday, October 2 **Monster Movie Club: *Carnival of Souls* and *Space Patrol***

- Wednesday, October 3 **Back to School Party**. "A new term begins at 'Swingin School' with Lulu, Bobby Rydell, Gene Pitney, and much more!"

- Thursday, October 4 ***They Eat Scum* by Nick Zodiak**. "With Donna Death, the Blessed, Arthur Wood. Nuclear sabotage, cannibalism, and Rock n' Roll. The violent story of a violent new breed of young people . . . the death rockers"

- Saturday, October 6 **Night at the Movies presents *College Confidential* with Mamie van Doren**

- Sunday, October 7 **Radio Free Europe**

- Tuesday, October 9 **Monster Movie Club: *Invasion of the Bee Girls* and *Space Patrol***

- Wednesday, October 10 **British Invasion** "With films of The Beatles @ Liverpool Cavern '62 Ed Sullivan '64, Dave Clark Five singing 'Glad All Over,' 'Bits and Pieces,' plus all the rest!"

- Friday, October 12 **Dada Disco: Xerox and Mykel Board's ART**. "We're all Boat People. Featuring Kimberly Davis on metronome, triangle and backing vocals, occasionally lead vocals. 'ART has attracted that portion of the audience which is attracted'—*N.Y. Rocker*"

- Saturday, October 13 **Night at the Movies presents *Hold On!* with Herman's Hermits**. With films by M. Henry Jones and Nick Zodiak

- Sunday, October 14 **The Happening: Au Glo-Go**

- Tuesday, October 16 **Monster Movie Club: *She-Demons* and final *Space Patrol*: Name the Planet Contest**. "Winners were PLANET MELONHEAD (Bruce Pross, member #133), RALSTONIA (N. A. Kintisch, #98), and ZECTRON (Keith Martin, #140)"

- Wednesday, October 17 **The Detroit Sound**. "Get down!"

Friday, October 19 **Container**

- Saturday, October 20 **Night at the Movies presents *The T.A.M.I. Show*.** Featuring the Rolling Stones, the Supremes, James Brown, Lesley Gore, Chuck Berry, Marvin Gaye, Smokey Robinson and the Miracles, Jan and Dean, and more

- Sunday, October 21 **Off Beat Expresso Bongo**

- Tuesday, October 23 **Monster Movie Club: *Hercules in the Haunted World***

- Wednesday, October 24 **Dick Clark Tribute**

- Saturday, October 27 **Night at the Movies presents *It's a Bikini World*.** Starring Deborah Walley and Tommy Kirk. With the Animals, the Castaways, the Toys, and the Gentrys

- Sunday, October 28 **Rockabilly Hootenanny Hayride**. "Special guest stars! Live chicken!"

- Wednesday, October 31 Closed for the **First Annual Monster Movie Club Costume Ball at Irving Plaza**. Featuring the Misfits, Snooky & Tish, the Mad, and Monster Movies

- Friday, November 2 **Night at the Movies presents *The Big T.N.T. Show*.** David McCallum hosts Donovan, the Byrds, Joan Baez, the Ronettes, Ike and Tina Turner, Ray Charles, Petula Clark, Roger Miller, and Bo Diddley

- Saturday, November 3 **Dada Disco**. "Following the success of October's HAPPENING, we are repeating the format on Saturday nights. These evenings DADA DISCO GO-GO CAVALCADE include live music, go-go's, varied multi-media presentations and general mania. The Man Rays return for your listening pleasure"

- Sunday, November 4 **Punk Resurrection**. "From the piss-coated walls of your personal hell comes a Punk Resurrection. Come dirty, dress 'punk,' scar faced; bring liquor, scuff tittied, cum guzzlen, drop [lipped], shit face, walrus pussy, junked out, bring beer! Revivalists: Scott Covert, Anthony Scibelli, Andy Rees"

- Tuesday, November 6 **Monster Movie Club: *Destroy All Monsters***

- Thursday, November 8 ***The Monkees* plus Cartoons**. "Take a trip down memory lane with Davey, Mikey, Peter and Mike"

- Friday, November 9 **Night at the Movies presents *Sex Kittens Go to College*.** "House favorite Mamie van Doren returns"

- Saturday, November 10 **The Model World of Glue**. "Bring your Aurora models. Breakthroughs in décor with Xerostallation by James and D. D. The Man Rays return"

● Film, video, and TV ● Performance, theater, poetry, and comedy ● Exhibitions ● Music, social events, and theme nights ● Events at other venues

● Sunday, November 11 **Swingin' Singles Party**

● Tuesday, November 13 **Monster Movie Club: *Frankenstein Meets the Space Monster***

● Thursday, November 15 **Cartoons You Won't See on TV**. "Including: *Russian Rhapsody, All This and Rabbit Stew, Scrap the Japs, Coal Black and De Sebben Dwarfs, Eliza on Ice, Scrap Happy Daffy, Out of the Inkwell, Uncle Tom's Cabana, Buried Treasure, Hot Lip Jasper, Tin Pan Alley Cats* and MORE! Featuring such cartoon favorites as Bugs Bunny, Betty Boop, Daffy Duck, Popeye, Mighty Mouse"

● Friday, November 16 **Night at the Movies presents *The Long Island Four* by Anders Grafstrom**. "Local independent epic starring David McDermott, Bradley Field, Kristian Hoffman, Lance Loud"

● Saturday, November 17 **Happening: Home Videos**. "Send home for your home movies . . . super and standard 8 and 16 projectors provided (slides too)"

● Sunday, November 18 **Putt-Putt Reggae 18-Hole Ska Party**

● Tuesday, November 20 **Monster Movie Club: *The Corpse Grinders***. "Story of a catfood company that boosts its sales by adding chopped up humans to its products. Happy Thanksgiving!!!!!!!!!!!!"

● Wednesday, November 21 **Free Multimedia Event TV and Jukebox**. "Experiments in normalcy—bring your set and Swanson Hungry Man"

● Friday, November 23 **Night at the Movies presents *The 10th Victim***. "Super Pop at Club 57!"

● Saturday, November 24 **Dada Go-Go Extravaganza**. Famed quartet ART returns

● Sunday, November 25 **Casino Royale**. "Proper Bond Attire Required. Gambling chips, dancing, music, screening of *Casino Royale*, and the most beautiful secret agents on screen and off"

● Tuesday, November 27 **Monster Movie Club: *Planet of the Vampires***

● Wednesday, November 28 **N. A. Kintisch Art Shebang**. "Paintings and other pictures by N. A. Kintisch"

● Friday, November 30 **Night at the Movies presents *Beyond the Valley of the Dolls* by Russ Meyer**

● Saturday, December 1 **Beer Bust**. "DJ, dancing and live entertainment by The Batusi Bros"

● Sunday, December 2 **Iran, Iraq, and Iroll: Free DJ Dance Party**

● Tuesday, December 4 **Monster Movie Club: *The Wasp Woman***

● Wednesday, December 5 ***The Long Island Four***. "Return by popular demand. *Soho News* calls it '*The Apocalypse Now* of Super-8 . . . entertaining and well made.' See for yourself at 9:00 or midnight"

● Thursday, December 6 **Russ Meyer's *Faster, Pussycat! Kill! Kill!*** "Also appearing is never before seen San Francisco produced independent film *Girls in the Future* by Eric Brogger."

● Friday, December 7 ***Bikini Girl* Magazine Film Program**. "Experience works by Kenneth Anger, Anney Bonney, Charles Braverman, David Cohn, Tony and Beverly Conrad, Jack Goldstein, M. Henry Jones, Manuel DeLanda, Francis Lee, Mark McGowan, Rachel Reichman, Elliot Rose, Rhody Streeter and Tony Ganz, Diana Toharina, Joel Winston. Deena Schwartzman—guest curator"

● Saturday, December 8 **Sock Hop Dance Romp with Buzz and the Flyers**

● Tuesday, December 11 **Monster Movie Club: *The Tingler***. "The original uncut version with color sequences"

● Wednesday, December 12 **Kenneth Anger Films**. "Magick Lantern Cycle, shown in its entirety": *Fireworks* (1947), *Puce Moment* (1949), *Rabbit's Moon* (1950), *Eaux d'artifice* (1953), *Inauguration of the Pleasure Dome* (1954), *Scorpio Rising* (1964), *Kustom Kar Kommandos* (1965), *Invocation of My Demon Brother* (1969), and *Lucifer Rising, Part I* (1974)

● Thursday, December 13 **Surf Soundz Party**. "Guest DJ George Scott (8 Eyed Spy, The Raybeats). Bring out the boards, bikinis, beachballs and Bain de Soleil"

● Friday, December 14 ***The Deadly Art of Survival* by Charlie Ahearn**

● Friday, December 14–Saturday, December 15 **B Movie Weekend**. "Scott and Beth B present *Black Box, G-Man* and *Letters to Dad* plus new work"

● Sunday, December 16 **Fashion Foto Fling**. "An open shooting session cocktail dance party affair featuring work by member and artist designer Christina Logan and Sherry Rosso. Photographer Jon Moore"

● Monday, December 17 **Benefit Reading for a New Magazine: *Undercity***

● Tuesday, December 18 **Monster Movie Club: *The Texas Chainsaw Massacre***

● Wednesday, December 19 **Amos Poe's *Unmade Beds***

● Thursday, December 20 **Jules Verne Astral Projection Party with Alexa Hunter**

● Saturday, December 22 **Ladies Auxiliary Holiday Dance**. "Music by The Furors, holiday formal wear required"

1980

● Tuesday, January 1 *Real Estate Show* leads to formation of ABC No Rio

● Tuesday, January 8 **Monster Movie Club: *1984***. "Every Tuesday this month Monster Movie Club gives you 'No Future.' George Haas' *American Shooting Series* #1-2-3 will be shown in serial form every Tuesday. And a NO FUTURE party!!"

● Wednesday, January 9 ***The Foreigner***. A film by Amos Poe

● Thursday, January 10 ***Ski Party***. "With Lesley Gore (singing Sunshine, Lollipops & rainbows!!!!), James Brown and his Famous Flames, Frankie Avalon, The Standells and more"

● Friday, January 11 **Amazon School of Modeling: Benefit Fashion Show and Dance Party**

● Saturday, January 12 "Performance Space 122 invites all club members to a party to commemorate the artists' opening exhibition at the space at First Avenue and Ninth Street"

● Tuesday, January 15 **Monster Movie Club: *Alphaville* and George Haas's *American Shooting Series***

● Wednesday, January 16 **Fab Four Fest '64–66: Films of the Beatles' Early Years**. "Discounts for those in fave Beatles garb"

● Thursday, January 17 ***The Jones* and Douglas Sirk's *Written on the Wind***. "Toast the American family!"

● Friday, January 18 **The Wild Wild World of Speed Party: Hi-Velocity Dancing Action!**

● Saturday, January 19 ***The T.A.M.I. Show***. "It's back!"

● Sunday, January 20 ***Liberty's Booty*: A New Film by Vivienne Dick**

● Tuesday, January 22 **Monster Movie Club: *World without End* and George Haas's *American Shooting Series***. "Celebrate 2600 early . . ."

● Wednesday, January 23 **Strangers in the Night: Frank Sinatra Tribute**. "Guest stars perform Frank's Greatest Hits"

● Thursday, January 24 **Cartoons You Won't See on TV Anymore!** "Sex, violence, racism, and good clean fun with Gumby, Betty Boop, Space Angel, Daffy Duck, and more!!!"

● Friday, January 25 **Twistin' in High Society**. "Cocktail wear requested / giant Twister game dance party"

● Sunday, January 27 ***Bikini Girl* Magazine presents Andy Warhol's *Vinyl* with Special Guest Ondine**. With *Iron Lung* by Peter Zaremba and *The Facts in The Case of M. Valdemar* by Janis Crystal Lipzin

● Tuesday, January 29 **Monster Movie Club: *Metropolis* with George Haas's *American Shooting Series***. Live score by Evan Lurie

● Wednesday, January 30 **Comic Testing Ground: Laugh-In**. "With Dale Ashmun, Tessie Chua, Michael Peppe, Bob Romagnoli, Duncan Smith, Dave Street and many more uncovered talents"

● Thursday, January 31 ***Mandingo***

● Friday, February 1 **Night at the Movies presents *Shellshock Rock***. "Punk in Northern Ireland"

● Saturday, February 2 **Groundhog Day: Soul Party**. "Motown night!"

● Sunday, February 3 **Double Feature: *I Am a Groupie* and *Satan's Cheerleaders***. "Rated R!"

● Tuesday, February 5 **Monster Movie Club: *The Undertaker and His Pals***

● Wednesday, February 6 **Leisure Time Lounge: Dancing and Muzak**

● Thursday, February 7 Closed. "Go see Wazmo Nariz at Irving Plaza tonight!"

● Friday, February 8 **Wild for Wheels presents *Hot Car Girl***. "Members are requested to sport their very best or worst leather and chain ensembles each Friday this month for this exciting head-bashing series!"

● Saturday, February 9 **Tribute to the Farfisa Sound: Beer Bust**. With guest DJ Deb O'Nair of Tina Peel

● Sunday, February 10 **Double Feature: Doris Day Tribute Night**. Featuring *Lover Come Back* and *Midnight Lace*. Accompanied by a slideshow

● Tuesday, February 12 **Monster Movie Club: *Manos: The Hands of Fate***

● Wednesday, February 13 ***They Eat Scum* by Nick Zodiak**. Benefit screening for *East Village Eye*

● Thursday, February 14 **Love in Light Show**. With Tammi Steve

● Friday, February 15 **Wild for Wheels presents *Naked under Leather***

● Saturday, February 16 **Island Rhythms**

● Sunday, February 17 **Double Feature.** "*Promises! Promises!*—the uncut, uncensored, unmissable European version—with Jayne Mansfield and *3 Nuts In Search of a Bolt* with Mamie Van Doren"

● Tuesday, February 19 **Monster Movie Club: *The Wizard of Gore*.** "New York Premiere! The genius behind last year's hit *Two Thousand Maniacs*! Expect the Worst!"

● Wednesday, February 20 **Video a Go-Go.** Videotapes by Kenny Scharf and Keith Haring

● Thursday, February 21 ***The Trip* and *Faster, Pussycat! Kill! Kill!***

● Friday, February 22 **Wild for Wheels presents *The Wild Angels***

● Sunday, February 24 **Double Feature: *Sign of the Gladiator* and *Siren of Atlantis***

● Tuesday, February 26 **Monster Movie Club: *Circus of Horrors***

● Wednesday, February 27 ***Beyond the New Wave*: An Exhibition of Representational Painting by Paul Bridgewater, Edward Brezinski, and Duncan Hannah.** Accompanied by a pamphlet with an introduction by Tim Dlugos. [David McDermott was announced but did not participate]

● Thursday, February 28 ***Myra Breckinridge***

● Friday, February 29 **Wild for Wheels presents *Motorcycle Gang***

● Saturday, March 1 Closed. "So all can see The Cramps at Irving Plaza"

● Sunday, March 2 ***The Glass Bottom Boat* and *Calamity Jane*.** "More Doris!"

● Tuesday, March 4 **Monster Movie Club: *The Blob***

● Wednesday, March 5 **The How-to Go-Go Show with the Cosmopolitans**

● Thursday, March 6 ***Bikini Girl* Magazine Begs You to Witness *The Loves of Ondine* by Andy Warhol.** With special guest Ondine. "Submissive attire suggested"

● Friday, March 7 ***Beyond the Valley of the Dolls***

● Saturday, March 8 **Manic Panic presents Glitter Rock Ballroom Blitz.** "Guest DJs Snooky, Joe, and Tish. NY Doll drag required"

● Sunday, March 9 ***99 Women*.** "Rated X! Women in prison!"

● Tuesday, March 11 **Monster Movie Club: *The Spider***

● Wednesday, March 12 **Ladies Auxiliary Gun Club Potluck Dinner**

● Thursday, March 13 ***Modesty Blaise*.** "Go 1966 two-tone!"

● Friday, March 14 **Gary Indiana Group presents *Ping Pong*.** "A film / video performance"

● Saturday, March 15 **ART: The Only Band in the World presents the Only Record in the World.** "Ides of March Singles Nite. Free Record with Every Admission"

● Sunday, March 16 ***The Girl Can't Help It***

● Tuesday, March 18 **Monster Movie Club: *Ghost of Dragstrip Hollow*.** "Monster Movie Club Costume Party with NewsCenter4. Come as your fave ghoul & be on network TV!"

● Wednesday, March 19 **Name That Noise: The Punk Rock Game Show.** "Host Lance Loud and the T.N.T. Orchestra match wits with contestants for big prizes w/ the big punk sound"

● Thursday, March 20 **Spring Comedy Special.** "Downtown personalities match uptown comic club regulars in this evening of stand-up and comedy entertainment. Featured performers include Dale Ashmun, Tessie Chua, Marjorie Gross, Felix Montez, Tom Murrin—The Suitcase Comic, Bob Romagnoli with his [Hooray] for Hollywood [puppet theater], Michael Peppe, David Street and famed Sic F*cks leader Russell Wolinsky"

● Friday, March 21 **Lady Wrestling**

● Saturday, March 22 **Bongo Voodoo.** "Special performance by Bradley Field just returned from Haiti"

● Sunday, March 23 **TV Night: Television Nostomania.** "Come over to our house and watch t.v. . . . Mom will serve popcorn and t.v. dinners while we watch *Lost in Space*, *Car 54 Where Are You?*, *My Favorite Martian*, *Super Car*, *Dark Shadows*, *Captain Nice*, *The Monkees*, and *The Man from U.N.C.L.E.* Plus vintage commercials!"

● Tuesday, March 25 **Monster Movie Club: *I Was a Teenage Werewolf* and *Blood of Dracula***

● Wednesday, March 26 **Let's Face the Music and Tap**

● Thursday, March 27 **Cartoons You Won't See on TV.** "An All-New Show! Including Porky Pig in the 1939 Warner Brothers Breakdowns blooper reel, *Draftee Daffy*, *Stratos-Fear*, *Boop-oop-a-Doop*, and *Beany Meets the Monstrous Monster*"

● Friday, March 28 ***57 Drawings* by D. E. Abraham.** "Works from Club 57 sketches. Daniel Abraham exhibition party, disc jockey Tom Scully"

● Saturday, March 29 **Japanese Pop.** "JapPop, Astro Boy & Starman films, import products and further esoterics"

● Sunday, March 30 **Fritz Lang's *Rancho Notorious* and Nicholas Ray's *Johnny Guitar***

● Tuesday, April 1 **Monster Movie Club: *Halloween*.** "Holiday special on April Ghouls"

● Wednesday, April 2 **Let's Face the Music and Tap!** "Bring your Shoes! Bring you records! Join our lineup of featured routines. Plus Debbie Reynolds in *What's the Matter with Helen?*"

● Thursday, April 3 **Unreal Time Animation and Film Graphics, Program I.** "Touring program from the American Federation of Arts"

● Sunday, April 6 **Easter Spectacle: The Resurrection of *Rome '78*.** A film by James Nares

● Tuesday, April 8 **Monster Movie Club: *The Brain That Wouldn't Die***

● Wednesday, April 9 **Lounge 57 presents Steve and Edie Look-a-Like Cocktail Party**

● Thursday, April 10 **Unreal Time: Animation and Film Graphics, Program II**

● Friday, April 11 **Decadent, Hi-Fashion, Bacchanal Party.** With *La Dolce Vita*

● Saturday, April 12 **Rapper Party Psycho-Disco.** "With special obnoxious guests"

● Sunday, April 13 **Films selected by Nick Zodiak.** Including *The Bogus Man*

● Monday, April 14 **Gala Academy Awards Party.** "Watch it with us for more laughs"

● Tuesday, April 15 **Monster Movie Club: *Earth vs. the Flying Saucers*.** With effects by Ray Harryhausen

● Wednesday, April 16 Closed. "Go see 999 at Irving Plaza tonight!"

● Thursday, April 17 **Unreal Time: Animation and Film Graphics, Program III**

● Friday, April 18–Saturday, April 19 **Sam Shepard's *The Tooth of Crime*.** Produced and directed by Gary S. Feldman. Music by Sam Shepard. Additional music by Pat D'Aguanno and performed by the Senders. Sets and lighting by Paul Campbell. Choreography by Debra Zalkind. Starring Sharon Niesp, Cly Fowkes, Taxi, Sweet William Edgar, Jason Harvey, Kathy Bonomi, Steven Kunz, Marie-Antoinette Rogers

● Sunday, April 20 **Film Mania! *Bikini Girl* Magazine Issue 5 Party.** "Films include *Slave Trade in the World Today*, spice from the 50's, slave films, s/m loops and *El (This Strange Passion*) by Luis Buñuel"

● Monday, April 21 **Memorial Screening.** "The friends of Anders Grafstrom request the pleasure of your company at a private screening of his greatest work *The Long Island Four*. You will also be pleased to see a previously lost Grafstrom short entitled *Some Boys*"

● Monday, April 21 **Timothy Dunleavy presents Barbie Fashion Show** at Hurrah

● Tuesday, April 22 **Monster Movie Club: *The Time Machine***

● Wednesday, April 23 **The Joe Show! A Cartoon Concert by *Punk* Magazine's John Holmstrom.** "A Live Cartoon Featuring Jazz and New-Wave Rock music by Blondie, Ramones, Iggy Pop, starring the creator of *Punk* magazine"

● Thursday, April 24 **Cartoons You Won't See on TV!!!** "All-New lineup with Daffy Duck, Betty Boop, Popeye and much more!"

● Friday, April 25 **Acts of Live Art.** Emceed by Drew Straub. With Dany Johnson, John Sex, Batusi Bros, Ann Magnuson, Shawn Salad, Al Diaz, Keith Haring, and others

● Saturday, April 26 **Las Vegas Excitement! Casino!**

● Sunday, April 27 **Salute to NASA: Dr. Navia or His Student Speaks**

● Monday, April 28 ***The Long Island Four*** screens at Mudd Club. With Klaus Nomi, the Swinging Madisons, and Broadway. A benefit hosted by David McDermott for the Anders Grafstrom Memorial Foundation

● Tuesday, April 29 **Monster Movie Club: *Invaders from Mars***

● Wednesday, April 30 ***Pictures You Can Dance Too*.** "Photo Dance Party. Exhibition featuring George Haas, Larry Meltzer, Eugene Merinov, Ebet Roberts, Trix Rosen, and Harvey Wang. Disc Jockeys Sean Cassette and Sara Salir." Organized by Haas

● c. May Danceteria opens on Thirty-Seventh Street

● Thursday, May 1 **Monster Movie Club 1-Year Anniversary Monster Party.** "Any Monsters or Fiends with photos, slides, or anything else pertaining to the MMC or Monsters in general are urged to call your President or Chairman or just to bring along your horrors that evening"

● Friday, May 2 **Amazon School of Modeling: Spring Meat Show.** "Clothes by Stacey Elkin, hats by Terry Parsons. The Amazons: Ande Whyland, Dany Johnson, Wendy Wild, John Sex, Min Thometz, Shawn AMMO. Drew Straub as Master of Ceremonies"

● Saturday, May 3 **Mofungo**

● Film, video, and TV ● Performance, theater, poetry, and comedy ● Exhibitions ● Music, social events, and theme nights ● Events at other venues

- Sunday, May 4 **Salute to Gloria Vanderbilt**. "It's birthday time for #35 Keith Haring and #133 Frank Holliday. Dress code enforced"

- Tuesday, May 6 **Monster Movie Club**: ***Cat-Women of the Moon* and *Invasion of the Bee Girls***. "To commemorate its anniversary, MMC presents the Best of their fare—Shock Shlock of '79. All double bills and even better the second time around"

- Friday, May 9–Saturday, May 10 **Return Engagement: Sam Shepard's *The Tooth of Crime***

- Sunday, May 11 **Jean-Luc Godard's *Masculin Féminin***

- Tuesday, May 13 **Monster Movie Club**: ***Astro Zombies* and *She Demons***

- Wednesday, May 14 **Samuel Fuller Film Festival presents *The Naked Kiss* and *Verboten***. Organized by Steve Brown. With Andrew Gurian's *That Rotten Teabag*

- Thursday, May 15 **Short Newz Shindig: Newspaper Dance Party**. "DJ #12 Nancy Breslow hosts"

- Saturday, May 17 **Members' Party**. With slideshows, videotapes, and films of past events. "Punch, free wine & beer, edibles, etc. Dance party with DJ Kristian Hoffman"

- Sunday, May 18 **Television Nostomania II**. "For the generation weaned on TV, Channel 57 presents Television-Nostomania II. Sunday's TV Guide reads: *Dobie Gillis*, *The Rifleman*, *The Donna Reed Show*, *He & She*, TV cartoons, commercials, and bloopers, *The Monkees*, *Rawhide*, *Gidget*, *77 Sunset Strip*"

- Tuesday, May 20 **Monster Movie Club**: ***Plan 9 from Outer Space* and *Frankenstein Meets the Space Monster***

- Wednesday, May 21 **Sam Fuller Film Festival presents *Underworld U.S.A.* and *House of Bamboo***

- Thursday, May 22 **Reader's Digest Theatre presents *The Professionals***

- Friday, May 23 **Lady Wrestling**. "Anne the Dread fighting Rasta. Naomi Cockroach Woman (unleashed by George Scott III) battles The Bag Lady. The Python Princess, Beate Nilsen, with extra rations of Victory Venom provided by manager Fred (not sonic) Smith and coach Commander Lewis Tropia. Bad Girl Cynthia Sley who slays *everybody* with not 1, not 2 but *3* managers (Dee Pop, Tim Wright and Lee 'Nuke the Whale' Penn). A million more stars to tantalize the eye and whet your lips . . . and perhaps a Freddie Blassie record or two"

- Saturday, May 24 **Brix Delux Barbeque Patio Party**. "Beer Bust Dance Party. Suburban patio porch wear appropo"

- Sunday, May 25 **5-Hour Cartoon Marathon**. "All your favorites!"

- Monday, May 26 **Dance Party for *Drawings of Abusive Tension* by Parker Dulany**. "Features scenes of local haunts—Stinky's, Kiev, etc"

- Tuesday, May 27 **Monster Movie Club**: ***Attack of the 50 Foot Woman* and *Queen of Outer Space***

- Wednesday, May 28 **Films Selected by M. Henry Jones: Serious Insanity**

- Thursday, May 29 **Club 57 Invitational and Xeroxes**. Organized by Keith Haring. With John Ahearn; Charles Stanley (Carlo Pittore), Bern Porter's Knees; Janice Eshelman-Koester, Baby Head in Plastic Bag; Death by Criminal Hands; Keith Haring, Fucking Himself; Biff, Plastic Sculpture; Marc Kehoe, Rhonda & Naomi; Jeff Turtletaub, Cards; William Moritz, Subway; Kermit Oswald, Albany, PA; Debbie Davis, Alimentos Felices; Brian Clark, Round Thing; Salvatore Principato; Richard McGuire, EE-00; Ixnae Nix (Richard McGuire), Sudden Anatomy; Jet Scharf, Fun Machine; Richard Toscano; Kitty Brophy; Lynn Hughes, Waiting for Godot; John Derespinis; Keith Glancy, Johnny Dodd Portrait; Herb / Manray / lation / Hack, Theatre Anorexia; Paris Raves, Paris Raves; Victor Alzamora; S. B. Vinita, The Final Elbow; Min Thometz, Sex Change Machine; Katherine Dumas, T.V. Static; Robert L. Seltman, Narcissistic Prima Donna; Claire Libin; Deb Manzella, Abstract; Alexa Hunter, Armies in the Night / Mohican Garden; Allen Frame, Money; Amy Sillman, Ooh . . . You're Such a Dreamboat; Tuck Davis; Be, Moral Gestures; Daria Deshuk, No. 1 USA; Eugene Lynch; Judith Wong, Fast Dancing N.Y.C.; Natalya Maystrenko, Handshake; Johnny Perfect, Native New Yorker; Robert Hawkins; Billy Jacobson, Self-Portrait 1980; Duncan Hannah, Rope; Mary Feaster, For Gill; Harvey Redding, Bagged Postcards; Peter Caine, Superdome; Joanne Kontopirakis, We Dream about Beautiful Houses; Frank Holliday, Have Another Martini, Darling; Denise; Luca Pizzorno; Kathy Ruttenberg, Sex; Joseph Drexel, Performance (60.00 per Hour); Pheesus Cunt, The Real Champion, Apollo; Barry Shils, Chair Globe; Valerie Haller, Dog with Bowl; Michael Holman; Georgio Rossomondo, 4 Nudes; Sur Rodney (Sur), Artworks; Rhonda Waggoner, Hexagon Series; Haoui Montaug, Bringing the War Horse. With Xeroxes by Drew B. Straub; Mike Selbach; Timna Grunwald; Evan Lurie; Martha Fishkin; Charles Stanley (Carlo Pittore); Parker Dulany, Broken Goosestep; Katy K, Elvis Jacket; Deb Parker (Debutante), Crucify Keith; Richard Toonkel; Cindy Schwab, Chess Pains; Joe Lewis, Guatemala '79; Bern Porter; Tseng Kwong Chi, Polaroid Performance; Mary Anne Russo-Makuta, Tires, Toilets, Toes / Scar; Mark Brady, Manicans from Outerspace; Ken Tisa; Guy Augeri, Go-Go; Bruno Testore Schmidt, Cargo; Ann Magnuson, Spider; Carmel, Fashions; April Palmieri; K; Johnny Rudo; Keith Haring; Wendy Andreiev; Coco Ugaz, Happy Birthday John; Jean-Michel Basquiat; Sur Rodney (Sur); Rodney Alan Greenblat, 2 Compasses; Anson Seeno, Meme; Shawn Salad, AMMO Fashions; Jet Scharf; Raulin Ogle Rogers, 57 Boys; D. E. Abraham, In with the In Crowd; Michael Roman, N; Leann Laverne; John Sex, Bull Whip; Adolfo Sanchez; Jayne Lewis (Kiev), Bacon 7 Eggs; Julie Wilson, Sometimes I Feel Like Smashing Things; plus anonymous and/or found drawings

- Friday, May 30 **Rock'n'Roll Memorial**: ***Don't Knock the Rock* and *Go, Johnny, Go!***

- Saturday, May 31 **Ladies Auxiliary Debutante Ball**. "Introducing the Action Combo. With special escort DJ Kristian Hoffman . . . The Ladies' Auxiliary present themselves to society. An event you won't want to miss!"

- Sunday, June 1 ***Times Square Show*** opens

- Tuesday, June 3 **Monster Movie Club**: ***The Mole People* and *At the Earth's Core***

- Thursday, June 5 **Fellini's *8½***. "Come and yell 'Marcello'—Italiano gear appropo"

- Friday, June 6 **Lana Turner in *The Big Cube* plus Maria Montez and Jon Hall Technicolor Trailers**

- Saturday, June 7 **Mortville Summer Party**

- Sunday, June 8 **The Super Heroes Show**. "Featuring your favorite Japanese superheroes: *Astro Boy*, *Starman*, *Gigantor*, and more!"

- Tuesday, June 10 **Monster Movie Club**: ***Tales from the Crypt***

- Wednesday, June 11 ***The Big Combo* and *The Steel Helmet***. "Brought to you by last month's Sam Fuller series"

- Thursday, June 12 ***Wild in the Streets***

- Friday, June 13 **Acts of Live Art II**

- Saturday, June 14 **UK Yuk**. "Our latest US show of strength with an All-American Flag Day Celebration. No British music! Dump the Limeys (except John Kemp)"

- Saturday, June 14 **Lady Wrestling** at Fashion Moda. "Featuring the Ladies Auxiliary Wrestling Team . . . Ann Magnuson, President; Dany Johnson, Vice President"

- Sunday, June 15 **Father's Day Celebration for Stanley**

- Monday June 16 ***The Blank Generation***. "A film by Amos Poe and Ivan Kral. Continuous shows start at 9 (10-11-12)"

- Tuesday, June 17 **Monster Movie Club**: ***The She-Creature* and *The Horror of Party Beach***. "Beach wear requested"

- Wednesday, June 18 ***The Phenix City Story* and *Shock Corridor***. "Brought to you by last month's Sam Fuller series"

- Thursday, June 19 ***Belle de Jour***. A film by Luis Buñuel

- Friday, June 20 **Lady Wrestling "The Video Tape" Premiere**. Autograph Party! Slides! DJ Dancin'!

- Saturday, June 21 **Salute to Lawrence Welk**. "Share in the middle class spirit of Bobby and Cissy, Anacani, and The Lennon Sisters. In the tunes of pablum self-pity, in this Wunnerful, Wunnerful celebration of suburban chic. Superstar, Tie a Yellow Ribbon 'Round the Old Oak Tree, Snowbird, Alone Again Naturally, Torn Between Two Lovers, There's Got To Be a Morning After, and Ben. Indeed, the height of musical mediocrity in a parade of well-heeled live performances which summarize the social climate of our past decade"

- Sunday, June 22 **Monkees Party**. "Brought to you by TV Nostomania. Rare films, TV episodes, Monkee-mania memorabilia! DJ Kristian Hoffman spins Monkee music"

- Tuesday, June 24 **Monster Movie Club**: ***Trog* and *The Creeping Terror***

- Thursday, June 26 ***Las Vegas Hillbillys* and *The Loves of Hercules***. "Jayne Mansfield and Mamie van Doren together!"

- Saturday, June 28 **Ethyl Eichelberger as Medea**. With John Heys as Nerris the Nurse and Agosto Machado as Hecate. Narrated by Sarah Jenkins-Jacob

- Sunday, June 29 **Cartoon-a-rama**. "Saturday morning on a Sunday night"

- Monday, June 30 **Reader's Digest Theatre presents *The Professionals: The Dentists***

- Tuesday, July 1 **Monster Movie Club**: ***Piranha***. "A bloody beach costume night which will be filmed for TV, so let's give them our worst Monsters!"

- Thursday, July 3 **Video Vision**. "Featuring local video visualists"

- Friday, July 4 **Closed for Fourth of July**. "Picnic at the Cloisters"

- Saturday, July 5 **The Baker Brothers' Dance Party**

● Monday, July 7 **Stefano Castronovo and Shawn Insalata present Sketch Show and Dance Party**

● Tuesday, July 8 **Monster Movie Club: *Suspiria* in Cinemascope!**

● Wednesday, July 9 ***The Pom Pom Girls***

● Thursday, July 10 ***Sleazoid Express* presents *Mondo Cane*.** "The legendary documentary of real life repulsions!"

● Friday, July 11–Saturday, July 12 **Closed.** "See James Brown at Irving Plaza this weekend!"

● Sunday, July 13 ***The Terror of Tiny Town* and *The Wizard of Oz* in Spanish.** Organized by Jeffrey Geiger

● Monday, July 14 **Kielbasa Lounge**

● Tuesday, July 15 **Monster Movie Club: *Forbidden Planet* in Cinemascope!**

● Wednesday, July 16 ***Mr. Lucky***

● Thursday, July 17 ***High School Hellcats* and *Dragstrip Girl*.** "50s punks on the loose"

● Friday, July 18 Closed. "Pere Ubu at Irving Plaza tonight!"

● Saturday, July 19 Closed. "See X-Slash at Irving Plaza"

● Sunday, July 20 **Brave Combo.** "A band live from Texas. Nuclear polka band! Nuclear polka fun!"

● Monday, July 21 **New Paintings by Keith Haring and Frank Holliday**

● Tuesday, July 22 **Monster Movie Club: *Freaks***

● Wednesday, July 23 ***Gun Crazy* and *Born Wreckless***

● Thursday, July 24 ***Murder at the Vanities* and *Cobra Woman*.** Organized by Jeffrey Geiger

● Friday, July 25 **Acts of Live Art III**

● Saturday, July 26 **Deck Party.** "Now you can take your fantasy CRUISE to excitement! Aboard the S. S. Fivtjisvenvson. Smorgesbord! Shuffleboard! On board pool! Dancing and scenic pleasures!"

● Sunday, July 27 **Beauty Pageant Exposé.** "Endorsed by the Ladies' Auxiliary. With a screening of *Smile*"

● Monday, July 28 **Bunny Lounge**

● Tuesday, July 29 **Monster Movie Club: *Death Race 2000***

● Thursday, July 31 **Cartoons You Won't See on TV Anymore!** "All-new cartoonal fare!"

● Friday, August 1 **San Francisco Independents: Mary Bellis, Richard Gaikowski, Marc Huestis**

● Tuesday, August 5 **Monster Movie Club: *Laserblast***

● Friday, August 8 Closed. "See Magazine at Irving Plaza"

● Sunday, August 10 ***The Blank Generation*.** "Return engagement!"

● Tuesday, August 12 **Monster Movie Club: *Homicidal* and *Strait-Jacket*.** Tribute to William Castle

● Wednesday, August 13 **Emergency Members Meeting**

● Thursday, August 14 **Bill Landis's *Sleazoid Express* presents *Manson*.** "Animal sacrifices! Interviews with all! Charlie sings! Sex games!"

● Friday, August 15 **Electric Renaissance.** Art by Stefano M. Castronovo. Sacrae Symphoniae by Heinrich Schütz (1585–1672). Performed by countertenor Julius Eastman

● Saturday, August 16 **Elvis Presley Memorial Party.** "Third anniversary of Elvis's death. Film: *King Creole*, with *One God, One Singer* by Ann Magnuson. Musical Tribute Performance: Elvis look-alike Jimmy Angel. DJ Kristian Hoffman. Elvis Shrine by Katy K. Contest, prizes for best look-alike"

● Sunday, August 17 **British Beat Bash: *Beat Girl* and *The Girl-Getters***

● Tuesday, August 19 **Monster Movie Club: *Dark Star***

● Wednesday, August 20 ***Sleazoid Express* presents *Villain***

● Thursday, August 21 **Monster Movie Club's Second Annual Field Trip to Great Adventure**

● Friday, August 22 **Beach Beer Bust.** With special guest DJ George Scott

● Saturday, August 23 **Exclusive Fashions by Amazon and AMMO.** With models Lisa Baumgardner, Kitty Brophy, Daria Deshuk, Ann Magnuson, John Sex, and Peter. Diana Lillig as the Mistress of Ceremonies. Musical direction by Dany Johnson

● Tuesday, August 26 **Monster Movie Club: *The Brain Eaters* and *Attack of the Giant Leeches*.** "Special request of #34 Frank Holliday"

● Thursday, August 28 **Bill Landis's *Sleazoid Express* presents *God Told Me To***

● Tuesday, September 2 **Monster Movie Club: *How to Make a Monster* and *Monster from the Surf***

● Thursday, September 4 ***Sleazoid Express*'s Sex, Sin, and Sadism Film Festival presents *Caged Heat***

● Friday, September 5 **Back to School Keg Party.** "All the beer you can stand. School teacher present"

● Saturday, September 6 Closed. "Go see Mo-Dettes at Irving Plaza"

● Sunday, September 7 **Rick McKoy Performance and JFK Party.** With *Zones*, a film by Vli Stern

● Tuesday, September 9 **Monster Movie Club: *Maniac!* and *Bowery at Midnight*.** "Psycho 30s"

● Wednesday, September 10 **Video Scotch-Guard.** "Featured are Barry Shils's documentation of the agony peculiar to delinquent youth, Steve Brown's Sumer documentary *The Black Headed People,* and tapes by Keith Haring, Bruce Birnbaum, Kenny Scharf and Target Video. Anyone arriving with a 3/4" tape can be assured of air time"

● Thursday, September 11 ***Sleazoid Express*'s Sex, Sin, and Sadism Film Festival presents *The Big Doll House***

● Friday, September 12 **Comedy Comatose**

● Saturday, September 13 ***Bikini Girl* and *Sleazoid Express* present *Chelsea Girls*.** "With guest speaker Ondine. A three and one half hour extravaganza involving double projection and double the fun"

● Sunday, September 14 **Juvenile Delinquent Film Pix presents *Young Savages* and *Blackboard Jungle***

● Sunday, September 14 **Club 57 Field Trip to Westpoint.** Please make your reservations with Andy Rees

● Monday, September 15 **Open Color Xerox Show.** Organized by Keith Haring. "Open to anyone: the largest collection of [Xeroxes] anywhere." With Xeroxes by Gervaise Soeurouge, Fanx Sham 69; Henny Garfunkel, Fast Food; Suzon; Bern Boyle, Mexican Wrestler, Public Toilet; John Berryhill, Self Portrait, Greetings from Times Sq.; Jean De La Fontaine, National Enquirer, March 25, 1980; Augie Tardy; Marlene Weisman, Numbers, Stevie & the Cars, Cocktail Picks; Sur Rodney (Sur), Clone; Lorraine Schein, Bibliomancy, Dimitri; Shmuel Thaler; John Comito, Artist at Work, Suite of Six; Fred M. Baca, Our Vanishing Indian Heritage; Dale Ashton, Toni Tennille and Amazing Animals, Marlon Brando; Keith Glancy, Nureyev Groupies / Torn Tulle, New York Gift / Not Returnable Statue of Liberty; David Barton, The History of Mankind, As Illustrated by the Necco Wafer, the Prehistoric Acropolis Is Extinct; Beth Lapides; Tony Redhead, Get a Head Kit; Sylvia Falcon; April Palmieri, Homage to Spaeth; Wendy Andreiev; John Sex; Drew B. Straub, My Girlfriends from Highschool; Seena Liff, They Punk by Night; K.; Steven La Forge; Randolph S. Black, The Ability to Massage; Adolfo Sanchez; Jennifer T. Ley, As Never Seen in Seventeen; Brian Butterick; David Wojnarowicz; Eva Machauf; P. O. (Oliver) Sanchez; Valery Oisteanu; Rumanian Folk Singer; Keith Derhammer; Martha Fishkin, T.V. Ruler; Richard Chevrolet; Todd Jorgensen; Stacey Elkin; Coco Ugaz; Tseng Kwong Chi, Slut for Art; Peter Cummings; Luca; Keith Haring, Portrait of Katy K, Post Pages; Paul Smith, Spinning; James Kling, Manhattan Jellybean; Richard Kurtz; Kara Westerman; Henry Benvenuti, Rockersize; Brookie Maxwell, Caresse and the Dog Suits; Sven Furberg; Robin Schanzenbach; Tim Miller; Kenny Scharf; Robert E. Warman; Ray, Farmer Brown; Julie Wilson; Donna Henes; Simon Peher; Chel White; Sharon Sandusky; Ann Magnuson; Larry Ashton; Zoe Leonard; Abby W.; Annette Vehwald-Riemschneider; Nancy Olivier; Richard Yodeo; Kai Eric; Karda Isler; Marie McAuliffe; Steve Holzer; Will Bennett; Janus Budde; Vernita Nemec; Harvey Wang; Judith Stiles, Red Banana Bride; Scarlatina Lust; Moana Haggard; Michael Biello; Anson Seeno; Debutante (Deb Parker); Alan Belcher; E. F. Higgins III; Buster Cleveland; Elmer Picasso; Gracie Mansion; Jeanne Mathew Young; Betty Good; Jeffrey Geiger; Daniel Abraham; Haoui Montaug; Jim Short (Nancy Breslow); Bruno Testore Schmidt; Paul Laster; Phillip Morrow; Peter McGrattan; Rick Krent; Maryanne Russo; Daria Deshuk; Judith Wong; Cindy Schwab; Alan Steinfeh; Robin Hauter; Yanna Trance

● Tuesday, September 16 **Monster Movie Club: *Cat Girl* and *She Devil***

● Wednesday, September 17 **Playhouse 57 presents Summer Repertory Workshop.** Produced by Scott Covert. Artistic direction by William Fleet Lively and Andy Rees. Musical direction by John Epperson. Technical direction by Tom Scully. ***Equus*.** By Peter Shaffer. Performed by Thomas Hawk / ***Valley of the Dolls*.** By Jacqueline Susann. Performed by Marjorie Gross / ***The Importance of Being Earnest*.** By Oscar Wilde. Performed by Jean Caffeine / ***A Telephone Call*.** By Dorothy Parker. Performed by Lauren Moon / ***The Madness of Lady Bright*.** By Lanford Wilson. Performed by Lazar Mintz / ***The Hunger That Dare Not Speak Its Name*.** By Peter Nolan Smith. Performed by Lazar Mintz and Felix Mintz / ***Candida*.** By George Bernard Shaw. Performed by Scott Covert / ***Bent*.** By Martin Sherman. Performed by Barry Shils and Scott Covert / ***Last Tango in Paris*.** By Bernardo Bertolucci. Performed by Matine Malle and Barry Shils / ***Scum Manifesto*.** By Valerie Solanas. Performed by Eileen Myles. "Don't let the Joans-es Get You Down" / ***Saint Joan of the Stockyards*.** By Bertolt Brecht. Performed by Tracy Brod / ***Saint Joan*.** By George Bernard Shaw. Performed by Barbara McCoy /

Joan of Lorraine. By Maxwell Anderson. Performed by Joanne Gries / ***The Lark***. By Jean Anouilh. Performed by Yvonne Fisher. "The Joan of Arc Bake-Off" / ***Who's Afraid of Virginia Woolf?***. By Edward Albee. Performed by Vicki Schrott and Ira Abramowitz / ***Macbeth***. By William Shakespeare. Performed by Asia Washington.

● Thursday, September 18 ***Sleazoid Express*'s Sex, Sin, and Sadism Film Festival presents *The Arena***

● Friday, September 19 **Playboy Bunny Club Party**. "A hip happening of gala entertainment excitement when Barbie and the Heftones groove along with their cocktail magic for your listening and dancing pleasure. Guest playboy DJ Tom Scully plays it real cool for the Manhattan sophisticate! And—the talk of the town—the beautiful 57 Bunnies"

● Saturday, September 20 **Debutante & Bruce present A Swank & Sleazy Saturday Night Affair!**

● Sunday, September 21 ***Bikini Girl* presents George Kuchar's *Portrait of Ramona***

● Tuesday, September 23 **Monster Movie Club: *The Flesh Eaters* and *The Frozen Dead***

● Thursday, September 25 ***Sleazoid Express*'s Sex, Sin, and Sadism Film Festival presents *Private Parts***

● Friday, September 26–Saturday, September 27 **Nicholas Ray Remembered: *Bigger Than Life, Rebel without a Cause*, plus *On Dangerous Ground, A Woman's Secret, Hot Blood***. Presented by Steve Brown

● Sunday, September 28 ***Reflections in a Golden Eye***

● Monday, September 29 ***At Long Last*: Photos by Anthony Scibelli and Katherine Dumas**

● Tuesday, September 30 **Monster Movie Club: Special Tribute to Richard Cunha with *Giant from the Unknown, Frankenstein's Daughter*, and *Missile to the Moon***

● Thursday, October 2 ***Sleazoid Express*'s the Other Sexes Film Festival presents Male Night**. The underground classics Jean Genet's *Un Chant d'Amour* and Kenneth Anger's *Fireworks, Scorpio Rising*, and *Kustom Kar Kommandos*. Guest speaker Kenneth Anger

● Saturday, October 4 ***Sleazoid Express* and *Bikini Girl* Magazine present An Evening with Gerard Malanga**. Films by Andy Warhol and Gerard Malanga. Featuring *Couch*, "The Gerard Malanga Story" from *Chelsea Girls, In Search of the Miraculous*, and *Vision*. Poetry reading by Malanga

● Saturday, October 4 Danceteria on Thirty-Seventh Street shuts down

● Sunday, October 5 **Five Poets: Rick McKoy, Helena Hughes, Chris Kraus, Jim Rydell, Jeff Wright**

● Tuesday, October 7 **Monster Movie Club: *Fiend without a Face* and *The Crawling Eye***

● Thursday, October 9 ***Sleazoid Express*'s the Other Sexes Film Festival presents Ladies Night**. "Radley Metzger's infamous *Therese and Isabelle*"

● Saturday, October 11 **Abel Ferrara directs live scenes from his upcoming film *Birds of Prey***

● Sunday, October 12 **John Epperson Piano Lounge on the Rocks**. Special guests for the evening Igor Stravinsky, Marvin Hamlisch, and Kay Thompson

● Tuesday, October 14 **Monster Movie Club: *Creature with the Atom Brain* and *The Astounding She-Monster***

● Thursday, October 16 ***Sleazoid Express*'s the Other Sexes Film Festival presents Sadism**. "Radley Metzger's rarely seen and beautifully executed S / M film *The Laughing Woman*"

● Thursday, October 16 Keith Haring's ***Open Studio Exhibition*** opens at Performance Space 122

● Friday, October 17 **Abel Ferrara directs live scenes from his upcoming film *Birds of Prey***

● Saturday, October 18 Closed. "The Stranglers at Irving Plaza"

● Sunday, October 19 **Judy Garland in *I Could Go on Singing***

● Tuesday, October 21 **Monster Movie Club: *Teenage Zombies* and *Curse of the Walking Dead***

● Wednesday, October 22 **Dany's Dance Party Supreme**. "Parquet punishment while Dany delivers music suitable for the Two-Step, Foxtrot, Samba, Waltz, Freak, Spank, Hustle, Pogo and Patty Duke. Join and compete in the 57 Fever Dance Contest"

● Thursday, October 23 ***Sleazoid Express*'s the Other Sexes Film Festival presents Odd Combos**. "Radley Metzger's notorious *The Lickerish Quartet*"

● Thursday, October 23 **Playboy Bunny Party** at Mudd Club. "Groove to the ear-stretching rock music of Barbie and the Heftones (their final farewell performance!) together with the lavish Galaxy Bunny Revue. Suggested attire is tie and jacket, tux or ascot for the Hefs and hi cocktail chic for their playmates"

● Friday, October 24 **Abel Ferrara directs live scenes from his upcoming film *Birds of Prey***

● Saturday, October 25 **The Smithereens: Super 8s by Justine Strait**

● Sunday, October 26 **Television Nostomania III**. "On Channel 57, Jerry Beck hues up again. *The Donna Reed Show*, Gumby and Pokey, *The Patty Duke Show, Batman, Land of the Giants, The Time Tunnel, The Partridge Family, The Twilight Zone, Amos 'n' Andy*"

● Monday, October 27 **Soft Sculpture and Video by Gerard Little**. "Surreal Still Lives, Otis and Marlena by the pool, babies and old folk. Vignettes ranging from the Bible Belt and *Ladies Home Journal*"

● Tuesday, October 28 **Monster Movie Club: *House on Haunted Hill* and *Burn, Witch, Burn***

● Wednesday, October 29 **The Groovy Dada Lounge presents Acts of Live Art**. Produced by Ann Eleanor Magnuson. With Bill Landis as the Rev. Jim Jones. **Strange Party Minus 8**. With Joey and Tony / **The Amazing Spiderboy**. Performed by Dale Ashmun / **Living Art**. Performed by Min and Van (Kenny) / **ART: The Only Band in the World** / **Patsy P. and Porter Parton Give You 'Jackson.'** Performed by Katy K and John Sex / **You'll Look Better in Jockeys Washed in Woolite**. Performed by Larry Ashton / **The Handy Man**. Performed by Robert Carrithers and Wendy Andreiev / **Wendy and the Roll Ons** / **Van Chrome Sings** / **Dean Jones**. With guest appearance by Anacani / **AMMO & the Puffs**. Featuring Angel, Lady, and Michelle. Music by D. E. Abraham / **John Sex Burlesque**. In the Room: Amazon designs by Stacey Elkin. Modeled by Daria and Janus. Patio Party by Diana Lillig (after Judy Chicago). Figurative installation by Daria Deshuk. Crickets in the stairwell by Man Parrish. Contemporary portrait painting by April Palmieri with Diana Lillig. Go-going by Charlotte, Brany, and Thomas Jefferson Oakman. Way-out light projection by Tom Scully. E Souix Meit Tzu (orb) by Kate Kennedy. *East Meets West* hosted by Tseng Kwong Chi. Red Tape by Bruno Testore Schmidt. DJ Dany Johnson. On the Walls: Lounge Murals by Keith Haring. Anonymous Art—Raw Art by Unknown Authors. Graffiti by Kenny Scharf. *Authorized Art Criminal* by Oliver Sanchez. *She Had a Checkered Past* by Dale Ashmun

● Thursday, October 30 ***Sleazoid Express*'s the Other Sexes Film Festival presents Transsexuals**. Irving Rapper's *The Christine Jorgensen Story*

● Thursday, October 30 **Parachute presents Modern Living 1981: A Fashion Performance** at 121 Wooster Street. Conceived and directed by Tseng Kwong Chi. Music by Man Parrish. "Television plays a key role in modern life and the runways of Parachute will be monitored by sets of pre-arranged color video images"

● Friday, October 31 Closed. "Go to Irving Plaza for The Monster Movie Club's 2nd Annual Halloween Ball. Screamin Jay Hawkins, The Misfits, Marilyn, Horror Movies, Guest Ghouls"

● Sunday, November 2 **Punk Rock Resurrection II**

● Tuesday, November 4 **Monster Movie Club: *Carnival of Souls* with Horror Trailers**

● Wednesday, November 5 **The Plague Years Party**

● Thursday, November 6 ***Don the Burp* Publication Party**. Hosted by Andrew Gurian. Featuring Arlene Ramsey, Minette, and *Clytemnestra* performed by Ethyl Eichelberger, Augusto Machado, and John Heys

● Saturday, November 8 Closed. "Ultravox at Irving Plaza"

● Sunday, November 9 **Dany Dance-a-Thon for MDA**

● Tuesday, November 11 **Monster Movie Club: *The Black Cat***

● Wednesday, November 12 **Marcus Leatherdale Twenty Photographs: *Urban Women***. "DJ Jean Caffeine featuring female vocalists"

● Thursday, November 13 Closed. "Gang of Four at Irving Plaza"

● Thursday, November 13 **Amazon Temptation** at Mudd Club. "Stacey Elkin presents her latest line of cocktail clothes"

● Saturday, November 15 Closed. "Slits at Irving Plaza"

● Sunday, November 16 **Pre-Vietnam Cabaret**. "Special Guest Stars! Video from Mississippi! Original Muzak"

● Tuesday, November 18 **Monster Movie Club: *Island of Lost Women* and *Mesa of Lost Women***

● Wednesday, November 19 **Playhouse 57's Dinner Theater presents *Boing Boing, or Passaic Perhaps***. Conceived and directed by Scott Wittman. Music by Marc Shaiman. Technical direction by Andy Rees. Cast: Bernard, a New Jersey bachelor / J. P. Dougherty. Bambi, a TWA stewardess / Ula Hedwig. Bertha, Bernard's domestic engineer / Tracy Brod. Robert, a friend of Bernard's / Scott Covert. Chantilly, an Air France stewardess / Georgia F. Wise. Mortidello, an Alitalia stewardess / Lisa Passaro. Joan Rivers, a Saint / Tracey Berg. Nightclub Singer, a winner / Bill Gallo

Wednesday, November 19 **Insectomania** at Mudd Club. Featuring the world premiere of a new videotape, *The Scary Truth about Cockroaches and Landlords*. Video by Neil Werde. Starring Tessie Chua with Robert Romagnoli, John Sex, Deb O'Nair, Dave Street, Stephano Robertino Caruso, Tish Bellomo, Sur Rodney (Sur), and Steve Mass

Thursday, November 20 **Rely, It Even Absorbs the Worry**

Friday, November 21 **Member's Art**

Sunday, November 23 **Television Nostomania 4**. "All new! *Gigantor*, *The Monkees*, *Amos 'n'Andy*"

Sunday, November 23 **Kenny Scharf presents *Carousel of Progress*** at Mudd Club

Tuesday, November 25 **Monster Movie Club: Salute to Herschell Gordon Lewis's *Two Thousand Maniacs!* and *Color Me Blood Red***

Wednesday, November 26 **Playhouse 57's Dinner Theater presents *Boing Boing***

Friday, November 28–Sunday, November 30 **A Night at the Opry: Country Round-Up!** With Country Music Stars. Styles by Katy K

Saturday, November 29 **The Cartoon Fantasy Organization of New York November Meeting**. "Cartoons! Fantasy films! From all over the world! Afternoon screening featuring *Astro Boy*, Hollywood cartoons, *Ultra Q*, and *Jack and the Witch*"

Tuesday, December 2 **Monster Movie Club: *The Thing***

Thursday, December 4–Saturday, December 6 ***Home Bodies***. A play by Michael Taav. Directed by Gordon Edelstein

Sunday, December 7 **Kiddie Matinee**

Monday, December 8 **Playhouse 57 presents *Boing Boing***

Tuesday, December 9 **Monster Movie Club: *The Fearless Vampire Killers*** "Uncut!"

Wednesday, December 10 **Slides of Politics and Fashion by David Schmidlapp with music by Walter Steding**

Thursday, December 11–Saturday, December 13 ***Home Bodies***

Sunday, December 14 **Free Lounge Night: DJ and Dancing**

Monday, December 15 **Playhouse 57 presents *Boing Boing***

Tuesday, December 16 **Monster Movie Club: *The Texas Chainsaw Massacre***

Wednesday, December 17 **Free Lounge Night: DJ and Dancing**

Wednesday, December 17 **ART** at Mudd Club

Thursday, December 18–Saturday, December 20 ***Home Bodies***

Sunday, December 21 **Soft Sculpture by Gerard Little**

Monday, December 22 **Rocky Horror Fan Club Christmas Party**

Tuesday, December 23 **Yuletide Carol Sing-a-long**

Sunday, December 28–Monday, December 29 **Painting Exhibition by Gene Gentile**

1981

Saturday, January 3 **The Waitresses**

Friday, January 9 Disturbed Furniture and John Sex open for Sector 27 at Irving Plaza

Friday, January 16 **Red Decade**. With Jules Baptiste, Brian Hudson, Jeffrey Glenn, and Fritz Van Orden

Tuesday, January 20 **Mudd Club Inaugural Ball**. "Featuring Ladies Auxiliary of the Lower East Side's Moral Majority Singers and their Salute to America"

Tuesday, January 20 ***It's War at No Rio*** at ABC No Rio

Sunday, February 1 **57 Lodge Meeting, Royal Order of the Groundhogs**. "The men's answer to the Ladies Auxiliary"

Monday, February 2–Tuesday, February 3 **Free Lounge Nite**

Wednesday, February 4 **Jungle Dance with DJ Dany**

Thursday, February 5 **Science Fiction Slideshow by Peter Grass**

Friday, February 6 **Radio Free Europe**. "An evening of Eastern European esoterica masterminded by Ann Magnuson. Featured are live music by Anoushka and Polska 81, with special guests Cyryl, Czyto Jest, Batuvski Brothers, the Olga Polonia Dancers & more. Free potato or beet at the door (while they last), and food catered by Leshko's"

Saturday, February 7 **Live Bands: Liquid Liquid and Dog Eat Dog**

Sunday, February 8 **Return Engagement: *Home Bodies***

Sunday, February 8 **Bill Landis's *Sleazoid Express* and the Ladies Auxiliary of the Lower East Side present *Satanis: The Devil's Mass***

Monday, February 9 **Mykel Board presents *Strictly Personal*: A New Cable TV Show Taping**. Come and be part of the studio audience or do a personal ad for yourself on camera

Tuesday, February 10–Wednesday, February 11 ***Home Bodies***

Wednesday, February 11 **Free DJ Nite with DJ Naomi of Club 57, Irving Plaza, Rock City, and WNYU fame**

Friday, February 13 **Mood Indigo: A Tribute to Duke Ellington**

Saturday, February 14 **Political Art Documentation presents All You Need Is Love**. "Art, Slides, discussion, dancing, and music by Noch Nichts"

Sunday, February 15 ***Home Bodies***

Sunday, February 15 **Bill Landis's *Sleazoid Express* and the Ladies Auxiliary of the Lower East Side present *Toys Are Not for Children***

Sunday, February 15 ***New York/New Wave*** opens at P.S. 1

Monday, February 16–Tuesday, February 17 ***Home Bodies***

Tuesday, February 17 **Haoui and Pals Perform Poetry**

Wednesday, February 18 **Truus de Groot and Instruments**

Friday, February 20 **John Sex Burlesque**

Saturday, February 21 **Greetings from Asbury Morgue: Mykel Board's ART, Death Movie, and an ART Death Set**

Sunday, February 22 ***Lower Manhattan Drawing Show* inaugurates Mudd Club's White Street Gallery**. Organized by Keith Haring

Monday, February 23 **Preview: *Trojan Women, or Hecuba to Block*, a New Play**. Artistic direction by Scott Wittman. Dances by William Fleet Lively. The Company: Ira Abramowitz, Tracey Berg, Jean Caffeine, Scott Covert, Cassandra Danz, J. P. Dougherty, Bill Gallo, Young Marge Gross, Ula Hedwig, Laura Kenyon, Lisa Passero, Sal Piro, Zora Rasmussen, Andy Rees, Vicki Schrott, Marc Shaiman, Arleen Sorkin, Cherry Vanilla, Georgia F. Wise, and Holly Woodlawn

Tuesday, February 24 **A Night of Idiocy with M. Henry Jones**

Wednesday, February 25 **Anti-Draft Bang to Benefit Mobilization for Survival**. With screenings of *The War Game* and *No Vietnamese Ever Called Me Nigger*. DJ Carol Black. "Draft counseling and first aid"

Thursday, February 26 **Home Movie Torture II**. "Bring anything—the film doesn't have to be your own but it must be amateur"

Friday, February 27 ***Erotic Art Show***. Organized by Keith Haring. With Kate Kennedy, Kit Robb & Parker Dulany, Jill Kimball, Gerald Ziegra, Nels Pierce, Cindy Schwab, Dan Stanger, Ken Tisa, Lynn Hughes, Marlene Weisman, Peter Cummings, Henny Garfunkel, John Monahan, Fred Baca, April Palmieri, Bronson Eden, Valery Oisteanu, Jon Stevens, Coco Ugaz, Judith Stiles, Valerie Haller, Angela Hans, Donald Baechler, Phyllis Bulkin, Lori Montana, Sur Rodney (Sur), G. H. Spencer, Frank Moore, Richard Taddei, Terri Zelig, Peter Hristoff, Mykel Board, Chip Duyck, Frank Holliday, David Wojnarowicz, Robin Fidoe, Buster Cleveland, Ande Whyland, James Brown & David Carrino, Peter Smith, David Spada, Rae Spencer-Cullen, AMMO, Phoebe Legere, Maryanne Russo, Judith Wong, Todd Jorgensen, Adolfo Sanchez, Oliver Sanchez, Vicki Schrott, Daria Deshuk, Sacco, Jean-Michel Basquiat, Richard Toscano, Christine Zounek, Ira Abramowitz, John Kelly, Ann Magnuson, Keith Haring, Bruno Testore Schmidt, Kenny Scharf, Chris Harkin, and Natalya Maystrenko

Saturday, February 28 **Live band: Y Pants plus Videotapes**

Sunday, March 1 **Jack Smith's Penguin Rustling out by the Old Archives**. "A Boiled Lobster color slide show with Sinbad Glick and Yolanda La Pinguina and Nazi Jacobs at the organ playing 'Ellen's Melons Are Missing Their Nipples'"

Monday, March 2 **Playhouse 57 presents *Trojan Women***

Tuesday, March 3 **Non-Writers Poetry Reading**. Featuring Ira Abramowitz, Robin Crutchfield, Bill Doherty, David Ebony, Duncan Smith, and Susan Springfield

Wednesday, March 4 **Playhouse 57 presents *Boing Boing***

Thursday, March 5 ***Sleazoid Express* presents *Sugar Cookies* with Mary Woronov**

Friday, March 6 **Katy K presents Truckers Ball**. "All Honky Tonk Angels and Truckers Welcome!"

Monday, March 9 **Playhouse 57 presents *Trojan Women***

Tuesday, March 10 **Dance Party with Certain Generals**

Wednesday, March 11 **Playhouse 57 presents *Boing Boing***

Film, video, and TV · Performance, theater, poetry, and comedy · Exhibitions · Music, social events, and theme nights · Events at other venues

Wednesday, March 11 **Ann Magnuson's Penelope and Her Exploding Mind Dimension** at Nobody's

Thursday, March 12 **Live Music from 3 Teens Kill 4 and Noch Nichts**. "Benefit for medical aid to El Salvador"

Saturday, March 14 **Radio Fire Fight: Dangerous Transmission with Jules Baptiste and Lefferts Brown**

Monday, March 16 **Playhouse 57 presents *Trojan Women***

Monday, March 16 **Monster Movie Club: *The Brain That Wouldn't Die*** at Mudd Club, kicking off a series of weekly screenings

Tuesday, March 17 **A Photography Show**. "Slides and prints by members of Club 57 and the Ladies Auxiliary." With April Palmieri, Ande Whyland, Robert Carrithers, Diana Lillig, M. Henry Jones, Kathy Cooke, Lori Montana, Robin Schanzenbach, Arunas Jankauskas, among others. [No comprehensive artist list has been found]

Wednesday, March 18 **Playhouse 57 presents *Boing Boing***

Saturday, March 21 **Appearing Live: Rhys Chatham with Scott Johnson and David Linton**

Sunday, March 22 and Monday, March 23 **Hotel Play**

Sunday, March 22 Tseng Kwong Chi's ***East Meets West*** exhibition opens at Mudd Club

Monday, March 23 **M. Henry Jones presents Independent New York Films at Cameron Public House, Toronto.** A replication of one of Jones's curated screenings at Club 57. Featuring Henry Jones, Rachel Reichman, Joey Ahlbum, Lisa Baumgardner, Judy Kamilar, Esther Regelson, Barry Masterson, and Susan Tremblay

Tuesday, March 24 **New York New Music: Snuky Tate**

Wednesday, March 25 **Appearing Live: Raw Adults with Paul Shapiro and Thunkaphonics**

Wednesday, March 26 **Rip-Offs Fashion show**

Friday, March 27 **Velvet Mania**. "Not the Velvets but an incredible simulation. With Ron Nemeth's film *Andy Warhol's Exploding Plastic Inevitable,* and a band including Ann Magnuson, Kai Eric, Bill Harris, Jean Caffeine. Guest DJ Bill Landis"

Saturday, March 28 **To Be Drugged, Gifted, and Dressed in Black: Soft Sculptures Fashion Party**

Monday, March 30–Tuesday, March 31 **Motive Dance Performance**

Tuesday, March 31 **Zoe's Unusual Entertainment**

Wednesday, April 1 **Elliott Sharp Trio**

Wednesday, April 1 **Open House** at Keith Haring and Kenny Scharf's. "All Day and Night"

Thursday, April 2 **Herbert Huncke Beat Poetry Reading and Films**

Thursday, April 2 **Ann Magnuson's A Lady Sings "She's Fit for Space"** at Mudd Club. "Taste the soothing sounds of Carol London (alias Penelope and Anouska)"

Friday, April 3 **Beth and Scott B present *Black Box, Letters to Dad,* and *G-Man***

Saturday, April 4 **The Bloods plus Poetry by Janet Hamill, Annie Toone, and Adele Bertei**

Sunday, April 5 **Super 8 Show by Dale Power**

Monday, April 6 **Playhouse 57 presents *Trojan Women***

Thursday, April 9 **M. Beach presents *F.U.R.* Magazine's Talent Hunt**. "Winner will be on the cover of *F.U.R.*"

Thursday, April 9 ***Beyond Words*** opens at Mudd Club. Organized by Fred Brathwaite and Futura 2000

Friday, April 10 **Wharton Tiers's Glorious Strangers**

Sunday, April 12 **Poetry Performance by Ira Brukner, Bob Holman, and David Wojnarowicz**

Monday, April 13 **Playhouse 57 presents *Trojan Women***

Tuesday, April 14 **Video Festival featuring Bernedette Stilletto**

Wednesday, April 15 **Revolution or Death Anti-Draft Benefit**

Friday, April 17 **Ladies Auxiliary Rites of Spring Fertility Bacchanal**. "Witness the debut performance of the Ladies' Auxiliary all-percussive orchestra Pulsallama"

Saturday, April 18 **Bill Landis's *Sleazoid Express* presents *The Laughing Woman***

Sunday, April 19 **Group Art Show**

Wednesday, April 22 **Celebrity Bingo**. "Jean Caffeine presents a star studded night, with Andy Rees and Vicki Schrott as your hosts"

Thursday, April 23 **Appearing Live: Group of Trees**

Friday, April 24 **Something with Richard Hell and Cookie Mueller**

Saturday, April 25 **Appearing Live: Glenn Branca**

Sunday, April 26 **Ondine Is Burr in Bill Landis's *The Life of Burr***. "See it with your own eyes—the life, the *Ironside* role and bizarre sexual practices of a sacred cow. With Ondine, Gerard Little as Marcus, Jimmy Joe, and Dany Johnson." [No comprehensive artist list has been found]

Monday, April 27 **Playhouse 57 presents *Trojan Women***

Monday, April 27 **Sleepers**

Tuesday, April 28 **Bill Landis's *Sleazoid Express* presents *Frustration***. "White Slaves!"

Wednesday, April 29 **Jam Session**

Wednesday, April 29 ***Ballgown Show*** opens at Mudd Club

Thursday, April 30 **Appearing Live: The Decals**

Saturday, May 2 ***Facere/Fascis*** opens at Group Material

Thursday, May 7 **Party for the Bush Tetras**

Friday May 8 **Poetry by Peter Cummings and Music by Sonic Youth**

Saturday, May 9 **Erotic Film Awards**

Sunday, May 10 **5700 Club: Mother's Day Special**

Monday, May 11 **Films by John Davis: *Shellshock Rock* and *Self Conscious over You***

Tuesday, May 12 ***Keith Haring New Drawings***

Wednesday, May 13 **Universal Interaction with AMMO**. Fifty simultaneous performances and total audience participation. With John Kelly, Tseng Kwong Chi, Bill Landis, Stacey Elkin, Keith Haring, Katy K, John Sex, and Daria Deshuk, among others. [No comprehensive artist list has been found]

Saturday, May 16 **Dress / Dance / Dazzle with Mundy McLaughlin**."Group Material fashion dance party in connection with *Facere / Fascis*. Dress: casually unique"

Saturday, May 16 ***The Monumental Show* opens at Gowanus Memorial Artyard**

Monday, May 18 **Anti-Ant Night**

Tuesday, May 19 **Sake Party by Debutante**

Wednesday, May 20 ***The Patriot Game* presented by Vivienne Dick**. "Movie Benefit for El Salvador"

Thursday, May 21 ***Mail Art Show*: Ray Johnson's Fun Club**. Presented by Valery Oisteanu. With May Wilson, Ray Johnson, Lightworks (Charlton Burch), E. F. Higgins III, Eddy Woods, Window Space, Vagrich Bakhchanyan, Deadley Lastname (Bradley Lastname), Chyrstal Feather, Ira Landgarten, Kasondra, Frizni (Sal Art), Scarlatina Lust, Eddy Rollins, Anna Banana, Alex TorridZone Igloo, B. C. Keech, Howard B. Stein, Joseph Nechvatal, S. Gustav Hägglund, Ray Kelly, A. M. Fine, Oleg Sohanievich, Roy Radio (Roger Stevens), Marcia Tucker, Charles Gatewood, Shel Silverstein, A. M. Pillar, Ira Cohen, Opal Louis Nations, Harry Pincus, Rolando Peña, Mario Lara, Carlo Pittore, Jon Stevens, Lon Spiegelman, Sur Rodney (Sur), Charles Henri Ford, R. Dick Trace It, Sabina Julick, Andrei Eyestone, Mark Rutkowski, Peter Frank, John Held Jr., Neil Sinall, Allen J. Sheinman, Ruth Friedman Oisteanu, David Ebony, Buster Cleveland, Coco Gordon, Spider Webb, Whitson Dada, Ted Jones, Gary Nagi, Sebastian Reichman, Jan van Raay, and Sheldon Polsky

Friday, May 22 **The Offs**. "Free 45"

Monday, May 25 **Bill Landis presents another play maybe with Ondine again**

Monday, May 25 **Club 57 Benefit** at Peppermint Lounge. With Katy K, Wendy Wild, John Sex, the Velvets, Anoushka, Barbie and the Heftones, Pulsallama, the Batusi Bros, and the Man Rays

Tuesday, May 26 **Two One-Act Plays by John Read**

Wednesday, May 27 **Poetry**

Thursday, May 28 **ART: The Only Band in the World**

Friday, May 29 **Tina Peel**. "Last show ever"

Saturday, May 30 **Liquid Liquid Album Party**

Sunday, May 31 **Word of Mouth Poetry by and Performance at Club 57**. Bob Holman, Rose Lesniak, Jeff McMahon, Joey Voitko, and Stephanie Skura

Tuesday, June 2 **Kathy Underhill Slideshow**

Wednesday, June 3–Thursday, June 4 **Second Annual Club 57 Invitational: Keith Haring's *Black Light Art Show* with Fab 5 Freddy**. With Haring, Fab 5, Kenny Scharf, John Sex, Michael Holman, Julie Wilson, Stacey Elkin, and Valery Oisteanu, among others. Music by DJ Afrika Bambaataa. [No comprehensive artist list has been found]

Friday, June 5 **Jerry Beck's Movie Madness**

Saturday, June 6 **Rummage Sale and Party**

Monday, June 8 **It's Dance Fever with Host Deney Terrio.** "Open Dance Competition: Couples Only"

Tuesday, June 9 **Johnny Cafeteria presents Trays: A Heterosexual Love and Eating Concept Unmatched by Horn & Hardart**. Original compositions by Sid Gilbert and Peter Kwaloff

Wednesday, June 10 James Nares's ***No Japs at My Funeral***

Thursday, June 11 **El Salvador???**

Friday, June 12 **Disco Italiano**. "La Dolce Vita! En persone: Giovanni Sexi, Anacani Magnanisoni, Bruno Testore, Katie Kalzone, April Palmieri, Ira Ai, Mortadella Velveeta, the Defranco Family, Topo Gigo, Lotsa Ronzoni, Pizza Di Stromboli, Joey Dante Orchestra, Spaghetti Garden, Tango Competition. With a screening of *Gidget Goes to Rome*"

Saturday, June 13 **Club 57 Bandstand**

Sunday, June 14 **Kenny Scharf Art Party: *Customized Appliances***

Tuesday, June 16 **Nell Campbell and the Return of the Cabaret of Fear**

Thursday, June 18 **Inner City Records Benefit**

Friday, June 19 **Live Lady Wrestling**

Saturday, June 20 **Psycho Comics Party**

Sunday, June 21 **LA Punk Party: An Evening with Chris Gremski**

Sunday, June 21 **Pulsallama Father's Day Dad-a-Rama** at Mudd Club. "All percussive, all bikini-clad"

Tuesday, June 23 **Universal Interaction #2.** "The second in a series of events produced by AMMO. This time, fifty participants (including many East Village celebrities) will move across a giant checkerboard performing a different activity in each square (such as: chanting, moaning, screaming, talking, laughing, crawling, rolling, walking, running, dancing, drumming, etc). The happening will build up to a wild frenzy and end with everyone collapsed on the floor. Spectators are encouraged to interact with the performers"

Wednesday, June 24 **Stella Que Linda's Posin' Party**

Thursday, June 25 **International Rap Night**

Friday, June 26 **Voodoo**

Saturday, June 27 **The Newest Romantics. ART: The Only Band in the World**

Sunday, June 28 ***Evasion***. A performance by Christian Joiris. Cameraman: Joel Cantor. Lighting: Michael Consance. Music and Voice: Robin Crutchfield. Performers: Josh and Dan Braun, Christian Joiris, Bill Sack. "**Scene 1**: Grey. Film: Super 8. 1. Image: The screen is divided-half black half white. 2. Action: The black surface will be painted white. The white surface will be painted black. Passage continues from each side to the other. Grey. **Scene 2**: Identical. 1. Image: 2 guys sitting on chairs, 1 of them is wrapped in gauze. 2. Action: The bandages of the first one will be removed from the feet up while the second one will be wrapped in bandages from the head down. The appearance of the two is identical (identical twins). Music: Xylophone. **Scene 3**: Reflection. 1. Image: Backstage the twins are standing up turning their backs to the audience. One is wearing a white overcoat; the other a black overcoat. Upstage 2 mirrors are set facing each other. 2. Action: The twins walk backwards upstage; when they get upstage they turn around revealing identical faces. They both move over to stand halfway behind mirrors. They create two singular images: half reality, half reflection. When this image is formed the two performers will be painted in grey"

Monday, June 29 **William Electric Black presents Romeo Rock and Juliet Jazzical**

c. Friday, July 3 **Classics of the New Cinema: Tina L'Hotsky's *Snakewoman* and John Lurie's *Men in Orbit***. "Romance and adventure. Guest DJ Anita Sarko"

c. Friday, July 10 **Classics of the New Cinema: New York Premiere of Harald Vogl's *Dear Jimmy***. With Anya Phillips, David McDermott, Becky Johnston, Eric Mitchell, James Chance, Patti Astor, James Nares, Tina L'Hotsky, Trixie Salke, Peter Wiese, Pat Place, Laura Kennedy, and Kathy Acker. "A vintage treasure from the hardcore cradle of the scene"—Edit DeAk. Cocktail piano: Steven Kramer

c. Thursday, July 16 FUN Gallery opens

Friday, July 17 **Classics of the New Cinema: James Nares's *Rome '78***. Starring the one and only David McDermott and a cast of thousands! Guest DJ Kristian Hoffman

Saturday, July 18 **Michael Holman Super 8 Film Loops Performance**. With Wayne Clifford

Thursday, July 23 **Calling on the Spirits: Voodoo Rhythms Night**

c. Friday, July 24 **Classics of the New Cinema: Anders Graftstrom's *The Long Island Four***. "'It was the perfect day to become Americans.' Guest DJ 'the famous' Jean Michel Basquiat"

Wednesday, July 29 **Reception for the Royal Wedding Party**. "For Topo Grajeda and Jimini Hignett of Christians from Outer Space with cake by Sur Rodney (Sur), films, music, tap dancer, poets, & DJs. Royal dress, drag preferred"

Wednesday, July 29 **Jim Fouratt and Rudolf Piper present a Modern Classix Event: The Royal Wedding Party** at Underground. "Live performance provided by Ms. Edith Massey (Polyester), Hibiscus and the Screaming Violets, DJ Mark Kamins. Coordinated by Lady Ann Eleanor Magnuson. Assisted by The Royal Manufacturer of Installations and Artistry, Brant Kingman, Esq., Numero Uno Lady-In-Waiting Kimberly Davis. Lady Diana portrayed by Baroness Wendylyn Wild of Psychedelia. Prince Charles portrayed by Kai Eric, Esq. Customized Cake by Appointment to the Royal Couple by Van Chrome. East Meets Royal West Tseng Kwong Chi, assisted by Sir Bruno of Capadocia, Cultural Attaché, Lady Samantha McEwen, Hostess of Edinburgh. High Tea Cakes Served by Lori "Bubbles" Montana and Min "Min" Thometz. Soft Court Sculpture and Gowns Created by The House of Westley-Little, Sir Gerald Westley-Little, Royal Purveyor of Couturie. Barbara Cartland Portrayed by The Grande Duchess of Doo-Wop Katy K, escorted by Sir John Sex, Esq. Princess Alexandra and the Hon. Angus Oglivy Portrayed by Lady April Palmieri and Sir Robert Carrithers, Esq. Fish And Chips by I.R.A.A. III. Bawdy Wench Scarlett is your Hostess of The Pirate Lounge. Royal SX-70s by Lord Alphonso, Duke of Gloucester, Royal Video courtesy of Sir Bruce Birnbaum. Visiting dignitaries: Contessa Stacey Elkin of Arizona, Sir M. Henry Jones, B.B.C, M.P. Belfast Chapter Patrick Quirk. Protests and Rioting by Dany Johnson, Coby Batty, Diana Lillig, Bruce Birnbaum, Barry Shils, Alexa Hunter. AP/UPI Coverage by Ande Whyland. By Appointment to Her Majesty the Queen, The Royal Purveyor of Protocol, Lord Drew Burns Straub"

Friday, July 31 **Classics of the New Cinema: Charlie Ahearn's *The Deadly Art of Survival***. Guest DJ Fab 5 Freddy

Sunday, August 2 **sCool Night: The New Beat Generation**. "Dig on Coby Batty, Randolph Hudson, Mark Kramer, and John Zorn's really gone sound. Interpretive dance by Ann Magnuson, Stacey Elkin, Charlotte Slivka, Wendy Wild, Kimberly Davis and other girls of being plus famous guest poets"

Saturday, August 8 **Lay Pray Die**. "Five musical theatre acts of prayer, tragedy, sin, evil and death choreographed by AMMO. Starring AMMO, Billy Harris, Lady, Jan Long, Ann Magnuson. Organ music by John Read"

Saturday, August 22 **Love Boat Cruise to Fantasy Island**. "Combining the best and worst of TV's soapy sitcoms. Captain Van Chrome welcomes you aboard. Top-line entertainment with Ann Magnuson as Carol London, Wendy Wild as Charo, and Tseng Kwong Chi at the blackjack table"

Friday, August 27 **Low Budget Luminary: A Lamp Show**. Organized by Diana Lillig and April Palmieri. With work by Jonathan Quinn, Gary Sherman, Deb O'Nair and Rudi Protrudi, M. Henry Jones from the Collection of D. B. Straub, Drew Straub for AMMO, Ann Eleanor Magnuson, Lisa Baumgardner, John Rosis, David Goode, Kim Schapich, Dan Stranger and Cindy Schwab, Tim Rollins, Kate Pierson, Fred Schneider, Gene Pragel, Patty Heffley, Barbara Wilson, M. Henry Jones, Ande Whyland, Richard Toonkel, Frank Correa and Mark Cronmiller, April Palmieri, Diana Lillig, David Lombard, Patrick Quirk, and Ann Levy

Wednesday, September 9 **Teenage Sex and Violence presents *Gun Crazy* and *Crime in the Streets***

Thursday, September 10 **Open Mic Audition Night**

Friday, September 11 **Mendel presents International Rap Night**

Saturday, September 12 **Pulsallama** at the Cavern. "The Ladies Auxiliary of the Lower East Side cordially invites you to attend their Rites of the Autumn Harvest Feast. Join Batusi Brother Host Van Chrome and rabid girls harvesting crops of dementia in savage seasonal pageantry! Free-from interpretive dance ceremonies choreographed by AMMO. Guest DJ Dany Johnson and house DJ Sara Salir. Coordinated by Ann Magnuson. Dress: Heathen"

Sunday, September 13 **Relax and Lounge, Group Discussion**

Monday, September 14 **Jelly Sessions with John Zorn, Coby Batty, Mark Kramer, Randolph Hudson, and Polly Bradfield**

Tuesday, September 15 **Stuck in Limbo Dance Party**

Wednesday, September 16 **Teenage Sex and Violence presents *Teenage Doll* and *High School Hellcats***

Wednesday, September 16 **Mykel Board's ART** at Carnegie Recital Hall

Thursday, September 17 **sCool Night**

Friday, September 18 **The National Geographics**. "A musical evening of socio-cultural presentations. The National Geographics are Ira Abramowitz, Christian Joiris and Gerard Little"

Saturday, September 19 **Psychedelic Freak-Out**. "The Mind-Expanding Fuzztones plus *Riot on Sunset Strip*. Formerly Tina Peel"

Sunday, September 20 **More Muzak**

Monday, September 21 **Preview of *Livin' Dolls***. The Who Family Presents: *Livin' Dolls*. A Musical by Scott Wittman and Marc Shaiman. Directed by Scott Wittman. Produced by Marc Shaiman and Scott Wittman, in association with Fran Pillersdorf. Midge / Donna Destri. Chatty Cathy / Zora Rasmussen. Barbi / Karon Bihari. Fifi / Young Marge Gross. Rip Curl / Bobby Siems. Poindexter / Scott Covert. Ken / James Rich. The Beast / Rob Walsh. Sets by Gallo's Humor and George Hurley. Costumes by Timothy Dunleavy. Assisted by William Fleet Lively. Hair by Baba. Lighting by Vince Lalomia. Sound by D. Perry Brandston. Music recorded at Man-Made Studios by Man Parrish. Music arranged and played by Marc Shaiman. Guitars played by Marc Ribot, David Acker, and Bruce Smith

Tuesday, September 22 **Preview of *Livin' Dolls***

Wednesday, September 23 **Teenage Sex and Violence presents *The Subterraneans* and *Beat Girl***

Thursday, September 24 **Comedy Night: Catch a Rising Reject**

Friday, September 25 **Freak Night: John Sex Side Show**

Saturday, September 26 **Local Rhythm Night: Elephant Dance**

Sunday, September 27 **5700 Club with Jim and Tammy Faye**. "New testimonial show. Rees, Magnuson, Lively Ent."

Monday, September 28–Tuesday, September 29 **Preview of *Livin' Dolls***

Wednesday, September 30 **Teenage Sex and Violence presents *City across the River* and *High School Confidential***

Thursday, October 1 **An Evening with Sal Piro**

Friday, October 2 **Living Debut**. With Terry Strecker and his SUNY Purchase group

Sunday, October 4 **Playhouse 57 presents Maxwell Anderson's *Bad Seed***. Adapted and directed by Andy Rees. Produced by Scott Covert. Sets by Frank Holliday. Sound by Tommy Hawk. Dances by William Fleet Lively. Miss Rockefeller's styling by Gerard Little. Cast: Rhoda Penmark / Becky Rockefeller (Scott Covert). Col. Kenneth Penmark, Richard Bravo / Lithgow Osborne. Christine Penmark / Georgia F. Wise. Monica Breedlove / Lisa Altomare. Leroy / Gerard Little. Emory Wages / Ira Abramowitz. Reginald Tasker / Anthony Scibelli. Miss Fern / Ann Magnuson and Lori Montana. Mrs. Daigle / Vicki Schrott. Radio Announcer / John Craig. Thank You Victor Carnuccio, Bruce Birnbaum, Richard Vasquez, David Richardson, Gabrielle Kelly, Marcus Leatherdale, Frances Pillersdorf, Scott Wittman, Staph of 57, Etan Patz, Joan Blondell, Robin Haislit, and Pepsi-Cola, Inc. "Watch for *Bad Seed* video trailer coming soon from Bruce Birnbaum Video Productions"

Monday, October 5–Tuesday, October 6 ***Livin' Dolls***

Wednesday, October 7 **Teenage Sex and Violence presents *Attack of the Puppet People* and *The Horror of Party Beach***

Thursday, October 8 **The John Sex Side Show**

Friday, October 9 **Subversive Activities Night: Regiment of Terror**

Friday, October 9 **Can Anyone Replace Crackers? What about Dale Ashmun? Come and See ART: The Only Band in the World** at 2+2. "Please dress for videotape"

Saturday, October 10 **Pulsallama Live**

Sunday, October 11 ***Bad Seed***

Monday, October 12–Tuesday, October 13 ***Livin' Dolls***

Wednesday, October 14 **Teenage Sex and Violence presents *Platinum High School* and *The Cool and the Crazy***

Thursday, October 15–Friday, October 16 **Jump Rope**. "A performance by Beth Lapides"

Thursday, October 15–Friday, October 16 **Two Guys: Songs from Shopping Centers**. Vocals by Chuck Tennis. Vocals and keyboards by Otis Telson. Saxophone by Jon Hagen. Slides by Rod Broadway

Sunday, October 18 ***Bad Seed***

Monday, October 19–Tuesday, October 20 ***Livin' Dolls***

Wednesday, October 21 **Teenage Sex and Violence presents *Hot Rod Gang* and *The Wild Angels***

Thursday, October 22 **Steve Strange New Romantic Memorial Party**. "Being that the Blitz surge is tired to the point of death, we at Club 57 feel that it is time for a wake. Complimentary Visage make-over, Bow Wow Wow group dance lessons, greatest hits sing-a-long, La Rock fashion show and special Renaissance East Village People set. Hosted by Drew Straub"

Friday, October 23 **Carrot Bottom and the Squeely-Weelies**. "A dance performance by Billy Harris"

Saturday, October 24 **Crazy Hearts**

Friday, October 23–Saturday, October 24 **Tom Scully Presents New York City's First Psychedelic Weekend** at the Cavern. "Certain Generals, They Came From Houses, the Fuzztones, Mental Floss, Exploding Mind Dimension. 5 bands, gogo girls, 16mm films, slide show, fluorescent light show"

Sunday, October 25 ***Bad Seed***

Monday, October 26–Tuesday, October 27 ***Livin' Dolls***

Wednesday, October 28 **Teenage Sex and Violence presents *Johnny Holiday* and *Girls in Prison***

Thursday, October 29 **Keith Haring Halloween Party**. "Another psychedelic Black-Lite fluorescent experience. 'Artists' are invited to come to the club between noon and 6pm to contribute 'art' to the walls. Fluorescent paint will be provided, the walls will be covered with paper. Costumes optional"

Friday, October 30 **A Swinging Soiree**. "A J. Ray Production. DJ M. Wheldon. Music by Manny-Mania"

Saturday, October 31 **Wendy Wild's Day-Glo Halloween Extravaganza**

Sunday, November 1 ***Gore Gazette* First Anniversary Party with Herschell Gordon Lewis in Person**. "*The Wizard of Gore* screens, with an excerpt of a new film by Frank Henenlotter, *Basket Case*"

Wednesday, November 4 ***Bad Seed***

Thursday, November 5 **Drew Straub's Show and Tell**

Thursday, November 5 **Pulsallama** at Club Negril

Saturday, November 7 **Limbo Party**

Sunday, November 8 **In Revival! *Boing Boing***. Directed by Scott Wittman

Monday, November 9–Tuesday, November 10 ***Livin' Dolls***

Wednesday, November 11 ***Bad Seed***

Thursday, November 12 **The USO Swing Show**

Friday, November 13 **Alien Comic Bad Luck Party**. Video by Merrill Aldighieri. Music by Richard Bone. Performance by Tom Murrin

Saturday, November 14 **Baseball Night**. The Confederation Courier Society presents A Fan's Night Out, a benefit evening for *Rundy's Journal*

Sunday, November 15 ***Boing Boing***

Monday, November 16–Tuesday, November 17 ***Livin' Dolls***

Wednesday, November 18 ***Bad Seed***

Thursday, November 19 **Artists Doing Comedy plus Fred Baker's film *Lenny Bruce without Tears***. Presented by ĕpoch. Featuring Barb Lafferty-Ferrari, Steve Durland, Bill Doherty, Buster Cleveland (assisted by Doherty, Durland, E. F. Higgins III, Sur Rodney (Sur), and Diane Sipprelle), Linda Frye Burnham. Hosted by Suzanne Glenn

Friday, November 20 **The M.D.A. Show**. With performance by AMMO

Saturday, November 21 **Dance Fever**

Sunday, November 22 ***Boing Boing***

Monday, November 23–Tuesday, November 24 ***Livin' Dolls***

Wednesday, November 25 ***Bad Seed***

Thursday, November 26 **Club 57's Thanksgiving Party**

Friday, November 27 **Spy Night at the Covert Club**. "Under Surveillance with Timothy Siciliano, Jennifer Q. Smith, Payton Wilkinson, Sandra McKee, Sarah Jenkins-Jacobs, Paul Serrato"

Friday, November 27 **Frankie Lymon's Nephew and the Bad Boys of 57** at the Cavern

Saturday, November 28 **Edith Head Is Dead: screening of *What a Way to Go***

Sunday, November 29 ***Boing Boing***

Monday, November 30–Tuesday, December 1 **Held Over! *Livin' Dolls***

Friday, December 4 **Eric Bogosian** "*Men Inside*, a solo performance consisting of a dozen characters out of Bogosian's mind – a bum, a nightclub entertainer, Superman – creating a composite of the American male. *On the Air* is a spoof of voice-overs, those ominous voices behind TV and radio advertising. Bogosian will create eighteen different voices in twenty minutes"

Sunday, December 6 **Art Exhibition**

Monday, December 7–Tuesday, December 8 **Held Over! *Livin' Dolls***

Thursday, December 10 ***Three Americans Address the World***. Paintings by Robert Hawkins, Edward Brezinski, and Brian Goodfellow. Organized and with a pamphlet by Ted Castle

Thursday, December 10 **On the Range Soirée** at Pyramid Club. Bobby Bradley, Alan Mace, and Vincent Sapienza inaugurate Pyramid Club programming under new management

• Monday, December 14–Tuesday, December 15 **Held Over! *Livin' Dolls***

• Wednesday, December 16–Friday, December 18 ***The Sound of Muzak***. Director: Scott Wittman. Choral master: Marc Shaiman. With Holly Woodlawn and a cast of dozens. Cast in order of number of rehearsals attended: Maria, a Pastulant at Ceasars Abbey / Holly Woodlawn. The Mother Abbess/ J. P. Dougherty. Captain Von Trapp / J. P. Dougherty. Sister Joey Heatherton / Young Marge Gross. Sister Morphine / Michael Musto. Sister Sledge / Linda Krauss. Sister Norma Kamali / L. A. Sank. Sister Record Deal / Wendy Wild. Sister Thing / John Sex. Sister Effie White / Lenny Dean. Sister Snooze / Jan Mohlan. Sister Conan / Vicki Schrott. Sister Twister / Scott Covert. Sister Sammy Davis Jr. / Gerard Little. Liesl / Wendy Wild. Rolf / John Sex. Gesundheit / Jan Mohlan. Pia / Michael Musto. Schnitzel / Lenny Dean. Schwartze / Gerard Little. Wilhemina / Young Marge Gross. Elite / L. A. Sank. Gestapo / Vicki Schrott. Guggenheim / Scott Covert. Elsa Dearest / Lisa Altomare. Adolf, the MC / Ira Abramowitz. Maurice the Fagula / Marc Shaiman. Diana Von Ross / Michael Musto. The Supreme Beings / Wendy and Madge. Yittle and Gittle / Haines and Pig. "Do-a-Deer" staged by Andy Rees. Sound by D. Perry Brandston. Sets by Woolworths. Assisted by Vicki Schrott. Costumes from the cast members' closets. Special thanks to Julie Andrews, Sally Field, Audrey Hepburn, Mary Tyler Moore, Debbie Reynolds, and Rosalind Russell

• Friday, December 18–Saturday, December 19 **A Christmas Special** at the Kitchen. Cast: Tammy Faye / Ann Magnuson. Van Chrome (Kenny Scharf) / Himself. Chorus / William Fleet Lively, Kathy Stephens, Frank Holliday, Billy Harris, Shawn AMMO. Written by Ann Magnuson and Andy Rees. Production management by Andy Rees. Sound by Tommy Hawk. Live selections played by Marc Shaiman. Slide reproduction by Tseng Kwong Chi. Lighting by Andy Rees. Costumes by Gerard Little. Crucifix gown designed by Stacey Elkin. Rhea's outfit designed by Carmel Johnson. Final "Trial" choreography by Shawn AMMO. Lena Häagendazsovitch choreography by William Fleet Lively. Lobby installation by Kenny Scharf. Shadow gods construction by Brant Kingman. Emmy courtesy of Melvyn Douglas. Special thanks to Susan Rose, Jim Fouratt, Peter Schuyff, Steve Mass, John Read, Richard Vasquez, M. Henry Jones, Joe Boyd, and Stanley

• Sunday, December 20 **International Super 8 Night**. Presenting films by Lisa Baumgardner, Edit DeAk, Manuel DeLanda, Richard Devereaux, Alexander Hahn, M. Henry Jones, Annebarbe Kau, Laura Kennedy / Pat Place, James Nares, Joe Nunes / Ted Cook, Amos Poe, Robert Hawkins & Patrick Fox, Arleen Schloss. Produced by Christian Joiris

• Monday, December 21 **Mendel's Chanukah Party**. "Bubby's dreydle table, Vegas style. Maurice Faygala on piano, Cantor Gerard Littlebaum, the comic genius of Giddle and Yiddle, Mendel and his Borscht Belt buddies. Dance the horah, holiday kvetch off"

• Wednesday, December 23 **Christmas Party**

• Saturday, December 26 **The Mr. Freeze Rap Show**. "Brooklyn's hottest rapper, Mr. Freeze with Dr. Jam, New Jersey's fastest cutting DJ"

• Thursday, December 31 **New Year's Party with Pulsallama**

1982

• c. 1982 Dan Asher solo exhibition

• c. January Ann Craig begins hosting weekly Cafe Iguana cabaret at Pyramid Club

• Thursday, January 7–Friday, January 8 **Robert Hawkins and Patrick Fox present the Haunted Nite Club**. With music by David Javelosa from Los Microwaves, the National Geographics, and Celeste Ries from Head Cheese

• Saturday, January 9 **John Sex Spins**

Wednesday, January 13 **Parts of the Moon**

• Thursday, January 14 ***4 Artists at Club 57***. Organized by Lisa Baumgardner. Featuring Joseph Ga Nun, Bernie Joelson, Jonathan Quinn, and Brian Spaeth

• Friday, January 15 **Women's Dance**. "Women Only Night"

• Sunday, January 17 **How to Be a Millionaire?** Amway meeting

• Monday, January 18–Wednesday, January 20 ***The Sound of Muzak***

• Thursday, January 21 **Bum's Benefit: The Warm Coat Variety Show**. "Films, dancing, song, comedy, magic. Admission: one warm coat"

• Friday, January 22 ***New Religious Directions for 1982: The Sacred and the Profane***. Organized by Jennifer T. Ley. Art by Vicky Alexander, Pieta; Myron Belger; Ronnie Cutrone; Heather Drake; Barbara Ess; Stephen Frailey; Jenny Holzer; Adrian Kellard; Jennifer T. Ley; Florian Michel; Paulette Nenner, Crucified Woman and Coyote; Italo Scanga; Lisa Stein; Edith Vonnegut; Nanette Vonnegut; Dragan Vukadinovic; Jeff Way, Head paintings; Douglas Wills. Performance by Ira Abramowitz, Hassidic Rap; Robert Carrithers; Kimberly Davis and Lori Montana, "The Vatican Rag," "An Ode to St. Aggie," and "The Barbie Doll Mass"; Daniel Faust; George Haas; Yolanda Hawkins and William Niederkorn, "The Further Adventures of Joan of Arc"; Jennifer T. Ley; Ann Wilson. Music programmed by D. Perry Brandston and Danny Kapilian

• Monday, January 25 **Monster Movie Club's Ed Wood Jr. Festival presents *The Bride and the Beast***

• Tuesday, January 26 **Tom Scully presents Chrystie Street Poets**. "Concretins in a reading of their own writing, selections from the soon to be published *New Facts About Cement*"

• Wednesday, January 27 **Drew Straub's Show and Tell**

• Thursday, January 28 ***Female Trouble***

• Friday, January 29 **Needles Jones presents Vamps: The Art of Seductive Performing**. Alexa Hunter, Brant Kingman, Kimberly Davis, Ann Magnuson, Lori Montana, Henny Garfunkel / Linda Farmer, John Sex, Needles Jones, Face Jones, Vicki Schrott, Jean Caffeine, Holly Woodlawn, Bob Fossil Dancers, Jennifer T. Ley, Diane Torr, Wendy Wild, the Westside Shirley Bassey Singers, Evan Lurie at the piano

• Saturday, January 30 **Van Chrome Variety Hour**

• Sunday, January 31 **Maria de Janeiro**. "A performance juxtaposing tribal minimalist dance, recorded electronics, and live vocal and percussive dub. Featuring Megan Haungs, a tap dancer native to Alphabet City, Pilar Limosner, a Costa Rican dancer with discarded Graham technique, and Meg Brazill, lead singer of Los Microwaves, with Todd Rosencrans from Los Microwaves on drums. Also performing: Bob Hoffnar and Fast Forward"

• Monday, February 1 **Monster Movie Club's Ed Wood Jr. Festival presents *Plan 9 from Outer Space***

• Tuesday, February 2 **Performance series by Los Microwaves**

• Wednesday, February 3 ***Michi's Blood***. A play by Franz Xaver

• Wednesday, February 3 Danceteria reopens on Twenty-First Street

• Thursday, February 4 ***Female Trouble***

• Friday, February 5 **Alien/Bone**. Alien Comic and Richard Bone

• Saturday, February 6 **Science Fair**. Organized by April Palmieri. Featuring George Stoll, Jonathan Quinn, Kimble Mead, Adrienne Leban, Kim Schapich, Gina Bianco, David Goode, Arunas Jankauskas, April Palmieri, M. Henry Jones, Chris Catania, Daniel Durning, Joanne Tolkoff, Sally Mason. A new film by Kathy Cooke plus slides. [No comprehensive artist list has been found]

Sunday, February 7 **Vivienne Dick, Louise Dovell, Greer Lankton, and Felice Rosser**

• Monday, February 8 **Monster Movie Club's Ed Wood Jr. Festival presents *Glen or Glenda***

• Tuesday, February 9 **Performance series by Los Microwaves**

Wednesday, February 10 **Blast with Green Ackerland, Era, Camier, and more**

• Thursday, February 11 **Poetes de l'invisible**. "An evening of poetry with Robin Crutchfield, Terri Hardin, Leslie LaRue, Rick McKoy, Marc Nasdor, Marc Penko, Jonathan Shipman, Joe Voitko. Produced by Christian Joiris"

• Friday, February 12 **ART: The Only Band in the World**. "Valentine's day show including love installation by Brant Kingman"

• Sunday, February 14 **Tribal Love Night with the National Geographics**. "With Al Diaz, Bill Sack, John Sex, Wendy Wild, Tom Murrin, Dany Johnson, Robin Crutchfield, Vicki Schrott, AMMO, Pilar Limosner, Billy Harris, Lori Montana, Stacey Elkin, Coby Batty, Kimberly Davis, April Palmieri plus surprise guests"

• Monday, February 15 **Monster Movie Club's Ed Wood Jr. Festival presents *Bride of the Monster***

• Tuesday, February 16 **Performance series by Los Microwaves**

• Thursday, February 18 **Preview of *An Evening with Nurse Strain***. A play directed by Robert I. Starring Penelope Rockwell

• Friday, February 19 **Women's Nite: Surgical Drag Ball**. "Post-Valentine's Broken Heart Surgery. Hosted by WOW. Women only"

• Saturday, February 20 ***NICE* Magazine Benefit Party**

• Sunday, February 21 **Rhythmic Interaction**. "A New Performance by AMMO. Featuring dance artists AMMO, Lady, Billy Harris, Lori Montana, and Drew B. Straub, and percussion music by Stacey Elkin, Dany Johnson, and Gerard Little. This all adds up to a totally unique evening of sensuous dancing and wild drumming."

Monday, February 22 **Red Red Trees**

• Film, video, and TV • Performance, theater, poetry, and comedy • Exhibitions • Music, social events, and theme nights • Events at other venues

• Tuesday, February 23 **Performance series by Los Microwaves**

• Wednesday, February 24–Thursday, February 25 ***An Evening with Nurse Strain***

• Friday, February 26 **Solid Gold.** Organized by Wendy Wild

• Saturday, February 27–Sunday, February 28 **Club 57 Performance Expo. Saturday night**: Ira Abramowitz, John Bernd, Charles Dennis, Bill Doherty and Barb Lafferty-Ferrari, Brant Kingman, Denis Kubyac, Pilar Limosner, Rick McKoy, Lori Montana and Coby Batty, Solomonoff & Von Hoffmannstahl. **Sunday night**: AMMO, Meg Brazill, Peter Cummings, Christian Joiris, Beth Lapides, Jennifer T. Ley, Bill Sack, Arleen Schloss, Paul Zaloom, and Payton Wilkinson and Timothy Siciliano. Produced by Christian Joiris. "This event will be videotaped for a show at the Cultural Center in Brussels"

• c. March Gracie Mansion inaugurates Loo Division in her apartment bathroom, a precursor to Gracie Mansion Gallery

• Wednesday, March 3–Thursday, March 4 ***An Evening with Nurse Strain***

• Friday, March 5 **NICE Magazine Benefit Party for *NICE* Issue 4.** "In performance and on display for *Sight & Sound* issue, the magazine you look at, read, then play on your phonograph. With Pop Decay, Gregory Fleeman, Solomonoff & Von Hoffmannstahl, DisloKate Klammer, Alex TorridZone Igloo, Standing Offer, Beth Lapides, Loi Kail, Amy Kaps, Lou Horvath, Ruby And The Roof Vandells, Theo Dorian, Erella Vent, S.T.O.P., Polly Wilkinson, Valerie Bart, Rick McKoy, Michael Hafftka, Daniel Abraham, Scarlatina Lust, Lisa Genet, and Gordon Blacker"

• Saturday, March 6 51X Studio / Gallery opens

• Sunday, March 7 ***This Object***. "A new film by Jacob Burckhardt"

• Monday, March 8 **Knife Dance, Denis De Visscher**

• Tuesday, March 9 ***Livin' Dolls* Cocktail Party**

• Tuesday, March 9 ***Livin' Dolls*** opens at Manhattan Theatre Club

• Wednesday, March 10–Thursday, March 11 ***An Evening with Nurse Strain***

• Friday, March 12 **John Sex's Burlesk Show.** "Live and uncensored!"

• Sunday, March 14–Monday, March 15 **I Crawled, I Walked, I Ran: New Wave Vaudeville.** With Sandra McKee, T. Hugill, Ron Littke, Phyllis Bulkin

• Tuesday, March 16 **57 Beat Cocktail Lounge**. "Snap Those Fingers!"

• Wednesday, March 17–Thursday, March 18 ***An Evening with Nurse Strain***

• Wednesday, March 17 **Pulsallama** at Mudd Club. "With special opening act AMMO"

• Friday, March 19 **Soul Party with Perry Homo**. "Motown Night!"

• Sunday, March 21 **An Evening with Jeanne Quinn and Bruce Tovsky**

• Tuesday, March 23 **57 Beat Cocktail Lounge**

• Wednesday, March 24–Thursday, March 25 **Jean Cocteau's *Antigone*.** Starring Louise Dovell. Directed by Liz Sheppard and Louise Dovell. Music by Wind of Codes: Michael Bezdrudczyk, Louis Lino, and Alfonse Manosalvas

• Friday, March 26 **Mee and Roland Young's I-Land**

• Saturday, March 27 **Chateau 57: An Evening of Bondage Comedy**. With Gerard Little, Sid Gilbert, Coby Batty, Chris Tanner, Wendy Wild, Kimberly Davis, Billy Bastiani, Vicki Schrott, John Sex, Lisa Baumgardner, Betsy Newman, Ellin Stein, Diane Torr, Marjorie Gross, Natasha Shulman, Bruno Testore Schmidt, Sur Rodney (Sur), Greer Lankton, Scott Lewis, Liz Sheppard, and Deb O'Nair and Master Rudy

• Sunday, March 28 **Poetes du silence**. An evening of poetry with Robin Crutchfield, Marc Penko, Marc Nasdor, Sandra McKee, and Peter Kwaloff. Produced by Christian Joiris

• Monday, March 29 **Academy Awards Night**

• Tuesday, March 30 **57 Beat Cocktail Lounge**

• Wednesday, March 31 **Jean Cocteau's *Antigone***

• Thursday, April 1 **Alien/Bone**. Alien Comic / Tom Murrin. Synthesist / Richard Bone

• Friday, April 2 **Open Party**

• Saturday, April 3 **Sleaze Party**

• Saturday, April 3 **Strange Party and Pulsallama** at Danceteria

• Sunday, April 4 ***Space Invaders*** opens at P.S. 1

• Monday, April 5 **Jean Caffeine's Celebrity Bingo II**. "We had so much fun last year, we decided to do it again. Your hosts Vicki Schrott and Andy Rees will lead you through a night to remember"

• Sunday, April 11 ***Performance Rites*** at P.S. 1. "Easter Sunday. The Word delivered to your spiritual doorstep by the Church of the SubGenius, Jill Kroesen with Joe Hannan, Krononauts, Gerard Little, Linda Montano with Pauline Oliveros, Ann Magnuson, Andy Rees, Kenny Scharf, M. Henry Jones, Tommy Hawk, and the Moral Majority Singers." Curated by Ann Magnuson. Assisted by Andy Rees

• Sunday, April 11 **Pulsallama** at the Underground. "With special performance by John Sex"

• Friday, April 16 **57 A-Go-Go**

• Saturday, April 17 **Freudian Slip/ Psychotic Underwear Bash**. "Women only, to benefit WOW. Another pure female production by Ruth Barone and Sherry Rosso. DJ Dany!"

• Sunday, April 18 **Three of Them: Dennis Cooper, Tim Miller, and Jeff McMahon Perform**. "Tim will: probably dance around a lot. He recently performed *Postwar* at Dance Theater Workshop and Beyond Baroque (LA). He's got the moves (and knows how to use them). Dennis will: read from his books *Idols* and *Tenderness of the Wolves*. He will probably hawk his magazine, *Little Caesar* and share some new stuff. He'll be fresh from a reading at St. Marks. Jeff will: indulge in the cult of personality. Or so he hopes. He recently performed with Tim at DTW and with Eric Bogosian at the Kitchen. He has some stories to tell. He also lies a little"

• Sunday, April 18 ***Performance Rites*** at P.S. 1. "The Flesh. Spring Bacchanal. Rampant Hedonism! With AMMO, Eric Bogosian, Johnny Dynell, Vincent Gallo, Ilona Granet, Michael Holman, Ginny King, William Fleet Lively, John Sex, Theodora Skipitares, Strange Party, Chi Chi Valenti, Ming Vauze." Curated by Ann Magnuson. Assisted by Andy Rees (see page 109)

• Tuesday, April 20 **57 Beat Cocktail Lounge**

• Wednesday, April 21–Thursday, April 22 **A Few Nights Out**. "With Nan Goldin, Max Blagg, David Massengill, Karen Maloof, Alfonse Manosalvas, C. P., Louise Dovell, Liz Sheppard, Gerard Little and Needles Jones. Includes *Postcards from Mexico* by Nan Goldin, Suzanne Fletcher, and Brian Burchill"

• Friday, April 23 **International Rap Night III**

• Sunday, April 25 ***This Object***. A film by Jacob Burckhardt screens with *Blips* by George Kuchar and Yoshiko Chuma's *Commercial Eruption*

• Sunday, April 25 ***Performance Rites*** at P.S. 1. "The Fracas. Wanton Maximalism, Unbridled Delirium! With Tracey Berg, Woofy Bubbles, Lizzy Mercier Descloux, Charles Dennis, Delia Doherty, Kai Eric, Mitchell Kriegman, Tom Murrin, Michael Peppe, Vicki Schrott, Wendy Wild, Hannah Wilke, Paul Zaloom, Zev." Curated by Ann Magnuson. Assisted by Andy Rees

• Monday, April 26 ***Gore Gazette* presents *The Worm Eaters***

• Tuesday, April 27 **Sing-a-long with Mitch**. "Mitch Millmer and the Mitch Millmer Singers"

• Wednesday, April 28–Thursday, April 29 **John Zorn Festival**

• Friday, April 30 **10 on 8 presents 100 Artists**

• c. May Civilian Warfare and Nature Morte galleries open

• c. May Haoui Montaug launches his weekly No Entiendes cabaret revue at Danceteria

• Saturday, May 1 **Fallout Shelter Party Cold Comedy**

• Sunday, May 2 ***Performance Rites*** at P.S. 1. "The Light. Atone with modern day visionaries. With Toby MacLennan, Mary de Blassio presenting Our Lady of Bayside—Ms. Veronica Lueken, brought to P.S. 1 by Andy Rees, Fran Lebowitz, Kazimir Passion, California Now! in protest of the Falklands with Frank Bednash, Tommy Geckle, Kimberly Davis, Ann Magnuson, and Billy Harris, Marty Watt, and Kenny Scharf." Curated by Ann Magnuson. Assisted by Andy Rees

• Monday, May 3 ***Found in the Street*: Sculpture Invitational.** Organized by Daniel Berglund. "Abstract, unaltered pieces preferred but will consider all gems of the gutter. However, all pieces must have been found—created by chance, not by will"

• Monday, May 3 **Lenny Dean's Miss Cheese of the Week Show** at S.N.A.F.U. "Monday is cheese day in May . . . a sure-fire cure for those Monday night blues this spring. Come cheese it up as New York City's favorite Cheese-Bombs: Donna Destri, Dori Hartley, Joyce Mandell, Vicki Schrott, Gerogia Wise, Holly Woodlawn vie for the coveted title. The girls will sing, dance, model, parade. . . . The winner is selected by the audience"

• Friday, May 7 **Sing-a-long with Mitch**

• Sunday, May 9 **57's Tribute to Motherhood with Downtown's Favorite Mother Cookie Mueller and Her Son Max**. "Queen for a day! House Dress Fashions! Shared Tender Moments with Mom and these wonderful sons and daughters: Haoui Montaug, Nan Goldin, Tom Murrin the Alien Comic, AMMO, Larry Ashton, Eric Smith, Needles

Jones / Ira Abramowitz, Solomonoff & Von Hoffmannstahl, Henny Garfunkel, Gerard Little, Greer Lankton, Becky Rockefeller, Merle Ginsberg, Christian Joiris, Lori Montana, Vicki Schrott"

● Wednesday, May 12–Thursday, May 13 **Jean Cocteau's *Antigone***

● Friday, May 14 **Frankie Lymon's Nephew and the Drugged Adults Dance Party**

● Wednesday, May 19–Thursday, May 20 **Jean Cocteau's *Antigone***

● Friday, May 21 **Needles Jones + Perry Homo's Sleaze Review**. "With Holly Woodlawn, John Sex, Diane Torr, Billy France, Sid Gilbert"

● Sunday, May 23 **Live and Animated Films by Emily Breer, M. Henry Jones, and Others**

● Wednesday, May 26–Thursday, May 27 **Jean Cocteau's *Antigone***

● Friday, May 28 **Rites of Spring Fertility Bacchanal**. "Pulsallama's first anniversary party! Musical guests: the Cowbells"

● Tuesday, June 1 **57 Beat Cocktail Lounge**. "Solomonoff & Von Hoffmannstahl with The Long Night's Eternal Dream"

● Friday, June 4 **Dance Party**

● Saturday, June 5 **Country Western Night**. "Eddy Dixon and Last Roundup featuring the Sugarmill Sisters: Michael McMahon, Garth Powell, Angela Jaeger, Amy McMahon, Amanda Uprichard and Sue Garner"

● Sunday, June 6 **Christian Joiris presents Nude Theology**. "An evening of music, comedy, performance and film featuring Ira Abramowitz, Peter Cummings, Stan Becker / Human Television, Christian Joiris, Brant Kingman, Greer Lankton, Sandra McKee, Arleen Schloss, Solomonoff & Von Hoffmannstahl performing *Swank: Oct. / Nov.*"

● Monday, June 7 **Andy Warhol's *Vinyl* with Ondine**. "Proceeds benefit *Before Stonewall*, a film by Greta Schiller, Robert Rosenberg, and Howard Petrick"

● Tuesday, June 8 **Beat Cocktail Lounge with the 57's Sedatives**

● Thursday, June 10–Friday, June 11 **57 Varieties**. "With Young Marge Gross, Betsy Newman, Ellen Stein, Vicki Schrott, Joel Winston, Billy Bat, Nancy Reagan, Needles Jones / Ira Abramowitz, John Sex, Michael Musto, Kimberly Davis, Nell Stewart, Peter Kwaloff, N.Y. Nicks, DJ Dany Johnson, Special K & Johnny Q"

● Sunday, June 13 **Scott Wittman and Marc Shaiman present 57 Goes to the Catskills**. "With your hosts Giddle and Yiddle, J. P. Dougherty, Mendel the Hasid Rocker, Sammy Davis Jr., Donna Destri, Michael Musto, John Sex, plus many more!"

● Tuesday, June 15 **57 Beat Cocktail Lounge**

● Wednesday, June 16 **Baby Face and the Boom Boom Saw** at Club Armageddon. "A performance by Christian Joiris to be aired on Channel D 'Art × 35' . . . artists step out for nuclear disarmament"

● Friday, June 18 **Alien/Bone, Susie Schneider, Alien Comic**

● Saturday, June 19 **WOW Benefit Party: The Party to End All Wars**. "Setting: The Officers' Club on Corregidor Island, 1945. Dany in the Radio Shack. Women Only. A Military Affair—Pure Female Productions"

● Sunday, June 20 **Garage Night with DJ Naomi**. "An evening of psychedelic punk"

● Monday, June 21 **Nervous Art Night**. "An evening of neurotic doodling and disco with DJs Jean Caffeine and Anita Sarko"

● Tuesday, June 22 **57 Beat Cocktail Lounge**

● Wednesday, June 23 **Art Exhibition**

● Thursday, June 24 **Post Modern Dance**. "With AMMO, Billy Harris, Lori Montana, Nell Stewart, Sent M'Ahesa, Ira Abramowitz, Eva Geueke"

● Thursday, June 24 **The June Bride Show** at Danceteria. "A Fashion Performance of Conceptual Bride Dresses by Animal and the Amazons. With Avant-Designers: Chris Bond, Katy K, Animal X, Ann Waldrop Burkhards, Ken Angelica of Jungle Red, Sonda, Maripol, Brian Damage, Layla, Patty Quinn, Judy Ross, Betsey Johnson, Angilique, Millie David, Kenny Valente, Ian's, Tim Dunleavy, Haruko, Tish Bellomo of Manic Panic, Sally Beers, Dianne Brill, Nona Hendryx, Jeannette Lee of Public Image Ltd., Anita Sarko. With celebrity models: Brenda Bergman, Cindi Lauper of Blue Angel, Patricia Field, Joey Arias and Janus of Strange Party, Holly Woodlawn, Alexa Hunter, Lisette of LaRocka, Liz Derringer, Michael Musto, Dovanna Dovanna, Wendy Wild of Pulsallama, Kathy of Avenue, Marilyn, Lori Eastside, Regina Richards, John Sex, Cheryl Wagoner, Marcia Resnick, Leia Ex Shangri-Las, Honi O'Rourke from Neon Leon Band, Karyn, Cynthia Ross from B-Girls, Stephanie Kaye from Shox Lumania, Tish and Snooky From Sic F*cks, Cookie Mueller, and Francine from Jungle Red"

● Friday, June 25 **The Dating Game: Swingin' Singles Party**. "Featuring Las Vegas type entertainment with the Fabulous Wantons, Gunnar Berglund the Swingin' Swede and Peter Brady. Dress to impress! Win a dream date with John Sex, Wendy Wild, Vicki Schrott, Needles Jones"

● Saturday, June 26 **Strange Party** at Pyramid Club

● Monday, June 28 **Color Xerox Art Show**. Organized by Jean Caffeine. With Xeroxes by Ira Abramowitz, Tom Bessoir, Nancy Brooks Brody, Jean Caffeine, Kjell Furberg, Ron Gault, Julie Hair, M. Henry Jones, Marcus Leatherdale, Robert Hawkins, Phil Lipchitz, Kano, Nene, Danny Plutzer, Futura 2000, Obdewl X (Kiely Jenkins), Sara Salir, Jon Sarkin, Julie Wilson, Jane Waltzer, Evan Shepherd, Kathy Underhill, Alex Vallauri, Zephyr, and others. DJs Anita Sarko and Jean Caffeine

● Tuesday, June 29 **57 Beat Cocktail Lounge**

● Wednesday, June 30 **Urban Primitives Party**. "Produced by Brant Kingman to benefit *the Monument Redefined*, the second Gowanus annual exhibition organized by Frank Shifreen and Scott Siken. Contributing artists and performers include AVANT, BARRY, Daniel Berglund, Beth Conard, Kimberly Davis, Tom Finkelpearl, Futura 2000, Andy Hammerstein, Keith Haring, Christian Joiris, Mary Jane Leach, Jennifer T. Ley, Michael Warren Powell, Brant Kingman, Layne Redmond, Alex Vallauri, Payton Wilkinson and Timothy Siciliano, and others. Music by the Angklung Brothers, Philip Johnston and friends"

● Friday, July 9–Saturday, July 10 **Pigbag, Pulsallama, and Last Roundup at Peppermint Lounge**

● Tuesday, July 27 ***Urban Primitivism* opens at White Columns**. "Organized by Jennifer T. Ley. With AMMO, Marla Buck, Jennifer T. Ley, Frank Shifreen, Timothy Siciliano, Nell Stewart, Payton Wilkinson, Doug Wills, Judith Wong"

● Sunday, August 22 **Summer's Cue with DJ Jean Caffeine** at Danceteria

● Friday, September 10 ***The Monument Redefined, Gowanus Annual II*** opens at Gowanus Memorial Artyard

● Monday, September 20–Tuesday, September 21 **Scott Wittman and Georgia F. Wise present *Sweet Blondes of Youth*** at Danceteria. "Loosely based on a Tennessee Williams classic." Starring John Sex and Alexis del Lago. With J. P. Dougherty, Georgia F. Wise, Burt Coleman, Susa Maher, and George Wrage

● Saturday, September 25 **Volatile Urban Monuments** at Westbeth. Organized by Brant Kingman. With Gina Wendkos, Ira Abramowitz, ART: The Only Band in the World, Ellen Ratner, Pool, Frankie Lymon and the Drugged Adults, AVANT, and Brant Kingman

● Wednesday, September 29 **Benefit Party for Club 57** at Danceteria. Organized by Susan Hannaford, Peter Kwaloff, and Patrick Quirk. With sections curated by Deb O'Nair, Lisa Baumgardner, Rich Colicchio, Andy Rees, and Scott Wittman. "This benefit will provide Club 57 with the necessary funds to suitably soundproof the club. The first 3 floors of Danceteria will feature a retrospective of four years of Club 57 activity in the fields of visual art, performance, music, film, video, fashion, and photography. In addition there will be an auction of valuable 57 memorabilia and art, a smorgasbord of Polish cuisine and t.v. dinners and polka dancing for fun and profit."

● Saturday, October 2 **Farewell Party for Pulsallama with Middle Class** at Danceteria. "To send these intrepid girls off as they go to perform in Europe"

● Tuesday, October 5 **The Tyrell Corporation presents Dark Amusements** at Danceteria. "The forgotten, decayed decrepitness of a top secret abandoned floor atop the gothic Danceteria complex. Post-apocalyptic exoticism with Vulcan Death Grip; John Sex and his Reptilian Replicant direct from the animoid mart; and the Brothers of Doom Choir. Functional DJ Roger Trilling. Dress: Harley-Davidson erotica. Genetic design and cloning by Ann E. Magnuson"

● Saturday, October 9–Sunday, October 10 **Psychedelic Fun House**

● Saturday, October 9 ***Keith Haring with LA2*** opens at Tony Shafrazi Gallery

● Thursday, October 14 ***Watch These Girls: 19 Women Who Do Copy Art***. Organized by Amy Chaiklin. With Emma Amos, Lisa Baumgardner, Doris Boris Berman, Kathy Caraccio, Amy Chaiklin, Sherry Edwards, Marie Favorito, Kirsten Hawthorne, Janet Henry, Miriam Jacobs, Kay Kenny, Kate Lambert, Ginny Lloyd, Dona Ann McAdams, Beverly Naidus, Pam Meyer, Erika Rothenberg, Esther K. Smith, and Barbara Wyeth

● Saturday, October 16 **On the Town with Tony Heiberg**. "Hosted by Tessa Hughes-Freeland and Irina Brook. Starring Mendel the Hasid Rocker, David Svitzer, Alison Gordy, Laura of Arabia, riveting new rapping / breaking sensations, and the On the Town band: Phoebe Legere (keys), Ernie Provincia (bass), Ed Steinberg (drums), Tony Heiberg (guitar), featuring Degan and Joal"

● Sunday, October 17 ***Beast: Animal Imagery in Recent*** opens at P.S. 1. With a presentation of ***Webelos***. Written and directed by Andy Rees. With Georgia F. Wise and Lisa Altomare

● Film, video, and TV ● Performance, theater, poetry, and comedy ● Exhibitions ● Music, social events, and theme nights ● Events at other venues

● c. Tuesday, October 19 **Nightshift presents Rancho Notorious** at Pyramid Club. With Lindzee Smith, Steve Wilkinson, Alexa Hunter, Jay Mark Johnson, John Lurie, Mark Boone Jr. "In three weekly episodes!"

● Thursday, October 21 **Gore Gazette presents *She Demons***

● Friday, October 22 **Upwardly Mobile: Close Encounters with the Very Few** at Danceteria. "Ann Magnuson in the blue elevator"

● Saturday, October 23 **On the Town with Tony Heiberg**. "Hosted by Tessa Hughes-Freeland. Starring David Svitzer, Laura of Arabia, Rockets Redglare, Double-Dutch Girls, T. X. Erbe, Keith Berger, Lucille, rapping and breaking, and the On The Town band"

● Thursday, October 28 ***Gore Gazette* presents *The Toolbox Murders***

● Saturday, October 30 **On the Town Halloween Cabaret with Tony Heiberg**. "Hosted by Tessa Hughes-Freeland. Starring Haoui Montaug singing "The Monster Mash" and more, temptress Tessa Hughes-Freeland spins the yarn of Hitchcock, the bewitching voodoo harmonies of the tropical trio Three Girls Spit-Fires, the horror stories of Ira Abramowitz, the evil puppet master and his toys of destruction, the impossible—a warm Italian—Vinnie Platatina, the seductive gyrations of Mutant Woman, Count David Svitzer—the boogeyman—sings, that sorcerous of song by Needles Jones, sinister Susan Israel, and the On The Town band"

● Sunday, October 31 **Halloween IV: The Party No One Came Home From**. "Solomonoff & Von Hoffmannstahl, Alien Comic, Voodoo Dancing Girls, the sick slides of Simone"

● Sunday, October 31 **Vampire Sex Girl** at Lucky Strike. "A night of horror and lust, paintings by Stefano Castronovo"

● Wednesday, November 3 **Hair Extravaganza: Get a Haircut, You Hippie**. "Performance, exhibits, audience participation. Club 57 or its subsidiaries are not responsible for reimbursement (monetary or otherwise) to losers of the 'Best do' contest"

● Thursday, November 4 ***Gore Gazette* presents David Cronenberg's *Rabid***

● Friday, November 5 **Circle Arts Performance Party**

● Saturday, November 6 **New York's Wildest Swingin' Beach Party**

Wednesday, November 10 **Two Red Heads**

● Thursday, November 11 ***Gore Gazette* presents *The Gore Gore Girls*.** "Herschell Gordon Lewis's depraved final release. NYC Premiere"

Sunday, November 14 **Quiet Riot**

● Saturday, November 20 **No Frills Party**

● Thursday, November 25 ***I Was a Teenage Frankenstein* and *I Was a Teenage Werewolf***

● Friday, November 26 **Bowery Benefit**

● Saturday, November 27 **Doctors Marv and Sid Friedman present Bellevue Night**. "Ward 57's Most Talented In-Patients, the Thorazine Players, Straight-Jacket Fashions, the Bellevue Revue, Rehab Arts and Crafts Display, Stand Up Catharsis"

● Monday, November 29 **Poetry Reading by Philip Dray / Art by Andrea Scrima**

● November 30 ***Vista*: Art by Jonathan Quinn**

● Thursday, December 2 ***Gore Gazette* presents *Andy Warhol's Bad*.** "Uncut and X-rated"

● Friday, December 3 **Circle Arts Performance Party**. With Julius Klein and others

● Sunday, December 5 **Scott Wittman and Marc Shaiman present *Trilogy of Terror***. With Laura Kenyon, Cameron Johann, and Vicki Schrott. Created by Laura Kenyon, Marc Shaiman, and Scott Wittman. Musical direction by Marc Shaiman. Directed by Scott Wittman

● Monday, December 6 **Performance by Pink Theatre Company / Art by Richard Rorne**

● Tuesday, December 7 ***Paintings at Club 57*: Bill Doherty presents 9 Artists**. With Angel Borrero, Brian Buczak, Nancy Clark, Bill Doherty, D. R. Jacobson, Kathy Johnson, Arina Malukova, Brad Melamed, and Claire Moore

● Wednesday, December 8 **Animation Night**

● Thursday, December 9 ***Gore Gazette* presents Herschell Gordon Lewis's *Color Me Blood Red***

● Sunday, December 12 ***Trilogy of Terror***

● Monday, December 13 **Poetry Reading by Tony Fowle / Art by John Rosis**

● Tuesday, December 14 **Paintings by Ellen Berkenblit**

● Thursday, December 16 ***Gore Gazette* presents *Two Thousand Maniacs*!**

● Friday, December 17 **Beat Night**. "Cool Daddy-o! Hipsville featuring Vinyl Syding and the Suburban Beat, Last White Poets, Laceration Team with Jonathan Prosser of Christa Gamper, Marta's Lucky Strike Movies, Mama Joy, Keiko, Christine Hatfull & company"

● Saturday, December 18 **Needles Jones's Red Light Café**. "From the heartland of America, from every roadhouse and Holiday Inn. With Miss Maggie, Tony Heiberg, Michael Chandler, Miss Joy Stick, Rob Hardon, Clitoris Gash, The Wild Women plus surprise guests from the dives and lounges of the Great Midwest"

● Sunday, December 19 **Z's Afternoon Christmas Tea**

● Sunday, December 19 ***Trilogy of Terror***

● Sunday, December 19 **WOW XXXMAS Benefit**. Hosted by Cathy Quinlan, Peggy Reynolds, and Diane Torr

● Sunday, December 19 **Pulsallama** at Jim Fouratt's Underground. "Having ravaged London, New York's own wild women return"

● Sunday, December 19 **Life Crusade** at Life Café. "Ann Magnuson invites you to her annual holiday performance . . . a free soup and bread line gospel revival for the wretched"

● Tuesday, December 21 **Rites of the Winter Sabbat** at the Clocktower. "The unveiling of Stefano Castronovo's new paintings of dark and light, and the incantations of the Holy Antiphony Choir"

● Wednesday, December 22 ***The Bank Show: A Show of Self-Portraits*** opens at SoHo Branch of Manufacturers Hanover Trust Co. Organized by ēpoch

● Thursday, December 23 ***Gore Gazette* presents *The Gore Gore Girls***

● Thursday, December 30 ***Gore Gazette* presents David Durston's *Stigma***

● Friday, December 31 **New Year's Is a Drag**. "On stage: Needles Jones, Glamourine, Leslie Coleman, James P. Richardson, Stephanie Fox, CC, Clitoris Gash, and surprise guests"

● Friday, December 31 **Garden of Fuzz New Years Eve**. "Live exotic entertainment. Ann Magnuson is Carol London, John Sex speaks his mind. Creative consultant: Dark Corp."

1983

● On Sundays **Reel Club**. Organized by Tessa Hughes-Freeland. "Free with your own Super 8 film"

● Sunday, January 2 **Wild and Wonderful** at Pyramid. "Hank appearing live at the Pyramid Ranch"

● Tuesday, January 4–Wednesday, January 5 ***New Year's Resolutions*.** Organized by Ira Abramowitz. Art by Victor Carnuccio, Not To Die; John Rosis, I'll Never Paint Again (in 1982); Amy Chaiklin; Daniel Berglund, The Resolute; Marissa Waichunas, Symbol for the New Year: I Will Fight the Darkness in '83; Carola von Hoffmannstahl, I Resolve to Give Up Smoking after Sex; Kate Kennedy, Good to the Last Drop; Carlo McCormick, I Will Never Pollute Again (limited edition print); Todd Jorgensen; Suzee Kendzulak, I Won't Fuck around w/ My TV, Herpes; John Sex; David Crocker; David Allen, Resolve; Tessa Hughes-Freeland, Grin & Bear It; Bill Paradise; Ellen Berkenblit; Brian Butterick, I Am a Country Singer; Mykel Board; Bayard Michael, Killing; Tessie Chua, Not to Waste Time; Merrill Aldighieri, To Wear More Sensible Shoes, Skin Deep from Outer Space; Françoise Marie, Light I Dark; Lisa Baumgardner, Lisa in Bondage; Tony Clay, Music, Man; Jonathan Quinn; Nancy Brooks Brody; Zoe Leonard; Ira Abramowitz; Richard Hambleton; Amy Masters, Wash the Dishes. Performances by Rockets Redglare, Peter Kwaloff, Tony Heiberg, M Drehd, Michael Chandler, Joy Stick, and special guests

● Thursday, January 6 ***Gore Gazette* presents *Caged Heat***

● Saturday, January 8 **Needles Jones's Red Light Café with Wild and Wonderful**

● Saturday, January 8 **Street Art Show with AVANT and Linus Coraggio: *Recent "Outstillations"***

● Saturday January 8–Tuesday, January 11 **Playhouse 57 presents Ibsen's *Ghosts*** at 18th Street Playhouse. "The domestic musical created by Andy Rees with Lisa Altomare, Scott Covert, Gregg Reel, Tony McKonly, Pepsi Togar. Sets and costumes by Dale Eliason. Music by Art Labriola, Tom Hawk"

● Tuesday, January 11 **Jonathan Quinn Invites 20 Artists**. Including art by Jonathan Quinn, Julia Wachtel, Peter Fend, April Palmieri, Lewis McDuffy, and Peter Dudek. [No comprehensive artist list has been found]

● Thursday, January 13 ***Gore Gazette* presents *The Last House on the Left*.** "Original uncut version not seen in NY since 1972!"

● Saturday, January 15 **Wild and Wonderful**

● Thursday, January 20 ***Gore Gazette* presents *Ilsa, She Wolf of the SS***

● Thursday, February 3 **Jim Mullen's Art Bar at Zippers presents *57 Varieties: Photographs by Robert Carrithers*.** "With performances by some of the 57: Kai Eric and Jeff Repella, Alexa Hunter, Gerard Little, Charlotte Slivka, Wendy Wild,

John Sex, Peter Kwaloff, the Fuzztones, Brant Kingman, Ann Magnuson"

• Saturday, February 5 **Needles Jones's Red Light Café**. "With Wild and Wonderful, Blackjack Savage, Last White Poets, Tony Heiberg, Michael Chandler. DJ Jim Marshall"

• Sunday, February 6 **Taxicabaret**. "A three act valentine's play starring Rockets Redglare, Mark Heidrich, Steve Buscemi, Anne de Bethune, Denise Tammaro & the comedy of Dan Vitale, Veronica Veiss. Music by Tony Heiberg"

• Monday, February 7 **Dry Ice Presents Bargain Monday**. Paintings by Brian Clark, Rodney Alan Greenblat, and Susan Karnet. Poetry by Frank Maya, Peggy McNaughton, and Frank Rubino

• Thursday, February 10 **Robert Patrick's *Pop People*** at Mudd Club. "Relive the 60s . . . The Chesterfield Kings, the Fuzztones, His Master's Voice. Guest DJ Peter Kwaloff. Kai Eric's Psychadelic Light Show"

• Friday, February 11 **WOW presents Debutantes on Parade Coming Out Ball**. "Women only"

• Friday, February 18 ***East Village Eye* Carnaval '83** at Mudd Club. "Produced by Alan Rish and Leonard Abrams. Hosted by David McDermott. Mr. and Mrs. *East Village Eye* pageant. Judges: Kathy Acker, Quentin Crisp, Fab 5 Freddy, Patricia Field, Rudolf Piper"

• Friday, February 25 **Anouschka Magnuson presents Depravnik Island** at Danceteria. "Where the high echelon party members and the privilegenzia find refuge from the winter doldrums, the depressed state-economy and the disintegrating morale. It's a pleasure zone. Hosted by your commissar Kestutis Nakas"

• Tuesday, March 15 **Contra** at Pyramid Club. "With Ralston Farina, Julius Klein, Jonathan Prosser"

• Saturday, March 19 **Stephen Tashjian**

• Sunday, March 20 **Dry Ice presents Non-Chang Pieces by John Jesurun**. "With 3-D Slide photos by Tina Paul"

• Thursday, March 24 **Pulsallama** at Danceteria. "Celebrating le debut for their nouvelle hit single 'Oui-Oui (A Canadian in Paris)'"

• Sunday, March 27 ***The Matchbook Show***. Organized by John Rosis. With matchbook art by Paul Duffy, Barnaby Ruhe, Janet Roller, Cindy Fusillo, Julius Klein, J. Pollock and Peggy G, Jonathan Quinn, Lill Luboya, Gracie Mansion, Richard Armijo, Michael Blaine, Michael Carter, Bill Vee, Stephen Lack, Pat Collins, Ken Hiratsuka, Katie Thamer, Peggy McNaughton, Tom Bulman, Peter Dudek, Jim Radakovich, Tress-Epstein, Roberto Olivo, David Hatchett, Dean Savard, Joe Herzfeld, Melanie Monios, Nancy Fischer, Mike Bidlo, Margaret Lanzetta, Liz n' Val, Elizabeth Grajales, Leslie Hopkins, Andreas Senser, Mundy McLaughlin, Vesna Golubovic, Ed Higgins, Sur Rodney (Sur), Eric Frye, John Rosis, and Nick Tobier

• Sunday, April 3 **Scott Wittman's *Les Girls*** at Danceteria. "Easter Sunday . . . live Burlesk starring John Sex, with the burley cuties Holly Woodlawn, Jayne County, Alexis del Lago, Ethyl Eichelberger; the top four bananas Tracey Berg, Laura Kenyon, Ula Hedwig, Georgia Wise; and J. P. Dougherty, George Wrage, Billy Gallo, The Ben Brothers, Vicki Schrott, and Maggie"

• Thursday, April 7 **On the Town Orchestra Superstar Jam with Tony Heiberg** at Mudd Club

• Friday, April 8 **Bikini Girl Doing Her Best on Bart's Show**

• Thursday April 21 **Joey Arias and Adrian Richards present a Benefit Concert for Klaus Nomi**. "With special performances by Brenda Bergman, Dave Street, David McDermott, Downtown Sissies, John Sex, Katy K, Little Ricky's Rockestra, Man Parrish, Marilyn and the Movie Stars, the Screaming Violets, Strange Party, the Swinging Madisons, Symbols, Tessie Chua, Valery Oisteanu & Yin Yang Gang. Nomi video presentation by Merrill Aldighieri and Joe Tripician. All proceeds from the door go to Klaus Nomi"

• Friday, April 22 **Ann Magnuson and Dany Johnson present the Battle of the Tribute Bands** at Danceteria. "Suburban splendor at its finest . . . a non-stop dance oriented rock-new-wave dance party with your MC and VJ Kestutis Nakas and your DJ Naomi"

• Thursday, April 28 ***The Brood***

• Friday, May 6 **Stefano Castronovo presents the Forgery Group Show: Mistaken Acquisitions** at Danceteria. "A selection of famous masterpieces faked by famous NY artists!"

• Saturday, May 14 ***Kenny Scharf*** opens at Tony Shafrazi Gallery

• Monday, May 23–Tuesday, May 24 **After Dante** at Danceteria. "Featuring Ann Magnuson, with Frank Holliday, William Fleet Lively & C. C. Williamson. An eighties style vaudeville revue: accompany TV evangelist Tammy Jan through the channels in her search for a 'format' in this television apotheosis"

• Wednesday, June 15 Tessie Chua at No Se No. "With Craig Backel on rod + hammer, Barry of Third Street on percussion"

• Saturday, June 18 **On the Town Orchestra** at Pyramid Club

• Monday, July 11 **Ann Magnuson: Riddles** at Pyramid Club."A performance every Monday in July!"

• Friday, July 15 **Wild and Wonderful** at Limbo Lounge

• Thursday, July 21 **Low Life** at Pyramid Club. "Ann Magnuson as Miss Vickie reveals the untold story—'I Was a Headless Body in a Topless Bar' featuring the music of Kristian Hoffman and Robert Maché"

• Monday, August 8 ***Titus Andronicus***. "Meat at the Pyramid." Directed by Kestutis Nakas. Cast: Chopped Hand / Bill Rice. Cut Trimmed / Ann Magnuson. Trim Sport For / William Allison, Steve Buscemi. Eats Pie / Catherine Tambini. Brains / Aric James. Stale / Randy Rollinson. Stab / John Kelly, John Sex. Pit / Mark Oates, Steven Keys. Neck / Dori Arnold, Nicky Paraiso. Meat / Rob Donaldson, Van Santvoord. Flesh / Mark Boone Jr., Tom Rubnitz. "Weekly serialized specials, Mondays through September 5"

• c. October Patrick Fox begins staging exhibitions in the Second Avenue Anderson Theater, a precursor to Patrick Fox Gallery

• Sunday, October 9 **Ann Magnuson, Kristian Hoffman, and Robert Maché Are Bleaker Street Incident**. "This is maybe a thought-provoking demonstration of the new survivalist ethics of doubt that are looming on the horizon of 1984! Remember: faith is out! Peace thru doubt! Be in and fall out!"

• Thursday, December 22 **Scott Wittman's *Peter Pan*** at Danceteria. John Sex as Peter Pan. Laura Kenyon as Captain Hook. With a cast of forty: Lisa Altomare, Jeorgia Anderson, Tracey Berg, The Ben Brothers, Brigitte Benmoha, Karon Bihari, Stefano Castronovo, Scott Covert, Jonathan Crow, Alexis del Lago, Donna Destri, J. P. Dougherty, Leigh Finner, Scott Flax, Mary Fulham, Billy Gallo, Tom Goldstein, Sandy Gray, Billy Harris, Linda Krauss, Karen Mandelbaum, Lyn Mandelbaum, Michael Musto, Miss April Palmieri, L. A. Sank, Vicki Schrott, Marc Shaiman, Wendy Wild, Joel Winston, Young Marge Gross, and Paul Zone

1984

• Friday, January 13 **Vulcan Death Grip** at Pyramid Club

• Sunday, April 15 ***The New Portrait*** opens at P.S. 1

• Wednesday, May 16 **Party of Life at Paradise Garage**. "Hosted by Keith Haring and Larry Levan. Music by Larry Levan and Juan Dubose. Art and Video by Keith Haring"

• Tuesday, June 5 **June Brides Fashion Party** at Limelight

• Tuesday, June 12 ***Made for TV*** at Limelight. "New York premiere of a video by Ann Magnuson and Tom Rubnitz"

• Wednesday, July 11 **Jackie Curtis in *Doris and Inez Speak the Truth*** at Danceteria. New York premiere of a film directed by James Ewing Murray with an original screenplay by George Haas

• Friday, July 13 **90 Miles "North!"** at Danceteria. "Rudolf invites you to a night of tropical celebration with an exhibition of the most recent works of Miguel Albear, Adolfo Sanchez, Oliver Sanchez"

• Monday, July 23 **Ann Magnuson and Joey Arias present Dali & Gala's Mad Tea Party** at Limelight. "With special guests Andy and Edie. Musical accompaniment Frederick Harris. Guest appearance: Philip Monaghan. Dress: Surreal"

• Thursday, August 2 **Dead Women: The Terminal Musical** at Palladium. "The march of skeletons: Eve, Mona Lisa, Joan Crawford, Marilyn, Judy Garland and many more! Featuring the International Chrysis, Teri Pars, Chi Chi Laverne, Alexa Hunter, Peter Kwaloff, Andriette Flemings, Marc Albam, Andy Valentin, Ron Witt, Kenny Usavage Gaylord, Chris Gallagher, Jimmy Mello, Chris Ianetta. Production and costumes by Gaylord. Directed by Andy Rees"

• Monday, August 13 **Vulcan Death Grip** at Limelight. "A demonic disco at the Limelight Memorial Coliseum"

• Thursday, September 8 **Lower East Side Polygon** at Danceteria. "A multimedia presentation that will take place on the 1st floor, side alley and basement of Danceteria; presented by Dry Ice, MC: Ann Craig. With bands: The Reformation of Certain Generals, Mistaken Identity, Wild and Wonderful. Performance: David Life, Kembra Pfahler, Pool, Jonathan Prosser. Art Show: Catacomb Art"

• Saturday, September 15 **Danceteria Lasciviously presents Island Recording Artist John Sex**. "Featuring the Montecarlo Rhinestone Orchestra with the Wedding Cake Fountain Chorus, directed by Scott Wittman"

• Saturday, December 1 **The Philosophy of Finism** at 163 Mercer Street. A performance by Ann Magnuson

1985

• Friday, March 15 **Joey Arias and Ann Magnuson Request the Pleasure of**

Your Company at a Mad Tea Party at Danceteria. "Hosted by Dali & Gala and their special guests of honor Andy and Edie and their hangers-on 'via satellite:' Murray & Gloria on cocaine from Los Angeles, Trevor & Fiona on fashion from London and Charlie & Squeaky on parole from maximum security. Musical accompaniment by Robert Arron and Ron Miller. Special appearance by Phil Monohue plus Dali & Gala's entrée into MTV Song's Video 45—Danspak II with Strange Party's 'Imitators'"

- Wednesday, May 15 **Rudolf presents Scott Wittman's *Nude Faces of 85*** at Danceteria. "One night only, around the world in sexty ways with an international cast of 80: Bill Anderson, Karon Bihari, The Ben Brothers, Burt Coleman, Jonathan Crow, Alexis del Lago, Evan, Scott Flax, Ellen Foley, Raymond Frankowski, Mary Fulham, Billy Gallo, Sandy Gray, Danny Irizary, Katy K, Mary Kaye, Laura Kenyon, Susa Maher, Karen Mandelbaum, Lyn Mandelbaum, Bucky Marino, Ken Miller, Michael Musto, Joe Niezes, April L. Palmieri, Lisa Pakulski, Zora Rasmussen, Stave Rowe, Eric Ryan, Vicki Schrott, Marc Shaiman, Bobby Siems, Trey Speegle, Walter Thomas, Craig Vandenburgh, Wendy Wild, Jeff Wilson, Matthew Williams, Joel Winston, Holly Woodlawn, Miki Zone, Paul Zone, and John Sex"

- c. July **Ann Magnuson performs *All Hail the Lizard King*** at Creative Time's Art on the Beach

- Wednesday, August 7 **Pagan Place at Palladium**. Produced by Scott Wittman. Starring Joey Arias, Ann Magnuson, and John Sex. With Miss April, Tracey Berg, Donna Bunte, Marc Cato, Alexis del Lago, J. P. Dougherty, Dovanna, John Epperson, Mary Fulham, Billy Gallo, Gaylord, Brian Hawks, Ian Hayslip, Barry Hendrick's Wigs, Danny Herman, Katy K, Gerard Little, Susa Maher, Karen Mandelbaum, Lyn Mandelbaum, Bucky Marino, Mikayla, Haoui Montaug, Michael Musto, Rick Negron, Leslie Neptune, John Isaac Nieto, Pony, Allen Robinson, Kristy Rose, Steve Rowe, Sheila, Mary Kay Shilling, Bobby Siems, Paula Swede, Stephen Tashjian, Craig Vandenburgh, Ming Vauze, Eugene Vincent, Wendy Wild, Joel Winston, Holly Woodlawn, Suzy Zabrowski, Miki Zone, and Paul Zone

- Friday, September 13 **Shawn McQuate presents Materialisations: Ideas in the Flesh** at Danceteria. "Fantasy evening gowns . . . models: Lady, Kitty, Carmel Johnson. MC and text by Richard Elovich, music arranged by Billy Harris, directed by Shawn McQuate"

- Thursday, December 5 **Club ETC presents *Ballet of the Dolls*, a Musical Parody** at Pyramid Club. Music and lyrics by John Epperson. Directed by Andy Rees and John Epperson. With John Kelly, Michael London, Meryl Goodfader, Marleen Menard, Mark Oates, Dan Taylor, Billy Basinki, Joey Smith, Kevin Malony and Stephen Pell as Susan Wayward. Choreography by Joey Smith. Sets by Andy Rees. Costumes by Pamela Goldman. Makeup by Paddy Crofton

1986

- Thursday, March 27 **The Saint presents a Gabriel Rotello Production of Scott Wittman's *Bye Bye Birdie*!** Cast: Ed Sullivan / Tracey Berg. Conrad Birdie / J. P. Dougherty. Rosie / Laura Kenyon. Albert / Craig Vandenburgh. Kim / Annie Golden. Hugo / John Sex. *Guys*: Harvey Johnson / Scott Covert. Rupert Maxwell / Stephen Paul. Huck Greenstreet / Rick Stanley. Rocky Preston / Paul Zone. *Gals*: Ann Margrock / Karen Bihari. Lucy Middleton / Lori Engelson. Lisa Rogers / Ellen Foley. Mary Fogbush / Tish Gervais. Neely Wonderkind / Meryl Goodfader. Summer Anderson / Wendy Wild. *Band*: Bobby Kent, Dick Gallagher, Arno Heckt, Paul Litteral, David Conrad, and David Gulyas. Costumes by Patricia Field. Wigs by Sture' Osten Designs. Makeup and hair by Harvey Livingston. Lights by Brian Lacosse. Assistant direction by Andy Rees. Musical direction by Dick Gallagher

- c. April Keith Haring opens Pop Shop

- Sunday, April 20 ***The Sound of Muzak***, a Scott Wittman production at Limelight [See entry for December 16–18, 1982. Cast additions to the Limelight production included Frank Holliday, April Palmieri, Tracey Berg, and Tom Rubnitz]

- Wednesday, August 6 **Standing Still** at Pyramid Club. "A dance premiere by choreographer / composer Shawn McQuate, dancing with Lady and Sean Kelly and instrumentalist Sylvia"

YOU ARE NOW ONE OF US: A CLUB 57 FILM AND VIDEOGRAPHY

This is a selective list of film and video created in New York's postpunk period, dating roughly from the late 1970s through the late 1980s—that is, during the heyday of Club 57 and the years directly following its closing. The list is organized by artist and includes not only works the artist directed, but also, in homage to the scene's collaborative spirit, works the artist shot, wrote, or performed in. For this reason, the same work may appear more than once, reflecting its shared authorship. Within a particular year, some titles appear in alphabetical order while others appear in the order sent to us by the artist.

The works herein were made by the era's better-known No Wave and Transgressive cinema artists, but also by its lesser-known ones, many of them students and amateurs whose moving-image works were exhibited in clubs and collectives, including New Cinema, Millenium, O-P Screening Room, and others. Many titles were distributed by Colab's Monday/Wednesday/Friday Video Club (c.1986–2003) before disappearing from view.

At the time, independent moving-image production was experiencing a shift, under way since the late 1960s, from Super 8 and 16mm film to a range of new prosumer and consumer video formats, including 3/4-inch reel-to-reel tape, U-matic, VHS, and Betamax.

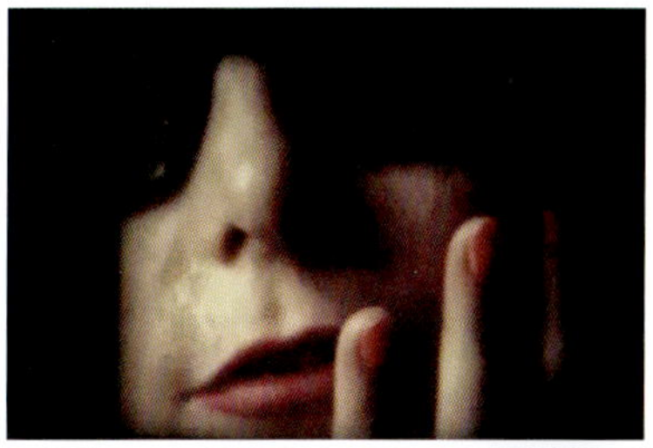

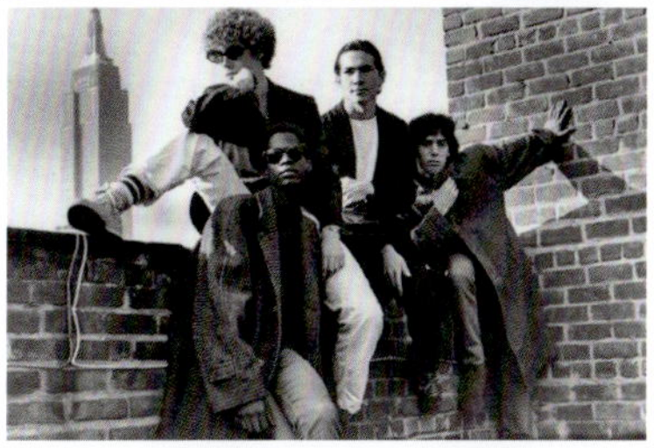

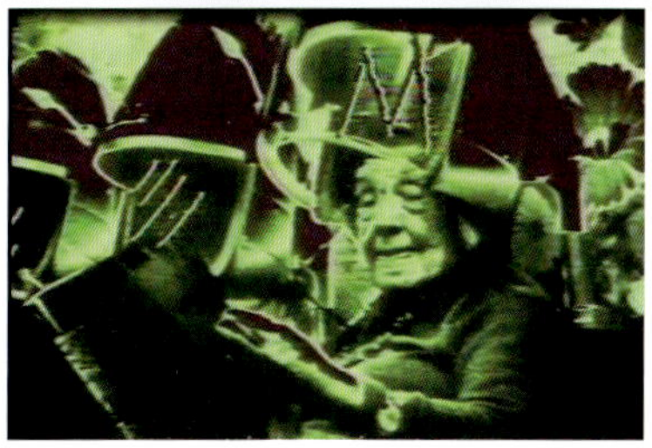

Sophie V.D.T, from Edit DeAk's *Beyond Genre* cycle, c. 1977–78
Shawn McQuate (second from right) in *Dancing Boys*, 1979. Directed by Esther Regelson
Still from *Skin Deep from Outer Space*, 1982. Directed by Merrill Aldighieri

Ahearn, Charlie
The Deadly Art of Survival. 1979. Super 8
Twins. 1980. 16mm
Wild Style. 1982. 16mm

Ahearn, John
Bronx Train. 1977. Super 8 *
Faces. 1977. Super 8 *
Distress. 1977–78. Super 8 *
Blizzard. 1978. Super 8 *
Shame. 1978. 16mm

Ahlbum, Joey
A Minute of Mystery. 1980. 16mm
Three Step. 1980. 16mm
Bandits. 1981. 16mm
Parade. 1986. 16mm

Aldighieri, Merrill
Alien Comic / Tom Murrin, performance at Club 57. 1981. Video *
Skin Deep from Outer Space. 1982. Video *
"Hip Hop Be Bop (Don't Stop)," with Man Parrish. 1984. Video *
"Imitators," with Strange Party. 1984. Video *

Aldighieri, Merrill, and Joe Tripician
Love among the Mutants. 1979. Video
Trojan Women, performance at Club 57. 1981. Video *

Amodeo, Rachel
What about Me. 1989–93. 16mm

Anderson, Jeorgia
The Visitor, directed by Andre Degas. 1979. Super 8 *
The Media Is My Masseur. 1982. Video

Andreiev, Glenn
Second Person. 1979. Super 8 *
Vlad Arnau. 1982. Super 8

Arias, Joey
Klaus Nomi, unreleased music video. c. 1979. Video *
Joey Arias and Janis Budde, screen test. 1980. 35mm *
Joey Arias and Mermaids on Heroin collaborators, screen test. 1985. 35mm *

B, Beth
"The Dominatrix Sleeps Tonight," with Dominatrix. 1984. Video *

B, Beth and Scott
G-Man. 1978. Super 8
NYPD Arson and Explosions Squad vs. FALN. 1978. Super 8
Black Box. 1979. Super 8
Letters to Dad. 1979. Super 8
The Offenders. 1979. Super 8
The Trap Door. 1980. Super 8
Vortex. 1982. 16mm

Baumgardner, Lisa
Girl Pack. 1978. Super 8 *
Lisa in Bondage. 1978. 16mm *
Plaza Party (aka 621). 1981. 16mm *

Bertoglio, Edo
Downtown '81, with Glenn O'Brien and Maripol. 1980–81/2000. 16mm

* MoMA Collection

Bonney, Anney
Shattered. 1978–79. Super 8

Borden, Lizzie
Born in Flames. 1983. 16mm

Brown, Steve
The Jones, with Barry Shils and Ellie Nagler. 1977. 16mm *
The Black Headed People (Sumer documentary). c. 1980. 16mm
Club 57 events, with Barry Shils. 1980. Video
Salute to Lawrence Welk *
Lady Wrestling *
Playboy Bunny Party, event at Mudd Club, with Barry Shils. 1980. Video *

Burns, Tim
Political Transmission. 1978. Super 8
WHY CARS?—CARnage!. 1979. Super 8
Against the Grain: More Meat Than Wheat. 1980. Super 8
Alphabet City / Thus Went to Phila. 1981. Super 8

Chua, Tessie
The Scary Truth about Cockroaches and Landlords, with Sur Rodney (Sur). 1980. Video *

Cooney, Robert
Alien Nation. 1979. Super 8
God's Police. 1980. Super 8

Crutchfield, Robin
Dead Dog Floating. c. 1980. Super 8
Fire in the Ashes. c. 1980. Super 8
Young Laundry. c. 1980. Super 8
Dark Day in Amsterdam. c. 1980. Super 8
General Accident. c. 1980. Super 8

DeAk, Edit
Beyond Genre cycle. 1977–86. Super 8

DeAk, Edit, Paul Dougherty, and Walter Robinson
"Frankie Teardrop," with Suicide. 1978. Video *

Degas, Andre
The Visitor. 1979. Super 8 *
Whatta Day. 1979. Super 8
Life and Death. 1980. Super 8
A Figment. 1980. 16mm
Open Window. 1981. 16mm
"Gangsters," with the Specials, performance. 1982. 16mm
First Coda. 1983. 16mm
American Autobahn. 1984. 16mm
Things Should Go on Like This Forever, with Paul Bowles. 1984–85. Video

DeLanda, Manuel
Incontinence: A Diarrhetic Flow of Mismatches. 1978. 16mm
Ismism. 1979. 16mm
Raw Nerves: A Lacanian Thriller. 1980. 16mm
Magic Mushrooms Mountain Movie. 1981. 16mm
Harmful or Fatal if Swallowed. 1982. 16mm
Judgement Day. 1983. 16mm

Dick, Vivienne
Guerillere Talks. 1978. Super 8
Staten Island. 1978. Super 8
She Had Her Gun All Ready. 1978. Super 8 *
Beauty Becomes the Beast. 1979. Super 8
Liberty's Booty. 1980. Super 8
Visibility: Moderate. 1981. Super 8
Loisaida. 1982. Super 8
Like Dawn to Dust. 1983. Super 8

Dobbins, Ray
Don the Burp publication party, event at Club 57. 1980. Video

Dougherty, Paul
"The Devil Lives in My Husband's Body," with Pulsallama. 1982. Video *
"Hangin'," with Chic. 1982. Video *
"Rap Machine," with Whodini. 1983. Video *

Doughton, Steve
Around Clown, with David Wojnarowicz. 1987. Super 8 *
Forming. 1987. Super 8 *
Betwixt. 1989. Super 8 *
Ferrum 5000. 1989/1995. 16mm *
Kembra Pfahler at Nice Chinese Restaurant. 1990. Super 8
Quagmire of Film. 1990. Super 8
Furkafall. 1991. Super 8
"Mr. Twilight," with the Voluptuous Horror of Karen Black. 1992.
"King of the Sea," with the Voluptuous Horror of Karen Black. 1992/2017.

Fessenden, Larry
The Eliminator. 1979. Super 8
White Trash. 1980. Super 8
The Field. 1980. Super 8
Lifeline. 1981. Super 8
A Face in the Crowd. 1981. Super 8
Habit. 1982. Video
Experienced Movers. 1985. Video

Fisher, Ellen
Black Goddess. 1986. 16mm

Grafstrom, Anders
Some Boys. c. 1979. Super 8
Klaus Nomi, screen test for Charles Ludlum. 1979. Super 8 *
Klaus Nomi, performance for Fiorucci Celebrates the New Wave. 1979. Super 8 *
The Long Island Four. 1979. Super 8 *
Anders Grafstrom benefit concert at Mudd Club. April 28, 1980. Video *

Haas, George
American Shooting Series. 1979. 16mm *
Romance. 1980–85. 16mm *
The Downtown Sissies in Revolt Ensemble, DSIRE, performance at Danceteria. 1983. Video *

Haring, Keith
Now Now Now. 1978. Video
Environments. 1978. Video
Bus Tape. c. 1978–80. Video
Keith's Face. c. 1978–80. Video
Untitled [Before and He Said]. c. 1978–80. Video
Untitled [Construction site music]. c. 1978–80. Video
Untitled [He Said That She Entering]. c. 1978–80. Video
Untitled [We Picked Up the Pieces]. c. 1978–80. Video
Analysis. c. 1979. Video
He Said I Have a Dream. c. 1979. Video
Video Tapes for Two Monitors. c. 1979. Video
SVA classroom, raw footage. c. 1979. Video
Lick, Fat, Boys. 1979. Video
Batusi Bros. Theme Song, with Kenny Scharf. 1979. Video
Open the Door. 1979. Video
His Nose. 1979. Video
Video Clones, with Molissa Fenley. 1979. Video
A Circle Play. 1979. Video
Boxes. 1979. Video
Painting Himself into a Corner. 1979. Video
Two handed white to black. 1979. Video
Mouth. 1980. Video
(F) Phonics. 1980. Video
Anal. 1980. Video
I was looking for my telephone book. 1980. Video
Machines. 1980. Video
People in the Elevator. 1980. Video
Tribute to My Father (Da-Di-Di-Da-Da). 1980. Video
Dedicated to Vincent van Gogh. 1980. Video
Tribute to Gloria Vanderbilt (Take One). 1980. Video
Tribute to Gloria Vanderbilt (Take Two). 1980. Video
Bang. 1980. Video
Times Square Animation. 1982. Video
Two-Sided. No date. Video

Harmel, Courtney
Andy & Edie Show, performance at Limelight. 1984. Video
Dali & Gala's Mad Tea Party, performance at Limelight. 1984. Video
June Brides, performance at Limelight. 1984. Video
007, with John Sex and Wendy Wild, performance at Limelight. 1984. Video
Party of Life, Keith Haring's birthday party at Paradise Garage. 1984. Video
Love Letters to Fiorucci, performance at Limelight. 1984. Video
Mermaids on Heroin, performance series at Danceteria. 1984–85. Video.
Mermaids on the Run
Mermaids Go Mardi Gras
Mermaids Do Retail
Robot Mermaid
Mermaids Go to Hell
Mermaids on Heroin, party at Asia Society
The Mega-Star book signing, event at Fiorucci. 1985. Video
The Fashion Moda press party, event at Fiorucci. 1985. Video
Fiorucci Fashion Moda / Sale, created for Fiorucci window monitor. 1985. Video
Halloween performance at Limelight. 1985. Video
Disco Hospital, performance at Limelight. 1985. Video
Fellini Party, with John Kelly, performance at Limelight. 1985. Video
New Year's Eve, with John Sex, performance at Limelight. 1986. Video
Fiorucci Classic Nouveau, created for Fiorucci window monitor. 1986. Video
Fiorucci Button Up Your Overcoat, with Joey Arias, created for Fiorucci window monitor. 1988. Video

Harris, Bill
Club 57 4th of July Picnic, Fort Tryon Park. 1980. Super 8 *

Harrison, Julie
Ladies Auxiliary Lady Wrestling, event at Fashion Moda. 1980. Video *

Hedwig, Ula
Livin' Dolls, performance at Club 57. 1981. Video

Holman, Michael
The Future of Vidal Sassoon. 1977. Video
Vincent Gallo as Flying Christ. 1980. Super 8
Bohack. 1980. Super 8
The Stranger, with Vincent Gallo. 1981. Super 8
Stilwend. 1981. Super 8
Catch a Beat, Rock Steady Crew, performance. 1981. Super 8
Untitled (PS1). 1981. Super 8
Negril. 1981. Video
Pesceador©, with Jean-Michel Basquiat. 1982. Super 8
TVNY. 1982. Video
On Beat TV cable series. 1983. Video
A7, Toxic & DJ High Priest, performance. 1983. Video
Bronx River Showdown, DJ Afrika Bambaataa, performance. 1983. Video
New York City Breakers, performance at Club New York. 1983. Video
Dream Crush. 1986. 35mm slideshow
Checkov Another One. 1986. Video
New York City Breakers, performance at Amnesty International Benefit. 1986. Video
Do the Right Thing. 1986. 16mm
Heads, You Win. 1986. 16mm
"All the Way to Heaven," with Doug E. Fresh. Animation by M. Henry Jones. 1986. Video and 16mm
Money Dog. 1987. 16mm
"Christmas in Hollis," with Run DMC. 1987. 16mm
Passion Play. 1987. 16mm

Horn, Andrew
Elaine: A Story of Lost Love. 1978. 16mm *
Doomed Love. 1983. 16mm

Hughes-Freeland, Tessa
Baby Doll. 1982. 16mm
Joker. 1983. Super 8
Graffiti Hall of Fame. 1984. Super 8
Play Boy. 1984. Super 8
Poppo at 8 B.C., Parts I–IV. 1984–85. Super 8
Bidlo Does Klein: Models in Blue. 1985. Super 8
Rhonda Goes to Hollywood. 1985. Super 8
Virginia Tripping Film. 1985. Super 8
Butthole Surfers. 1986. Super 8

* MoMA Collection

Rat Trap, with Tommy Turner.
1986. Super 8
Jane Gone, with the Workdogs. 1987.
Super 8 and video
The Story of the Little Green Man.
1989. Super 8

Hunter, Alexa
Columbia scratch film. 1979. Super 8 *
Casino Royale and Iran, Iraq, and Iroll, events at Club 57; Madness concert footage. 1979. Super 8 *
Hit or a Miss/Information, with Disturbed Furniture, in collaboration with Geoff O'Connor. 1979/2017. Video

Johnston, Becky
Sleepless Nights. 1978. Super 8

Jones, M. Henry
The Fleshtones, performance at SVA, with Manuel DeLanda. 1977. Video *
Pat Oleszko commercial. c. 1978. 16mm *
"Soul City," with the Fleshtones. 1977–79. 16mm *
"Go-Go Girl," with Nervus Rex. 1978–81. 16mm
"Brand New Cadillac," with the Zantees. 1979/2010. 16mm *
"A Beautiful Light," with the Fleshtones. 1993. Video *

Kern, Richard
Goodbye 42nd Street. 1984. Super 8
Zombie Hunger. 1984. Super 8
Zombie Hunger 2. 1984. Super 8
The Right Side of My Brain. 1984. Super 8
The Manhattan Love Suicides. 1984. Super 8
Thrust in Me, with Nick Zedd
Stray Dogs
Woman at the Wheel
I Hate Your Now
Submit to Me. 1985. Super 8
You Killed Me First. 1985. Super 8
Death Valley '69. 1986. Super 8 *
Fingered. 1986. Super 8
Pierce. 1986. Super 8

The Kitchen
A Christmas Special, with Ann Magnuson. 1981. Video

Klein, Julius
On the Town, with Tony Heiberg, performance at Club 57. 1982. Video *
Big Wack. 1983. Super 8 *
Sylvester's Light, performance. 1984. Video *
Dig. 1985. Super 8 *

Kleman, Richard
A Suicide. 1978. Super 8

Ley, Jennifer T.
Avoid Living the Lyric. 1980. 16mm *
Such Sweet Dreams. 1981. 16mm *

Joe Lewis
Pyramid Sweet / You Don't Love Me. 1979. Video *
Lewis & Lewis, performance at Fashion Moda. 1979. Video *

L'Hotsky, Tina
Barbie. 1977. Super 8 *
Snakewoman. 1977. Super 8 *

Lung Leg
Untitled (Worm Movie). 1985. Super 8
The Black Monster. 1986. Super 8

Lurie, John
Hell Is You. 1979. Super 8
Men in Orbit. 1979. Super 8

Magnuson, Ann
The Wallet Exercise. 1976. Super 8
The Indoor Lighting Exercise. 1976. Super 8
One God, One Singer. 1976. Super 8
Made for TV, with Tom Rubnitz. 1984. Video *

Marciano, Eric
The Jimmy Donahue Story. c. 1981. Super 8 *
Plain. 1981. Super 8 *
Bad Seed trailer. 1981. Video
Ghosts, performance at 18th Street Playhouse. 1983. Video *
The Age of Insects. 1983/1990. Super 8 *
Ballet of the Dolls, performance at Pyramid Club. 1985. Video *
Spin Cycle. 1986. 16mm *
Narrowcast. 1996. 35mm *

Masterson, Barry
Devil Movie. c. 1978. 16mm
Bad Brains. c. 1979. 16mm

Mitchell, Eric
Mass Homicide (aka Car Crash). 1977. Super 8
Kidnapped. 1978. Super 8
Red Italy. 1979. Super 8
Underground U.S.A. 1980. 16mm *
The Way It Is, or Eurydice in the Avenues. 1985. 35mm

Montag, Haoui
Chant Chant Amour Amour. 1984. Super 8

Moore, Frank, and Jim Self
Beehive. 1985. 16mm

Murray, Jimmy
Doris and Inez Speak the Truth, with George Haas. 1984. 16mm *

Nagler, Ellie
The Jones, with Barry Shils and Steve Brown. 1977. 16mm *

Nakas, Kestutis
Your Program of Programs, cable series. 1982. Video *

Nares, James
Suicide? No, Murder. 1977. Super 8
TV Faces. 1977. Super 8
Rome '78. 1978. Super 8
No Japs at My Funeral. 1980. Video
Waiting for the Wind. 1982. Super 8

Nicolayevsky, Ricardo
Lost Portraits. 1982/1985. Super 8 and 16mm *
Lost City. 1982. 16mm *

Scratches on My Brain. 1982. 16mm *
Bauhaus. 1983. Super 8 *
NYC '83. 1983. 16mm *
A Letter to Katia. 1984. 16mm *
Luminocri. 1985. 16mm *

Oblowitz, Michael
Portrait of Tina L'Hotsky. 1977. Super 8 *
Table Conversation. 1979. 16mm *
X-Terminator. 1979. 16mm *
Minus Zero. 1979. 16mm *
Too Sensitive to Touch, with Sylvère Lotringer. 1981. 16mm *
King Blank. 1983. 16mm *

O'Brien, Glenn
TV Party, cable series. 1978–81. Video
Downtown '81, directed by Edo Bertoglio, with Maripol. 1980–81/2000. 16mm

Patterson, Clayton
Peter Kwaloff and Gerard Little (Mr. Fashion), with Daphne Hellman, performance at Pyramid Club. 1986. Video
Peter Kwaloff and Kennon Raines, performance at Pyramid Club. 1987. Video
Peter Kwaloff as Nacha Cheap, performance at Pyramid Club. 1987. Video
Peter Kwaloff and Lady Bunny, performance at Pyramid Club. 1987. Video
Peter Kwaloff, Gerard Little (Mr. Fashion), and Stephen Tashjian (Tabboo!), performance. 1988. Video
Peter Kwaloff and Gerard Little, performance. 1988. Video
Peter Kwaloff, performance at Pyramid Club. 1988. Video
Tompkins Square Park Police Riot. 1989. Video

Perlman, Cara and Jane Sherry
Topless. 1979. Super 8

Pfahler, Kembra
Mild Seven: The Cowboy Stories. 1986. Super 8
Cornella: Story of a Burning Bush. 1985. Super 8
Pussycat Bladder Waste. 1987. Super 8
Straight Jackie. 1987. Super 8

Poe, Amos
My, My Michelangelo. 1974. 16mm
Unmade Beds. 1976. 16mm
Alphabet City. 1985. 35mm

Poe, Amos, and Johanna Heer
The Foreigner. 1978. 16mm
Subway Riders. 1981. 16mm

Poe, Amos, and Ivan Kral
Night Lunch. 1975. 16mm
Blank Generation. 1976. 16mm

Protrudi, Rudi, and Deb O'Nair
"The Witch," with the Fuzztones, directed by Andrew Christiansen. 1983. Video *
"Ward 81," with the Fuzztones. 1984. Video *

Quinn, Jonathan
Over Water. c. 1985. Super 8
You'll Get Yours. 1986. Super 8 *
Liberty, Queen of the Statues. 1989. Super 8 *

Rees, Andy
New Wave Vaudeville and East Village Home Movies. c. 1978. Super 8 *
Alexa Hunter / Disturbed Furniture performance, with Barry Shils. 1980. Video
Danceteria / Mass Hysteria *
Breakdown *
Bobby Beausoleil *
Alors Allez *
Dead Woman, performance at Palladium. 1986. Video

Regelson, Esther
Dancing Boys. 1979. Super 8 *
Dear Cousin. 1979. Super 8 *
Stop Action. 1980–81. 16mm *
Blih-Ah. 1981. 16mm *
WMEN. 1981. 16mm *
Catharsis. 1982. 16mm *

Roebling, Christian
Unique New York, cable series. 1983. Video
The Joe Blow Show, cable series. 1984. Video

Rubnitz, Tom
Reverend Howard Finster: Man of Vision. 1980. Video
Midnight Lullaby. 1980. Video
From the Files of the Pyramid Cocktail Lounge. 1983. Video
Chicken Elaine. 1983. Video
John Sex: The True Story. 1983. Video *
Made for TV, with Ann Magnuson. 1984. Video *
Psykho III: The Musical. 1985. Video
Hustle with My Muscle. 1986. Video
Bump and Grind It. 1986. Video
Drag Queen Marathon. 1986. Video
Wigstock: The Movie. 1987. Video *
Undercover Me. 1988. Video *
Pickle Surprise. 1989. Video
Strawberry Shortcut. 1989. Video
The Fairies. 1989. Video
Summer of Love PSA, with MICA TV. 1990. Video *
Listen to This, with David Wojnarowicz. 1992. Video *

Rubnitz, Tom, Tom Koken, and Barbara Lipp
Frieda! (The Movie). 1980. Video
Plastic Rap with Frieda. 1983. Video
The Mother Show. 1991. Video

Scharf, Kenny
Avon Freakout. 1979. Video *
Belly Button. 1979. Video *
Delta Sex. 1979. Video *
Give Me Television. 1979. Video *
Green Snowballs. 1979. Video *
The Hanging of Joe Tynan. 1979. Video *
I'm So Tired. 1979. Video *
Radiation Family Dinner Murder. 1979. Video *
Acts of Live Art. 1980. Video *
Boy from the City. 1980. Video *
Hydrogen Is God. 1980. Video *

The Klaus Nomi Show. 1980. Video *
The Sparkl End. 1980. Video *
Sugar. 1980. Video *
Suicide Can Be Fun. 1980. Video *
The Tales of Bardrochat. 1980. Video *
Television. 1980. Video *
You Really Turn Me On. 1980. Video *
Your Show of Shows, with Kestutis Nakas. 1980. Video *
Carousel of Progress. 1981. Video *
Dr. Navia Speaks at Club 57. 1981. Video *
Country Fume. 1982. Video *
The Philosophy of Finism. 1984. Video *

Schanzenbach, Robin A.
Teen Etiquette. 1980. Video
Chapter 1: Rockabilly Romance
Chapter 2: Ska Head Crush
Chapter 3: The Obscure Tea Party
Berlin. 1980. Video
Happy Birthday Emily. 1980. Video
John Sex Burlesque, performance at Club 57. 1981. Video
Boys Backs. 1981. Video
"Sleepwalking through Life," with Strange Party. 1981. Video
King Pins. 1982. Video
Solid Gold Show, performance at Club 57. 1982. Video
Portraits. 1983. Video
Partyline. 1983. Video

Schloss, Arlene
Lewis, Eastman & Lewis, performance at A's. 1981. Video *
How She Sees It by Her. 1983. Super 8
Glenn Branca: Symphony No. 4. 1984. Super 8 and 16mm

Schmidlapp, David
Fas Gas. 1979. 35mm slideshow
State of State. 1979. 35mm slideshow
What of the City Is Left Naked to the Night. 1980. 35mm slideshow
Which Thoughts Actually Do the Counting. 1981. 35mm slideshow
Not Quite Love, with Walter Steding. 1981. 16mm
I Magi. 1982. Video
Facts of Life. 1982. Video
world war. 1982. Video
Ode. 1982. Video
Party Tar. 1982. Video
War Years. 1983. 35mm slideshow

Shils, Barry
The Jones, with Steve Brown and Ellie Nagler. 1977. 16mm *
Club 57 events, with Steve Brown. 1980. Video
Salute to Lawrence Welk *
Lady Wrestling *
Playboy Bunny Party, event at Mudd Club with Steve Brown.1980. Video *
Alexa Hunter / Disturbed Furniture performance with Andy Rees. 1980. Video
Danceteria / Mass Hysteria *
Breakdown *
Bobby Beausoleil *
Alors Allez *
Love Comix. 1983. Video *

Siems, Bobby
Boing Boing, performance at Club 57. 1980. Video *

Smith, Kiki
Poofo, with Cara Perlman. 1979. Super 8
Cave Girls. 1982. Super 8

Squat Theatre
Andy Warhol's Last Love. 1981. Video
Pig, Child, Fire!. 1981. Video
Mr. Dead and Mrs. Free. 1982. Video

Steinfeld, Alan
A Walking Tour of the East Village. c. 1985. Video

Sullivan, Nelson
Peter Pan, performance at Danceteria. 1983. Video
Bye Bye Birdie, performance at Danceteria. 1983. Video
Nude Faces of 85, performance at Danceteria. 1985. Video
The Sound of Muzak, performance at Limelight. 1986. Video
Rauncho Notorious, performance at Palladium 1986. Video
The Disney Show, performance at Limelight. 1986. Video

Sur Rodney (Sur)
Corridor. 1973. Video
Conversation with Luc Beland. 1973. Video
Silkscreen Video. 1974. Video
Mannequin. 1974. Video
Security Rick. 1974–76. Video
Taking Care of Business (Destruction Event at Montreal Museum of Fine Arts). 1976. Super 8
Untitled (Opera). 1977. Super 8 *
The Invocation of Lawanda Rose. 1979. Super 8
Untitled (Animal Hospital with Larry Shox). 1979. Super 8 *
Untitled (Wax). 1980. Super 8 *
Untitled (Kenny Scharf Installation / Watermelons). 1980. Super 8 *
The Scary Truth about Cockroaches and Landlords, with Tessie Chua. 1980. Video *
The Sur Rodney (Sur) Show, cable series. 1980–82. Video

Sussler, Betsy
Tripe. 1980. Video
Menage. 1981. Super 8

Troyano, Ela
Totem of the Depraved, with Nick Zedd. 1983. 16mm

Turner, Tommy
Simonland. 1984. Super 8
Where Evil Dwells, with David Wojnarowicz. 1985. Super 8
Rat Trap, with Tessa Hughes-Freeland. 1986. Super 8

Vieille, Sophie
Four Fashion Horses. 1982–84. Video
Woman and Whale. 1985. Video
Sarabande. 1986. Video

Vogl, Harald
Dear Jimmy. 1978. Super 8 *
Only You. 1981. Super 8 *
OK Today Tomorrow. 1982. Super 8 *
Measure Taken. 1983. Super 8 *

Vogl, Harald, and Andrew Bergen
Candide in America. 1986. Video

Wojnarowicz, David
Heroin. 1981. Super 8
Where Evil Dwells, with Tommy Turner. 1985. Super 8
A Fire in My Belly. 1987. Super 8 *
Fear of Disclosure. 1989. 16mm

Zaremba, Peter
Iron Lung. 1975–76. 16mm
Miracle Film (Suicide). 1977. Super 8 and 16mm

Zedd, Nick
They Eat Scum. 1979. Super 8
The Bogus Man. 1980. 16mm
Geek Maggot Bingo. 1983. 16mm
The Wild World of Lydia Lunch. 1983. Super 8
Totem of the Depraved, with Ela Troyano. 1983. 16mm
School of Shame. 1984. Super 8
Thrust in Me, with Richard Kern. 1984. Super 8
Kiss Me Goodbye. 1986. Super 8

Cable TV Programs
Colab c. 1977–91
All Color News. 1977–78
Nightwatch. 1979
Red Curtain. 1979–83
Potato Wolf. 1979–86
Downtown Tonight. 1988
Colab News Live. No date
Greg Masters and collaborators. Public Access Poetry. 1977–78
The Coca Crystal Show: If I Can't Dance, You Can Keep Your Revolution. 1977–95
Glenn O'Brien. TV Party. 1978–82
Jaime Davidovich. The Live! Show. 1979–84
Liza Béar, Milly Iatrou, Terese Svoboda, and Betsy Newman. Communications Update / Cast Iron TV. 1979–91
The Sur Rodney (Sur) Show. 1980–82
Kestutis Nakas. Your Program of Programs. 1982 *
Walter Robinson. The Love Show. 1982
Michael Holman. On Beat TV. 1983
Michael Holman. TVNY. 1983. Video
Christian Roebling. The Joe Blow Show. 1984
Christian Roebling. Unique New York. 1983
Willoughby Sharp's Downtown New York. 1985–86
REHAB. Rehab Video.1987–89

INDEX OF NAMES

* MoMA Collection

Page numbers in italics denote illustrations.

Page numbers in italics denote illustrations.

Contributors

Ron Magliozzi is Curator, Department of Film, The Museum of Modern Art, New York.

Sophie Cavoulacos is Assistant Curator, Department of Film, The Museum of Modern Art, New York.

J. Hoberman has written and edited thirteen books, including *On Jack Smith's Flaming Creatures*, and was the film critic at the *Village Voice* from 1977 to 2012.

Jenny Schlenzka is artistic director of Performance Space 122 in New York.

Laura Hoptman is Curator, Department of Painting and Sculpture, The Museum of Modern Art, New York.

Lucy Gallun is Assistant Curator, Department of Photography, The Museum of Modern Art, New York.

Ann Magnuson is a writer, musician, actress, and part-time performance artist living in Los Angeles and Joshua Tree, California.

Published in conjunction with the exhibition *Club 57: Film, Performance, and Art in the East Village, 1978–1983*, organized by Ron Magliozzi, Curator, and Sophie Cavoulacos, Assistant Curator, Department of Film, with Ann Magnuson, guest curator, at The Museum of Modern Art, New York, October 31, 2017–April 1, 2018

Major support for the exhibition is provided by the Keith Haring Foundation.
Generous funding is provided by mediaThe foundation inc.
Additional support is provided by the Annual Film Fund.

Produced by the Department of Publications, The Museum of Modern Art, New York

Christopher Hudson, Publisher
Chul R. Kim, Associate Publisher
Don McMahon, Editorial Director
Marc Sapir, Production Director

Edited by Sarah Resnick
Designed by Geoff Kaplan, General Working Group

Production by Matthew Pimm
Color separations by Evergreen Colour Management Ltd., Hong Kong
Printed and bound by Gorenjski Tisk Storitve, Slovenia

This book is typeset in Univers, Benton, and Cooper Black.
The paper is 135 gsm Magno Matt.

Published by The Museum of Modern Art, New York
11 West 53 Street
New York, New York 10019
www.moma.org

Distributed in the United States and Canada by ARTBOOK | D.A.P.
75 Broad Street, Ste. 360
New York, New York 10004
www.artbook.com

Distributed outside the United States and Canada by Thames & Hudson Ltd.
181A High Holborn
London WC1V 7QX
www.thamesandhudson.com

Library of Congress Control Number: 2017950637

ISBN: 978-1-63345-030-1

Printed in Slovenia

Front cover: John Sex. *Acts of Live Art*. 1980. See page 45.

Endpapers: Covers from the *New York Post*, 1978–83

Half-title page: Club 57 logo, c. 1978. Design by Stanley Strychacki. The Museum of Modern Art, New York. Department of Film Special Collections

Frontispiece: John Sex. *Untitled (Jayne Mansfield)*. c. 1980. Silkscreen and spray paint on paper, 24 × 15" (61 × 38.1 cm). Collection the Keith Haring Foundation. This work was exhibited in the *Black Light Art Show* organized by Keith Haring at Club 57 in June 1981.

Opposite table of contents: East Village Students Club Pot-Luck Picnic menu, c. 1982. Design by Peter Kwaloff for a Club 57 benefit at Danceteria. The Museum of Modern Art, New York. Department of Film Special Collections

Back cover: Original collage for issue two of Lisa Baumgardner's zine, *Bikini Girl*, 1979 (detail). See page 17.

Primary credits and courtesies: © Keith Haring Foundation: 72–73, 87; 113, top left; 124, fig. 1; 127, fig. 3. Photo Jean Vong: 4; 53; 56; 57; 60; 61; 65; 66; 67; 69; 72–73; 76; 77; 78; 79; 80, top; 87; 88; 92; 93; 117; 119; 124, fig. 1. Digital Image © The Museum of Modern Art, New York. Photo John Wronn: 13, fig. 3; 14, fig. 4; 17, fig. 6; 26, fig. 3, fig. 4; 30, fig. 9; 31, fig. 10; 32, fig. 12; 38, fig. 20; 39, fig. 21; 44; 45; 46; 74; 95, fig. 2; 96, fig. 3; fig. 4; 97, fig. 5; 102, fig. 1; 103, fig. 2; 109, fig. 5; 110, fig. 6; 118; 120; 121, both; 123; 127, fig. 3; 144, fig. 1; 158, fig. 8, Digital Image © The Museum of Modern Art, New York. Photo Peter Butler: 68. © 2017 Muna Tseng Dance Projects, New York: 32, fig. 11; 47; 138; 139; 155, fig. 4 (photograph); 158, fig. 7.

Additional credits and courtesies (plates): Photo Joshua White: 43. Photo Mark Reinertson: 48, both. Courtesy School of Visual Arts: 49. © 2017 Kenny Scharf/ Artists Rights Society (ARS), New York: 50; 51, all. Courtesy Honor Fraser Gallery: 50, middle. Courtesy Gordon Robichaux, New York. Photo Max Lee: 58, 59. Courtesy Video Data Bank, School of the Art Institute of Chicago: 62, 63. Photo Monica McGivern: 64, 70–71, 91. Photo Pat Carney: 75. Photo Bill Massey: 80, bottom, Courtesy Anton Kern Gallery, New York. Photo Object Studies: 81, bottom. Photo D. James Dee, courtesy Alexander and Bonin, New York: 83. © A. T. Willett Photographer 2016: 84, 85. Photo Bill Orcutt: 89. Photo Wes Magyar: 90 © The Estate of Jean-Michel Basquiat/ ADAGP, Paris/ARS, New York 2017: 117. © Estate of Katherine Dumas: 143.

Additional credits and courtesies (essays): Courtesy Billy Rose Theatre Division, The New York Public Library for the Performing Arts: 10, fig. 1. Courtesy Video Data Bank, School of the Art Institute of Chicago: 21, fig. 10. Courtesy © Timothy Greenfield-Sanders: 25, fig. 2. © Andreas Sterzing: 34, fig. 15. Courtesy The Museum of Modern Art Library, New York: 31, fig. 10; 103, fig. 2. Courtesy The Museum of Modern Art Archives, New York: 109, fig. 5; 110, fig. 6; 128, fig. 5. Photo Jeff McLane: 156–57, fig. 5. Endpapers: Use of the *New York Post* courtesy NYP Holdings, Inc.

Trustees

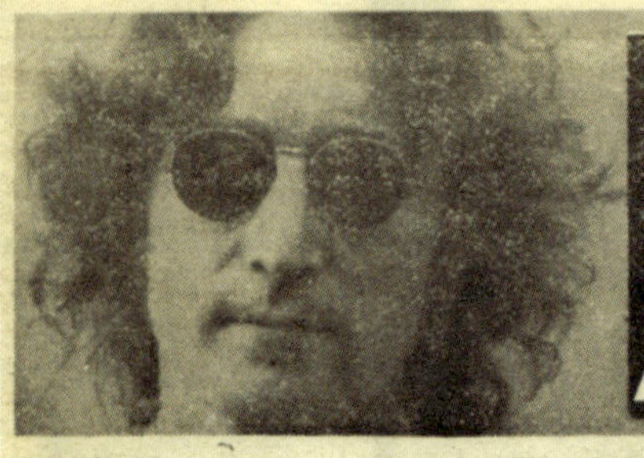

WORLD MOURNS A MAN OF PEACE

Ten pages of stories and tributes start on Page Two

TONIGHT
Rain, 30-35

TOMORROW
Partial clearing, 35-40

Details, Page 2

NEW YORK POST

FINAL
LATEST PRICES

TV listings: P. 63 TUESDAY, DECEMBER 9, 1980 25 CENTS

 Vol. 180, No. 20

AMERICA'S FASTEST-GROWING NEWSPAPER

AVERAGE DAILY SALES EXCEED 700,000

FIRST PICTURE

'I JUST SHOT JOHN LENNON'

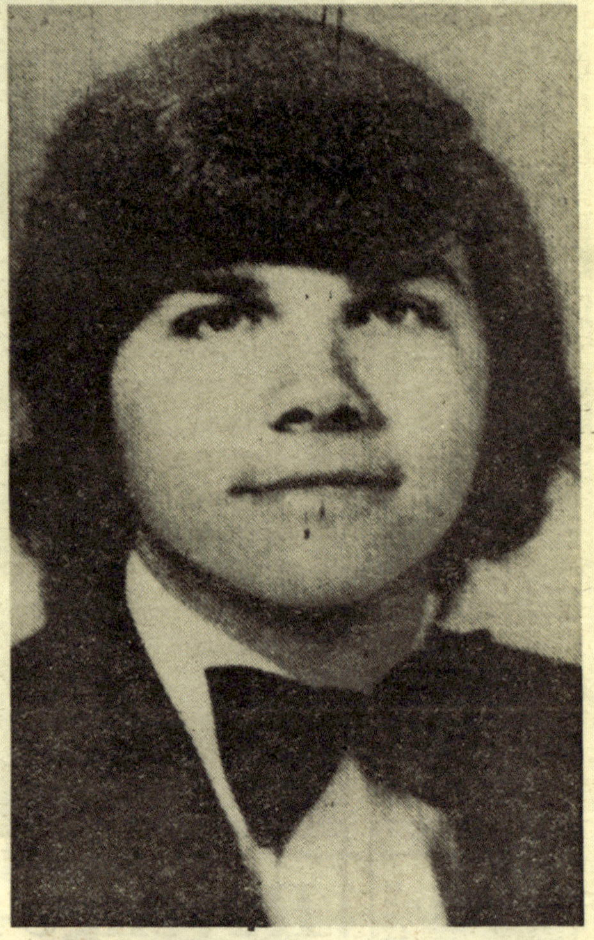

THIS is Mark David Chapman, the 25-year-old accused of killing ex-Beatle John Lennon in New York last night. "I just shot John Lennon," he is alleged to have yelled, seconds after the shooting.

Chilling eyewitness story of murder: P2